BUSINESS PLANNING AND CONTROL

BUSINESS PLANNING AND CONTROL

Integrating Accounting, Strategy and People

Bruce Bowhill

John Wiley & Sons, Ltd

Other Wiley Editorial Offices

John Wiley & Sons Inc., 111 River Street, Hoboken, NJ 07030, USA

Jossey-Bass, 989 Market Street, San Francisco, CA 94103-1741, USA

Wiley-VCH Verlag GmbH, Boschstr. 12, D-69469 Weinheim, Germany

John Wiley & Sons Australia Ltd, 42 McDougall Street, Milton, Queensland 4064, Australia

John Wiley & Sons (Asia) Pte Ltd, 2 Clementi Loop #02-01, Jin Xing Distripark, Singapore 129809

John Wiley & Sons Canada Ltd, 6045 Freemont Blvd, Mississauga, ONT, L5R 4J3

Wiley also publishes its books in a variety of electronic formats. Some content that appears in print may not be available in electronic books.

Library of Congress Cataloging in Publication Data

Bowhill, Bruce.
   Business planning and control : integrating accounting, strategy, and people / Bruce Bowhill.
     p. cm.
   Includes bibliographical references and index.
   ISBN 978-0-470-06177-0 (pbk. : alk. paper)
   1. Business planning. 2. Managerial accounting. 3. Strategic planning. 4. Cost control.
   I. Title.
   HD30.28.B6847 2008
   658.4′012—dc22

                                                      2008039324

British Library Cataloguing in Publication Data

A catalogue record for this book is available from the British Library

ISBN: 978-0-470-06177-0

Typeset in 10/12pt Goudy by Integra Software Services Pvt. Ltd, Pondicherry, India
Printed and bound in Great Britain by Bell & Bain Ltd, Glasgow
This book is printed on acid-free paper responsibly manufactured from sustainable forestry in which at least two trees are planted for each one used for paper production.

CONTENTS

Preface

Introduction

In planning for the future and in an attempt to influence an organization's development, successful managers are likely to need to draw on a range of skills and knowledge. These include accounting and finance, business strategy and the management of people.

On many academic courses, topics such as management accounting and business strategy are taught in separate modules. The result can be that the relevance of theory to the specific problem area of planning and control is not always obvious. This book aims to overcome this problem by integrating relevant material from the various disciplines into a single text.

The Market

This book has been written for both academic courses and practicing managers.

For academic courses, the book is intended as a core text for a wide range of postgraduate and undergraduate courses related to business planning and control. For specialist accounting degrees and professional courses, the book provides an opportunity for students to gain an understanding of the business context in which management accounting methods can be used. This also means that there is a greater opportunity to explore the strengths and weaknesses of such approaches than is possible in many traditional management accounting textbooks.

For managers, the text can be a reference and working guide to management accounting and strategic management techniques and to current developments in management control.

Scope

The book is divided into four parts with five or six chapters in each part, covering the following key areas:

Part 1 – Information for decision-making and financial reporting requirements
Part 2 – Traditional accounting controls
Part 3 – Strategic management
Part 4 – Issues in management control

Part 1 focuses on management accounting information for decision-making and financial reporting requirements. Chapters cover short-term decision-making topics, such as cost–volume–profit analysis, approaches to pricing and the evaluation of different marketing plans as well as the appraisal of investments in new projects that will have an impact on the business over a number of years. Traditional and activity-based approaches to costing are also considered.

Part 2 explores the use of traditional accounting techniques to achieve control in organizations. Chapters consider approaches to budgeting and budgetary control, the preparation of budgets, control in manufacturing and in divisionalized organizations and the use of ratio analysis in the interpretation of performance. Funding the business, both long and short term, including the control of working capital, is also covered.

Part 3 of the book deals with aspects of strategic management. This includes the appraisal of the threats and opportunities in the external environment, the review of organizational strengths and weaknesses and consideration of strategic options to meet objectives. The role of management accounting information in the strategic management process will also be explored.

Part 4 develops from the material considered in the previous three parts of the book. This is used to investigate criticisms of traditional accounting approaches to control and to investigate potential solutions to such problems. Issues include:

- People and control.
- Monitoring performance against strategic objectives and strategy.
- The measurement of shareholder value.
- Measuring and improving business processes.
- Controls in a complex and changing environment.

In relation to academic courses, Parts 1 and 2 broadly cover material that would be covered in an introductory management accounting course, with further information provided on areas such as control through the use of accounting ratios. Part 3 can be used on introductory courses to strategic management and underpins courses of study investigating the role of accounting information in strategic analysis and the evaluation of strategic options. Part 4 is appropriate for a wide range of courses concerned with management control in organizations.

A key purpose of the book is to provide a text that covers key issues of business planning and control, but one which is also readily accessible to the target audience. To improve the readability of the book, some specialist technical areas are not developed in depth in individual chapters. However, additional information on a number of techniques is available on the web site for the book. Lecturers are also invited to write to the author if they would wish to see specific techniques or topics developed in more depth on this site.

Features of the text

Theory and practice and use of case material

The text takes a practical approach and wherever possible examples are used to illustrate key learning points. For instance, in Part 2 of the book, planning and control for one organization is explored over several chapters. In Part 3, several chapters relate to a single industry, with theoretical and real organizations considered. Chapter exercises in Parts 3 and 4, in particular, draw on material from a limited number of short case scenarios that are provided at the end of the book.

Questions and answers

Self-assessment questions

Throughout each chapter, self-assessment questions are set, which test understanding of the key learning points covered in the previous section of the text. Answers to the self-assessment questions are provided at the end of each chapter.

End-of-chapter questions and answers

End-of-chapter questions and answers cover both discussion and, where relevant, numerical questions. Answers to some of the questions are provided at the back of the book. Answers to other questions are found on the student and lecturer areas of the web site.

INFORMATION AVAILABLE ON THE WEBSITE

Access to the web site can be found at www.wileyeurope.com/college/bowhill
The students' web site includes:

(i) Answers to a number of the questions set at the end of each chapter.
(ii) Multiple choice questions.
(iii) A full version of the book's glossary.
(iv) Supplementary reference material on some key issues, including web links to resources.

The lecturers' web site includes:

(i) PowerPoint slides of the lecture material.
(ii) Excel spreadsheets of exercises that have been used to illustrate key points in the chapters of the book, which can be downloaded. Students can use these spreadsheets to help develop an understanding of the relationship between key variables and to assess the impact of changes in input values.
(iii) Additional questions and answers.
(iv) Answers to a number of questions set at the end of each chapter (where not included on the student website).

Additional information on accounting 'techniques'

A key purpose of the book is to provide a text that covers key issues of business planning and control in a manner that is readily accessible to the target audience. Accordingly, in order to improve the readability of the book, some specialist technical topics are not developed in depth in individual chapters. Management accounting courses for specialist accounting degrees however, may require greater consideration of some techniques and to cater for this requirement further information has been provided on the student website for the book. Topics covered include:

Further decision-making problems

- Linear programming

Capital investment decisions

- Decision rule for mutually exclusive projects
- Capital rationing

– Taxation
– Dealing with inflation

Standard costing and manufacturing methods

– Volume capacity and volume efficiency variances
– Material mix and yield variances
– Market share and size variances
– Ex post and ex ante variances

Evaluating options

– Minimax regret

Process costing assuming:

– No losses; normal losses; abnormal losses with a scrap value; abnormal gains no scrap value; abnormal losses with a scrap value; different degrees of completion; beginning and ending work in progress

Joint and by-product costing

– allocation of costs using: physical measures; sales value at split off point; net realisable value method

Lecturers are invited to write to the author if they would wish to see specific techniques or topics developed in more depth on this site.

ACKNOWLEDGEMENTS

My thanks to my family and colleagues who have helped in the writing of this book. To my family, Janet, Gareth, Philip and Sally, who between them read the first draft of the book. To my colleagues at the University of Portsmouth, especially those who made the mistake of calling in at my room at the wrong time and found that they were walking out with a chapter for review. Even more so to those who made the mistake a second time.

Thanks go to Gerry Banks, Clare Callaghan, Richard Christie, Lynne Conrad, Arief Daynes, Sue Davey-Evans, Chris Fill, Alan Graham, Robert Major, Richard Noble, Doug Richardson, Rob Thomas, Richard Tonge, Richard Trafford, Caroline Willett and Michael Wood. Thanks also to Bill Lee of the University of Sheffield (chapter 9 in particular, drew on articles that we have written together in the area of control in manufacturing organisations) and to the external reviewers of the initial chapters of the book. The advice I received from everyone has been invaluable and any errors of the book remain mine. Further thanks to Adrian Williams of Pashley Cycles and last but not least to Steve Hardman, Emma Cooper, Vidya Vijayan and all the team at John Wiley & Sons for their help and support.

PART 1

INFORMATION FOR DECISION-MAKING AND FINANCIAL REPORTING REQUIREMENTS

This section of the book considers the use of financial information for the evaluation of a number of typical planning and short-term decision-making problems.

Chapter 1 explains the need to analyse costs in terms of cost behaviour and the importance of cost–volume–profit analysis for decision-making.

In Chapter 2, the focus moves to a consideration of the pricing of goods and services. Traditional approaches to pricing placed emphasis on identifying the cost of a product or service and adding a mark-up to allow for profit. A key disadvantage with this approach is that many organizations operate in a highly competitive environment and the cost plus approach ignores a number of significant issues. A range of alternative approaches that take into consideration the competitive environment are therefore also explained in this chapter.

Chapter 3 considers a range of decisions that are typically faced by organizations. For example, whether to drop a product or service from the mix of products sold by an organization; assessing the return from different marketing plans; assessing whether to make or buy a product; identifying the optimum production plan given specific constraints. The importance of identifying relevant costs in order to evaluate these decisions is explained and illustrated.

In order to survive and grow, organizations often need to invest in new projects that will have an impact on the business over a number of years. Chapter 4 is concerned with the financial evaluation of capital investment decisions.

Chapter 5 considers traditional approaches to identifying the 'full' cost of a product or service, i.e. a cost which includes a proportion of overhead cost. As well as for pricing, full cost information is required for financial accounting reasons in order to value stock and determine profit.

A criticism of the traditional approaches to costing that are covered in Chapter 5 is that the overhead cost is assigned to products and services on an arbitrary basis that does not reflect the extent to which they consume resources. Chapter 6 explains the approach of activity-based costing, which does attempt to more accurately allocate costs using cause and effect relationships.

COST BEHAVIOUR AND CONTRIBUTION

Objectives

When you have completed this chapter you should be able to:

- Describe different types of cost behaviour, including fixed and variable costs.
- Explain and undertake key aspects of cost–volume–profit (CVP) analysis, including:

  - Contribution analysis and how to prepare a contribution statement.
  - Break-even analysis, including the preparation of a break-even chart and calculation of the break-even point.
  - Operating gearing and its relevance to decision-making.

- Describe the assumptions that underpin cost–volume–profit analysis.

Introduction

Organizations are interested in planning for the future and understanding how revenue and costs will change when different decisions are made. Cost–volume–profit analysis examines the relationship between volume of activity, revenue, costs and profits.

The classification of costs into fixed and variable costs is discussed in the first part of the chapter. Essentially, variable costs are those that vary according to the volume of activity. The concept of contribution (revenue minus variable cost) and the preparation of a contribution statement are then explained. Break-even analysis is also discussed, and this is demonstrated by both a graphical approach and a mathematical method for calculation.

Another type of decision in a firm concerns the scale of investment in fixed costs that will be undertaken. For example, is it better to employ expensive machinery to manufacture a product, which will involve high fixed costs, or to use lower technology, which will require less expenditure on fixed costs, but higher variable costs? Operating gearing concerns the relationship between total fixed costs and total variable costs.

In the final part of the chapter, the assumptions of cost–volume–profit analysis are reviewed. It is important to realize that the classification of costs into fixed and variable costs may be too simplistic in many organizations; for example, step fixed costs and semi-variable costs may also exist.

Cost behaviour

In order to plan for the future, it is important to understand how costs will change given different decisions made by an organization. A common method of classification is according to whether costs are variable or fixed.

Variable costs

Variable costs are those that change in relation to the level of activity. Variable cost information for the manufacture of a single size of metal tube is provided in Figure 1.1.

Sherman Ltd manufactures a single type of metal tube that would be used in the production of bicycle frames.[1] The cost information is as follows:

1. The material cost of the metal tube is calculated at £5.
2. The work force is paid £1 to manufacture each metal tube.

Figure 1.1 Variable costs of manufacturing metal tubes

Examining the scenario in Figure 1.1, if one unit of metal tube is manufactured, the material cost is £5. Each metal tube requires material and if two tubes are manufactured, then the total material cost will be £10 and so on. In this example, the labour cost is also a variable cost as workers are paid £1 for every tube that is manufactured. These are the only costs that increase as output increases, so the total variable costs are £6 per unit (£5 per unit for the material and £1 per unit for the labour). See Figure 1.2, which illustrates graphically the manner in which total variable costs vary in relation to output of metal tubes.

---

[1] For a number of the examples in this book we will use, as illustration, companies related to the manufacture of bicycles and bicycle frames. The web site for this book has reference to web sites that will describe in more detail the manufacturing process for bicycle frames. At its simplest, a bicycle frame can be considered to consist of a number of metal tubes, which are cut to size, bent and welded together.

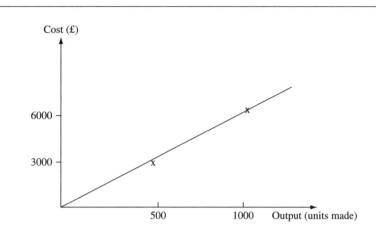

The variable costs are £6 per unit. The table below identifies the material, labour and total variable cost at different levels of activity. For example, for 500 units, the variable cost will be 500 units multiplied by £6 a unit = £3000.

	1 unit	100 units	500 units	1000 units
	(£)	(£)	(£)	(£)
Material	5	500	2500	5000
Labour	1	100	500	1000
Total variable costs	6	600	3000	6000

Figure 1.2   Variable costs

Activity 1.1

(a) Calculate the total variable cost for 600 units.
(b) Calculate the total variable cost for 900 units.

Fixed costs

A **fixed cost** does not vary with the output level. For example, cost of rent for premises, lease payment on equipment and items such as rates and standing charges on utilities have to be paid regularly regardless of the activity being carried out within the business. In Sherman Ltd, to manufacture the metal tubes, it has also been necessary to lease a machine at £1200 per month. Other costs are also £800 per month and these must be paid whether or not components are made. This gives a total cost of £2000 per month that must be paid each month. See Figure 1.3, which plots fixed costs in relation to output.

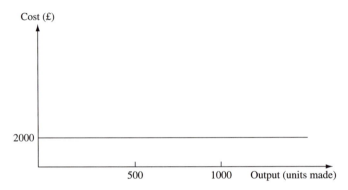

Whether 1 unit, 500 units or 1000 units are made, the cost of the lease of the machine, rent of the building and other costs remains constant at £2000.

Figure 1.3   Fixed costs

Total cost

For Sherman Ltd, it is possible to identify the total cost by adding the variable costs to the fixed costs. This is demonstrated in Figure 1.4.

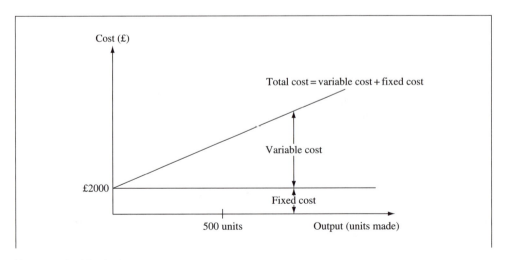

Figure 1.4   Total costs

	1 unit (£)	100 units (£)	500 units (£)	1000 units (£)
Material	5	500	2500	5000
Labour	1	100	500	1000
Total variable costs	6	600	3000	6000
Fixed cost	2000	2000	2000	2000
Total cost	2006	2600	5000	8000

The total cost = variable cost + fixed cost.
So for 500 units:
Total cost = variable cost (500 units × £6 per unit = £3000) + fixed costs of £2000
= £5000

Figure 1.4 (*Continued*)

Contribution and the contribution statement

Cost–volume–profit (CVP) analysis is based on the relationship between sales volume (in units) and sales revenue, costs and profit. Once an organization has identified its variable and fixed costs, given the knowledge of its revenue at different levels of sales, it is also possible to calculate the profit at these different levels. Table 1.1 shows the total revenue, variable and fixed costs and profit or loss given different sales of 1, 500, 1000 and 1500 units sold.

Table 1.1 Revenue, cost and profit statement for Sherman Ltd

	1 unit (£)	500 units (£)	1000 units (£)	1500 units (£)
Total sales revenue	8	4,000	8,000	12,000
Variable cost	6	3,000	6,000	9,000
Fixed cost	2,000	2,000	2,000	2,000
Total cost	2,006	5,000	8,000	11,000
Profit/(loss)	(1,998)	(1,000)	0	1,000

Note that if a loss is made this is shown in brackets.
Profit = total sales revenue – total cost
Total sales revenue = sales price per unit multiplied by number of units sold
Total cost = variable cost plus fixed costs
Variable cost = variable cost per unit multiplied by number of units sold

Activity 1.2

Prepare a profit statement for Sherman Ltd if:

(a) 600 units are sold.
(b) 900 units are sold.

Rather than showing information in tables, many managers like to view information in a graphical format. An example is the profit/loss chart shown in Figure 1.5, which shows the profit or loss generated at different levels of output.

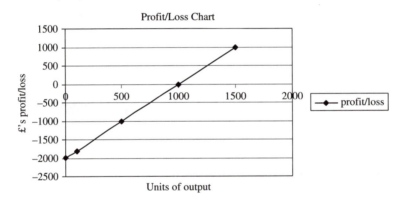

Figure 1.5   Profit/loss chart for Sherman Ltd

Table 1.1 and Figure 1.5 have been helpful in identifying the profit and loss at various levels of activity. For example, it is possible to see that at 1000 units of output the company is in a break-even situation, i.e. total costs are equal to the revenue. Above 1000 units a profit is made and below 1000 units there will be a loss.

The contribution statement

In order to more clearly identify the impact of changes in volume on costs and profits, it is usually considered helpful to produce a contribution statement as well as a profit statement. **Total contribution** is defined as the total sales revenue less total variable costs. The **contribution per unit** is the sales revenue per unit – the variable cost per unit.

The format of a contribution statement is as follows:

Total sales revenue
Less   variable costs
= contribution

Less   fixed cost
= Net Profit

The contribution statement shows the contribution that is made after variable costs are deducted from sales. Fixed costs are then deducted from the contribution to show the net profit or loss that is generated. A contribution statement for Sherman Ltd is shown in Table 1.2. This highlights that the break-even point occurs at 1000 units, with profits generated above that point.

Table 1.2   Contribution statement for Sherman Ltd

	1 unit (£)	500 units (£)	1000 units (£)	1500 units (£)
Total sales revenue	8	4,000	8,000	12,000
Variable cost	6	3,000	6,000	9,000
Contribution	2	1,000	2,000	3,000
Fixed cost	2,000	2,000	2,000	2,000
Profit/(loss)	(1,998)	(1,000)	–	1,000

Activity 1.3

Prepare a contribution statement for Sherman Ltd if:

(a) 900 units are produced.
(b) 1200 units are produced.

Break-even analysis

Break-even analysis is a business tool that can help to identify at what activity level the business will move from making a loss to a profit. The moment that this happens is known as the **break-even point**.

The break-even chart provides more information than the profit volume chart, by identifying revenue, fixed costs and variable costs at different volumes of output and sales. The charts also highlight the break-even point. See Figure 1.6.

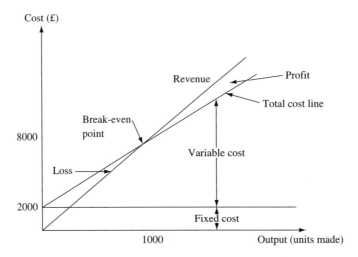

From the graph it can be seen that the break-even point is at 1000 units. Below 1000 units, the business will make a loss. Above 1000 units, the business will make a profit.

Figure 1.6   Break-even chart

An alternative chart that is sometimes used is known as the contribution chart. The difference from the break-even chart is that the variable cost line is drawn first and then the fixed cost line is added. See Figure 1.7.

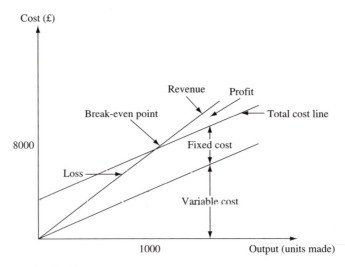

Figure 1.7   Contribution chart

Calculating the break-even point

The break-even point can also be calculated using the contribution approach. For the worked example above, the contribution earned for every unit sold would be:

		£
	Selling price per unit	8
Less	Variable cost per unit	6
	Contribution per unit	2

The revenue increases by £8 for every extra unit sold while costs increase by £6 if one additional unit is made. Therefore the net effect on the business of making and selling an additional unit is £2. This additional £2 is called the contribution per unit (selling price per unit – variable cost per unit).

Given the contribution per unit, it is possible to identify the number of units needed to cover the fixed overheads of the business. If every unit sold provides a contribution of £2 and if the fixed overheads are £2000, then 1000 units need to be sold to make a contribution of £2000.

The break-even point can be calculated using the formula:

$$\text{BEP} = \frac{\text{Fixed cost}}{\text{Contribution per unit}} = \frac{£2000}{£2} = 1000 \text{ units}$$

To see how the formula is derived, see the explanation in Figure 1.8.

Profit = total sales revenue – total costs
i.e. Profit = sales price per unit × number of units sold – (fixed costs + variable cost per unit × number of units sold)

Note that this calculation can be expressed as a mathematical equation:

i.e. $\text{Profit} = PX - (a + bX)$

where

P = sales price per unit
X = number of units sold
a = fixed cost
b = variable cost per unit

The break-even point occurs when there is no profit:

$$0 = PX - (a + bX) = PX - a - bX$$

This formula can be rearranged as:

$$a = PX - bX \quad \text{or} \quad a = (P - b)X$$

This formula in turn can be rearranged as:

$$X = \frac{a}{(P - b)}$$

i.e.

$$\text{Break-even point} = \frac{\text{Fixed cost}}{(\text{Sales revenue per unit} - \text{variable cost per unit})}$$

Figure 1.8   Deriving the formula to calculate the break-even point

---

Activity 1.4

Assume that a company sells a product with a variable cost of £6. The product can be sold for £12 and the fixed costs are £3000.

(a) How many products need to be sold in order that the break-even point is reached?
(b) If the price went up to £14 and fixed costs increased to £4000, what would be the new break-even point?

Calculating the sales to earn a set profit

If Sherman Ltd wanted to earn a profit of £1000 a month then it would be necessary to sell enough units to make a contribution that would cover the overheads and earn a further £1000.

Units to be sold to make £1000 profit =

$$\frac{\text{Fixed cost} + \text{target profit}}{\text{Contribution per unit}} = \frac{(£2000 + £1000)}{£2} = 1500 \text{ units}$$

Activity 1.5

(a) How many units would need to be sold to generate a profit of £1500?
(b) How many units would need to be sold to generate a profit of £3000?

Calculating the margin of safety

The **margin of safety** is the extent to which sales are above the break-even point. For Sherman Ltd, the break-even point is 1000 units. If actual units sold were 1500, then there would be a margin of safety of 500 units. This means that sales can fall by up to 500 units before the organization would incur a loss. For an organization it would generally be considered that the larger the margin of safety, the better!

The margin of safety is also often expressed as a percentage of expected sales, and the calculation of the margin of safety for Sherman Ltd is shown in Figure 1.9.

To calculate the expected margin of safety it is necessary to identify the expected sales and the break-even sales. For Sherman Ltd:

Expected sales in units – break-even sales in units = Margin of safety (units)

1500–1000 = 500 units.

The margin of safety is often expressed as a percentage of expected sales:

$$\text{Percentage margin of safety} = \frac{\text{Expected sales units} - \text{break-even sales units}}{\text{Expected sales units}} \times 100\%$$

So for Sherman Ltd

$$\text{At 1500 units} = \frac{1500 - 1000}{1500} = 33\%$$

This means that sales could fall by up to 33% before a loss was experienced.

Figure 1.9 Calculation of margin of safety of Sherman Ltd

Activity 1.6

The break-even point for an organization is 1200 units.

(a) Calculate the percentage margin of safety if the expected sales are 2000.
(b) Calculate the percentage margin of safety if the expected sales are 3000.

An example of an organization that failed to sell a sufficient volume of its product is discussed in Figure 1.10.

In July 2006, *The Sportsman*, the first national daily newspaper to be launched for two decades, fell into administration.

When *The Sportsman* was launched at the beginning of 2006, its backers said that the paper would appeal to a new generation of sports and poker players, as well as traditional horseracing fans. The paper indicated that it needed to sell 40,000 copies to break even.

The paper initially sold 65,000 copies, however by May 2006 the average daily sale was 12,762.

Figure 1.10 Launch of *The Sportsman* newspaper
Source: *The Times*, 21 July 2006.

In the case of *The Sportsman* newspaper initial sales were 65,000 units. Since only 40,000 units were required to break even, the management may have felt some confidence that they could compete on a profitable basis, because sales would have to fall by 25,000 before a loss situation would occur. Unfortunately, this margin of safety was only temporary and when sales fell to about 13,000 units, the administrators were called in.

Operating gearing

Often an organization has a choice on whether to invest heavily in fixed costs and incur lower variable costs per unit, or to invest less in fixed costs and incur higher variable costs per unit. **Operational gearing** is the relationship between fixed and variable costs.

Organizations which are capital-intensive and where fixed costs are high as a proportion of total costs are considered to have high operational gearing. Organizations where fixed costs are low as a proportion of total costs have low operational gearing. Consider the example in Figure 1.11.

The lease of the machine that is involved in the manufacture of metal bicycle tubes is up for renewal. It is possible to manufacture bicycle tubes by using a labour-intensive process and this would avoid the cost of leasing the machine. The labour cost per tube would, however, rise to £2 per unit. The management of Sherman Ltd are considering which process to adopt.

The total cost of each process can be calculated at different volumes.

With the machine (higher operational gearing)

	1 unit (£)	500 units (£)	1000 units (£)	1500 units (£)
Sales	8	4,000	8,000	12,000
Variable cost	6	3,000	6,000	9,000
Contribution	2	1,000	2,000	3,000
Fixed cost	2,000	2,000	2,000	2,000
Profit/(loss)	(1,998)	(1,000)	–	1,000

Without the machine (lower operational gearing)

	1 unit (£)	500 units (£)	1000 units (£)	1500 units (£)
Sales	8	4,000	8,000	12,000
Variable cost	7	3,500	7,000	10,500
Contribution	1	500	1,000	1,500
Fixed cost	800	800	800	800
Profit/(loss)	(799)	(300)	200	700

Figure 1.11   Profit/(Loss) given different operating gearing

With the lease of the machine Sherman Ltd becomes more highly geared. This means that at low volumes of sales, e.g. under about 1000 units, larger losses are incurred than would be the case without the machine. At 500 units, for example, the loss with the machine is £1000, while without the machine the loss is £300.

At 1000 units, a profit of £200 per month would be generated if no machine was leased, while with the leased machine, the company is only in a break-even situation.

At a production level of 1500 units, the company is generating a profit of £1000 with the machine, while it would only be £700 without the machine.

In deciding whether to lease the machine or not, the company needs to consider the likely level of sales. If there is a significant chance that sales will fall to low levels, then it might be best to keep a low operational gearing, even though this will mean a higher level of variable costs.

Figure 1.11 (*Continued*)

In recent years a number of organizations have adopted a policy of low gearing to limit the potential losses, if sales fall. For example, rather than employing full-time training staff, they might buy in training staff when required and pay them a daily rate for their work.

Activity 1.7

An organization is considering alternative policies for the future. It can sell a product for £20 and is not sure whether to invest heavily in new technology or to choose a less capital-intensive option.

(a) If it invests in the heavily capital-intensive option, the fixed costs per month will be £5000 and the variable cost per unit will be £8.
(b) If it invests in the less capital-intensive option, the fixed costs per month will be £2000 and the variable cost per unit will be £12.

Advise the company on the circumstances in which each option should be chosen.

Activity 1.8

AB Ltd currently employs three full-time trainers who earn £35,000 each. Overheads involved with the training department are £50,000 per year. It currently runs 300 training days of courses a year and is considering whether to subcontract the training to freelance trainers. It would have to pay these trainers £400 per day. Overheads would reduce to £30,000 if outside trainers were employed. Advise the company on what it should do.

Assumptions of break-even analysis

It is vital that the individual preparing or interpreting information on costs and revenue is aware of the assumptions that have been made, otherwise errors can occur. Assumptions in CVP analysis that need to be tested include:

1. Fixed costs will stay the same for any given level of output.
   In the example of Sherman Ltd, it has been assumed that the fixed costs will be £2000 whether one metal bicycle tube is manufactured or 1500 units are manufactured.
2. The sales price is constant whatever the sales volume.
3. The variable cost per unit is constant whatever the level of output.
4. Costs can be accurately divided into fixed or variable elements.

Considering these assumptions in more detail

(1) Fixed costs will stay the same whatever the level of output

In many instances this is unlikely to be the case. Fixed costs may only be fixed within a certain level of activity and beyond that level, fixed costs will need to increase; these are **step-fixed costs**. For example, it might be that Sherman Ltd can make 1500 units of output in its current premises, with the existing machine. Above that production level, it might be necessary to lease an additional machine and rent additional floor space at an additional cost of £1500 per month, as illustrated in Figure 1.12.

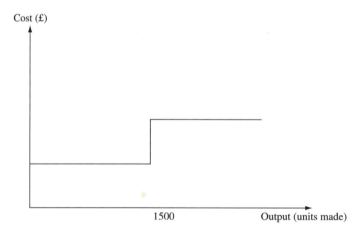

Figure 1.12   Step-fixed costs

Given this knowledge of step-fixed costs, it is possible to produce a revised contribution table for Sherman Ltd to cover a larger range of output. See Table 1.3.

Table 1.3   Contribution statement for 1 unit, 1500 units, 1750 units and 2500 units sold

	1 unit (£)	1000 units (£)	1500 units (£)	1750 units (£)	2250 units (£)
Sales	8	8,000	12,000	14,000	18,000
Variable cost	6	6,000	9,000	10,500	13,500
Contribution	2	2,000	3,000	3,500	4,500
Fixed cost	2,000	2,000	2,000	3,500	3,500
Profit/(loss)	(1,998)	–	1,000	–	1,000

An analysis of this table reveals that there are two break-even points. If production of bicycle tubes goes above 1500 units a week, then the increase in fixed costs of £1500 will mean that the company must achieve sales of 2250 units before the same profit is generated from sales as is achieved at 1500 units.

A break-even chart can also be produced for Sherman Ltd, which will reflect the revenue, costs and profit for a range in output from 0 to 3000 units. This is illustrated in Figure 1.13.

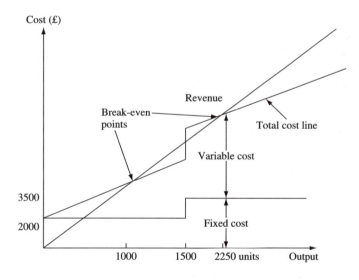

This chart indicates the two break-even points, the first when sales are 1000 units and the second at sales of 1750 units.

Figure 1.13   Break-even chart

The term 'relevant range' is used to indicate the range over which cost and revenue assumptions are valid. For example, the assumption is made in the break-even chart for Sherman Ltd that up to 3000 units, the increase in variable costs is linear, i.e. it increases by £6 per unit whether 1 unit is made or 3000 units are made. Fixed costs are assumed to increase only once at 1500 units. If above 3000 units these assumptions are no longer valid, then the relevant range for this analysis is between 0 and 3000 units.

(2) The sales price per unit is constant, whatever the sales volume

In the example of Sherman Ltd, it is assumed that the sales price per unit remains at £8 per unit, whatever the level of activity. To achieve a volume greater than 1500 units it might be necessary to discount this price. This is discussed further in Chapter 2, when demand-based pricing is considered.

(3) The variable cost per unit is constant, whatever the volume of output

(a) The variable costs per unit might change. For example, if the company purchases additional raw material, it may be possible to arrange additional discounts to allow for bulk buying. At higher levels of output, it might be possible to achieve a lower variable labour cost per unit, for example due to efficiency improvements. Alternatively, it could be necessary to work overtime, which would mean that variable labour cost per unit would increase.

Figure 1.14 demonstrates a graph showing the marginal cost per unit decreasing at higher volumes for 'company X'.

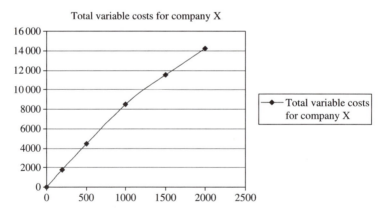

In the above diagram it can be seen that the increase in the marginal cost for an organization is not linear, since at higher volumes it has been possible to achieve cost savings per unit.

Figure 1.14   Total variable costs assuming efficiency improvements

(b) Some costs may change in proportion to an activity other than output. For example, costs of purchasing might change in proportion to the number of purchase orders raised rather than the number of units produced. Dealing with this problem will be considered in more detail in Chapter 6.

(c) A company is likely to produce a number of products, which earn different contributions. If the sales mix of the company changes, then this is likely to change the average cost, sales value and contribution per unit sold. This is illustrated in Figure 1.15.

Demand for the metal tube size 1 has fallen to 500 units per month and Sherman Ltd is considering manufacturing a second size of tube that can be sold for £10.50. It is estimated that 500 size 2 tubes could also be sold per month.

Cost information for tube size 2 is as follows:
1. Material cost per tube is £6.
2. Labour cost per tube is £1.50. (The tube takes 15 minutes to manufacture.)
3. Fixed overheads at the factory remain at £2000 per month.

The management of Sherman Ltd wish to know the impact on their profits of making this decision.

The contribution for 500 units for metal tube size 1 is:

	500 units (£)
Sales	4000
Variable cost	3000
Contribution	1000

The variable cost for metal tube size 2 is £7.50 (material of £6 and labour of £1.50). Also given a selling price of £10.50 per tube, the contribution for 500 tubes is:

	500 units (£)
Sales	5250
Variable cost	3750
Contribution	1500

The analysis below shows the contribution that is earned from both the sale of 500 units of size 1 tubes and 500 units of size 2. A total contribution can then be calculated.

If fixed costs are deducted from the total contribution this will give the net profit.

	Tube size 1 500 units (£)	Tube size 2 500 units (£)	Total (£)
Sales	4000	5250	9250
Variable cost	3000	3750	6750
Contribution	1000	1500	2500
Fixed cost			2000
Profit/(loss)			500

It is possible to tell the management of Sherman Ltd that tube size 1 makes a contribution of £1000 to overheads, while tube size 2 makes a contribution of £1500. Both therefore make a positive contribution to overheads.

The contribution of tube size 1 is £2 per unit and the contribution of tube size 2 is £3 per unit.

If equal numbers of both products are sold then the average contribution per unit sold would be £2 × 50% + £3 × 50% = £2.50 and the break-even point at low volumes would be £2000/£2.50 = 800 units.

If the proportion of each product changes then so will the average contribution per unit and the number of units required to break even. For example, assume that the sales mix changes so that 75% of units sold are of type tube size 1, which earn a contribution of £2 and 25% are of tube size 2, which earn a contribution of £3. Then the average contribution sold would

Figure 1.15   Break-even point given multiple products

be £2 × 75% + £3 × 25% = £1.5 + £0.75 = £2.25. To break even it would be necessary to sell £2000/£2.25 = 889 units. On the other hand, if more of the units that earn a contribution of £3 per unit were sold, the average contribution per unit would increase and the number of units that need to be sold to break even would reduce.

Note the cost assumptions:
1. That fixed costs will not change, with the increased complexity of making two products.
2. That variable costs and revenue are constant per unit of output.

Figure 1.15 (*Continued*)

Activity 1.9

What is the average contribution per unit and how many units need to be sold to cover fixed costs of £2000 if:

(a) 60% of units made and sold are of type tube size 2, earning a contribution of £3 and 40% are of type tube size 1, earning a contribution of £2.
(b) 45% of units made and sold are of type tube size 2, earning a contribution of £3 and 55% are of type tube size 1, earning a contribution of £2.
(c) Other variables change, e.g. production efficiency and production methods, which in turn may cause a change in the variable costs per unit.

(4) Costs can be accurately divided into fixed or variable elements

This is not always the case as costs can change in more complex ways. A number of costs also have both a fixed and a variable element and are **semi-variable costs**, as illustrated in Figure 1.16. An example is the electricity charge paid by many people.

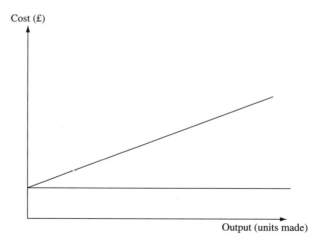

Figure 1.16 A semi-variable cost

Summary

Fixed costs are those that do not change in relation to changes in output. Variable costs vary directly in proportion to output.

Cost–volume–profit analysis is concerned with identifying the changes in cost and revenue at different levels of output.

Contribution is revenue minus variable costs and a contribution statement shows the contribution generated from sales for a particular product or organization before deducting fixed costs.

A break-even chart illustrates the loss or profit earned at different levels of activity and the point at which costs equal revenue, i.e. the break-even point. The break-even point as well as margin of safety and sales required to generate a certain level of profit can also be calculated.

Low operating gearing occurs where fixed costs form a low proportion of the total costs of a firm. If there is a significant chance that sales will fall to low levels, then it will be easier for a firm to reduce costs if it has low operational gearing. However, if sales are high then profits are likely to be less than for a firm with high operational gearing.

Cost behaviour and contribution analysis is only valid given the validity of the assumptions on which the calculations are based. It is not always possible to classify costs as purely fixed or variable. Fixed costs for example may only be fixed within a certain level of activity and beyond this level an increase is required (a step fixed cost), while other costs may have a fixed and a variable element (a semi-variable cost).

Answers to activities

Activity 1.1

	600 units (£)	900 units (£)
Total variable costs	3600	5400

Activity 1.2

	600 units (£)	900 units (£)
Sales	4800	7200
Variable cost	3600	5400
Fixed cost	2000	2000
Total cost	5600	7400
Profit/(loss)	(800)	(200)

Activity 1.3

	900 units (£)	1200 units (£)
Sales	7200	9600
Variable cost	5400	7200
Contribution	1800	2400
Fixed cost	2000	2000
Profit/(loss)	(200)	400

Activity 1.4

(a) The contribution per unit is £12 − £6 = £6.
The break-even point = £3000/6 = 500 units
(b) The contribution per unit is £14 −£6 = £8.
The break-even point = £4000/8=500 units

Activity 1.5

$$\frac{\text{Fixed cost} + \text{target profit}}{\text{Contribution per unit}} = (\pounds 2000 + \pounds 3000)/\pounds 2 = 1750 \text{ units}$$

$$\frac{\text{Fixed cost} + \text{target profit}}{\text{Contribution per unit}} = (\pounds 2000 + \pounds 3000)/\pounds 2 = 2500 \text{ units}$$

Activity 1.6

$$\text{Percentage margin of safety} = \frac{\text{Expected sales} - \text{break-even sales}}{\text{Expected sales}} \times 100\%$$

(a) $\dfrac{2000 - 1200}{2000} \times 100\% = 40\%$

(b) $\dfrac{3000 - 1200}{3000} \times 100\% = 60\%$

Activity 1.7

Option (a)

$$\text{Break-even point} = \frac{\text{Fixed cost}}{\text{Contribution per unit}} = \frac{\pounds 5000}{\pounds 12} = 417 \text{ units}$$

With the new technology

	1 unit (£)	250 units (£)	500 units (£)	750 units (£)	1000 units (£)
Sales	20	5,000	10,000	15,000	20,000
Variable cost	8	2,000	4,000	6,000	8,000
Contribution	12	3,000	6,000	9,000	12,000
Fixed cost	5,000	5,000	5,000	5,000	5,000
Profit/(loss)	(4,988)	(2,000)	1,000	4,000	7,000

Option (b)

$$\text{Break-even point} = \frac{\text{Fixed cost}}{\text{Contribution per unit}} = \frac{£2000}{£8} = 250 \text{ units}$$

With the less capital intensive option

	1 unit (£)	250 units (£)	500 units (£)	750 units (£)	1000 units (£)
Sales	20	5,000	10,000	15,000	20,000
Variable cost	12	3,000	6,000	9,000	12,000
Contribution	8	2,000	4,000	6,000	8,000
Fixed cost	2,000	2,000	2,000	2,000	2,000
Profit/(loss)	(1,992)	–	2,000	4,000	6,000

The two projects generate the same return at 750 units. Below that level, option (b) is more profitable/has a lower break-even point. Above 750 units, option (a) is more profitable. The management of the company need to consider the likelihood of sales being above or below 750 units.

Activity 1.8

Three full-time trainers at £35,000 = £105,000

	Overheads	£50,000
	Total costs	£155,000

300 training days at £400 per day = £120,000

	Overheads	£30,000
		£150,000

It seems that it is £5000 cheaper to subcontract the training to outside trainers.

The assumption on the expected number of training days should be checked. If the days required increases above 306, then it may be worthwhile continuing with the existing three trainers. Cost assumptions need to be checked, including the impact on overheads and possible costs of redundancy.

Non-financial factors should also be considered; for example, are the outside trainers of equal quality to the internal staff and will the organization be losing a resource that does more than just provide the 300 training days.

Activity 1.9

(a) $£3 \times 60\% + £2 \times 40\% = £1.80 + £0.80 = £2.60$. To break even it would be necessary to sell $£2000/£2.60 = 770$ units.
(b) $£3 \times 45\% + £2 \times 55\% = £1.35 + £1.10 = £2.45$. To break even it would be necessary to sell $£2000/£2.45 = 817$ units.

Discussion questions

1. What information does a break-even chart show?
2. Explain the difference between profit and contribution.
3. Explain the following terms:

   Relevant range
   Operating gearing
   Margin of safety.

4. In what circumstances might a break-even chart provide misleading information?
5. Why might an understanding of the margin of safety be of interest to managers?
6. What is the difference between a profit–volume chart and a break-even chart?
7. When deciding to start a business, why might it be important to take into consideration the proposed operating gearing?

Exercises

(Questions in bold have answers at the back of the book.)

Q1.1 Read the following descriptions and match the description with the graphs shown beneath.

  (i) Rent on a factory is £2000 per month.
 (ii) An additional supervisor is needed for every 1000 units produced.
(iii) A telephone bill consists of a standing charge of £10 per month and then a charge per minute.

(iv) A supplier charges £25 per kg of raw material for the first 1000 kgs, then £18 per kg for the next 1000 kgs and £16 per kg for all kgs ordered over 2000.

(v) Material costs of a product are £5 per unit.

(vi) Labourers are paid a flat wage for the first 2000 units that they work. For all units over that volume they are paid a bonus of £1 per unit.

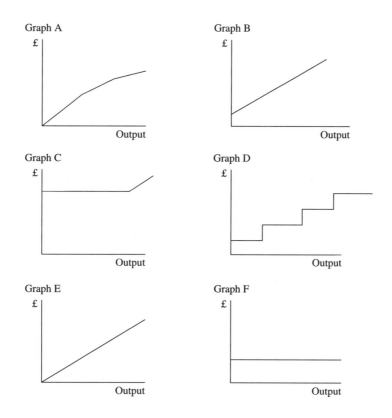

Q1.2 A company produces a single product – the Widget.

Selling price is £15 per unit.

Variable costs are £10.

Fixed costs are £40,000 a month.

Expected sales are 10,000 units per month. Maximum capacity is 12,000 units.

Required:

1. Draw a break-even chart, showing the break-even point.
2. Calculate the break-even point and the margin of safety if expected sales are achieved.

Q1.3 The company in Question 1.2 above is considering introducing a second product – the Didget. Anticipated selling price and costs are as follows. Selling price is £20 per unit, variable costs £14 and fixed costs will remain at £40,000. It is expected that sales of the Didget will be 2000 units per month. Sales of the Widget will, however, reduce to 9000 units.

Required:

Calculate the break-even point given this product mix and the margin of safety.

Q1.4 Company X expects to sell 1500 shirts a month at £10 per shirt. The purchase price is £5 and overheads are £5000 a month.

Required:

(i) How many shirts are needed to break even and what is the margin of safety?
(ii) How many shirts does the company need to sell to make a profit of £2000 per month?
(iii) The marketing manager suggests that the price per shirt be reduced to £9. He believes that this will result in an additional 400 shirts being sold. Is the marketing manager correct in believing that the sales price reduction would be worthwhile?

Q1.5 Company Y expects to sell 12,000 shirts a month at £22 per shirt. The purchase price is £13 per shirt and overheads are £60,000 a month.

Required:

(i) How many shirts need to be sold to break even and what is the margin of safety given the existing level of sales?
(ii) How many shirts does the company need to sell to make a profit of £20,000 per month?
(iii) The sales manager suggests that the price per shirt be reduced to £19.50. He believes that this action will result in an additional 2000 shirts being sold. Advise whether this would be a worthwhile initiative.

Q1.6 Apple Ltd produces a single product – the 'Peardrop'.

The selling price of a Peardrop is £20 per unit.
The Peardrop can be made using a manual process or using machinery.
If made manually:

The variable cost per unit will be £13 and the fixed costs will be £40,000 per month.

If the machinery is leased:

The variable cost per unit will fall to £10 per unit, but fixed costs will increase to £60,000 per month.

Expected sales are 10,000 units per month. Maximum capacity with both processes is 12,000 units.

Required:

(i) Calculate the likely contribution if the Peardrop is made manually and if the machinery is leased.
(ii) Identify the break-even point and margin of safety given both options.
(iii) Would you advise the management of Apple Ltd to lease the machinery or to continue to use the manually intensive process?

PRICING AND COSTING IN A COMPETITIVE ENVIRONMENT

2

Objectives

When you have completed this chapter you should be able to:

- Calculate a selling price using a traditional full cost-based approach.
- Explain the deficiencies of a traditional cost-based approach to pricing.
- Describe the approach and calculate the selling price given alternative methods of pricing that take into consideration market factors, including:

  - The contribution approach.
  - Demand-based pricing.
  - Target costing.
  - Pricing strategies.
  - The product lifecycle and pricing.

- Describe lifecycle costing.

Introduction

A traditional method of pricing used by organizations is to identify the full cost per unit and then add a mark-up on this cost to allow for profit. In the first part of the chapter, the full cost method is explained along with potential deficiencies of this approach.

A key weakness of the full cost plus mark-up approach is that it takes inadequate account of market conditions. The second part of the chapter considers alternative approaches that do take these into consideration. These include:

- Accepting prices that generate a contribution to overheads.
- Taking account of the demand curve for the product or service and by doing so, identifying the price at which profits are maximized.

- Identifying the market price at which it is likely that the product can be sold. By deducting a target profit margin from this price, a target cost can be identified.
- Pricing strategies for new products, including penetration pricing or price skimming and for existing products including price leader, price taker or predatory pricing.
- Pricing policies at different stages of the lifecycle of a product.

In the final section of the chapter, lifecycle costing is reviewed. Product-related costs can change substantially throughout the life of a product, and the importance of this for planning and accounting for costs is discussed.

Identify the full cost per unit of a product or service

Identifying the full cost per unit

In the previous chapter, Figure 1.4 showed total costs for Sherman Ltd given different volumes of production. This was for a company where material costs were £5 per unit, labour cost was £1 per unit and fixed costs were £2000. This information is recreated in Table 2.1.

Table 2.1 Total costs of bicycle tubes at different levels of output

	1 unit (£)	100 units (£)	500 units (£)	1000 units (£)
Material	5	500	2500	5000
Labour	1	100	500	1000
Total variable costs	6	600	3000	6000
Fixed cost	2000	2000	2000	2000
Total cost	2006	2600	5000	8000

The total variable costs can be seen to increase as the volume of production increases. The total fixed costs, however, remain the same. The **total** or **full cost per unit** is the variable cost per unit plus the fixed cost per unit at a given level of output. At different levels of output the fixed cost per unit and therefore the full cost per unit will change. This is illustrated in Table 2.2.

From Table 2.2 it can be seen that the variable cost per unit remains constant, whatever the level of activity, while the fixed cost per unit reduces as the fixed costs are shared across more units. The manner in which fixed cost per unit declines is illustrated in Figure 2.1.

Table 2.2   Cost of a single bicycle tube at different levels of activity

	1 unit (£)	100 units (£)	500 units (£)	1000 units (£)	1500 units (£)
(1) Material cost per unit	5	5	5	5	5
(2) Labour cost per unit	1	1	1	1	1
(3) Total variable cost per unit (note 1)	6	6	6	6	6
(4) Fixed cost per unit (note 2)	2000	20	4	2	1.33
(5) Full or total cost per unit (note 3)	2006	26	10	8	7.33

Note 1. Total variable cost per unit = material cost per unit + labour cost per unit.
Note 2. Fixed cost per unit = fixed cost divided by the number of units manufactured.
Note 3. Full or total cost per unit = variable cost per unit + fixed cost per unit.

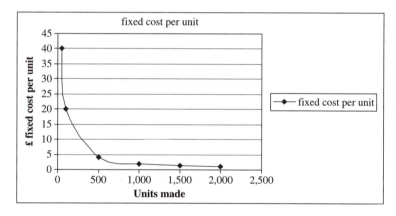

Figure 2.1   Graph of the fixed cost per bicycle tube given different volumes of output

Activity 2.1

Zebra Ltd manufactures a product with a variable cost of £7 per unit. The fixed costs are £3000.
   Calculate the full cost per unit at 100, 200 and 500 units.

Full costing – a traditional approach to pricing

Using full cost in order to identify the selling price of a product or service

Cost plus pricing involves the identification of the full cost of a product or service and the addition of a mark-up to allow for profit.

The use of a full costing approach to pricing is illustrated in Figure 2.2.

Portland Ltd produces three products, M, N and O. Below the calculated selling price for product M is shown, if a full costing plus mark-up approach to pricing is followed.

(i) For product M the variable costs involved in manufacturing the product are material and labour.

	£
Material	21
Labour	<u>15</u>
Total variable costs	36

An amount of overhead is added in order to identify the full cost per unit.

Fixed overheads for Portland Ltd were budgeted at £180,000 for the coming year. It is expected that 12,000 units *in total* of product M, N and O will be produced. The method of charging overheads to products used in Portland Ltd is a budgeted rate per unit.

The fixed cost per unit was therefore $\dfrac{£180,000}{12,000 \text{ units}} = £15.00.$

Accordingly, the full cost of product M is the variable cost plus the fixed cost per unit of £15.

	£
Material	21.00
Labour	15.00
Fixed cost per unit	<u>15.00</u>
Full cost per unit	51.00

(ii) Adding a mark-up. Assume that Portland Ltd wished to charge a price that will lead to a 20% mark-up on full cost. The calculation will be as follows.

	£
Material	21.00
Labour	15.00
Fixed cost per unit	<u>15.00</u>
Total cost per unit	51.00
Add 20% mark-up	<u>10.20</u>
Selling price	61.20

The selling price per unit for product M is therefore £61.20.

Figure 2.2 Selling price per unit of product M using a full costing approach to pricing

Activity 2.2

The selling price per unit for product M in Portland Ltd, using a full cost plus mark-up approach, has been calculated at £61.20. Identify reasons why this might not always be a good method for setting prices.

Activity 2.3

Able PLC produces a product Z. The material cost of Z is £10 per unit, the labour cost is £8. Overheads for the coming period are budgeted to be £200,000 and 20,000 units are expected to be produced in that time period.

Identify the price that would be charged for each product Z if full cost plus a mark-up of 10% is used as the basis for setting prices.

Criticisms of the full costing approach to pricing

Given the changes that have occurred in the environment, a number of concerns have been raised about the suitability of the use of full costing as a basis for pricing.

(1) Full cost plus a mark-up may lead to an uncompetitive price

In an increasingly competitive environment, a calculated full cost per unit may be uncompetitive and could lead to falling sales. This could lead to a dangerous spiral effect, as illustrated in Figure 2.3.

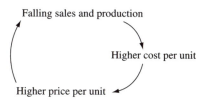

Falling sales and production

Higher cost per unit

Higher price per unit

Figure 2.3   Spiral effect of falling sales and pricing based on a full cost per unit

(2) The method of apportioning overheads does not necessarily reflect the extent to which individual products use or cause overheads costs

The increasing complexity of products and increased proportion of costs that are overheads has meant that the method of allocating fixed overheads to products will have a major impact on the full cost per unit. A complex product or service may require considerably more use of overhead resources than one that is simple to make or provide. A costing system that allocates an equal charge per unit, for example, will not reflect this usage. This problem is considered further in Chapters 5 and 6.

(3) Budgeted production or costs may be incorrectly assessed

In many instances, organizations calculate the overhead cost per unit, based on assumptions about budgeted costs and production. In the example of Portland Ltd in Figure 2.2, it was estimated that the fixed cost per unit would be £15 based on budgeted overheads of £180,000 and a budgeted output of 12,000 units. If the forecast of either the budgeted costs or the budgeted units is incorrect, then the forecast overhead cost per unit will be inaccurate.

Approaches to pricing that take into consideration market factors

To overcome the disadvantages of the traditional full costing approach to pricing, a number of alternative approaches that take account of market factors have been suggested (see Figure 2.4). These are discussed in more detail below.

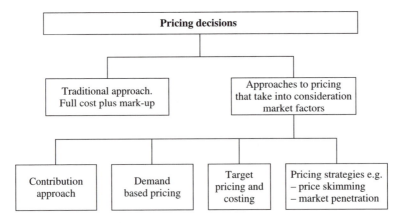

Figure 2.4   Different approaches to pricing

Contribution approach to pricing

For Portland the following variable costs were identified for product M.

	£
Material	21.00
Labour	15.00
Total variable costs	36.00

A **contribution approach to pricing** involves the identification of the variable cost and adding a mark-up. For product M, any price above £36.00 would make a contribution to overheads. If the company sold each unit of product M for £50, for example, there would be a contribution of £14 per unit. If the company received an order for 200 units of product M, at a sales price of £50, the contract would make a contribution of £2800 (200 units ×£14 contribution unit) towards the overheads of the company. In practice, when organizations follow a contribution approach to pricing, it will often mean that the price set is below full cost plus mark-up.

Activity 2.4

(1) Albert Ltd supplies two products.

Product	A	B
	(£)	(£)
Labour £6/hr	9	6
Material	4	10

It is expected that 100 units of A will be produced and 60 units of B will be produced in the month.

Overheads per month   £3200

Required:

(a) What prices should be charged for products A and B, if the organization operates a pricing policy of full cost plus 10%.
(b) If a customer offered to buy 5 units of product A for £18 each, would you agree to sell the product at this price?

Benefits of the contribution approach to pricing

There may be circumstances when the contribution approach makes sense, particularly to meet short-term requirements. For instance:

(a) When there is spare capacity. In the short term a company may have spare capacity and it may be possible to produce more products or provide more services with no additional fixed costs. As long as an order only utilizes this unused capacity for a short period, then *some* contribution to overheads may be better than none.

(b) If the company is not committing itself to repeat longer-term business at this low price.

(c) As a means of getting entry to a particular customer or market.

(d) For a large order. Orders, whether they are large or small, often require a similar amount of effort by overhead departments; for example, the same amount of order documentation is required for both.

(e) When some existing customers are more important to the company. The company may be prepared to accept a low contribution on one order for a customer who currently purchases a large volume of other goods.

Dangers of using the contribution approach to pricing

It should be noted that there are significant dangers of following a contribution approach to pricing for all contracts. If insufficient contribution is generated to cover fixed costs, then the company will be making losses. Before following the contribution approach a range of factors should be considered:

(a) Future customer reaction. For example, customers might be resistant to paying higher prices, once lower prices have been offered.

(b) Competitor reaction. Competitors may retaliate by also reducing their prices and this could lead to a price war.

(c) Incorrect cost assumptions. As with all contracts, care should be taken to ensure that cost assumptions are correct. It is often easy to assume that fixed costs will not change and variable costs will only increase in proportion to output. This may be a simplistic view of cost behaviour. Some products might require greater use of overhead costs. Setting up machinery for one product may be particularly time-consuming or require specialist engineering time. Some customers may also cause particular problems, while others may be very easy to work with. A company may again wish to take this into consideration when costing and pricing.

Judging the contribution that is likely to be acceptable for an order

The contribution or variable cost plus approach to pricing is a flexible tactic that may be worthwhile to follow for the short term. In the longer run a company must cover fixed costs and make a profit. Following a contribution approach for all contracts for the longer term may be dangerous.

If the contribution approach to pricing is used, managers will need to judge the level of contribution that is acceptable. There is no precise formula that can be used. It will be necessary to consider the size of the order, with greater discounts likely to be permitted on large rather than small orders. It will also be necessary to then consider the range of factors discussed above in the sections on the benefits and dangers of contribution pricing.

Activity 2.5

A sales representative of Portland Ltd has been asked to provide a quote for 100 units of product M. He feels that he can get the order at a price of £50. Advise him on the points for and against proceeding with a quote based on this price.

Demand-based pricing

In Chapter 1, the assumption was made that the price per unit would remain constant, at any level of output. This is not always the case and to achieve higher volumes of sales it may be necessary to reduce the price.

Ideally the managers of the firm should have a clear idea of the likely sales given different prices and also the cost behaviour of their own products or services at these different levels of activity. **Demand-based pricing** is an approach that will take into consideration prices and costs at different volumes of sales in order to identify the point at which profit is maximized.

Figure 2.5 reflects an estimated demand curve for product M, showing a trade-off between sales volume and price.

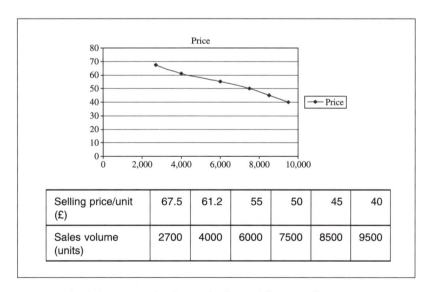

Selling price/unit (£)	67.5	61.2	55	50	45	40
Sales volume (units)	2700	4000	6000	7500	8500	9500

Figure 2.5   Graph of the expected volume of sales at different selling prices

Demand falls as the price rises. At £61.20, an expected 4000 units will be sold. It is expected that sales volume will rise to 9500 units, at a selling price of £40.

It is also possible to calculate the total revenue at different levels of demand and prices. The total revenue curve in Figure 2.6 shows the impact of a lower price per unit at higher volumes of units sold.

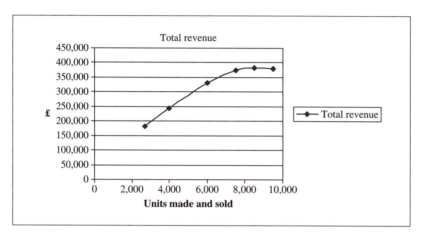

Figure 2.6   Graph of total expected revenue given different levels of units sold

In order to work out the optimum pricing policy it is now necessary to identify the costs and then the contribution of producing product M at these different output levels. The calculation of revenue, variable cost and contribution, along with a graph representing this data, is shown in Figure 2.7. The assumption is made that variable cost per unit remains constant. Accordingly, total variable costs increase in proportion to the increase in number of units made.

Based on the expectation of demand at different price levels, the best profit is generated at a selling price of £55. The price of £61.20 (based on full cost plus mark-up) led to a contribution to overheads of £100,800, while a price of £55 results in a contribution to overheads of £114,000. Note that fixed overheads are not deducted from contributions as they are considered to be general overheads and therefore do not change in relation to the level of output of product M.

Obviously, the analysis is only as good as the assumptions underpinning it. If the assumptions concerning demand at different prices and variable and fixed costs are incorrect, then the expected contributions and profits at these different prices will also be incorrect. As an example, fixed costs might in practice increase at a certain level of output (step-fixed costs). If this did occur then in order to identify the optimum price, this increase in fixed costs should be taken into account.

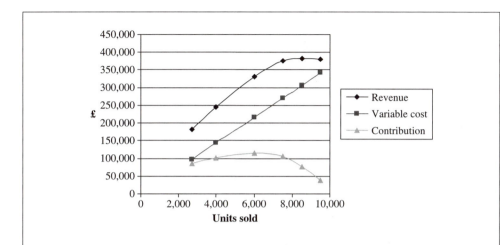

Selling price/unit (£)	67.5	61.2	55	50	45	40
Contribution/unit (£) (note 1)	31.5	25.2	19.0	14.0	9.0	4.0
Sales volume (units)	2,700	4,000	6,000	7,500	8,500	9,500
Revenue (£) (note 2)	182,250	244,800	330,000	375,000	382,500	380,000
Variable cost (£) (note 3)	97,200	144,000	216,000	270,000	306,000	342,000
Total contribution (£) (note 4)	85,050	100,800	114,000	105,000	76,500	38,000

Note 1. Contribution per unit is calculated by taking the selling price per unit and deducting the variable cost per unit of £36.00.

Note 2. Total revenue is calculated by multiplying the selling price per unit by the sales volume (units).

Note 3. Total variable cost is calculated by multiplying the variable cost per unit by the sales volume.

Note 4. Total contribution is calculated by multiplying the contribution per unit by the sales volume.

Figure 2.7 Graph and table showing revenue, variable costs and contribution at different level of sales

---

Activity 2.6

Apricot Ltd sells a number of products. The following information about product Y is available.

Selling price/unit	£42	£37
Expected sales volume (units) per month	3700	6000

The variable cost per unit of manufacturing product Y is £28.

Required:

(a) Identify the total contribution if the product is sold at £42 per unit and £37 per unit and on the basis of the contribution alone, advise which price should be set.
(b) Identify any further factors that should be taken into consideration.

Activity 2.7

Refer to the information in Activity 2.6. Would the management of Apricot Ltd make a different decision if it was necessary to employ an additional foreman at a cost of £2000 a month, when production rises above 5000 units.

In practice, it is often difficult to identify the slope of the demand curve. Because of this a number of alternative pricing strategies might be tried for existing and new products. Some of these strategies are discussed later in the chapter.

Target pricing/target costing

For many goods, often high-volume products, there is a market price above which sales volume is likely to fall sharply. For example, at the time of writing, many basic version small family cars are sold for just under £8000. If a company is launching a car which is very similar to others in the market segment, then the price needs to be set at a similar level. With **target costing**, a target selling price is first established, the desired profit margin of the company is then deducted to leave the target cost at which the product should be made. The actual estimated cost must then be compared with the target cost and where actual is greater than target, ways of driving down actual costs must be investigated. In Figure 2.8 the steps traditionally followed when undertaking a full costing approach to pricing new products and a target costing approach are compared.

Steps followed when undertaking a full costing approach to pricing new products	Steps followed when undertaking target costing
Step 1 – *Market research to identify customer requirements takes place.*	Step 1 – *The target selling price of the product is identified.*
Step 2 – *Product specification and design.* In many cases the design process is undertaken in the following steps, with each step following on from the other. 1. The product to meet the identified customer needs is specified. 2. The designers produce a product design to this specification. 3. The production engineers are provided with the design and specify how this design is to be manufactured.	Step 2 – *Target costs are identified.* The desired profit margin is deducted from the target selling price to identify the target cost. The process of identifying the target cost is illustrated in Figure 2.9.
Step 3 – *Costs are estimated.* If the costs seem high, the designers will be asked to look for cost savings in the product design.	Step 3 – *Actual costs will be estimated.* Rather than a separation of designers, engineers and other functional areas, each completing their own specific functions, under target costing a more multidisciplinary team-based approach is encouraged.
Step 4 – *The expected selling price is established.* This is often achieved by adding the desired profit margin to the estimated costs.	Step 4 – *Where costs are higher than target costs, the multidisciplinary teams will be asked to look for cost savings in the product design.*

Figure 2.8   A comparison of a traditional cost plus approach to setting prices with a target costing approach

Figure 2.9 shows the process of identifying the target cost.

There are a number of differences in the activities undertaken under target costing.

Market research

Market research is important in identifying the target price early in the process, along with the anticipated volume of sales that will be achieved at this price. Market research

XY Ltd wishes to produce and sell a new product. Market research indicates that similar products are in the market for sale at just over £50 per unit and XY Ltd thinks that it could sell approximately 10,000 units at £50. Above £50, it believes there would be a sharp fall in demand.

XY Ltd has a target profit to sales of 20%. The target cost of developing and producing the new product can now be calculated.

TARGET COSTING

1. Market price   £50 × 10,000 units = £500,000
2. Less required profit   £10 × 10,000 units = £100,000
   Target cost   £40 × 10,000 units = £400,000

The firm must ensure that the total cost of producing the 10,000 units does not exceed £400,000.

Figure 2.9 Setting a target cost

should also be an ongoing activity, rather than being a one-off event, as information is needed on the value of specific product features to the customer. If a new model of a car is launched with new features, such as four-wheel drive or active suspension, for example, then the value to the customer of such features should be identified. Changes in price to that of the existing model should be in accordance with the value of features added or dropped.

Estimating actual costs

Rather than a separation of designers, engineers and other functional areas each completing their own specific functions, under target costing a more multidisciplinary team-based approach is encouraged in the design and costing process. If designers, engineers, purchasing and manufacturing operations work together on common problems, it is more likely that they will take account of each other's needs. Thus, rather than designers purely focusing on design features that may not be desired by the customer or that may be difficult and expensive to engineer, a multidisciplinary approach is more likely to bring greater focus on the cost-effective achievement of customer requirements. The approach should also enable the design to take into consideration lifecycle costing implications. Lifecycle costing is discussed later in the chapter.

Looking for cost savings in the product design

The aim of the product specification and design phase is to design a product that will meet target cost and provide the product functions desired by the target market. Where expected cost is above target cost then techniques such as tear-down analysis and value engineering will be used to reduce costs and achieve target cost.

Tear-down analysis involves examining a competitor's product in order to identify opportunities for improvement in the design of the firm's own product.

Value engineering involves an examination of each component to see if it is possible to reduce costs without losing functionality. For example, if the cost of a component is 10% of the total cost of a product, but market research identifies that the value added for the customer is only 5% of the total, then this would indicate a need to reduce the cost of the component. This might be achieved through means such as reducing the number of parts, simplifying assembly or using cheaper materials.

Activity 2.8

A new product is being introduced by a company. It is anticipated that at £80, 100,000 units could be sold. It is expected that total costs will be £6 million. The company is aiming for a return on sales of 30%. Will it achieve the return on current estimates?

Pricing strategies

In competitive markets a number of pricing strategies may be followed by firms. These may vary according to whether an existing or a new product is being priced.

Pricing strategies for existing products

(a) Price leader

If a company is a **price leader** it sets the pricing benchmark for the rest of the market. If the product is superior to its competitors in some way, e.g. quality, particular features, then this may mean that the company can also charge a premium price.

(b) Price taker

A company that is a **price taker** must price the product or service at the market price. This will occur in a market where there are a large number of companies supplying similar products. In such a situation it is difficult for a company to differentiate the company's product or achieve a different price from that of the competition.

(c) Predatory

Predatory pricing involves undercutting the competition in order to gain market share. Although short-term profit is sacrificed because low contribution contracts are accepted, the strategy is followed because the company feels it can gain market share in the future and hence generate future profits. Predatory pricing can also be used to prevent new entrants into the market. If new entrants are aware that if they enter a new market, existing competitors will drive down the price, then it is likely that they will be less enthusiastic about following the option.

Pricing strategies for new products

Price skimming

Price skimming involves the charging of high prices to take advantage of a novelty appeal of a new product, e.g. new computer consoles and games. This is usually used at the early stage of the product lifecycle, when there is no competition. The price can be lowered if competitors enter the market or demand is insufficient.

Penetration pricing

With **penetration pricing** a company will launch a product at a low price to get market share and discourage potential competitors from entering the market. Penetration pricing for new products and predatory pricing for existing products are strategies more normally followed where the level of competition is high.

Pricing and the product lifecycle

The theory of the **product lifecycle** (see Figure 2.10) is that all products progress through a similar cycle of development, introduction, growth, maturity and decline:

- *Development.* Market research takes place to identify potential market size, product features that are desired by the target market and price they are likely to pay. The product must be designed, prototypes developed and then facilities prepared for the product launch.
- *Introduction.* When products or services are first launched, market growth is slow as there is little consumer awareness and often prices are high.
- *Growth.* Sales increase as more consumers become aware of the product and increased competition from suppliers is likely to lead to price reductions.
- *Maturity.* Sales have now levelled off. Competition means that prices are under even more pressure.
- *Decline.* The market for the product or service is declining and the company will be considering how to generate the maximum profit from the remaining time that the product or service will be offered in the market place. High expenditure on advertising and other forms of promotion is less likely.

In recent years the length of the product lifecycle of most new products has been reducing. Computers and associated hardware, for example, can become out-of-date within months of their launch as newer and better models are released. Many new products also have high development costs and at the end of the product lifecycle there may be disposal costs to consider. Profits generated during the period in which products are sold must be sufficient to offset the costs associated with development and abandonment.

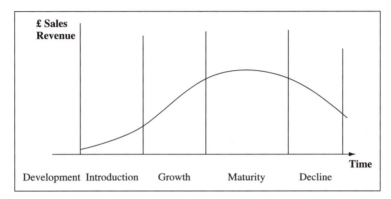

Figure 2.10   The product lifecycle

The product lifecycle and the pricing decision

Different pricing strategies may be appropriate at different stages of this lifecycle.

Introduction

At the introduction phase, market penetration or price skimming policies may be followed depending on competitive circumstances.

Growth

During the growth stage, there is increasing competition as new competitors enter the market. If a company has been an early entrant to the market, it may be able to take advantage of economies of scale and therefore generate greater profits than competitors charging a similar price. Alternatively, it may be able to afford to adopt a predatory pricing policy that will discourage new entrants.

Maturity

As the product matures, a firm may act as a price-taker if there are a large number of competitors and the market is no longer growing. It may be possible to also differentiate the product from its competitors by widening the range of options offered and sell different versions at different prices. For example, in the car industry there is often a range of different models with different product features and prices, for each type of car. While the basic version of a car might be say, £8000, different options may have significantly higher prices.

Lifecycle costing

Lifecycle costing is concerned with the estimation of costs of a product over its entire lifecycle.

From the perspective of the producer of a product, three key stages in the lifecycle can be identified, from conception through to the post-manufacturing stage. The type of cost incurred will change throughout this lifecycle:

1. *Pre-production/development.* This is the planning and design stage in which market research activities take place and a new product idea is designed and developed.
2. *Production and sales stage.* During this phase, the product is manufactured and sold (introductory, growth, maturity and decline stages of the product lifecycle). Costs will be incurred in:

    (a) The manufacturing process.
    (b) Outside the manufacturing process, for example in dealing with warranty claims and other customer service requirements.

3. *Post-manufacturing phase.* Costs of this stage can be high in some industries, for example, nuclear power plants in the UK will need to be decommissioned and this will cost many millions of pounds. Other industries such as chemical plants, quarrying and mining also need to consider the costs required at the end of the production and sales process.

The amount of costs incurred at these three stages can vary according to industry.

Committed and incurred costs

A key lesson of lifecycle costing is that, in some organisations, possibly up to 80% of costs are *committed* at pre-production stage even though a large proportion of the costs have not been *incurred*. Although in designing a product it may be possible to reduce the costs of the pre-production/development phase, this may mean that costs at the manufacturing and post-manufacturing stage are higher than necessary. Although process efficiency improvements will be possible during the production and sales phase, savings will be relatively minor compared with the costs that are 'locked-in' by the design decisions.

A target costing approach is important in order to highlight the potential cost impact of different designs. Multidisciplinary teams should be working together to ensure that costs are reduced throughout the lifecycle.

The contrast between costs committed and incurred is illustrated in Figure 2.11.

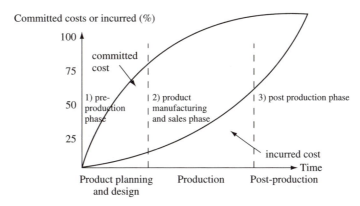

Figure 2.11 Committed and incurred costs during different stages of the product lifecycle

---

Activity 2.9

Richmond PLC is considering launching a new product, product D. Sales over the coming years are expected to be as follows:

	2007	2008	2009	2010	2011
	£'000	£'000	£'000	£'000	£'000
Sales	0	400	2000	2000	600
Variable costs	0	200	1000	1000	300
Identifiable fixed costs	1000	200	300	300	500

What would be the expected contribution (after deducting identifiable fixed costs) generated by the product in each of the years of its product life?

Advise, as far as possible given this information, on the viability of progressing with this project. (Ignore the time value of money.)

Whole lifecycle costing – a purchaser perspective

Whole lifecycle costing considers the cost of a *purchase* over its life. As an example, a purchaser might have the choice of buying two products that in theory can do the same job. The temptation may be to buy the product with the lowest purchase price, however, the upfront costs might not lead to the cheapest alternative in the long run. This is illustrated in Figure 2.12.

James has the choice of purchasing one of two printers.

Either:

Printer 1, which will cost £120 to purchase and is expected to have a life of 6 years at which point it will have no value. Ink cartridges are expected to cost £30 a year.

Or:

Printer 2, which will cost £40 to purchase and will last for 2 years at which point it will have no value. Ink cartridges are expected to cost £60 a year.
  Which would be the best machine to purchase?

Answer:

A review of the cash flows shows that machine 1 will cost £300, while machine 2 will cost £480 over the 6 years. Although the initial purchase cost of machine 2 is less, the lifecycle cost of choosing this option is more expensive.

Figure 2.12   Two products with different lifecycle costs

Inter-company sales

In large organizations, individual sections or divisions will often provide goods or services for other parts of the organization. A problem that arises is the method of allocating resources between the different parts. One approach, which will be considered further in Chapter 10, is the use of a pricing system.

Full cost and profit/loss per unit

Managers sometimes like to quote whether a profit or loss is being earned per unit of a product or service. In order to calculate the profit or loss from the sale of a product, an overhead cost must be deducted from the contribution per unit. The example of Sherman Ltd, which was illustrated in Tables 2.1 and 2.2, is considered further in Table 2.3.

While the contribution per unit will remain constant at £2 per unit, the profit or loss per unit will change depending on the level of output. At low volumes a very high loss per unit results, as output increases, the fixed overheads are spread across more units, so the cost per unit becomes lower and the product will eventually make a profit per unit. At 1000 units a break-even is achieved while with 1500 units produced and sold, the product makes a £0.67 profit per unit.

Table 2.3   Profit/(loss) per unit at different levels of sales

	1 unit (£)	100 units (£)	500 units (£)	1000 units (£)	1500 units (£)
(1) Selling price per unit	8	8	8	8	8
(2) Variable cost per unit	6	6	6	6	6
(3) Contribution per unit (note 1)	2	2	2	2	2
(4) Fixed cost per unit	2000	20	4	2	1.33
(5) Profit/(loss) per unit (note 2)	(1998)	(18)	(2)	–	0.67

Note 1. Contribution per unit = selling price – variable cost.
Note 2. Profit/(loss) per unit = contribution per unit – fixed cost per unit.

Summary

A traditional approach to pricing is to identify the full or total cost of producing a product and add a mark-up.

Full cost plus a mark-up may not be an appropriate approach to pricing in competitive market conditions. Alternative approaches include:

- Accepting prices that generate a contribution to overheads.
- Demand-based pricing.
- Target pricing combined with target costing.
- Pricing strategies for new products, including penetration pricing or price skimming and for existing products including price leader, price taker or predatory pricing.
- Different pricing policies may be appropriate for different stages of the lifecycle of a product.

In developing new products, it is important to take into consideration lifecycle costs, i.e. pre- and post-production costs as well as costs incurred during the manufacturing phase. Higher expenditure at the development stage may result in lower costs over the entire lifecycle of the product.

Purchasers of goods should also consider the whole lifecycle cost.

Further reading

For a further insight into the practical application of target costing:

Atkinson, A.A., Kaplan, R.S., Matsumara, E.M. and Youngs, S.M. (2007) *Management Accounting*, 5th edn. Prentice-Hall.
Swenson, D., Ansari, J., Bell, J. and Kim, I.-W. (2003) Best practices in target costing. *Management Accounting Quarterly* **4**(2): 12–17.

For a more detailed marketing perspective of pricing policy:

Wilson, R.M.S. and Gilligan, G.C. (2004) *Strategic Marketing Management: Planning, implementation and control*, 3rd edn. Butterworth-Heinemann, Oxford.

Answers to activities

Activity 2.1

Units	100	200	500
	(£)	(£)	(£)
Variable costs £7/unit	700	1400	3500
Fixed costs	3000	3000	3000
Total cost	3700	4400	6500
Total cost per unit	37	22	13

Activity 2.2

There are many potential reasons, some of which are discussed later in the chapter. For example, customers may not be prepared to pay this price.

Activity 2.3

	20,000 units	1 unit
	(£)	(£)
Variable costs £18/unit	360,000	18
Fixed costs	200,000	10
Total cost	560,000	28
Mark-up @ 10%		2.80
Selling price per unit		30.80

Activity 2.4

(a)

	Product A	Product B
	1 unit	1 unit
	(£)	(£)
Variable costs	13.00	16.00
Fixed costs (note 1)	20.00	20.00
Total cost	33.00	36.00
Mark-up @ 10%	3.30	3.60
Selling price per unit	36.30	39.60

Note 1. Fixed costs $= \dfrac{£3,200}{160} = £20$ per unit.

(b) At £18 the selling price of product A is well below the full cost plus mark-up of £36.30.

The contribution per unit is, however, £18 − £13, i.e. £5 a unit. A sale of 5 units at £5 contribution would therefore generate a contribution of £25.

The arguments for and against accepting a contribution are reviewed in the chapter. Unless there are strong commercial arguments for accepting the contract, however, this seems to be a very large discount on the cost-plus price for a small contract that is generating little contribution.

Activity 2.5

The arguments are reviewed in the chapter. In this case the contribution is £14 a unit and 100 units are sold, leading to an overall contribution of £1400. This may well be a sufficient contribution to justify a discount against the full cost mark-up price.

Activity 2.6

(a)

Selling price/unit	£42	£37
Contribution/unit	£14	£9
Expected units sold	3,700	6,000
	£51,800	£54,000

A price of £37 leads to a contribution of £2200 greater than will happen at £42 and therefore on the basis of contribution, £37 should be the price set.

(b) Other factors to consider include:

  (i) The assumptions – how confident is the company about the level of demand at the different prices? Would a higher contribution be earned at a different price? It is also necessary to check that variable costs will remain constant per unit and that fixed costs will not change.
  (ii) The company might also need to consider competitor and customer reaction to the different price levels. The company might also have problems with capacity constraints, taking on higher levels of sales may also mean that more profitable options have to be turned down because an additional 2300 units of this product are being manufactured.

Activity 2.7

	(£)	(£)
Selling price/unit	42	37
Total contribution	51,800	54,000
Less identifiable fixed costs	0	2,000
Contribution after deducting identifiable fixed costs	51,800	52,000

The contribution after deducting fixed costs that are identifiable to the increase in production and sales volume is only £200 a month greater at a price of £37 per unit. On the basis of contribution alone it is still very marginally worthwhile reducing the price, however, other factors need to be reconsidered. For example, will the foreman be solely involved with supervising this additional production or will this employee be able to carry out other work as well? The company should also consider the contribution that could be earned at a volume of between 3700 and 5000 units. The increase in fixed costs does not occur until an output level of 5000 units is achieved.

Activity 2.8

Revenue   £8,000,000
Costs   £6,000,000
Profit   £2,000,000

Return on sales $\dfrac{£2,000,000}{£8,000,000} = 25\%$

Therefore the required return on sales is not achieved.

Activity 2.9

	2007	2008	2009	2010	2011	Total
	£'000	£'000	£'000	£'000	£'000	£'000
Sales	0	400	2000	2000	600	5000
Variable costs	0	200	1000	1000	300	2500
Identifiable fixed costs	1000	200	300	300	500	2300
Contribution	(1000)	0	700	700	(200)	200

Over the period from 2007 to 2011 the product makes a contribution of £200,000 to general overheads.

It is difficult to advise fully on whether to progress with the product as some contribution is generated, however, it does seem to be a fairly limited contribution towards general overheads, given the time period over which sales take place. The company should investigate in more depth assumptions on sales and costs.

Discussion questions

Alpha Ltd is launching a new product and the management team have come to a meeting to discuss the launch of the product including pricing policy and the budget for its product launch. The following comments have been overheard.

'I think that we should launch this product at a very low price to ensure that the market is unattractive for competitors to even consider launching their own versions of the product.'

Managing Director of Alpha Ltd

'We need to identify the demand curve for the product and ensure production is at the optimum level to ensure profits are maximized.'

Management Accountant

'To use full costing is foolish, it will lead this organization to ruin.'

Sales Director

'If things go well, this product will ensure the profitability of Alpha Ltd for the next 20 years.'

Financial Director

'The development budget for this product is excessive, it should be cut back by 20% immediately.'

Chief Accountant

'The purpose of a business is to maximize profits and our price should aim to do this.'

Research Manager

Required:

Critically evaluate the merits of each of these comments.

Exercises

(Questions in bold have answers at the back of the book.)

Q2.1 The following information about product N is available.

Selling price/unit	£36	£30
Expected units sold	4300	5800

The variable cost per unit of manufacturing product N is £21.

Required:

(a) Identify the total contribution if the product is sold at £36 per unit and £30 per unit and on the basis of the contribution alone, advise which price should be set.
(b) Identify any further factors that should be considered.

Q2.2 Alpha Ltd uses cost plus a mark-up to set its prices. Overheads are expected to be £1000 for the coming month and 200 units in total will be produced (150 of product A and 50 of product B).
The direct costs of manufacturing product A and B are shown below.

Product	A	B
	(£)	(£)
Labour £5/hr	10	5
Material	5	6

Required:

(a) Calculate the selling price per unit if a mark-up of 20% on full cost is used.
(b) You have been approached by a customer who has offered to buy 10 units of product A for £20 each. Would you agree to sell the products at this price?

Q2.3 Mr Jones is a painter and decorator. His overheads are £200 a week and he expects to work on average 40 hours in any week.

He has been asked to quote for a job which he estimates will take him 20 hours to complete. The material cost for the job will be £100.

Required:

Calculate the quote for the job that Mr Jones should give the customer, if he includes a pay rate of £10 an hour for himself and builds in a 20% profit margin on full cost.

Q2.4 The marketing manager of Division A of your company has estimated the monthly demand for a new product, with a marginal cost of £20, would be as follows:

	(£)	(£)	(£)	(£)	(£)	(£)	(£)
Price	40	38	36	34	32	30	28
Demand	2000	2400	3000	3800	4800	6000	7500

Machines will be required to each produce 1000 units per year at an annual monthly fixed cost of £4000 per machine.

Required:

Identify how many machines should be acquired and at what price should the product be sold?
   Comment on any concerns that you would have about your answer.

Q2.5 A new product is being introduced for a company. It is anticipated that at £50, 25,000 units could be sold. It is expected that total costs will be £1 million. The company is aiming for a return on sales of 30%.

Required:

(a) Will it achieve this target rate of return on current estimates?
(b) The managing director has asked you to indicate action that could be taken to investigate how cost can be reduced. Indicate potential alternative courses of action.

FURTHER DECISION-MAKING PROBLEMS

3

Objectives

When you have completed this chapter you should be able to:

- Describe an approach to decision-making.
- Undertake an appraisal of a range of different decision problems:

  - Dropping a product or service.
  - Assessing the return from different marketing plans.
  - Assessing whether to make or buy a product.
  - Identifying the optimum production plan given specific constraints.

- Explain key costing terminology used in relation to decision-making.
- Identify relevant costs for decision-making, including the importance of opportunity costs.

Introduction

The chapter begins with an outline of one approach to assessing decisions. It then looks at a number of short-term decisions that might typically face an organization and have a financial impact. These include identifying the implications of dropping a product or service, assessing the return from different marketing plans, assessing whether to make or buy a product and identifying the optimum production plan given specific constraints.

The chapter introduces some of the terminology often used when assessing the financial viability of different decision-making situations. A number of problems involving relevant and opportunity costs are then considered.

Short-term decision-making in organizations

A decision-making approach

When faced with a decision it is necessary to:

1. Identify the objective to be achieved.
2. Identify the alternatives for achieving the objective.
3. Evaluate the alternatives.

Steps to be followed in the process of evaluating short-term financial decisions are considered in Figure 3.1.

In order to evaluate each alternative, three steps or stages of analysis can be identified. These are listed below:

Step 1. Identify the revenue and cost that will change if a particular alternative is chosen. Check for the existence of constraints

Costs that will change include:

  (i) Costs that change in proportion to output, i.e. the variable costs.
 (ii) Identifiable fixed costs. These are the fixed costs that change because of a decision, for example the cost to lease a machine required for the manufacture of a product. Identifiable fixed costs are different from general fixed overheads, which do not change following a particular decision.

Constraints will affect the ability to undertake a particular option and will impact on the financial evaluation of different options. Where there is a single constraint, then it is necessary to focus on maximizing the contribution that is generated by that constraining factor.

Step 2. Evaluate the change in costs and revenue

Given the information identified at step 1, evaluate the financial impact of each alternative in terms of additional costs and, where relevant, contribution.

Step 3. Identify the non-financial or qualitative factors

An option might be financially preferable, but there might be a range of other reasons why it should not be followed. For example, if a company is considering subcontracting the provision of a product or service to an outside supplier it might wish to consider:

  (i) Quality. Will the quality of the product or service be the same?
 (ii) Time. If it is a product, will the product be delivered on time?
(iii) Future costs. Having subcontracted a product or service, will the supplying company be able to raise the price in the future? By this time it may be too difficult to reverse the policy.
(iv) Whether the product or service is of key strategic importance and subcontracting will mean that crucial information or knowledge is lost by the company.

Figure 3.1   An approach to decision-making

With the short-term decision problems considered in this chapter, the objective will be to identify the alternative that generates the greatest contribution to overheads.

Some typical short-term problems in organizations

Managers face a range of potential problems in organizations. Typical problems can include whether:

1. A service or product should be withdrawn from the market or whether a segment of an organization should be closed?
2. The most profitable sales plan is being followed or whether alternatives will lead to higher profits.
3. A component should be made (or service provided) by the company or whether it should be bought in from another supplier?
4. The optimum sales and production plan is being followed, given a shortage of a key resource such as labour skills, raw materials or machine capacity?

Illustration of problem types

The above problems will be illustrated using the following information on Richmond PLC.

Richmond PLC manufactures and sells three products. The company is in the process of preparing a budget for the forthcoming year. The accountant has produced a statement showing the profit and costs for the forthcoming budget year, based on the first round of discussions. See Figure 3.2.

Revenue	1,581,500
Total costs	1,487,750
Profit	93,750
The total costs include fixed costs of £247,250.	

Figure 3.2   Richmond PLC – budgeted profit and loss for the period 20X0

As well as producing a summary budget for the coming year, the accountant has prepared a detailed analysis of the budgeted volume of sales, the sales price, cost and profit per unit for each product. See Figure 3.3.

The senior management of the company have met to review the above information and identify alternative policies that may lead to an increase in the profit for the coming year. Four existing policies have been questioned.

1. The sales manager has asked whether production and sale of product X should stop since it appears to make a loss.
2. The marketing director and sales director are suggesting different marketing strategies, in order to increase sales. Should either be accepted?

Budgeted sales (units)	6500	8000	7000
Product	X	Y	Z
	(£)	(£)	(£)
Sales price per unit	45	78	95
Variable cost per unit	39	56	77
Fixed overhead per unit (note 1)	11.5	11.5	11.5
Total/full cost per unit	50.5	67.5	88.5
Profit per unit	−5.5	10.5	6.5

Note 1. Calculation of the fixed overhead per unit.
  (i)   Budgeted fixed overheads are £247,250.
  (ii) Budgeted output is 21,500 units sold (6500 units of product X, 8000 units of product Y, 7000 units of product Z).
  (iii) To calculate the fixed cost per unit, the fixed overheads of £247,250 have been divided by 21,500 units. This gives a fixed cost of £11.50 per unit.

Given this method of assigning fixed costs to units, it can be seen that while products Y and Z make a 'profit', product X makes a 'loss' per unit of £5.50. However, the overheads of £247,250 are general fixed overheads and will not change given any changes in output of products X, Y or Z.

Figure 3.3   Budgeted sales price, costs and profit for each of the products sold by Richmond PLC

3. Able Engineering has offered to make product Z for £87 for the forthcoming year. The purchasing manager has questioned whether this offer should be accepted.
4. At present it is difficult to recruit appropriately skilled staff. The production manager has asked about the best sales and production plan to follow, if there is a shortage of labour in the current year.

Evaluation of whether a service or product should be withdrawn from the market or a segment of an organization closed

Question 1: Should production of product X be discontinued because it is making a loss?

This problem is analysed in figure 3.4.

Step 1. Identify the revenue and cost that will change if a particular alternative is chosen. Check for the existence of constraints

The costs that change if product X is manufactured are the variable costs, i.e. material, labour and variable overhead.

There will be no change in the fixed cost incurred by the company as the fixed overhead cost per unit is an allocation of general overheads. If production of product X ceases, then the overheads currently borne by product X will be reassigned to products Y and Z.

No constraints on resources have been identified.

Figure 3.4   Financial evaluation of the contribution generated by product X

Step 2. Given the information identified at step 1, evaluate the financial impact of each alternative in terms of additional costs and, where relevant, contribution

To evaluate this option, the contribution per unit can first be identified. Having identified the contribution per unit, the total contribution generated from sales of product X can be calculated.

Product	X
Budgeted sales (units)	6500
	(£)
Sales price per unit	45
Variable cost per unit	39
Contribution per unit	6

Product X generates a contribution of £6 per unit towards general overheads. Since 6500 units are sold, a total contribution of £39,000 is generated.

Note that as an alternative, a total contribution statement can be produced. This will show the total revenue, variable costs and contribution for the 6500 units of product X.

A total contribution statement for product X:

Product	X
Budgeted sales (units)	6,500
	(£)
Revenue	292,500
Total variable cost	253,500
Total contribution	39,000

Step 3. Identify the non-financial or qualitative factors

No information is provided about non-financial factors to take into consideration.

Conclusion

Whichever method is used, it can be seen that product X generates a significant positive contribution of £39,000 to general overheads. The company should consider continuing with its production and sales unless better options are available.

Figure 3.4 (*Continued*)

Activity 3.1

Apple Ltd operates in three regions. The following 'Profit and Loss' statement has been produced.

Region	North	East	West
	£'000	£'000	£'000
Revenue	600	750	1000
Costs	650	700	850
Profit/(loss)	(50)	50	150

The management of the company are considering shutting down the North region as it is making a loss.

Required:

(a) Before proceeding with the closure, what further information is required?
(b) Advise the management of the company on the proposal to shut the region.

You are advised that Head Office costs of £450,000 have been included in costs. £150,000 has been charged to each of the three regions.

Evaluating alternative marketing strategies

Question 2: The marketing director and sales director of Richmond PLC are suggesting different marketing strategies, in order to increase sales. Should either be accepted?

The objective is to identify the alternative that will lead to the greatest financial return to the organization. The alternatives to consider are:

(a) Continue with the existing marketing strategy and sales plan.
(b) The marketing director's proposal: a special advertising campaign costing an additional £120,000 should be undertaken. This will increase sales of all products by 25% for the year.
(c) The sales director's proposal: introduce a sales commission scheme, which would increase the sales volume by 20% for a year, but would also result in a selling commission that was 5% of sales.

These alternatives need to be compared with the profit generated given the existing policies.

Alternative (a): the existing sales policy is budgeted to result in a profit of £93,750. See Figure 3.2.

Alternative (b): for an evaluation of the marketing director's proposal, see Figure 3.5.

Step 1. Identify the revenue and cost that will change if a particular option is chosen. Check for the existence of constraints

Variable costs are assumed to be material, labour and variable overheads and will change in proportion to output. As before, fixed costs are general overheads and therefore will remain the same whatever the level of output.

No constraints on resources have been identified.

Figure 3.5   Financial evaluation of the marketing director's proposal

Step 2. Evaluate the financial impact of the marketing director's proposal

To evaluate this proposal, the contribution per unit and for the budgeted sales should be identified.

Product	X	Y	Z	Total
Budgeted sales (units) (note 1)	8,125	10,000	8,750	
	(£)	(£)	(£)	
Sales price per unit	45	78	95	
Variable cost per unit	39	56	77	
Contribution per unit	6	22	18	
Total contribution (note 2)	48,750	220,000	157500	426,250
General fixed overheads				247,250
Additional advertising campaign				120,000
Net Profit				59,000

Note 1. The budgeted number of units sold have been increased by 25%. For example, the budgeted sales of product X were originally expected to be 6,500 units, a 25% increase would lead to revised budgeted sales of 8125 units.

Note 2. Budgeted contribution per unit remains the same for product X at £6 per unit. The sales of 8125 units multiplied by the contribution per unit will lead to a contribution of £48,750 from the sale of product X.

Using the same method for products Y and Z, total contribution increases from £341,000 to £426,250, i.e. an increase of £85,250.

This suggestion of the marketing manager involved an increase in advertising of £120,000, so the overall impact is a reduction in the overall profit from £93,750 given the existing marketing strategy to £59,000, i.e. a reduction of £34,750.

Figure 3.5 (*Continued*)

Activity 3.2

Evaluate the proposed marketing plan of the sales director.
What assumptions might you wish to question in your analysis?

Activity 3.3

Which of the three alternatives will lead to the best financial return?

Evaluating whether a component be made (or service provided) by a company or bought in from another supplier

Organizations are often faced with decisions where they can make or do something themselves or they can subcontract it. Many organizations have traditionally subcontracted the manufacture of non-core product components. Non-core services, such as cleaning or catering services, have also often been subcontracted and increasingly organizations are looking to subcontract services such as computing or accounting.

Again it is vital to identify which costs and revenue flows will change if the decision to buy in a product or service is made.

Question 3: Able Engineering have offered to make product Z for £87. Should this offer be accepted?

The objective is to identify whether making or buying product Z leads to the best financial return to the company, see example in Figure 3.6.

Step 1. Identify the revenue and cost that will change if a particular option is chosen. Check for the existence of constraints

The additional cost of making one unit of product Z is the variable costs of £77. The buy-in price from Able Engineering is £87.

Again, there will be no change in the fixed cost incurred by the company as the fixed overhead cost per unit is an apportionment of general overheads. If product Z is bought in, then the overheads currently borne by product Z will be reapportioned to products X and Y.

No constraints on resources have been identified.

Step 2. Evaluate the financial impact of buying in rather than making the product

Since it would cost Richmond PLC £87 to buy in product Z and £77 to manufacture it (if the only extra costs are the variable costs), the company would be £10 per unit worse off if it decides to buy in the product from Able Engineering.

Step 3. Other 'non-financial' considerations

Consider Activity 3.4.

Figure 3.6   Financial evaluation of making or buying in product Z

Activity 3.4

Identify possible reasons why Richmond PLC might wish to buy in product Z, even though the additional variable costs of manufacturing the product are less.

Activity 3.5

Alpha Computing Ltd has recently approached Richmond PLC and offered to take over some of the provision of key computing services for £50,000 per year. Richmond has calculated its own costs of providing these services as being £60,000. This cost includes £40,000 in direct wages, and a further £20,000 for a share of the overheads of the company.

(a) On the basis of cost, should the computing services work be subcontracted?
(b) What other factors should be taken into account?

Identifying the optimum product or service mix given a constraint in resources

If there are no constraints in operation then all work that increases contribution is worthy of consideration. However, often there are constraints operating on businesses and in such an instance it is necessary to consider undertaking the work that maximizes the contribution earned relative to that constraint.

An example of a company with two products and a constraint on the labour time is illustrated in Figure 3.7.

Alpha Ltd sells two products, product A and product B. The following information is available about sales price and variable costs.

	Product A		Product B	
	(£)	(£)	(£)	(£)
Sales price		15		12
Material cost	4		6	
Labour cost	6		3	
Total variable cost		10		9
Contribution per unit		5		3

All the fixed costs are general overheads. Product A takes one hour to manufacture and product B takes 30 minutes.

Figure 3.7 Example of a limiting factor problem

Both products generate a contribution, so given no constraints on labour, it would be worthwhile making and selling both products. However, the company has had problems with recruiting staff, and can only make and sell one of the products. Which product should it make and sell?

Answer:

The contribution per labour hour is £5 for product A and £6 for product B. Assuming that the only factor to consider is the contribution, then given the above assumptions on price and costs, it would be more profitable to make and sell product B.

Figure 3.7   (*Continued*)

Activity 3.6

Referring to the information in Figure 3.7, if the price of product A could be raised to £17, which product should be sold? What other factors should he take into account?

A fuller analysis will now be undertaken for the problem identified for Richmond PLC.

Question 4: If there is a shortage of labour in the current year, which would be the best sales and production plan to follow?

The objective is to identify the production plan that will lead to the highest profits. It is possible to manufacture any number of products X, Y and Z subject to the volume of sales identified in the sales forecast. This problem is analysed in Figure 3.8.

Step 1 Identify the revenue and costs that will change.
The assumptions on costs and revenue remain the same. It is necessary to identify whether there is a constraint and if so what the optimum production plan should be.

1.1 Identify whether there is a constraint on labour
You are advised that product X requires 2 labour hours of work, product Y 3 hours and product Z 6.5 hours and that the production managers fears that only 70,000 labour hours will be available in the coming year.

The calculation of the total labour hours required is as shown in the next table:

	Budgeted sales	Hours per unit	Hours required	Cumulative hours
Product X	6,500	2	13,000	13,000
Product Y	8,000	3	24,000	37,000
Product Z	7,000	6.5	45,500	82,500

The budgeted sales volume is multiplied by the number of hours required per unit to give the total hours required for each product.

Figure 3.8   Optimum production plan for Richmond PLC given a limiting factor

82,500 labour hours are required to produce the existing sales budget. If only 70,000 hours are available, it will not be possible to produce the expected volume required. Accordingly, it is necessary to identify the contribution per labour hour in order to identify which products will generate the most contribution to overheads.

1.2 Identify the contribution generated per labour hour for each product and rank the products according to their relative profitability

Product	X	Y	Z
Contribution	6	22	18
Hours	2	3	6.5
Contribution per hour	3.00	7.33	2.77
Ranking	2	1	3

Product X generates a contribution of £6. It takes 2 labour hours to manufacture product X, so the contribution per hour is £3.00. The contribution per hour for product Y is £7.33 and for product Z, £2.77. This analysis would indicate that, given a shortage of labour, product Y generates the highest contribution per labour hour, followed by product X and then product Z.

Step 2. Evaluate the financial impact on the organization in terms of additional costs and, where relevant, contribution

Optimum production plan if the business is to maximize its profits

	Budgeted sales	Hours per unit	Hours required	Cumulative hours	Contribution (£)
Product Y	8,000	3	24,000	24,000	176,000
Product X	6,500	2	13,000	37,000	39,000
Product Z	5,076	6.5	32,994	69,994	91,368
Total					306,368

Since product Y generates the highest contribution per labour hour, the hours required to manufacture the budgeted sales volume of this product is first calculated. Since 24,000 hours are required and the total available is 70,000, this will mean that 46,000 hours remain for the production of the other two products. Product X makes the next highest contribution per hour and therefore should be manufactured next.

The analysis shows that it would be best to produce and sell the full allocation of products X and Y and as many units as possible of product Z. Given the limitation on labour hours, only 5076 units of the least profitable product, product Z, can be made.

The total contribution that can be generated is £306,368.

Given fixed costs of £247,250 this will lead to a revised budgeted profit of £59,118.

Step 3. Identify the non-financial or qualitative factors that should be taken into consideration

Customers who purchase products X and Y might also wish to purchase product Z. If Richmond PLC is unable to meet this demand, customers may go elsewhere to purchase all the products. The management should assess the likelihood of this occurring.

Figure 3.8   (*Continued*)

Activity 3.7

The sales manager of Richmond PLC is interested in identifying what would be the likely production plan and profit if the expected sales price of product X were to decrease to £42. Provide an evaluation of this scenario.

Cost terms and further consideration of relevant costs

A number of terms, often used by accountants and others when decision-making calculations are completed, are considered below.

Incremental costs

Incremental costs are those that change as a result of a decision and include identifiable fixed costs. See the example in Figure 3.9.

XYZ Company is considering increasing the output of product A from 1000 to 2000 units. The variable cost per unit is £5 and additional expenditure on fixed cost of £2000 is required. The accountant wishes to identify the incremental costs if output is increased from 1000 to 2000 units.

Answer:

The incremental costs are the variable costs of 1000 units at £5 per unit (£5000) plus the additional fixed costs of £2000, giving a total additional or incremental cost of £7000.

Figure 3.9   Incremental costs

Relevant and irrelevant costs

In decision-making, **relevant costs** are the costs that change because of a decision. **Irrelevant costs** are general overheads and other costs that do not change.

Sunk costs

Sunk costs are those that have already been spent or the commitment has been made to spend them. Sunk costs are not relevant to a decision.

For example, assume that Richmond is considering introducing a new product. The product development manager has undertaken a costing exercise (shown in Figure 3.10), which suggests that the product should not be launched.

Re: Profitability of Product A
From: Product Development Manager
To: Managing Director

An analysis of the profitability of product A suggests that it will lead to a loss of £7000 (see below). The recommendation is therefore to not proceed with the launch of the product.

		Profitability of product A	
		£	£
Revenue	(note 1)		40,000
Variable costs	(note 2)	20,000	
Lease of machine	(note 3)	5,000	
Overheads	(note 4)	8,000	
Market research	(note 5)	5,000	
Product development	(note 6)	9,000	
Total cost			47,000
Loss on product A			(7,000)

Note 1. Revenue based on estimated sales of 2000 units at £20 per unit.
Note 2. Variable cost per unit estimated at £10.
Note 3. A machine will need to be leased for £5000.
Note 4. General overheads are allocated to projects on the basis of 20% of revenue.
Note 5. The cost of the market research exercise carried out earlier this year.
Note 6. £4000 on product development has already been spent and a further £5000 is committed.

Figure 3.10   Memo from product development manager on profitability of product A

The managing director has asked the accountant to critically examine these figures and this has been provided in Figure 3.11.

From: Accountant
To: Managing Director
Re: Profitability of Product A

The analysis by the product development manager does not provide a true picture of the impact on Richmond PLC if it decides to progress with the development and launch of product A. In his analysis, a number of irrelevant costs have been included. The market research expenditure of £5000 has already been spent, as has £5000 on product development. A further £4000 has also been committed on product development, whether the product is or is not launched. These are sunk costs and are irrelevant to the decision. The share of general overheads is also an irrelevant cost, as these costs will be incurred whether the product is produced or is not produced. A revised contribution statement shown below will more accurately illustrate the impact on the company of the decision to launch product A.

Figure 3.11   Analysis of project considering relevant costs

	Contribution with launch of product A	
	£	£
Revenue		40,000
Variable costs	20,000	
Lease of machine	5,000	
Total additional cost		25,000
Contribution from sale of product A		15,000

The decision to progress with the sale of product A should therefore lead to a contribution to overheads of £15,000 based on the assumptions provided.

Figure 3.11 *(Continued)*

Activity 3.8

XYZ Company has undertaken a market research exercise for £5000 to investigate the viability of a project. Having undertaken this exercise it has identified that the project will generate extra sales of £100,000 and additional variable costs will be £20,000. Fixed costs that will increase because of the project will be £30,000. The company has already committed itself to legal fees of £10,000 on an exercise to patent the new product and general overheads that will be apportioned to the product are £20,000.

Identify the additional contribution that will be generated by this project and identify whether it is worth progressing the project to the next stage.

Opportunity cost

Opportunity cost is a cost that measures the opportunity that is lost or sacrificed when an opportunity is foregone.

For example, assume a catering company has been asked to quote for a contract. It is a busy time of the year and if this contract is won then other work, which contributes £300 to overheads, will have to be foregone. This £300 foregone is an opportunity cost and should be taken into consideration when decisions are made.

Activity 3.9

The variable cost of the contract for which the catering company has been asked to quote is £1000. What is the minimum price that should be quoted for the contract?

Avoidable and unavoidable costs

Avoidable costs are the same as relevant costs. If the decision is made not to proceed with the sale of a product, then the costs saved would be avoidable costs. Costs that cannot be saved are unavoidable costs.

Relevant cost of material

The relevant cost of material depends on the circumstances. In the exercises considered to date, the relevant cost of material has been the purchase cost of that material. If material is in stock, then the original purchase cost is not the relevant cost as it is a sunk cost.

(a) If the material is in constant use and more material will be purchased to replace the existing material in stock that is used on a particular job, then the relevant cost is considered to be the cost to *replace* the material used.

(b) If the material is not required for any other contract and the only option available is to resell the material, then the relevant cost is the resale value. The original cost of the material is again irrelevant as it is a sunk cost. This is illustrated in Figure 3.12.

XYZ Company has 100 kgs of material A in stock. This material originally cost £300 to buy. If it is not used in any existing product then the material could be resold to the wholesaler for £200. To purchase an extra 100 kgs of material from the wholesaler would cost £400.

What is the relevant cost assuming:

(a) Material A cannot be used on any other contract?
(b) Material A is in constant use on a range of contracts?

Answer:

(a) If material A cannot be used on any other contract then the relevant cost is the best alternative, which is the resale value of £200.
(b) If material A is in constant use on a range of contracts then the 100 kgs of material will have to be replaced at a cost of £400. £400 is therefore the relevant cost.

Figure 3.12   Relevant cost of material

Activity 3.10

ABC Ltd has 50 kgs of material D in stock. This material originally cost £400 to buy.
    100 kgs of material are required on a contract. There is no other use for the material.
    What is the relevant cost of 100 kgs of material D if the resale value is £3 per kg and the replacement cost is £5.50 per kg?

Summary

In considering different options it is helpful to follow a decision-making approach. The objective of a study should be stated, and alternatives identified. In undertaking a financial evaluation, relevant costs and revenues are those that change because of a decision.

Managers face a range of decisions that have implications for the short and for the longer term. In this chapter the focus was on decisions that affect the short-term future. Such decisions might include:

- Whether to drop a product or service.
- Assessing the return from different marketing plans.
- Considering whether to make or buy a product.
- Identifying the optimum production plan given a constraint in a resource.

A range of terminology is used by managers and accountants, including avoidable and unavoidable costs; incremental costs; marginal costs; opportunity cost; relevant and irrelevant costs; sunk costs.

Further reading

Drury, C. (2004) *Management and Cost Accounting*, 6th edn. Thomson Learning, Chapter 9 and 26.

Robinson, M. (1990) Contribution Margin Analysis: No longer Relevant/Strategic Cost Management; The New Paradigm *Journal of Management Accounting Research*, **2**, 1–32. This article focuses on a panel discussion on relevant costs, involving a number of academics including Kaplan, Shank and Horngren.

Answers to activities

Activity 3.1

(a) It is necessary to identify the costs that will be saved if the region is closed.
(b) Assuming that no Head Office costs will be saved by the closure of the region, then closure of the North region could lead to a loss in contribution to the company overheads of £100,000.

A number of assumptions need to be tested. For example, it is assumed in this analysis that all regional costs can be saved with the closure of the region. This might not be the case. Also, it is assumed that all revenue is lost. In practice, the East and West regions may be able to undertake some of the work previously undertaken by the North region.

Region	North £'000	East £'000	West £'000
Revenue	600	750	1000
Regional costs	500	550	700
Contribution to Head Office costs	100	200	300
Costs	150	150	150
Profit/(loss)	(50)	50	150

Activity 3.2

The analysis of the sale's directors proposal is shown below

Product	X	Y	Z	Total
Budgeted sales (units)	7,800	9,600	8,400	
	(£)	(£)	(£)	(£)
Sales price per unit	45.00	78.00	95.00	
Variable cost per unit	39.00	56.00	77.00	
Selling commission	2.25	3.9	4.75	
Total variable costs	41.25	59.9	81.75	
Contribution	3.75	18.1	13.25	
Total contribution	29,250	173,760	111,300	314,310
Fixed costs				247,250
Net Profit				67,060

The proposal results in a contribution of £314,310 and a profit of £67,060, which is less than expected without the sales commission.

It might be questioned whether the price per unit will remain the same if the volume of sales increases 20%. Will the cost assumptions still be valid; for example, will there be no increase in fixed costs, despite the increase in the volume, and will the variable cost per unit remain the same?

Activity 3.3

The existing marketing and sales plan would seem to lead to the highest financial return.

Activity 3.4

- Will the quality of product Z be the same if Able Engineering manufacture it?
- Will the product be delivered on time to customers?
- If the work were subcontracted to Able Engineering is there a danger that it would raise the price at a later date? At that point Richmond PLC may find that it is difficult to take back the work.
- What is the impact on the workforce of Richmond PLC? For example, will there be redundancies and the loss of skilled labour from Richmond PLC? Also, what will be the effect on morale from lost sales and redundancy of colleagues?

Activity 3.5

(a) It is necessary to investigate the cost savings that could be made if Richmond PLC subcontracted its computing work. Could the £40,000 wages be saved? Would there be redundancy costs? Would any of the general overheads be saved? Assuming that the wages could be saved, but the general overheads could not, then the company would be £10,000 worse off from subcontracting.

(b) The company would need to consider the quality of the service of the contractor vs. in-house. If additional services are required, will this mean that additional costs have to be incurred to obtain them from outside? An employee may be able to answer certain questions on an ad-hoc basis without an additional charge being incurred by the company.

Activity 3.6

If the price of product A were £17, then the contribution per unit and per hour for product A would be £7. This would compare with a contribution per hour for product B of £6. It would therefore be financially better to produce and sell product A. It would be necessary to consider the likelihood of the price changing again.

Activity 3.7

The expected production plan and contribution would be as shown below.

Product	X	Y	Z
contribution £	3	22	18
hours	2	3	6.5
contribution/hour £	1.50	7.33	2.77
Ranking	3	1	2

	Budgeted sales	Hours per unit	Hours required	Cumulative hours	Contribution (£)
Product Y	8,000	3	24,000	24,000	176,000
Product Z	7,000	6.5	45,500	69,500	126,000
Product X	250	2	500	70,000	750
Total contribution					302,750
Fixed costs					247,250
Profit					55,500

Activity 3.8

Additional revenue	£100,000
Additional future costs are variable cost	£20,000
Additional fixed costs	£30,000
Total additional future costs	£50,000

The additional contribution that will be generated from this project will be £50,000.

The market research exercise of £5000, the legal fees of £10,000 are sunk costs as the money on the first has already been spent and the legal fees are a committed cost. The general overheads are irrelevant as they are apportioned overheads.

Activity 3.9

The additional variable costs of the contract are £1000 and the contract must also generate a contribution of at least £300 as that is the opportunity cost of not progressing with the best alternative. The minimum price that should be quoted is therefore at or above £1300.

Activity 3.10

If the company proceeds with the contract, it will have to purchase 50 kgs of material A at a cost of £5.50 per kg. This is a cost of £275.

The relevant cost of the existing stock of 50 kgs is the resale value of £3 per kg, i.e. a cost of £150.

The relevant cost of 100 kgs of material A is therefore £275 + £150 = £425.

Discussion questions

1. What 'non-financial' reasons are there for making rather than buying a product or service?
2. Dropping a product or segment may result in people losing their jobs. How should this be taken into account by an organization?
3. What is an opportunity cost and why is it important for decision-making.
4. When is the purchase price of material irrelevant for decision-making purposes? Explain when replacement cost or resale value is the relevant cost.

Exercises

(Questions with numbers in bold have answers at the back of the book.)

Q3.1 Android Ltd supplies two products, product M and product N. The following information is provided on the cost of these two products.

Product	A	B
	(£)	(£)
Labour £5/hr	10	5
Material	5	6
Overhead	5	5
Total cost	20	16
Mark-up 25%	5	4
Selling price	25	20

It is expected that 150 units of M and 50 units of N will be produced. Overheads of £1000 are general overheads and are fixed costs. The overhead per unit is calculated by dividing the expected overheads for the forthcoming month by the total number of units. The overhead cost per unit will be the same whether it is product M or product N.

Overheads per month £1000 = £5/unit
Expected output per month 200 units

(a) The marketing manager has suggested that the price of product A be reduced from £25 to £23. He suggests that this will result in an additional 20 units a month being sold.

Is this proposal worthwhile?

(b) As an alternative to (a) above, the marketing manager has suggested that an advertisement be placed in a local newspaper, which will cost £200. This advert will result in an extra 25 units of product A being sold each month.

Is this proposal worthwhile?

Q3.2 The summarized 'Profit and Loss' statement for Able PLC for the last year is as follows:

	£'000	£'000
Sales (25,000 units)		100
Direct materials	35	
Direct labour	25	
Production overhead	15	
Administration overhead	20	
Total Cost		95
Profit		5

Labour and material costs are assumed to be variable and the production and administration costs are assumed to be fixed.

Required:

(a) Calculate the break-even point and margin of safety.
(b) The sales manager has suggested reducing the price by 10%, which he believes will result in an increase in sales volume of 25%.

Is this proposal worthwhile?

(c) The personnel manager has suggested a productivity agreement. With this agreement, wages will increase by £0.20 per unit and production can be increased by 20%. Production was previously a constraint and so sales volume can also be increased by 20%. Advertising costs would increase by £10,000.

Q3.3 The management of AB Ltd is considering making

Either:

Component Q, for which the production cost is as follows:

	£
Raw materials	6
Direct labour	6
Fixed overhead	16
Total cost	28

Component Q could be bought from an outside supplier for £19.

Or:

Product Z, for which the normal selling price is £17 and the production cost of one unit of Z is

	£
Raw materials	8
Direct labour	4
Fixed overhead	8
Total cost	20

It cannot make both products because of a shortage of labour. The workforce is paid £4 an hour.

Identify which of the two contracts should be accepted on financial grounds. Identify other factors that should be considered.

Q3.4 Product A can be sold for £65. Adams Ltd can buy product A for £60 from a supplier or it can make the product at a variable cost of £50 per unit. The product requires 4 hours of labour per unit and the wage rate is £7 per hour. There is a shortage of labour to make product A and so Adams Ltd is considering bringing in agency staff. What is the maximum wage per hour that the company would be prepared to pay for this agency staff?

Q3.5 Edam Ltd can sell product M for £45. It can buy product M for £40 per unit or it can make it at a variable cost of £30 per unit. To make the product it will also be necessary to lease a machine for £4000. How many units need to be sold to justify making the product rather than buying it?

Q3.6 Eldon Ltd can sell a second-hand machine now for £2000. Alternatively it could repair the machine and sell it for £2500.

To repair the machine would require 30 hours of a skilled maintenance engineer who is paid £12 an hour. If the engineer works on the machine it will not be possible to accept a contract which will generate a contribution to overheads of £250.

Required:

Should the machine be sold for £2000 or should it be repaired and sold for £2500? Show calculations to support your argument.

Q3.7 The summarized 'Profit and Loss' statement for Beta PLC for the last year is as follows:

	£'000	£'000
Sales (30,000)		90
Direct materials	30	
Direct labour (10 minutes per unit)	20	
Fixed production overhead	15	
Selling and administration overhead (note 1)	20	
Total Cost		85
Profit		5

Note 1. Selling and administration costs are considered to be 50% variable and 50% fixed.

1. Calculate the break-even point and margin of safety.
2. The sales manager has suggested reducing the price by 5%, which he believes will result in an increase in sales volume of 20%.

Is this proposal worthwhile?

3. Evaluate a proposal to implement an agreement on working hours. With this agreement labour cost will increase by 10p per unit but production can be increased by 25%. Production was previously a constraint and so sales volume can also be increased by 25%. Advertising costs would increase by £5000.

Q3.8 The following information is provided about Sentinel Ltd:

Product	A	B	C
Budgeted sales (units)	2500	3000	3000
	(£)	(£)	(£)
Sales price per unit	40	39	75
Variable cost per unit			
Material (1 kg of material costs £6)	12	6	8
Labour (pay is £8 per hour)	12	20	32
Variable overheads	5	4	13
Fixed overhead per unit	6	10	16
Total cost per unit	35	40	69
Profit per unit	5	−1	6

(a) Provide a statement that will show:

  – The contribution per unit by product.
  – The total contribution by product and in total.
  – The total profit.

(b) The management of Sentinel Ltd are considering dropping product B, as it is making a loss. Evaluate the merit of this proposal.

(c) An outside contractor has offered to manufacture product A for £31.
Should Sentinel accept this offer? Discuss both financial and non-financial considerations.

(d) Two alternatives have been recommended.

- The managing director has proposed that a marketing campaign costing £30,000 be undertaken. This will increase sales by 20%.
- The personnel director has suggested that an incentive scheme worth £2 an hour be introduced. He believes that this policy will enable productivity and sales to increase by 15%.

Evaluate these two proposals and advise whether either is worthwhile.

(e) It is estimated that the maximum number of labour hours available is 25,000 and the maximum amount of material will be 10,000 kgs. All three products use only one type of material and the cost per kg is £6.

Identify the optimum production plan and the profit that will be generated given this production plan and sales.

Q3.9 Home Carers Ltd has been set up to provide services to old people so that they can remain living independently. At present the company is totally dependent on social services departments for payments. The company is currently operating in three locations and has a Head Office in Portsmouth. The income statements for the latest quarter for each location are as follows:

	Area 1	Area 2	Area 3
No. of clients	200	150	120
Average billing/client/qtr	£1,680	£1,400	£1,800
	(£)	(£)	(£)
Billings to SS departments	336,000	210,000	216,000
Less Costs			
Carers' wages	120,000	90,000	72,000
Consumables	40,000	30,000	24,000
Supervisors' salaries	9,360	8,100	8,160
Office costs	92,000	64,000	59,200
Share of central overheads	38,000	38,000	38,000
Net Profit	36,640	−20,100	14,640

Carers' wages and consumables are variable costs. Supervisors are paid a salary of £6000 per quarter plus a bonus of 1% of total billings. Office costs have a variable element of £250 per client per quarter.

The proprietors, Mr and Mrs Bumble, are dissatisfied with overall performance and are considering closing Area 2 office. Two alternatives have been suggested.

Alternative 1

The company could move into the private care market by introducing a premium service for clients, whose relatives could afford to pay a top-up payment. The quarterly billing would be £2000 per client, but the cost of carers' wages would increase by 50% and consumables would increase by 100%. It is estimated that the number of clients would remain the same.

Alternative 2

Billings to social services departments could be increased by paying for independent reassessments of clients' needs. There would be additional fixed costs per location of £5300 per quarter, but the billing fee per client would increase by 5%.

Required:

(a) Redraft the income statements in contribution format.
(b) Should the Area 2 location be closed?
(c) Are alternatives 1 and 2 worthwhile in each location?

Q3.10 The accountant of Lyon Gate PLC has prepared a quote for a contract:

	£
Revenue from the contract	
Labour cost	12,000
Material	10,000
Depreciation of machinery	1,000
Product development	6,000
General overhead 100% of labour	12,000
Total costs	39,000
Mark-up at 10%	3,900
Recommended quote for the contract	42,900

The following information is available:

(i) The labour cost of £12,000 consisted of £3000 for grade A labour and £9000 for grade B labour. There is no other work for grade A labour at present. Grade B labour is in scare supply and if not used on this contract this labour will be subcontracted to an outside company at a charge of £10,000.

(ii) The material cannot be used on any other contract and the only alternative is to sell the material for £6000.

(iii) Depreciation of machinery is based on a conventional straight-line method of calculation. The production manager considers that the value of the equipment used will fall in value regardless of the use to which it is put. There is no alternative use for this machinery.

(iv) The product development cost has already been spent.

Required:

The commercial manager has commented that this quote is totally unrealistic and has asked you to re-examine the work of the accountant in order to identify the true cost of undertaking the contract.

Q3.11 Appledore Ltd is considering tendering for a job which will take three months to complete. If the job is taken it will not displace another one. The accountant has submitted the following estimate:

	£
Direct materials	
Material A	12,000
Material B	10,200
Material C	10,800
Direct labour	40,000
Manufacturing overheads	
Depreciation of equipment	4,000
(straight line)	
Salary of supervisors (2)	14,000
General fixed overheads	20,000
(50% on direct labour)	
Total manufacturing cost	111,000
Administration overhead	22,200
(20% of manufacturing cost)	
Total cost	133,200

The following additional information is available:

(1) The cost of all materials is shown at their purchase cost. Material A was purchased a year ago, is not in common use and would fetch about £6000 if sold. If not used on this job it could be used in the next few months on another contract as a substitute for a material that costs approximately 20% of the cost of material A. Material B is in common use, the purchase price has risen 50% since the current stock of material B was purchased. Material C has not yet been ordered.

(2) Labour costing £20,000 will be recruited for this contract. The remaining labour will be employed from the existing workforce. Currently there is spare capacity, with some idle time for the workforce; however, this contract will use up this spare capacity and in fact an estimated £4000 will need to be worked on overtime.

(3) The equipment cost £50,000 some eight years ago and is planned to be kept for another four years, after which it will be sold for an expected £2000. The depreciation charge is based on this expectation. The equipment is currently valued at £5000 and is expected to be worth £4000 after the contract. If not used on the contract the value would be £4500.

(4) One foreman will be employed specifically for this contract. The other supervisor is currently underemployed and undertaking clerical duties that could be completed by a new recruit on a salary of £4000.

(5) General fixed overheads and administration costs will not be affected by this contract.

Required:

(a) A revised cost estimate for the job. Calculations should be explained.

(b) What factors should the company be taking into account when deciding on the price to tender for the contract?

Capital Investment Decisions

4

Objectives

When you have completed this chapter you should be able to:

- Explain and undertake an investment appraisal using four techniques.

  - Payback.
  - Accounting Rate of Return.
  - Net Present Value.
  - Internal Rate of Return.

Introduction

In order to survive and grow, organizations often need to invest in new projects that will have an impact on the business over a number of years. Such projects can involve the acquisition of new assets such as building and machinery for expansion, cost reduction, asset replacement or sometimes even non-profit-earning purposes. This chapter is concerned with the financial evaluation of such investments.

In order to decide whether it is worthwhile acquiring an asset it is necessary to identify the cash flows that are expected to occur. A means of appraising these cash flows is then required and four commonly used methods are explained, namely payback, Accounting Rate of Return, Net Present Value, Internal Rate of Return. More complex problems, which require the information to be first sorted into a cash flow table, are identified in the second part of the chapter. Problems arising from the need to deal with risk, inflation, taxation and non-financial issues are noted.

Financial evaluation of the investment decision

On many occasions, organizations will wish to evaluate new options which involve the purchase of fixed/non-current assets such as land, buildings, machinery and other equipment. These investments can be for:

1. Expansion
   Additional investment might be necessary for a range of purposes, for example:

   - Market penetration through increased sales of existing products.
   - Sales of new products in existing markets.
   - Sales of new products in new markets.
   - Mergers with other organizations.

2. Cost reduction
   For example, the building of new manufacturing plant to deliver economies of scale.
3. Replacement of existing assets
   Assets that have reached the end of their life will need to be replaced.
4. Non-profit-earning projects
   These may be for one of two purposes:

   (i) Statutory requirements, for example the construction of safety or pollution control equipment following new legislation on such areas.
   (ii) 'Altruistic' purposes, for example the construction of medical facilities for the staff of employees or for the community.

Consideration of cash flows

In order to undertake an appraisal it is necessary to identify the cash inflows and outflows that will occur when an investment takes place. Cash flows will involve:

(i) Investment in new assets.

   (a) Fixed/non-current assets. If certain assets are also being sold as a result of an investment then these cash flows should be included in the appraisal.
   (b) There may also be a need to invest in additional working capital, i.e. inventory (stock) and trade receivables (debtors). With the launch of a new product, for example, it will most probably have been necessary to have previously built up a holding of stock/inventory in order to meet the expected level of sales demand.

(ii) Operating cash flows. For a replacement project, there may be savings in costs, for example, labour, materials and maintenance costs. For an expansion project, there will be an additional contribution due to increased revenue flows less additional costs of labour, materials and overheads.
(iii) Tax effects. Tax will need to be paid on profits, although there are offsetting benefits with a tax allowance for any capital investment. In the examples included in this chapter, the impact of tax is ignored.
(iv) Recoveries at the end of a project. At the end there may be some cash recoveries if land, buildings or equipment can be sold. Also, at the end of the product life, there will be a reduction in working capital when production ceases and the remaining stocks of the product are sold.

Consideration of cost of capital

If a capital investment is undertaken then there will be a funding cost involved. Calculation of the weighted average cost of capital will be considered in Chapter 12.

Stages in the appraisal of investments

The financial appraisal of an investment will require a number of stages.

(1) As identified above, the first part of an appraisal exercise is to identify the cash flows that change as a result of the investment. Only future cash flows should be considered and non-cash items, such as depreciation, should not be included in the analysis.
(2) The second part of the exercise is to apply the appraisal techniques used by the organization to the data that has been collected.

There are four main appraisal techniques used in organizations. Two traditional appraisal techniques that do not take into consideration the cost of capital are payback and accounting rate of return (ARR). Appraisal techniques that do take account of the cost of capital are net present value (NPV) and internal rate of return (IRR).
(3) The final stage is the application of the decision rule. For example, the decision rule used by an organization may be that the cash inflows must be equal to the cash outflows within a certain period of time. This is the payback criterion.

Illustration of the use of four appraisal techniques for three investment projects

To illustrate the use of the appraisal techniques, three projects will be considered.
The net cash flows for these projects are shown in Figure 4.1.

Three projects, A, B and C, are being considered by XY Ltd. Each of the projects is expected to involve an initial investment in new machinery of £1,000,000, with a nil scrap value at the end of five years. Net cash flows (i.e. the net effect of both cash inflows and outflows) from the trading activities for the next five years are shown below.

Year	A £'000	B £'000	C £'000
0	−1000	−1000	−1000
1	0	200	200
2	100	200	300
3	300	300	500
4	600	400	400
5	1300	1150	400

The requirement is to identify the preferred investment.

Note that in this table year 0 refers to the time when the initial investment takes place. Year 1 is the cash flows in the first year, which for simplicity in the examples in this chapter are assumed to occur at the end of the year.

Figure 4.1 Net cash flows of projects A, B and C

To decide which investment to undertake, it is necessary to know the criteria used by the organization. Four possible criteria are usually used, payback period, accounting rate of return, net present value and internal rate of return.

Payback period

The **payback period** is the number of years it takes to recover the initial investment. This occurs when the cumulative cash inflows equals the cumulative cash outflows.

Organizations will have a decision rule on the payback time that is acceptable. For example, with a three-year payback requirement,it would be necessary for cash inflows to be equal to outflows within three years.

The calculation of the payback for projects A and B is shown in Figure 4.2.

	Project A cash flow			Project B cash flow	
Year	In year	Cumulative	Year	In year	Cumulative
	£'000	£'000		£'000	£'000
0	−1000	−1000	0	−1000	−1000
1	0	−1000	1	200	−800
2	100	−900	2	200	−600
3	300	−600	3	300	−300
4	600	0	4	400	100
5	1300	1100	5	1150	1250

The payback for project A is 4 years.

The payback for project B is 3 years 9 months. At the end of year 3, £300,000 still needs to be paid back. At the end of year 4, after a cash repayment of £400,000 in the year, there is a cash surplus of £100,000.

The investment is paid back in $\dfrac{£300,000}{£400,000} = 0.75$ of a year.

That is, 9 months through the fourth year. Note that it is assumed that cash flows evenly throughout the year rather than in one single cash flow amount.

If XY Ltd required a three-year payback, then neither of these investments would be accepted.

Figure 4.2 Payback for projects A and B

Activity 4.1

Calculate the payback of project C.

The advantages and disadvantages of payback

Advantages

Payback is popular because:

1. Cash flow is crucial to many companies and payback measures the net cash generated by the project in the shorter term.
2. It can be used as a filter to reject projects, without the need to consider all the cash-flow implications.
3. It is a simple and easy-to-understand rule and can be used for *small projects* where a simple decision rule is adequate.

Disadvantages

1. It does not consider the cash flows after the payback cut-off point. After four years for project A, for example, there will be a major cash inflow, but this has been ignored.
2. Ignores the timing of cash flows and the cost of capital. Cash flows in later years are treated as being as important as the cash flows in earlier years.

Accounting Rate of Return

The **Accounting Rate of Return (ARR)** is the average annual profit divided by the initial investment. An investment would be accepted if its ARR was equal to or greater than a minimum 'hurdle' rate set by the organization.

Profit is different from net cash flow. Profit = cash flows from trading activities − non-cash items such as the cost of depreciation.

$$\text{Average annual profit} = \frac{\text{Profit}}{\text{Number of years of the project}}$$

The calculation of the accounting rate of return for project A is shown in Figure 4.3.

(i) Calculating average profit

For project A the first step is to work out the average annual profit. The cash inflows from trading over the five years are $0 + £100,000 + £300,000 + £600,000 + £1,300,000 = £2,300,000$.

The asset cost £1,000,000 to purchase. The value at the end of the project was zero (nil residual value). Depreciation on the project is therefore £1,000,000.

	£
Net cash flow from trading	2,300,000
Depreciation	1,000,000
Profit over the five years	1,300,000

$$\text{Average profit} = \frac{£1,300,000}{5} = £260,000.$$

(ii) Calculate the ARR

Divide the average profit by the investment, in this case £1,000,000.

$$\text{Therefore ARR} = \frac{£260,000}{£1,000,000} = 26\%.$$

If the 'hurdle' rate ARR of the organization was 25% then using this criterion in isolation, the investment would be acceptable.

Figure 4.3   Accounting rate of return for project A

Activity 4.2

Calculate the ARR of projects B and C.

Note that some organizations quote the accounting rate of return by dividing the average accounting profit by the average capital investment rather than the initial capital investment. For project A:

$$\text{Average capital investment} = (\text{initial value} + \text{ending value})/2$$

$$= (£1,000,000 + 0)/2 = £500,000.$$

$$\text{Accounting rate of return would be } \frac{£260,000}{£500,000} = 52\%.$$

The advantages and disadvantages of accounting rate of return

Advantages

The ARR technique is popular because:

1. It is familiar to many managers, for example, divisional managers are often assessed on accounting measures such as return on capital employed or return on investment. These accounting measures are very similar to ARR.
2. It considers the whole life of the project.

Disadvantages

ARR treats all cash flows as being equally important, even though early cash flows are 'worth' more than later cash flows.

Net Present Value

The next two appraisal techniques, Net Present Value (NPV) and Internal Rate of Return (IRR) take into consideration the cost of capital using a technique called discounting.

Discounting is based on the principle that £1 in a number of years' time is worth less to the investor than £1 now. For example, if an investor has some funds and is considering an investment in a new building project, then cash flows to be earned in the future would be worth less than current cash because of:

1. Interest. The funds could be invested in a bank and earn interest.
2. Risk. The higher the risk involved in an investment, the higher will be the return that will be required by the investor to compensate for the risk.
3. Inflation. With inflation, future cash flows will purchase less than cash available now.

The present value approach aims to discount future cash flows to their equivalent value now by taking account of the 'time value' of money. **Net present value** is the sum of the present values of the future cash flows.

For a company considering its cost of capital, the rate of discount should reflect the requirement of investors to be compensated for interest, risk and inflation. Calculating the cost of capital is illustrated in Chapter 12.

Compound interest and discounting is discussed further in Figure 4.4.

Compound interest

Compound interest is interest based not only on the original (principal) sum invested, but also on any unpaid interest that has been added to the principal. To find out the future value of an investment the formula $S = P(1 + i)^n$ can be used, where S is the future value of the investment, P is the principal invested, i is the interest earned on this investment and n is the number of years.

Assume £1 is invested and earns 10% interest payable at the end of the year. Using the formula, at the end of year 1 the value of the investment $S = £1(1 + 0.1) = £1.10$.

If the £1.10 was reinvested at 10%, then at the end of year 2, $S = £1.10(1 + 0.1) = £1.21$ (i.e. £1.10 × 1.1).

If the £1.21 was reinvested at 10%, then at the end of year 3, the investment will be worth £1.331 (i.e. £1.21 × 1.1).

Activity 4.3

If £909.10 is invested at 10%, how much would it be worth at the end of years 1, 2, 3, 4, 5?

Figure 4.4 Compound interest and discounted cash flow

Discounting

If the rate of discount is known, the expected cash flow in the future can be expressed in terms of its value to the business now. For example, if it is known that £1 will be earned in 1 year's time, then at a discount rate of 10%, it would be necessary to invest approximately 91 pence now. This can be calculated by reversing the compound interest calculation, i.e. $P/(1+i)$, where the principal sum P in this example is £1 and i is 10%. To be precise: $\dfrac{£1}{(1+0.1)} = £0.9091$.

The *discount factor* is the factor by which future cash flows are discounted to arrive at today's monetary value. In this example, if the discount rate is 10%, then the discount factor to be applied to bring cash flows received in 1 year's time to present value is 0.9091.

Similarly, £1 earned at the end of year 2 is the equivalent of having approximately £0.8264 today, i.e. invest £0.8264 at 10% over two years and this will result in an investment of approximately £1. Therefore:

If £1 is to be received in 1 year's time and the cost of capital is 10%, then the 'present value' of that £1 is £0.9091.

If £1 is to be received in 2 years' time and the cost of capital is 10%, then the 'present value' of that £1 is £0.8264.

Discounting is a technique which enables organizations to take account of the cost of capital. If future cash flows are identified then it is possible to discount these future cash flows in order to identify their *present value*.

It is possible to calculate the discount factor given different discount rates. Appendix (Present value table) at the back of the book provides a summary of the present values of receiving £1 in a number of years' time given different discount rates.

Figure 4.4 (*Continued*)

The net present value of project A is shown in Figure 4.5.

The cost of capital of the company (the rate of discount) is 10%. Future cash flows of the project are therefore discounted using the discount factor for 10%.

	Project A cash flow		
Year	Cash flow in year £'000	Discount factor	Present value £'000
0	−1000	1	−1000
1	0	0.9091	0
2	100	0.8264	83
3	300	0.7513	225
4	600	0.6830	410
5	1300	0.6209	807
			525

At a discount rate of 10% the project earns a net present value of £525,000. Since this is positive, the investment creates value for the investors.

Figure 4.5 Net present value of project A

Activity 4.4

Calculate the NPV of projects B and C.

The advantages and disadvantages of net present value

Advantages

1. NPV takes into account the amount and timing of all cash flows.
2. Undertaking a positive NPV project is the same thing as adding to shareholders' wealth.

Internal Rate of Return

The **Internal Rate of Return (IRR)** is the discount rate that gives an NPV equal to zero. An investment would be accepted if its IRR was equal to or greater than a minimum 'hurdle' rate set by the organization.

IRR can be calculated using a computer spreadsheet or programmable calculator. If either of these is not available it can be found by trial and error, with the net cash flows discounted using different discount rates until NPV comes to zero. A 'short cut' method to calculate the approximate value of the IRR, called linear interpolation, is shown in Figure 4.6.

Year	Cash flow in year £'000	Discount factor 10%	Present value £'000	Year	Cash flow in year £'000	Discount factor 25%	Present value £'000
0	−1000	1	−1000	0	−1000	1	−1000
1	0	0.9091	0	1	0	0.8000	0
2	100	0.8264	83	2	100	0.6400	64
3	300	0.7513	225	3	300	0.5120	154
4	600	0.6830	410	4	600	0.4096	246
5	1300	0.6209	807	5	1300	0.3277	426
			525				−111

The net present value is £525,000 at a 10% discount factor and −£111,000 at a 25% discount factor. The discount rate must therefore be closer to 25% than 10%.

The formula to be followed with linear interpolation is shown below:

$$\text{IRR} = \text{lowest discount rate} + \text{difference in discount rate} \times \frac{\text{NPV at lowest discount rate}}{\text{difference in NPVs}}$$

For this example:

$$\text{IRR} = 10\% + 15\% \times \frac{£525,000}{(£525,000 + £111,000)}$$

$$= 10\% + 12\% = 22\%.$$

Figure 4.6   Internal rate of return for project A

Activity 4.5

Calculate the IRR of projects B and C.

The advantages and disadvantages of internal rate of return

Advantages

1. For most projects IRR actually gives the same project selection as NPV.
2. IRR may be better for communicating than NPV. A comment such as 'the internal rate of return is 22% on this project' may seem more meaningful than 'the NPV of this project is £525,000'. Note that the percentage return is not the same as the ARR.

Disadvantages

The IRR technique can have more than one IRR, also some projects have no IRR.

Activity 4.6

It has been argued that in order to evaluate a project to see if it leads to an increase in shareholder wealth, it is necessary to satisfy the following criteria:

1. The amount of all cash flows should be considered.
2. The timing of the cash flows should be considered.
3. The risk of the cash flows should be considered.

Which technique(s) satisfy the three criteria identified above?

Decision rule for accepting projects

It is possible to accept any combination of projects as long as they comply with the decision rules of the organization (unless the projects are mutually exclusive, i.e. it is only possible to accept one of the options).

Payback method: Each organization should decide on how quickly an investment must pay back its cash. If payback must be within 3 years, then 3 years is the cut-off point for the organization. Any investment which took longer than 3 years to pay back would not be accepted.

ARR method: Projects with ARRs greater than or equal to the organization's hurdle rate should be accepted. As an example, if an organization requires all investments to have an ARR of greater than 12%, then 12% is the hurdle rate.

NPV method: Accept all positive NPV projects.

IRR method: Accept all projects with IRRs greater than or equal to the organization's hurdle rate.

The results of the appraisal of the three investments for XY Ltd are shown in Table 4.1.

Table 4.1   Appraisal of three investments for XY Ltd

	Project A	Project B	Project C
Payback	4 years	3.75 years	3 years
ARR	26%	25%	16%
NPV	£525,000	£559,800	£327,000
IRR	22.40%	24.50%	21.50%

Activity 4.7

Which projects would be accepted if the criteria are that all projects must have a:

(a) Minimum of a 3-year payback.
(b) Minimum of a 25% accounting rate of return.
(c) Positive net present value.
(d) Minimum IRR of 20%.

Many organizations use a number of investment criteria in order to judge which projects to accept. Increasing shareholder wealth might be a key objective of the organization and accordingly a project should have a positive net present value. However, other financial objectives might be important, for example it might be important to the organization that cash is paid back quickly or to the manager that a high accounting rate of return is generated.

Activity 4.8

Which project should be accepted given that the organization will only accept projects that meet criteria of a payback equal to or less than 3 years and a positive net present value?

If projects are mutually exclusive

If more than one project satisfies the minimum criteria set by the organization, then management must make a judgement on which is the best project.

Activity 4.9

Assume that the following are the minimum criteria for XY Ltd:

- A payback of 4 years.
- A positive net present value.
- An ARR of 15%.
- An IRR of 20%.

Which project should an organization accept if the three projects are mutually exclusive?

A further example of a choice between two mutually exclusive projects is considered in Figure 4.7.

Sad Ltd is considering purchasing one of two machines to manufacture a new product.

	Machine 1	Machine 2
	(£)	(£)
Capital cost	−460,000	−400,000

Expected cash inflows from operations by year

	(£)	(£)
1	190,000	160,000
2	130,000	120,000
3	130,000	120,000
4	130,000	120,000
5	130,000	110,000
6	130,000	110,000

The expected scrap value of machine 1 is £30,000 and machine 2, £20,000. Each machine is expected to last 6 years.

The cost of capital is 14%.

Required:

Which machine should the company purchase given the net present value criterion?

Answer:

Each project can be evaluated individually and the net present value of each identified. If this is done then the NPV of machine 1 is £111,800 and the NPV of machine 2 is £101,100; machine 1 is preferable as it provides a higher NPV.

An incremental analysis can also be undertaken with a comparison of the two cash flows, as illustrated below.

Figure 4.7   Choosing between two projects

Year	Cash flow machine 1 £'000	Cash flow machine 2 £'000	Difference £'000	14% discount factor	Present value £'000
0	−460	−400	−60	1	−60.0
1	190	160	30	0.8772	26.3
2	130	120	10	0.7695	7.7
3	130	120	10	0.6750	6.7
4	130	120	10	0.5921	5.9
5	130	110	20	0.5194	10.4
6	*160	*130	30	0.4556	13.7
				Net present value	10.7

The cash flow in year 6 represents the cash flow from trading plus the scrap value of the machine.

The above analysis shows that the NPV of investing in machine 1 is £10,700 greater than the NPV for machine 2 and therefore machine 1 is preferable.

Figure 4.7 (*Continued*)

Consideration of a problem requiring a more detailed analysis of cash flows

To date in this chapter, the focus has been on understanding the appraisal technique and so a summary cash flow has been provided. A question which first requires the identification of cash flows into a cash flow table is considered in Figure 4.8.

Appledore Ltd is considering a proposal to manufacture a new product. Market research suggests that 600 units of the product could be sold each year for the next 5 years.

The accountant of Appledore has produced the following estimate of the selling price and costs (excluding machinery) per unit.

	£	£
Selling price		42
Less		
Materials – 4 kgs @ £4	16	
Labour – 2 hours @ £4	8	
Variable overhead	4	
Depreciation of machinery per unit (note 1)	4	
Design costs (note 2)	3	
Other fixed overhead (based on 100% labour) (note 3)	8	
		43
Loss per unit		1

Note 1. The product can be manufactured using a machine already owned by Appledore Ltd. It was purchased 3 years ago for £18,000 and currently stands in the firm's Balance Sheet at £13,000 (after deducting depreciation). It is expected to last a further 5 years and a scrap value of £1000 is expected.

Figure 4.8 Preparation of a cash flow table

The asset value will decrease from £13,000 down to £1000, so that the depreciation will be £12,000. 600 units will be made per year for 5 years, i.e. a total of 3000 units. Therefore:

$$\text{Depreciation per unit} = \frac{£12,000}{3,000 \text{ unit}} = £4 \text{ per unit.}$$

Note 2. The company has just spent £9000 on a design study for the product. Given expected sales of 3000 units, this would mean a cost per unit of £3. Contribution per unit is selling price (£42) less the variable costs of material (£16), labour (£8) and variable overhead (£4), i.e. a contribution per unit of £14. Total contribution per annum = 600 units ×£14 = £8400.

Note 3. The company policy is to absorb overheads to products on the basis of 100% of direct labour cost.

In view of the loss per unit, the managing director of the company has asked for an appraisal in order to identify whether production and sale of this product should proceed. The NPV technique is to be used as the method of appraisal.

Answer:

To answer this question, it is first necessary to identify the cash flows that will result from the decision to proceed.

An investigation has led to the following further information being made available:

(i) Appledore has no other use for the machine that would be used to manufacture the product and it could be sold for £12,000, if the proposal to manufacture the new product is rejected. If the machine is not sold now, it could be sold for £1500 at the end of year 5.
(ii) Maintenance costs of the machine would be £500 a year for the first two years and £600 for years 3, 4 and 5. Other fixed costs are general overheads, which are absorbed on the basis of 100% of labour.
(iii) The company cost of capital is 12%.

Stage 1. Prepare a cash flow table

Year	Machine (note 1)	Contribution (note 2)	Maintenance (note 3)	Net cash flow
0	−12,000			−12,000
1		8,400	−500	7,900
2		8,400	−500	7,900
3		8,400	−600	7,800
4		8,400	−600	7,800
5	1,500	8,400	−600	9,300

Note 1. The book value of the investment is irrelevant. If the decision to manufacture and sell the new product is made, then it will not be possible to sell the machine for £12,000 (this is the opportunity cost that should be taken into account). The project will continue for 5 years and at the end of the fifth year it will be possible to sell the machine for £1500.

Note 2. The cash flow impact needs to be identified.
– Depreciation of the machine is not a cash flow.
– The design costs have already been incurred and are therefore a sunk cost.
– The fixed costs are absorbed on the basis of 100% of overheads and are not relevant to the decision.

Note 3. The maintenance costs are the only fixed costs that change because of the decision to manufacture the product.

Figure 4.8 (*Continued*)

Stage 2. Identify the net present value of the investment

Net cash flow (£)	12% discount factor	Present value (£)
−12,000	1	−12,000
7,900	0.8929	7,054
7,900	0.7972	6,298
7,800	0.7118	5,552
7,800	0.6355	4,957
9,300	0.5674	5,277
	Net present value	17,158

Stage 3. Apply decision rule to make the choice

Since the decision to manufacture and sell the new product results in a positive net present value, it is worthwhile progressing with the decision.

Figure 4.8 (*Continued*)

An advantage in laying out the cash flow information in the form of a cash flow table is that managers can review the information and consider the validity of the assumptions.

Non-financial considerations

In the analysis undertaken to date, only financial factors have been taken into consideration. Non-financial factors may also be important; for example, one option might involve greater pollution to the environment or be unacceptable to key stakeholders of the organization. An option may also provide a lower financial return, but provide a better fit with the strategy of the organization than another alternative. This is considered further in Chapters 17 and 18.

Consideration of risk

The financial analysis is only as good as the assumptions that underpin it. In forecasting future cash flows that could be several years into the future, there are likely to be a number of items where it is difficult to be certain of likely events. A small change in assumptions on some key variables may lead to a large difference in the financial return. Risk techniques such as sensitivity analysis can be used to assess the impact of changes on such variables. A number of risk techniques are considered further in Chapter 18.

Dealing with inflation

There are two ways to deal with inflation.

1. The first is to build inflation into the cash flow forecasts. For example, if it was assumed that 5% inflation were to occur each year over the life of the project, then this could be built into the cash flows and the discount rate would be the cost of capital of the organization.

2. The second is to ignore the effect of inflation and to use an adjusted discount rate. For example, if the money cost of capital to the organization was 15% a real cost of capital would be 5% less than this if inflation was approximately 5%.

It has been suggested that many firms overstate the cost of capital. Often a rate of 15–20% is used for discounting purposes, however, this is above the real cost of capital of many companies where a rate of 8–10% would be more appropriate. The reason is to allow for risk.

Taxation

In the examples considered in this chapter, no provision has been made for taxation. In real examples, this should be taken into account. Organizations may also be able to claim some capital allowances for new investments, which will reduce the taxation that they have to pay.

Summary

Four investment appraisal techniques were introduced.

The payback period is the number of years it takes to recover the initial investment. This occurs when the cumulative cash inflows equal the cumulative cash outflows.

ARR is the average annual after-tax profit divided by the initial investment. An investment would be accepted if its ARR was equal to or greater than a minimum 'hurdle' rate set by the organization.

NPV takes into account the **amount and timing** of all cash flows. Undertaking a positive NPV project is the same thing as maximizing the value of shareholders' wealth.

IRR is the discount rate that gives an NPV equal to zero. An investment would be accepted if its IRR was equal to or greater than a minimum 'hurdle' rate set by the organization.

Further reading

Arnold, G. (2005) *Corporate Financial Management*, 3rd edn. FT/Prentice-Hall, Chapters 2, 3, 4.

Drury, C. (2004) *Management and Cost Accounting*, 6th edn. Thomson Learning, Chapter 16.

Answers to activities

Activity 4.1

Payback for project C is 3 years.

Activity 4.2

ARR of project B is 25% and project C, 16%.

Activity 4.3

£1000; £1100; £1210; £1331; £1464.

Activity 4.4

£559,800; £327,000.

Activity 4.5

24.5%; 21.5%.

Activity 4.6

Net present value is the only appraisal technique that can take account of all three factors. Internal rate of return takes account of all cash flows and the timing of these flows, however, it does not take into consideration a different discount rate given different levels of risk.

Activity 4.7

None of them. Only project C meets the minimum criteria on payback, however, it does not meet the minimum criterion for ARR.

Activity 4.8

Project C.

Activity 4.9

All the three projects exceed the minimum target on each of the criteria. If they are mutually exclusive then a new rule needs to be identified to help choose the best option. If an expected increase in shareholder wealth was the most important then project B is preferable. In Chapter 17, the importance of taking into consideration the suitability of a project from a strategic perspective is discussed.

Discussion questions

1. The Net Present Value of a project in theory measures the change in shareholder wealth. Explain why this is the case.
2. Why is it necessary to discount future cash flows when considering long-term investments?
3. What is the difference between compounding and discounting?
4. Why might a manager prefer ARR or IRR to NPV?
5. Why do many organizations require an assessment of a project using a number of appraisal techniques?

Exercises

(Questions in bold have answers at the back of the book.)

Q4.1   Happy Ltd is considering investing £5 million in new production facilities. The expected cash inflows from the project are as follows:

Year	Cash inflow (£'000)
1	1600
2	1700
3	1660
4	2400
5	1400

The company's cost of capital is 15%.

Required:

Calculate the payback, accounting rate of return and net present value of this investment.

Q4.2   Milton PLC is considering an investment in a machine that will reduce labour costs. The following information relates to this machine:

Cost	£600,000
Salvage value in 5 years	£0
Estimated life	5 years
Annual reduction in existing cash costs	£160,000
Cost of capital	14%

Required:

(i) Calculate the following in respect of the above investment:

- Accounting rate of return (based on initial cost of capital).
- Net present value.
- Payback period.
- Internal rate of return (to nearest 0.5%).

(ii) Discuss how each of the above should be used to determine whether an investment proposal should be accepted and explain, with reasons, which of the above appraisal approaches you favour.

Q4.3   The Richmond Company is preparing its capital budget for the year. A question has arisen as to whether or not to replace a machine with a new and more efficient machine. An analysis of the situation reveals the following based on operations at a normal level of activity:

	Old machine (£)	New machine (£)
Cost new	160,000	200,000
Book value	56,000	–
Estimated physical life remaining	10 years	10 years
Depreciation per year	16,000	20,000
Labour cost per year	30,000	20,000
Material cost per year	720,000	690,000
Power per year	9,000	4,000
Maintenance per year	15,000	10,000

The expected scrap value of both the new and the old machine in 10 years' time is estimated to be zero. The old machine could be sold now for £40,000.

The cost of capital for the Richmond Company is 10%. The company uses net present value and payback as its two main methods for evaluating projects.

Required:

Advise the company as to whether it should purchase the new machine.

Q4.4   Jones Ltd is considering investing in an advanced manufacturing machine.

An initial appraisal of the investment has indicated the following.

The capital costs will be £4,000,000 and the machine is estimated to have a life of 6 years, after which time its disposal value will be £1,000,000. Disruption to production facilities will result in lost production, costing £2 million in lost sales in year 1, on which a contribution of 20% of sales would have been made. Costs of retraining staff to work the new machinery would be £20,000 in year 1.

There will be a number of benefits resulting from the use of this machinery. The equipment will enhance the quality of the company's products. This will lead to less reworking of products and a subsequent reduction in warranty costs. The annual cost saving will be £1.2 million. The new equipment will also use less floor space than the existing machinery. As a result, one floor of the existing factory will no longer be needed. It is estimated that this floor can be let at an estimated annual rental of £200,000.

The directors of Jones Ltd currently require all investments to generate a positive net present value at a cost of capital of 14%.

Required:

(a) Give calculations to show whether purchase of the new machine would be worthwhile.
(b) Discuss any concerns that you may have with the assumptions used in your analysis and note any other factors that should be taken into consideration.

Q4.5   Tilsbury supermarkets are considering purchasing a supermarket from another organization for the remainder of a 5-year lease. Consultancy fees of £100,000 have been spent to date. The cost to purchase the lease is £5,500,000 and a further £1,500,000 will need to be spent immediately in refurbishing the store. New equipment and fixtures will also be purchased at the beginning of year 2 for the sum of £1,300,000. In addition, fixed asset equipment which is surplus to requirements in other stores, but which has no scrap or resale value, will be transferred to the store at a written down value of £275,000.

A senior management team will be deployed from other stores to manage the store at a gross salary cost of £165,000 per annum. New managers will be recruited externally to replace them in current branches at an anticipated replacement annual cost of £120,000. Other staff costs will be £3,800,000 per year. Other operating costs are expected to be £1,500,000 in years 1 and 2 and £2,000,000 for years 3, 4 and 5.

Sales are forecasted to be £20,000,000 in year 1, growing at £1,000,000 per annum to year 5, when it will be £24,000,000. The gross trading margin will be 35% of sales. Head office fixed costs will be reapportioned over the expanded store group with this store absorbing an annual charge of £500,000 as an allocation of the current fixed cost base of head office.

At the end of the five years, the property will be returned to the landlord and there will be redundancy and other terminal costs of £1,000,000. Fixtures and fittings worth £100,000 can be transferred to other stores, though the cost of moving them will be £10,000.

The company's cost of capital is 9%.

Required:

Advise the company whether it should proceed with the lease of the property and the development of the store.

TRADITIONAL APPROACHES TO FULL COSTING

Objectives

When you have completed this chapter you will be able to:

- Describe the difference between direct and indirect costs.
- Explain three possible reasons for calculating the full cost of a product or service.
- Explain the full costing approach to cost analysis and calculate the full costs of a product or service using traditional costing approaches, including:

    – A blanket overhead rate.
    – A rate for individual departments or cost centres.

- Describe the treatment of manufacturing and non-manufacturing costs in the Profit and Loss Account and Balance Sheet.
- Explain the need for different costing systems in order to cost jobs, batches, services, contracts and processes.

Introduction

In previous chapters, the importance of classifying costs as fixed or variable was reviewed. This chapter begins with an explanation of an alternative approach of classifying costs as either direct or indirect. Reasons for this approach are discussed.

Traditional methods for identifying how indirect costs (or overheads) should be assigned or identified to a particular product or service are then explained.

The treatment of manufacturing and non-manufacturing costs in the Profit and Loss Account and Balance Sheet is discussed, as is the need for different costing systems for different industries and circumstances, including for individual jobs, batches of products, services, contracts and processes.

Cost recording and classification

Costs incurred in an organization should be recorded. Having been recorded, this information can be used for different purposes. In previous chapters, it has been noted that in order to make decisions, it is important to understand and classify costs according to how they change in relation to activity, e.g. into fixed or variable costs. This is not necessarily easy to do, as costs cannot always be clearly identified as fixed or variable. The way costs change can also vary over time; for example, a cost may be fixed in the short term, but can be eliminated over a longer time period. An alternative method is to classify costs as either direct or indirect.

Direct costs are those costs that can be exclusively identified with a particular cost object.[1] These are generally the costs of the material that are used on each job or unit of production and the cost of the labour that is involved in making a product. It can also include other expenses. The **prime cost** is the total of all the direct costs of a product or service.

Indirect costs or **overheads** are those costs that cannot be exclusively identified with a particular cost object. They are incurred by manufacturing departments and also non-manufacturing departments (such as administration and selling) and include expenditure on items such as rent and rates, lighting and heating and depreciation.

Cost recording and classification of the costs of Appleman Engineering Ltd is considered in Figure 5.1.

Appleman Engineering has a contract to repair some electronic equipment for a customer.

Cost recording
1. The material cost used on the contract is £500.
2. The wages of engineers working on the contract are £1000.
3. The company owns a building and the costs of this building and wages of administrative staff at this building are £3000 per month. The administrative staff work on a range of activities, not necessarily on specific contracts.

Cost classification
The material and labour costs can be identified directly to the contract and can therefore be classified as direct costs.

The cost of the building and administrative staff cannot be identified to the contract (the cost object in this case) and can therefore be classified as overheads or indirect costs.

Figure 5.1 Cost recording and classification for Appleman Engineering Ltd

---

[1] A cost object is any activity for which a separate measurement of cost is desired. This could be a range of entities such as a product, a service or a department.

Activity 5.1

A company identifies its costs according to the following six categories.
Direct costs
Direct materials
Direct labour
Direct expenses
Indirect costs
Indirect manufacturing costs/manufacturing overheads
Administration expenses
Selling and distribution

Classify the following costs according to each of the above categories.

(a) Cost of raw materials.
(b) Wages of assembly worker.
(c) Wages of cleaners in the factory.
(d) Repairs to factory plant and equipment.
(e) Depreciation of delivery vans.
 (f) Depreciation of office equipment.
(g) Cost of hiring equipment for a specific job.
(h) Managing director's salary.
 (i) Production manager's salary.

Figure 5.2 Shows an analysis of the cost structure for a manufacturing company.

	£'000
Direct material	150
Direct labour	170
Direct expenses	30
Prime cost	350
Manufacturing overheads	110
Manufacturing costs	460
Administration costs	90
Selling costs	100
Total costs	650

Figure 5.2   An analysis of costs

Consideration of fixed, variable, direct and indirect costs

Classifying costs as fixed and variable is often more difficult to do and more subjective than classifying costs as direct or indirect. Whilst direct costs will often be variable and indirect costs may be fixed, this is not necessarily the case. In a number of examples used in previous chapters, it has been assumed that the direct labour and material costs have been variable. The labour was variable because the workforce was assumed to be paid piece-rate, i.e. each worker is paid a wage for each unit produced. In many organizations, labour is employed and paid a weekly wage, which will be paid irrespective of the volume of units produced. In such an instance direct wages could be considered to be fixed costs. In other circumstances they might also be considered to be stepped fixed costs, as it might only be when the existing workforce is working at full capacity that another member of staff is employed.

Indirect costs can also be variable or fixed. Costs such as depreciation of equipment, rent and rates of the building and indirect and supervisor wages are all fixed (at least in the short term), however, cost of power (e.g. the cost of the electricity to run the machinery) is likely to change to some extent in relation to output.

Activity 5.2

As far as it is possible, classify the costs identified in Activity 5.1 according to whether they are fixed or variable costs.

Purposes of full/total costing

In order to provide a full cost of a single product or service, it is necessary to:

 (i) Identify the direct costs.
(ii) Assign *a proportion* of the indirect costs to each product or service.

There are three main possible reasons for undertaking this activity.

(1) *Profit determination.* If goods or services are sold then, in order to determine whether a profit has been made, a proportion of the overheads should be included in the cost of those goods or services.
(2) *Pricing.* Some organizations use the full cost of a product or service as a basis for pricing. This topic was considered in more detail in Chapter 2.
(3) *Inventory valuation.* For manufacturing organizations, the financial accounting regulations (Statement of Standard Accounting Practice 9) mean that inventories should be valued at the lower of full *manufacturing* cost or the net sales value.

Costing products and services

The process of identifying costs, classifying them as direct and indirect and then identifying these costs to products or services is illustrated in Figure 5.3.

Direct costs can be traced directly to individual cost objects such as a product or a service. This is not possible with indirect costs or overheads and therefore a method of assigning overheads to cost objects needs to be devised.

One method of assigning a proportion of the overhead to an individual cost object is to use a 'blanket overhead rate'. A **blanket overhead rate** is a single overhead rate established for an organization. Refer to the example of Richmond Ltd, which was considered in Chapter 3 (see Figure 3.3). Budgeted total overheads were £247,250 and budgeted output was 21,500 units. In order to identify an overhead cost per unit, a blanket overhead rate per unit was used. The budgeted total overheads of £247,250 were divided by the budgeted output to identify an overhead cost recovery rate per unit of £11.50. The use of a blanket overhead rate, given different methods of assigning overheads to cost objects, is discussed in more detail in the next section.

A second method involves the calculation of an overhead rate assigned from individual departments of an organization which is illustrated in Figure 5.7. This will be explained in more detail later in the chapter.

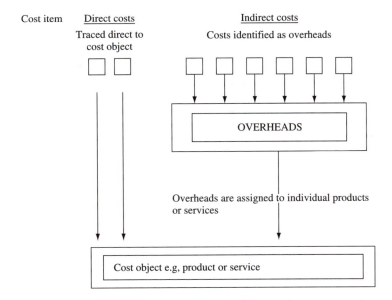

Figure 5.3   Tracing direct costs and assigning overheads to products or services

Using a blanket overhead rate

Alternative methods for assigning overheads to products and services

A number of different methods can be used for assigning overheads to products and services. These include:

(a) A cost per unit.
(b) A cost per labour hour. This is used where the process is labour-intensive.

(c) A cost per £ of labour. Some employees are paid substantially more per hour than others and it can be argued that the overhead charged per hour of a highly paid employee should be higher than for a lower paid employee.

(d) A cost per machine hour. This is used where the manufacturing process is machine-intensive. Rather than dividing factory overheads by the number of labour hours, the number of machine hours will be used.

The first three approaches are considered for Appleman Engineering in Figure 5.4.

The overheads in Appleman Engineering are £4000 per month. The following time is spent by the engineers of the company on four jobs that were undertaken in the month:

	Hours worked
Job 1	25
Job 2	75
Job 3	125
Job 4	25

The following methods are illustrated below:

(a) *A cost per job*

If the overheads are £4000 and four jobs were undertaken in the month, a cost per job would be £1000. In this example, this method does not seem to be a very satisfactory method of charging overheads to jobs as jobs 1 and 4 only took 25 hours to complete, while job 3 took 125 hours.

If this method was used as a basis for pricing, it seems unlikely that Appleman Engineering would gain many orders for small contracts!

(b) *A cost per hour*

Rather than charging an equal amount per contract, an hourly rate could be charged out to each job.

250 hours were worked in total, so if the overhead costs were £4000, a charge of $\frac{£4000}{250 \text{ hours}} = £16$ an hour could be charged.

Accordingly, the overhead charged to job 1 would be only 25 hours $\times$ £16 = £400, while for job 3 the charge would be 125 hours $\times$ £16 = £2000.

(c) *A cost per £ of labour*

Appleman Engineering employs a senior consultant who is paid £5000 a month and a junior consultant who is paid £3000 a month, i.e. a total of £8000. Both consultants are expected to work 125 hours each month on chargeable work. No other costs are anticipated.

The overhead cost is £4000 a month.

Using a cost per £ of labour the company would charge out overheads at the rate of $\frac{£4000}{£8000} = £0.50$ per £ of labour.

In order to calculate the overhead to be assigned to each job, it is necessary to know the wages that should be charged to the job. Assume job 1, which required 25 hours work, was completed by the senior consultant.

Figure 5.4   Three methods of assigning overheads to jobs

(i) The labour cost of the senior consultant is £5000 per month and 125 hours are charged to clients, i.e. £5000/125 hours = £40 per hour. Therefore 25 hours × £40 per hour, i.e. £1000, should be charged to job 1 for wages.
(ii) If overheads are assigned at a rate of £0.50 per £of labour then £500 should be assigned to job 1 to cover overheads.

Figure 5.4 (*Continued*)

Activity 5.3

Consider the information for Appleman Engineering Ltd, illustrated in Figure 5.4.

Required:

1. Excluding direct material costs, what is the charge-out rate per hour for (i) the senior consultant and (ii) the junior consultant, if the company bases its charges on full cost (using method c) plus 40% mark-up?
2. Assuming that the method outlined in (1) above is used, what would be the fee for a job that is anticipated to require 40 hours work by the senior consultant and 90 hours work by the junior consultant? Material costs are estimated at £2000.

Costing of overheads to products – using a different cost recovery rate for different areas of an organization

In recent years, it has been recognized that using a single blanket overhead rate may lead to an inaccurate cost. The costs that are incurred by different departments can vary considerably. For example, one department might use expensive automated machinery, while another might be labour-intensive. An alternative to assigning overheads using a blanket rate is to calculate an overhead rate for each of the different production departments. The steps to be followed in order to calculate a cost rate by department are discussed below.

Calculating the departmental overhead rate

Step 1. Indirect/overhead costs need to be identified by department to create a cost centre. Some costs can be **allocated** directly to a single department, for example a supervisor might work for only one department. Other costs cannot be identified directly to a department and so will have to be **apportioned** on some agreed basis to a number of departments. For example, rent may be paid on a building and if a number of departments occupy the building, then some method for sharing the cost across these departments must be agreed. See illustration in Figure 5.5.

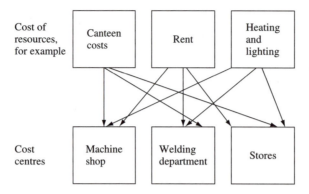

Figure 5.5 Allocating and apportioning indirect costs/overheads to departments

The basis for apportioning costs can vary. For example, for rent the usual method for allocating costs is on the basis of the floor area of each department. Other common methods are shown in Figure 5.6.

Cost	Basis of apportioning costs to cost centres
Supervision (if supervising a number of departments)	Number of employees
Heating	Floor areas
Insurance	Cost of assets in the department

Figure 5.6 Bases for apportioning overheads

Step 2. Costs of service departments need to be reallocated to production departments. Sections such as the stores section are not involved in providing services to the public, but only provide a support or service function to the production departments of machining and welding. The cost of these support departments needs to be reallocated to the production departments before overhead rates can be calculated. Recharging service department costs also needs to be undertaken using an agreed fair method.

Step 3. A separate overhead rate needs to be calculated for each production cost centre. This would most likely be one of the overhead recovery rates discussed above. For a department (or cost centre) that provides a labour-intensive service then the method of cost recovery is likely to be a cost per labour hour or per £ of labour. If the department is machine-intensive, the charge-out rate might well be a rate per machine hour.

Step 4. An overhead rate can be assigned or charged to each product. For example, if the overhead rate in the department was £5 an hour and a product required 1.5 labour hours, then the overhead rate charged from the department to that product would be $1.5 \times £5.00$ per hour $= £7.50$.

A diagrammatic overview of the steps required to cost a product or service in an organization, using a cost recovery rate for individual departments, is shown in Figure 5.7.

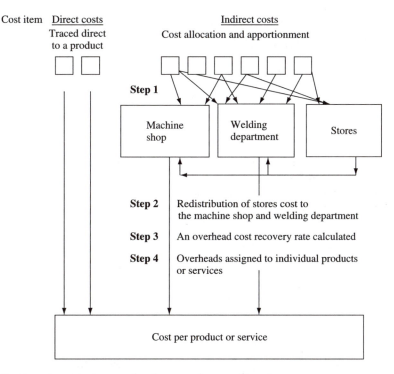

Figure 5.7 **Steps in assigning overheads to products and services**

Costing in service organizations

The same process of costing can take place in service organizations or in the public sector. Appleman Engineering was a small engineering company and a blanket overhead rate was acceptable. If it had been a larger consulting company with a number of departments that work for clients, then the company might have decided to use different charge-out rates for each department.

Using predetermined or actual rates

In charging overheads to products it is possible to use an actual overhead rate or a predetermined rate.

To calculate an actual overhead rate it is necessary to wait until the accounting period has taken place, identify the actual overheads that have occurred and then calculate a cost per unit. Given changes in volumes of production and overheads each month, this would mean that the cost per unit would change each month. It would also be a time-consuming process to calculate the overhead rate.

The most common method used in organizations is to calculate a **predetermined overhead rate**, which is calculated by dividing the budgeted overhead cost by the budgeted output.

A comprehensive example – calculating the overhead recovery for Milton Ltd

Further information is provided in Figure 5.8 for Milton Ltd. A comprehensive illustration showing the calculation of the overhead recovery rate is then provided.

Milton Ltd manufactures bicycle frames, which is the main component of a bicycle, onto which wheels and other components are fitted.

A bicycle frame consists of a number of metal tubes that are cut and bent to the shape needed and holes cut as appropriate (mitred), so that the various tubes can fit together to form the specific frame required. These tubes are then welded together.

Source: Reproduced by permission of Craig D. Calfee of Calfee Design (www.calfeedesign. com).

Departments of Milton Ltd

A simplified version of the manufacturing process can be considered to involve two main stages, machining and welding. In Milton Ltd, these two activities take place in the machine shop and the welding department respectively. There is also a stores section, which provides a support service to the production departments. This cost centre is staffed by one individual who is involved in the purchase, receipt of raw materials from suppliers and issue of materials to the factory floor.

Figure 5.8   Cost and operational information for Milton Ltd

Products

Milton Ltd produces two types of bicycle frame:

- The 'Alto' requires 1.5 hours in the machine shop and 2 hours in the welding department.
- The 'Special' requires 2 hours in the machine shop and 3 hours in the welding department.

Costs

A number of costs are incurred by the company. As well as direct costs of material and labour there are a number of indirect costs or overheads. A detailed analysis of the overhead costs of Milton Ltd is shown in Table I. Operational information which can be used to allocate costs across the departments is shown in Table II.

Table I Budgeted overheads for 20X8

Indirect wages	£	
Machine shop*	8,000	
Welding*	10,000	
Stores	14,000	32,000

Table I Budgeted overheads for 20X8

Other overheads		
Power	10,600	
Rent	36,400	
Depreciation of machinery	25,000	
Heating and lighting	10,000	
Supervision	27,000	109,000
Total overheads		141,000

* The two products Alto and Special are made in batches, for example typically 50 units of the bicycle frame Alto will be made as a batch and then the production process will need to be changed in order to manufacture the Specials (usually a batch of 2 units). The labour cost involved in changing over from producing the Alto to producing the Special has been identified separately as indirect wages.

Table 2 Operational information on departments

The following operational information is provided:

	Employed numbers	Floor area (m²)	Book value of machinery	Power (metered usage)	Material issues	Labour hours
Machine shop	3	350	£25,000	30%	80%	4,700
Welding	4	450	£20,000	70%	20%	6,400
Stores	1	400	£5,000			
Total	8	1,200	£50,000	100%	100%	11,100

Figure 5.8 (*Continued*)

Steps 1–4 noted above will now be carried out, using Milton Ltd as illustration.

Step 1. Overhead costs need to be identified by department to create a cost centre

Overhead costs have been analysed by department as shown in Figure 5.9. Indirect wages can be allocated directly by department, other costs need to be apportioned.

Cost	Basis of allocation or apportionment	Total	Machine shop	Welding	Stores
		£	£	£	£
Indirect wages	Direct	32,000	8,000	10,000	14,000
Power	Metered usage	10,600	3,180	7,420	0
Rent	Floor area	36,400	10,617	13,650	12,133
Depreciation of machinery	Book value of machinery	25,000	12,500	10,000	2,500
Heating and lighting	Floor area	10,000	2,917	3,750	3,333
Supervision	Number of employees	27,000	10,125	13,500	3,375
	Total	141,000	47,338	58,320	35,342

Figure 5.9   Analysis of overhead costs by department

Step 2. The cost of the support departments needs to be reallocated to the productive cost centres

After some discussion in Milton Ltd, the value of material issues was used as a basis for allocating the costs of the stores between the machine shop and the welding cost centre. See Figure 5.10.

		Total (£)	Machine shop (£)	Welding (£)	Stores (£)
Total		141,000	47,338	58,320	35,342
Reallocation of stores	Material issues		28,274	7,068	−35,342
Total costs (after reallocation)		141,000	75,612	65,388	

Figure 5.10   Reallocation of stores costs

Step 3. Calculate a rate for each cost centre for assigning overheads to products

In *this* organization both the machine shop and the welding department are labour-intensive and a labour hour rate would seem to be the most appropriate method for calculating the absorption rate. To work out the labour hour rate that will be charged for overheads, it is necessary to divide the budgeted cost of the department by the budgeted labour hours it is expected will be worked in each department.

Machine shop:

(1) Budgeted overhead	£75,612
(2) Budgeted labour hours	4,700

Budgeted labour hour rate = (1) divided by (2) = £16.09 per hour.
The welding cost centre is also labour-intensive and it is expected that 6400 labour hours will be worked in the year. To work out the labour hour rate it is again necessary to divide the budgeted cost of the department by budgeted labour hours.

Welding department:

(1) Budgeted cost	£65,388
(2) Budgeted labour hours	6,400

Budgeted labour hour rate = (1) divided by (2) = £10.22 per hour.

Step 4. Assign cost centre costs to individual products

The costing exercise can now be completed, with a rate per hour absorbed to each product depending on the hours worked on each product in each cost centre.

Cost of Alto

The average full cost of making one Alto is:

	£	£
Machine shop labour 1.5 hrs @ £6 per hour	9.00	
Welding cost centre labour 2 hrs @ £8 per hour	16.00	
Materials	50.00	
Direct costs		75.00
Overhead:		
1.5 hrs in machine shop @ £16.09 per hour	24.13	
2 hrs in welding department @ £10.22 per hour	20.44	
Overhead cost		44.57
Total cost		119.57

Cost of Special

The average full cost of making one Special is:

	£	£
Machine shop labour 2 hrs @ £6 per hour	12.00	
Welding cost centre labour 3 hrs @ £8 per hour	24.00	
Materials	60.00	
Direct costs		96.00
Overhead:		
2 hrs in machine shop @ £16.09 per hour	32.18	
3 hrs in welding department @ £10.22 per hour	30.66	
Overhead costs		62.84
Total cost		158.84

Period and product costs and the calculation of profit

Period and product costs

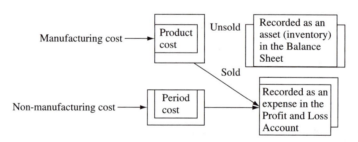

Figure 5.11   Treatment of manufacturing and non-manufacturing costs

Manufacturing costs and non-manufacturing costs are treated differently in calculating the profit of a company. Manufacturing cost is treated as a **product cost** and only the cost of products sold are recorded as an expense of the business. Unsold product is recorded as an asset (inventory) in the Balance Sheet. Non-manufacturing cost is treated as a **period cost** and is written off in the period in which the expense occurs. This is illustrated in Figure 5.11.

An example of Sherman Ltd when it produced a single product will be considered in Figure 5.12.

The **Profit and Loss Account** shows revenue, expenditure and the profit and/or loss resulting from operations for a given period of time. In Figure 5.13 the budgeted Profit and Loss Account is shown for Sherman Ltd, given two different assumptions:

(a) 1500 metal tubes are manufactured and sold in a month at £10 each and the costs are as identified in Figure 5.12.
(b) 600 metal tubes sold given the same price and costs.

Sherman Ltd is budgeted to produce and sell 1500 units of the size 1 metal tube in the month of January. The budgeted cost is as shown below:

		£
Direct labour	(£5 a unit)	7,500
Direct material	(£1 a unit)	1,500
Prime cost		9,000
Indirect overheads		1,500
Total production costs		10,500
Administration costs		500
Total cost		11,000

The product cost of each metal tube is expected to be:

	£
Direct labour	5
Direct material	1
Production overhead (note 1)	1
Full manufacturing cost per unit	7

Note 1. $\dfrac{£1500}{1500 \text{ units}} = £1$ per unit.

Figure 5.12   Product cost of metal tube for Sherman Ltd

(a) 1500 units sold at £10 each

	£
Sales	15,000
Less	
Cost of Sales (note 1)	10,500
Gross Profit	4,500
Less	
Administration expenses	500
Net Profit	4,000

Note 1. The cost of sales is calculated by multiplying the budgeted manufacturing cost per unit of £7 by budgeted sales of 1500 units.

(b) 600 units sold at £10 each. 1500 units manufactured, so 900 units are in inventory at the end of the month.

	£
Sales	6,000
Less	
Cost of Sales (note 2)	4,200
Gross Profit	1,800
Less	
Administration expenses	500
Net profit	1,300

Figure 5.13   The budgeted Profit and Loss Account for Sherman Ltd for given different assumptions

Note 2. In preparing a Profit and Loss Account, a number of accounting conventions are followed. The **matching** principle requires that expenses are matched with revenues. In this example, 600 units have been sold, so the cost of sales should also be for 600 units.

900 units of stock are unsold and these are also valued at £7 per unit, which is £6300 and is treated as an asset of the business and will be shown in the Balance Sheet.

The administration expenses of £500 are treated as a cost of the accounting period and written off to the Profit and Loss Account in both instances.

Figure 5.13   (Continued)

Different costing methods for different industries

Different costing methods may be used for different industries.

Job costing

Job costing is required where each unit of a product or service is unique and costs are accumulated for each job. For example, the cost of repairing a car or providing a consultancy service.

Batch costing

A company might make two or three products, which are made as a batch of say 10, 20 or 50 units in one production run. **Batch costing** is used where costs are accumulated for the batch and then a cost per unit is calculated by dividing this cost by the number of units in the batch.

Contract costing

Contract costing is a system of job costing that is used for long-term contracts. In ship building or construction, for example, a contract may last a number of years. The company needs to identify how much profit should be declared in each year. Recognized practice is that losses should be recognized when they occur, while if it is considered that the company is likely to make profits on the contract, then a proportion of profits should be taken in each year, reflecting how much of the total contract has been completed. An example is shown in Figure 5.14.

Southsea ship builders has a contract to manufacture a cargo ship. The contract price is £12 million and the budgeted cost is £10 million. The contract is expected to last 2 years.

At the end of the first year:

	£million
Certified work completed is valued at	7.0
Costs to date	6.0
Profit	1.0

The profit on the work certified to date on the contract is £1.0 million.

At the end of the second year:

	£million
Certified work completed is valued at	12.0
Costs to date	10.5
Profit	1.5

Profit in second year = £1.5 million − £1.0 million = £500,000.

Figure 5.14   Contract costing

Process costing

Process costing is used in industries where identical units are produced and these products pass through the same stages (examples include oil refining and beer production). A problem is to identify a cost per unit, when there is opening and closing stock of partly completed units. The **equivalent completed units** method converts partly completed units into completed units, for example two units that are 50% complete is equivalent to one completed unit. An example is shown in Figure 5.15.

Ellesmere Chemicals produces a chemical product.

Step 1. Calculate the equivalent number of litres processed in a period

(i)   4000 litres are completed in the month.
(ii) 300 litres of partly completed chemical (25% complete) were available at the beginning of the month. This is equivalent to $300 \times 25\% = 75$ completed units.
(iii) 500 litres of partly completed chemical (50% complete) were available at the end of the month. This is equivalent to $500 \times 50\% = 250$ completed units.

Figure 5.15   Process costing

The equivalent completed units are therefore:

	Litres
Competed units	4000
Add equivalent completed units at end of month	250
	4250
Less equivalent completed units at beginning of month	75
Equivalent completed units in month	4175

Step 2. Identify the costs in the month

The costs of production were £41,750 in the month.

Step 3. Identify the cost per litre

The cost per litre of chemical is $\dfrac{£41,750}{4,175 \text{ litres}} = £10$.

Figure 5.15   (*Continued*)

Summary

Costs should be recorded and can then be classified according to:

(i) How they change in relation to activity or
(ii) Whether they are direct or indirect.

Full costing is used for profit determination, inventory valuation and, in some organizations, pricing purposes.

To identify the full cost of a product or service, indirect costs need to be assigned to cost objects. In a small single product or service organization, a blanket overhead rate may be used. In larger organizations a blanket overhead rate may lead to inaccurate costs and an analysis by department may be more appropriate.

Different methods of assigning overheads may be used. Commonly used methods are a rate per unit (if units are identical), a rate per labour hour (if the process is labour-intensive) or a rate per machine hour (if the process is machine-intensive).

In preparing the Profit and Loss Account for a manufacturing organization, indirect manufacturing overheads are treated as part of the cost of a product and along with the direct manufacturing costs need to be charged to products on an agreed basis. Other overheads are treated as a period cost and are written off in the period in which the costs are incurred.

Different costing systems are required for different circumstances, including for individual jobs, batches of products, contracts and processes.

Further reading

The topics covered in this chapter are covered in more depth in a number of other books. For example:

Drury, C. (2004) *Management and Cost Accounting*, 6th edn, Thomson Learning, Chapters 3, 4, 5, 6.
See also website for this book.

Answers to activities

Activity 5.1

Classify the following costs according to each of these categories:

(a) Cost of raw materials – direct material.
(b) Wages of assembly worker – direct labour.
(c) Wages of cleaners in the factory – indirect manufacturing.
(d) Repairs to factory plant and equipment – indirect manufacturing.
(e) Depreciation of delivery vans – selling and distribution.
(f) Depreciation of office equipment – administration.
(g) Cost of hiring equipment for a specific job – direct expense.
(h) Managing director's salary – administration.
(i) Production manager's salary – indirect production.

Activity 5.2

(a) Variable.
(b) This depends on circumstances facing the organization. In the event of spare capacity this could be considered to be a fixed cost. In other circumstances it could be variable cost.
(c) Fixed.
(d) Further information is required. It is likely that there would be some increase in repair costs given an increase in output.
(e) Fixed.
(f) Fixed.
(g) Fixed.
(h) Fixed.
(i) Fixed.

Activity 5.3

(i)

	Senior engineer (£)	Junior engineer (£)
Labour cost per hour	40	24
Overhead at £0.50 per £ of labour	20	12
Full cost	60	36
Mark-up @ 40%	24	14.4
Hourly rate	84	50.4

(ii)

	Fee (£)
Senior consultant 40 hours @ £84/hr	3360
Junior consultant 90 hours @ £50.40	4536
Material	2000
	9896

Discussion questions

1. Why is it necessary to classify costs as direct and indirect, if they have already been classified as variable and fixed?
2. Why are overhead rates for each department preferable to a blanket overhead for the organization?
3. Why is a predetermined overhead rate preferable to an actual overhead rate?

Exercises

(Questions with numbers in bold have answers at the back of the book.)

Q5.1 Provide an analysis of the cost structure of Hines Ltd (see Figure 5.2 for an example of the required format) given the following information.

	£
Direct materials	400,000
Direct labour	325,000
Salaries:	
Sales staff	82,000
Administration staff	65,000
Managing Director	50,000
Works manager	40,000
Depreciation:	
Plant and equipment	46,000
Office equipment	2,000
Power cost:	
3/4 factory, 1/4 administration office	20,000
Rent and rates:	
4/5 factory, 1/10 administration office, 1/10 sales office	60,000

Q5.2 Southton council charge for the services of their engineering department.

The overheads of the department are calculated at £400,000.
   The salaries of the department are £200,000 and the method of charging out the work of the staff of the department is at a rate of 200% on direct labour.
   There are two categories of employees:

(i) Senior engineers, who are paid £48,000 a year. It is expected that on average such staff will work for 1200 hours on contracts in the year.
(ii) Junior engineers, who are paid £28,000 a year. On average such staff will work for 1400 hours on contracts in the year.

Required:

Calculate the cost of a contract which will require 100 hours of the senior engineer and 200 hours of the junior engineer.

Q5.3 Harold Ltd produces a product that requires material costing £50. Direct labour is required from two departments: 1.5 hours are worked in department A where the workforce earns £10 an hour and 1 hour is worked in department B where the workforce earns £12 an hour.

Overhead:

Department A is labour-intensive and overhead is recovered to units at the rate of £15 per labour hour. Department B is machine-intensive and overhead is recovered to units at the rate of £25 per machine hour. 1/2 machine hours are worked on this product.
   The company policy is to set prices based on cost plus 20%.

Required:

The selling price for this product.

Q5.4 The following information relates to a four-week accounting period for Foster Engineering Ltd.

	Total	Machining	Assembly	Finishing	Stores
Source information:					
Area occupied – square feet	40,000	12,000	18,000	8,000	2,000
Plant and equipment – at cost	£835,000	£700,000	£100,000	£30,000	£5,000
Number of employees	47	15	20	10	2
Direct labour hours	6,300	2,100	2,800	1,400	
No. of stores requisitions	1,812	400	1,212	200	
Machine hours		4,800			
Traced costs	Total (£)	(£)	(£)	(£)	(£)
Indirect wages	17,000	4,500	7,500	2,000	3,000
Power	3,300	2,400	600	300	0
	20,300	6,900	8,100	2,300	3,000
Other costs	(£)				
Rent and rates	7,800				
Lighting and heating	2,400				
Depreciation – plant and equipment	50,100				
Factory administration	21,300				
Insurance – plant and equipment	5,010				
Canteen subsidy	10,650				
	97,260				

Required:

(i) Prepare an overhead analysis sheet showing the basis for allocation of the other costs to departments.
(ii) For each item you have allocated, briefly explain the reason.
(iii) If the absorption method is machine hours for the machining department and labour hours for the assembly and finishing departments, identify a rate per hour.

Q5.5 Albion Ltd manufactures three products, X, Y and Z, in two production departments (machining and assembly) and a service department, a maintenance section.

Shown below are next year's budgeted production data and manufacturing costs for the company.

	Product X	Product Y	Product Z
Production (units)	2,100	3,450	850
Prime cost:			
Direct materials (per unit)	£11	£14	£17
Direct labour:			
Machining	£6	£4	£2
Assembly	£12	£3	£21
Machine hours per unit	2 hours	1 hour	1.3 hours

Labour in both the machining and assembly department is paid at £6 an hour.

The following information relates to a four-week accounting period for Albion Ltd:

	Total (£)	Machining (£)	Assembly (£)	Maintenance (£)
Costs				
Indirect wages	43,000	15,600	23,400	4,000
Other costs:				
Rent and rates	12,000			
Depreciation – plant and equipment	14,400			
Factory administration	15,300			
Canteen subsidy	3,600			
	88,300			

Source information:

	Total	Machining	Assembly	Maintenance
Area occupied – square feet	32,000	12,000	18,000	2,000
Plant and equipment – at cost	805,000	£700,000	£100,000	£5,000
Number of employees	75	25	48	2
Direct labour hours	13,592	4,692	8,900	
Maintenance hours	320	260	60	
Machine hours		8,755		

Required:

(i) Prepare an overhead analysis sheet showing the basis for allocation of the other costs to departments.

(ii) For each item you have allocated, briefly explain the reason.

(iii) If the absorption method is machine hours for the machining department and labour hours for the assembly departments, identify a rate per hour.

(iv) If the company used cost plus 25% as its basis of pricing, identify the price for each of the products.

Q5.6 Reesdale Breweries produces a brand of beer:

(i) 14,000 litres of beer are completed in the month.
(ii) 6000 litres of partly brewed beer (30% complete) were available at the beginning of the month.
(iii) 700 litres of partly brewed beer (40% complete) were available at the end of the month.

The cost of production was £9360.

Required:

The cost per litre of beer.

Q5.7 Enterprise Ltd manufactures chairs and expects to manufacture and sell 1000 units a month. Budget costs are as follows:

Material costs per unit   £20
Labour cost per unit   £30

Production overheads are expected to be £2000 a month and administration costs £1000 a month.
    The budgeted selling price per chair is £70.

Required:

(i) A budgeted production cost statement.
(ii) A budgeted Profit and Loss Account.

Q5.8 Assume that costs are as per the budget shown in Question 5.7, but actual sales in a month are 700 units at £70 per chair. Produce a Profit and Loss Account for the month.

ACTIVITY-BASED COSTING

6

Objectives

When you have completed this chapter you should be able to:

- Describe key elements of the value chain and its use.
- Describe the key steps followed in undertaking an activity-based costing (ABC) exercise.
- Calculate the cost of a product or service using an ABC approach.
- Explain when ABC might be most appropriate and why it does not always provide an accurate method of costing.

Introduction

In Chapter 5, traditional approaches to costing products and services were introduced. This included the analysis of costs to departments or costs centres and from there to products or services. The most common method of charging overheads to products or services was based on volume-related methods, such as the number of labour or machine hours required to manufacture each unit or provide a service.

Rather than identifying the costs of departments, an alternative is to cost the different activities undertaken in an organization. Potentially the latter will be more accurate and therefore more relevant for costing and cost management purposes.

In the first section, the idea of an organization as a linked set of activities that forms a 'value chain' is introduced. In the second section, activity-based costing (ABC) is explained and illustrated. ABC is concerned with identifying the costs of activities, the key factors that cause those costs to change and the calculation of product or service costs. Also discussed are the conditions in which ABC is likely to be most relevant and some of the potential problems in identifying costs accurately using activity-based costing.

Activity analysis and cost behaviour

Value chain analysis

The **value chain** of an organization consists of the resources and activities that link an organization together and together produce a product or service.

Primary activities

Some of these activities will directly involve the transformation of raw materials into a finished product and the delivery of these products to the customer. Porter (1980) refers to these as the primary activities of an organization and suggests that a broad category of primary activities for organizations consists of inbound logistics, operations, outbound logistics, marketing and sales and service.

1. *Inbound logistics.* The activities that are involved in receiving raw materials, such as the transport, sorting and storing of the materials that are brought into a factory.
2. *Operations.* The raw materials then need to be transformed into the finished product. Different products will go through different processes.
3. *Outbound logistics.* These are concerned with the distribution of the product to the customer.
4. *Marketing and sales.* This includes promotion, pricing, sales force activities and other means by which consumers are made aware of the product and are able to purchase it.
5. *Service.* This involves installation, repair, spares, warranty and training for use.

Secondary activities

As well as these primary activities, there will also be a range of secondary activities carried out in organizations. These support the primary activities and include the firm's infrastructure, human resource management, technology development and procurement or purchasing activities.

1. *Firm infrastructure.* This includes the planning, information and quality control systems.
2. *Human resource management.* This incorporates the recruitment, training, development and rewarding of people within the organization.
3. *Procurement/supplier relationship development.* This is concerned with the interaction between the firm and its suppliers to ensure that raw materials and services purchased are of the right quality, price and where appropriate delivered on time. Activities include design collaboration (jointly designing new services or products with suppliers), the sourcing process (selecting and evaluating suppliers), the negotiation process (obtaining a contract that meets requirements in terms of price, quality and delivery requirements), the buying process (the creation, management and approval of purchase orders).
4. *Technology development/new product or service development.* Current R&D projects and product design innovations should be assessed in order to consider their relevancy to the marketing programme. As well as product development, organizations are

concerned with process development, i.e. with improving the manufacturing or service processes. With process development, it should be possible to produce or provide products or services more efficiently and effectively.

An illustration of the value chain is shown in Figure 6.1.

Figure 6.1   The value chain
Source: Porter, M.E. (1985) *Competitive Advantage: Creating and Sustaining Superior Performance*. © 1985, 1988 by Michael E. Porter. Reprinted with the permission of the Free Press, a Division of Simon and Schuster Adult Publishing Group.

Cost behaviour and the value chain

Historically, costs in organizations were mainly associated with the operations activity and the manufacturing process was labour-intensive. There was little need for sophisticated product design facilities or marketing and sales activities.

As markets and products have become more complex, so has the value chain of many organizations. Many manufacturing processes have become more capital-intensive and firms have had to increase expenditure on a range of secondary or support activities, such as research and development of new products and firm infrastructure (e.g. IT systems), as well as on primary activities such as marketing and after-sales service.

In many organizations therefore:

(i) The cost structure has changed with the proportion of direct costs falling and that of indirect costs rising.
(ii) While historically most of the cost of an organization was incurred during the operations stage, in modern organizations significant costs are involved in 'upstream' activities, e.g. research development and design or in 'downstream' activities such as distribution, marketing and customer service.
(iii) Different products and services are also likely to make different demands of the various activities and a large number of costs do not necessarily change in proportion to volume of products or services produced.

The above factors mean that traditional full costing systems that charge overheads to products or services using a volume-related measure of activity may provide an inaccurate product or service cost. A more accurate method of allocating the costs of the various activities in the value chain to individual products and services that use those activities is required.

Activity-based costing

Activity-based costing allocates costs to products and services using cause and effect relationships to identify the resources that are consumed.

Steps taken in an activity-based costing exercise

With activity-based costing (ABC), while the recording and classification of direct costs is as for the traditional approach to costing, the treatment of overheads is different.

Rather than identifying overhead costs by department or cost centre and then identifying an overhead cost per unit using a single method such as cost per unit or per labour or machine hour, activity-based costing attempts to use a more accurate cause and effect cost allocation method. The following steps are undertaken.

Step 1. Identify activities

As indicated in Figure 6.1, various activities are undertaken at different stages of the value chain. For a manufacturing organization, primary activities can include receiving raw materials, issuing materials to the production departments, inspecting materials, changing over (setting up) activities from manufacturing a batch of one product to manufacturing another, processing customer orders. There can also be a number of support activities, such as organizing the purchase of raw materials, product development, information technology support and other infrastructure requirements and human resource management.

Step 2. Assign costs to activities

Rather than identifying a cost for each department, the focus is on identifying the cost of carrying out an activity, for example, the costs involved in purchasing raw materials. The term **cost pool** describes the costs assigned to an activity, for which there is a single cost driver, on the basis of a cause-and-effect relationship. If costs are assigned using arbitrary apportionments, then the ABC information will be less reliable for decision-making purposes.

Step 3. Identify cost drivers and identify a cost driver rate

Cost drivers need to be identified for each activity and are factors which provide a good explanation of cost change. They should also be easily measured. For some activities a volume base might be appropriate, for example for a production department, a labour or machine hour rate, or for a purchasing activity, the number of purchase orders. A simple volume measure might be insufficient for other activities.

The most commonly used type of cost drivers are:

1. *Transaction drivers*. These drivers assume that costs increase in proportion to the *number* of transactions that take place. If number of purchase orders was considered to be the cost driver for the purchasing function, then this would be an example of a transaction driver.

2. *Duration drivers.* These drivers might be necessary if the amount of *time* varies according to the type of transaction. For example, if some purchases required considerably more time than others, then it might be considered that a transaction-based driver is not sufficiently accurate and that some form of time measurement should be incorporated.

Step 4. Compute the cost per unit

Having identified the cost of each activity, a further analysis can identify the cost to be assigned to each product type and from there a cost per unit can be calculated.

Figure 6.2 provides a diagrammatic representation of an activity-based costing system.

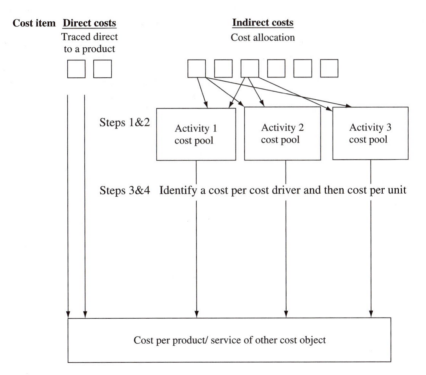

Figure 6.2 Steps taken in undertaking an ABC exercise

The diagram above illustrates the need to undertake:

- Steps 1 and 2 – identify the activities and allocate costs to identify the cost pool.
- Steps 3 and 4 – identify the cost drivers for each activity and calculate a cost per cost driver and then a cost per unit.

Example of an ABC exercise for Milton Ltd

In Chapter 5, a costing exercise was undertaken for Milton Ltd, using the traditional approach to costing. Direct labour and material costs were first identified to the two products. Overheads costs were then charged to units from the machining and welding department using departmental labour hour rates.

An ABC costing exercise will now be undertaken with Milton Ltd. Key information from Chapter 5 is used, along with supplementary information provided in Figure 6.3.

In Chapter 4, three main departments were identified: the machine shop, the welding department and the stores.

The accountant of Milton Ltd has undertaken an analysis of the time spent by the staff of these three departments in order to identify the activities undertaken and the time spent on these activities:

Machine shop
80% of the time of the workforce is spent on machining the bicycle tubes that are used in the manufacture of bicycle frames. This time has previously been identified as direct labour.

The Alto bicycle frames are made as a batch of 50 and 'Specials' are made as a batch of two. At the end of each batch of production, the completed metal tubes are carried by the workforce of the machine shop to the welding department. Materials for the next batch of units are then brought into the metal shop and the material specifications checked. Approximately 20% of the time of the workforce is spent on this 'set-up' activity. The cost of this activity was previously identified as indirect machine shop wages (see costs in table 1 of Figure 5.8).

Welding department
80% of the time of the workforce is spent on welding the bicycle frames. The remaining 20% of their time is spent on a set-up activity, preparing for the next batch of goods to be produced. As with the machine shop, the labour cost of these two activities was previously identified as direct and indirect wages, respectively.

Stores department
The storekeeper/purchasing officer spends 40% of her time on the purchasing activity, 30% of her time in receiving goods from suppliers and 30% of her time in issuing materials to the machine shop and welding departments.

Figure 6.3   Additional operational information for Milton Ltd

---

Activity 6.1

What are the main activities for Milton Ltd, as identified in Figure 6.3?

Step 1. Identifying the activities

From Figure 6.3 it can be noted that the main activities undertaken in the company are machining, welding, setting up for production of the next batch of goods, purchasing of raw materials, and receipt of materials and issue of materials to the factory.

The labour time spent on each activity in each department is summarized in Figure 6.4.

Cost pools for each of these activities should now be calculated.

Activity	Machine shop	Welding department	Stores
Machining	80%		
Welding		80%	
Set-up	20%	20%	
Purchasing			40%
Receiving materials			30%
Issuing materials			30%
Total	100%	100%	100%

Figure 6.4 Identifying percentage time by activity for each department

Step 2. Assigning costs to activities

Rather than analysing costs by department, with activity-based costing the purpose is to identify the costs of activities. Accordingly, in addition to the identification of costs by the productive cost centres of machining and welding, the accountant of Milton Ltd has assigned costs to activities that are not directly involved in converting raw materials into products.

As far as possible, costs should be assigned on a cause-and-effect basis. Personnel costs can be assigned using time, while for non-personnel costs, such as power, computers, direct measurement or estimates of the resource used by each activity should be employed. For the exercise of Milton Ltd, the accountant (after discussion with operational staff) has decided that in the absence of further operational data, the analysis of labour time by activity is also an adequate basis for non-personnel costs and this is reflected in the cost analysis shown in Figure 6.5.

Activity	Machine shop	Welding department	Stores	Total of cost pool
	£47,338	£58,320	£35,342	**£141,000**
Machining	£37,871			£37,871
Welding		£46,656		£46,656
Set-up	£9,468	£11,664		£21,132
Purchasing			£14,137	£14,137
Receiving materials			£10,603	£10,602
Issuing materials			£10,603	£10,602

Figure 6.5 Cost analysis by cost pool

It is important to recognize that if arbitrary apportionments have been employed and the assignment of costs does not accurately reflect the resources consumed, then an ABC product costing will be provided that will be adequate for stock valuation and profit determination purposes, but not for decision-making requirements. The use of activity-based costing information for decision-making purposes will be considered in more detail, later in the chapter.

Step 3. Identify cost drivers for each of the activities and a cost driver rate

In the traditional approach to costing, previously illustrated for Milton Ltd, it was assumed that production overheads of themachine shop and welding department should be assigned to products on the basis of hours worked on each product. Discussions with the staff of Milton Ltd have identified cost drivers for each activity as shown in Figure 6.6.

Activity	Cost driver
Machining	Labour hours worked machining the metal tubes for the bicycle frame.
Welding	Labour hours worked welding tubes to form the frame.
Set-up/progress chasing	Number of batches. 'Altos' are always made as a batch of 50 bicycle frames, while 'Specials' are made as a batch of two bicycle frames and an equal set-up cost should be charged to each batch.
Purchasing	The number of purchase orders. There is one purchase order for each batch of material required.
Receiving	The number of material receipts.
Issuing	The number of material issues.

Figure 6.6   Cost driver for each activity

Information is available on cost driver usage, see Figure 6.7.

Activity	Alto (use of driver)	Specials (use of driver)	Total of cost driver
Machining	2600× 1.5 hours = 3900 hours (note 1)	400× 2 hours = 800 hours	4700 labour hours
Welding	2600× 2 hours = 5200 hours	400× 3 hours = 1200 hours	6400 labour hours
Set-up	2600 units/50 units per batch = 52 set-ups	400 units/2 units a batch = 200 set-ups	252 set-ups
Purchasing	52 purchase orders	200 purchase orders	252 purchase orders

Note 1. A budget for 2600 Altos and 400 Specials has been set.

Figure 6.7   Cost driver usage

| Receiving | Material sufficient for 100 bicycle frames is delivered = 2600/100 = 26 receipts | 1 material receipt for material sufficient for 4 bicycle frames = 100 receipts | 126 material receipts |
| Issuing | 1 issue per 25 frames = 2600/25 = 104 issues | 1 issue per batch = 200 issues | 304 issues |

Figure 6.7   (*Continued*)

Activity 6.2

(a) Are the cost drivers identified for set-up, purchasing and issuing activities transaction or duration cost drivers?
(b) What are the potential limitations of the cost driversused for the set-up/progress chasing, purchasing and receiving and issuing cost pools?

Figure 6.8 shows details of the activity; the cost pool associated with that activity; the cost driver for each activity; the quantity of each cost driver; and finally the rate per unit of cost driver or the activity cost driver rate.

Activity	Activity cost pool (from Figure 6.5)	Activity cost driver	Quantity of activity cost driver	Activity cost driver rate (£)
Machining	£37,870.70	labour hours	4700	£8.06
Welding	£46,656.00	labour hours	6400	£7.29
Set-up/progress chasing	£21,131.70	number of batches	252	£83.86
Purchasing components	£14,136.70	number of purchase orders	252	£56.10
Receiving components	£10,602.50	number of material receipts	126	£84.15
Issuing components	£10,602.50	number of issues	304	£34.88
	£141,000.00			

Figure 6.8   **Analysis of cost driver rate**

The activity cost driver rate = activity cost pool divided by the quantity of the activity cost driver. For example, for the machining activity this is £37, 871 divided by 4700 hours = £8.06.

Step 4. Identify the cost per item

The calculation of the total activity cost and cost per unit of Altos and Specials is shown in Figure 6.9.

To obtain a cost per unit of an Alto and a Special, it is first necessary to work out the total cost of each activity that should be assigned to each product and then divide by the number of units manufactured.

Activity	Activity cost driver rate	Alto		Special	
		Use of cost driver	Cost for Altos	Use of cost driver	Cost for Specials
	£		£		£
Machine shop	8.06	3,900	31,425	800	6,446
Welding	7.29	5,200	37,908	1,200	8,748
Set-up	83.86	52	4,361	200	16,771
Purchasing	56.10	52	2,917	200	11,220
Receiving	84.15	26	2,188	100	8,415
Issuing	34.88	104	3,627	200	6,975
		Total Cost	82,425	Total Cost	58,575
		Cost per unit	£31.70	Cost per unit	£146.44

Explanation of the costing for the Alto:

The cost of each activity for each product = activity driver rate x the usage of that cost driver rate. For example, the hourly assignment rate from the machining department is £8.06 per hour and 3,900 hours are required to manufacture 2,600 'Altos'. This gives a total machining cost for the product of £31,425.

The total cost assigned to Altos is £82,425 and so the cost per unit is £31.70.

Figure 6.9   Activity-based costing of the 'Alto' and the 'Special'

The table in Figure 6.9 shows the activity cost to be assigned to each unit of Alto or Special. This is shown to be £31.70 for the Alto and £146.44 for the Special. A total cost for the two products is shown below.

Cost of Alto

	£
Machine shop labour 1.5 hrs @ £6 per hr	9.00
Welding cost centre labour 2 hrs @ £8 per hr	16.00
Materials	50.00
Direct costs	75.00
Overhead assigned	31.70
Total cost	106.70

Cost of Special
The average full cost of making one Special is:

	£
Machine shop labour 2 hrs @ £6 per hr	12.00
Welding cost centre labour 3 hrs @ £8 per hr	24.00
Materials	60.00
Direct costs	96.00
Overhead assigned	146.44
Total cost	242.44

Activity 6.3

The managing director of Milton Ltd has noticed that the cost per set-up is nearly £84. He has therefore proposed that there be longer production runs in order to reduce set-up costs.

Critically evaluate this proposal. What issues would you wish to bring to the attention of the managing director?

Problems with identifying an accurate product or service cost for decision-making purposes

The proponents of activity-based costing argue that it provides more accurate cost information. There are, however, a number of practical issues that may result in concerns about the accuracy of the analysis and its potential use for pricing and other decision-making purposes.

Identifying activities

An organization consists of many hundreds of activities. To collect information it is usually necessary to interview staff and/or ask for completion of timesheets for a period of time. From this process a number of main activities will emerge. Initial ABC studies often resulted in large numbers of activities; however, in more recent times, activity analysts undertaking costing exercises have tried to limit the number of activities to between 20 and 30. A key problem is to identify an activity of sufficient size to justify separate treatment and for which a single cost driver can be identified. There may be a trade-off between accuracy and the cost of a very detailed analysis.

Costing the activities

If the costs of activities include expenditure such as general overheads, then changes in the level of activity will not lead to a proportionate change in costs. In the example of Milton Ltd, the cost pool for the set-up cost activity included a share of the rent of the factory, depreciation of machinery and supervision costs. When the managing director recommended a decision to reduce the number of set-ups as he thought that each set-up would cost an additional £88, he was demonstrating a lack of understanding of the costs that were included in the £88. Cooper (1990) recommended that for decision-making purposes, costs should be analysed according to a cost hierarchy. This hierarchy should be identified at four different levels: unit, batch, product-sustaining and facility-sustaining.

Unit level

These are costs that increase in proportion to the number of units manufactured, for example direct labour.

Batch level

These are costs that increase as a result of batch of units being manufactured. The exercise on Milton Ltd illustrates a number ofactivities where costs are considered to vary in relation to number of batches, for example the set-up and purchasing activities.

Product-sustaining level

These are incurred irrespective of the number of batches or volume of products produced and might include technical support for a particular product. This support can be the same whether the level of production of the product is high or low.

Facility-sustaining level

Facility-sustaining activities include general administration and management of the organization. The costs involved in such activities cannot be accurately assigned to products as they are incurred irrespective of the production of individual product lines.

When costs are analysed in this manner, it should be easier to better understand the impact of different decisions. Note that in order to analyse costs in different ways for different purposes, it is necessary to provide an appropriate cost coding system.

Activity 6.4

How do you consider the costs of Milton should be classified, using the hierarchy identified by Cooper?

Selecting appropriate cost drivers and identifying a cost per cost driver

The extent to which individual cost drivers provide a good explanation of cost behaviour for each activity should also be questioned. A number of factors may cause costs to change, however, practical limitations may lead to those that are easily measured being chosen.

In the analysis for Milton Ltd, even when unit-level and batch-level costs are considered, care should be taken in the analysis. For example, if labour is paid a weekly wage rather than an hourly rate, then even this cost is unlikely to change in direct proportion to the number of set-ups, as a small reduction is likely to be insufficient to justify releasing a member of staff. In the short term, significant change in the level of activity is often required before action is taken to change both staffing levels and the labour cost of the organization.

Kaplan (1994) differentiates between the cost of resources supplied and the cost of resources used. He suggests that the cost of resources supplied = the cost of resources used + the cost of unused capacity. In the example of the set-up activity for Milton Ltd, if employees are not fully occupied, there is likely to be a cost of unused capacity.

Activity 6.5

Why is it important to distinguish between the cost of resources supplied and the cost of resources used?

Conditions in which ABC may be appropriate

Although ABC has been applied in a large number of organizations throughout the world, it is not necessarily appropriate for all organizations.

It appears to have been most successful where:

1. Indirect costs are a high proportion of total costs and a significant proportion of these costs do not vary in relation to volume produced, but rather in relation to other factors.
2. There is a diverse range of products or services provided, which all consume resources in different proportions.
3. There is intense competition and a more accurate costing system is needed in order to eliminate non-value-adding activities and obtain a more 'accurate' measurement of product and service costs that can be used for pricing and other purposes.

Activity analysis can be a time-consuming activity. If competition is not intense, indirect costs are not a significant proportion of total costs and there are not a wide variety of different products and services, this cost is probably not justified.

Applications of ABC

Profitability analysis given a cost hierarchy

Given that costs can be identified at different levels, then the contribution can be identified at different levels as well. See Figure 6.10 for the format for an analysis of a company with two main products.

Profitability analysis by product and in total

	Product 1	Product 2	Total products
Sales by product	xxx	xxx	xxx
Less unit-level costs	xxx	xxx	xxx
Contribution after deducting unit-level costs	xxx	xxx	xxx
Less batch-related costs	xxx	xxx	xxx
Contribution after deducting batch-level costs	xxx	xxx	xxx
Less product-sustaining expenses	xxx	xxx	xxx
Contribution after deducting product-sustaining expenses	xxx	xxx	xxx
Less facility-sustaining expenses			xxx
Plant profitability			xxx

Note that as the facility-sustaining costs cannot be identified to product level, the profitability analysis will be at plant level after the deduction of these costs.

Figure 6.10   Profitability analysis by product and in total

Profitability analysis for different cost objects, e.g. customer account profitability

The analysis can also be undertaken for different cost objects where a cost object is anything for which cost data is desired. In the examples that have been considered to date, the purpose of most of the exercises has been to identify the cost of a product or service or job. An organization might also wish to identify the cost and profitability of a range of other objects, for example customers and organizational subunits such as departments and divisions.

Customer account profitability analysis is the assessment of the profitability to the business of individual customers or groups of customers. In supporting a customer, as well as the manufacturing cost of a product, a number of other activities are undertaken, such as order-taking, packing, dispatch and warehousing. ABC analysis by customer may highlight more or less profitable customers.

Activity-based management

In recent years, increasing emphasis has been placed on the management use of activity information. This is discussed further in Chapter 22.

The use of ABC in organizations

The initial applications of ABC were in the manufacturing sector. In more recent times, it has been most widely used in service organizations, where indirect costs are a high proportion of total costs. A survey by Drury and Tayles (2000) found that only 15% of manufacturing organizations had implemented ABC as opposed to 51% of financial and service organizations.

Summary

The value chain of an organization consists of the resources and activities that link an organization together. Primary activities transform inputs into outputs, for example raw materials into a finished product. Secondary activities provide support to the primary activities.

With activity-based costing, it is necessary to identify key activities of the business, assign costs to these activities to form cost pools, determine the cost driver for each activity and thus calculate a cost per unit.

There are a number of practical issues that may lead to concerns about the accuracy of an ABC analysis. These relate to the identification of appropriate activities and cost drivers and the accurate assignment of costs to activities.

Care should also be taken in using ABC information for decision-making and general overheads, such as facility-sustaining costs should not be identified to product level.

Activity-based costing systems are likely to be most relevant where:

- The proportion of indirect costs is high.
- There are a diverse range of products which do not necessarily consume resources in proportion to units of output.
- The organization operates in a competitive environment.

Further reading

Drury, C. (2004) *Management and Cost Accounting*, 6th edn. Thomson Learning, Chapter 10.

Glad, E. and Becker, H. (1995) *Activity Based Costing and Management*. John Wiley & Sons Ltd.

Kaplan, R. and Anderson, S. (2007) *Time-driven Activity Based Costing*. Harvard Business School Press.

Kaplan, R. and Cooper, R. (1998) *Cost and Effect: Using integrated cost systems to drive profitability and performance*. Harvard Business Press.

Turney, P.B. (1996) *Activity Based Costing: The performance breakthrough*. Kogan Page.

Answers to activities

Activity 6.1

In Milton Ltd the key activities were identified as machining, welding, set-up/progress chasing, purchasing components, issuing components.

Activity 6.2

(a) All the cost drivers are transaction cost drivers.
(b) Duration cost drivers might be more accurate for Milton Ltd. For example, the set-up time for Altos may be different from that for Specials.

Activity 6.3

Given the ABC analysis undertaken for Milton Ltd, a change in the level of activity will not lead to a reduction in the set-up cost of £84 per unit because of the inclusion of costs that do not change given a change in the number of set-ups. Increasing the production run will also lead to an increase in batch size, which will in turn result in an increase in stock holdings and investment in stock.

In contrast to reducing the number of set-ups, reducing the time spent on each set-up should be a positive step, since the time and cost spent in setting up for a new batch of production does not add value to the customer.

Activity 6.4

Direct wages can be identified at unit level, indirect wages at batch level. Factory rent, heating and lighting, supervision are product-sustaining costs. Power and depreciation are difficult to identify without further information. A machine may be bespoke to an individual product or it may be used for the production of many hundreds of products; similarly power might be monitored by machine but the information may also only be available at the product-sustaining level.

Activity 6.5

A decrease in the usage of activities does not necessarily mean that the resource usage will decrease. Where many overheads are fixed, although the usage of the resource may decline, it might not be able to reduce its 'supply'. The cost per cost driver can be a long-term average and a reduction in the use of the cost driver can result in an increase in the unused capacity.

Discussion questions

1. What are the key differences between activity-based costing and traditional approaches to costing?
2. Why can the traditional costing system lead to the costs of high-volume products being overstated while the cost of low-volume products is understated?
3. Discuss why activity-based costing might be more appropriate for some organizations than for others.
4. Why is the identification of an ABC cost hierarchy important?
5. Identify the dangers of using activity-based costing for decision-making purposes.
6. Critically evaluate why a number of organizations have employed activity analysis to take a process view of activities, rather than used it for cost ascertainments purposes.
7. How might activity analysis lead managers to take action that is against the interests of the organization?
8. Describe the value chain for a university. Would activity-based costing be an appropriate system for a university?

Exercises

(*Questions with numbers in bold have answers at the back of the book.*)

Q6.1 Eddy Ltd produces two products, Alpha and Beta. The profits of the company have been decreasing in recent years, with sales of Beta increasing and sales of Alpha declining. Prices are set using full cost plus 10%. The costs for materials and labour of the two products are as follows:

	Alpha (£)	Beta (£)
Direct materials	56	75
Direct labour	4	8

This system assigns overheads to products on the basis of direct labour hours. In 2008 the company has estimated that £2,000,000 in overhead costs will be incurred and 5000 units of the Alpha and 40,000 units of the Beta will be produced. The Alpha requires 0.8 hours of direct labour per unit and the Beta needs 1.6 hours.

Further information:

Activity centre	Costs (£)	Cost driver
Purchase orders	84,000	Number of purchase orders
Scrap/rework orders	216,000	Number of scrap/rework orders
Product testing	450,000	Number of tests
Machinery	1,250,000	Machine hours
Total overheads	2,000,000	

Operational information:

	Total	Alpha	Beta
Purchase orders	1,200	400	800
Scrap/rework orders	900	300	600
Product tests	15,000	4,000	11,000
Machine hours	50,000	20,000	30,000

Required:

Calculate a product cost using:

(a) A traditional full costing method using direct labour hours as the basis for assigning overheads to products.
(b) Activity-based costing. *Hint:* With this question the first two of the four steps described in the chapter for the calculation of the cost per unit have been completed, i.e. the activities have been identified and a cost pool for each activity has been calculated. For this exercise, the remaining two steps now need to be undertaken: first the calculation of the activity cost driver rates (see Figure 6.8 for an example) and then the calculation of the cost per unit (see Figure 6.9).
(c) From the costs calculated in (a) and (b) above, identify factors which may account for the company's declining profits.

Q6.2 Albat Ltd uses activity-based costing. A component is processed through four manufacturing activities: materials handling, machinery, assembly and inspection. Costs from each cost pool are recovered to products using the activity cost driver rate multiplied by the usage of that cost driver. The following information is available:

Manufacturing activity	Cost driver	Activity cost driver rate (£)
Materials handling	Number of parts	0.90
Machinery	Number of machine hours	2.00
Assembly	Number of parts	5.70
Inspection	Number of finished units	60.00

Albat has just completed 120 units of a component for a customer. Each unit required 115 parts and 4 machine hours. The direct costs of production are £1100 per unit.

In addition to the manufacturing costs, the firm has identified that the total cost of upstream activities including research and development amount to £140 per unit. The downstream activities of distribution, marketing and customer relations are £200 per unit.

Required:

(i) Calculate the total manufacturing cost and the unit cost of the 120 units completed.
(ii) Calculate the total cost per unit.

Q6.3 Havelock Ltd manufactures types of kitchen appliance, one of which is more complex to manufacture than the other. The simpler, higher production volume appliance, the Snappit, is manufactured in longer runs on machine A. The more complex appliance, the Badger, is manufactured in short production runs on machine B. Budgeted overheads are £360, 000 and currently the overheads are absorbed to products on the basis of labour hours. Price is then calculated using total cost plus a 25% mark-up.

The accountant of Havelock Ltd has suggested that the current costing system is inaccurate and is leading to a set of prices that are out of line with those of competitors. She has suggested that an activity-based costing exercise be undertaken and has collected the information below. This exercise has identified costs by area of activity and the driver of these costs.

	Analysis of overhead costs	
	Costs per month (£)	Monthly volume (£)
Machine A	150, 000	500 machine hours
Machine B	75, 000	1250 machine hours
Set-up costs	30, 000	250 set-ups
Handling charges	50, 000	400 movements
Other overheads	55, 000	
Total overheads	360, 000	

5000 direct labour hours are available each month and it has been decided that other overheads should be assigned to products based on labour hours.

Details of the current volume of goods produced and production parameters are shown below.

Operational information:

	Total	Snappit	Badger
Set-ups	250	50	200
Movements	400	200	200
Labour hours	5,000	3,500	1,500

The direct labour cost of the Snappit is £16 and the material cost is £20.
   The direct labour cost of the Badger is £22 and the material cost is £25.
   The wage rate is £8 per hour.

Required:

(a) Identify the total cost and price of each product using a traditional full costing method, using direct labour hours as the basis for assigning overheads to products.
(b) Identify the total cost and price of each product using activity-based costing.
(c) From the costs calculated in (a) and (b) above, identify factors which may account for the company's declining profits.

Q6.4 A company manufactures cookers. There are three models, A, B and C, each aimed at different markets. Product costs are computed on a blanket overhead rate basis using a labour hour method. The price as a general rule is set based on cost plus 20%. The following information is provided:

	A	B	C
Material cost (£/unit)	25	62.5	105
Direct labour hours (per unit)	0.5	1	1
Budgeted production/sales (units)	20,000	1,000	10,000

The budgeted overheads amount to £4,410,000. Direct labour cost is £8 an hour.
   The company is currently facing increased competition – especially from imported goods. As a result, the selling price of A has been reduced to a level which reveals very little profit margin.
   Activity-based costing has been suggested as a method that should be employed in order that the selling price more accurately reflects the cost. The overheads have been examined and it is found that they are grouped around the main business activities of machining (£2,780,000), logistics (£590,000) and establishment costs (£1,040,000). It is argued that these costs should be traced based respectively on cost drivers of machine

hours, material orders and space to reflect the use of resources in each of these areas. After analysis, the following proportionate statistics are available related to the volume of products:

	A (%)	B (%)	C (%)
Machine hours	40	15	45
Material orders	47	6	47
Space	42	18	40

Required:

(a) Calculate for each product the full cost and selling price determined by:

   (i) The original costing method.
   (ii) The activity-based costing method.

(b) What are the implications of the two systems of costing in the situation given? What business options exist for the company in the light of the new information?
(c) Comment on the use of activity analysis for decision-making purposes.

PART 2

TRADITIONAL ACCOUNTING CONTROLS

Part 2 of the book focuses on the use of traditional accounting controls in organizations.

The first two chapters consider the design of budgetary control systems and the preparation of budgets. Chapter 7 provides an overview of the budgetary control process. The benefits of budgeting are discussed and the operation of a budgetary control system is explained. Chapter 8 describes in detail the preparation of key budgets of an organization. Initially, a cash flow budget is illustrated followed by a consideration of alternative approaches to budgeting for overhead departments. Finally, a comprehensive example of a full set of budgets for an organization is provided.

Chapter 9 focuses on control in manufacturing organizations. It considers the use of a system of control called standard costing, alternative production management systems and the relevance of standard costing to such systems.

Chapter 10 reviews specific issues related to the control of divisional organizations. Control in large and complex organizations is often difficult and one approach that can be employed to cope with this complexity is to change the organizational structure. With the divisional structure, a company is organized into a number of individual divisions, each looking after a separate product, market or geographic area. Accounting information is often used to measure the performance of these divisions and their managers, with accounting ratios being a frequently employed method. The chapter will look at problems that arise with the use of accounting information to report performance, including issues related to the use of return on investment measure of profitability, the pricing of goods that are sold between divisions and the design of control reports.

Chapter 11 explores in more detail the use of the financial ratios to assess performance in organizations' statements, while Chapter 12 will consider the funding of organizations to meet both short-term and long-term requirements.

Illustrating a budgeting and accounting system using a case scenario

In order to help illustrate the various techniques introduced in this part of the book, a number of examples will be used. A particular case that is used in the initial chapters is a fictitious organization called Dundee Bicycle Division. Some initial information on this organization and key elements of the budgeting and accounting system are provided in the case scenarios provided in a separate section at the end of the book. To provide an overview of the problems that will be considered, this case information should be read before beginning the chapters. The information includes:

(i) The procedures followed in preparing the budget for each financial year, by the organization and individual departments.

(ii) The budgetary control system. With this system, actual results are compared with budget. In the factory a standard marginal costing system is in operation.

(iii) The review process that takes place every three months throughout the year, when a revised forecast for the financial year is identified.

A number of problems and issues that arise as a result of the use of a budgetary control system are also discussed.

BUDGETARY CONTROL SYSTEMS

7

Objectives

When you have completed this chapter you should be able to:

- Describe key stages that may be followed in the planning process of an organization.
- Identify the potential benefits of budgeting and budgetary control systems.
- Explain key principles of budgetary control systems.

    - Budgetary control as a feedback and feedforward control system.
    - The meaning of responsibility accounting and the main types of responsibility centres.
    - Using best practice in the design of budgetary control reports, including:

    The use of comparison with flexed budget.
    Management by exception.
    Whether to separate controllable from non-controllable expenditure.
    Frequency of reporting.
    Presentation of information.

- Explain key features of a reward system based on budgetary control information.

Introduction

Chapter 7 initially reviews some of the main steps that are undertaken by organizations in the planning process. It then focuses on the design of budgetary control systems, key features of which are explained below, including:

- Feedback and feedforward control.
- Providing accounting reports for individual responsibility centres within an organization.
- Identifying current best practice in the design of budgetary control reports. This includes the use of flexible budgeting where variable costs are involved, the need to

separate controllable from non-controllable costs and revenues and the presentation of information.

• The use of budgetary control information as a basis for the reward/incentive scheme.

A number of organizations have found various problems with the operation of budgetary control systems. Detailed consideration of problems and potential solutions will take place in Part 4 of the book.

Stages in the planning process

The diagram in Figure 7.1 indicates some of the processes that organizations might undertake in planning and controlling their operations. Steps 1–5 in Figure 7.1 identify

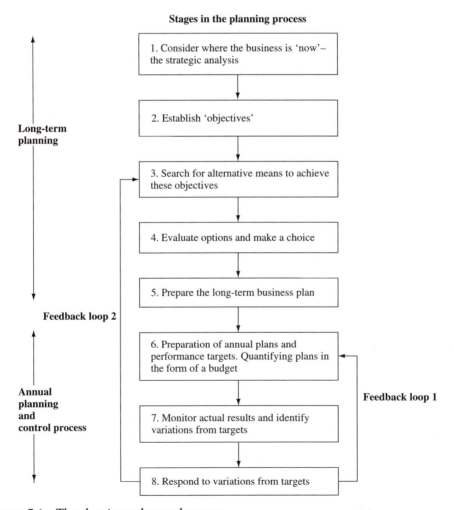

Figure 7.1 The planning and control process

activities that might be undertaken by organizations wishing to plan and manage for the longer term (say three to five years). These include an analysis of the organization in comparison with its competitors and the environment in which the organization operates; the identification of objectives for the longer term; the identification and evaluation of alternative options that might be followed in order to reach these objectives. These issues are considered further in Part 3 of the book.

As well as planning for the longer term, many organizations plan for the medium term (for example the coming year) and operate control systems in order to help identify whether these plans are being achieved and take corrective action if they are not (steps 6, 7 and 8 in Figure 7.1). Accounting-based systems have traditionally been used to assist in planning and control activities for the medium and shorter term and are the subject for examination in this part of the book. In this chapter the operation of a budgetary control system is explained.

The budget

Key objectives of organizations are often related to cash flow and profit and many organizations spend a considerable amount of time and effort in planning how cash flow and profit targets for the coming year will be achieved. If an organization has identified and agreed a profit objective for the coming period and a plan for achieving this objective, then a budgeted Profit and Loss Account will provide the detail of the expected revenue that will be generated and the expenditure that will be incurred. A **budget** is a quantification of a plan, for a defined period of time and in Table 7.1 the budgeted Profit and Loss Account for the year April 20X8 to March 20X9 is shown for

Table 7.1 Budgeted Profit and Loss for Dundee Bicycle Division for the period April 20X8 to March 20X9

	(£)
Sales	2,460,000
Labour	872,182
Material	603,818
Fixed production overhead	540,000
Production cost	2,016,000
Gross profit	444,000
Accounting	144,000
Commercial	75,000
Net profit	225,000

Dundee Bicycle Division. Background information to Dundee Bicycle Division (parts 1 and 2) is provided in the case material provided at the back of the book.

The budgeted Profit and Loss Account and also the budgeted cash flow statement are usually seen as crucial documents by senior management.

Budget reviews

On a regular basis (probably every three months) most organizations review the actual outcome for the year to date and the budget for the remainder of the financial year, in order to identify whether the original budget will be achieved. If it is not likely to be achieved then corrective action may be taken. This is known as feedforward control and is discussed in more detail later in the chapter, with an illustration from Dundee Bicycle Division.

Rolling budgets and flash forecasts

Some organizations operate a **rolling budget**, which is a budgeting system in which budgets are updated on a continuous basis to ensure that a 12-month budget is always available. For example, after the first quarter of the financial year (April to June 20X8), the budget for the remaining 9 months may be revised and a further budget for the first quarter of the following year (April to June 20X9) added.

In recent years an increasing number of other organizations have reconsidered the benefit of the annual budgeting process and rather than prepare an annual budget, the use of a flash forecast for the coming short term (say the next three months) has been recommended. The 'beyond budgeting' debate is considered in Chapter 23.

The potential benefits of budgeting

If an organization introduces or uses budgeting, then there are a number of potential benefits.

(i) Improved planning

The process of planning forces managers to consider the objectives to be achieved and the resources that will be required to reach these objectives. It will also be necessary to consider how environmental conditions might change in the future and the financial impact of these changes. Some options might initially seem attractive, but may actually be risky given possible adverse trading conditions.

(ii) Improved coordination and communication between business units and departments

In planning, managers are able to examine the relationships between their own operations and those of other departments. For example, in a manufacturing organization, the production department will need to be aware of expected sales and the required levels of finished goods in order to plan for potential changes in production facilities. The sales department will need to be aware of potential constraints on the production process that will limit the level of sales. If the production department needs to recruit additional staff, in order to meet an expected increase in sales, then the personnel department should be aware of this in order to advise on recruitment. Increased sales at certain times of the year might mean additional marketing resources are required in order to achieve the increased sales.

Given the discussions involved in preparing the annual budget, everyone in the organization should have a clear understanding of the part they are expected to play in its achievement. Appropriate individuals are then made accountable for implementing and achieving the budget.

Administration of the budget

In order to coordinate the activities of a potentially large number of different managers who are involved in the budgeting process, it is necessary to identify a proposed timetable for receipt of information.

If different managers within an organization are preparing budgets, then it is also important that they are working to common assumptions. Accordingly, communication of budget parameters, such as likely price and wage increases and any expected major environmental change, is required. For example, if a senior manager was reviewing a budget, it would be extremely difficult to judge different budget submissions by two subordinate managers, if one budget had been calculated assuming a 10% wage increase in April and a downturn in sales demand, while the second budget assumed a 5% increase in June with an increase in sales demand.

Information about any factor that restricts performance should also be communicated to relevant operational managers at an early stage. For example, if there is a constraint on production then there is very little benefit in the marketing department forecasting sales of 2000 units a month and preparing a marketing plan to meet such a sales level, when the maximum number of units that can be manufactured is 1500 units a month.

(iii) Improved control of the actions of organizations

Budgetary control involves the use of the budgets as a method of comparison with actual financial results in order to identify any differences and whether corrective action may be required.

(iv) Improved evaluation of the performance of managers

The comparison of actual performance against budget can also be used in the evaluation of management performance. Where financial results are better than expected this may be interpreted as an indicator of good performance, while adverse results against budget may indicate the reverse.

(v) Higher motivation of staff

In theory, the budgeting system may provide a means of motivating staff through providing:

(i) A *target*. This may be expressed in terms of sales, costs, profits or other financial objectives.
(ii) A basis for rewarding staff who achieve budget target.

The 'behavioural' implications of budgetary control systems, including the use of budgets to assist in the evaluation of the performance of managers and to achieve higher motivation of managers, are discussed further in Chapter 19.

Budgetary control

As indicated in Figure 7.1 (steps 6, 7 and 8), the budgetary control process can be considered to have three steps in the process:

1. Following agreement of the plan, the budgets are prepared. The budget provides a target in financial terms. For some departments or organizations the budget target might be expressed in terms of profits or a return on investment, for others it might be revenue or costs.
2. Actual results are compared with budget and differences are identified. Causes of variance are determined and corrective action proposed.
3. Corrective action should be implemented. Managers may also be rewarded or punished based on the level of achievement of actual result against target.

This form of control is called feedback control and is illustrated in Figure 7.2.
    Further key aspects that are central to the effective performance of a budgetary control system are discussed below.

Feedback control information – variance analysis

Table 7.2 shows the budget for Dundee Bicycle Division for the first quarter (April–June) of the financial year April 20X8 to March 20X9.
    During the period April 20X8 to June 20X9, actual results are recorded on a monthly basis by the accounting system and a comparison against budget reported. Any difference between actual and budget is called a variance. As well as comparing actual with budget

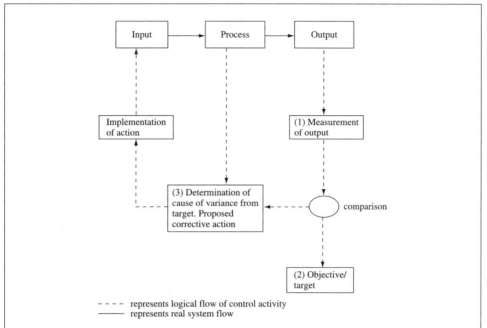

Organizations are involved in producing an output. For example, a manufacturing company produces manufactured goods. Raw materials, labour and overheads are input into a process and the finished product is the output.

With a budgetary control process, the objective/target (box 2 above) is measured in financial terms. The output that is measured (box 1) is the actual financial results (this might be measured in terms of cost, revenue or profit). Where there is a difference (variance) between actual output and the target, the cause of the variance is investigated and corrective action proposed and then implemented.

Figure 7.2   Illustration of a feedback control process

Table 7.2   Budget for the period April–June 20X8

Sales units		6,000
	(£)/unit	£
Sales	110	660,000
Labour	39	234,000
Material	27	162,000
Fixed production overhead		135,000
Production cost		531,000
Gross profit		129,000
Overheads		
Accounting		36,000
Commercial		18,000
Net profit		75,000

for the month, cumulative actual with budget is also often shown. Table 7.3 shows the actual results for the three months from April to June 20X8, compared with the budget for the same period.

Table 7.3   Comparison of actual results against the budget target

	£/unit	Budget	Actual	Variance	
		* Accounts for the period April–June 20X8			
Sales units		6,000	5,200	(800)	(A)*
		(£)	(£)	(£)	
Sales	110	660,000	598,000	(62,000)	(A)
Labour	39	234,000	211,558	22,442	(F)
Material	27	162,000	143,240	18,760	(F)
Fixed production overhead		135,000	132,000	3,000	(F)
Production cost		531,000	486,798	44,202	(F)
Gross profit		129,000	111,202	(17,798)	(A)
Accounting		36,000	35,000	1,000	(F)
Commercial		18,000	43,000	(25,000)	(A)
Net profit		75,000	33,202	(41,798)	(A)

* In the table above (A) stands for an adverse variance. An adverse variance is also shown in brackets. (F) stands for a favourable variance.

Reviewing the variance report in Table 7.3, it can be seen that actual profit for the quarter April to June 20X8 is £41,798 adverse, i.e. less than budget profit.

Key variances causing profit to be lower than expected are:

(i) Gross profit is £17,798 less than budget. This was due to an adverse sales variance of £62,000, only partly offset by a favourable production cost variance of £44,202.
(ii) A £25,000 adverse variance for the commercial department.

These variances should be examined in order to identify why actual results are different from budget. Corrective action can then take place if this is considered necessary.
Note that:

• If actual revenue is less than budget then this is an adverse variance.
• If actual revenue is greater than budget then this is a favourable variance.
• If actual cost is greater than budget then this is an adverse variance.
• If actual cost is less than budget then this is a favourable variance.

Further refinements to the control report, when some costs are variable, are considered in the section on flexible budgeting that is covered later in the chapter.

Responsibility accounting

As well as providing a budgetary control report for the organization as a whole, a **responsibility accounting** system will provide control reports for individual responsibility centres of an organization. A **responsibility centre** is a unit of an organization where a manager is held responsible for the performance of the unit.

Responsibility centres can be treated as profit, cost, revenue or investment centres.

(i) *Profit centres.* Some units of an organization will be involved in the sale of goods and services to customers. A responsibility centre can be treated as a **profit centre** where a manager is held accountable for both the revenue and the costs of the centre.

(ii) *Cost centres.* Some departments will not be selling their services to others. **Cost centres** are responsibility centres where managers are held accountable for the expenses under their control.

In manufacturing organizations where it is possible to measure outputs and the input required for this output then it is possible to introduce a standard costing system. This system is explained in depth in Chapter 9.

A **discretionary cost centre** is one where the manager is responsible for expenses, but the optimum relationship between input and output is difficult to judge. Overhead departments such as accounting and marketing are often considered to be discretionary cost centres.

(iii) *Revenue centres.* A unit will be treated as a **revenue centre** when the manager is held responsible for the sales revenue that is generated.

(iv) *Investment centres.* An **investment centre** exists where managers have responsibility for revenue, costs and investments. Measures of performance are return on the capital employed and residual income. These measures are discussed further in Chapter 10.

Activity 7.1

Accounting information (budget and actual) is provided for the Dundee Bicycle Division as a whole and also for individual departments (commercial, accounting, production and engineering). The division and individual departments are therefore treated as separate responsibility centres.

Advise whether the various responsibility areas are being treated as cost, profit, revenue or investment centres; see Dundee Bicycle Division – Part A.

Identifying best practice in the design of budgetary control reports

Budgetary control information is usually provided to management in the form of a formal report provided on a regular basis, for example, monthly or quarterly. Over time, discussions on best practice in the design of control reports have referred to:

(i) The use of comparison of actual results against flexible budget.
(ii) Management by exception.

(iii) Whether to separate controllable from non-controllable expenditure.
(iv) Frequency of reporting.
 (v) Presentation of information.
(vi) Reporting non-financial information.

(i) Comparison of actual against flexible budget

In the variance reports that we have looked at to date for Dundee Bicycles Ltd, the actual result has been compared with original budget in order to identify a variance. For example, for the period April to June 20X8, budgeted sales and production were for 6000 bicycle frames and budgeted raw material cost was £162,000. The actual material cost of £143,240 was therefore £18,760 favourable.

Question

Since there is a favourable material variance of £18,760, does that mean that the production department has been efficient and achieved a good result?

Answer

The actual cost was for 5200 units, but the budget was for 6000 units. To provide a more meaningful control report, where costs are variable it would be better to compare actual costs against a **flexible budget**, which is the original budget adjusted for the change in the actual level of activity. In this example, assuming costs vary in relation to output, it would be better to compare actual material costs for 5200 units against a flexible budget for 5200 units, see Table 7.4.

Table 7.4 A comparison vs. flexible budget for raw materials

Units	Original budget	Flexible budget	Actual	Variance
	6000	5200	5200	
	£	£	£	£
Material	162,400	140,400	143,240	(2,840) (A)

Each bicycle frame is budgeted to need raw material costing £27 (a variable cost) and if 5200 units were manufactured, the expected cost of the materials should be 5200×£27=£140,400. Since the actual material cost of manufacturing 5200 units was £143,240, material costs were in fact £2840 more than might have been expected.

A full variance report for the company including revenue, labour, material and fixed costs and incorporating the use of comparison vs. flexed budget is shown in Table 7.5. Note that this analysis separates variable from fixed costs.

This analysis shows that the company originally budgeted to make a profit of £75,000. It actually generated a profit of £33,202 (a difference of £41,798). The original variance report, however, was not as helpful as it could have been, as it did not separately identify the variance that was due to a lower number of units being sold (a sales volume variance) from other operational variances.

Table 7.5   Accounts for the period April–June 20X8

		Accounts for the period April–June 20X8			
		Original budget	Flexed[1] budget	Actual	Variance
Sales units	Per unit £	6,000	5,200	5,200	£
		£	£	£	
Sales	110	660,000	572,000	598,000	26,000 (F)
Labour	39	234,000	202,800	211,558	(8,758) (A)
Material	27	162,000	140,400	143,240	(2,840) (A)
Total variable cost	66	396,000	343,200	354,798	(11,598) (A)
Contribution	44	264,000	228,800	243,202	14,402 (F)
Fixed costs:					
Production		135,000	135,000	132,000	3,000 (F)
Accounting		36,000	36,000	35,000	1,000 (F)
Commercial		18,000	18,000	43,000	(25,000) (A)
Net profit		**75,000**	39,800	**33,202**	(6,598) (A)

[1] In order that an accurate flexible budget can be produced, it is important to:

(a) Identify the basis on which costs vary. In the examples in this chapter it will be assumed that level of output is the cost driver. In Chapter 6, it was identified that costs may in fact vary in relation to a range of different cost drivers and the potential use of activity-based budgeting will be discussed in Chapter 8.

(b) Recognize that fixed costs will remain the same despite changes in activity level. In reality, organizations should be continuously working to reduce 'fixed' costs, through a process of continuous improvement.

1. The sales volume variance is £75,000−£39,800 = £35,200.

   (i) Each unit sold is expected to generate £44 contribution (a selling price of £110 less variable cost of labour of £39 and material cost of £27). If sales are 800 units less than expected the adverse variance due to lower sales is £44 × 800 units = £35,200 adverse.

   (ii) Note that budgeted fixed costs do not change given changes in output and therefore do not impact on the sales volume variance.

2. The remainder of the variance of £6598 (£39,800−£33,202) is due to operational reasons.

   1. The sales variance of £26,000 favourable has occurred because the average selling price per unit is greater than expected (£115 rather than the budgeted £110 per bicycle frame). 5200 bicycle frames have been sold for £5 more than had been expected.

   2. Adverse labour and material variances of £8758 and £2840 respectively.

   3. Favourable fixed production and accounting expenditure (total £4000) offset by a substantial adverse variance of £25,000 by the commercial department.

Many companies also provide:

(a) A monthly summary document reconciling the difference between the original budgeted profit and the actual profit. See Table 7.6.

Table 7.6 Reconciliation budget to actual profit April–June 20X8

	Favourable	Adverse	Reconciliation budget to actual profit April–June 20X8	
			£	£
Original budgeted profit				75,000
Sales volume variance				35,200 (A)
Budgeted profit at actual sales volume				39,800
Operational variances:	Favourable	Adverse		
Sales price	26,000			
Labour		(8,758)		
Material		(2,840)		
Fixed production overhead	3,000			
Accounting	1,000			
Commercial		(25,000)		
				(6,598) (A)
Actual profit				33,202

(b) A written report that explains the reasons for the variances. The format of a written report is discussed further in Chapter 9, which additionally explains the operation of a system of control called standard costing.

(ii) Management by exception

A large organization can consist of a number of hierarchical layers with many departments. It would not be practical or helpful to provide detailed information about all departments to the top management of the organization. If that happened, senior management would soon become overloaded with information. An easier approach is to operate a system of **management by exception** in which the attention of managers is focused on those departments and account items where there is a significant variance from budget. In the control report shown in Table 7.7, it can be seen that the actual expenditure by the commercial department was £25,000 above budget for the period April–June 20X8. Mr Jones could ask the commercial manager for the reasons, or indeed could ask for a review of the accounting report for the commercial department.

The detailed accounts for the commercial department are shown in Table 7.7. These accounts indicate that actual expenditure is £25,000 over budget. The general manager can see that all costs are above budget. The main cause is the above-budget expenditure on advertising. Attention would be particularly focused on the reason for this variance.

Table 7.7   Accounts for the commercial manager

	Accounts for the commercial manager April–June 20X8		
	Budget £	Actual £	Variance £
Wages	11,100	13,100	(2,000) (A)
Travel	3,100	3,700	(600) (A)
Share of company			
Advertising costs	3,000	23,100	(20,100) (A)
Other costs	800	3,100	(2,300) (A)
	18,000	43,000	(25,000) (A)

In this case it is found that the division has been charged a share of central advertising costs and that expenditure is above budget because the advertising campaign has occurred earlier than expected.

(iii) Separation of controllable and uncontrollable costs

Conventional wisdom is that **controllable costs** are those costs which are the responsibility of a manager and can be controlled by that manager. The report of the Committee of Cost Concepts and Standards in the United States in 1956 suggested the following:

(i) If a manager can control the quantity and price paid for a service then the manager is responsible for all the expenditure controlled by the service.
(ii) If a manager can control the quantity of the service, but not the price paid for the service, then only the amount of difference between the actual and budgeted expenditure that is due to usage should be identified to the manager.
(iii) If the manager cannot control either the quantity or the price paid for the service then the expenditure is uncontrollable and should not be identified with the manager.

In reality it is not always possible to clearly follow the guideline. Merchant (1985) has made a partial move away from the principle that the manager should only be accountable for items that they can control to the suggestion that they should be held 'accountable for the performance areas that you want them to pay attention to'. Accordingly, even if some costs are not fully controllable by a manager, Merchant argues that they should be included in the departmental report, as he/she will at least pay attention to these costs and attempt to bring pressure to bear to reduce them. If the cost is excluded from the departmental report, then there may be a lack of concern about the control and potential misuse of this expense or asset.

One option is to include all items in the control report that are not controllable, under the heading of 'uncontrollable costs'. This does mean that even if the manager cannot control the costs, he is at least aware of them and can draw the attention of senior management to any possible overspend.

Activity 7.2

Review the cost information shown in the accounting report of the commercial manager provided in Table 7.7. Identify those costs that might be considered controllable by the manager and those that are uncontrollable.

(iv) Frequency of reporting

Many organizations provide budgetary control information on a monthly basis. Some accounting systems can provide real-time information on expenditure to date against budget.

(v) Presentation of information

In the examples considered above the cumulative results for the first quarter (April to June) of Dundee Bicycle Division have been reviewed. Many monthly accounting packages would provide a report of the monthly accounts and a cumulative comparison of actual results and budget. See, for example, Table 7.8. Some organizations also report variances compared with last year.

A further refinement often included in many reports is an indication of the percentage variance that has occurred. Some organizations may investigate variances if they have

Table 7.8   Accounts for the commercial department

	Accounts for the commercial department							
	June Month				April–June Cumulative			
	Budget (£)	Actual (£)	Variance (£)	%	Budget (£)	Actual (£)	Variance (£)	%
Controllable costs								
Wages	3,500	4,450	(950)	(27)	11,100	13,100	(2,000)	(18)
Travel	1,100	1,500	(400)	(36)	3,100	3,700	(600)	(19)
Other costs	300	200	100	33	800	3,100	(2,300)	(288)
	4,900	6,150	(1,250)	(25)	15,000	19,900	(4,900)	(33)
Uncontrollable costs								
Advertising	4,000	18,100	(14,100)	(352)	3,000	23,100	(20,100)	(670)
	8,900	24,250	(15,350)	(172)	18,000	43,000	(25,000)	(139)

exceeded a certain monetary sum or a certain percentage, while others will leave it to individual managers and accountants to investigate.

Table 7.8 shows a more detailed accounting report for the commercial department for the month of June and for the quarter April to June 20X8. Expenditure that is controllable by the commercial manager is shown separately to the uncontrollable expenditure, this being the advertising costs authorized by head office. Variance information is also shown, with an adverse variance shown in brackets. The percentage that the variance represents from the budget is also indicated. For example, wages in the month of June were £950 above the budget of £3500. This is an adverse variance of 27% and has been shown as (27) on the accounting statement.

Looking at the statement it is possible to identify some large differences from budget. Wages and travel costs are significantly over budget in June and to a lesser extent over budget for the quarter. This may reflect the recruitment of an additional member of staff in the last two months. Although other costs are in line with plan in June, they are significantly greater for the quarter and therefore some large expenditure appears to have occurred in earlier months. Advertising costs are regarded as uncontrollable. It is clear that over-expenditure in this area has caused the majority of the overall variance above budgeted expenditure.

(vi) Reporting non-financial variances

In recent years, it has been recommended that increasing emphasis be placed on the reporting of non-financial performance measures. This will be discussed further in Chapters 20 and 22.

Compliance with guidelines

It should be noted that these frameworks should only be used as guidelines, there are no accounting standards that dictate that organizations produce their reports strictly according to these guidelines. Individual organizations do not strictly follow the guidelines, often for very valid reasons.

Feedforward control

As well as monitoring actual results against plan using feedback control, organizations often undertake reviews of what they expect to happen for the year ahead. **Feedforward control** occurs where a revised forecast of future performance takes place, is compared with the original plan and action is taken to deal with likely divergences. These reviews could be held every month, however, it is likely that they will be held less frequently, say once every three months. For example, if the financial year runs from April 20X8 to March 20X9, the first review might take place in July 20X8. This is the process that took place in the Dundee Bicycle Division.

Such reviews:

1. Identify the financial performance of the organization for the year to date.
2. Reassess the expected financial performance for the year ahead. By adding the actual performance achieved in the year to date to the expected performance for the remainder of the year it is possible to identify a revised estimate of financial performance for the year.
3. Compare the revised estimate for the budget year to the original budget for the year, in order to identify any differences.
4. If the expected financial performance for the year ahead is not as good as the original budget then corrective action may be taken to try to bring expected future performance back into line with plan.

To illustrate this process, an *abbreviated* version of the Profit and Loss Account of Dundee Bicycle Division, showing just the sales revenue, total costs and profit will be considered.

As previously illustrated, at the end of the period April 20X8–June 20X8, the actual results were published showing an adverse profit variance of £41,798. See summarized information in Table 7.9.

Table 7.9   Dundee Bicycle Division

	April–June 20X8		
	Budget £	Actual £	Variance £
Sales	660,000	598,000	(62,000) (A)
Costs	585,000	564,798	20,202 (F)
Profit	75,000	33,202	(41,798) (A)

In July, the accountant and management of Dundee Bicycles Ltd reviewed expected performance for the remainder of the financial year and produced a revised sales, cost and profit estimate for the period July 20X8 to March 20X8, as shown in Table 7.10.

Table 7.10   Dundee Bicycle Division

Revised Profit and Loss Account estimate July 20X8–March 20X9	
	£
Sales	1,700,000
Costs	1,610,000
Profit	90,000

Taking actual results for the year to date (Table 7.9) and adding the expected results for the remainder of the financial year (Table 7.10), a revised forecast of expected revenue, costs and profit for the year April 20X8 to March 20X9 can be produced as shown in Table 7.11.

Table 7.11   Dundee Bicycle Division

	(1) Actual April–June 20X8 £	(2) Revised forecast July 20X8–March 20X9 £	(3) = (1) + (2) Revised forecast April 20X8–March 20X9 £
Sales	598,000	1,700,000	2,298,000
Costs	564,798	1,610,000	2,174,798
Profit	33,202	90,000	123,202

Table 7.12 shows the original budget for the financial year April 20X8–March 20X8 (summarized from Table 7.1) compared with the revised estimate shown in Table 7.11.

Table 7.12   Dundee Bicycle Division

	Original budget 20X8/9 £	Revised forecast 20X8/9 £	Variance £
Sales	2,460,000	2,298,000	(162,000) (A)
Costs	2,235,000	2,174,798	60,202 (F)
Profit	225,000	123,202	(101,798) (A)

As a result of this exercise, the organization needs to consider the action that it should take. It should either accept that the actual profit for the year will most likely be £101,798 less than originally budgeted or it should take action to increase revenue or reduce costs, in order to bring actual back into line with budget.

Activity 7.3

Jack Jones has reviewed the information in Table 7.12 and noted the expected shortfall in profit for the coming year of £101,798. His reaction was to say that a shortfall was not acceptable and that all managers will have to reduce their costs by just over 4% on budget in order that this is achieved. List potential disadvantages of this approach to control.

Budgetary control and reward systems

Financial incentive schemes can be provided at all levels of the organization and for many managers such schemes are linked to performance of their responsibility centre against budget, particularly where the centre is a profit centre. In most organizations there is a linear link between the reward and the result, with the reward usually promised over a restricted performance range. This is illustrated in Figure 7.3.

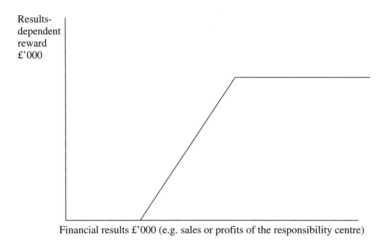

Figure 7.3   Budgetary control information and rewards

Below a certain level of performance no additional reward is given. At a certain point, say 80% of budget performance, an incentive reward will be given and this will increase, usually to a maximum level. In a study of 12 organizations, Merchant (1989) found that nine of the organizations set a maximum reward level. Reasons suggested included:

1. Higher payments might not be justified.

   (i) If favourable results are the result of a windfall gain, e.g. demand has increased more than expected because of an unexpected rise in consumer demand or an exceptionally large order that was achieved through luck rather than management effort.
   (ii) Managers might be encouraged to take inappropriate action, e.g. by cutting costs that will increase short-term profits but at the expense of long-term profits.
   (iii) The target set in the plan may be too low, resulting in a reward being given for little effort on the part of the manager.

2. Lower-level managers may be paid more than senior-level managers.
3. A desire to adhere to industry norms.

Any financial reward will often be awarded based on performance over a year, although some reward systems may be based on performance over a number of years.

As well as financial rewards there may be non-financial rewards and some form of recognition, e.g. small prizes may be given in some organizations.

Linking reward to performance

If rewards are linked to performance then it is likely that the attention of employees will be further attracted to the different aspects of performance that are rewarded. A guide is being given by the organization about the amount of time that should be given to the different areas of performance. Rather than just being told which are the important areas, rewards such as promotion and bonuses are being provided.

Having a reward can be motivational. An employee may put in extra time and effort in order to gain a reward. An inappropriately designed reward system can, however, negate the potential benefits of an otherwise well-designed performance measurement system as managers may spend excessive time on improving performance in areas that are not central to the desired objectives and strategies of the organization. This issue is considered further in Chapter 19.

Summary

A formal model of the planning and control process identifies a number of steps that can be undertaken in relation to the longer term (say 3–5 years) and medium term (for example 1 year).

Key principles of a budgetary control system include:

- Feedback control in which actual results are compared against budget.
- Responsibility accounting. The provision of accounting reports for various responsibility centres within an organization. These can be cost, revenue, profit or investment centres.

Guidelines on best practice for reporting information often recommend:

- The use of comparison vs. flexible budget.
- Separating controllable from non-controllable costs.
- Employing management by exception.
- Reporting of actual and percentage variances against budget for the month, cumulative, compared with last year.
- Reporting of non-financial results.

As well as feedback control, feedforward control is also used by many organizations. This involves the reassessment of the expected financial performance for the future (e.g. remainder of the financial year), identifying any variation to original budget that seems likely to occur and taking corrective action.

A number of organizations link rewards to the achievement of financial results. An inappropriately designed system can lead to inappropriate action being taken by managers.

Further reading

Anthony, R. and Govindarajan, V. (2004) *Management Control Systems*, 11th edn. Irwin.

Merchant, K. A. (2003) *Modern Management Control Systems: Performance measurement, Evaluation and Incentives: Text and Cases*, Prentice-Hall.

Emmanuel, C., Otley, D. and Merchant, K. (1990) *Accounting for Management Control*, International Thompson Business Press.

Answers to activities

Activity 7.1

The division as a whole is treated as an investment centre with the requirement to achieve a target return on the investment in the division.

The accounting, engineering and production departments are treated as cost centres. The commercial department is being treated as:

(i) A revenue centre. The commercial manager has been given a target level of sales to achieve and actual sales will be reported with a comparison made against target.

(ii) The department is also treated as a cost centre in that the commercial manager department is also accountable for the costs of his department.

Note that this would probably not be considered a profit centre as only a limited proportion of the costs of sales are identified and under the control of the commercial manager. However, if it was assumed that goods sold were transferred at the standard cost, then it would be technically possible to measure performance based on profit.

Activity 7.2

Table 7.8 provides an illustration of the type of report. In this table, controllable costs are clearly separated from non-controllable costs. The overall adverse variance is £25,000 but it can be clearly seen that £20,100 of this is caused by the overspend on the share of central advertising costs, which cannot be controlled by the commercial manager (head office just make an allocation of their central costs).

Activity 7.3

A potential problem disadvantage of any approach is to ensure a balance between long-term and short-term gains in profit. It may be possible to cut some costs that will improve short-term profits, but will hamper longer-term success. For example, cutting training or research and development.

Discussion questions

1. What is the difference between feedforward and feedback control?
2. An engineering consultancy company consists of three departments that work directly for clients – roads, buildings and sewage construction sections. As well as these sections there is an administration department and a canteen. The managing director of the company has asked your advice about setting up a responsibility accounting and budgetary control system. You should advise on:

    (a) The types of responsibility centres that could be established.
    (b) The key features of a budgetary control system.

3. A major problem with an accounting system based on flexible budgeting is in identifying the basis for flexing the budget. Discuss.
4. For a budgetary control system to operate successfully, is it necessary to have accounting reports provided for all different departments of the organization? Discuss.
    Particular reference should be made to the Dundee Bicycle Division when answering the remaining discussion questions.
5. You are advised that sales for Dundee Bicycle Division are £70,000 lower than budgeted in July. There is an adverse sales price variance of £25,000 and an adverse sales volume variance of £45,000.

    (i) List the possible reasons for these variances.
    (ii) Why might the reporting system be providing a misleading picture of the performance of the sales manager and his sales team?
    (iii) You are advised that sales for Dundee Bicycle Division are £70,000 lower than budgeted in July. There is an adverse sales price variance of £25,000 and an adverse sales volume variance of £45,000.

6. The works manager has approached Jack Jones and requested that £100,000 be spent on a quality improvement programme. Although there will be no benefit from this expenditure in the current year, he anticipates that it will lead to a net improvement in profits of £50,000 in all subsequent years.

    (i) Should Jack Jones authorize the expenditure on the quality improvement programme?
    (ii) Why might he not take this action?

Note that the impact of accounting reports on human behaviour is considered further in Chapter 19.

Exercises

(Questions with numbers in bold have answers at the back of the book.)

Q7.1 'Sound Sleepers' Ltd manufactures a single product, a comfortable mattress. In February 20X8, the following information was available:

	Original budget	Actual	Variance
Sales units	1,000	1,100	
	£	£	£
Sales	100,000	107,800	7,800 (F)
Direct material	50,000	57,475	(7,475) (A)
Direct labour	12,000	15,750	(3,750) (A)
Total variable cost	62,000	73,225	(11,225) (A)
contribution	38,000	34,575	(3,425) (A)
Fixed overheads	6,000	7,000	1,000 (A)
Profit	32,000	27,575	4,425 (A)

Actual sales and production were 1100 units.

Required:

(i) Provide a revised variance report that you believe will be more meaningful for the management of the company. (See Table 7.5 for an example.)
(ii) Provide a reconciliation between the original budgeted profit and the actual profit. (See Table 7.6.)
(iii) Comment on possible reasons behind the causes of the variances reported in (i) above. What further information do you require for a full analysis?

Q7.2 Elba Ltd uses variance analysis as a method of cost control. The following information is available for the year ended 31 March 20X7:

	£/unit	Original budget	Actual
Sales units		12,000	11,500
		£	£
Sales	75	900,000	851,000
Direct material	30	360,000	350,000
Direct labour	24	288,000	310,000

Total variable cost	648,000	660,000
Contribution	252,000	191,000
Fixed overheads	96,000	100,000
Profit	156,000	91,000

Required:

(i) Provide a variance report that you believe will be meaningful for the management of the company.
(ii) Provide a reconciliation between the original budgeted profit and the actual profit.
(iii) Comment on possible reasons behind the causes of the variances reported in (i) above. What further information do you require for a full analysis?

Q7.3 Seaworth Ltd runs ten garages based in the South of England. Each garage has three departments:

(i) A department that sells new cars.
(ii) The servicing department, which undertakes services and minor repairs for customers.
(iii) The parts department, which sells car parts to the public and also provides parts to the servicing department.

The company has decided to implement a system of responsibility accounting for the financial year April 20X7 to March 20X8 and the accountant of the company has prepared a budget for each garage. Every month a set of accounts will be sent to the garage manager showing budget and actual revenue and costs for the garage. The accounts for May, for the Portston branch, are shown below.

**Portston Garage
Accounts for the month of May
20X7**

	Budget (£)	Actual (£)	Variance (£)
Sales	370,000	310,000	60,000 (A)
Cost of new cars	170,000	130,000	40,000 (F)
Cost of parts	40,000	38,000	2,000 (F)
Showroom staff	40,000	35,000	5,000 (F)
Service department staff	25,000	26,000	1,000 (A)
Parts department staff	15,000	14,000	1,000 (F)
Garage overhead costs	18,000	20,000	2,000 (A)
Allocated head office costs	20,000	30,000	10,000 (A)
Profit	42,000	17,000	25,000 (A)

Required:

An evaluation of how the accounting statement provided above could be improved in order that it is more useful for the management of Seaworth Ltd and the manager of the Portston Garage. Identify the further information that you require in order to fully answer this question.

Q7.4 The Empire Corporation manufactures a range of kitchen equipment. The management had been very concerned with the financial losses incurred in the previous period and as a result decided to improve the management accounting control system to ensure that the situation did not occur again. As a result the following report was submitted to the management team for the first quarter ending 31 March 20X8.

Profit statement – as at 31 March 20X8

	Original budget	Actual	Variance
	£'000	£'000	£'000
Sales Revenue	1,200	1,100	100 (A)
Less:			
Expenses			
Direct labour costs	(400)	(378)	22 (F)
Direct materials	(300)	(260)	40 (F)
Production overheads:			
Variable	(100)	(92)	8 (F)
Fixed	(50)	(58)	8 (A)
Allocated head office costs	(50)	(80)	30 (A)
Profit	300	232	68 (A)

Additional information:

Direct labour hours worked	100,000	95,000
Units produced/sold	10,000	9,000

All the members of the management team are concerned by the content of the report shown above, not only with respect to the poor profit performance shown, but also with regard to how the information is presented.

You are required to:

- Redraft the statement in a way that will provide more relevant information to the management team.
- Identify why your revised statement is an improvement on the original presentation.

- Identify issues that you would ideally wish to consider further before continuing with the provision of a revised report.
- Identify any further information, whether financial or non-financial, that you consider would be helpful for management.

Q7.5 Advise the management of Coopers Leisure Resorts Ltd on the design of an appropriate budgetary control system for the Dorset holiday home and campsite, 'Sunshine Site' described in the short case scenario 'Cooper Leisure Resorts Ltd' at the back of the book.

PREPARING THE MASTER BUDGET

8

Objectives

When you have completed this chapter you should be able to:

- Prepare a cash flow budget.
- Identify and describe alternative approaches to planning for overhead costs:

    - Incremental budgeting.
    - Activity-based budgeting.
    - Zero and priority-based budgeting.

- Prepare key operational and summary financial budgets.
- Describe the use of computer-based budgeting.

Introduction

This chapter considers the preparation of the budgets of an organization. The preparation of a cash flow budget is illustrated first. Alternative approaches to budgeting for overhead costs are then discussed; these include approaches such as the use of financial ratios, incremental, zero-based and activity-based budgeting. This is followed by a review of the key operational budgets that feed into the summary financial budgets, the Profit and Loss Account, the cash flow statement and the Balance Sheet. The chapter ends with a comprehensive illustration of a budgeting exercise for Dundee Bicycle Division and a brief discussion of the benefits and dangers of computer-based budgeting.

Preparation of the cash flow budget

Managing the flow of funds through a business

Figure 8.1 illustrates that a business can be considered to consist of a range of cash inflows and outflows.

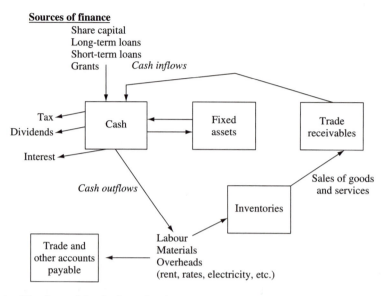

Sources of finance
Share capital
Long-term loans
Short-term loans
Grants

Figure 8.1   **The flow of funds through a business**

A key aim of financial management is to ensure that there is sufficient cash available to fund cash outflows required for:

1. Operating costs including labour, materials and overheads such as electricity, rent, rates and marketing expenditure.
2. Non-current (fixed) assets such as land, buildings and equipment.
3. Payments to other key stakeholders including dividends to shareholders, interest on loans and tax.

Cash inflows will be received from payments for goods and services by customers and in the short term it may be possible to delay payments to suppliers. If these inflows are insufficient to fund the business then alternative sources of cash need to be found and can include:

1. Long-term sources of finance including share capital from investors; long-term loans from a bank or finance institution; occasionally it may be possible to obtain a government grant.
2. If the requirement for cash is only for the short term, then short-term loans may be obtained.
3. Some companies raise cash by selling existing assets, such as land and buildings in order to fund activities in different areas.

The cash flow forecasts and the cash flow budget

A cash flow forecast is a forecast of future cash requirements and identifies:

  (i) The opening cash balance at the beginning of a trading period.
 (ii) Cash inflows from sales and sources of finance.

(iii) Cash outflows.
(iv) The closing cash balance at the end of a trading period. Opening cash balance + cash inflows − cash outflows.

A cash flow forecast will be produced on a regular basis by most businesses and is considered to be a key forecasting document that is required for a range of purposes. In the short term it is necessary to know whether the business will have a cash flow problem over the coming months. For the long term it is important to know whether the business will have a funding problem in future years.

A cash flow budget is the statement produced following the formal (often annual) budgeting process. As an illustration, in Table 8.1 the cash budget is shown for Alpha Ltd for the first few months of the forthcoming year.

Table 8.1 Cash flow budget for Alpha Ltd

	January	February	March	April	January–April
	£'000	£'000	£'000	£'000	
(1) OPENING CASH BALANCE (note 1)	10	21			
(2) ADD CASH INFLOWS					
Receipts from sales (note 2)	54	45			
TOTAL CASH AVAILABLE (1)+(2)	64	66			
DEDUCT CASH OUTFLOWS (PAYMENTS)					
Wages and salaries (note 3)	10	10			
Payments to suppliers (note 4)	27	22.5			
Overheads (note 5)	6	6			
Capital expenditure (note 6)					
(3) TOTAL CASH OUTFLOWS (PAYMENTS)	43	38.5			
CLOSING CASH BALANCE (1)+(2)−(3)	21	27.5			

The cash flows for the months of January and February have been completed in the table above. Explanation is provided in the notes below.

Note 1. The opening cash balance is £10,000.

Note 2	December	January	February	March	April
	£'000	£'000	£'000	£'000	£'000
Budgeted sales for Alpha Ltd are	54	45	47	52	47

All sales are on credit and these trade receivables are assumed to be paid *one month* after the sale occurred.

Note 3. Wages and salaries are budgeted to be £10,000 per month, payable in the same month as they are earned.

Note 4	December	January	February	March	April
	£'000	£'000	£'000	£'000	£'000
Budgeted purchases for Alpha Ltd are	27	22.5	23.5	26	23.5

Payments to suppliers occur *one month* after the goods have been purchased.
Note 5. Overheads are £6000 per month payable in the same month.
Note 6. Capital expenditure of £15,000 takes place in March payable in April.

Activity 8.1

Complete the budgeted cash flow statement for the months of March and April and in total for the period January to April.

Management will be concerned about the cash flows for the coming period in order to know whether cash flow objectives are likely to be met. For example, assume a target cash surplus of £150,000 has been set and the cash budget indicates that there will be a shortfall. Management will either need to revise their target downwards or consider corrective action to ensure that it is achieved.

Budgeting for overheads

Overhead departments, such as the accounting and marketing departments, are also known as discretionary cost centres as the level of expenditure is at the discretion of managers. The effect on profitability that is due to an increase or decrease in expenditure on overheads is often a matter of judgement. A number of methods, including incremental budgeting, the use of ratios, activity-based budgeting and zero-based budgeting are discussed below.

Incremental budgeting

A traditional approach to budgeting for overheads is called incremental budgeting. With **incremental budgeting**, the current level of expenditure is taken as the base/starting point for next year's annual budget and then an allowance is made for inflation. Figure 8.2

The accounting department of Dundee Bicycle Division consists of five members of staff. The Chief Accountant and four others. The Chief Accountant and two members of staff prepare the accounts and undertake sales and purchase ledger activities as well as looking after the cash book.

The remaining two members of staff are involved with management accounting activities such as preparation of the budget, reporting on causes of variances to budget and undertaking costing and other miscellaneous activities. The lead member of the management accounting team reports to the Chief Accountant and is particularly concerned with the development of a computer-based decision support system.

In 20X7/8 the Chief Accountant was paid £36,000, the lead member of the management accounting team was paid £26,000 and the other three members of staff were paid £20,000 each. The management of Dundee Ltd used an incremental approach to budgeting and assumed that the existing use of resources would be the same in 20X8/9 as in 20X7/8, but that there would be an inflationary impact of 5% for all costs. This is reflected in the expected expenditure for 20X7/8 and the budgeted expenditure for 20X8/9 shown below.

Figure 8.2 Budget for the accounting department of Dundee Bicycles Division

	Expected 20X7/8 £	Budget 20X8/9 £
Wages	122,000	127,900
Expenses	5,100	5,600
Travel	6,000	6,300
Training	4,000	4,200
Total	137,100	144,000

Figure 8.2   (*Continued*)

provides an illustrative example of using an incremental approach to budgeting in Dundee Bicycle Division.

In the public sector, the above type of analysis is known as a *line item* budget. It identifies the line items of wages, expenses, etc., without identifying the cost of the activities that are completed by the department.

Use of ratios

A quick method to check whether the budget put forward by an overhead department appears reasonable is to use ratio analysis. There may be little point in departments budgeting for a large increase in costs if sales are only increasing at a marginal rate or are even declining. Many senior managers expect a year-on-year increase in profits and accordingly an overhead department that showed an increase in costs as a percentage of revenue might find itself subject to close review. If the revenue for Dundee Bicycles was forecast to remain the same or decrease in the coming planning period, for example, then senior management may be reluctant to allow any increase in expenditure and a real cut in resources may be required. Other comparisons might also be helpful and identify unusual trends, for example a large increase in the budget over current expenditure. The use of ratio analysis as a means of control will be discussed further in Chapter 11.

Approaches that aim to quantify inputs and outputs

If a departmental manager wishes to increase the level of resources then it is likely that a financial case will be needed. Additional resources will often be justified in terms of the additional outputs that will be achieved.

Activity-based budgeting and zero-based budgeting are two approaches that aim to bring a more formal method of justifying the funding needed.

Activity-based budgeting

In Chapter 7, the use of flexible budgeting was explained. The assumption was made that variable costs would vary in relation to the volume of output. However, in Chapter 6 it was noted that costs may in fact vary in relation to a range of other cost drivers.

Activity-based budgeting is budgeting by activities rather than by cost elements. The budgeted output is determined in order to decide how much resource should be allocated to each activity. ABB has been described as 'ABC in reverse' and incorporates the following steps:

1. Production and sales volume for the next period should be identified.
2. The demand for activities to meet this volume is forecast.
3. The demand for resources to perform these activities is calculated.
4. An estimate for each resource to meet the demand can then be made.
5. The actual resource supply based on spending patterns and the activity capacity can then be calculated.

An example is considered in Figure 8.3.

Appledore Ltd is preparing its budgets for the coming year and is currently considering the level of expenditure in the credit control department.

(i) Budgeted sales to be approximately £1,000,000 a month for the coming year.
(ii) The key activity in the credit control department is the raising of invoices and collection of money related to these invoices. The average order is for £100 and it is estimated that the company will therefore need to raise 10,000 invoices a month along with the associated credit control activity.
(iii) On average it is estimated that credit control staff need to work for 6 minutes per invoice.
(iv) This means that 60,000 minutes or 1000 hours of work is required by credit control staff in the invoicing and credit control activity. If members of staff work on average 140 hours a month (allowing for sickness and holidays) this is the equivalent of 7.14 members of staff required.
(v) 10 members of staff are employed in the invoicing and credit control department. Assuming that each member of staff is paid £1000 a month, the actual cost of resources on this activity is £10,000. In theory, only 7.14 members of staff are required in order to complete the budget activity, which should cost £7140.

Given valid assumptions and an even volume of sales throughout the year, this analysis would suggest a reduction or redeployment of staff would be possible in the credit control department.

Figure 8.3   Using ABB to estimate budget cost

Zero-based budgeting

Zero-based budgeting is a comprehensive approach to budgeting that requires an organization to build up overhead budgets from a zero base as if the organization were starting from scratch. It involves a three-stage process:

(i) Each organizational activity is identified and a number of decision packages developed.
(ii) Each decision package is ranked in order of priority.
(iii) The allocation of resources based on the order of priority up to the spending cut-off point.

Stage 1. Each organizational activity is identified and a number of decision packages developed. The types of question that will be asked are:

  (i) Should the function be performed at all?
 (ii) What should the quantity level be? Are we doing too much?
(iii) How much should it cost?

The process of undertaking a zero-based approach to budgeting will be illustrated for the accounts department of Dundee Ltd.

Stage 1 of the process is illustrated in Figure 8.4.

In Dundee Ltd, the accounting department has two main sections, financial accounting and management accounting. With zero-based budgeting, each activity should be considered in turn.

Management accounting section
  (i) Should the function be performed at all?
      The work of the financial accounting section is essential for the company to fulfil its statutory requirements of producing a set of annual accounts. The work of the management accounting department, which might involve the production of costing information, budgets and budgetary control reports, is only required for management information purposes. The management of the division should consider how valuable this information is and if it is valuable, whether the functions should be undertaken by a specialist management accounting section or whether operational managers could do the work themselves!
 (ii) What should the quantity level be? Are we doing too much?
      Differing amounts of input resources can result in different outputs. The managers of the department might decide that it was possible to identify two different levels of activity. For example:

      'Management accounting' package 1. This might involve a limited service, possibly providing some basic information and the coordination of budget preparation, which could be achieved with the employment of one of the assistant accountants.

      'Management accounting' package 2. This could involve the provision of a service to develop the decision support system and an improved budgetary control system. To provide this package, it might be necessary to continue with the employment of the lead management accountant in addition to the assistant accountant.
(iii) How much should it cost?
      Management accounting package 1 is budgeted to cost £24,000 (the salary of the assistant of £20,000 plus other related expenses of £4000).

      Management accounting package 2 would cost <u>an additional</u> £29,000 in total (the salary of the lead management accountant of £26,000 plus other related expenses of £3000).

The same exercise would be carried out for the financial accounting section. Possibly a reduced service could be carried out with just the chief accountant and one assistant accountant at a cost of £66,000 (financial accounting package 1). The appointment of an additional assistant would be in financial accounting package 2.

Figure 8.4 Preparing decision packages

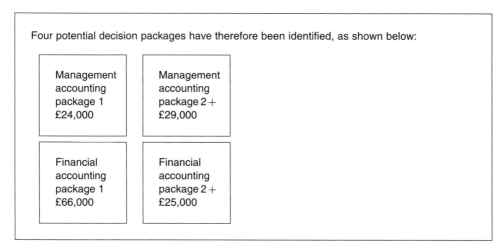

Four potential decision packages have therefore been identified, as shown below:

Management accounting package 1 £24,000	Management accounting package 2 + £29,000
Financial accounting package 1 £66,000	Financial accounting package 2 + £25,000

Figure 8.4 (*Continued*)

Stage 2. Each decision package is ranked in order of priority. This is illustrated in Figure 8.5.

The organization would need to consider the most important functions, in order that they can be ranked. It might be that it has been decided that the most important activity is represented by financial accounting package 1, the next most important being management accounting 1, then financial accounting package 2 and so on.

The most important package is therefore shown at the bottom of the column and the least important at the top.

Management accounting package 2 + £29,000
Financial accounting package 2 + £25,000
Management accounting package 1 £24,000
Financial accounting package 1 £66,000

Figure 8.5   Ranking decision packages

Stage 3. The allocation of resources based on the order of priority up to the spending cut-off point. If the organization had £144,000 available then it could continue to employ all the existing resources. If the organization only had £66,000 available then it would only be possible to fund financial accounting package 1. If £115,000 were available it would be possible to fund financial accounting package 1 and package 2 plus management accounting package 1. If more funds than £144,000 were available it would also be possible to look at producing additional decision packages.

The supporters of zero-based budgeting argue that:

(a) It is a systematic/fundamental review, which does not assume that expenditure in the last year is necessarily a good guide to the optimum level of expenditure.
(b) Specific objectives are set, with costs and outputs quantified.
(c) Lower-level managers are involved in preparing the different decision packages.
(d) Since the priorities for expenditure have already been set, it is possible to quickly make adjustments given changes in the availability of funds.

However, when zero-based budgeting has been used, a number of problems or disadvantages have also been experienced.

(i) It can be a very time-consuming exercise. Rather than delivering the outputs that they are meant to achieve, many managers have complained that excessive time is involved in preparing different decision packages and in identifying priorities.
(ii) The relationship between input and output is often not clear and assumptions made may be unrealistic.
(iii) It is not possible to consider all alternatives. There could even be a danger that viable alternatives will be ignored with managers limiting the analysis by only comparing a preferred option against others that are inferior.
(iv) Different managers and decision-makers will have different priorities and this will have an influence on the ranking of the packages. 'Pet' packages may be placed above essential programmes.

Activity 8.2

Consider the zero-based costing analysis for the accounting department that has been completed above. Provide a critical review of the analysis that has been undertaken.

Zero-based budgeting became popular in a number of government and local government bodies in the 1970s, however, its popularity has fluctuated over the years as those organizations that try to undertake the exercise struggle with the disadvantages. Rather than undertaking a zero-based approach every year, a number of organizations undertake the exercise on different departments every few years. Alternatively, a less exhaustive exercise can be carried out on an ad-hoc basis, such as priority-based budgeting. With **priority-based budgeting**, a more modest review might be undertaken, e.g. what changes would occur if there was a 10% increase or decrease in the budget?

Preparing the master budget

The master budget provides senior management with an overall picture of the firm's planned performance for the budget period. The **master budget** includes the budgeted income statement, the budgeted balance sheet and the cash budget. For small organizations, it is possible to prepare the master budget without the involvement of many other members of staff or departments. However, as organizations become larger, more people and departments need to be involved and a number of **operational budgets**, which include the sales, production and departmental overhead cost budgets, will need to be produced prior to the production of the summary financial documents. The logical order in which they should be prepared is shown in Figure 8.6. A comprehensive example illustrating the preparation of these budgets will be illustrated later in the chapter.

Sales budget

In commercial organizations, the sales budget is normally produced first. The reason is that other departments need to know the level of likely sales before they begin their planning.

The sales team or manager will often produce the sales budget, based on a best estimate of likely sales. Other techniques that might be used in organizations to identify expected sales include statistical techniques (based on the identification of past trends) or market research estimates. The sales team will also need to be aware of any constraints in the system. There is little point in budgeting for a level of sales for a service or product if there is a production or other constraint that will mean this level of sales cannot be achieved.

The sales budget is likely to be prepared many months in advance of the start of the budget period in order to allow time for other departments to prepare their own budgets. In many industries, the level of sales will change throughout the year, for example sales of products such as toys will be high at Christmas. Companies then have to make the choice of how to deal with these changing volumes of sales. Retail organizations are likely to work closely with their suppliers to advise them of likely requirements over the coming months, in order that the manufacturing companies can be prepared for the expected level of demand.

Production budgets

Manufacturing organizations will need to identify their strategy for dealing with expected demand. Some manufacturing companies are able to be very flexible in their manufacturing processes and respond quickly to demand. This is in line with a just-in-time philosophy. This approach, however, can be expensive, as it may be necessary to work overtime in peak periods, while when sales are low there may be spare capacity and workers may not be fully occupied. Ideally, manufacturing companies would like to aim to maintain a relatively stable level of production, though this gives the problem of inventory levels increasing during periods of low sales. An example in the UK is the car industry. Sales are much lower at the times of the year prior to changing the vehicle

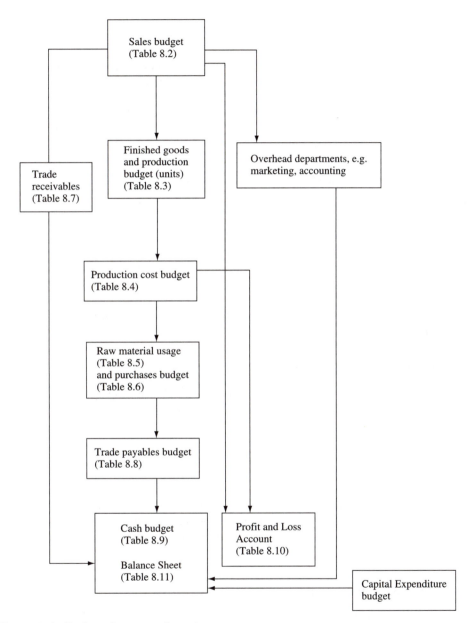

Figure 8.6 Budgets for a manufacturing company

licence registration numbers and the inventory of most car manufacturers increases prior to those times.

Based on the expected sales and inventory policy, a manufacturing plant can identify the budgeted resources in terms of material, labour and production capacity that will be required.

Capital expenditure budget

Where it is identified that additional facilities are required to meet the budget requirements for the coming year, managers will put forward proposals for new capital equipment. These bids for new resources will be appraised by the financial staff and senior management. Individually each proposal should meet the criteria for new investments (reviewed in Chapter 4) and collectively the total value of the proposals should be affordable. If the total value of the bids will result in the organization not meeting expected cash flow targets then only the most important bids can be accepted.

Trade receivables and trade payables budgets

Trade receivables (debtors) are customers who have bought on credit and not yet paid. **Trade payables** (creditors) are trade suppliers from whom the organization has bought on credit and not yet paid. In order to prepare the cash flow statement it is necessary to not only prepare a sales budget and a purchases budget, but also allow for the delay in customers paying their bills or the organization paying its suppliers. This information, along with details of amounts owing from customers and owed to suppliers, is also needed for the Balance Sheet.

Note that for non-manufacturing organizations, it will not be necessary to produce the production budgets (units and cost) or the raw materials budget.

The budgeted Profit and Loss Account

To calculate the budgeted Profit and Loss, budgets should have been prepared for sales, the cost of production of those sales (if it is a manufacturing organization) and the level of expenditure on other overheads.

The cash flow budget

For the cash flow budget, assumptions will have been made as to when cash payments will be received from trade receivables and when payments will be made to suppliers (trade and other payables). All cash expenditure in the production and overhead departments as well as the capital expenditure that is to be undertaken by the organization will need to be taken into consideration.

The budgeted Balance Sheet

This can be drawn up after the completion of the budgeted Profit and Loss Account and the cash flow statement.

A comprehensive budgeting exercise

In this section the preparation of the operational budgets will be illustrated using information from the case, Dundee Bicycle Division.

The sales budget

The budget period of Dundee Bicycle Division runs from April 20X8 to March 20X9, and initial discussions of the sales budget started in November 20X7. This would be necessary, in order to allow plenty of time for the other departments to prepare their own budgets and for the budget review to take place. A partially completed sales budget in units and revenue is shown in Table 8.2.

Table 8.2   Sales budget

	April	May	June	July
Units to be sold	1500	2000	2500	2500
Sales revenue at £110 per bicycle frame	£165,000	£220,000		

Activity 8.3

Calculate the sales revenue budget for June and July 20X8.

Production-related budgets

Finished goods/production budget in units

In a manufacturing environment the budgeted level of sales is required in order for the production department to identify required staffing levels; the production facilities required and inventory of finished goods can also be planned. The relationship between budgeted production, finished goods and sales can be expressed by the equation:

> Units to be sold + units to be in closing stock − units in opening stock
> = Units to be produced

The finished goods/production budget for Dundee Bicycles is considered in Table 8.3.

Table 8.3   Production budget (units)

Dundee Bicycles planned to sell and manufacture 24,000 bicycle frames in the year. It decided to budget for constant production at 2000 frames per month, even though sales were planned to vary on a monthly basis. Opening stock of finished goods at the beginning of April was budgeted at 1000 bicycle frames and sales in April were budgeted at 1500 units. Applying the equation for the month of April:

Units to be sold	+ units in closing stock (at end of month)	− units in opening stock	= Units to be produced
1500	+ units in closing stock at the end of April	− 1000	= 2000

Table 8.3   (*Continued*)

Rearranging the equation:

Budgeted units in closing stock at the end of April	= Units to be produced	+ units in opening stock	– units to be sold
	= 2000 units	+ 1000 units	– 1500 units
	= 1500 units		

A partly completed finished goods/production unit budget for Dundee Bicycles is shown in the table below.

Finished goods/production budget (units)

	April	May	June	July
Units to be sold (see Table 8.1)	1,500	2,000	2,500	2,500
+ units in closing stock	1,500	1,500		
= Required units	3,000	3,500		
– units in opening stock	1,000	1,500	1,500	
= Units to be produced	2,000	2,000	2,000	2,000

Note that although it may be desirable to maintain production at 2000 units per month, given sales above this level during peak periods, some increase in production might be required in order to ensure that a certain minimum level of closing stock is maintained.

Activity 8.4

Calculate the planned closing stock for the number of components that should be available in June and July, given planned sales and production.

Production cost budget

Having identified the expected level of production for each period, it is possible to calculate a budgeted cost of production. The production cost budget for Dundee Bicycles is shown in Table 8.4.

Table 8.4   **Production budget (cost)**

Standard cost per unit
The standard variable costs of making an individual bicycle frame are:

	£
Direct material	27
Direct labour	39
Variable cost per unit	66

Fixed production costs are expected to be £45,000 per month. This includes £10,000 depreciation on fixed assets.

Production cost budget
Given equal budgeted production of 2000 units a month, assuming no cost increases occur throughout the year, the monthly production cost budget for each of April, May and June will be:

	2000 units £	
Variable costs		
Materials	54,000	(2000 units × £27)
Labour	78,000	(2000 units × £39)
Total variable cost	132,000	
Total fixed cost	45,000	
Total production cost	177,000	

Raw material usage and purchases budgets

Raw material usage budget

Given the budgeted level of production and knowledge of the material usage per unit of product it is possible to budget for the total material usage by month. The raw material usage for Dundee Bicycle Division is shown in Table 8.5.

Table 8.5   Raw material usage budget

The material required for each bicycle is 3 kilograms (kgs) of material A

The raw materials usage budget for material A in April is therefore:

Units of production for April	2000
Quantity of material required per unit (kgs)	3
Material usage for production (kgs)	6000

Raw material purchases budget

If the company needs to order raw materials some time in advance of usage, then there may be a difference between the amount of material used in the month and the amount of material purchased as it will be necessary to make an allowance for opening and closing stock of raw material:

Material usage for production (kgs) + closing inventory (kgs) − opening inventory (kgs) = Purchase requirement (kgs)

To calculate the cost of the raw material purchased, it will be necessary to multiply the purchase requirement in kgs by the cost per kg.

The opening inventory at the beginning of April for Dundee Bicycle Division is 2000 kgs and this will be increased by 1000 kgs in April and by a further 1000 kgs for May. It will then be maintained at 4000 kgs of raw material.

The purchases budget is therefore as shown in Table 8.6.

Table 8.6   Purchases budget

	April	May	June	July
	(kg)	(kg)	(kg)	(kg)
Units to be used in production (kgs)	6,000	6,000	6,000	6,000
+ units in closing stock (kgs)	3,000	4,000	4,000	4,000
	9,000	10,000	10,000	10,000
− units in opening stock (kgs)	2,000	3,000	4,000	4,000
= Purchase requirement (kgs)	7,000	7,000	6,000	6,000
£ purchase cost per kg	9	9	9	9
Purchases in month £	£63,000	£63,000	£54,000	£54,000

Budget for overhead departments – marketing and accounting departments

Both the marketing and the accounting departments are treated as cost centres. In the first three months costs for the commercial department are budgeted at £6000 per month and for the accounting department at £12,000 per month.

Trade receivables budget

Once a company has identified the expected sales by period, it will need to consider the assumptions on when payments will be received from customers. The trade receivables budget for Dundee Bicycles is shown in Table 8.7.

Table 8.7   Trade receivables budget

	April	May	June	July
	(£)	(£)	(£)	(£)
Opening trade receivables	365,000	350,000	385,000 (note 1)	495,000
Sales (Table 8.2)	165,000	220,000	275,000	275,000
	530,000	570,000	660,000	770,000
Cash received from trade receivables	180,000	185,000	165,000 (note 2)	220,000
Closing trade receivables	350,000	385,000	495,000	550,000

Dundee Bicycles finds that on average customers take two months to pay their debts. Accordingly, the explanation of the budget that is provided below will be for June.
Note 1. The opening trade receivables balance at the beginning of June will be the sales for April and May.
Note 2. The cash receipts in June will be the sales for April (paying two months after sale).

Trade payables budget

An organization may take time to pay its suppliers and this delay factor should also be taken into account when preparing the trade payables budget. The trade payables budget for Dundee Bicycles is shown in Table 8.8.

Table 8.8   Trade payables

	April	May	June
	(£)	(£)	(£)
Opening trade payables (note 1)	60,000	63,000	63,000
Purchases of raw materials (Table 8.6)	63,000	63,000	54,000
Amount owed before payments	123,000	126,000	117,000
Cash payments to trade payables (note 2)	60,000	63,000	63,000
Closing trade payables	63,000	63,000	54,000

Dundee Bicycles pays its suppliers on average one month after receipt of the goods. The explanation that is provided below is for June.

Note 1. You are advised that the opening trade payables balance at the beginning of April is £60,000.

Note 2. The cash payment in the month will be the purchases for the previous month.

Capital expenditure budget

Managers of the organization will bid for expenditure on new capital equipment. These requests will be reviewed by senior management and if it is accepted that the investments are worthwhile, the proposed expenditure will be included in the budget.

In Dundee Bicycles £20,000 will be spent on new capital equipment in June.

Preparing the cash flow budget and the budgeted Profit and Loss Account and Balance Sheet

Cash flow budget

Information on cash receipts and payments can be extracted from the operational budgets, i.e. trade receivables, trade payables, production cost, overhead expenditure and capital expenditure budgets. These will be incorporated into the cash flow budget.

Table 8.9 shows the cash budget for April and May for Dundee Bicycle Division. Assumptions related to payments are included in the notes to the cash budget.

Table 8.9 Cash budget

	Budgeted cash flow	
	April	May
	£'000	£'000
Opening balance (note 1)	63,000	52,000
Add receipts		
Trade receivables (note 2)	180,000	185,000
Cash available	243,000	237,000
Less payments		
Materials (note 3)	60,000	63,000
Labour (note 4)	78,000	78,000
Fixed production costs (note 5)	35,000	35,000
Other fixed (note 6)	18,000	18,000
Capital expenditure	0	0
Total payments	191,000	194,000
Closing balance	52,000	43,000

Note 1. Opening cash balance at the beginning of April is £63,000.

Note 2. Cash is received two months after sale. Cash collected is shown in the trade receivables budget – Table 8.7.

Note 3. Purchases of raw materials are identified in the purchases budget. Cash payments are highlighted in the trade payables budget – Table 8.8.

Note 4. It is planned that labour costs will be paid in the same month as the costs are incurred. These costs can be identified in the production cost budget – Table 8.4.

Note 5. All overheads are also to be paid in the same month as the costs are incurred. Production overheads were £45,000 (see the production cost budget – Table 8.4). However, depreciation of £10,000 a month is included in this figure. Depreciation is not a cash flow and should be excluded from the cash budget, so the cash outflow is £35,000.

Note 6. You are advised that the costs of the accounting (£12,000 per month) and commercial departments (£6000 per month) are all cash items and will be paid in the same month as the costs are incurred.

Activity 8.5

Calculate the cash flow budget for June.

Budgeted Profit and Loss Account

The budgeted Profit and Loss Account for April for Dundee Bicycle Division is shown in Table 8.10.

Table 8.10   Budgeted Profit and Loss Account

	April	May	June
Sales units	1,500	2,000	2,500
	(£)	(£)	(£)
Sales value (£110 per unit)	165,000		
Less cost of sales (note 1)	132,750		
Gross Profit	32,250		
Commercial department (note 2)	6,000		
Accounting department	12,000		
Net profit	14,250		

Note 1. 1500 bicycle frames were sold in April and so, applying the matching principle, the cost of 1500 bicycle frames should be deducted in order to identify the gross profit. See Chapter 5 for a further discussion of the matching principle.

(a) As a first step it is necessary to identify the budgeted full cost per bicycle.

For Dundee Bicycles, the budgeted manufacturing overheads of the company are £45,000 per month or £540,000 for the year.

Budgeted output for the year was 24,000 bicycle frames.

$$\text{Budgeted overhead per unit} = \frac{£540,000}{24,000} = £22.50.$$

Full manufacturing cost per unit is therefore:

	£/unit
Material cost	27
Labour cost	39
Fixed overhead per unit	22.50
Full cost per unit	88.50

(b) To calculate the cost of sales it is necessary to multiply the number of units sold by the full cost per unit. For April this is $1500 \times £88.5 = £132,750$.

Note 2. The costs of the accounting and commercial departments should be written off to the Profit and Loss Account in the same month as the expenditure is incurred.

Activity 8.6

Calculate the Profit and Loss Account for May.

Budgeted Balance Sheet

The **Balance Sheet** shows the assets and liabilities of a business at a moment in time. The budgeted Balance Sheet for Dundee Bicycle Division is shown in Table 8.11.

Table 8.11 Budgeted Balance sheet

	Balance Sheet as at 31 March 20X8		Balance Sheet as at 30 April 20X8	
Non-current assets at cost		2,080,000		2,080,000
Less accumulated depreciation		1,130,000		1,140,000
Net book value (note 1)		950,000		940,000
Current assets				
Inventory of finished goods (note 2)	88,500		132,750	
Inventory of raw materials (note 3)	18,000		27,000	
Trade receivables (note 4)	365,000		350,000	
Cash (note 5)	63,000		52,000	
	534,500		561,750	
Current liabilities				
Trade payables (note 6)	60,000		63,000	
Net current assets (note 7)		474,500		498,750
Net capital employed (note 8)		1,424,500		1,438,750
Share capital and reserves (note 9)	1,350,000		1,350,000	
Retained Profit (note 10)	74,500		88,750	
		1,424,500		1,438,750

Note 1

March. The cost of the fixed assets of Dundee Bicycles at March 20X8 was £2,080,000. Depreciation on these fixed assets was £1,130,000 so the net book value of these assets was £950,000.

April. No fixed assets were purchased in April 20X8, so the original cost remains the same. Additional £10,000 depreciation was charged to the Profit and Loss Account, so the accumulated depreciation was £1,140,000, leaving a net book value at the end of April of £940,000.

Note 2. Finished goods at the end of March were 1000 bicycle frames and at the end of April were 1500 units. (See Table 8.3.) The full cost of each bicycle frame is £88.50 (see Table 8.10), so for 1000 bicycle frames the inventory value is £88,500 and for 1500 bicycle frames the inventory value is £132,750.

Note 3. Stocks of raw materials held by Dundee Bicycles at the beginning of April were £18,000 (2000 kgs @ £9 per kg, see Table 8.6).

Note 4. See trade receivables budget (Table 8.7).

Note 5. See cash budget (Table 8.9).

Note 6. See trade payables budget (Table 8.8).

Note 7. Current assets less current liabilities, i.e. for month ending March 20X8 the current assets are £534,500 and the current liabilities are £60,000. Accordingly, net current assets are £474,500.

Note 8. Net capital employed = Fixed assets plus net current assets.

Note 9. Issued share capital is £1,350,000 and retained profits to the end of March 20X8 are £74,500. Profits in the month of April are £14,250 (see Table 8.9).

Note 10. Retained profits in April were the retained profits cumulative to 31 March 20X8 plus the profits in April 20X8, i.e. £74,500 + £14,250 = £88,750.

Using a computer-based decision support system

Completing a budgeting exercise can be considerably eased if a spreadsheet or other computer-based model is developed.

With a computer-based model it is possible to:

(i) Ensure mathematical accuracy.
(ii) Undertake 'what-if' and sensitivity analysis questions to see the impact that changes in the assumptions will bring.
(iii) Have graphical and presentation facilities.
(iv) Interface with other databases and spreadsheets so that other information can be imported and exported, e.g. sales forecasts.

However, it is important to realize that many planning models used by organizations contain errors. If any of the assumptions are incorrect or not updated, as changes occur in the organization, then the models can become wildly inaccurate. As a simple example, in preparing the budget forecast of Dundee Bicycle Division, the assumption has been made that wages are variable with output. If the contracts of the employees change, so that they are employed on a full-time basis rather than being paid piece-rate, i.e. a fixed amount per unit produced, the wage costs will not change directly in relation to output. Care should be taken to examine the assumptions that have been built into the model, to ensure that they are still valid.

Summary

Key summary financial budgets are the Profit and Loss Account, the cash flow statement and the Balance Sheet.

In setting overhead department costs it is possible to use an incremental approach or more formal methods that attempt to quantify inputs and output relationships, such as activity-based costing and zero-based budgeting.

Before the summary financial statement can be drawn up a number of operational budgets should be produced including sales, production (production units, costs, raw material usage, material purchases), other overhead costs, capital expenditure, trade receivables and trade payables.

Further reading

For a discussion of the use of zero-based budgeting and other planning and control approaches in the public sector see:

Jones, R. and Pendlebury, M. (2000) *Public Sector Accounting*, 5th edn. FT/Prentice Hall.

Answers to activities

Activity 8.1

	January	February	March	April	January–April
	£'000	£'000	£'000	£'000	£'000
(1) OPENING CASH BALANCE	10	21	27.5	35	**10**
(2) ADD CASH INFLOWS					
Receipts from trade receivables	54	45	47	52	**198**
TOTAL CASH AVAILABLE (1)+(2)	64	66	74.5	87	**208**
DEDUCT CASH OUTFLOWS (PAYMENTS)					
Wages and salaries	10	10	10	10	**40**
Payments to suppliers	27	22.5	23.5	26	**99**
Overheads	6	6	6	6	**24**
Capital expenditure				15	**15**
(3) TOTAL CASH OUTFLOWS (PAYMENTS)	43	38.5	39.5	57	**178**
CLOSING CASH BALANCE (1)+(2)−(3)	21	27.5	35	30	**30**

Activity 8.2

The zero-based budgeting exercise might help the company in formally considering the outputs that can be achieved with different levels of staffing. The analysis is only as good as the assumptions on which it is based. For example, it is assumed that the development of the decision support system and improved budgetary control can only take place with the appointment of a lead management accountant. Possibly, if the work is required, then it could be undertaken by other members of the organization or through means of a short-term consultancy contract.

Activity 8.3

Calculate the sales revenue budget for June and July 20 × 8.

	April	May	June	July
Units to be sold	1500	2000	2500	2500
Sales revenue at £110 per bicycle frame	£165,000	£220,000	£275,000	£275,000

Activity 8.4

Calculate the number of components that should be produced in June and July.

	April	May	June	July
Units to be sold	1500	2000	2500	2500
+ units in closing stock	1500	1500	1000	500
= Total units required	3000	3500	3500	3000
− units in opening stock	1000	1500	1500	1000
= Units to be produced	2000	2000	2000	2000

Activity 8.5

Calculate the cash flow budget for June.

	Budgeted cash flow		
	April	May	June
	£'000	£'000	£'000
Opening balance	63,000	52,000	43,000
Add receipts from debtors	180,000	185,000	165,000
Cash available	243,000	237,000	208,000
Less payments			
Labour	78,000	78,000	78,000
Materials	60,000	63,000	63,000
Fixed production costs	35,000	35,000	35,000
Other fixed	18,000	18,000	18,000
Total payments	191,000	194,000	194,000
Closing balance	52,000	43,000	14,000

Activity 8.6

Calculate the Profit and Loss Account for May.

Sales units	2,000
	(£)
Sales value (£110 per unit)	220,000
Less cost of sales	177,000
Gross Profit	43,000
Commercial department	6,000
Accounting department	12,000
Net profit	25,000

Discussion questions

The accountant at Dundee Bicycle Division decided that she would need to approach Jack Jones and request that he reconsider the budget preparation process that he was proposing to follow. She feels that there are a number of issues that need to be considered. She has identified these issues below and since she knows that you are studying accounting at the moment has asked you to comment. As well as information from this chapter, you should refer to the case Dundee Bicycle Division (section 1).

1. What do you think are the main purposes of budgeting at Dundee Bicycle Division, from the perspective of Jack Jones?
2. Textbooks identify a range of potential benefits of budgeting. What are these? From the description of events and the proposed approach to budgeting at Dundee Bicycle Division (section 1), do you feel these benefits will be achieved at the division? If not, why not?
3. A clear timetable and set of procedures are required for the budget-setting process at the division. Can you advise on these details?
4. Do you consider it is necessary for the division to use zero-based budgeting every year for allocating resources in the commercial and accounting departments?

Exercises

(Questions with numbers in bold have answers at the back of the book.)

Q8.1 Milton Ltd, a subsidiary of Richmond, is preparing a cash flow forecast for the next few months. The opening cash balance on 1 May was expected to be £20,000. The sales budgeted were as follows:

	£
March	145,000
April	155,000
May	195,000
June	120,000

Analysis of the records shows that 55% of debtors settle in the month that the sales take place and the remainder settle in the next month, though bad debts of 1% are anticipated.

Extracts from the purchases budget were as follows:

	£
March	80,000
April	100,000
May	85,000
June	90,000

All purchases are on credit and the firm takes one month to settle its debts.

Wages are £30,000 per month and overheads are £30,000 per month (including £10,000 depreciation) and are settled in the same month.

In June, payment of £100,000 will be made for a new machine.

Required:

(a) Prepare a cash budget for May and June.
(b) Comment on any action that the company should consider taking if a likely overdraft situation is identified.

Q8.2 Money PLC is preparing a cash flow forecast for the next few months. The opening cash balance on 1 July was expected to be £2000. The following information is provided:

Sales

	May	June	July	August	September	October
Units sold	200	150	120	260	270	280

All goods are sold at £20 per unit on credit and trade receivables take on average two months' credit.

Production

	May	June	July	August	September	October
Units produced	230	220	200	220	220	220

(i) Direct labour is £8 per unit payable in the same month as production.
(ii) Raw materials are £7 per unit. Trade payables are paid one month after receipt of goods. The company operates a just-in-time system so materials are received immediately prior to production.

Fixed costs
Fixed costs are £1000 per month. This includes £200 depreciation.

Capital expenditure
In September there will be capital expenditure of £10,000 with payment expected in the following month.

Required:

Comment on action that management can take to eliminate any cash overdraft situation.

Q8.3 Venus Ltd is a company manufacturing a single product, which sells for £100 per unit. Budgeted sales (in units) are as follows: 4000 for May, 5200 for June and 7200 for July, 7500 for August and 8000 for September.

Venus Ltd has decided that they should maintain a closing stock of finished goods equal to 50% of the next month's budgeted sales.
　　Each unit of output requires:

　2 kgs of material at a cost of £12 per kl.
　3 hrs of labour at a cost of £14.00 per hr.

Fixed overheads per month (including £8000 depreciation) are £40,000. Assume that these are all administrative overheads.
　　Cash payments by Venus Ltd are made during the month in which they are incurred. Venus Ltd has found that 60% of the cash from sales is received during the month of sale, and 40% of the cash from sales is received during the following month.
　　The cash balance at the end of business on 31 May was £30,000.

Required:

(i) Complete the production budget (units).

	May	June	July	August
Units to be sold	4000	5200	7200	
+ units in closing stock (note 1)	2600			
= Required units	6600			
− units in opening stock (note 1)	2000			
= Units to be produced	4600			

Note 1. Stock is 50% of the next month's sales.

  (ii) Production cost budget for June (note 2).
  (iii) Budgeted Profit and Loss Account for June.
  (iv) Budgeted cash flow statement for June (note 3).

Note 2. To simplify the problem, it has been assumed that there are no fixed production overheads. All overheads can therefore be treated as period costs.

Note 3. In the comprehensive example in the chapter, trade receivable and trade payable budgets were prepared. Cash receipts from trade receivables and payments to trade payables can be calculated without completing these budgets for this exercise.

Q8.4 Able components division plans to sell the following number of units:

	Units
June	1,400
July	1,300
August	1,300
September	1,200
October	1,200

Stocks of finished goods at 1 June are expected to be 140 units. From then on the company's stockholding policy is for the finished goods stock at the end of each month to represent 10% of the following month's sales requirement.

The production costs per unit are:

Direct material (20 kgs at £2.50 per kg)	£50.00
Direct labour (2 hrs at £6.00 per hr)	£12.00

The standard selling price of the product is £100.

Fixed administrative costs were expected to be £18,000 per month. This includes £1000 for depreciation.

Labour and fixed overheads are paid in the same month as the expenditure was incurred. Debtors take two months to pay and the company pays its creditors after one month. The opening cash balance is £10,000 as at August.

Required:

Produce for the month of August:

  (i) Production budget (units).
  (ii) Production cost budget.
  (iii) Budgeted Profit and Loss Account.
  (iv) Budgeted cash flow statement.

Q8.5 XY Ltd plans to sell the following:

	Product A (units)
June	1200
July	1800
August	2800
September	3200
October	3200

Stock of finished goods at 1 June was 240 units and the company's stockholding policy is for the finished goods stock at the end of each month to represent 20% of the following month's sales requirement.

Each unit of product A uses two units of a component X1. On 1 June there were expected to be 264 units of X1 in stock. The desired closing stock of X1 is 10% of the next month's production.

Each unit of component X1 costs £5.

Each unit of product A requires £6 of labour.

Fixed administration overheads in each month are budgeted to be £5000 (and include a charge of £1000 depreciation). Product A can be sold for £26 each.

Labour and fixed overheads are paid in the same month. Debtors take two months to pay and the company pays its creditors after one month. The opening cash balance is £10,000.

Required:

  (i) The production budget (in units) for June, July and August.
 (ii) The production cost budget for June, July and August.
(iii) The raw material purchases budget (in units and £'s) for June, July and August.
 (iv) The budgeted Profit and Loss Account for August.
  (v) The budgeted cash flow for August.

Q8.6 Prepare the budgeted Profit and Loss Account for Dundee Bicycle Division for June. The relevant information is provided in the chapter.

Q8.7 Prepare the budgeted Balance Sheet for Dundee Bicycle Division for:

 (i) May.
(ii) June.

STANDARD COSTING AND MANUFACTURING METHODS

Introduction

An accounting system that has been commonly used in organizations employing both mass and batch production methods is called standard costing. The main part of the chapter examines this system and considers:

(i) The potential benefits of standard costing.
(ii) The 'technical aspects' of operating a standard costing system. This includes the preparation of a standard cost card, how to analyse labour and material variances, reconciling original budget to actual profit, and interpreting and reporting variance information. A final section considers key differences between standard marginal and standard absorption systems.

In recent years, standard costing systems have been widely criticized as being irrelevant for the modern competitive environment. These criticisms are reviewed in the next section of the chapter.

In the final part of the chapter, the main production strategies employed in manufacturing organizations are considered. Traditionally, these were mass and batch production, though in recent years alternative production strategies such as just-in-time have been increasingly introduced. The relevance of standard costing to such systems is reviewed.

Standard costing

Standard costing is a system in which it is assumed that each unit of a product will require the exact same inputs of labour, materials and other resources at all stages of a standard production process. It is predominantly used in manufacturing organizations involving repetitive operations.

Establishing the standard cost of a product

The example of Dundee Bicycle Division manufactures will be continued in this chapter. The division manufactures a single type of bicycle frame and a cost to make each frame has been calculated and is detailed in the standard cost card seen in Table 9.1. The standard cost card shows for a single bicycle frame:

- The expected material usage, cost per kilogram of material and therefore expected cost for each material.
- The labour hours worked by each grade of labour, the expected wage rate per hour and therefore the expected labour cost.

In this example, no variable overheads are anticipated and the company operates a standard marginal costing system, so there is no calculated fixed cost per unit.

Table 9.1 Standard cost card for bicycle frame

	£	£
DIRECT MATERIAL		
Material X – 3 kgs @ £8 per kg	24	
Material Y – 0.5kg @ £6 per kg	3	
Total material cost		27
DIRECT LABOUR		
Machining – 1 hour at £10.00 per hour	10	
Welding – 2 hours at £14.50 per hour	29	
STANDARD DIRECT COST		39
		66

The standard materials price is likely to be determined by the purchasing staff, who will take into account the likely impact of inflation, bulk buying discounts and volumes of material ordered. The quantity of material to be used will be determined by the production department, taking into account existing standards and improvements that can be achieved over the coming period.

The time taken to manufacture each part will usually be determined by the production department. The wage rate per hour may be determined in conjunction with the personnel department, again taking into consideration likely wage rate changes expected for the coming period.

Attainable and ideal standards

In setting a standard, many companies use **attainable standards**. These assume efficient operation, but include allowances for normal loss, waste and machine downtime. Many organizations build in target improvements that they would expect as a result of continuous improvement.

An alternative is to set **ideal standards**, which make no allowances for inefficient operation and assume most favourable conditions. The danger of setting ideal standards is that the workforce might be unable to achieve such standards and could become demotivated.

Purposes of standard costing and variance analysis

A number of potential benefits can arise from the introduction of a standard cost system. These can include:

1. *Stock valuation.* It is an easy method to use in order to arrive at a valuation of the stock holdings of the business.
2. *Planning.* It can be used to help in determining future costs, budgets and selling prices.
3. *Motivation.* A standard can be used as a target, which workers can strive to achieve.
4. *Control.* By identifying and investigating variances from standard, it is possible to highlight areas of activity that may be out of control.
5. *Performance evaluation.* It is one measure of the performance of members of staff. Any variances from standard, either positive or negative, can be measured and used to define additional rewards or penalties for the operators or departments responsible.

Variance analysis

The chart in Figure 9.1 identifies the key variances that can be calculated using standard costing and marginal costing principles.

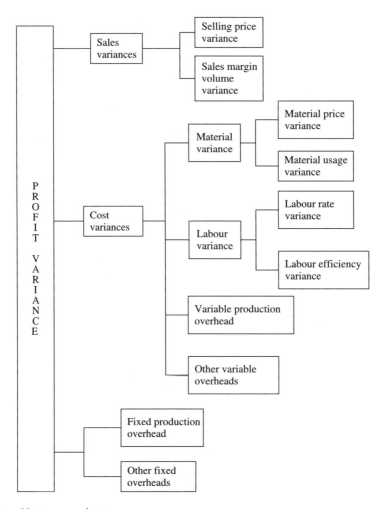

Figure 9.1 Variance analysis

The main standard costing variances will be illustrated using the example of the accounts of Dundee Bicycle Division for the period April–June 20X8.

In Chapter 7, the budgeted Profit and Loss Account for 6000 bicycle units and the actual Profit and Loss Account for 5200 units was shown for the period April–June 20X8. Further information on the budget and actual revenue and costs is shown in Table 9.2.

In Chapter 7 it was argued that a more meaningful control report would show the difference between actual revenue and expenditure and a flexible budget for the *actual* number of units. A more detailed analysis of the comparison vs. flexible budget produced in Chapter 7 (Table 7.5) is reproduced in Table 9.3.

Table 9.2   Budget and actual Profit and Loss Account for Dundee Bicycle Division for the period April–June 20X8

Sales units		Budget 6,000 (£)		Actual 5,200 (£)
Sales	6000 units at £110 per unit	660,000	5200 units sold at £115 per unit	598,000
Less costs				
Material				
— material X, 6000 units × 3 kgs/unit × £8 per kg		144,000	16,520 kgs used at £7.5 per kg	123,900
— material Y, 6000 units × 0.5 kgs/unit × £6 per kg		18,000	3393 kgs used at £5.7 per kg	19,340
Labour				
— machine shop 6000 units × 1 hour/unit × £10/hour		60,000	5512 hours at £10.5 per hour	57,876
— welding 6000 units × 2 hours/unit × £14.5/hour		174,000	9915 hours at £15.5 per hour	153,682
Fixed production overhead		135,000		132,000
Production cost		531,000		486,798
Gross profit		129,000		111,202
Accounting		36,000		35,000
Commercial		18,000		43,000
Net profit		75,000		33,202

Table 9.3   Variance report for the period April–June 2008

Sales units		Variance report for the period April–June 2008				
		Original 6,000 (£)	Flexed 5200 (£)	Actual 5200 (£)	Variance (£)	
Sales	110	660,000	572,000	598,000	26,000	F
Material X	24	144,000	124,800	123,900	900	F
Material Y	3	18,000	15,600	19,340	(3,740)	A
Labour: machining	10	60,000	52,000	57,876	(5,876)	A
Labour: welding	29	174,000	150,800	153,682	(2,882)	A
Variable cost		396,000	343,200	354,798	(11,598)	A
Contribution		264,000	228,800	243,202	14,402	F
Production		135,000	135,000	132,000	3,000	F
Accounting		36,000	36,000	35,000	1,000	F
Commercial		18,000	18,000	43,000	(25,000)	A
Net profit		75,000	39,800	33,202	(6,598)	A

Sales variances

For Dundee Bicycle Division, the standard contribution per bicycle frame was £44 (£110 – £66) and budgeted sales were 6000 units. The budgeted contribution was therefore £264,000 (6000 units × £44).

The actual contribution may be different from budget because of two reasons related to sales:

1. A selling price variance if the goods and services are sold at a different price from the standard.
2. The sales margin volume variance due to the actual volume of sales being different from budget.

Note that where there is more than one product sold, there may also be a variance due to the sales mix being different from budget.

Sales price variance

The **selling price variance** is the difference between the actual selling price per unit (AP) and the standard selling price per unit (SP) times the sales volume in units:

$$(AP - SP) \times SV$$

At Dundee Bicycle Division the actual selling price per bicycle frame was £115 and the standard selling price was £110. The actual sales volume was 5200 units. Accordingly, the selling price variance = (£115 – £110) × 5200 = £26,000 favourable.

Sales margin volume variance

The **sales margin volume variance** is the difference between the budgeted sales volume (BV) and the actual sales volume (AV) multiplied by the standard contribution per unit (SC):

$$(BV - AV) \times SC$$

At Dundee Bicycles the budgeted volume was 6000 units, the actual volume was 5200 units and the standard contribution per unit was £44. The sales margin volume variance therefore is (6000 – 5200) × £44 = (£35,200) adverse. (Since actual sales were lower than budget sales the variance is adverse.)

A review of the two variances shows that although a favourable variance of £26,000 was achieved through a higher sales price, this was more than offset by a lower volume of sales that resulted in an adverse sales margin volume variance of (£35,200).

Labour and material variances

In Chapter 7, Table 7.5, the comparison vs. flexible budget identified the labour and material variances in total, with material showing an adverse variance of £2840 and labour an adverse variance of £8758. Table 9.3 analysed these variances by component, i.e. by type of material and grade of labour. These variances will now be examined in further detail.

Material variances

The total material variance of £2840 was due to an adverse variance on material Y of £3740, partly offset by a favourable variance of £900 for material X (see Table 9.3).

In this section the material Y variance will be analysed.

(i) The standard cost per unit of material Y is £3 and so the standard cost of 5200 bicycle frames (the flexible budget) is £15,600.
(ii) 3393 kgs of material Y were actually used in production at a cost per kg of £5.70, giving an actual cost of £19,340.
(iii) The total material Y variance was £15,600 − £19,340 = £3740 adverse.

It would be helpful to know how much of this variance was due to a different number of kilograms of material being used than the standard for 5200 bicycle frames and how much is due to the price per kilogram being different. This can be identified by subdividing the variance into a material usage variance and a material price variance.

Material usage variance

A **material usage variance** is equal to the difference between the standard quantity of material (SQ) that should have been required for the actual production compared with the actual quantity (AQ) of material used multiplied by the standard price (SP) per kilogram:

$$(SQ - AQ) \times SP$$

The material usage variance for material Y is shown in Table 9.4.

Table 9.4 Material Y usage variance

Standard quantity (SQ) 5200 bicycle frames @ 0.5 kgs per frame	Actual quantity (AQ) of material for 5200 frames	Variance in kgs of material SQ − AQ	Standard price per kg (SP)	Variance in cost (SQ–AQ)×(SP)
2600 kgs	3393 kgs	793 kgs (A)*	£6	£4758 (A)

* Note that (A) is shown for an adverse variance and (F) is shown for a favourable variable.

A comparison of usage according to the standard with the actual amount of material used shows that 793 more kilograms of material were used than the standard expected for 5200 units. Given a standard price per kilogram of £6, the adverse usage variance = £4758 (adverse). Note that since the actual quantity of material used was more than the standard usage expected, then the variance is adverse.

Activity 9.1

Calculate the material usage variance for material X.

Material price variance

The **material price variance** is equal to the difference between the standard price (SP) per kilogram of material and the actual price (AP) per kilogram multiplied by the actual quantity (AQ) of material used:

$$(SP - AP) \times QP$$

The material price variance for material Y is shown in Table 9.5.

Table 9.5   Material price variance for material Y

Standard price (SP) per kilogram of material	Actual price (AP) per kilogram of material	Variance in cost per kg SP – AP	Actual quantity (AQ) of material used for 5200 bicycle frames	Variance due to difference between standard and actual price per kilogram (SP–AP)×AQ
£6 per kg	£5.7 per kg	£0.3 (F)	3393 kgs	£1018 (F)

The actual price paid per kilogram was less than the standard price per kilogram that was originally set, so the variance is favourable. The actual variance has been calculated by multiplying the difference between the standard and actual price of each kilogram by the number of kilograms that have been used.

Note that some companies calculate the material price variance at the time the materials are purchased, i.e. the difference between the actual and standard price per kilogram multiplied by the number of kilograms purchased.

Activity 9.2

Calculate the material price variance for material X (based on actual kilograms of material X used).

Reconciliation of the material usage and price variances for material Y to the total material variance for material Y and interpretation of these variances

The total material variance (flexible budget compared with actual) for material Y was £3740 (adverse).

The calculations of the price and usage variances for material Y shown above are:

Material usage	£4758 (adverse)
Material price	£1018 (favourable)
Total variance	£3740 (adverse)

This reconciliation shows the overall variance for material Y of £3740 (adverse). This was due to 793 kgs more material used than the standard (£4758 adverse). This excess usage variance was only partly offset by a favourable price variance of £1018 due to the standard price per kilogram being £0.30 less than standard.

Activity 9.3

Reconcile the material usage and price variances for material X to the total variance.

Labour variances

In Table 9.3, the total labour variance of £8758 was further analysed by grade of labour. £5876 was due to an adverse variance on the machine shop labour and £2882 adverse for the welding labour.

The labour for the machine shop will now be examined in more detail.

(i) The standard cost per hour for machinists is £10 and so the standard cost for 5200 bicycle frames (the flexible budget) is £52,000.

(ii) 5512 hours were worked at £10.50 per hour, giving an actual cost of £57,876.

(iii) The total labour variance for the machine shop was £52,000 − £57,876 = £5876 (adverse).

It would be helpful to know how much of this variance was due to a different number of hours being worked than the standard for 5200 bicycle frames and how much is due to the rate per hour being different. This can be identified by subdividing the variance into a labour efficiency variance and a labour rate variance.

Labour efficiency variance

The **labour efficiency variance** is the difference in the standard number of hours that would have been expected (SH) for the actual production and the actual hours worked for each grade of labour (AH) multiplied by the standard rate (SR) per hour:

$$(SH - AH) \times SR$$

The labour efficiency variance for the machine shop is calculated in Table 9.6.

Table 9.6   Machine shop labour efficiency variance

Standard hours (SH) of labour for 5200 bicycle frames (1 hour per frame)	Actual hours (AH) of labour used in the manufacture of 5200 bicycle frames	variance in hours (SH – AH)	Standard rate per hour of labour (SR)	Variance in cost due to hours worked being different from standard (SH–AH)× SR
5200	5512	312 (A)	£10 per hour	£3120 (A)

Note that since the actual hours worked was more than the standard hours expected, the variance is adverse.

Activity 9.4

Calculate the labour efficiency variance for welding.

Labour rate variance

The **labour rate variance** is calculated by identifying the difference between the standard rate per hour (SR) and the actual rate (AR) per hour of labour multiplied by the actual hours worked (AH):

$$(SR - AR) \times AH$$

See Table 9.7 for a calculation of the labour rate variance of the machine shop.

Table 9.7   Machine shop labour rate variance

Standard rate per hour of the machine shop grade of labour to manufacture one component SR	Actual rate per hour of the machine shop grade of labour (AR)	Variance in rate per hour (SR – AR)	Actual hours worked in the machine shop to produce 5200 bicycle frames (AH)	Variance due to difference between standard and actual rate per hour = (SR–AR) × AH
£10 per hour	£10.5 per hour	£0.5 adverse per hour	5512 hours	£2756 (A)

Note that since the actual cost per hour was more than the standard cost per hour that was originally set, then the variance is adverse.

Activity 9.5

Calculate the labour rate variance for welding labour.

Reconciliation of the labour rate and labour efficiency for the machine shop labour to the total labour variance for the machine shop

The total labour variance (flexible budget compared with actual) for machining labour was £5876 (adverse).

The calculations of the price and usage variances for machining labour shown above are:

Labour efficiency	£3120 (adverse)
Labour rate	£2756 (adverse)
Total variance	£5876 (adverse)

This reconciliation shows that the overall variance for machining labour of £5876 was due to both an adverse labour efficiency variance and an adverse labour rate variance. The labour rate variance is due to the rate per hour paid to the machining labour being £0.50 greater than the standard that was set. The labour efficiency variance was adverse due to 312 hours more than the expected 5200 hours that should have been worked in the machine room if the standard had been achieved. This is approximately 6% above expected and may not be considered excessive, though management may well wish to keep this under observation in case this is a continuing trend.

Activity 9.6

Reconcile the labour efficiency and the labour rate variances for welding labour.

Fixed overhead variances using a standard marginal costing system

Under a standard marginal costing system, the fixed overhead variances will be the difference between the fixed overhead that was budgeted and the actual fixed overhead expenditure.

In Dundee Bicycles, for example, budgeted fixed production overheads were £132,000 while the actual fixed overheads were £135,000. The variance is therefore an adverse expenditure variance of £3000.

Reconciling budgeted profit to the actual profit and reporting on the variances

In Chapter 7 a reconciliation from original budgeted profit to actual profit for Dundee Bicycle Division for the period April to June 20X8 was provided. This can now be expanded to show the additional labour and material variances. See Table 9.8.

Table 9.8   Reconciliation of budgeted to actual profit

		F		A		
Original budgeted profit						75,000
Sales margin volume variance						(35,200) (A)
Budgeted profit at actual sales volume						39,800
Operational variances:		F		A		
Sales price		26,000				
Material – usage variance	(note 1)			(12,118)		
– price variance	(note 2)	9,278				
Labour – efficiency variance	(note 3)	3,913				
– rate variance	(note 4)			(12,671)		
Fixed cost		3,000				
Accounting		1,000				
Commercial				(25,000)		
						(6,598) (A)
Actual profit						33,202

Note 1. The material usage variance is £12,118 adverse due to £7360 adverse for material X, plus £4758 adverse for material Y.

Note 2. The material price variance is favourable due to £8260 favourable for material X, plus £1018 favourable for material Y.

Note 3. The labour efficiency variance is £3913 favourable, due to £7033 favourable for the welding department, though this has been partly offset by £3120 adverse for the machining department.

Note 4. The labour rate variance is £12,671 adverse due to £2756 adverse for machinists, plus £9915 adverse for welders.

Activity 9.7

What issues do you think would need to be investigated following the provision of this information?

A review of the statement shown in Table 9.8 highlights a number of variances where further investigation would be of interest. For example:

- *Sales.* A higher than budgeted sales price has been achieved of £26,000. However, this has been offset by a high adverse sales volume variance of £35,200.
- *Materials.* Material costs per kilogram were less than expected for both material X and material Y, leading to a favourable variance; however, has this had an adverse impact upon material usage?
- *Labour.* What has caused the adverse labour efficiency variance in the machining department?
- An adverse variance of £25,000 on the commercial department has already been discussed in Chapter 7 and is caused by the allocation from head office for advertising costs.

Writing a report on the variance statement for the period April to June 20X8

As well as providing an analysis of variances for the period, a written report is often provided. The accountant or other reporting officer would be expected to search for reasons for the variances. A summary of key findings is provided in Figure 9.2.

---

1. In February 20X8, the commercial manager decided that given favourable trading conditions, it would be a good time to raise the average price of each bicycle frame by an average of £5 per unit. The sales team have since expressed the belief that if the price rise had not occurred then sales would have been in line with budget.
2. During the three months April to June 20X8, a number of problems occurred in the manufacturing process. The purchasing officer had agreed to purchase raw materials from a new supplier, at a lower price than standard. The production department has complained about the quality of these new raw materials and claim that because of an inferior quality, material wastage is much higher than expected and additional time has been required in the machine department. The production supervisor considers that with the old supplies, material costs would have been less than standard.
3. Following negotiations, a pay increase for production staff took place in March rather than in July, which had been expected in the original plan.
4. McLoed Ltd (the holding company of the division) has charged a share of central advertising costs to Dundee Bicycle Division because it feels that the division benefits from central advertising. Expenditure is principally above budget because the advertising campaign has occurred earlier than expected.

Figure 9.2 Findings on investigation of variances

An example of a report for Dundee Bicycles is shown in Figure 9.3.

Report on variance report of Dundee Bicycle Division for the period April to June 20X8

Actual profit for the period April to June 20X8 at £33,202 was nearly £42,000 less than the original budgeted profit of £75,000.

Although the average £5 per unit increase in prices above standard sales price produced a favourable sales price variance of £26,000, this was more than offset by an adverse sales volume variance of £35,200. This adverse sales margin volume variance is due to 5200 units sold in the period compared with a budgeted 6000 units. Discussions with the sales team support the view that the original budget would have been achieved if the sales price had been maintained at the original standard price. A review into pricing policy is to be undertaken by the commercial manager.

An adverse total material variance of £2840 is caused by an adverse material usage variance of £12,118 being only partly offset by a favourable price variance of £9278. Discussions with the production department indicate that the reason for the adverse material usage variance is due to higher wastage following the use of inferior quality raw material. It is considered by the

---

Figure 9.3 Variance report

production supervisor that costs would have been less than standard if the materials had been sourced from the previous supplier. An investigation of the costs and benefits of sourcing from the new supplier is to be undertaken.

The adverse variance of £8758 for labour is mainly due to an adverse labour rate variance of £12,671 following an earlier than expected pay rise. Overall there was a favourable efficiency variance of £3913, with a favourable variance of £7033 in the welding department only partly offset by an adverse labour efficiency variance in the machine department of £3120. It is reported that the latter was caused by additional work due to inferior quality material.

The adverse variance on the commercial department accounts of £25,000 is primarily due to the charge for advertising by head office.

Figure 9.3 (*Continued*)

The above discussion highlights that:

1. The accounting variance statement shown in Table 9.8 does not provide the reasons for variances, all it does is highlight the areas where further investigation is required – the principle of *management by exception*.
2. It can also be difficult to use standard costing variances as a means of evaluating the performance of managers as:

    (i) There may be an interrelationship between variances. Individual variances may be influenced by decisions made by other managers; for example, the purchase of cheap raw materials may result in a favourable material price variance, but may lead to greater material usage.
    (ii) The information on which the standards are based may be out of date. For example, if the economy has deteriorated since plans were prepared, the budgeted sales volume may now be over-optimistic.

Standard absorption costing

For those requiring a deeper technical knowledge of standard costing, it will also be necessary to understand standard absorption costing. If this is not required, move on to the next section.

With a standard absorption costing system, there are two main fixed overhead variances that are identified: the fixed overhead expenditure variance and the fixed overhead volume variance.

Fixed overhead variances

1. *Expenditure variance.* As with a standard marginal costing system, the **fixed overhead expenditure variance** is the difference between the budgeted fixed cost and the actual fixed cost. The variance for Dundee Bicycles was £3000.
2. *Fixed overhead volume variance.* Accounting standards identify that fixed production overheads should be treated as a product cost. With a standard absorption costing system there will be a variance if there is a difference between the actual and the budgeted level of production. For example, if Dundee Bicycles operated a standard absorption costing system:

(i) From Table 9.2, it can be noted that the budgeted fixed production overhead for the three months April to June 20X8 was £135,000.
(ii) The original budgeted production was 6000 units so that the standard fixed overhead to be absorbed (assigned) to each unit was £135,000/6000 = £22.50. For the actual three months April to June, 5200 units were produced, so that the actual fixed overhead absorbed into products was 5200 × £22.50, i.e. £117,000.
(iii) The **fixed overhead volume variance** (also called the production volume variance) is the difference between the budgeted production (BP) and the actual production (AP) multiplied by the standard fixed overhead rate (SR):

$$(BP - AP) \times SR$$

For Dundee Bicycles the fixed overhead volume variance = (6000 − 5200) × £22.5 = (£18,000) adverse. The variance is adverse because actual production (AP) is less than budgeted production (BP).

This under-absorbed overhead will need to be written off to the Profit and Loss Account and is called an adverse fixed overhead volume variance. An effect of a fixed overhead volume variance can be to encourage some factory managers to increase production to avoid under-absorbed overhead being charged against profits. This may not be in the interests of the organization as it will mean that additional funds are tied up in inventory.

Activity 9.8

Budgeted fixed overhead cost was £49,000.
Budgeted production was 7000 units.
Actual fixed overhead cost was £50,000.
Actual volume was 6300 units.

(a) What was the fixed overhead expenditure variance?
(b) What was the fixed overhead volume variance?

Sales margin volume variance under an absorption costing system

It should be noted that the introduction of a system based on absorption costing will mean that the sales volume variance is now based on the standard profit per unit rather than the standard marginal cost.

For Dundee Bicycle Division the contribution per unit was £44.00 and the fixed cost per unit was £22.50. Therefore the profit per unit was £21.50.

The **sales margin volume variance** under an absorption costing system is the difference between the budged sales volume (BV) and the actual sales volume (AV) multiplied by the standard profit per unit (SP):

$$(BV - AV) \times SP$$

$$(6000 - 5200) \times £21.50 = £17,200 \text{ (adverse)}$$

The revised reconciliation of budgeted to actual profit is as shown in Table 9.9.

Table 9.9 Reconciliation of original budgeted profit to actual profit under an absorption costing system

	F	A		
Original budgeted profit			75,000	
Sales margin volume variance			(17,200)	(A)
Budgeted profit at actual sales volume			57,800	
Operational variances:	F	A		
Sales price	26,000			
Material – price variance	9,278			
– usage variance		(12,118)		
Labour – rate variance		(12,671)		
– efficiency variance	3,913			
Fixed overhead expenditure	3,000			
Fixed overhead volume variance		(18,000)		
Accounting	1,000			
Commercial		(25,000)		
			(24,598)	(A)
Actual profit			33,202	

Where sales and production are the same, the only difference from the reconciliation shown in Table 9.8 for the marginal costing system is that the sales margin volume variance is now separated into a sales margin variance (based on a profit per unit) and a fixed overhead volume variance.

Relevance of standard cost systems in the new competitive environment

In recent years standard costing has been criticized on the grounds that while it is adequate for stock valuation purposes, it is not always relevant for other purposes. In particular, standard costing systems may in some circumstances:

1. Provide an incomplete set of performance measures.
2. It may not be possible to set an accurate standard or appropriate performance target.
3. Managers may be encouraged to make decisions that are contrary to the objectives of the organization.

Standard costing systems provide an incomplete set of performance measures.

(i) Measures should be relevant to issues that are of value to customers. If speed of delivery or quality is more important to the customer than cost, then a standard costing system will provide only part of the information needs of the company.

(ii) Standards incorporate an allowance for scrap and poor quality work. This may mean that inefficiencies in the production process become accepted rather than being separately identified and eliminated.

(iii) Manufacturing cost is only part of the cost of the finished product. Expenditure in other parts of the value chain may be significant.

(iv) Many standard costing systems may only provide summary information at the end of the month. This is inadequate for operational managers wishing to identify specific causes of variances.

It may not be possible to set an accurate standard or appropriate performance target.

(i) Standard costs may be established annually or biannually and therefore are not sufficiently up-to-date and do not set a sufficient target for an organization wishing to achieve continuous improvement.

(ii) Most standard costing systems charge overheads to products on the basis of a standard rate per labour or machine hour rate. If a significant proportion of costs vary in relation to other activity drivers, activity-based costing may provide a more accurate indication of costs.

(iii) If costs are used as a basis for setting prices then standards based on the traditional costing method will potentially lead to prices that bear little reflection to a 'true' cost of the product.

Standard costing variances can provide the wrong message and incentive to managers.

(i) Goldratt and Cox (1984) and Goldratt and Fox (1986), in discussing the theory of constraints, argue that the traditional cost accounting and variance reporting systems are responsible for many of the problems that factories experience.

Labour efficiency variances may be of relevance in areas where there are bottlenecks, as any inefficiency in such areas will result in a reduction in factory throughput. In non-constraint areas, a focus on efficiency variances may in fact encourage inappropriate action. If a report shows an adverse labour variance against a specific cost centre and idle time occurring, there may well be an incentive to encourage production to eliminate such a variance. If the non-constraint areas do produce output faster, the inevitable result is that cash will be tied up as there will be unnecessarily high levels of inventory. As discussed earlier, the reporting of a fixed overhead production volume variance may also encourage factory management to increase production in all areas of the factory, when this is not desired. While a buffer of inventory may be required for the constraint resources to ensure that they are operating to capacity, stocks do not need to be held in non-constraint areas, as any increase in demand can easily be handled.

Activity 9.9

Hamble Ltd produces a number of products using several machines. It operates a standard absorption costing system. Machine 1 manufactures a component (component A) that is used in one of the products of the company. In the current week, machine 1 is only expected to be in operation for 20 hours given the preliminary production schedule. This means that the machine is not in use for the remaining 20 hours that are available. The works manager has decided to use the free time by producing extra units of component A.

Discuss the advantages and disadvantages of this decision.

Johnson and Kaplan (1987) have argued that new manufacturing techniques also make variances, such as labour efficiency, less useful. When companies mass-produced large volumes of standard units, using labour-intensive processes, it was possible to identify poorly performing employees and departments by comparing their actual output against a standard. However, as companies increasingly automate production, the need for direct labour input diminishes. Attention may be given to labour variances that are of minor importance when compared with other areas that need to be controlled.

(ii) Standard cost variances can be caused by decisions taken elsewhere in the company. For example, an adverse material usage variance and an adverse labour efficiency variance might occur due to the purchase of inferior quality materials causing production problems. The production manager might have responsibility for the material usage and labour efficiency variances and be judged as achieving poor performance due to the adverse variances. In reality, the performance might have been good, given the quality of the raw materials. Similarly, the purchase of poor quality raw materials might result in an adverse impact on the level of sales and the price at which goods can be sold and again this poor performance might not reflect the efforts of the sales manager.

With inappropriate management styles and pressures, the potential problems identified above are likely to be increased. For example, pressure to achieve budget on the purchasing manager may increase the likelihood that she or he will purchase cheaper and poorer quality materials, which may be at the expense of the overall profitability of the organization.

The issues raised in this section will be considered further in later chapters of this book, when alternative approaches that may help overcome the limitations of traditional accounting controls will be considered.

It should be noted that despite the potential limitations, standard costing systems remain in widespread use in manufacturing organizations. For example, Drury *et al.* (1993) found that 76% of organizations responding to his survey operated a standard cost system and 72% of those respondents considered that such a system was either 'above average' or of 'vital' importance to their ongoing success. Reasons can vary by organization, though may include the continued use for stock valuation, one basis of pricing and production control requirements. Some cost variance information may also be relevant, particularly for mass production organizations following a competitive strategy of low cost.

Alternative production strategies

This section of the chapter reviews alternative production strategies. The implication of such strategies on accounting information systems is also considered.

Traditional production strategies

Historically, a company's choice of production strategy revolved around mass production of a single product, or batch production of a specific selection of type and layout of machinery.

Mass production

Mass production utilizes a series of single-purpose machine tools organized into a linear sequence that mirrors the order in which operations have to be performed in the progressive conversion of raw materials into finished products. Mass production is particularly appropriate for large-volume production of a relatively few number of products.

Figure 9.4 illustrates the factory layout for a company manufacturing two types of bicycle frame and employing a mass production or flow line production strategy.

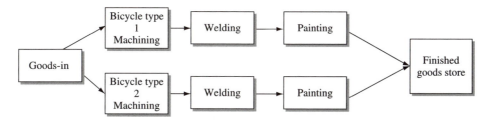

Figure 9.4 **Simplified layout of a factory employing mass production/flow production layout**

The main manufacturing processes illustrated are:

1. Goods received. Raw materials required for the manufacture of bicycle frames and assembly of completed bicycles into this store received into a raw materials store.
2. Machining.
3. Welding.
4. Painting.
5. Storing of finished goods. There will need to be a store where the completed bicycle frames are kept before assembly of the completed bicycle takes place, i.e. wheels, gears and other components of a bicycle are added.

Using this manufacturing system, raw materials for each product would go to an appropriate product line and then identical products would go through identical processes on each product line. In a mass production system there would be separate sections and machines for each of the two bicycle frames. The completed frames are sent to the finished goods store ready for despatch to the customer.

Johnson (1992) suggests that a key to low cost in many American companies in the 1950s to 1980s was to undertake large-scale capital investment in dedicated machinery. These were kept busy producing a high volume of output by workers performing highly programmed tasks. A problem occurs with this system when an increasingly competitive environment leads to customer demands for increased variety of products. Mass production can be inflexible and to introduce a new variety it is necessary for the production line to stop many times. In order to cope with this problem, many companies decoupled the production process – with different processes operating at different rates. This meant that inventories increased with buffers of stock at each stage of the production process. In theory, low cost can be achieved if each process achieves economies of scale and speed. In practice, for many organizations there were increased costs of carrying inventory, additional warehousing and transportation costs, as well as increased overheads in the form of additional production controllers and schedulers due to the requirement to manage the production flow.

Batch production

Batch production employs general-purpose machines and functional layout, see Figure 9.5. Batch production is a flexible system, which allows for different types of product to be made, in batches of, for example, 10 or 100 units.

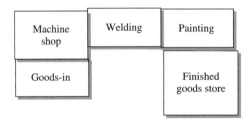

Figure 9.5 Functional layout of department with batch production

Given the functional departments indicated in Figure 9.5, raw materials (the metal tubes used in each bicycle frame) for each batch will be first supplied to the machine shop from the goods-in store. Once work on the batch in the machine shop has been completed, it will be sent to the welding section. When capacity is available or the due date for production arrives, the machined tubes will be welded together to form the bicycle frame. Having completed the welding, the batch can be sent to the paint shop for painting. From there the batch will go into the finished goods store ready for despatch to the customer.

This layout permits high levels of flexibility because machines can be reset to machine different parts (in this case different bicycle frames). The functional layout allows parts to progress through different routes according to design specifications.

A key disadvantage of batch production is the potential loss in efficiency as time is lost with batches being moved from one location to another and machine settings changed to meet the needs of the next batch of products. Inventories also accumulate at intervening stages of the process in batch production because the functional layout means that products are rarely assembled in the most efficient order. Batches of products often wait for some time to be moved from one area of the plant to another and may then wait a further length of time to be processed further.

New production strategies

Just-in-time production

A number of writers (e.g. Womack and Jones, 1990) have argued that batch and mass production are being superseded by a new option, just-in-time production (JIT).

Just-in-time (JIT) employs a factory layout which moves away from batch production to one in which products are split into families of similar products each of which is manufactured in a small manufacturing cell (see Figure 9.6). The production system works on flow line principles, so that batches of products can be made from start to finish, without the long wait between stages that often occurs with batch production.

The advocates of JIT claim that its simplified routing of products through the use of linear organization helps realize the productivity of mass production. The employment of multipurpose machines facilitates the flexibility of batch production, by allowing firms

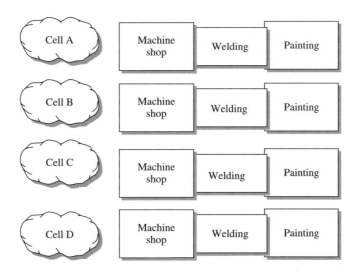

Figure 9.6   Just-in-time production – factory layout

to change production to manufacture something else whenever demand drops. This flexibility should also lead to a reduced order-to-delivery time.

A further benefit of JIT is to reduce inventories, one of the major costs of both mass and batch production strategies. JIT production's use of linear organization allows parts to progress through the factory via simplified routes, eliminating the accumulation of many stocks while the introduction of associated practices, such as the emphasis on zero defects, eliminates the need for stocks to be held at intervening stages.

In order for the theoretical benefits of JIT to be achieved, a range of process improvements are essential.

1. Set-up time reduction is required in order that very small batches can be made if necessary.
2. The manufacturing process must be synchronized so that sub-assemblies and components are available just when they are needed and not before or after.

In traditional manufacturing processes, ensuring that sub-assemblies and components are available has often involved 'sophisticated' (and expensive) information systems, which organize the scheduling of different products. This has been termed 'push manufacturing' as the individual production areas are told by the *information system* to produce parts, whether or not the next process has indicated a requirement for those parts. In JIT systems this has been simplified with the introduction of 'pull manufacturing'. This uses a much simpler method of employing *visual* signalling techniques such as the use of kanban containers or racks, which hold materials or parts to be transferred to the next work centre. When the container or rack is full, no further parts will be manufactured, when the number of parts stored in the kanban rack is reduced to a certain level, this is a visual signal to refill the container.

3. A change in vendor relationships.

Continuity of supply of high-quality raw materials and components is essential, as any disruption to supply will lead to substantial disruption to the production process. To 'guarantee' this, rather than focusing on achieving lowest prices from a wide range of suppliers, it is particularly important that companies in a JIT environment focus on the development of long-term supplier relationships.

Computerized manufacturing technology

Computerized manufacturing technology involves the use of computers to regulate production processes in industry. In the 1970s and 1980s authors such as Jaikumar (1986) suggested that with the development of computerized manufacturing technology, it would be possible to lower the costs of adding to a company's range. The 'knowledge' to manufacture parts and products could be stored in computer programs. This would mean that it would be as cheap to machine batches of one as it is to mass produce and this would mean that mass production systems would no longer be necessary. In practice, these economies have not yet materialized in many organizations.

Manufacturing strategies and the new competitive environment

There remains a considerable body of literature that questions the extent to which mass production was either dominant in manufacturing in the past, or has been superseded by a new manufacturing environment markedly different from the past (e.g. Wood, 1989). Mass production still provides economies of scale when large-volume production is required, while batch production can still be appropriate where flexibility, in order to produce a wide product range, is required.

Manufacturing strategies and the role of accounting information

Given the continued use of traditional forms of manufacturing, it may be argued that there remains a role for standard costing. As already suggested, this may be particularly true for organizations which retain mass production and for which low cost is crucial in order to remain competitive. The role of standard costing for organizations employing new manufacturing strategies is more open to doubt.

Just-in-time and the accounting system

JIT is not a cost management technique, but has potentially great significance in terms of cost and the cost management techniques that might be appropriate when this production management system is used.

1. Decentralization of activities with support staff appointed to look after specific product lines means a fall in overheads involved in large central support departments. This in turn reduces the requirement for complex allocation of costs using systems such as activity-based costing and activity-based management.
2. With a full JIT system, stock movement through the factory is not recorded and this will mean that insufficient information is available to calculate standard costing variances. A simplified accounting system called backflush accounting has been recommended when this occurs.
3. Variance information provided by standard costing systems, such as labour efficiency and material price and usage variances, may not be relevant. For a JIT system to operate, much of the control is maintained through observation and the personal intervention of the workforce.
4. Production decisions are signalled by systems such as an empty kanban rack.
5. In a JIT environment it is preferable for the staff to be 'idle' (be involved in non-production activities) than building for stock. A standard costing system might highlight apparent inefficiencies through an indication of adverse labour and production volume variances.
6. High-quality production is essential as (at least in theory) 'just-in-time' production will mean zero stock levels and any poor quality will cause the production line to stop. In such an environment, it is essential that individual workers have responsibility for quality at each workstation.

Despite the apparent lack of relevance for companies operating a JIT system, Cobb (1993), in a review of ten companies that had implemented JIT, found that the companies continued to use work-in-progress accounts for both financial and more importantly production control procedures. Existing accounting software was also identified as a constraint on the ability of a company to change its accounting system.

Summary

A standard costing system assumes that each unit of a product will require the exact same inputs of labour, materials and other resources at all stages of a standard production process.

The potential benefits of standard costing include its potential use as a basis for stock valuation; as an aid to planning; as a method of motivating managers; a method of control; and as a means of performance evaluation.

With standard marginal costing variance analysis it is possible to identify more detailed variances, including:

- *Sales price variance.* Difference between the actual sales revenue and the actual volume of sales at the standard price per unit.
- *Sales margin volume variance.* (Budgeted sales volume − actual sales volume) × standard contribution per unit.
- *Direct material price variance.* (Standard price per unit of material − actual price per unit of material) × actual amount of material used.
- *Direct material usage variance.* (Standard quantity of material used for actual output − actual quantity of material) × standard price per unit of material.
- *Direct labour rate variance.* (Standard rate per hour − actual rate per hour) × actual hours worked.
- *Direct labour efficiency variance.* (Standard hours expected for the actual output − actual hours worked for the actual output) × standard rate per hour.
- *Fixed expenditure variance.*

A summary report can be produced reconciling variance causing the difference between original budgeted profits and actual profits.

Many organizations would expect a written report to be provided, which would explain causes of variance. Care should be taken in interpreting variance reports as there may be interdependencies between variances and standards may be out of date.

Standard absorption costing systems identify a proportion of fixed production overhead to each unit. Production above or below budget will result in an over- or under-absorption of overheads which will be credited or charged to the Profit and Loss Account.

Traditional production systems employed mass or batch production. A new production strategy of just-in-time production is being increasingly employed in many organizations. Computerized manufacturing technology is also being increasingly used, though the economies of full automation have not been achieved in many organizations.

The relevance of standard costing has been questioned in the new production environment, although a large number of organizations still use the technique.

Further reading

Further issues related to management control are discussed in Part 4 of this book.

For information on further standard costing variances:

Drury, C. (2004) *Management and Cost Accounting*, 6th edn. Thomson Learning, Chapters 18, 19 and 22.
Horngren, C., Bhimani, A., Foster, G. and Datar, S. (2005) *Management and Cost Accounting*, 3rd edn. FT Prentice Hall, Chapters 16 and 17.

Answers to activities

Activity 9.1

Material X – usage variance

Standard quantity (SQ) (5200 × 3) kgs	Actual quantity (AQ) kgs	SQ – AQ (kgs)	Standard price (£)	Variance (£)
15,600	16,520	920 (A)	8	7,360 (A)

Activity 9.2

Material X – price variance

Standard price (£)	Actual price (£)	SP – AP (£)	Actual quantity (AQ) kgs	Variance (£)
8	7.5	0.5 (F)	16,520	8,260 (F)

Activity 9.3

Reconciliation of variances for material X to the total variance.

Material usage	£7360 (adverse)
Material price	£8260 (favourable)
Total variance	£900 (favourable)

Activity 9.4

Labour efficiency variance for welding.

Standard quantity (SH) (5200 × 3) hrs	Actual quantity (AH) hrs	SH – AH (hrs)	Standard rate/hour (SR) (£)	Variance (£)
10,400	9,915	485 (F)	14.5	7,032.5 (F)

Actlvlty 9.5

Labour rate variance for welding.

Standard rate per hour (SR) (£)	Actual rate per hour (AR) (£)	SR – AR (£)	Actual hours (AH) (hrs)	Variance (£)
14.5	15.5	1 (A)	9915	9915 (A)

Activity 9.6

Reconciliation of labour variances for welding.

The calculations of the price and usage variances for welding labour shown above are:

Labour efficiency	£7033 (favourable)
Labour rate	£9915 (adverse)
Total variance	£2882 (adverse)

Activity 9.7

See discussion after Activity 9.7.

Activity 9.8

Fixed overhead expenditure variance $=£50,000$ actual $-£49,000$ budget $=£1000$ (adverse).

Fixed overhead volume variance $=7000$ units $\times £7$ per unit -6300 units $\times £7$ per unit $=£49,000 - £44,100 = £4900$ under-absorption of overhead.

Activity 9.9

It depends on the situation. If this is not a constraint machine and there is sufficient stock of component A, then it would not seem a good idea. Presumably the works manager would feel that he is benefiting as the accounts would show a favourable labour and fixed overhead volume variance, however, the impact on the business is to tie up funds in unnecessary inventory.

  If the machine is often operating at full capacity and there is a shortage of component A, then it would make sense to increase production of the component.

Discussion questions

1. What is the difference between original budget costs and standard costs?
2. What would be the best basis for setting standards – ideal or attainable standards?
3. What are the potential benefits of standard costing systems?
4. Why is a variance statement that reconciles original budgeted to actual profit inadequate in isolation? Why do most organizations expect a written report as well?
5. What are the potential benefits of labour rate and efficiency variances, why might they provide the wrong incentive in the management of production activities?
6. What are the potential benefits of material usage and price variances, why might they provide the wrong incentive in the management of production activities?
7. Why are many organizations introducing new production management systems that are consistent with just-in-time principles?
8. In what type of organizations would standard costing be of little use?
9. Standard costing is considered by some to be a control technique that is of little relevance to manufacturing organizations of the twenty-first century. Explain why this might be so and to what extent do you agree?

Exercises

(Questions with numbers in bold have answers at the back of the book.)

Q9.1 'Sound Sleepers' Ltd manufactures a single product, a comfortable mattress. In February 20X7 the following information was available.

Standard costs:

Direct material (10 m² at £5.00 per m²)	£50.00
Direct labour (3 hours at £4.00 per hour)	£12.00
Fixed overheads (3 hours at £2.00 per hour)	£6.00
The standard selling price of the mattress is £100.00	
The budgeted production for the month was 1000 mattresses	

Actual figures for February:

Sales: 1100 mattresses at £98.00

Production: 1100 mattresses

Direct material: 12, 100 m² at £4.75 per m²

Direct labour: 3500 hours at a total cost of £15,750

Fixed overhead: £7000

For reporting purposes ABC Ltd uses a standard marginal costing system.

Required:

(i) For the month of February, compute two variances for each of material, labour, the sales price and volume variance and also the fixed overhead expenditure variance.

(ii) Provide a reconciliation between the original budgeted profit and the actual profit.

(iii) Comment on possible reasons behind the causes of the variances reported in (i) above.

Q9.2 Elba Ltd uses variance analysis as a method of cost control. The following information is available for the year ended 31 March 20X7.

Budget:
Standard cost per unit

Direct material (3 kgs at £10.00 per kg)	£30.00
Direct labour (4 hours at £6.00 per hour)	£24.00
The standard selling price per unit was £75	
The budgeted sales and production for the year was 12,000 units	
Fixed overheads £96,000	

Actual results for the year ended March 31:
Sales and production 11,500 units

	(£)
Revenue	851,000
Material cost (37,300 kgs)	350,000
Labour cost (43,800 hrs)	310,000
Fixed overhead £100,000	

For reporting purposes Elba Ltd uses a standard marginal costing system.

Required:

(i) For the year, compute appropriate sales variance and two variances for each of material and labour and also the fixed overhead expenditure variance.

(ii) Provide a reconciliation between the original budgeted profit and the actual profit.

(iii) Comment on possible reasons behind the causes of the variances reported in (i) above.

Q9.3 Tootles PLC manufactures and sells a single product and operates a standard marginal costing system.

The trading results for April are as follows:

	Budget		Actual	
Sales (units)		10,000		11,200
	£	£	£	£
Sales		95,000		100,800
Operating costs				
Material	20,000		23,500	
Labour	45,000		53,428	
Fixed overhead	18,000		19,600	
		83,000		96,528
Profit		12,000		4,272

Budgeted standard cost per unit is shown below:

		£
Material X	1 kg at £2 per kg	2.00
Labour	0.75 hrs at £6 per hr	4.50

The company produces to order and holds no stocks of product or material. The following factors have affected April's costs and revenues:

1. In March the sales manager decided to cut selling prices by 50 pence per unit. He argued that the company had capacity available and ought to take the opportunity to increase its market share. In the original forecast it had been estimated that Tootles would achieve a 20% market share of a market of 50,000 units sold in the month. In fact, 55,000 units were sold.
2. In order to reduce operating costs the works manager decided to change his supplier of material X and obtained a 20% price reduction compared with the standard cost per kilogram. The quality of the product is inferior to that delivered by the previous supplier. If the previous supplier had been retained then the cost per kilogram would have been in line with plan.
3. At the beginning of April the company granted a 5% pay increase. This compared with an industry average of 4% and a planned pay rise of 3%.

Required:

(a) Produce a statement showing variances for the above organization against planned performance.
(b) Prepare a report highlighting key points that emerge from the statement. What implications about the operating performance of this organization could be drawn from this information?

For Questions 9.4 and 9.5 calculate the fixed overhead volume and the fixed overhead expenditure variances.

Q9.4 Budgeted production volume 5000 units.
    Budgeted fixed overhead £50,000.
    Actual production volume 4800 units.
    Actual fixed overhead £47,000.

Q9.5 Budgeted production volume 8000 units.
    Budgeted fixed overhead £64,000.
    Actual production volume 7500 units.
    Actual fixed overhead £63,000.

Q9.6 Assume that Sound Sleepers Ltd (Exercise 9.1) operated a standard absorption costing system. Provide a revised reconciliation between the original budgeted profit and the actual profit.

Q9.7 Assume that Elba Ltd (Exercise 9.2) operated a standard absorption costing system. Provide a revised reconciliation between the original budgeted profit and the actual profit.

CONTROL IN DIVISIONALIZED ORGANIZATIONS

10

Objectives

After studying this chapter you should be able to:

- Describe the advantages and disadvantages of divisional and functional organizational structures.
- Explain potential issues in measuring the financial results of divisions, including:

    - The transfer pricing problem.
    - Measuring divisional profits in order to assess the performance of the divisional management and the division.

- Explain alternative approaches to measuring divisions as investment centres.

    - The use of return on investment as a measure of divisional performance.
    - The benefits of an alternative measure of performance, residual income.
    - Determination of the investment base.

Introduction

Divisions are often created in large organizations in which many people are employed, significant revenues generated, costs incurred and assets used. An initial section of the chapter considers reasons for organizations to create a divisional structure.

The chapter then progresses with a consideration of the role that accounting information might play in measuring the performance of a division and its management. Issues that need to be considered – if a division is to be treated as a profit or investment centre – are reviewed, including:

 (i) The transfer pricing problem. This occurs when goods or services are sold to other divisions and an agreed selling price has to be set. Different transfer pricing methods will have an impact on the profitability of divisions.
(ii) Measuring divisional profit.
    The analysis of expenses and profits. It will be necessary to decide whether divisional managers should be responsible for all costs that are charged to their division or just those that they can control.

(iii) Treating divisions as investment centres.

    (a) The potential benefits and problems of using return on investment and an alternative measure of residual income.

    (b) The method of treating asset values, for example whether at book value or original cost.

Controlling a business through developing new organizational structures

Organizations tend to change organizational structure as they grow. The functional structure is operated by many smaller organizations, with different departments specializing in specific areas of the business, such as production, marketing and finance, as illustrated in Figure 10.1.

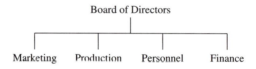

Figure 10.1 **A functional organisational structure**

With further growth and development, control through means of the functional structure became more difficult and the divisional structure is an alternative to consider. This can be particularly the case when organizations operate in a complex environment.

    With the divisional structure, there might be a number of corporate functions provided at a head office level, for example central finance or legal services. The management of the operations of the business, however, is organized into divisions. Each division would deal with the production, marketing and accounting for a specific product area. See Figure 10.2.

Figure 10.2 **A divisional organisational structure**

The potential advantages of the divisional structure are:

1. The decision-making process may be improved. Divisional managers have detailed local information and specialist knowledge and so can make informed decisions while top managers can be too far removed from events to understand all the implications of different decisions. Decisions can also be made more quickly, as the number of layers of management who should be informed and involved in the decision-making process is reduced.
2. Empowering divisional and junior management with decision-making responsibility provides motivation to junior management. This experience also provides valuable management training for those who will gain future responsibilities in more senior positions.
3. Top management are freed from operational decision-making and can spend more time on strategic decision-making.

There are also potential disadvantages when power and decision-making is delegated to divisional staff and top management have incomplete information about the conditions facing the divisional managers and the various options that can be chosen.

1. Divisional managers may use their position of greater independence from the control of head office staff to pursue their own goals at the expense of the objectives of the organization.

   (a) It may be possible to ensure easy targets are set, which will mean that they are rewarded for little effort.
   (b) Action may be taken which results in additional profits for the division but lower profits for the whole organization. For example, a division might buy goods and services from external companies because they are cheaper, rather than purchasing from other divisions of the company.

2. Divisional managers may be averse to taking risky decisions. A risky decision will have a high potential payoff, however, there is also a chance that low profits or even losses will occur. A divisional manager may prefer to ensure that his/her division enjoys slow, but steady, growth rather than run the risk of making heavy losses and being 'punished' by senior management. A large corporation can afford to take risks as a loss in one area is likely to be offset by profits elsewhere.
3. Top managers may lose touch with the detail of the market and competition and start to operate as a remote and ineffective bureaucracy.
4. Some costs may be duplicated. For example, there may be accounting costs at divisional level and at head office level. Mini empires may develop which have marginal benefits (if any) in improving customer satisfaction or increasing the profits of the business.

The remainder of this chapter considers the measurement of the financial results of divisional organizations, using traditional accounting controls.

Transfer pricing in divisional organizations

With the divisional structure, the different divisions of an organization may provide manufactured products or services for each other. If divisions are to be accountable for profits or a return on investment, then a **transfer pricing mechanism** needs to be in place in order that a price can be established for the goods and services that are transferred.

Consider the problem in Figure 10.3.

(i) Division B of Abingdon Ltd manufactures component W. Total cost is:

	£
Variable cost per unit	5
Fixed cost per unit	6
Total cost per unit	11

Division B sells the component to external customers and to Division A at £12 per unit.

(ii) An overseas company has offered to supply component W to Division A for £11.50.

Questions

(a) What action should the management of Division A take? Should they continue to buy the component from Division B and if so at what price?

(b) If the management of Division A decide to purchase the component from outside the company, what action should be taken by the management of Division B or the management of the head office of Abingdon Ltd?

Figure 10.3   A transfer pricing problem

Where the volume of goods sold between divisions is low, then the decision to buy internally or externally and a transfer price for internal sales is not important. However, when it is high, there can be a major impact on the profits of both the selling and buying division. Although the transfer price will not affect overall income of the company (since costs and revenues of buying and selling divisions exactly cancel out), the price can lead divisional managers to make decisions that may not be in the best interests of the company and overall company profit may suffer.

In the remainder of this section the objectives/criteria required for an efficient and effective transfer pricing system are clarified. Alternative bases for setting transfer price are then identified and evaluated in terms of whether they meet the required criteria.

Criteria for a transfer pricing system

It should:

(i) Encourage decisions made by the divisional managers to be in the interests of both the company and each individual division. This is often called **goal congruence**.

(ii) Allow the divisions to be evaluated as independent companies.

(iii) Be fair to the management of the divisions and easily understood. Systems that are cumbersome will lead to inefficiencies and confusion.

Bases used

A number of bases are used by different organizations in setting transfer prices, the three main methods being cost-based, market-based and negotiated, see Figure 10.4.

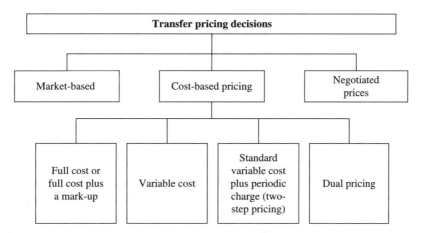

Figure 10.4 Alternative approaches to setting transfer prices

Market prices

Generally, market price is considered the best method where:

 (i) There is a competitive and active market.
(ii) The division selling the goods is operating at full capacity.

Given these two conditions then market price is usually the only situation which fully meets the three criteria of a transfer pricing listed above. The example of Abingdon Ltd is considered in Figure 10.5.

> If Division B of Abingdon Ltd is operating at full capacity and can sell all units of component W for £12 externally, then unless there are strategic reasons for the goods to be bought internally, it should not reduce the price. Any reduction will lead to a fall in profit for both the division and the company.
>
> Division A should be allowed to purchase the components from the external company as its costs will be reduced and there is no adverse impact on other divisions of the company.

Figure 10.5 Selling division operating at full capacity

Problems with market-based pricing as a basis for the transfer price

There are limitations to market-based prices in certain conditions.

(i) Where there is unused capacity in the selling division.

If the selling division has spare capacity then it should consider selling its products or services at less than the market price. Any price above marginal cost will lead to the generation of a contribution to overheads. If an order is accepted that makes a contribution to overheads, then as long as other orders are not lost because of this decision, the company as a whole will generate additional profits. Consider the problem of Abingdon Ltd in Figure 10.6.

The total cost of the component W was identified in Figure 10.5 as:

	£
Variable cost per unit	5
Fixed cost per unit*	6
Total cost per unit	11

* Assume that fixed costs are general overheads and that these will not change if a decision to stop production is made.

If Division B is unable to sell this product elsewhere, since the only additional cost of making one unit of component W is £5, any price above this amount will lead to a contribution and an increase in profits for both the division and Abingdon Ltd.

Figure 10.6   Selling division with unused capacity

(ii) Another problem occurs when there is no external market price for a product.
(iii) A company may not wish to deal with an outside company because of concerns about the quality of competing products or services, the reliability of supply or protection of trade secrets.

Activity 10.1

Assume that market demand for the products of Division B of Abingdon Ltd has fallen so that it is no longer operating at full capacity and therefore any reduction in sales to other divisions cannot be replaced by other opportunities, i.e. there is no opportunity cost.

Division A currently purchases 5000 units of component W a month and has advised Division B that unless the price per unit of component W is reduced to £9, it will purchase its supplies from another company.

(i) What would be the financial impact on the profits of Division A if it purchases components from an outside company for £9 per unit rather than £12 per unit from Division B?
(ii) What will be the impact on the profits of Abingdon Ltd following the decision to purchase the components from the outside company?

Cost-based transfer prices

Market-based pricing might be seen as the ideal basis for transfer pricing, given certain conditions – e.g. there is an external market price and the selling division is operating at full capacity. However, due to the potential problems of market pricing, some firms use cost as a basis for the transfer price.

Four cost-based transfer pricing systems are considered below:

- Full costs or full cost plus a mark-up.
- Variable costs.
- Two-step pricing.
- Dual pricing.

Full cost or full cost plus a mark-up

If full cost or full cost plus a mark-up are used, then given sufficient sales, the selling division will cover its fixed costs. A disadvantage of this method is that the transfer price may be higher than the market price and there is a potential for a lack of 'goal congruence' between divisional and corporate objectives. If the selling division insists on selling at full cost or full cost plus a mark-up, the buying division may find it unprofitable to manufacture a product or provide a service, even though from the company's point of view it is worthwhile. See the example in Figure 10.7.

Division C can sell a product for £18 per unit. Component W is a key component for this product and Division B has offered to sell component W to Division C for £12 per unit. The costs of a product manufactured by Division C are as follows:

	£
Component W	12
Additional costs of Division C	8
Total cost of product to Division C	20

Since the cost to Division C is higher than the price it can obtain for the product, it decides to not proceed.

From the company's point of view, if Division B has spare capacity, the additional cost to Division B and the company is the variable cost of £5. If the transfer had been made at £5, then the total cost of the product would be £5 + £8 = £13. At this cost the sale would have generated a positive contribution.

Figure 10.7 Example of a full costing approach to setting transfer prices

Variable cost

As illustrated in Figure 10.7, a benefit of the method is that where a selling division is not selling at capacity (i.e. there is no opportunity cost), it is possible to view a sale from the point of view of the contribution earned by the company as a whole.

The problem of using variable cost as a basis, however, is that the selling division will not obtain any contribution from the transfer, so that the divisions cannot be treated as independent companies and there is no incentive or reward to the selling division. In the example in Figure 10.7, Division B would only receive £5 for each unit that it transfers to Division C.

Both marginal and full cost systems therefore have disadvantages. To try to overcome some of these problems, two other cost-based alternative mechanisms have been suggested.

Two-step pricing (e.g. standard variable cost plus periodic charge)

With this method the buying division is charged with:

(i) A standard variable cost for each unit transferred.
(ii) A fixed amount per month. This should be equal to the fixed costs associated with the facilities required to provide the products reserved for the buying division.

Figure 10.8 provides an example of the use of standard variable cost plus a periodic charge.

> Division A expects to purchase 5000 units of component W a month. If the company decided to operate a policy of charging variable cost plus a periodic charge for overheads, an agreement would need to be signed between Division A and Division B. This would identify that Division A would purchase component W from Division B at £5 per unit plus pay an agreed monthly charge. The monthly charge would be based on an estimate of the use of fixed overheads involved in manufacturing 5000 units.

Figure 10.8   Standard variable cost plus a periodic charge

The main advantage from the point of view of the buying division is that the fixed cost is a sunk cost and it will make decisions based on the marginal cost of the units. The selling division will make a contribution equal to the fixed charge per month.

Dual pricing

Dual pricing occurs when buying divisions are charged with the marginal costs of goods transferred, but the revenue will be shown in the accounts of the selling divisions at an agreed higher amount. The main advantage is that managers in the division buying goods will make a decision based on the incremental costs to the business, though a danger is that opportunity costs may be ignored. The selling division will be receiving the full cost for each unit and this may discourage it from looking for other alternatives. Figure 10.9 provides an example of the use of dual pricing at Abingdon Ltd.

> Division A would be charged £5 for every unit of component W that it purchases. It might be agreed with the senior of management of Abingdon Ltd that the revenue per unit could be shown in the accounts of Division B at, say, the full cost of £11 per unit plus a mark-up of £1, i.e. a total of £12 per unit.

Figure 10.9   Example of dual pricing

Note from the example in Figure 10.9 that since the cost per unit to Division A would be £5 while the revenue for Division B would be £12 per unit, the combined profits of the divisions would be £7 per unit greater than the actual profit earned by the organization as a whole. This effect will be removed when the accounts of the various divisions are consolidated at head office.

Negotiated transfer prices

Given the problems that occur with a pricing system based on both market prices and costs, an alternative is for divisional managers to **negotiate** transfer prices in order that an acceptable solution can be found. A disadvantage is that the negotiation process can be time-consuming and there may be a need for an appeal system to higher management.

Identification of revenue in divisional operating statements

If revenue is being shown in a divisional operating statement, then it would be helpful for sales to external customers and sales to other divisions to be shown separately. The method of valuing the transfers is important, if the report is to be used to interpret performance of either the manager or the division, a transfer price based on variable cost is likely to reflect adversely on the performance of that division. An argument can be made that an adjustment should also be made in the report to reflect the market price. The problem is illustrated in Figure 10.10.

Division B of Abingdon Ltd expects to sell 5000 units of component W a month to Division A. Assume that the sales value of component W is currently shown in the accounts at variable costs. It has now been decided that a policy of dual pricing should be implemented, with the selling division being credited with the full cost of each unit. Sales to external and internal customers are also to be shown separately.

(i) Identify external sales:
Current sales shown in the accounts of Division B are £18,000,000.
This includes internal sales of 5000 units a month or 60,000 units a year of component W.
60,000 units at £5 per unit = £300,000.
External sales are therefore £17,700,000.

(ii) Identify the value of internal sales at the agreed price set at the full cost of manufacturing the component:

The full cost of manufacturing a unit of component W is £11. Internal sales value should therefore be restated at £11 × 60,000 units = £660,000.

(iii) Prepare a revised analysis of revenue, showing separately sales to external customers and inter-divisional transfers.

	£'000
Sales to external customers	17,700
Inter-divisional transfers	660
Total sales	18,360

Figure 10.10   Revised analysis of sales

Analysing divisional profits

Divisional profit statements

The structure of a potential divisional profit statement is shown in Figure 10.11.

Revised Divisional Profit Statement	
Sales to external customers	xxx
Inter-divisional transfers	xxx
Total sales	xxx
Less variable expenses	xxx
Controllable contribution (1)	xxx
Less controllable divisional overheads	xxx
Controllable profit (2)	xxx
Less non-controllable divisional fixed expenses	xxx
Divisional profit before deducting	
central allocated overheads (3)	xxx
Less allocated central management expenses	xxx
Divisional net profit(loss) (4)	xxx

Figure 10.11   Revised divisional profit statement

Controllable contribution

In Chapter 1, the concept of the contribution statement was introduced. Producing a contribution statement may help highlight the high level of fixed costs in one division compared with another and also the importance of contribution to decision-making.

Controllable profit

Controllable profit is the profit that can be identified after deducting controllable costs from divisional revenues. Controllable costs can include fixed costs.

Divisional profit after deducting non-controllable avoidable costs

Non-controllable avoidable costs are those that the divisional managers do not control, but they are costs which would be saved if the division were to be closed down. The following are examples:

(i) The divisions may be charged for certain central services such as computing or legal services. Head office may insist that the divisions use and pay for these services. As an example, one division might use an estimated 20% of the time of the legal department and so head office charge 20% of the costs of this department.

(ii) Depreciation of fixed assets. Many of the fixed assets will have been purchased prior to the appointment of the existing divisional management. Performance of the division will therefore in part depend on the impact of past decisions and the divisional management have had no control over these costs.

Divisional net profit/(loss)

Divisional net profit/(loss) is calculated after deducting costs that are charged to the division on an arbitrary basis. They are costs that would continue, even if a division were closed down, and are the general overheads of a company.

Evaluating the performance of managers and divisions

Different measures of profit may be appropriate for the assessment of performance of the manager and the division. Applying the theory that the manager should be held responsible for the revenue and expenditure that they can control, it can be argued that divisional managers should be held responsible for the controllable profit of a division.

In evaluating the performance of a division, either the profit before or after deducting all costs including central overheads might be used. The latter might be used if an organization wishes to compare the performance of a division with a competing firm. The competing firm will have to pay for the services currently carried out by the head office of a divisional organization (e.g. central accounting services, cost of audit fees, costs of the board of directors), so for a like-for-like comparison, a share of these costs should be apportioned to each division.

Example of divisional profit statement

In Figure 10.12, further information is provided about Division A of Abingdon Ltd. The Profit and Loss Account of Division A is reanalysed according to the format shown in Figure 10.11.

The Profit and Loss Account of Division B of Abingdon Ltd

	£'000
Sales	18,000
Cost of sales	13,500
Gross profit	4,500
Marketing costs	1,500
Other costs	1,000
Divisional profit	2,000

The following further information has been provided:

(i) Information on internal transfers is as provided in Figure 10.10.

(ii) 40% of the cost of sales is expected to be variable costs, while the balance is considered fixed. Marketing and other costs are considered to be fixed.

(iii) Included in the marketing costs is an allocation from head office to cover the costs of an advertising campaign. The charge was for £500,000. Other costs cover expenditure controlled by Division B.

(iv) Included in 'other costs' is a share of the cost of running the head office of Abingdon Ltd. This is apportioned to divisions on the basis of the sales revenue of each of the divisions and amounts to a charge of £550,000 to Division B.

Figure 10.12 Revised profit and loss account of division B of Abingdon Ltd

Revised Divisional Profit Statement for Division B

	£'000
Sales to external customers	17,700
Inter-divisional transfers	660
Total sales	18,360
Less variable expenses	5,400
Controllable contribution (1)	12,960
Less controllable divisional fixed expenses:	
Fixed production overheads	8,100
Controllable marketing costs	1,000
Controllable other costs	450
Controllable profit (2)	3,410
Less non-controllable divisional fixed expenses:	
Allocation of advertising costs	500
Divisional profit before deducting central allocated overheads (3)	2,910
Less allocated central management expenses:	
Apportionment of head office costs	550
Divisional net profit (loss) (4)	2,360

Figure 10.12   (*Continued*)

Practical issues in producing the revised profit statement

In practice, many organizations do not produce this level of analysis or apply the principle of holding managers solely responsible for items they can control. Firstly, it is not always possible to clearly classify costs either as fixed and variable or as controllable and non-controllable. Secondly, some organizations feel that it is important for a divisional manager to take responsibility for performance after deducting all costs. Even if a manager cannot control certain costs, it may be important that they pay attention to those costs in order that they might bring influence to bear on them. This is particularly the case when a division is treated as an investment centre and the manager is considered to have responsibility for investments.

Treating divisions as investment centres

Return on investment

A common method traditionally used in the assessment of performance in investment centres is return on investment (ROI), which expresses the divisional profit as a percentage of the assets employed in the division.

$$ROI = \frac{\text{Divisional profit}}{\text{Investment in net assets}} \times 100$$

The return on investment measure considers the divisional profit compared with the investment in assets. Assume that Abingdon Ltd has decided to treat its divisions as investment centres, with the measure of divisional profit as the profit before deducting central allocated overhead. Information on the level of divisional net assets and the calculated return on investment is shown in Figure 10.13.

	Division A £'000	Division B £'000
Divisional profit	1,000	2,910
Net assets	4,000	29,100
ROI	25%	10%

Figure 10.13   Return on investment for Divisions A and B of Abingdon Ltd

Problems with the return on investment measure

A number of problems with the use of ratios for assessing performance will be discussed further in Chapter 11. A particular problem, that will be illustrated in Figure 10.14, can arise when investment decisions are being evaluated.

Investment decisions

The general managers of the two divisions of Abingdon Ltd are facing separate investment decisions. Project X for Division A and project Y for Division B. The following information has been provided:

	Division A Project X	Division B Project Y
Investment project available	£100,000	£100,000
Additional average profit	£17,000	£11,000
Accounting rate of return on the proposed project	17%	11%
Net present value of project at a cost of capital of 16%	+£27,024	−£433
Correct investment decision	Invest in project	Do not invest

Project X is worthwhile as it generates a positive net present value of £27,024.
Project Y is not worthwhile as the net present value of the project is −£433.

However
The return on investment measure potentially provides an incorrect incentive to managers.
 (i) The return on investment of project X at 17% is lower than the current return on investment of the division of 25%. The new investment will therefore reduce the overall return on investment of the division and because of this the divisional manager may be unwilling to invest.
 (ii) For project Y, the return on investment of 11% is above the return on investment of Division B, which is currently 10%. It will therefore increase the overall return on investment of the division and may provide an incentive for the investment.

Figure 10.14   Assessing investment divisions for Abingdon Ltd

The information in Figure 10.14 highlights how the measurement system may not encourage managers to take action in the interests of the organization. Return on investment is a relative measure of performance, i.e. profit is considered as a percentage of the investment. Particularly if divisional managers are rewarded on the basis of achieving a certain return on investment, there is a danger that action will be taken that is inconsistent with organizational objectives such as increasing shareholder wealth.

Activity 10.2

The following information is relevant to divisions of Alpha Ltd:

(i) Division M is considering an investment of £200,000 at the beginning of the budget year. It expects that this investment will generate an average profit of £40,000 a year for four years. The asset will have no value at the end of the four years.

(ii) Without the investment, at the end of year 1, Division M is budgeted to generate a profit of £500,000 with capital employed to be £2,000,000.

(iii) The weighted cost of capital that Alpha use is 15%.

Calculate the budgeted return on investment for Division M of Alpha Ltd at the end of year 1 assuming:

(a) The investment has not taken place.
(b) The investment has taken place.

Assets are valued at original cost in calculating the return on investment.
    Would it be in the interests of Alpha Ltd for the investment to be undertaken? Would the performance measurement system provide the correct incentive to the divisional managers of Alpha Ltd?

Residual income

To overcome the problems found with the use of the return on investment measure, an alternative measurement called residual income has been suggested. Net residual income for a division can be calculated using the following formula:

Divisional net residual income = Divisional profit – interest charge for using the capital invested in the division

The interest charge is calculated by multiplying the net investment in the organization (e.g. division) by the cost of capital. It has been argued that this measure is more likely to result in managers taking action that is in line with the objectives of both the organization and the division. Figure 10.15 illustrates the impact of the investment decisions discussed in Figure 10.14 on the two divisions of Abingdon Ltd.

Residual income of Divisions A and B before taking account of the investments

	Division A £'000	Division B £'000
Divisional profit	1000	2910
Interest charge (note 1)	640	4656
Divisional residual income	360	(1746)

Note 1. Interest charge for Division A is £4,000,000 @ 16% = £640,000.
Interest charge for Division B is £29,100,000 @ 16% = £4,656,000.

Division A generates a positive residual income of £360,000, while Division B generates a negative residual income of £1,746,000.
Investment decision – the residual income of the two projects considered by Divisions A and B

	Project X £100,000	Project Y £100,000
Investment project available	£	£
Additional profit	17,000	11,000
Interest charge (16%)	16,000	16,000
Residual income	1,000	−5,000

A calculation of the residual income shows that having taken account of the cost of capital it is not worth investing in project Y, but it is worth investing in project X as it will increase divisional residual income by £1,000. The measure therefore provides the correct incentive to make a decision in the interests of both the division (and its managers) and the organization.

Figure 10.15 Residual income of Divisions A and B, before and after taking account of the investments

Activity 10.3

Refer to the exercise in Activity 10.2. Calculate the residual income for Division M of Alpha Ltd before and after the proposed investment. On the basis of this analysis, should the manager of Division M proceed with the investment and would it also be in the interests of Alpha Ltd for him to proceed?

There are a number of further advantages of residual income:

(a) Different cost of capital percentages could be applied to different investments that have different levels of risk.
(b) In considering the performance of a company or division, it is possible to compare performance against budget, previous year, other companies in a similar industry, other divisions in the same company.

Despite these advantages, there are a number of potential problems with residual income and it was not a widely used performance measure until recent years, when a version of residual income called economic value added was promoted. The use of residual income and economic value added is discussed further in Chapter 21.

The investment base

When an organization is treated as an investment centre then it is necessary to consider.

(i) The assets that should be included in the investment base. The choice should be consistent with the choice of profit measure. If controllable profit is included then this should be compared with controllable investments. As with profits, there can be considerable difficulty in deciding which assets are controllable and which are not controllable.

   If divisional managers are responsible for all investment decisions then all investments should be included in the asset base and used for calculating the divisions' ROI.

(ii) The valuation of the assets. The choice of valuation method can result in a considerable difference in the apparent return generated by a division. A number of organizations use the original cost or the replacement value of fixed assets. The reason is that if a manager is assessed or division measured on the basis of return on investments which are valued at net book value, there can be an incentive to delay replacing old assets. The replacement of assets will result in an increase in the value of the asset base and a reduction in the return on investment.

When comparing divisions against other divisions or against other companies, it is crucial that comparison is made on a consistent basis. Different methods should not be used for different organizations. Care must still always be taken in evaluating the meaning of any information. As discussed above, if net book value is used then divisions with old and heavily depreciated assets are likely to appear more profitable than those with new assets. A guide to future profitability will not necessarily be provided.

Further issues in measuring and managing performance

The measurement of performance of organizations, in particular decentralized organizations, will be considered further in Parts 3 and 4 of the book. Alternative financial measures are reviewed as well as performance measurement systems that evaluate a broader range of measures than just financial performance.

Summary

Different organizational structures may be appropriate for different environmental and organizational circumstances. The divisional structure is often used in larger organizations and in complex and fast-changing environments. A number of potential advantages can occur with this structure, although there are also potential disadvantages.

Divisional organizations may be treated as profit centres. When goods and services are sold between divisions, a transfer price should be established and ideally such a pricing mechanism should encourage managers to act in the interests of both the company and the division, be fair and easily understood and allow the division to be treated as an independent company. A range of alternative transfer pricing approaches can be used and may be appropriate for different circumstances. Market price is considered to be the best mechanism, although this is only the case when there is a competitive and active market and the selling division is operating at full capacity.

Conventional wisdom is that where divisions are treated as profit centres then divisional profit statements should separate controllable from non-controllable costs in order that divisional managers can be measured on controllable contribution or controllable profits.

Divisions can also be treated as investment centres. A common measurement used is return on investment, though a criticism of this measure is that management action may be encouraged and rewarded that is not in line with organization objectives such as an increase in shareholder wealth. Other measures, such as residual income, may be more appropriate in certain circumstances.

The method used to value assets will lead to differences in the return generated by a division and may impact on decisions made by divisional managers.

Further reading

Anthony, R. and Govindarajan, V. (2004) *Management Control Systems*, 11th edn. Irwin.
Merchant, K. A. (2003) *Modern Management Control Systems: Performance Measurement, Evaluation and Incentives: Text and Cases*, Prentice-Hall.
Drury, C. (2004) *Management and Cost Accounting*, 6th edn. Thomson Learning, Chapters 20, 21.
Emmanuel, C., Otley, D. and Merchant, K. (1990) *Accounting for Management Control*, International Thompson Business Press.

Answers to activities

Activity 10.1

(i) There will be a benefit of £3 per unit to Division A, i.e. an increase on its profits of £15,000 per month.
(ii) For Abingdon Ltd, there would be a negative effect of £20,000 a month.

Since the variable cost per unit of making component W is only £5, if the price was reduced to £9 a unit, a contribution of £4 per unit sold would be earned by Division B. Division B is unable to sell this product elsewhere and has spare capacity. The loss to the company is therefore 5000 units a month @ £4 a unit = £20,000.

Activity 10.2

(i) If investment has not taken place:

$$\text{Return on investment (ROI)} = \frac{£500,000}{£2,000,000} \times 100\% = 25\%$$

(ii) If investment has taken place:

$$\text{ROI of new investment} = \frac{£40,000}{£200,000} \times 100\% = 20\%$$

$$\text{Divisional ROI given new investment} = \frac{£540,000}{£2,200,000} \times 100\% = 24.5\%$$

The new investment will lead to a fall in the return on investment of the division, so the divisional manager may be motivated to avoid the investment even though it leads to a positive net present value and is worthwhile.

The net present value of the investment is +£56,948.

Year	Cash flow (£)	Discount factor	Present value (£)
0	−200,000	1	−200,000
1	90,000	0.8696	78,261
2	90,000	0.7561	68,053
3	90,000	0.6575	59,176
4	90,000	0.5718	51,458
			56,948

Note that straight line depreciation is assumed in calculating the cash flow.

From this analysis it can be seen that a positive net present value is generated for the project. However, the project leads to a lower ROI, so that the divisional management may be motivated to not undertake the investment.

Activity 10.3

Residual income before the investment:

	£
Divisional profit	500,000
Interest charge 15% × £2,000,000	300,000
Residual income	200,000
Residual income of the investment	£
Profit from the investment	40,000
Interest charge 15% × £200,000	30,000
Residual income	10,000

The residual income method would indicate that the investment is worthwhile.

Discussion questions

1. Dundee Bicycle Division is one of the divisions of McLoed Ltd. Another division of the company is the assembly division, which completes a range of bicycles. Discuss the advantages and disadvantages of the decision to form two divisions to cover the activities of manufacturing bicycle frames and assembling bicycles.
2. Discuss key problems that are inherent to the return on investment measure.
3. Discuss why residual income has often been recommended as an alternative to return on investment as a measure of divisional performance.
4. Discuss why there is no one best transfer pricing system.
5. Discuss whether replacement cost or net book value should be used with the measure of return on investment.

Exercises

(Questions with numbers in bold have answers at the back of the book.)

Q10.1 Aldo Ltd is a large public company which is organized in a divisional structure. The divisional managers are measured on the return on investment (ROI), where return is net profit and the investment is considered to be fixed assets (at cost) plus current assets. The company estimates that its cost of capital is 15%.

Extracts from the budgets of Divisions A and B for the coming year are shown below, assuming that no projects are implemented.

	Division A £'000	Division B £'000
Net profit	480	130
Current assets	280	400
Fixed assets (at cost)	1,840	2,200

Division A is considering undertaking project X and Division B is considering project Y. The following information is provided about these two projects.

(i) Project X
Additional sales are expected to be £600,000 per annum for the next four years and contribution is expected to be 20% of sales. To achieve these additional sales an advertising campaign costing £84,000 per annum is required.
An additional £200,000 will need to be invested in current assets, which will be recovered at the end of the project in four years' time.
(ii) Project Y
Investment in new machinery will cost £500,000 and result in annual cash savings (i.e. before taking account of depreciation) of £140,000. It is expected that the new machinery will last five years and have no residual value.

Required:

(a) The budgeted ROI for each division assuming fixed assets are included at original cost:

   (i) Before the two proposals are incorporated.
   (ii) If the two proposals are adopted.

(b) Comment on the results produced in (a) and how the divisional management and head office are likely to react.
(c) How should any problems be rectified?
(d) The head office of Aldo Ltd is considering changing the method of valuing fixed assets from cost to net book value. Discuss the merits of this proposal.
(e) The head office of Aldo Ltd is considering changing the measurement method to residual income. Calculate the budgeted residual income for each division:

   (i) Before the two proposals are incorporated.
   (ii) If the two proposals are adopted.

Q10.2 The 'A' division of Aldo Ltd currently buys a component from the 'B' division of Aldo Ltd, and the current contract is up for renewal. It has asked two other companies, Cheapbuy Ltd and Fairdoo Ltd, to quote for the contract. Details of the three quotes are as follows:

 (i) Cheapbuy Ltd has quoted £85. Cheapbuy will not purchase any raw materials or supplies from Aldo Ltd.
 (ii) Fairdoo Ltd has quoted £90 a component. If it supplies the component it would purchase a subcomponent from the 'C' division of Aldo Ltd. The subcomponents would be sold by 'C' division for £40. The 'C' division earns a 40% contribution margin (40% of sales) and is currently working at 80% capacity.
(iii) The 'B' division has quoted £95. The division is currently working at full capacity. Division B does not purchase any components from other divisions.

Required:

(a) Which quote should the general manager of the 'A' division accept if acting in the interests of himself and Division A?
(b) Which quote will be best from the point of view of Aldo Ltd?
(c) If Division A were to choose the option that is not best from the point of view of Aldo Ltd, what should the management of Aldo do to rectify the problem?

Q10.3 Milton PLC is a group of companies consisting of autonomous, profit-motivated divisions A, B, C, D.

Division A has received two quotes for a subassembly it requires.

(i) Apple PLC, an external company, has quoted £7200 for each subassembly. Apple will buy various electrical components from Division C for £2000. The variable costs of Division C are £1400.

(ii) Division B has quoted £9200. Its costs include the following:

  – Division B will also purchase electrical components from Division C for £2000.
  – It will subcontract some work to Division D for £2700. Division D can earn a 50% contribution margin on this subcontracted work.
  – The balance of the costs considered is the variable costs of Division B. The quote of £9200 was based on its expected costs plus a 25% mark-up.

Required:

Advise the management of Milton PLC on which contract should be accepted by Division A, if it is to act in the interests of the organization, assuming:

(a) There is spare capacity in Divisions B, C and D.
(b) There is spare capacity in Divisions B and C, but Division D is working at full capacity.

Q10.4 A division of a large organization has just produced its budget for the next year, key summary information is provided below:

	£'000
Net profit	450
Fixed assets at cost	1000
Accumulated depreciation	475
Net book value	525
Net current assets (average for the year)	500

The division is reviewing a number of different decisions that could be made at the beginning of the budget year, but have not yet been included in the above summary information.

(a) Machinery to be purchased for £240,000 with resulting cash savings expected to be £70,000 a year. The machine is expected to have a six-year life.

(b) Offer discounts to customers. This is expected to cost £6000, but reduce trade receivables by £36,000.

(c) Sell a machine that cost £400,000 three years ago for £40,000. The machine was expected to last four years and would have been scrapped at the end of the budget year for nil scrap value. It was budgeted to have made a contribution to profit of £60,000.

The division is measured on the basis of return on investment with fixed costs valued at net book value (at year end). The cost of capital of the division is 14%.

Required:

(a) Calculate:

  (i) The current budgeted ROI of the division.
  (ii) The ROI of the division given each of the above decisions took place. Note that there should be three calculations as each decision should be treated separately.

(b) Comment on the results produced in (a) and how the divisional management and head office are likely to react.
(c) How should any problems be rectified?

Q10.5 The budget review of Dundee Bicycle Division of July 20X8 identified the revised forecast for the period April 20X8 to March 20X9 as shown in Figure 1.

	April–June 20X8 £	July 20X8– March 20X9 £	Revised estimate April 20X8–March 20X9 £
Sales	598,000	1,700,000	2,298,000
Labour	211,558	623,400	834,958
Material	143,240	417,600	560,840
Fixed production overhead	132,000	237,000	369,000
Production cost	486,798	1,278,000	1,764,798
Gross profit	111,202	422,000	533,202
Accounting	35,000	115,000	150,000
Commercial	43,000	217,000	260,000
Net profit	33,202	90,000	123,202

Figure 1 Budget review for Dundee Bicycle Division

Budgeted and revised estimates for profits, capital employed and return on capital employed (return on investment) are shown in Figure 2.

	Budget 20X8/9	Revised estimate 20X8/9
Profit	£225,000	£123,202
Capital employed		
Fixed assets	£1,000,000	£1,100,000
Current assets	£200,000	£250,000
Total capital employed	£1,200,000	£1,350,000
Return on capital employed	23.3%	9.1%

Figure 2 Budget and revised estimate ROI for Dundee Bicycle Division

The following further information is available:

(i) Jack Jones, the general manager of Dundee Bicycle Division, is considering investing in some new automated machinery. The machinery is expected to cost £50,000 with a zero scrap value at the end of the five years. The average profit over the life of the project is expected to be £6000 per annum, with the expected cash flows that will be generated from the investment as follows:

Year	£'000
0	(50)
1	10
2	10
3	10
4	25
5	25

The company cost of capital is 10%.

(ii) Labour and material costs can be treated as variable costs and the remainder are fixed costs.

Commercial costs for the period April–June 20X8 include £20,000, which is a share of the advertising costs for the corporate advertising campaign.

Required:

1. Provide arguments for and against Jack Jones investing in the new capital equipment.
2. Re-analyse the actual information for the period April–June 20X8, using the format shown in Figure 10.11 in the chapter.

CONTROL USING ACCOUNTING RATIOS

Objectives

After studying the material in this section you will be able to:

- Describe the financial information needs of key stakeholders of the business.
- Compute key financial ratios, using the accounting statements of the Profit and Loss Account and the Balance Sheet, that can help inform key stakeholders of the performance of an organization. These include measures of:

  - Profitability.
  - Efficiency, including measuring the working capital operating cycle time.
  - Liquidity (ability to meet short-term cash commitments).
  - Solvency (ability to meet long-term cash commitments).
  - Investment.

- Interpret the meaning of these ratios.
- Explain the key limitations of financial ratios in assessing performance.

Introduction

In the first part of this chapter, the financial information needs of key stakeholders of an organization are considered. The calculation and interpretation of financial ratios that can be extracted from the financial statements, the Profit and Loss Account and the Balance Sheet, are then considered. Financial ratios do not necessarily provide a good indicator for future performance, however, and the limitations of this information are also reviewed.

The information needs of stakeholders

A number of key stakeholders are interested in the financial health of a company. These would include present and potential:

1. Suppliers.
2. Lenders to the company, e.g. banks.

3. Shareholders.
4. Competitors.
5. Customers.
6. Managers of the company.
7. Other employees.
8. Employee representatives.

The various stakeholders will be interested in the ability of the business to fund itself in the short and longer term, i.e. its cash flow situation and in the profits and profitability of the business.

Suppliers will be particularly interested in the ability of a business to pay its short-term debts. They will not wish to sell goods or services, if the business is unable to pay for them, and will be reluctant to supply them if the company is a very slow payer.

The banks will be interested in the ability of the business to meet the loan and interest payments, both in the short and longer term. For the longer term, its ability to fund any expansion or asset replacement plans, given loan and interest payments and any potential downturn in trading conditions, will also be a concern.

Shareholders are likely to be particularly interested in past and future profits, as high profits are likely to lead to good dividend returns. However, shareholders will also be interested in long-term solvency. If a business has a high level of loan capital, then the requirement to fund these loan repayments will provide an increased risk to the dividend payments and the potential claim that shareholders might have on the business.

Competitors will be interested in the ability of the firm to fund competitive strategies. As part of a strategy a competitor might be considering developing into a new geographical area or launching a product that will bring it into direct competition with the business. They will be interested in the ability of that business to defend itself against such a development. If the firm had a strong financial situation, it will have a greater ability to survive a protracted price war, which will squeeze both profit margins and cash flows. Competitors might be less willing to consider an aggressive competitive stance if this was the case.

Customers will not wish to buy a product or service from a company if it is likely to cease trading because of poor profitability or cash flows.

Managers and employees are obviously interested in both profitability and cash flow strength from the viewpoint of the ability of a company to support ongoing employment and in its ability to support pay increases.

Comparative analysis using ratios

Financial ratios can be calculated using information extracted from the Profit and Loss Account and the Balance Sheet and can provide an indication of the financial health of an organization. An example of a ratio was given in Chapter 10, where it was noted that a popular measure of divisional performance is return on investment. For Division A of Abingdon Ltd, for example, the divisional profit was £1,000,000, the net assets invested in the division were £4,000,000 and the return on investment was 25%. In order to identify whether this ratio is good or not it is important to compare it against another standard. For example:

1. Comparison could be made with the return that could be generated if the funds invested in the division could be released and invested in a bank or other financial institution. A bank might be able to offer a return of 5% and the board of directors might consider whether the return currently generated by the division is sufficient to justify the investment.
2. Comparison can be made with other divisions within the company or with similar companies or the industry average. If ratios are worse than those of other similar organizations then it might be necessary to investigate why this is the case.
3. Comparison with the ratios of the same company or division over the previous three to five years, so that the *trend* in the ratios can be analysed. If the company is showing a decline over time and probably in particular from last year, then again reasons should be investigated.
4. Comparison of ratios with plan.

As discussed in Chapters 7 and 10, many commercial organizations use accounting ratios to help in planning and control. For example, if the budgeted return on investment of a division was 25% and the actual return on investment was 15% then questions might be raised about the performance of the managers and the division.

Key financial ratios

This chapter will consider ratios that may help in the interpretation of the financial performance of the organization. This will cover measures of profitability, whether too much money is tied up in working capital (liquidity and efficiency ratios), the longer-term solvency of the company and finally some key investment ratios. In order to illustrate the calculation and interpretation of ratios that relate to these areas, a comprehensive example will be used.

Bramble Ltd

The accountant of a company 'Bramble Ltd' has consolidated the information received from managers and prepared a budgeted Profit and Loss Account and Balance Sheet for the year 20X7/8. The actual Profit and Loss Account and Balance Sheet for Bramble Ltd for the financial year to March 2008 and the proposed budgeted statements for the year 20X8/9 are shown in Tables 11.1 and 11.2.

The senior management of Bramble Ltd have asked for a copy of these accounts along with some key summary ratios that compare actual results for the year 20X7/8 with budget for 20X8/9. They have also asked for information on key ratios of competitors over the last year.

The calculation of the actual financial ratios for 20X7/8 is explained in the next section and using the same method, the reader is expected to calculate the budgeted

Table 11.1   Profit and Loss Account for Bramble Ltd

Bramble Ltd
Profit and Loss Account for the year to 31 March

	Actual 20X7/8 £'000	Budget 20X8/9 £'000
Sales	**2,030**	2,370
Cost of sales	1,120	1,302
Gross profit	910	1,068
Less:		
Administration expenses	248	355
Selling and distribution expenses	237	348
Profit before interest and tax	**425**	365
Interest	7	55
Profit before tax	418	310
Taxation	160	96
Profit after tax	258	214
Dividends	140	144
Retained profit for year	118	70
Retained profit b/f	294	412
Retained profit c/f	412	482

Table 11.2   Balance sheet for Bramble Ltd

Bramble Ltd
Balance Sheet as at 31 March

	Actual 20X7/8 £'000	£'000	Budget 20X8/9 £'000	£'000
Non-current assets				
Cost	1,964		2,864	
Less depreciation	(550)		(750)	
		1,414		2,114
Current assets				
Inventories	266		512	
Trade receivables	174		325	
Bank	64		–	
	504		837	
Less current liabilities:				
Amounts due in less than one year				
Trade payables	106		185	
Dividend	140		144	
Tax	160		96	
Bank overdraft	–		44	
	406		469	
Working capital		**98**		368

Net capital employed	**1,512**	2,482
Less non-current liabilities:		
Debenture loans (2011)	100	1,000
Total net assets	1,412	1,482
Financed by:		
Ordinary shares @ £1 each	1,000	1,000
Retained profits	412	482
	1,412	1,482

financial ratios for 20X8/9. Having calculated the ratios for both the budget and actual past year, the relevance of information provided will be reviewed.

Some terminology

Current assets are the assets which are expected to be sold or otherwise used up in the near future and include cash, inventories (stock) and trade and other receivables (debtors).

Current liabilities are the company's debts a obligations that are due within one year. They include short term debt, trade and other payables (creditors).

Working capital (also often called net current assets) = current assets − current liabilities.

Net capital employed = fixed assets + working capital.

Calculating and interpreting key profitability ratios

Profitability ratios

Three key ratios often calculated to obtain a first indication of the profitability of a business are return on capital employed, net profit margin and capital turnover. Table 11.3 shows the actual return on capital employed for 20X7/8 and industry averages for 20X7/8. The net profit margin and the capital turnover ratio are also shown. Further information about the ratios is provided after the table.

Return on capital employed

Although the term 'return on investment' is usually used when referring to divisional organizations, a more commonly used term in relation to all organizations is 'return on capital employed'. The ratio of profits to the investment or capital employed has often been considered to be a key ratio that can be used in order to judge whether an investment is worthwhile or a company is generating sufficient profits.

Table 11.3   Key profitability ratios

Ratio	Formula	Actual 20X7/8		Industry average
		(£)	(%)	(%)
Return on capital employed	$\dfrac{\text{Net profit (BIT)}}{\text{Net capital employed}} \times 100$	$\dfrac{\text{£425,000}}{\text{£1,512,000}} \times 100$	28.1	25
Net profit margin	$\dfrac{\text{Net profit (BIT)}}{\text{Sales}} \times 100$	$\dfrac{\text{£425,000}}{\text{£2,030,000}} \times 100$	20.9	20
Capital turnover	$\dfrac{\text{Sales}}{\text{Net capital employed}}$	$\dfrac{\text{£2,030,000}}{\text{£1,512,000}}$	1.34 X	1.25 X

For the calculation of return on capital employed, there are a number of alternative profit measures that could be used. If the aim is to judge how well trading, i.e. operational activities, have been performed then the net profit *before* tax and interest is recommended. If a business raises funds through issuing loan capital during the year, then net profit *after* interest will be a result that has been affected by *both* operational and financing decisions. Net profit margin before interest and tax in 20X7/8 was £425,000 (shown in bold on the Profit and Loss Account in Table 11.1).

Net capital employed = fixed or non-current assets (£1,414,000 in 20X7/8) + working capital (£98,000 in 20X7/8), i.e. £1,512,000 in total for 20X7/8 (shown in bold on the Balance Sheet in Table 11.2).

Working capital or (net current assets) = current assets (£504,000) − current liabilities (£406,000). This information is again shown in bold on the Balance Sheet.

The implication is that a higher ratio should reflect better performance, although reasons why this might not always be the case were discussed in Chapter 10.

As well as having the primary return on capital employed ratio, it is also helpful to have supplementary information explaining how a return on capital employed target has been achieved. It can either be through a change in the profit margin on sales (the profit margin ratios) or it can be through sales changing at a different rate to the change in capital employed (the capital turnover ratios).

Profit margin ratios

The **net profit margin** is the net profit as a percentage of sales and again the net profit is the net profit before interest and tax. Information on sales is available in the Profit and Loss Account.

As well as identifying the net profit to sales, other useful information can be gained by a further analysis of the elements that make up the net profit margin. For example, having identified the net profit to sales percentage it would also be of interest to identify the gross profit to sales percentage and also the relationship of costs, such as administration as a percentage of sales. This will be covered in a later section.

Capital turnover ratios

Another method of increasing the return on capital employed is to increase the **capital turnover** ratio, which is the level of sales in relation to the capital employed in a business. This ratio is usually quoted as a ratio rather than a percentage. It indicates the number of times that sales are greater than net capital employed. In this instance, sales in the year were 1.34 times more than the net capital employed.

Generally speaking, firms like to increase capital turnover. If sales are higher, overall profits will increase and therefore the higher sales are in relation to the capital employed, the higher will be the return on capital employed.

Activity 11.1

Are the following organizations likely to achieve a high return on capital employed by achieving a high profit margin or a high capital turnover?

1. A dealership for luxury cars.
2. A supermarket.

Activity 11.2

Calculate for 20X8/9:

 (i) The budgeted return on capital employed.
 (ii) The budgeted net profit margin percentage.
 (iii) The budgeted capital turnover ratio.

The pyramid of ratios

The key profitability ratios have been identified and it has been noted that return on capital employed can be increased if the profit margin is increased or the capital turnover is increased. It can also be noted that:

Return on capital employed = Net profit margin × capital turnover

$$\frac{\text{Net profit}}{\text{Net capital employed}} = \frac{\text{Net profit}}{\text{Sales}} \times \frac{\text{Sales}}{\text{Net capital employed}}$$

For 2007:

$$\frac{£425,000}{£1,512,000} = \frac{£425,000}{£2,030,000} \times \frac{£2,030,000}{£1,512,000}$$

$$28.1\% = 20.94\% \times 1.34$$

Reference is sometimes made to the 'pyramid of ratios', see Figure 11.1. At the top of the pyramid is the return on capital employed (often called the primary ratio), which identifies *what* has happened. As the pyramid is descended, greater explanation is obtained as to *why* any change has happened. At the first level from the top, the explanation might be that it is due to a change in profit margin or capital turnover. As the pyramid descends further details can be identified.

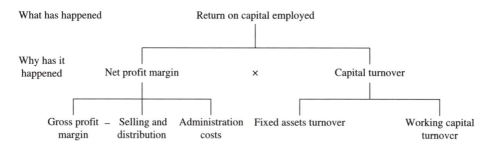

Figure 11.1 The pyramid of ratios

Commentary on changes in profitability ratios between actual results for 20X7/8 and budget for 20X8/9

The analysis indicates that there is expected to be a reduction in the return on capital employed (ROCE) from 28.1% in 20X7/8 to a proposed budget of 14.7% for 20X8/9. The industry average for similar companies to Bramble Ltd in the past year was 25%.

The budgeted return on capital employed is lower than the actual for 2007/8 because of a reduction in the budgeted net profit margin, which is expected to decline from 20.3% down to 15.4% and an expected fall in the capital turnover from 1.34 X down to 0.95 X. It would be helpful to analyse in more detail the change in the profit margins and capital turnover, and this is done in the next sections.

Further analysis of the profit margin ratio

The net profit margin has been calculated above and it would be useful to know what has caused this change, for example, is it because of a change in the gross profit margin earned by the business or is it because some of the costs, such as selling and distribution and administration, have increased as a percentage of sales? A number of actual ratios for 20X7/8 are shown in Table 11.4.

Table 11.4   Net profit margin ratios for 20X7/8

Ratio	Formula	Actual 20X7/8		Industry average (%)
			(%)	
Gross profit margin	$\dfrac{\text{Gross profit}}{\text{Sales}} \times 100$	$\dfrac{£910,000}{£2,030,000} \times 100$	44.8	45.0
Administration costs to sales	$\dfrac{\text{Administration}}{\text{Sales}} \times 100$	$\dfrac{£248,000}{£2,030,000} \times 100\%$	12.2	12.0
Selling and distribution costs (S and d) to sales	$\dfrac{\text{S and d}}{\text{Sales}} \times 100$	$\dfrac{£237,000}{£2,030,000} \times 100\%$	11.7	10.0

Activity 11.3

Calculate for 20X8/9

(a)

  (i)   The budgeted gross profit margin percentage.
  (ii) The budgeted administration costs to sales percentage.
  (iii) The budgeted selling and distribution cost to sales percentage.

(b) Identify possible reasons for the percentages between 2007/8 and discuss the implications of this analysis.

Further turnover ratios

Sometimes organizations like to analyse the capital turnover ratio in more detail, for example, it is possible to look at the relationship between sales and fixed assets and between sales and working capital to see if the change in turnover has been caused by either of these factors. Turnover ratios for the actual results for 20X7/8, along with industry averages, are shown in Table 11.5.

Table 11.5   Capital Turnover ratios for 2007/ 08

Ratio	Formula	Actual 20X7/8		Industry average
Fixed assets turnover	$\dfrac{\text{Sales}}{\text{Fixed assets}}$	$\dfrac{£2,030,000}{£1,414,000}$	1.44 X	1.5 X
Working capital turnover	$\dfrac{\text{Sales}}{\text{Working capital}}$	$\dfrac{£2,030,000}{£98,000}$	20.7 X	9 X

Activity 11.4

Calculate for 20X8/9

(a)

    (i) The budgeted fixed asset turnover ratio.
    (ii) The budgeted working capital turnover ratio.

(b) Identify possible reasons for the percentages between 2007/8 and discuss the implications of this analysis.

Review of key comments

So far the comments made have focused on identifying the changes between the actual results for 20X7/8 and the budgeted results for 20X8/9. It is important to recognize that the ratios in themselves are not necessarily a sign of good or bad performance. If the capital turnover ratio has declined because of investment in fixed assets and working capital that is required for the launch of a new product, for example, then a temporary decline in the ratio and in the overall return on capital employed may in fact be a 'necessary evil'. If the managers of the business are penalized for taking action that is in the best long-term interests of the business, then there is a danger that managers will focus on short-term results at the expense of the longer term. This issue is subject to further discussion in later chapters of the book.

A key lesson of ratio analysis is that it provides an indication of areas where further investigation is required. It is only after further investigation has taken place that an informed judgement can be taken.

Return on shareholders' funds

A further profitability ratio that is often calculated is return on shareholders' funds.

$$\text{Return on shareholders' funds} = \frac{\text{Net profit after taxation and preference dividend}}{\text{Ordinary share capital plus reserves}} \times 100\%$$

For 20X7/8

$$\text{ROSF} = \frac{£258{,}000}{£1{,}412{,}000} \times 100\% = 18.3\%$$

Net profit used for this ratio is after deducting tax and preference dividends (if any) as this is the profit that is available to the shareholders. Reserves in this case means retained profits, though there can be other forms of reserves shown as part of the equity. Shareholders can compare this return to the return from other investments.

Activity 11.5

Calculate the budgeted return on shareholders' funds for 20X8/9.

Using accounting ratios to assess whether too much or too little money is tied up in working capital

As well as profitability, different stakeholders will be interested in the ability of an organization to fund short-term and long-tem cash requirements. Two groups of accounting ratios can be used to help with the assessment of this area, the first group are known as the liquidity ratios and the second group are called efficiency ratios.

Liquidity ratios

The liquidity ratios compare the amount invested in different types of current assets and compare this to the current liabilities. If current liabilities are high compared with current assets, then potentially the business may have a problem in paying its short-term debts. Two ratios will be calculated, the current ratio and the quick ratio.

To illustrate the ratios, information will be used from the accounts of Bramble Ltd, with actual results for 20X7/8 and the industry average shown in Table 11.6.

Table 11.6 Liquidity ratios

Ratio	Formula	Actual 20X7/8		Industry average
Current ratio	$\dfrac{\text{Current assets}}{\text{Current liabilities}}$	$\dfrac{£504,000}{£406,000}$	1.24:1	1.9:1
Quick ratio	$\dfrac{\text{Current assets−inventory}}{\text{Current liabilities}}$	$\dfrac{£238,000}{£406,000}$	0.59:1	0.9:1

Current ratio

The current ratio measures the organization's ability to pay its way in the medium term and is the relationship between current assets and current liabilities.

Current assets at the end of 20X7/8 totalled £504,000. Current liabilities totalled £406,000 in 20X7/8. They included money owed to suppliers (trade payables) of £106,000, dividends declared by the company but not yet paid to the shareholders of £140,000 and £160,000 owed to the government in tax. The current assets are 1.24 times greater than the current liabilities.

It was traditionally a rule of thumb that the correct level of the current ratio should be around 2:1, i.e. current assets should be approximately twice as great as current liabilities. The argument is that if the ratio is lower than 2:1 then the company may have difficulty in paying its current liabilities. However, if the ratio is higher than 2:1 the argument is that the company has too many resources tied up in short-term assets. Normally investment in current assets does not yield such a high rate of return as investment in fixed assets, so the company should have as little as possible invested in current assets.

There are, however, many exceptions to the 2:1 rule. For example, large supermarket chains often have current ratios of around 0.6:1. This is not risky for them because nearly all sales are cash sales and inventory is sold very quickly. As large amounts of cash are being generated all the time, it is possible to have a lower current ratio. The current ratio should therefore be compared with the industry average (benchmark norms) and the trend over time should be examined.

Quick ratio

The quick ratio is also called the *acid test* and *liquid ratio*. **Quick assets** include cash and trade and other receivables. These can be turned into cash quickly, while inventories may take some time to sell and then even longer for the debts to be collected. The quick ratio therefore measures an organization's ability to pay its way in the short term, i.e. over the next few months.

Using the same reasoning as in the discussion of the current ratio it can be argued that the quick ratio should not be too low or too high. A traditional 'rule of thumb' was that the correct level of the ratio is 1:1. However, the 1:1 rule is only a very rough guide and there are many exceptions to it. The quick ratio should be compared with the industry average and managers should be aware of the trend of the ratio for their company over several years.

Activity 11.6

Calculate for 20X8/9

(i) The budgeted current ratio.
(ii) The budgeted quick ratio.

Having calculated the liquidity ratios it is possible to comment on whether these ratios indicate a situation where too much or too little money is tied up in the various categories of working capital.

Commentary on liquidity ratios

The proposed budget indicates an improvement in the current ratio for Bramble Ltd from 1.24:1 in 20X7/8 to 1.8:1 in 20X8/9, the industry norm is 1.9:1. The liquid ratio is expected to improve from 0.59:1 in 20X7/8 to 0.67:1 in 20X8/9, the industry norm is currently 0.9:1.

The budget indicates a planned improvement in both the current and quick ratios for the year 20X8/9, with both ratios moving towards the average for the industry. The liquidity of the company should be kept under review.

Efficiency ratios

The efficiency ratios examine the efficiency of a business to collect and pay its debts or achieve suitable inventory levels. Actual results for 20X7/8 and industry averages for the trade receivables, trade payables and inventory ratios are shown in Table 11.7.

Table 11.7 Efficiency ratios

Ratio	Formula	Actual 20X7/8		Industry average
Trade receivables ratio	$\dfrac{\text{Trade receivables}}{\text{Credit sales}} \times 365$	$\dfrac{£174,000}{£2,030,000} \times 365$	31 days	45 days
Trade payables	$\dfrac{\text{Trade payables}}{\text{Purchases of materials}} \times 365$	$\dfrac{£106,000}{£600,000} \times 365^*$	64 days	45 days
Inventory ratio (days)	$\dfrac{\text{Inventory}}{\text{Cost of sales}} \times 365$	$\dfrac{£266,000}{£1,120,000} \times 365$	87 days	50 days

* Details of purchases are not available on the financial statements provided for Bramble Ltd. You are advised that purchases in 20X7/8 were £600,000 and are assumed to be £720,000 in 20X8/9.

Trade receivables ratio

This ratio measures the average time it takes for the company to collect a debt. The trade receivables at the end of the year are divided by the *credit* sales in the year and multiplied by the number of days to calculate an average for the number of days of trade receivables outstanding at the end of the year. If a comparison is being made with competitors, then it will be necessary to estimate the level of credit sales for those competitors. For Bramble Ltd, it is advised that all sales are on credit.

Normally there will be an accepted average within the industry, say 60 days. The business should compare its ratio with the industry average and again also observe the trend of its ratio over time.

Trade payables ratio

This measures the average time it takes the company to pay its trade payables. It is important to compare like with like, daily purchases should not be compared with all current liabilities, since this will also include other payables such as dividends that have been declared, but not yet paid.

In identifying the appropriate level of trade payables a balance should be maintained. It should not be too high so that the company risks damaging its relationship with its suppliers, nor too low so that the company is paying out valuable cash before it is really necessary.

Sometimes it is not possible to identify the trade purchases from the annual accounts of organizations. In that case analysts might try to identify an approximation based on the cost of sales for the year, although such an approximation must be treated with care.

Inventory turnover (days)

This indicates the amount of inventory that is held in relation to the daily demand. Again, any ratio in isolation is not meaningful and should be compared with the industry average. If the ratio is too high it means that too much cash is tied up in stocks. There is also an increased risk that the firm has damaged or obsolete goods that it cannot sell. If the ratio is too low it means that the firm may not have enough stock available to satisfy customer demand. Most companies are very conscious of the amount of money tied up in inventory and try to reduce the amount by increasing the inventory turnover.

Often in manufacturing organizations, the inventory turnover is commonly quoted. This is the number of times that inventory is turned over in the year and can be calculated by dividing the cost of sales by the inventory holding:

$$\text{For } 20X7/8 = \frac{1,120,000}{266,000} \times 365 = 4.2 \text{ X}$$

Activity 11.7

Calculate for 20X8/9:

(i) The budgeted trade receivable days.
(ii) The budgeted trade payable days.
(iii) The budgeted number of days' stock held and also the budgeted inventory turnover.

In a number of textbooks it is suggested that the average inventory figure is used (average of opening and closing values) rather than just the year-end value in the Balance Sheet. If the information on opening inventory is not available however, then as illustrated in this chapter, just the closing balance can be used.

Calculating the operating cycle time

Having calculated the days outstanding for trade receivables, inventory and trade payables, it is possible to calculate the number of days it takes from the time that an organization pays for its raw materials to the time that it collects its debts from its customers. This period of time is known as the **operating cycle time** and can be calculated by adding: the number of days that material is held in inventory, plus the average number of days that it takes trade receivable to pay their debts, less the time that the organization takes to pay its own debts. The actual and budgeted operating cycle times for Bramble Ltd for 20X7/8 and 20X8/9 are shown in Table 11.8.

Table 11.8   Operating cycle time

	2007	20X8/9	Industry norm
Average holding of stock Plus	87	144	50
Average days trade receivables Less	31	50	45
Average days trade creditors	62	94	45
Operating cash cycle	56	100	50

Efficiency of management of working capital at Bramble Ltd

It is of concern that there has been a significant deterioration in both the trade receivables and inventory ratios, with debtor payments increasing from 31 to 50 days and stock holdings increasing from 87 to 144 days. Trade creditors have also increased from 62 to 94 days. The operating cycle time in 20X8/9 is planned to be substantially above that of the current industry average.

The management of Bramble Ltd should closely examine the assumptions of the budget that have led to this deterioration. If the high expected increase is due to a build-up of inventory for a new product that is about to be launched on the market, then the explanation for the increase in stock may be acceptable. The increase in trade receivables is also of concern unless this can be explained by a change in general terms of trade in the industry, e.g. competitors are allowing customers to take a longer time to pay their debts. At 94 days, the average time for the company to pay its suppliers seems very high and the company may find that these suppliers are reluctant to allow debts to continue at this level for a prolonged period. An investigation of the ratios might indicate that action is required to reduce the level of working capital. A checklist of potential areas of action is discussed in Chapter 12.

Overtrading

Overtrading can occur, when there are inadequate funds to finance the level of trade receivables and inventory. This can easily happen in businesses which are expanding fast. As sales increase, so do costs, the amounts owing to suppliers, inventory of work in progress and finished goods. These outflows of cash may not be balanced by inflows of cash from customers. A careful eye must therefore be kept on trends in the efficiency and liquidity ratios to identify potential indicators that a business is losing control of its cash flow.

Long-term solvency ratios – gearing

Banks and other investors use guideline ratios to help identify whether a company is at risk of being unable to pay its debts in the longer term. These are known as the gearing ratios. A company might be able to pay its debts in the short term, but there is also a concern about the longer term if profits were to fall in future years. If a company has borrowed money through raising loans and if profits are falling, it may struggle to repay the interest on those loans and the capital repayments.

Actual results for 20X7/8 and industry averages for the debt to equity and interest cover ratios are shown in Table 11.9.

Table 11.9   Solvency ratios

Ratio	Formula	Actual 20X7/8		Industry average
Gearing ratio	$\dfrac{\text{Long-term liabilities}}{\text{Equity} + \text{long-term liabilities}}$	$\dfrac{100{,}000}{(1{,}412{,}000 + 100{,}000)} \times 100\%$	6.6%	40%
Interest cover	$\dfrac{\text{Net profits (BIT)}_*}{\text{Interest paid}}$	$\dfrac{£425{,}000}{£7000}$	61:1	10:1

* BIT stands for 'before interest and tax'.

Gearing ratio

The **gearing ratio** calculates the relationship between long-term liabilities and shareholders' funds. Long-term debt includes debentures and other long-term loans which are falling due after one year. **Equity** is the owner's interest in a business and includes share capital and retained profits. A number of other reserves, including revaluation reserves (created when assets are revalued) and share premium account (created when shares are issued at a higher price than the nominal share price), are also included in the equity of a business.

Although the ratio can vary from industry to industry, a traditional guideline is that if long-term liability is greater than 50% of the total of the equity + long-term liability, then the company is beginning to have a high level of gearing. The gearing ratio for Bramble Ltd is considerably less than 7% of the total of equity + long-term liability, so this business would be seen to be low geared. Banks and shareholders would be likely to have less concern about longer-term solvency problems.

Interest cover

The **interest cover** ratio compares the net profit before tax and interest with the interest paid. If the net profit figure was less than the interest being paid, then creditors would be likely to feel concerned about the security of the interest payments. It is likely that they would wish that the interest cover is 2:1 and preferably higher.

The interest cover is very high and therefore the creditors would have little concern about the potential risk to the interest payments in the future, unless there was a serious reduction in the profitability of Bramble Ltd.

Activity 11.8

Calculate for 20X8/9:

(i) The budgeted gearing ratio.
(ii) The budgeted interest cover.

Commentary on solvency issues

The gearing ratio has increased from a low level of 6% to a much higher level of 40%. The interest cover is also reduced from 61:1 to 6.6:1. Although these levels are acceptable, it is unlikely that Bramble Ltd should expect to raise substantial funds in the immediate future through the issue of further loan capital.

Investment ratios

A final set of ratios to consider in this chapter are the investment ratios, which are of particular relevance to the shareholder. These include:

(i) The earnings per share.
(ii) Dividend yield.
(iii) Dividend cover.
(iv) The price/earnings ratio (P:E ratio).
(v) The earnings yield is the inverse of the price/earnings ratio.

Actual results for 20X7/8 and industry averages for the investment ratios are shown in Table 11.10.

Earnings per share

The **earnings per share** (EPS) can be calculated by dividing the profits after tax by the number of shares. The earnings per share are used in other ratios for comparison purposes.

Table 11.10   Investment ratios

Ratio	Formula		Actual 20X7/8 £'000	Industry average
Earnings per share	$\dfrac{\text{Profit after tax}}{\text{Number of shares}}$	$\dfrac{£258,000}{1,000,000}$	25.8p	23p
Dividend yield	$\dfrac{\text{Dividend per share}}{\text{Market price of the share}} \times 100$	$\dfrac{14.0 \text{ pence}}{210 \text{ pence}} \times 100$	9.3%	7%
Dividend cover	$\dfrac{\text{Earnings per share}}{\text{Dividend per share}}$	$\dfrac{25.8 \text{ pence}}{14.0 \text{ pence}}$	1.84:1	0.9:1
P:E ratio	$\dfrac{\text{Market price per share}}{\text{Earnings per share}}$	$\dfrac{210 \text{ pence}}{25.8 \text{ pence}}$	8.14:1	9:1
Earnings yield	$\dfrac{\text{EPS}}{\text{Market price per share}}$	$\dfrac{25.8 \text{ pence}}{210 \text{ pence}}$	12.3%	11.1%

Dividend yield

Dividends are payments made by a company to its shareholders. The shareholder will be concerned with the likely dividend payments and the risk to these payments. The dividend for 20X7/8 (see Profit and Loss Account for Bramble Ltd) was £140,000. 1,000,000 £1 shares have been issued (see Balance Sheet). Therefore for 20X7/8 the dividend per share is 14.0 pence.

Each share has a nominal value of £1, however, this is not the same as the market price at which the share is traded. For this example, it will be assumed that the shares are currently traded at £2.10 per share.

The dividend yield ratio is the dividend as a percentage of the market price of the share. Some shareholders will hold shares because of the dividend yield. The shareholder (or prospective shareholder) can identify this dividend yield and decide whether it is sufficient when compared with a potentially safer investment such as a building society or bank.

Dividend cover

As well as identifying the return, a shareholder will be concerned with the risk associated with an investment in Bramble Ltd. If the earnings per share are much greater than the dividend per share, then a shareholder may have more confidence that the company will continue to be able to fund a dividend payout in the future. However, if the earnings per share are only a little more than the dividend per share, then investors may be more concerned for the future. For Bramble in 20X7/8, the earnings per share are 1.84 times greater than the dividend per share.

Price/earnings ratio

The **price/earnings ratio** is the relationship between the market price per share and the earnings per share. The P:E ratio can be used to give an indication as to whether this is a cheap or an expensive share. For example, if the P:E ratio for similar companies to Bramble Ltd, operating in the same industry was on average 9:1, this might be an indication that the share price of Bramble Ltd is a bargain. However, this can be a dangerous assumption.

Firstly, the EPS calculation will be based on the last published financial reports, so although the share price may be the current share price, the EPS figure can be a year out of date.

Secondly, Bramble Ltd may be seen as a poorly managed company. If investors anticipate that profits and return on capital employed will decline between 20X7/8 and 20X8/9, other companies in the industry may be seen as a better investment.

Earnings yield

The earnings yield is the inverse of the price/earnings ratio and is the amount of earnings for every pound of the market price of the share.

Activity 11.9

Calculate for 20X8/9:

(i) The earnings per share.
(ii) The budgeted dividend yield assuming a market price per share of £2.00.
(iii) The budgeted dividend cover for 20X8/9.
(iv) The P:E ratio given the assumed share price.
(v) The earnings yield.

Commentary on the investment ratios

In 20X7/8 the dividend yield and dividend cover were higher than the average for competitors. This indicates that investors wishing to invest in order to gain an annual income are achieving a better return than can be obtained elsewhere, and the company has a better cover on this dividend than other companies. The P:E ratio for 20X7/8 was lower than for key competitors. This may indicate that the shares of Bramble Ltd are relatively cheap. The management of Bramble Ltd should consider action to counteract the impression that the company is an inferior investment to competitors.

Note that it is often suggested managers in the UK and USA are more concerned with short-term financial performance than managers in other countries such as Germany and Japan. A key reason given is the higher proportion of funds raised in the form of share capital in the UK and USA. Managers in these countries are therefore more concerned about shareholder reaction and shareholders usually take a shorter-term view of investments.

Limitations of ratio analysis

Ratio analysis can potentially be useful in identifying areas where further investigation is required. However, the limitations of ratio analysis should also be considered. A number of these issues will be considered further in later chapters of the book, however, a brief review is included below.

1. Ratios provide a restricted vision of the performance of an organization. They provide information on financial performance over the past. This can be a poor indicator of performance in the future.
2. Ratios provide a relative rather than an absolute measure of performance. In Chapter 10, the problems associated with a relative measure of performance – such as return on investment/capital employed – were illustrated with an example of investments being considered for Divisions A and B of Abingdon Ltd.
3. Balance Sheet ratios are based on the balances at period ends. An organization might take special action to reduce the balances for these single time periods and they might not be representative for the rest of the year. If a comparison is being made between companies, a further complication can arise if they have different year ends (e.g. in one company the accounting year runs from January to December, while in another it runs from April to March).
4. Comparisons between companies and between years are sometimes difficult because of the problem of obtaining like-for-like information. In calculating the trade receivables or trade payables figure, for example, it is necessary to know the credit sales and credit purchases. This information is likely to be difficult to obtain for different organizations.
5. Book value may be significantly less than market value. Much of the value of some businesses is in the form of intellectual capital such as patents and trademarks and in the skills of employees, yet these items are excluded from the Balance Sheet. The prudence concept means that a number of items of expenditure such as marketing and basic research are also treated as expenses to be charged to the Profit and Loss Account, while it could be argued that at least part of such expenditure should be treated as assets of the businesses. Calculations based on the net capital employed, as represented by the Balance Sheet value, can therefore give a misleading idea of the true return being generated by the business. The implication of following Generally Accepted Accounting priniciples (GAAP) will be discussed further in Chapter 21. Although accounting standards provide strong guidance on the way in which assets and expenditure should be treated, some flexibility can still exist and this can mean that a true comparison between organizations on a like-for-like basis can be difficult.

6. Some organizations may indulge in creative accounting. This can occur when directors deliberately set out to manipulate the financial statements through, for example:

  (i) Overstatement of revenue. This can happen in a number of ways, such as two companies selling goods to each other or pre-dispatching goods (for example as soon as an order is received, therefore inflating sales and profits).
  (ii) Treating expenses of the business as assets, thus increasing profits.
  (iii) Overstating the value of assets, through obtaining a revaluation of assets at artificially high values.

Following the scandals in a number of public companies in recent years, including Enron and World Com in America, corporate governance procedures have been tightened in many countries and it is to be hoped that there is less scope for irregularities in the future.

Summary

A range of stakeholders, shareholders, managers and workers, suppliers, lenders to the organization, employee representatives, competitors and customers all have an interest in the performance of an organization.

  Ratios extracted using information from the financial accounting statements, the Profit and Loss Account and the Balance Sheet can help provide an indication of performance in terms of profitability, liquidity, efficiency and solvency, and as an investment. Ratios provide only a partial view of performance and must be treated with care. They provide an indication of areas where further investigation and explanation might be required, in isolation they should not be used to provide a final judgement on performance.

Further reading

Holmes, G., Gee, P. and Sugden, A. (2004) *Interpreting Company Reports & Accounts*, 9th edn. FT/Prentice-Hall.

Answers to activities

Activity 11.1

  (i) A dealership of luxury cars may not sell many cars, but on those that it does, it should make a high profit margin.
  (ii) A supermarket should achieve a high return on capital employed through achieving a high capital turnover, even if the profit margins on the items it sells may not be great.

Activity 11.2

The budgeted return on capital employed	14.7%
The budgeted net profit margin percentage	15.4%
The budgeted capital turnover ratio	0.95 X

Activity 11.3

The budgeted gross profit margin percentage	45.1%
The budgeted administration costs to sales percentage	15.0%
The budgeted selling and distribution cost to sales percentage	14.7%

Discussion of the net profit margin ratios

The proposed budget net profit margin percentage has fallen from 20.9% in 20X7/8 to 15.4%. Although the budgeted gross profit margin is expected to be similar to the actual for 20X7/8, there is a substantial increase expected in both administration costs as a percentage of sales (12.2% increasing to 15%) and selling and distribution costs as percentage of sales (11.7% increasing to 14.7%). The reasons for these increases should be identified to see if they can be justified. The management might consider requesting some sort of analysis (e.g. zero-based budgeting) that demonstrates the additional benefits gained from the extra expenditure should be undertaken. The gross profit margin has not changed significantly, but further understanding of cost and price changes in the company and in the market place would be helpful.

Activity 11.4

The budgeted fixed asset turnover ratio	1.12 X
The budgeted working capital turnover ratio	6.4 X

Discussion of turnover ratios

Budgeted capital turnover declines substantially from 1.34 X down to 0.95 X. Although sales are budgeted to increase by 17% from the level in 20X7/8, net capital employed is expected to increase by 64% (£1,512,000 in 20X7/8 to £2,482,000 for 20X8/9). Looking at the Balance Sheet, it is possible to see that the largest increase has been a substantial increase in fixed assets, with an increase in net book value from £1,414,000 to £2,114,000.

If the benefit of the additional investment is to be gained over the next few years, then this will have been worthwhile. An understanding of the business plans which would give an insight into future expected trends would be helpful.

Activity 11.5

Return on shareholders' funds for 20X8/9 = 14.4%.

Activity 11.6

The budgeted current ratio	1.8:1
The budgeted quick ratio	0.7:1

Activity 11.7

The budgeted trade receivable days	50 days
The budgeted trade payable days	94 days
The budgeted number of days' stock held	144 days
The budgeted inventory turnover	2.54 X

Activity 11.8

The budgeted gearing ratio	40%
The budgeted interest cover	6.6 X

Activity 11.9

Earnings per share	21.4p
The budgeted dividend yield	7.2%
The budgeted dividend cover	1.49 X
The P:E ratio	9.3:1
Earnings yield	10.7%

Discussion questions

1. In order to increase the profitability of a company it is important to increase the capital turnover.
2. Profitability ratios are more important than liquidity ratios.
3. Why might it be acceptable for there to be an increase in debtors days and inventory days.
4. Explain the difference between liquidity and solvency.
5. What is the benefit of the P:E ratio? Will all the companies in a particular industry have a similar P:E ratio?
6. Accounting ratios are of little value to managing a business.

Exercises

(Questions with numbers in bold have answers at the back of the book.)

Q11.1 Digiprint Ltd is a producer of electronic and electrical products which are sold through a number of retail outlets such as Comet, Currys and Dixons. The market has expanded by 10% over the last year and the company says it has increased its market share while improving profit margins. To support the increase in production needed to meet the demand, the company has made substantial investments in new automated manufacturing systems. The number of employees is expected to decline from 250 in 200X7/8 to 200 in 20X8/9.

Required:

 (i) Calculate key profitability, liquidity, efficiency and solvency ratios.
 (ii) As far as the information allows, provide an analysis of the performance of Digiprint over the last year. Identify further information that would be helpful for a complete analysis to be made.

	Digiprint Ltd Profit and Loss Account for the year to 31 March	
	20X6/7	20X7/8
	£'000	£'000
Sales	2,400	2,880
Cost of sales	1,200	1,500
Gross profit	1,200	1,380
Less:		
Operating expenses	590	800
Profit before interest and tax	610	580

Interest	50	90
Profit before tax	560	490
Taxation	224	150
Profit after tax	336	340
Dividends	134	150
Retained profit for year	202	190
Retained profit b/f	308	510
Retained profit c/f	510	700

Purchases of raw materials were £800,000 in 20X6/7 and £1,050,000 in 20X7/8.

Digiprint Ltd
Balance Sheet as at 31 March

	20X6/7		20X7/8	
	£'000	£'000	£'000	£'000
Fixed assets				
Cost	1,640		1,920	
Less depreciation	(450)		(580)	
	1,180	1,190		1,340
Current assets				
Inventories	320		445	
Trade receivables	500		940	
Bank	45		0	
	865		1,385	
Less current liabilities:				
Amounts due in less than one year				
Trade payables	137		195	
Dividend	134		150	
Interest payable	50		90	
Taxation	224		150	
	545		585	
Working capital		320		800
Net capital employed		1,510		2,140
Less non-current liabilities:				
Debenture loans (2010)		300		740
Total net assets		1,210		1,400
Financed by:				
Ordinary shares @ £1 each		700		700
Retained profits		510		700
		1,210		1,400

Q11.2 Anglesea Ltd has launched a new range of sea food and has sold this range heavily to supermarkets. The accounts for 20X7/8 have just been published.

Required:

Using ratio analysis as a basis for assessing performance, provide an analysis of the company over the last year. What further information is required for a fuller assessment?

Anglesea Ltd
Profit and Loss Account for
the year to 31 March

	20X6/7 £'000	20X7/8 £'000
Sales	2,880	3,744
Cost of sales	1,320	1,950
Gross profit	1,560	1,794
Less:		
Administration expenses	450	600
Selling and distribution expenses	258	440
Profit before interest and tax	852	754
Interest	50	105
Profit before tax	802	649
Taxation	321	260
Profit after tax	481	389
Dividends	120	156
Retained profit for year	361	233
Retained profit b/f	480	841
Retained profit c/f	841	1,074

Purchases of raw materials were £650,000 in 20X6/7 and £950,000 in 20X7/8.

Anglesea Ltd
Balance Sheet as at 31 March

	20X7/8 £'000	£'000	20X8/9 £'000	£'000
Fixed assets				
Cost	1,968		2,496	
Less depreciation	(506)		(696)	
		1,462		1,800
Current assets				
Inventories	416		667	
Trade receivables	600		1,363	

Bank	68		40
	1,084		2,070
Less current liabilities:			
Amounts due in less than one year			
Trade payables	151		254
Dividend	120		156
Tax	50		105
Bank overdraft	384		331
	705		846
Working capital		379	1,224
Net capital employed		1,841	3,024
Less non-current liabilities:			
Debenture loans (2009)		500	1,450
Total net assets		1,341	1,574
Financed by:			
Ordinary shares @ £1 each		500	500
Retained profits		841	1,074
		1,341	1,574

Q11.3 The current equity of Empire PLC is £2,800,000. This consists of issued share capital of 1,000,000 shares at a nominal value of £1 each and general and other reserves of £1,800,000. The current market price per share is £3.20. A dividend totalling £100,000 for the year has been declared. A 6% debenture loan of £500,000 has been issued. The profit before interest and tax is £400,000 and tax is £185,000.

Calculate the following ratios and discuss what implications may be drawn:

(i) The earnings per share.
(ii) The gearing ratio.
(iii) The interest cover.
(iv) The dividend cover.

FUNDING THE BUSINESS

Objectives

When you have completed this chapter you should be able to:

- Prepare a cash flow budget.
- Explain the need for permanent and temporary funding requirements.
- Describe the main sources of long-term finance and calculate the weighted average cost of this finance.
- Describe the benefits of alternative capital structures.
- Explain the need for temporary sources of funds and describe the main sources of such funds.

Introduction

This chapter considers alternative methods of funding the business, either through raising new funds or through improving controls on the use of existing assets, in particular working capital.

In Chapter 8, the preparation and importance of cash budgeting was explained. In Chapter 11, the use of accounting ratios as a means of assessing performance was illustrated with the example of Bramble Ltd. This chapter reviews the cash budget for Bramble Ltd and considers the different forms of funding and controls that might be used to overcome a cash flow shortfall.

In some instances there is a need to fund investments of a long-term nature, for example non-current (fixed) assets or a permanent increase in current assets (e.g. inventory and accounts receivable). Where this is the case, then it is generally considered that long-term sources of funds, such as share capital or long-term loans, should be raised. The various sources of long-term funds and the cost of such funds are identified in this chapter.

Other cash requirements are of a more temporary nature, for example sometimes sales are seasonal in nature. When sales are low or prior to a high period of sales, the level of inventories may increase and cash balances may fall. The problem should eventually be resolved when sales increase and the cash from these sales is collected, but in the short term there may be a cash shortfall. Short-term funding solutions may involve releasing funds through improving the control of working capital by reviewing the management of trade receivables, inventory or trade payables. It may also be possible to make use of short-term loans or a bank overdraft.

Identifying the funding requirement

From the Balance Sheet of Bramble Ltd, shown in Chapter 11 (Table 11.2), it can be seen that the cash balance moved from a positive £64,000 at the end of 20X7/8 to a budgeted overdraft of £44,000 at the end of 20X8/9. In Table 12.1 the forecast cash inflows and outflows for Bramble Ltd are shown in detail, by quarter for the forthcoming year. The opening cash balance, cash inflows, cash outflows and closing cash balance for each quarter are shown. The last column shows the summary cash flow forecast for the year.

Table 12.1 Cash budget 20X8/9 for Bramble Ltd

	April– June 2008 £'000	July– September 2008 £'000	October– December 2008 £'000	January– March 2008 £'000	April 2008– March2009 £'000
(1) Opening cash balance	64	(148)	(29)	241	**64**
(2) Add cash inflows					
Receipts from sales	535	440	795	449	**2,219**
Long-term loan		900			**900**
Total cash available (1)+(2)	599	1,192	766	682	**3,183**
Deduct cash outflows (payments)					
Wages	101	107	110	116	**434**
Materials	146	175	160	160	**641**
Production overheads	46	52	56	57	**211**
Administration	67	85	95	97	**344**
Selling and distribution	85	85	86	86	**342**
Dividends	140				**140**
Taxation	160				**160**
Interest	2	17	18	18	**55**
Capital expenditure		700		200	**900**
(3) Total cash outflows (payments)	747	1,221	525	734	**3,227**
Closing cash balance (1)+(2)−(3)	(148)	(29)	241	(44)	**(44)**

Given the assumptions in the plan, additional funding is required in order to avoid a substantial negative cash balance in the quarter July to September 2008, due to the purchase of a fixed asset for £700,000, as well as relatively low cash receipts compared with the expenditure on wages, materials and overheads. The latter is due to a decision to build inventories prior to a high sales period in the third quarter.

The assumption in the plan is that the funding problem will be overcome through means of a long-term loan of £900,000 in July. It is expected that this will mean that the requirement for a bank overdraft can be kept at a relatively low level.

It can be noted that cash receipts from sales are lower than the sales revenue in the year shown in the Profit and Loss Account of Bramble Ltd (Table 11.1). This is because the level of trade receivables (amounts owed by customers) is budgeted to have increased by the end of the year. The level of cash expenditure is also different from the costs, since depreciation is recognized as a cost of the business but is not a cash flow, and there are also changes in the level of inventory and accounts payable. A cash flow statement in the format required for a published set of accounts is shown at the end of this chapter.

Identifying and meeting the permanent and temporary funding requirement

If the business is expanding and requires a long-term investment in additional non-current and current assets then there will be a permanent requirement for additional funds to finance this investment. If demand for current assets increases for temporary reasons, for example prior to a high sales period, there will be a requirement for funding on a temporary basis.

Permanent funding

Additional permanent funds are required when:

(a) The business is first established, in order to acquire any necessary non-current (fixed assets), such as land and building and to provide the initial working capital, in the form of inventories and trade receivables.
(b) Expansion and increased investment in assets is required at a greater rate than can be financed out of retained profits.

Traditional guidance is that where the requirement for funds is of a permanent nature and for the longer term, an organization should look to finance this requirement through long-term sources of finance. The reason is that this is seen as less risky. If a company were to borrow money using a bank overdraft, the bank can demand repayment of the overdraft at very short notice. If a business has invested its funds in, for example, fixed assets, then it may be extremely difficult to meet any demand for immediate repayment of the loan.

A number of long-term sources of finance have been identified previously and are discussed further below. These include share capital, loan capital, government grants, and sale and leaseback of assets. It should also be noted that rather than purchasing assets outright, some organizations lease or acquire assets on hire purchase.

Share capital

One method of raising finance is to sell a share of the business to a third party. For young businesses including business start-ups, finance can be raised from venture capitalists. Venture capitalists are interested in businesses that have high growth and profit potential and are usually looking to invest several hundreds of thousands of pounds, in return for shares in the business. For investments of less than £250,000, it may be possible to interest a 'business angel'. Business angels are wealthy individuals who invest in high-growth businesses in return for equity. They also often make their own skills, experience and contacts available to the company. Some business angels invest on their own, while others are part of a network.

For larger businesses, it may be possible to raise funds from the issue of shares on the stock exchange. The issue of share capital is usually in the form of ordinary shares, and this can be expensive for the firm. If the business grows and significant profits are generated, ordinary shareholders will expect to receive a portion of these profits in the form of dividends. Ordinary shareholders should also expect a higher rate of return to allow for the risk that the company is wound up. In the event of that occurring, they will only receive a payment after the lenders and creditors have been paid. As the long-term cost of equity finance can be high, the issue of ordinary shares is not always popular with owners of a business. However, a benefit of ordinary share capital to a business is that if it does not generate profits, then the company can avoid paying a dividend, so ordinary share capital does not involve the burden of debt that occurs with loans.

Although gaining a stock market quotation gives greater access to external sources of capital, the actual process of raising money on the stock exchange is very expensive. To gain a quotation on the exchange can cost up to 10% of the initial amount raised by the share issue. Gaining a public quotation also means that the rights of the existing shareholders are reduced considerably and there is a danger of being taken over. There are also strict regulations concerning the disclosure of financial and other information.

As well as ordinary shares, a firm may issue preference shares. These shares will normally pay a fixed percentage rate of dividend to investors each year, although this is at the discretion of the directors. If the company is wound up, then preference shareholders will have priority for payment over ordinary shareholders. Because the risk is higher for the company than ordinary shares (and less for the investor), the cost to the company is normally less.

Long-term loans

With **loan capital**, the lender will enter an agreement with the company to lend a sum of money in return for regular, fixed amounts of interest on the debt and agreed capital repayments. A term loan is offered by a bank or other financial institution to an organization. A **debenture** is a loan that is frequently divided into a number of units and investors are invited to purchase the number of units they require.

Lenders have priority over shareholders as the loans are usually secured on the assets of the business and if the company fails to repay the loan, then assets can be seized. Loans are a very important source of finance for many companies and are also often cheaper than equity capital as interest on loan capital is tax deductible.

Retained earnings

When a business earns profits, it has a choice to distribute these profits to shareholders, for example in the form of dividends, or to retain the profits in the business. Retained profits represent a major source of long-term finance for many organizations and although they are not cash, they do represent the cash dividends that could have been paid to shareholders.

Grants

Grants may be provided in some circumstances by the government and the EU.

Sale and leaseback

This occurs when a business sells its assets to a leasing company and then leases it back. Sale and leaseback will release funds that can be used for other purposes. See Figure 12.1.

Sale and leaseback has not always been judged a total success. During its ownership of Center Parcs, Deutsche Bank sold off the combined property assets in a £465 million sale-and-leaseback deal. In 2006 the new owners decided to reunite the operating company with the assets. Analysts suggested that problems had occurred because the assets were not owned. It had been found to be more difficult to fund improvements and because of onerous leases only 10 per cent of the funding was in the form of equity, which meant that any trading problems had a disproportionate impact.*

Source: Reported in *The Times*, 4 May 2006.

* The problems that can arise when a high proportion of capital is raised from non-equity sources are discussed later in the chapter.

Figure 12.1 Sale and leaseback at Center Parcs

Hire purchase or leasing

Hire purchase and **leasing** are means of obtaining the use of an asset before payment is completed. They are similar insofar as payment for the use of the asset is spread over a period of time, rather than being made in a lump sum with the assets acting as security on the debt. With HP, the hiree becomes the owner of the equipment at the end of the HP agreement. With leasing, the lessee has no automatic ownership right of the asset. Usually leasing is a cheaper option because favourable tax breaks allow the lessor to charge lower rentals.

In deciding which source of funds to use, it will be important to consider the cost and the risk that is associated with each source of capital.

Costs and risks of different capital structures

Businesses have a choice over the capital structure that they employ. They can either decide to raise funds predominantly through debt finance by the raising of loans or through issuing share capital. Different capital structures will involve different costs and different risks.

Cost of capital

The cost of each source of long-term finance can be expressed as a rate of return that the firm needs to pay the providers of the funds.

Cost of debt

The **cost of debt** is the interest that needs to be repaid on the loan capital divided by the market value of that loan capital. Interest is tax deductible so the amount of tax that is saved should be taken into account in the cost of the interest payment. The cost of debt of Bramble Ltd is considered in Figure 12.2.

Bramble Ltd, at the end of 20X7/8, has £100,000 of debt on which interest of 7% is paid. Interest is tax deductible and the rate of tax is 30%. The market value of this debt has fallen to £80,000.

Step 1. To calculate the cost of interest to the business:

- Interest of 7% is paid on £100,000, so £7000 is payable.
- If the tax rate is 30% the true cost of interest is £7000 × (1−0.3) = £4900.

Step 2. Calculate the cost of the debt given a market value of the loan of £80,000:

If the market value of the debt has fallen to £80,000, then the cost of debt is

$$\frac{£4900}{£80,000} = 6.1\%.$$

Figure 12.2   Cost of debt for Bramble Ltd

Activity 12.1

Alpha Ltd has £500,000 of debt on which interest of 5% is paid. The market value of this debt has fallen to £400,000. The tax rate is 30%.
   Calculate the cost of debt.

Cost of equity

$$\text{The } \textbf{cost of equity} = \frac{\text{Dividend per share}}{\text{Current market price per share}} + \text{growth rate of dividends}$$

The cost of equity capital for Bramble Ltd is illustrated in Figure 12.3.

Bramble Ltd has 1,000,000 shares, which at the end of 20X7/8 are quoted on the stock exchange at £2.10 per share. A dividend of 14p per share is currently paid. The cost of capital is

$$\frac{14p}{210p} \times 100\% = 6.7\%^*$$

* For the exercises in this chapter, it will be assumed that there is no growth in dividends expected.

Figure 12.3   Cost of equity for Bramble Ltd

Activity 12.2

Alpha Ltd has 1,000,000 shares, which are quoted on the stock exchange at £3.00 per share. A dividend of 30p per share is paid.
    What is the cost of equity?

Weighted average cost of capital

The **weighted average cost of capital (WACC)** is calculated by multiplying the cost of each capital component by its proportional weight and then summing. The weighted average cost of capital of Bramble Ltd is as shown in Figure 12.4.

Source of finance	Market value	Proportion (%)	Cost of capital (%)	Weighted average cost of capital (%)
Equity	£2,100,000	95.9	6.7	6.42
Debt	£80,000	4.1	6.1	0.25
	£2,180,000	100.0		6.67

The market value of the equity is 1,000,000 shares at a market value of £2.10 per share.

Figure 12.4   Weighted average cost of capital for Bramble Ltd

---

Activity 12.3

Given the information in Activities 12.1 and 12.2, calculate the weighted average cost of capital of Alpha Ltd.

Financial and investment risk

In raising finance, it is important to consider:

1. The financial risk.
2. The investment risk.

Financial risk is the additional risk a shareholder bears when a company uses debt in addition to equity financing. Share capital is considered to be low risk because dividends do not need to be paid if profits are low. Loan capital is a higher-risk form of funding as interest must be paid whether or not the firm is earning profits.

The **investment risk** is the risk that a company or project will not have adequate cash flow to meet financial obligations.

Financial risk

Figure 12.5 illustrates the earnings per share for Bramble Ltd given different levels of profit and capital structures.

With funds raised through loan capital there is a much greater variation in the earnings per share. Although it is higher given high profits, if profits fall to £100,000, the earnings per share will be only 3 pence.

In 20X8/9 Bramble Ltd is considering raising a further £900,000 in order to fund an investment and is considering whether it should raise this finance through either:

(a) A 7% debenture loan (this would give a total loan of £1,000,000 as the company currently has issued loan capital of £100,000).
(b) The issue of a further 450,000 shares, which will be issued at a price of £2 per share.

The management would like to consider the effect of the alternative methods of raising finance given three different scenarios on the level of profits that will be earned in 20X8/9:

- Scenario 1. Profits before interest and tax will be £600,000.
- Scenario 2. Profit before interest and tax will be £365,000 (this is the current plan).
- Scenario 3. Profits before interest and tax will be £100,000.

Figure 12.5   Earnings per share given different levels of profit and capital structure

If funds are raised through a loan

	Scenario 1 (£)	Scenario 2 (£)	Scenario 3 (£)
Profit before interest	600,000	365,000	100,000
Interest (on loan of £1,000,000)	70,000	70,000	70,000
Profit after interest (in full year)	530,000	295,000	30,000
Number of shares	1,000,000	1,000,000	1,000,000
Earning per share	53 pence	29.5 pence	3 pence

If funds are raised through issuing further share capital

	Scenario 1 (£)	Scenario 2 (£)	Scenario 3 (£)
Profit before interest	600,000	365,000	100,000
Interest (on existing loan)	7,000	7,000	7,000
Profit after interest (in full year)	593,000	358,000	93,000
Number of shares	1,450,000	1,450,000	1,450,000
Earning per share	40.9 pence	24.7 pence	6.4 pence

Figure 12.5   (*Continued*)

Gearing and the cost of capital

The traditional view of gearing is that as more debt is introduced into the capital structure of an organization, the WACC will fall because debt charges are less than the cost of share capital and there is a tax benefit as interest is tax deductible. However, as gearing increases, equity holders will ask for higher returns to offset the increased risk and a point is reached when the WACC starts to rise, so there is therefore an optimum point at which WACC is minimized. This is illustrated in Figure 12.6.

It is not only the shareholders who will be concerned if firms take on very high levels of loans. Customers, suppliers and employees may all have increased concerns because of the fear of a default on interest payments. A further argument against high borrowing can also occur when a firm is investing heavily in new assets. When this happens, capital allowances granted on the purchase of these assets may reduce the tax bill to the point that interest charges cannot be offset against chargeable income. Capital structure theory, including that of Modigliani and Miller, can be reviewed in textbooks such as Arnold (2005).

Given the above discussion, it should be noted that when undertaking an investment appraisal, individual sources of finance should not be linked to individual projects. Raising debt or equity, even if it is for a specific project, will have an impact on the overall weighted average cost of capital.

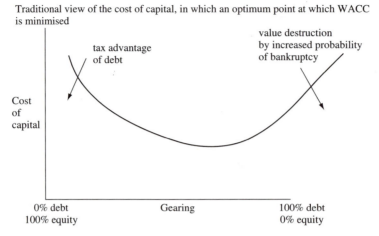

Figure 12.6 Weighted average cost of capital

Investment risk

Some investments may have the potential of a high return, but there may be a high risk of non-achievement of the targets.

A general guideline is that *if an investment is high risk*, then it would be safer to consider *low-risk funding*, e.g. raising equity capital. Although high profits may be earned, there is also a considerable risk that if the investment fails, then the long-term future of the business is at risk, as it will not be able to fund the interest payments. Firms such as new biotechnology companies, which are undertaking very high-risk investment, have almost universally raised money from a share issue. This can be through a sale to a venture capital company or, if the company is listed on a stock exchange, through the issue of further shares.

If an investment is *low risk* then *higher-risk funding* could be considered. Utility companies, such as water or electricity and gas, have traditionally been considered to be safe investments. They are assured a steady flow of cash payments from consumers. Much of their funding is raised through the issue of loan capital.

Temporary funding requirements

It has been noted above that businesses may require long-term sources of finance to fund permanent increases in assets. A distinction can be made between 'permanent' and 'temporary' funding requirements. The level of investment in assets such as inventory and trade receivables can vary over the year. For example, in Bramble Ltd a high sales period occurred in the period October to December with cash receipts from sales of £795,000, while sales and cash receipts in the period July to September were much lower. It might be possible to keep the levels of inventory constant by producing goods 'just-in-time' to meet customer requirement. For many businesses, however, this is likely to be difficult and is certainly likely to be expensive. Bramble Ltd, for example, might have to employ a very large workforce to meet demand on a just-in-time basis during the period October to December, and the workforce would be underemployed during the period July to September.

Figure 12.7 illustrates the concept of permanent and temporary funding requirements. The bottom sloping line represents the permanent fixed plus permanent working capital held by the business. The top sloping line reflects the maximum level of assets held by the company. The amount of assets will fluctuate between minimum and maximum levels. At certain periods, due for example to adverse trading conditions, the level of working capital, e.g. inventory and trade receivables, will increase. At other times, with high cash sales, the level of inventory and trade receivables will fall. The x's on the diagram in Figure 12.7 represent the balance of total assets at the end of each month with the variation due to changes in the level of working capital held.

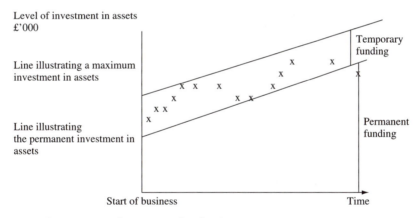

Figure 12.7   Permanent and temporary levels of investment in assets

The type of funds that are required will depend on whether the funds are needed for a long or a short period of time. Where there is a temporary funding requirement, it would be very expensive to raise long-term sources of finance. This would be expensive both in terms of the cost of raising the finance and then in funding the interest or dividend payments during periods when this level of funding was not required. If the funding requirement is for the short term, for example funding a temporary increase in stock during a low period of sales, then it would be far cheaper to look to raise or release funds from working capital or use short-term loans.

In the next section, a number of methods for releasing funds are considered, including action to increase cash inflows by increasing sales and reducing the level of debts or by short-tem borrowing and actions to reduce cash outflows by taking appropriate action on stocks and trade payables.

Increasing cash inflows

Action to increase cash inflows by increasing sales and reducing the level of debtors

Such action could include:

(i) Improving credit management. Ensuring invoices despatched on time, the age of debts are identified and debts collected promptly.
(ii) Providing discounts to customers who pay promptly.
(iii) Discounting prices to generate additional sales and reduce stocks.
(iv) Debt factoring. This involves a factoring company taking over the management of a company's trade debt in return for commission. The factor will charge an administration fee of between 1% and 4% of sales turnover to manage and collect debts. Where finance is advanced the charge will be a charge of between 3% and 5% above base rate.
(v) Invoice discounting. The factoring company will again provide an advance on the debts of a company, however, management of those debts is retained by the seller. Since the factoring company is not administering the debt collection process the administrative charge is lower, say 0.5% to 1% of turnover. On top of that, the financing charge on the advance will again be 3% to 5% above base rate.

The first two of these actions are considered in more detail below.

(i) Improve credit management

It is important to ensure that invoices are despatched on time, the age of debts are identified and debts collected promptly.

Businesses should ensure that trade receivables are invoiced as soon as possible. A delay in sending out invoices is likely to lead to delay in payment by customers. Where debts are slow in being paid, then phone calls to the customer, personal visits, final demand letters, turning the account over to a debt collection agency and as a final act legal action may be necessary. It is also important that trade receivables are kept under continuous review and that an aged analysis of debts is maintained. For example, assume that an aged analysis of the trade receivables balance for Bramble Ltd at the end of 20X7/8 has produced the details shown in Figure 12.8.

Age of debts (months) payment by end of month						
1–2	2–3	3–4	4–5	5–6	6+	Total
£'000	£'000	£'000	£'000	£'000	£'000	£'000
120	20	10	10	5	9	174

Figure 12.8 Aged trade receivables analysis

From this analysis it can be seen that debts worth £120,000 are between 1 and 2 months old, while £64,000 are over 2 months and debts from 5 and 6 months ago are still outstanding. Urgent action is needed on the older debts.

Another reason for poor debt collection might be due to a business allowing credit for high-risk customers. Before selling to a new customer, the company ought to make every effort to check the credit rating. This can be undertaken through a number of sources:

1. *Bank references.*
2. *Trade references.* Suppliers who already deal with the potential customer can be used as a means of verifying whether the customer is a good payer.
3. *Credit agencies.* There are a number of agencies, such as Dunn and Bradstreet, that will provide a credit rating of companies.
4. *Published information.* Completing an analysis of the accounts of the potential customer, e.g. calculating the current, quick and debtors ratios described above, will provide an indication of the likelihood of payment.

(ii) Provide discounts to customers who pay promptly

To generate additional cash, a business might offer a cash discount. Before offering a cash discount, the cost of this discount should be evaluated. For example, consider the example in Figure 12.9.

Assume that Bramble Ltd thinks that the trade receivable profile will be similar to that shown in Figure 12.8 for the next few months, unless it introduces a new discount policy. It considers that if a 1% discount policy was introduced:

- 50% of those customers who currently pay by the end of month 2 would pay by the end of month 1.
- 50% of those customers who pay in month 3 would pay by the end of month 1.

It wishes to know whether this policy would be worthwhile to the company. Assume the cost of capital of Bramble Ltd is 10%.
    An evaluation of this policy shows the following.

(a) *Additional cost of introducing the policy*

		Debtors paying within one month after introduction of the policy	Cost of policy 1% of sales lost due to discount
Month 2	£120,000	£60,000	£600
Month 3	£20,000	£10,000	£100
			£700

(b) *Saving resulting from the policy*

  (i) £60,000 is paid one month earlier. Cost of capital is 10% per annum

  or $\dfrac{10\%}{12}$ for one month $= 0.83\%$ per month

  $= £60,000 \times 10\%/12 = £500$

  (ii) £10,000 is paid two months earlier. Cost of capital is 10% per annum and

  for 2 months $= £10,000 \times 10\% \times \dfrac{2}{12} = £166.67$

Figure 12.9   Evaluating the cost of providing a discount on sales

Therefore saving in interest due to earlier
payment of debts = £500 + £166.67 = £666.67

Net effect of policy	£
Revenue loss due to providing a 1% discount	700
Saving on interest payment due to earlier payment of debts	666.67
Net loss due to introducing the discount policy	−33.33

Accordingly, there is a net loss if the discount policy is introduced to the company. However, there will be a benefit in terms of reducing the amount of money tied up in working capital. Where organizations have a cash flow problem, then it will often be necessary to sacrifice profit in favour of cash.

Figure 12.9 (*Continued*)

Activity 12.4

XY Ltd has the following profile of outstanding debts:

Debtor age (months)	1–2 £'000	2–3 £'000	3–4 £'000	4–5 £'000	5–6 £'000	6+ £'000	Total £'000
	75	20	15	5	5	5	125

The company considers that if it gave a 2% discount, 75% of the customers who currently pay in the second month would pay by the end of the first month. 50% of those who pay in the third month would also pay by the end of the first month. There would be no change on other debtors. The company's cost of capital is 15%.
    Calculate whether offering this discount is worthwhile.

Consider raising finance through means of a short-term loan or bank overdraft

A bank overdraft is a very flexible form of finance. A bank grants the organization a facility of an overdraft to an agreed limit and interest is only paid on the amount borrowed. Disadvantages of an overdraft are that the bank can call it in at any time and the rate of interest can also change at short notice.

Bank loans are generally for 3 to 10 years, though it is possible to obtain a short-term loan that can mature in as little as 90–120 days. In general, banks require very specific repayment plans for their short-term loans, for example if a company takes out a loan to even out cash flow until a customer pays a debt, the lender would expect repayment of the loan as soon as the company received its money.

Reducing cash outflows

Reduce inventory

Carrying insufficient stock carries the risk that the company will need to stop production if it cannot get quick deliveries of replacements, with consequent loss in sales and goodwill of customers. Holding too much inventory, however, is expensive. These costs include the cost of interest paid or opportunity cost of money tied up in stock; cost of obsolescence or deterioration and damage that can occur when stocks are held for a lengthy period of time; cost of storage for the materials.

Companies need to review inventory management policies, for example by moving towards the adoption of just-in-time stock management.

Increase amounts owed to suppliers

(i) Delay payment of bills.
(ii) Negotiate more credit from suppliers.

Again companies want to hold accounts payable at appropriate levels. If payment is delayed too long, then there is a danger that suppliers will refuse to sell goods to the purchaser in future and will take legal action to recover goods. A good payer is also likely to be favoured if supplies are low. Purchasers, however, will wish to take advantage of the credit period that is granted to them and if the normal term of trade is to allow 30 days' credit, then they would not normally wish to pay before this time.

Just as a company may consider offering customers discounts if they pay quickly, suppliers may well offer incentives for quick payments. The calculation is similar to that shown for the assessment of trade receivables. See Figure 12.10.

AB Ltd currently takes an average of approximately 61 days to pay its creditors.

It buys on average £2000 a month from X Ltd and has been offered a 2% discount if it pays within 31 days. The cost of capital of AB Ltd is 10%.

The management wish to calculate whether to take the discount and pay early.

(a) Saving from accepting the discount is: £2000 × 2% discount = £40
(b) Additional cost resulting from the policy: £2000 is paid one month earlier.

$$\text{Cost of capital is 10\% per annum} = \frac{10\%}{12} \text{ for one month} = £2000 \times \frac{10\%}{12} = £16.67$$

Saving due to earlier payment of debt = £40 − £16.67 = £23.33.

If AB Ltd can fund the quicker repayment of goods then it is financially worthwhile.

Figure 12.10   Taking a trade discount

Cash flow statement and cash ratios

In published accounts, a cash flow statement is produced in a format that complies with International Accounting Standard 7 (IAS 7). This format identifies the cash generated from operations; increases or decreases in the amount of money tied up in working; expenditure on dividends, tax and interest; expenditure on fixed assets and other investments; and funds raised for long-term loans or issues of share capital. A cash budget for Bramble Ltd is produced in Table 12.2 using the format for IAS 7.

Table 12.2   Budgeted cash flow statement for year to 31 March 20X8/9

	£'000	£'000
Net profit before tax (note 1)		310
Adjustment for:		
Depreciation (note 2)		200
Interest expense		55
Operating profit before working capital changes (note 3)		565
(Increase)/decrease in trade and other receivables (note 4)		−151
(Increase)/decrease in inventories (note 5)		−246
Increase/(decrease) in trade and other payables (note 6)		79
Cash generated from operations		247
Interest paid (note 7)	−55	
Taxation paid (note 8)	−160	
		−215
		32
Cash flow from investing activities		
Sale of fixed assets		
Purchase of fixed assets (note 9)		−900
Cash flow from financing activities		
Proceeds from long-term borrowings		900
Dividend paid (note 10)		−140
Note 11		−108
Cash and cash equivalents at the beginning of the period (note 12)		64
Cash and cash equivalents at the end of the period		−44
		−108

Note 1. The cash flow statement starts with the identification of net profit *after* deducting interest, but before tax.

Note 2. Cumulative depreciation for the year 20X8/9 is budgeted to be £740,000 and actual cumulative depreciation for 20X7/8 is £540,000 (see Table 10.2 in Chapter 10). Assuming no disposals of assets, the depreciation in the year is the difference between the two, i.e. £200,000.

Note 3. To identify the cash impact from operating profit *before* interest charges and working capital changes, it is necessary to add back interest. Depreciation is an expense of the business and should be deducted from revenue in calculating profit, however, it is not a cash flow so the depreciation in the year of £200,000 should also be added back.

    The budgeted cash flow statement shown in Table 12.1 showed cash receipts from sales and cash expenditure on labour and materials as well as on overheads. This is not the same as the revenue and expenditure shown in the accounts because of timing differences in customers paying their bills and Bramble Ltd paying its suppliers. There may also be a difference due to a change in the inventory holdings of Bramble Ltd. In order to identify the cash generated from operations, it is therefore necessary to make an adjustment for changes in trade receivables, trade payables and the level of inventory.

Table 12.2   (Continued)

Note 4. Trade receivables increased from £174,000 in 20X7/8 to £325,000 in 20X8/9, an application (i.e. increase) of £151,000. (The cash receipts were £151,000 less than sales.)

Note 5. Inventories increased from £266,000 in 20X7/8 to £512,000 in 20X8/9, an application (i.e. increase) of £246,000.

Note 6. Trade payables increased from £106,000 in 20X7/8 to £185,000 in 20X8/9. This is a source of funds of £79,000 as Bramble Ltd is delaying paying its suppliers.

Note 7. Interest payments are budgeted to be paid at £55,000.

Note 8. The cash flow statement (Table 12.1) identifies that taxation to be paid was £160,000. The amount paid could also have been calculated given the information in the Balance Sheet and Profit and Loss Account for Bramble Ltd (Tables 10.2 and 10.1).

	£
Opening balance of taxation owed at the end of 20X7/8 (Table 10.2)	160,000
Add taxation due for 20X8/9 (see Table 10.1)	98,000
Total amount due for payment	258,000
Closing balance of taxation owed at the end of 20X8/9 (Table 10.2)	98,000
Amount paid in 20X8/9	160,000

Note 9. Two investments were made, one for £700,000 in quarter 2 of 20X8/9 and the second for £200,000 in quarter 4.

Note 10. The cash flow statement (Table 12.1) identifies that dividend to be paid was £140,000. The amount paid could also have been calculated given the information in the Balance Sheet and Profit and Loss Account for Bramble Ltd (Tables 10.2 and 10.1).

	£
Opening balance of dividend owed at the end of 20X7/8 (Table 10.2)	140,000
Add taxation due for 20X8/9 (see Table 10.1)	144,000
Total amount due for payment	288,000
Closing balance of dividend owed at the end of 20X8/9 (Table 10.2)	144,000
Amount paid in 20X8/9	140,000

Note 11. There has been a net application of funds of £108,000. This is reflected in a movement in the cash balance from +£64,000 at the end of 20X7/8 to a proposed −£44,000 at the end of 20X8/9 (£8000 in the bank less £52,000 bank overdraft).

Cash or profit as a measurement of performance

In recent years, many companies have paid increased attention to the importance of cash as a measure of performance rather than profit. A cash measure of return on capital employed is:

$$\frac{\text{Net cash flow from operations}}{\text{Net capital employed}} \times 100\%$$

The budgeted cash return on capital employed (20X8/9) is:

$$\frac{£247,000}{£1,482,000} \times 100 = 16.7\%$$

A range of other measures that focus on cash flow rather than profit are discussed in Chapter 21.

Note that the cash return on capital employed can also be calculated using the average of the opening and closing net capital employed. Where comparisons are used, it is important to be consistent and use the same method.

Summary

In this chapter key sources and applications of funds in a business have been discussed.

In order to identify potential cash shortfalls or surpluses it is important to produce a cash flow statement for both the short and longer term.

Where the requirement of funding is of a long-term or permanent nature, it is important to raise funds through long-term sources of finance. If the funding need is of a temporary nature, it is possible to use short-term sources of finance.

Long-term sources of finance include the issuing of share capital and loan capital. Given knowledge of the cost of capital of each of these sources of funds, it is possible to calculate a weighted average cost of capital.

It is also possible to fund investments through sale and leaseback of existing assets and through use of lease or hire purchase for new fixed assets.

In considering whether to raise funds from the issue of share capital or from issuing loan capital, both financial and investment risk should be considered.

Further reading

For a more detailed discussion of the sources of finance and the cost of capital, the reader is referred to:

Arnold, G. (2005) *Corporate Financial Management*, 3rd edn. FT/Prentice-Hall. Sources of finance – Chapters 10, 11, 12, 13; Cost of capital – Chapter 19; Capital structure – Chapter 21.

Answers to activities

Activity 12.1

The interest paid per year will be 5% of £500,000 = £25,000 per annum. Interest is tax deductible, so if the tax rate is 30% the true cost of interest is £25,000 × (1 − 0.3) = £17,500.

If the market value of the debt has fallen to £400,000 then the cost of capital is £17,500/£400,000 = 4.4%.

Activity 12.2

Cost of equity is $30p/£3.00 = 10\%$.

Activity 12.3

The weighted average cost of capital of Alpha Ltd is as follows.

Source of finance	Market value (£)	Proportion (%)	Cost of capital (%)	Weighted average cost of capital (%)
Equity	3,000,000	88.2	10.0	8.82
Debt	400,000	11.8	4.4	0.52
	3,400,000			9.34

Activity 12.4

(a) Additional cost of introducing the policy:

		Debtors paying within one month after introduction of the policy	Cost of policy 2% of sales lost due to discount
Month 2	£75,000	£56,250	£1,125
Month 3	£20,000	£10,000	£200
			£1,325

(b) Saving resulting from the policy:

  (i) £56,250 is paid one month earlier. Cost of capital is 15% per annum or $\frac{15\%}{12}$ for one month $= 1.5\%$ per month $= £56,250 \times 1.25\% = £703.13$

  (ii) £10,000 is paid two months earlier. Cost of capital is 15% per annum and for 2 months $= £10,000 \times 15\% \times \frac{2}{12} = £250.00$

Therefore saving in interest due to earlier payment of debts $= £703.13 + £250.00 = £953.13$.

Net effect of policy	£
Revenue loss due to providing a 2% discount	1,325
Saving on interest payment due to earlier payment of debts	953.13
Net loss due to introducing the discount	371.87

Discussion questions

1. 'If additional funds are required then a business should always obtain long-term sources of funds.' Critically evaluate this statement.
2. Should a company raise finance through the issue of share capital or loan capital? Evaluate the advantages and disadvantages of both methods of financing a business.
3. 'Financing decisions and investment strategy are unrelated.' Critically evaluate this statement.
4. A manager of a local company has approached you for your advice. His company is experiencing a cash flow problem and the company is unable to currently raise any long-term sources of finance. Identify key ways in which this problem can be overcome without resorting to raising long-term sources of funds.
5. 'A company should always try to reduce its investment in working capital'. To what extent do you agree with this statement?

Exercises

(Questions with numbers in bold have answers at the back of the book.)

Q12.1 2,000,000 £1 shares have been issued for Milton PLC and are currently trading at £1.50 a share. A dividend of 10p per share was recently paid. Assume the level of dividend will stay the same.

A £1,000,000 debenture loan, on which interest of 8% is payable, has also been issued. The current market value of the loan is £1,200,000. The tax rate for the year is 35%.

Required:

Work out the weighted average cost of capital of Milton PLC.

Q12.2 3,000,000 £1 shares have been issued for Frewen Ltd and are currently trading at £2.00 a share. A dividend of 15p per share was recently paid. Assume the level of dividend will stay the same.

A £1,500,000 debenture loan, on which interest of 6% is payable, has also been issued. The current market value of the loan is £1,400,000. The tax rate for the year is 30%.

Required:

Work out the weighted average cost of capital of Frewen Ltd.

Q12.3 CD Ltd is considering introducing a 2% discount on sales if a debt is paid within 30 days. If a 2% discount policy was introduced then the impact on trade receivables is expected to be:

(a) 60% of customers who currently pay by the end of month 2 (£130,000) would pay by the end of month 1.
(b) 40% of customers who currently pay in month 3 (£25,000) would pay by the end of month 1.

Required:

Advise the company whether this policy would be worthwhile. Assume the cost of capital of CD Ltd is 12%.

Q12.4 CD Ltd buys on average £4000 a month from X Ltd and has been offered a 2.5% discount if it pays within 31 days. The cost of capital of CD Ltd is 15%.

Required:

Advise the management whether it is worthwhile taking the discount and paying early.

Q12.5 Refer to the information in Question 11.3. The management of Empire PLC is considering raising further funds of £1,000,000 and is wondering whether this should be in the form of loan or share capital.

Required:

Advise the management on the appropriate source of funds.

PART 3

STRATEGIC MANAGEMENT

In Part 2 of the book, the emphasis was on planning and control for the short to medium term, particularly for the next year and the next few months. As well as planning for the next year, most organizations also need to undertake a more fundamental type of review, which is concerned with the strategic direction of the business. While it is possible to just plan for the year ahead, the danger is that an organization will continue to sell products and services that have proved successful in the past, but may now be becoming out-of-date.

Strategic management is concerned with the long-term objectives of the organization and how it is proposed that these objectives be achieved, i.e. the strategy. Issues related to strategic management are the subject of this third part of the book, with individual chapters explaining key stages of the process.

Johnson and Scholes (1998) proposed a model involving three interrelated stages of strategic analysis, strategic choice and strategy implementation.

Strategic analysis

The purpose of strategic analysis is to form a view of key influences on the organization and on the choice of strategy. It involves an understanding of:

1. The aims and objectives of the various stakeholders of the organization and the culture of the organization.
2. The external environment in which the organization operates and the threats and opportunities existing in this environment.
3. The resources and capabilities of the organization.

Chapters 13, 14, 15 and 16 deal with these issues. Chapter 16 focuses on the potential use of accounting information in the strategic analysis process.

Strategic choice

Strategic choice leads on from the analysis stage. It involves the generation of strategic options, the evaluation of these options and the selection of a strategy. Chapter 17 is concerned with the development of suitable strategic options, drawing on the analysis of the threats and opportunities in the external environment as well as the resources and capabilities of the organization. A particular focus of chapter 18 is on the financial evaluation of different options taking into consideration risk and uncertainty. Other issues related to evaluation are also covered, for example does the organization have the resources to implement the plan (feasibility) and are the options in line with the objectives of the key stakeholders of the organisation (acceptability).

Strategic implementation

Strategic implementation is concerned with translating strategy into action, for example with resource planning, changes in the organizational structure needed to carry through strategies and with the management of change. Resource planning in the form of budgeting was considered in Part 2 of the book. In Part 3 there is only a limited consideration of this topic area, with Chapter 18 providing an outline of the structure that would be appropriate for a business plan.

OBJECTIVES, STRATEGY AND INFLUENCES

13

Objectives

At the end of this chapter you should be able to:

- Describe the need for and method of writing a mission statement and organizational objectives.
- Describe the meaning of the planning gap.
- Explain the key features of and alternative approaches to strategy formulation.
- Explain key influences to be taken into consideration when writing a mission statement, objectives and evaluating strategies:

  - Different stakeholders of the organization.
  - Organizational culture.
  - Business ethics.
  - Corporate social responsibility.
  - Corporate governance.

Introduction

This chapter first reviews the need for and method of writing a mission statement and organizational objectives. The identification of the planning gap between actual performance and objectives and the need for strategies to close this gap is then discussed.

When drawing up objectives and strategies, stakeholders, business ethics, corporate social responsibility and the organizational culture are all factors that should be taken into consideration.

Mission statements and objectives

The mission statement

Before detailed objectives are set, many organizations feel that it is important to prepare a mission statement.

The **mission statement** is a statement of the purpose of the organization. It should provide a vision or desired future state of the organization and it is against this vision that more detailed objectives can be written. It can also provide a statement of the key values of the organization and attitudes towards key stakeholders.

Many organizational mission statements provide specific details about the organization. For example, a description of the products/services, the target market, geographical domain in which it will operate and expectations of growth and profitability.

Mission statements for two contrasting organizations, EasyJet and the British Embassy in Madrid, are included in Figure 13.1.

EasyJet
To provide its customers with safe, good value, point-to-point air services. To effect and to offer a consistent and reliable product and fares appealing to leisure and business markets on a range of European routes. To achieve this they will develop their people and establish lasting relationships with their suppliers.

British Embassy Madrid
To deliver client-driven support both to companies in the UK wishing to develop their international trade into the Spanish market and to Spanish enterprises seeking to locate in the UK.

Figure 13.1   Examples of mission statements

Activity 13.1

To what extent does the EasyJet mission statement comply with the guideline provided?

Objectives

The traditional theory of the firm assumes that shareholder value maximization is the goal of the firm. **Shareholder value** refers to the concept that the primary goal for a company is to enrich its shareholders (owners) by paying dividends and/or causing the stock price to increase. A number of organizational mission statements, however, indicate a need to pursue *multiple objectives*. The EasyJet mission statement, for example, implies that it is necessary to consider the pursuit of goals related to customer safety and the development of people and supplier relationships. Many organizations have also felt that for control purposes a range of performance areas or 'dimensions' should be monitored. For example, early in the 1950s, General Electric in the USA initiated an extensive decentralization of authority and responsibility for the operation of the company. The company recognized that if this decentralization was to be successful it would need an improved system of control. As a result, it was decided that detailed consideration was required of eight areas of performance:

1. Profitability.
2. Market position.
3. Productivity.

4. Product leadership.
5. Personnel development.
6. Employee attitudes.
7. Public responsibility.
8. Balance between short-range and long-range goals.

Setting objectives

Having identified the areas or performance dimensions to be monitored, appropriate measures of these dimensions need to be agreed and then objectives set. When writing objectives, care must be taken to ensure that they are understandable and clearly communicated. If an objective is to be used in a performance measurement system then it should comply with 'SMART' principles, in that it should be specific, measurable, achievable, relevant and timely.

Specific. Each objective should relate to a specific/single performance dimension, for example financial performance.

Measurable. It should be possible to state an objective in quantitative rather than in descriptive terms. Profit or return on capital employed might be an appropriate measure of financial performance.

Achievable. An objective should be challenging but achievable, a target that is not achievable may well lead to loss of motivation by managers.

Relevant. Measures should be of key importance to the manager.

Time. There should be a time deadline.

As an example, an objective to 'maximize profits' would not comply with SMART principles as there is no time deadline and it is not specific. What is the size of 'maximum' profits? If a review was taking place at a later date, how could anyone tell whether profits had been maximized or not?

Assuming a budgeted profit of £200,000 is achievable for a business unit, then an objective that would comply with SMART principles could read, 'to achieve profits of £200,000 for the year ended 2009'. Profit is a specific/single performance dimension; it is measurable; a profit of £200,000 is achievable; it is relevant (of key importance); a time deadline is identified.

Activity 13.2

The managers of AB Ltd have set the following objectives:

(a) To increase sales revenue.
(b) To reduce the number of items that are scrapped.

Required:
Rewrite the two objectives applying SMART principles given the following information.
  An achievable sales revenue target for 2009 is £2,000,000.
  Currently 5% of stock is scrapped because of failures in the production process.
  A 90% reduction in scrap levels in 2009 is achievable.

Hierarchy of objectives

Many organizations distinguish between corporate objectives and unit objectives. Corporate objectives will be those that influence the strategic thrust of the whole organization. Below the corporate level, each *subsidiary and department or unit* should have its own objectives, with achievement of subsidiary or department objectives leading to the achievement of corporate objectives.

A simplified diagram illustrating the relationship between mission and objectives is shown below in Figure 13.2.

Figure 13.2   Relationship between mission statement and objectives

This diagram suggests how the mission statement provides the overall vision from which detailed corporate and then subsidiary or unit objectives would be set.

When a range of objectives are set, some may conflict; for example, increasing short-term profits and gaining market position or share. The former could be achieved through reducing expenditure on discretionary areas such as marketing research and development and training, though this would be likely to be at the expense of the longer-term development of the business. The organization will need to decide how these objectives will be prioritized.

Objective-setting and its role in the performance management system of an organization will be considered in more detail in Part 4 of the book.

Gap analysis

Gap analysis is a method for determining the difference between an organization's objectives and its future level of attainment if present strategies and policies continue.

In Figure 13.3 the planning gap is illustrated for a profit objective. The bottom line reflects a forecast of profits given existing strategies for the next few years. The top line represents profit objectives that have also been set for the next few years. The difference between the two is called the planning gap.

In order to close the planning gap, new strategies must be formulated and implemented.

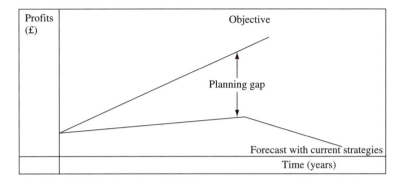

Figure 13.3   Identifying the planning gap

Strategic management

Strategy formulation is the process of determining appropriate courses of action for achieving organizational objectives and thereby accomplishing organizational purpose. Johnson and Scholes (1989) propose a model of the strategic management process involving three interrelated stages of strategic analysis, strategic choice and strategy implementation. The introduction to Part 3 of this book reviewed key aspects of the strategic management process that will be covered in this part of the book.

Alternate approaches to strategy formulation

Strategy formulation may be achieved in a number of ways.

Planned strategies. A number of models of strategy formulation suggest that the process takes place in a planned fashion. For example, the model shown in Figure 13.4 indicates a linear model of planning that starts with the identification of objectives and ends with the choice of strategy.

The diagram suggests that planners would first identify objectives, then the external environment would be assessed in order to identify strengths and weaknesses, next an internal evaluation of the organization and its capabilities, and so on. In practice, the process is unlikely to develop in this way and it is much more likely that it will develop in an iterative manner, with ongoing reviews of the external environment and internal strengths and weaknesses occurring. The model also suggests a very rational process, with groups of staff meeting to complete set stages of action. It is unlikely that events will unfold in this way in all organizations, and a number of other approaches to strategy development and planning have been observed.

Emergent strategies. Some strategies may develop unintentionally. Environmental change can occur rapidly and opportunities or threats may result where an immediate strategic response is required and can be taken.

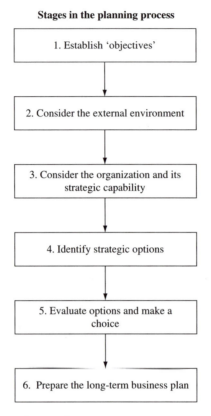

Stages in the planning process

Figure 13.4   The planning and control process

Incrementalism. Sometimes the environment is so complex and changes so fast that a formal planned strategy becomes difficult to formulate. The situation can be further complicated when there are a number of powerful interest groups with different objectives, for example organizations operating in local or national government often have conflicting political pressure groups trying to influence decisions. An incrementalist approach that involves short-term targets and continuously adapting to the needs of the environment may be appropriate. A danger of this approach is that it may also lead to an organization losing sight of overall objectives.

Realized strategies are the result of both intended strategies that have been implemented and unplanned emergent strategies that have occurred spontaneously. In Part 4 of the book (Chapter 20), consideration is given to control system design given alternative approaches to formulating strategy. Simons (1995) highlights the need for a control system that can monitor performance against planned strategies. However, he also highlights a need for a system to identify key strategic changes that are occurring in order that management may recognize such changes and be able to adapt strategies at short notice.

Influences on the mission statement, corporate goals and strategies

In this section influences on the mission statement, corporate goals and strategies will be considered.

Firstly, the extent to which the stakeholders of an organization should be taken into consideration.

Secondly, the influence of the organizational culture.

Thirdly, a 'boundary system' that can help managers identify the specific actions and behaviours that are 'off limits'. Three elements to this boundary system will be considered:

(i) Business ethics.
(ii) Corporate social responsibility.
(iii) Corporate governance.

Stakeholders

Stakeholders are the different groups of people who are affected by, or can have an effect upon, the company's strategies.

Identifying stakeholders and their objectives

Figure 13.5 identifies a list of potential stakeholders that might exist in a private-sector organization and the goals or objectives that they might wish to achieve from their association with the organization.

Stakeholder group	Objective
Shareholders	Shareholders will be concerned with the increase in wealth, i.e. future cash inflows, in the form of annual dividends and in the movement in the share price. They will also be concerned with the risk that dividends and share price will not grow at the expected rate.
Managers	Salaries, bonuses, status, security, challenge, responsibility.
Employees	Probably similar issues to the managers. However, potentially employees have a different view of the impact of policies than the managers.
Customers	Quality of the product or service, the price.
Suppliers	Prompt payment, consistent orders, price paid.
Lenders	Interest payments, loan repayment, security.
Government	Tax payment, provision of employment, compliance with law.
Pressure group	Compliance with interests of the pressure group.
Local community	Employment opportunities, pollution of the environment.

Figure 13.5   Potential stakeholders of an organisation

Taking account of stakeholder objectives

Stakeholders can have very different and potentially conflicting goals. For example, while shareholders might be interested in a business increasing profits in order that dividends and/or the share price will increase, the local community might be concerned to preserve the local environment.

There are different views on the extent to which an organization should take account of the objectives of stakeholders. If 'shareholder value maximization' is to be the key objective of the firm, then it might be argued that the only relevant objective is that of the shareholders. A second view is that to achieve shareholder value maximization, highly successful companies will take into consideration the objectives of a range of other stakeholders since this will also lead to the achievement of the main organizational objectives. A third view is that all stakeholders' interests have value and therefore an organization has a duty to take these into account.

Stakeholder management – considering the interests and power of stakeholders

Mendelow (1991) supported the argument that if an organization wished to achieve certain objectives, then it was important to take particular account of those stakeholders who have an *interest* in particular issues being affected by a firm's objectives and strategies and also those with a *level of power* that they can exert.

Mendelow suggested that stakeholder influence can be mapped using a power/interest matrix. See Figure 13.6.

		LEVEL OF INTEREST	
		Low	High
LEVEL OF POWER:	Low	A (Minimal effort)	B (Keep informed)
	High	C (Keep satisfied)	D (Key players)

Figure 13.6 Stakeholder mapping
Source: Adapted from A. Mendelow, Proceedings of 2nd International Conference on Information Systems, Cambridge, MA, 1991.

If an organization has an objective and strategy that is of interest to a particular set of stakeholders who also have the power to prevent or impede its successful implementation, then the organization needs to recognize these stakeholders as key players (cell D). The organization will need to consider how to deal with these key players in order that its objectives can be achieved. If stakeholders have little power and/or influence then it is possible that the organization will need to make minimal effort to take account of their objectives (cell A). Where stakeholders have high power, though little interest in specific objectives, then it is necessary to keep these stakeholders satisfied (cell C). Where they have low power, but high interest, it is necessary to keep them informed (cell B).

To use stakeholder analysis in isolation could lead an organization to take action on the basis of power. As a simple example, assume that one way to increase profits in an organization would be to reduce expenditure on pollution controls to the minimum level required in order to comply with legal requirements. This would have a favourable impact on profits, but an adverse impact on the local environment. Using the mapping system of Mendelow this policy might be followed if the shareholders were seen as key players and the local community or environmental pressure groups seen as having little power. Later in the chapter, the need to consider ethics, corporate social responsibility and governance issues will be discussed.

It should also be noted that an incomplete or inaccurate stakeholder analysis can prove costly to an organization. See Figure 13.7.

In 1995 Shell decided to destroy the oil platform Brent Spar by dumping it at sea. Although Shell considered this proposal to be environmentally safe, this decision caused a major reaction from the environmentalist movement and Greenpeace occupied Brent Spar to prevent Shell going through with their original plan. Revenue was lost throughout Europe as the adverse publicity led to motorists boycotting Shell petrol stations and Shell was forced to revise its plans. As well as lost sales, the destruction of the rig eventually cost Shell over £40 million, compared with the £4.5 million cost of dumping.

Figure 13.7   The destruction of the Brent Spar oil platform

The influence of organizational culture

A further influence on both the purpose and strategies of an organization can be the cultural context. This can follow on from influences that are both internal and external to the organization.

Internal influences

Organizational culture is the key values, beliefs and assumptions that underpin the way each organization operates. Individuals in an organization will tend to be influenced by the culture of the internal groups to which they belong. Different organizational cultures are therefore also likely to have an influence on the objectives set, the strategies followed and the way that organizations organize their activities. Some organizations, for example, may have a market-oriented culture, in which case they will be outward-looking and will most likely be flexible in meeting a changing environment, while other organizations may be very conservative in setting objectives and remain averse to taking risks. See Figure 13.8. A number of authors have suggested organizational 'typologies'.

In 1971, a liquidator was appointed to take on the affairs of Rolls Royce. The company had collapsed due to heavy expenditure on the development of a new airplane engine, the RB 211, which had resulted in the company running out of cash. A key reason, suggested by investigators into this event, was that the main board was dominated by engineers and this had significantly influenced the decision-making process in the organization. Although excellent work had been undertaken on the engine contract, financial and managerial control had been lacking. The drive for engineering excellence had taken precedence over other objectives, including the key objective of the financial survival of the company. Different organizational cultures may well be appropriate in different circumstances. In the case of Rolls Royce, the pursuit of engineering excellence was a key driving force.

The airplane engine business of Rolls Royce was successfully refloated in 1971. It is a highly successful company to this day and a world leader in the sales of airplane engines. Its engineering excellence has ensured that it maintains this leadership status. The collapse in 1971, however, highlighted the dangers of a culture that was so focused on the achievement of engineering excellence that other objectives may have been insufficiently considered.

Figure 13.8 The collapse of Rolls Royce

Miles and Snow: defender, prospector, analyser and reactor cultures

Miles and Snow (1978) suggested that the culture of organizations can be classified into four different types: defenders, prospectors, analysers and reactors (see Figure 13.9).

Organizational culture	Typical features
Defender	Conservative, often inward-looking and risk-averse.
Prospector	Innovative organizations prepared to take a risk and to consider change.
Analyser	Rational analysis and planning is considered important.
Reactor	Tend to live from crisis to crisis, reacting to events rather than planning for them.

Figure 13.9 Typologies of culture
Source: Miles and Snow (1978).

Organizations with a defender culture are more likely to follow a strategy involving strict cost control maintained through a centralized organization. Prospector companies, on the other hand, are likely to set objectives and strategies that emphasize new product and service development and innovation to meet new and changing customer needs and demands. A prospector organization is likely to be decentralized and have few levels of management, encouraging collaboration among different departments and units.

Analyser organizations share characteristics with prospector and defender organizations. They will tend to try to match new ventures to the existing business and will tend to be followers in the market. They will try to maintain the efficiency of established products or services, while remaining flexible enough to pursue new business activities. Reactor organizations do not have a systematic strategy, design or structure, and do not make long-term plans.

Miles and Snow do not suggest that one particular organizational culture is best. In a stable environment, for example, a firm can be successful through means of low costs and strict cost control and a defender culture may indeed be the most appropriate for the organization. This style of management, however, may not be appropriate in a fast-changing environment requiring entrepreneurial expertise to develop new products and adapt to change. To thrive in such an environment, a prospector culture may be more appropriate as creativity may be more important for success than efficiency.

Activity 13.3

Using the typology of Miles and Snow, would a prospector or defender culture be appropriate for:

(a) A company designing and selling fashion clothing?
(b) A company selling school uniform clothing?

In both circumstances explain why this would be the case.

Handy: power, rule, task and person cultures

A second way to classify organizational culture was proposed by Handy (1976), who suggests that organizations can have one of four types of culture: power, rule, task and person (see Figure 13.10).

Organizational culture	Typical features
Power	The organization is dominated from the centre.
Rule	The organization is dominated by rules and is rather bureaucratic in its operations, working through committees and the hierarchy.
Task	The emphasis is on solving problems and producing.
Person	The culture is people-oriented.

Figure 13.10 Typologies of culture
Source: Handy (1976).

Using the Handy typology in a power culture, the dominant force in setting objectives is the centre and less attention will be paid to pluralism, i.e. taking into account objectives of the different stakeholders. In a task-oriented culture, the objectives would be related

Organizational Culture in British Airways

In the 1980s, British Airways was transformed from a loss-making state enterprise, into the world's largest and most profitable international airline. Much of this turnaround was attributed to BA's own cultural change, which 'remodelled' staff attitudes. From having a hierarchical and militaristic culture, which existed in BA at the time, it is claimed the culture of BA was changed to one that was oriented towards the meeting of customer needs. Using Handy's method of classification, it could be argued that this was a move from a power- and/or rule-based to a more task-based culture. It has been argued that this cultural change was achieved through a wide range of methods, including attendance at training courses (including the 'Putting People First' programme), the introduction of team briefing, Total Quality Management, autonomous team working and multi-skilling in many areas. Cabin crew rosters were also changed in order to create 'families' of staff, and new appraisal and rewards systems introduced.

It should be noted that other authors, e.g. Grugulis and Wilkinson (2002), question the extent that cultural change led to the improved performance. They point out that during the 1980s and 1990s a number of other factors led to the improved performance. These included: little competition, as the European markets were still tightly regulated; control of 60% of the UK domestic market, with competition experienced on only 9% of routes; and a series of strategic alliances that further increased its market power. British Airways also invested heavily in its infrastructure of control systems, terminal facilities and aircraft.

Figure 13.11   Organizational culture in British Airways

more to achievement of specific tasks and the mode of operation is likely to be more through team work. See Figure 13.11.

External influences

As well as the existing internal culture of the organization, it is also necessary to consider external influences.

  (i) External values and beliefs of society that can change
      The influence of the external values and beliefs of society should be considered. This is particularly true as they can change over time and therefore policies may need to change as well. Increasing public support for environmentally friendly policies, for example, has been taken into account by many organizations in setting objectives. Corporate social responsibility has been more widely considered and reported by companies in recent years.
 (ii) National and regional cultures
      Attitudes to work, authority and equality differ from location to location. Stakeholders in different societies will have different expectations. Employees, for example, may have a different attitude to work, working practices, authority and equality. A set of objectives and strategies that might be successfully pursued in a culture where the decisions of a higher authority tend to be automatically accepted and employment laws are weak may not be acceptable in another society, where employment practice and legal safeguards are different.

Ethics

Ethics is about right and wrong. Business ethics can provide businesses with moral guidance in conducting their affairs and can be considered at three levels: the level of society; the individual level; and the corporate level.

Societal view

The societal level is the extent to which society considers that businesses should take account of the views of different stakeholders.

As discussed earlier, the orthodox view among free market economists was that organizations should only take into account the objectives of the owners of the business and should aim to maximize the wealth of the shareholders. An alternative view is that there are a number of stakeholders who are affected by the decisions of organizations and the objectives of this broader range of stakeholders, including customers, employees, the public and local communities, should be taken into account by organizations.

Different societies might have alternative views on how the various stakeholders should be treated. It would now be a widely held view in many societies that a basic employee right is the right to work without being injured. The public attitude to companies that employ child labour or have unacceptable working conditions for their staff has also altered in many countries, though such conditions still exist in others. Similarly, the attitudes of the public to organizations that cause harm to the environment has changed with, in many societies, a much less tolerant view taken of companies that cause damage and adversely affect the consumer and local communities.

Individual perspective

Ethics also needs to be considered at an individual level. When encountering a situation, an individual needs to:

1. Identify whether there is an ethical dimension to the problem.
2. Analyse the problem using available principles, rules and norms, which might help clarify whether a decision can be considered to be morally correct. These might be found from within or external to the organization.
3. Propose a response.

Every individual needs to consider his or her own position. In some instances it should be recognized that individual values may be causing an ethical dilemma, however in others, more fundamental issues are at stake. As a last resort, employees may decide that it is necessary to 'whistle blow' to outside authorities.

De George (1999) proposes a five-stage test that can be used in order to decide whether to 'whistle blow'. He argues that whistle blowing is morally permitted if:

(a) Serious harm to the public is involved.
(b) The situation has been reported to the immediate supervisor of the employee.
(c) All other internal procedures have been exhausted.

Whistle blowing is morally required if:

(i) Convincing documentary evidence is available to justify the concern.
(ii) 'Going public' will bring about the necessary change.

Activity 13.4

You are part of a team developing a process to manufacture a new product for an organization.

Two alternative methods have been identified, the first is cheaper, but will result in the release of some toxic chemicals into the atmosphere, which will not occur with the second method.

(a) What factors should be taken into account by the team in arriving at a decision?
(b) The organization has decided that the cheaper method should be adopted. What action should you take as an individual?

Corporate social responsibility

A business affects many different people – employees, customers and suppliers, and the local community – and it should deal with these stakeholders in a socially responsible manner. Johnson, Scholes and Whittington (2005) define **corporate social responsibility** as the 'ways in which an organisation exceeds its minimum obligations to stakeholders specified through regulation and corporate governance'.

In dealing with the environment an organization acting socially responsibly can aim to minimize possible damage by, for example, using sustainable raw materials. It can minimize packaging, source materials responsibly (e.g. use recycled materials), buy locally and work with suppliers who take steps to minimize their environmental impact. B&Q systematically analyse the products they sell against a list of a dozen social issues from climate change to working conditions at its suppliers' factories. The purpose is to determine which products pose potential social responsibility risks and how the company might take action before any external pressure is brought to bear.

An organization should also deal responsibly with customers and suppliers, compete fairly and avoid collusion or other anti-competitive practices. In addition, it can consider ways to work with the local community.

Strategic benefits of corporate social responsibility

Porter and Kramer (2006) argue that corporate social responsibility is much more than just good public relations, it can also provide strategic benefits and a competitive advantage. In response to public concerns about the adverse impact of automobile emissions, Toyota developed the 'Prius' which is a hybrid electric and petrol car. This has given Toyota a competitive lead and a unique position with consumers. The Credit Agricole bank in France has differentiated itself from competitors by offering specialized financial products for energy-saving home improvements. A high proportion of customers of 'The Body Shop' are reported to have been influenced in the past by the natural ingredients and the company's environmental aims and ban on animal testing. Microsoft and Marriott (the hotel chain) have provided financial support for schools and colleges in the USA, but have also benefited from employing the students trained there.

Being perceived as a moral organization promotes a positive image in the eyes of customers, particularly if it is difficult to differentiate products in other ways. It should be noted, however, that there is also a danger of promoting the business as an ethical business – if the media or key pressure groups can reveal that this is really just a superficial public relations exercise, the consumer backlash can be punitive.

Corporate governance

Experience of inappropriate action by corporations and the managers that work within them has provided evidence that a number of formal controls are required to ensure that there is appropriate governance and accountability in organizations. Governance means the strategy, method and manner in which a group of people direct, control and manage the organization. Accountability is the responsibility of those charged with governance to account for their choices, decisions and actions. Over the years, a mix of company law, stock exchange listing rules and self-regulatory codes has developed, with the aim of ensuring that governance and accountability is occurring within organizations.

Corporate governance is a term that refers to the rules, processes or laws by which businesses are operated, regulated and controlled. It is concerned with the relationship and responsibilities between the board, management, shareholders and other relevant stakeholders. The aim is to protect shareholder rights, enhance disclosure and transparency, facilitate effective functioning of the board and provide an efficient legal and regulatory enforcement.

The culture and values of the organization must support corporate governance principles. Key elements include honesty, trust and integrity, openness, performance orientation, responsibility and accountability, mutual respect and commitment to the organization. The conduct of senior executives is essential for the achievement of such a culture. Employees should also feel confident about reporting unethical or illegal acts by the company or its employees.

Summary

A mission statement should provide an overall vision for the relevant organization. Objectives should then follow from and be consistent with the mission statement. They should comply with SMART principles.

The planning gap is the difference between objectives and expected results given existing strategies.

Strategy formulation is the process of determining appropriate courses of action for achieving organizational objectives and thereby accomplishing organizational purpose. The way that strategies are developed may vary in different organizations. In some it may be the result of a logical linear planning process being followed, in others they may emerge as environmental changes take place or may develop as a series of incremental and short-term steps.

A number of factors can influence the goals and strategies of organizations. These can include the stakeholders of the organization, organizational culture, ethical, corporate social responsibility and corporate governance considerations.

Stakeholders are groups or individuals who have a stake and an interest in the objectives and actions of an organization. Organizations may hold different views of the extent to which stakeholder objectives should be taken into consideration.

Organizational cultures are built on shared traditions, norms, beliefs, values, ideologies, attitudes and ways of behaving.

Ethics are a code of behaviour considered to be morally correct and business ethics can provide businesses with moral guidance in conducting their affairs. An organization might feel that it should exceed minimum obligations to stakeholders, and the extent to which it does so is a reflection of *corporate social responsibility*. There can be strategic benefits of corporate social responsibility.

The formal system by which organizations are directed and controlled is called corporate governance. This is concerned with the relationship and responsibilities between the board, management, shareholders and other relevant stakeholders.

Further reading

Johnson, G., Scholes, K. and Whittington, R. (2005) *Exploring Corporate Strategy: Text and cases*, Prentice-Hall, 7th edn. FT/Prentice-Hall.

Organizational culture:
Miles, R.E. and Snow, C.C. (1978) *Organization Strategy, Structure and Process*. McGraw-Hill.
Handy, C.B. (1976) *Understanding Organisations*. Penguin Books.

Ethics:
Crane, A. and Matten, D. (2007) *Business Ethics*, 2nd edn. Oxford.
Porter, M.E. and Kramer, M.R. (2006) Strategy and Society: The link between competitive advantage and corporate social responsibility. *Harvard Business Review*.

Answers to activities

Activity 13.1

The EasyJet statement does include a number of areas suggested in the guidelines considered:

(a) Its market covers Europe. A good value service should be provided.
(b) The service must be safe for customers and be consistent and reliable in order to appeal to its target customers (the leisure and business market).
(c) To achieve these market goals, EasyJet mentions the need to 'develop its people' and establish 'lasting relationships with its suppliers'.

Activity 13.2

(a) Sales revenue: £2,000,000 in 2009.
(b) Scrap level: 0.5% or less in 2009.

Activity 13.3

A company designing and selling fashion clothing will need to be able to respond to changing fashions and quickly bring out new products that better meet market needs. Using the Miles and Snow typology, a prospector culture might be appropriate.

If the company is selling school uniform clothing then it will be necessary to sell the goods at a cheap price and therefore a cost leadership strategy is most likely required and a defender culture may be appropriate.

Activity 13.4

(a)

(i) The current and future legal position in relation to health and safety standards.
(ii) Cost of each project. Potential costs in the light of future action to tighten pollution controls.
(iii) Business ethics at a societal, corporate and individual level.
(iv) Stakeholder analysis. Who are the key stakeholders and what interest/power do these stakeholders have that could act for or against either of the strategies. Consider also the commercial benefits of an ethical stance.

(b) Review the implications of the four questions noted in the section on ethics at the individual level.

Exercises

Q13.1 Provide a detailed review of key issues to consider in answer to Activity 13.4.

Q13.2 To what extent is it appropriate for a political party to follow a planned, emergent or incremental strategy.

Questions 13.3 to 13.5 draw on a case scenario from Dundee Bicycle Division Part A and Dundee Bicycle Division Part B.

Q13.3 Identify the stakeholders of Dundee Bicycle Division. How should the views of these stakeholders be taken into account when developing the mission statement and objectives for the organization.

Q13.4

(a) Identify the issues that you consider should be included in a mission statement for the division.
(b) Write a mission statement that you consider would be suitable for the division, which meets the issues identified in (a) above.

Q13.5 Write objectives for the budget year 20X9 in relation to profitability, quality and on-time delivery to customers in a manner that complies with the SMART principles. Make 'reasonable' assumptions in the preparation of these objectives, e.g. assume a certain performance measure and target for each area of performance.
Hint: Some information on existing quality and delivery time performance is provided at the end of part B of the case scenario. Information on budgeted and revised estimate profitability is provided in part A.

Questions 13.6 to 13.7 draw on a case scenario from Dundee Bicycle Division Part B.

Q13.6 What action would you advise the works manager to take in relation to the proposal that no repair work should be undertaken to the damaged wall of the factory? What action would you advise if the condition of the wall deteriorated and Jack Jones still refused to authorize any repairs?

Q13.7 Are the typologies of (a) Handy and (b) Miles and Snow appropriate for analysing the organizational culture of Dundee Bicycle Division? What changes in the culture appear to be occurring and what are the implications of this change? How could the management of the organization attempt to rectify any potential adverse consequences of the change in culture?

Questions 13.8 to 13.10 can be answered using the case scenarios of (a) Siegmund Ltd and/or (b) McLoed Ltd – Assembly Division. In answering the questions for either company, make any assumptions that you feel are appropriate.

Q13.8 Identify the stakeholders of the company. How should the views of these stakeholders be taken into account when developing the mission statement and objectives for the organization?

Q13.9

(a) Identify the issues that you consider should be included in a mission statement for the company.
(b) Write a mission statement that you consider would be suitable for the company, which meets the issues identified in (a) above.

Q13.10 Choose three dimensions of performance and write objectives for them in a manner that complies with SMART principles. You will need to make assumptions in the preparation of these objectives on an appropriate measure of performance for each dimension and an acceptable target for this performance measure.

STRATEGIC ANALYSIS – THE EXTERNAL ENVIRONMENT

Objectives

When you have completed this chapter you should be able to:

- Explain the importance of organizations undertaking an appraisal of the external environment.
- Use the following techniques:

    - PESTEL analysis, which involves an analysis of the general environment.
    - Competitor analysis, using Porter's five forces model.
    - Market analysis, which is concerned with identifying specific market segments in which the organization might wish to compete.

- Draw on the PESTEL, market and competitor analysis to produce a summary of key opportunities and threats in the environment.

Introduction to environmental appraisal

In considering alternative strategies, it is important that an organization takes into account events and potential changes in the environment. As an example, launching a new product that requires considerable amounts of cash may be an appropriate strategy if the economy is in a growth situation and funding is easily available. It is likely to be a riskier strategy if the economy is heading for a depression and obtaining funds is difficult.

An external environment can be considered to operate at three levels:

1. *The general or macro-environment.* Changes here affect the whole economy and not just a specific market and can be political, economic, social, technological, ecological or legal (PESTEL). The chapter will explain the use of PESTEL analysis.
2. The *competitive forces* that exist in specific industries and markets. To help identify the sources of competition, the use of Porter's (1980) five forces model will be reviewed.

3. The specific *market* in which the organization operates. Market analysis identifies consumers as market segments and is concerned with estimating the size of particular market segments and the most appropriate product or service features that should be promoted for each segment.

The analysis of the macro-environment, the competitive environment and the market place will all help identify threats and opportunities that are external to the organization. Strategies that are chosen by the organization should take advantage of these environmental opportunities and/or combat the environmental threats.

As illustration, an analysis of the external environment faced by airline companies will be undertaken in this chapter.

Macro-environmental changes

General or macro-environmental changes affect the whole economy and not just a specific market. They can be political, economic, social, technological, ecological or legal:

Political	Government policies towards industry, taxation, foreign trade regulations.
Economic	Interest rate changes, inflation levels, energy costs, economic growth, unemployment, money supply, disposable income.
Social	Population changes, income distribution, education level, attitudes to work and leisure, level of education.
Technological	New discoveries, speed of technological transfer, rate of obsolescence.
Ecological	Environmental protection, energy consumption, pollution.
Legal	Monopoly and merger legislation, employment law, product safety, health and safety.

Different environmental changes are likely to be important for different organizations. A manufacturing organization might be particularly interested in changes in technology, for example a manufacturer of videotape recorders should have been concerned with the developments in digital technology, which eventually led to the sharp decline in demand for video playing equipment. The owner of a small grocers shop would be particularly concerned about planning laws, which might allow large out-of-town supermarkets to be built. Local consumer tastes and behaviour would also be important. If consumers start to demand higher-quality goods or more organic fruit and vegetables, then the grocer should be aware of how such changes could impact on demand for existing produce that is sold in the shop; it might also highlight to the grocer the need to change the range of products currently offered. All organizations are likely to be affected by economic changes, for example rises in interest rates and taxation are likely to affect consumer demand and the cost of borrowing.

An example of a PESTEL analysis undertaken for the airline industry is considered in Figure 14.1.

Political

Politicians have exercised control over the sector in a number of ways:

(P1) Traditionally, governments provided subsidies to most national airlines. Without this aid, several of the airlines would not have been able to continue trading. More recently, trade agreements have prevented governments from continuing to provide the same level of financial support and this has meant that the airline companies have no longer been able to rely on the government to subsidize loss-making routes.

(P2) The policy in many countries throughout the world has been to privatize the national airline. Once a company has been privatized, it is likely that it will have more freedom to operate and make decisions without interference from government.

(P3) For many years, governments maintained strict regulations on the airline industries. In 1997 the European Union established a single aviation market in Europe, which freed airlines to make their own decisions on access, capacity and fares. Similarly, liberalization has occurred in other areas of the world such as the USA and Australasia.

(P4) Demand for flights appears to be highly elastic in relation to incomes and any changes in taxation could have a major impact on income.

(P5) Increased concerns on the environmental damage caused by the airline industry may result in increased taxation in the future.

Economic factors

(E1) The effect of economic cycles. The early 1990s saw a major downturn in a number of economies around the world. This in turn led to a sharp fall in passenger numbers, in particular the demand for premium services such as business and first class, which are primarily used by business passengers. This decline led to a major adverse impact on airline profitability, with many recording substantial losses. Since many airlines lease their aircraft, a sharp downturn in passenger demand and profitability also had a quick impact on the demand for, and costs of, leased aircraft.

(E2) Changes in foreign exchange rates. Some airlines can earn up to half their revenues in foreign currencies and in such an instance any fluctuation in the exchange rate will have a big impact on earnings.

(E3) A rise in interest rates can reduce consumer and business spending. It can also reduce business investment by raising the cost of borrowing.

(E4) Rising unemployment and increased concerns over consumer debt and a need to save for pensions could have an impact on the use of flights for leisure purposes.

Social factors

A range of changes in demographic and social and cultural factors can also have an impact on the main airline markets.

(S1) There are a number of demographic changes that are having an impact on the number and demands of leisure travellers.

   a. An increasing number of retired people.
   b. A decline in the average family size should encourage a shift from surface to air travel for leisure. This segment of the population is likely to be very cost-conscious.
   c. An increasing student population, with leisure time. Again this segment of the population is likely to be cost-conscious.

Figure 14.1 Pestal analysis of the airline industry

(S2) Changing holiday patterns.

    a. An increasing trend for younger people to take a number of short leisure breaks a year and to travel by air.

    b. Changing fashions in holidays. An increasing number of holidays are now to more distant locations.

    c. Ownership of holiday homes in other countries.

    d. Willingness to organize own holidays and not use 'packages'.

(S3) Changing work patterns.

    a. Work pressures have increased and business travellers are often expected to conduct their business as soon as they arrive at their destination. This has meant that such travellers value, and are prepared to pay for, extra comfort on long-haul flights.

    b. Migrant workers travelling between their European home and the UK.

Technological factors

(T1) The impact of the internet.

    a. The internet has had a major impact on the way that many businesses interact with consumers (B2C). Employees from the same organization can use video conferencing and alternative electronic approaches rather than flying to attend meetings. For contact with external customers, face-to-face contact still appears to be important.

    b. Airlines can now establish web sites for their own business. Direct selling and paperless ticketing has also meant that companies can reduce selling costs by bypassing travel agents.

(T2) Impact of technological change on aircraft design. In previous decades, technological improvements have led to substantial cost savings. This fall in costs has mainly come through the increase in the size of aircraft, with some technological leaps. While there is still some potential for technological improvements, it is felt that these will have a more marginal impact on running costs. In recent years a new trend has emerged, with aircraft being withdrawn from service due to age rather than technological obsolescence.

(T3) Investment in road and rail transport. Additional investment is taking place in many countries on faster roads and high-speed rail links. This is likely to draw traffic away from air transport, particularly for short journeys.

Ecological

(Eco1) Greater concerns about the environmental impact of increased numbers of aircraft. Aircraft manufacturers are reported to be designing aircraft that will do less damage to the environment. A new generation of jets will fly more slowly than existing jets but have more efficient engines that use up 20% less fuel and are half as noisy.

(Eco2) Planning constraints on expansion of airports. The expansion of services at some airports is limited due to planning constraints.

(Eco3) Impact of world terrorism. Following 11 September 2001, airline travel fell significantly for a period of time.

Figure 14.1 (*Continued*)

Legal

(L1) EU legislation. EU legislation sets limits on the level of state aid provided to European airlines.

(L2) Monopolies and mergers legislation. Potential mergers that might result in individual airlines controlling too great a proportion of a market might be referred to organizations such as the monopolies and mergers commission in the UK.

(L3) Employment legislation. Maximum flight hours allowed for airline pilots in set periods of time.

The information in Figure 14.1 and other figures on the airline industry in this and two subsequent chapters has been informed by the work of several writers (see Doganis 2006, Hanlon 1999, Shaw 2007, Gittel 2002) a number of newspaper and journal articles and web based sources. The level of analysis on the airline industry provided is limited in scope and detail, however sufficient for illustrative purposes.

Figure 14.1 *(Continued)*

A consideration of the changes in the macro-environment of the airline industry, identified in Figure 14.1, will highlight events that could have a significant impact on the success of a commercial airline.

Activity 14.1

Identify general or macro-environment changes that may lead to an expansion in the number of flights of a low-cost airline.

Activity 14.2

Identify potential changes in the general or macro-environment that are likely to have a detrimental impact on a strategy of expanding the number of flights of a low-cost airline.

A further use of PESTEL analysis is in scenario analysis. A range of scenarios can be built up based on possible future situations. Strategic options can then be tested against the scenarios to help construct strategic plans and develop contingency plans to meet different possible environmental outcomes.

Competitor analysis

Organizations are likely to prefer to operate in an industry or market where there are weak competitive forces. In such an environment it will be easier to dominate and increase sales and profits. If the competitive forces are strong it will be much more difficult to be successful.

Five forces analysis

Porter (1980) identified five forces that will influence the competitive position of an organization. These include:

(a) The intensity of the rivalry of existing competitors.
(b) The threat of potential entrants to the market.
(c) The bargaining power of suppliers of raw material to the organization.
(d) The bargaining power of buyers of the organization's products and services.
(e) The threat of substitute products being developed and introduced to the market.

Ideally an organization would like to operate in a competitive environment where:

- There is little existing competitive rivalry.
- There are high barriers[1] to entry and few potential entrants are likely to enter and compete through lower costs or other means.
- The suppliers of raw materials to the organization have weak bargaining power and are therefore unable to command a premium price for their products or services.
- Buyers of the products or services of the organization have weak bargaining power and so are unable to exert any power to demand lower prices or higher quality or other performance attribute.
- There is a low threat of substitute products being used through technological or other breakthroughs.

If a firm is able to operate in such an environment, it should mean that it will earn high profits. Such conditions, however, are unlikely to exist for any length of time as the high profit potential will attract new firms into the market segment. If the reverse conditions exist in a market segment then the business will be operating in a very competitive environment, profits are likely to be low and survival a struggle.

Each of the five forces will now be considered in turn, with a discussion of the key factors that influence the strength of each force. As illustration, the short-haul low-cost market in the airline industry (e.g. 300 miles–1000 miles in Europe) will be considered.

Competitor rivalry

Competitive rivalry may take the form of price competition, product differentiation, advertising battles and increased customer service and is likely to be stronger with:

- Many or equally balanced competitors.
- Slow industry growth. If there is slow industry growth, then to increase sales, firms need to fight over market share.

---

[1] **Barriers to entry.** Sometimes there may be strong barriers preventing a new firm entering an industry or market. Reasons can include the high level of investment required or the fact that existing firms in the market are achieving economies of scale, which a new entrant cannot match.

Barriers to exit. There can also exist barriers to organizations leaving a market segment. For example, it may be necessary to write off asset value or there might be high closure costs.

- High fixed costs in the industry. If fixed costs are high, then firms need to sell more to break even and make a profit.
- Low switching costs for the buyer.
- Widely differing objectives and strategies of competitors.
- High exit barriers. Given high costs of leaving, competitors may decide to continue in the market segment.

See Figure 14.2.

Competitor rivalry in the airline industry

Until the latter part of the twentieth century, governments maintained close regulatory control on the airlines in terms of what routes they were allowed to fly, the frequency of flights and prices. With the deregulation of the industry, airlines have been able to identify particular routes and then start new services on routes of their choice. Where new low-cost airlines have started services they have been able to gain market share relatively quickly, meaning that competitive rivalry has increased substantially on many routes.

Factors that have led to this competitive rivalry include a number of equally balanced competitors on specific routes and low switching costs of the buyers (increasingly individual buyers who are buying direct from the airlines on-line).

For the 'leisure' market segment, price is the key competitive factor on the short-haul routes and lower prices have generated substantial growth in this sector. Product features such as in-flight service are important on longer routes, however, they are of less concern to customers – whether they are business or leisure travellers – on shorter routes.

Business travellers will be particularly concerned with punctuality, timeliness and frequency of service.

Figure 14.2   Competitive rivalry in the airline industry

Potential entrants

Potential entrants are more likely to enter if *barriers to entry* are low. The seven main barriers to entry are:

1. Economies of scale occur where large-scale production has led to a low cost per unit. Where the existing competitors have already achieved economies of scale, this acts as a high barrier to new competitors entering the market. There can be a number of reasons for economies of scale, including:

   - Technical economies, for example larger plant size being used more economically.
   - Managerial economies, where specialist staff can be employed more efficiently.
   - Purchasing and marketing economies. With bulk buying, raw materials can be purchased more cheaply and the cost of the sales force and other marketing costs do not need to increase in relation to sales.
   - Financial economies. Small firms find it difficult to finance new investments. Larger firms have a much greater choice for finance.

2. Large capital requirements. These may be required to finance research and development, an initial advertising campaign or high start-up losses.
3. High costs to the buyer if they switch suppliers.
4. Access to distribution channels.
5. Non-scale cost disadvantages such as patents, location, favourable access to materials, monopoly control of a resource.
6. Government regulation or licensing.
7. Product differentiation. This is the degree to which a product is regarded by a user as different from, and of higher value than, a competitor.

See Figure 14.3.

Threat of new entrants in the airline industry

There are low barriers to entry in this industry as:

- There are low economies of scale. If a new company wishes to start a single point-to-point route, for example from one of the regional airports in the UK to a European location, the start-up costs are low. It is relatively easy to lease aircraft, hire crews and buy support services at similar cost to those already in use on different routes.
- Low capital requirement. It is possible to lease rather than purchase aircraft.
- Consumers and agencies who buy airline tickets can easily change from purchasing tickets from one airline to purchasing from another.
- Regulations preventing access to individual point-to-point short-haul routes have been removed.

Although there has been a high mortality rate of low-cost airlines, the low barriers to entry seem to have encouraged many new entrants into the market.

Figure 14.3   Threat of new entrants in the airline industry

Suppliers bargaining power

A company is more likely to be in a weak bargaining position relative to suppliers when:

1. Suppliers are dominated by a few companies.
2. The industry is a minor customer for the product and therefore not important to the suppliers. In such an instance, the supplier may be unwilling to give concessions on price.
3. A supplier's product is an important input to the product or service of the buyer, who cannot risk losing this input.
4. There are few substitutes for the product or service provided by the supplier and the buyer has to incur high switching costs in moving to another product. For example, if it was necessary to redesign the product to accommodate a change.
5. Suppliers' products are differentiated and specific features offered by particular suppliers are of added value to the buyer.

See Figure 14.4.

Suppliers' bargaining power in the airline industry

The bargaining power of suppliers can vary according to market conditions and location. New airlines, however, are often in a strong position compared with a number of their suppliers, which include aircraft leasing companies, airports, engineering support services and the providers of a range of distribution services.

Boeing and Airbus are the two major aircraft manufacturers, however, there are also a number of leasing organizations that purchase aircraft from manufacturers and then lease them to the airlines. The bargaining power of suppliers of aircraft is strongly influenced by the economic cycle. During recessionary periods, the suppliers of aircraft in particular are in a relatively weak position and with many aircraft not flying, it is possible to either lease or purchase airplanes under very favourable conditions. During boom periods, suppliers are in a considerably stronger position.

Access to the major airports, such as London (Heathrow) and London (Gatwick), can be difficult for new airlines and they are in a weak position in negotiating terms with such airports. However, in most locations around the world, major cities have a number of satellite airports, which are keen to offer good terms to airlines. For example, Ryanair (at Stansted) and EasyJet (at Luton) have managed to negotiate good terms with two London satellite airports.

Aircraft support services are readily available at competitive rates. A number of the major airlines are prepared to service aircraft for other airlines. Although they are providing a service to competitors, the logic for doing this is that the work will provide a contribution to the overheads of the supplier organization and if they do not provide the service, then another competitor will.

There are a limited number of providers of distribution services. When travel agents book tickets they can compare prices and book the tickets using a global distribution system (GDS). Traditional airlines have sold up to 85–90% of tickets through GDS systems and this has meant that the companies running the GDS systems have had great power in negotiations. With the advent of the internet, low-cost airlines have been able to sell direct to customers and thus bypass the GDS suppliers.

Overall then, the suppliers do not have a strong bargaining position in relation to the airline industries, unless the airlines are negotiating aircraft purchases or lease acquisition during periods of strong economic activity.

Figure 14.4 Suppliers bargaining power in the airline industry

Buyers' bargaining power

A market is less attractive to a company when it has a weak bargaining position relative to buyers of its products or services due to conditions such as:

1. The buyer group is concentrated.
2. A given buyer buys a major proportion of output.
3. The product is a major cost element for the buyer.
4. The buyer earns low profits.
5. The buyer faces low switching costs. Alternative products can be purchased with no or little requirements for redesign or development costs.
6. Buyers pose a threat of backward integration, i.e. the buyer can take over the supplier.

7. The product is unimportant to the buyer.
8. The buyer has full information about the supplier's cost structure and competitive position.

See Figure 14.5.

Buyers' bargaining power

It is necessary to identify the buyers. In the airline industry, traditionally most airline tickets have been purchased through travel agents and bucket shops and for the leisure market from tour operators, rather than through individual customers. This has meant that these buyers have had a great deal of power to negotiate lower prices from the airlines. There has also been a risk of backward integration with large tour operators also acquiring or establishing their own airlines to deliver their own customers to the tourist locations.

More recently, the advent of direct selling has meant that increasingly individual customers are also the purchasers of the tickets. Some low-cost airlines do attract a significant proportion of business travellers, where timing and location are particularly suitable, although many leisure customers are flexible as to the tourist destination and are sensitive to price.

Figure 14.5   Buyers bargaining power

Threat of substitute products

Substitute products are often not easy to identify, but there must be a search for other products that can carry out the same function, however dissimilar they may appear. See Figure 14.6.

Threat of substitute products

In the short-haul market, substitute products include car, train and boat services. Travelling by train is a clear substitute when high-speed train access is available for the whole journey, while improved motorway links are also likely to have an impact.

There is also the potential for new technology to reduce business travel, for example increased use of video conferencing facilities.

Figure 14.6   Threats of substitute products

Activity 14.3

(a) A large number of new airlines have started trading in recent years.
(b) A number of traditional airlines have withdrawn from flying on certain routes on which low-cost airlines have opened services.

For both (a) and (b), use the five forces model to explain why this is the case.

As with any framework, care should be taken in using and interpreting the results of the five forces analysis. Firstly, it is a static model and in practice the competitive environment can change, often quite rapidly. Secondly, an assumption is made that the environment is a threat, for example the suppliers to the organization, however a number of organizations engage in close cooperation with suppliers.

Market analysis

Market analysis identifies consumers into market segments and then tries to identify the needs of each market segment. This analysis can help the company in deciding the product attributes that it will promote and the means for promoting these attributes in the market place.

Market segmentation

Market segmentation is the process of dividing a varied and differing group of buyers or potential buyers into smaller groups within which broadly similar patterns of buyers' needs and behaviour exist. By doing this it is possible for the marketer to target the specific market segments more precisely. In general, large organizations concentrate on market segments with high existing or potential sales. Small organizations, by contrast, often ignore such markets because of the level of resources needed to compete and the pressures from large competitors.

The majority of markets can be segmented in a variety of ways, see for example Figure 14.7.

	Consumer market	**Industrial/organization market**
Characteristics of people or organizations	Age, sex, race Income Family size Lifecycle stage Location Lifestyle	Industry Location Size Technology Profitability Management
Purchase/use situation	Size of purchase Brand loyalty Purpose of use Purchasing behaviour Importance of purchase Choice criteria	Application Importance of purchase Volume Frequency of purchase Choice criteria Distribution channel
User needs and preferences for product characteristics	Product similarity Price preference Brand preference Desired features Quality	Performance requirements Assistance from suppliers Brand preference Desired features Quality Service requirements

Figure 14.7 Segmentation of markets
Source: Market segmentation, Johnson, G., Scholes, K. and Whittington, R. (2005). *Exploring Corporate Strategy: Text and Cases.* 7th edn., p. 94, FT/Prentice-Hall.

Having segmented the market it is possible to identify the key features of these segments and then identify the size and growth potential of each market segment.

A market analysis for the airline industry is considered in Figure 14.8.

It is possible to analyse the airline industry into a number of segments. Many airlines would identify at least two key categories for segmentation, the business and the leisure markets. They would also recognise that there are further differences between the short and the long haul markets.

Business market

Characteristics of people

Business travellers are predominantly wealthy, male and middle-aged, although the proportion of women business travellers is increasing

Purchase/ use situation

A business trip could be on a short haul route of 500 miles (800 kilometres) or so or a long haul route of several thousand miles.

User needs and preference for product characteristics

In chapter 15, the need to identify the attributes that customers value will be discussed in more depth. Desired attributes on an airplane might include the service features that are offered such as the leg room, cabin service or the frequent flyer points. It might also include other features such as the price of the ticket or the reliability of the airline to arrive and depart on time. The attributes that provide value and accordingly the market segment size may vary according to circumstances.

Gittell (2002) reports that Southwest Airlines have noted that cabin service may be less important than reliability for many business people on short haul routes. A business person may be prepared to have fewer comforts for a short journey as a key requirement is that a meeting is attended on time. On the other hand on a long haul route the requirement for product attributes such as service and facilities provided might be more important. For in-flight services, traditional airlines have provided first class and business class services, which provide extra space, free food and drink and leisure activities. At airports, separate lounges and quicker check-in procedures may be provided. A number of airlines have announced the launch of a business class only plane to fly from New York to London to start in 2008. This reflects a growing market for business-class-only travel. It should be noted however that it would be incorrect to assume that the whole business market is insensitive to price, as business people who are self employed are likely to be influenced by the relative prices offered by different airlines.

Leisure market

Characteristics of people

Again consumers can be segmented according to a range of categories including age, sex, income, family size and life cycle stage. The demand for leisure travel, for example, varies through the life cycle of people. Young adults fly frequently. During child rearing years, disposable income is reduced and the needs of families are considered, so that the frequency of holidays declines. Finally when children have left home, subject to pension concerns, disposable income again increases and combined with increased leisure, more holidays can be taken.

Figure 14.8   Market segmentation analysis of the airline industry

Purchase/ use situation

In recent years there has been a major increase in short haul holidays, for example from the UK to various European destinations. There has also been an increase in holidays taken at more distant locations.

User needs and preference for product characteristics

The low cost market has expanded at a fast rate. Most leisure travellers are paying for their own flights and are usually price sensitive. The main purpose of the trip is to enjoy a holiday at the destination and a lower standard of service provision is acceptable. There does seem however to be a growing market, particularly on the longer haul routes, for a premium service at the top end of the leisure market. Airlines are starting to cater for this segment with, for example, the introduction of a 'premium' economy service.

Knowing the size of market segments and the attributes that are important for those segments is crucial to marketing management in order that they can identify the marketing mix that can best achieve the desired level of sales. For further discussion of market segmentation and marketing management in the airline industry see, for example, Shaw (2007). Market segmentation analysis is also relevant for the accounting function, as managers will wish to understand the profitability of individual segments. This is discussed further in chapter 16.

Figure 14.8 (*Continued*)

Activity 14.4

Given the market analysis, which market segments would be of particular interest to a low-cost airline and what are the important features of an airline service for those market segments?

Identifying threats and opportunities

- *An opportunity* – a change in the external environment that might help to advance the organization.
- *A threat* – a change that may destabilize and/or reduce the potential of the organization.

Having undertaken an appraisal of the wider external environment using PESTEL analysis, market analysis and an analysis of the competitive environment using the five forces model, it is possible to summarize the main opportunities and threats.

Activity 14.5

From a review of the environment (PESTEL), market and competitive forces analysis, identify the opportunities and threats in the environment for a traditional airline company.

Analysis of individual competitors and identification of strategic options

Having understood the threats and opportunities in the environment, organizations also need to understand their strengths and weaknesses compared with major competitors. This analysis is considered in the next chapter.

In Chapter 17, ways in which a company might use this information to identify suitable strategic options that take into consideration strengths and weaknesses of the organization and take advantage of opportunities and threats of the environment are considered.

Summary

In considering different strategies, it is important that an organization takes into account potential changes in the environment that could have a large impact on the success of that strategy. These include:

- General or macro-environment factors, including political and economic events, social change, technological, innovations, ecological and legal factors (PESTEL).
- The competitive pressures in the industry. Competitor analysis can be undertaken using Porter's five forces analysis.
- The changing size and needs of individual market segments.
- Using the analysis of the macro-environment, the market place and the competitive environment will all help identify threats and opportunities in the environment.

Further reading

Johnson, G., Scholes, K. and Whittington, R. (2005) *Exploring Corporate Strategy: Text and Cases*, 7th edn. FT/Prentice-Hall.

For a further analysis of the airline industry:

Doganis, R. (2006) *The Airline Business*, Florence, KY, USA: Routledge.
Hanlon, P (1999) *Global Airlines*, 2nd edn, Butterworth Heinemann, Oxford.

Gittell, J. H. (2002) *Southwest Airlines Way: The Power of Relationships for Superior Performance*, McGraw-Hill.

Shaw, S. (2007) *Airline Marketing and Management*, 6th edn, Ashgate.

For in depth studies of the airline industry, a number of reports are available from Mintel.

More in-depth review of the business environment:

Kew, J. and Stredwick, J. (2005) *Business Environment: Managing in a strategic business context*. CIPD, London.

Morrison, J. (2006) *The International Business Environment: Global and Local Marketplaces in a Changing World*, 2nd edn. Palgrave Macmillan, Basingstoke.

Answers to activities

Activity 14.1

A number of favourable economic factors could have a beneficial impact on a strategy of expanding the number of flights. An upturn in the general economy, a favourable exchange rate for the main customers of the airline, a fall in interest rates, which will boost consumer and business spending and mean that borrowing is lower, falling unemployment. As well as such economic factors, a range of political, social and legal factors are likely to have a favourable impact. For example, those labelled P1, P3, S1, S2, L1, L2 in Figure 14.1.

Activity 14.2

The opposite economic factors will have a detrimental effect on the strategy, e.g. a downturn in the economy, a deterioration in exchange rates for the main customers of the airline, a rise in interest rates, which will depress consumer and business spending and mean that borrowing is more expensive, rising unemployment. Issues related to the ecological environment labelled eco1, eco2, eco3 as well as P5 and L3 could result in an adverse impact.

Activity 14.3

(a) Reasons can be identified in the review of competitive forces carried out in the chapter. In particular, there are weak barriers to entry with low economies of scale, low capital investment and suppliers' bargaining power at regional airports is often weak.

(b) Many competitors also leave the industry and the five forces analysis of the airline sector suggests that a reason could be the strong competitive forces in the short-haul market segment.

- Increasingly there are a number of airlines competing on price and on features such as frequency and punctuality rather than in-flight service.
- There are low barriers to entry for competitors and new entrants are attracted to the industry (although there is also a high failure rate).
- The bargaining position of suppliers varies according to economic conditions. During slump periods such as the early 1990s, for example, there were many aircraft available for lease at low rates. The bargaining power of airports varies according to location. Some satellite airports have weak bargaining power and will offer competitive rates to low-cost airlines willing to use their airport.
- Bargaining power of buyers. Traditionally, most airline tickets have been purchased through travel agents and bucket shops and these buyers have had a high bargaining power. The low-cost airlines have not used these agents and have sold tickets direct to customers. These customers have low power to reduce prices on specific routes, although there are low switching costs for these customers who are often flexible on the date of flights and to some extent on location.
- Substitute products, such as fast trains and improved motorway connections, will have some impact on some routes.

The conditions necessary for airlines to exist in the low-cost market are considered in more detail in the next chapter. The impact of fast turn-around and 'no-frills', in particular, has meant that many traditional airlines have struggled to compete and have withdrawn from a number of short-haul routes.

Activity 14.4

A number of different ways of segmenting the market were discussed in Figure 14.8. Two major segments are leisure and business travellers. These can be subdivided into further categories. For leisure travellers, low cost appears to be a main feature. Business travellers are likely to be more concerned with reliability. It is important that they arrive at a meeting at the scheduled time.

Activity 14.5

A review of key threats and opportunities in the environment is likely to identify the following.

Threats

1. Ending of subsidies means that the airline cannot look to the government to solve its financial problems.
2. Ending of regulation means that all routes may be subject to competition.
3. Substantial losses in the airline may occur during economic downturns.
4. Strong financial management skills are required to ensure that losses are not incurred due to foreign exchange fluctuations.
5. Introduction of technology such as video conferencing may have an adverse impact on the number of business travellers.

6. Investment in road and rail transport and the development of high-speed train links is likely to adversely affect air travel on short-haul routes.
7. World terrorism is likely to adversely affect air travel.
8. There are potential constraints on capacity due to planning restrictions at the main airports.
9. Consideration of the five forces model indicates that the short-haul market segment is likely to remain competitive on a number of routes, particularly due to high competitive rivalry and low barriers to entry.

Opportunities

1. Increasing demand for high-quality service on long-haul flights by business travellers provides an opportunity to meet a new consumer demand.
2. Rising incomes plus changing demographics and social and cultural factors also provide an opportunity to meet a new consumer demand. In particular, the demand for 'exotic' (i.e. long distance) as well as short-haul holidays is increasing.
3. Wide customer use of the internet means that direct selling of tickets is increasingly possible.

Exercises

Q14.1 Conduct a PESTEL analysis, a competitive analysis (using the five forces model) and a market analysis for the Assembly Division of McLoed Ltd (see case scenario material). Identify those environmental factors that could be considered to be threats and those that are opportunities. Identify the further information that you would need in order to complete a fuller market analysis.

You can refer to the information on the UK bicycle industry in the section of this book containing the case information.

Q14.2 Conduct a PESTEL analysis; market analysis; competitive analysis for Siegmund Ltd. Identify those environmental factors that could be considered to be threats and those that are opportunities. Identify the further information that you would need in order to complete a fuller market analysis. Consider the implications of your analysis for Siegmund Ltd and identify the key environmental threats and opportunities identified.

Refer to the case scenario provided on Siegmund Ltd in the section on case information.

Q14.3 Conduct a PESTEL analysis; competitive analysis (using the five forces model) and a market analysis for one of the following industries. Identify those environmental factors that could be considered to be threats and those that are opportunities.

 (i) A holiday home and campsite resort such as 'Sunshine Sites' mentioned in the case scenario Coopers Leisure Resorts Ltd.
 (ii) A chain of shops selling expensive fashion clothing.

(iii) The motor car industry.

(iv) An industry/market sector of your choice.

Note that information on a range of market sectors is available in market research provided by organizations such as Mintel, which can be accessed through a number of libraries.

Q14.4 Would farmers or the supermarkets buying their produce have the higher bargaining power? Explain why.

INTERNAL APPRAISAL OF THE ORGANIZATION

15

Objectives

At the end of this chapter students should be able to explain key principles of undertaking an internal appraisal of the organization, including:

- Undertaking a market analysis and appraisal of products and services employing

  - Profitability and sales analysis by market segment.
  - Product lifecycle analysis.
  - Portfolio analysis.

- How to achieving competitive advantage through

  - Identifying the attributes that add value for customers.
  - Strategic positioning of the organization.

- Identifying the sources of competitive advantage through

  - Undertaking a resource audit.

    - Financial resources and performance.
    - Physical resources.
    - Personnel resources.
    - Intangible assets.

  - Identifying organizational capabilities.

    - Value chain analysis.

- Benchmarking.

Introduction

In Chapter 14, the importance of general, market and competitor analysis for the strategic management process was reviewed. This chapter investigates the need for an *internal appraisal* of the organization and an assessment on how well the organization is performing in its chosen markets and in comparison with competitors.

The first section of the chapter considers the appraisal of the performance of the products and services of the company in terms of the level of sales and stage in the product lifecycle. A comparative analysis can also be made to the products and services of competitors.

The identification of the attributes of products and services that provide value is fundamental to strategic management and will be considered in a second section. If an organization can provide some feature that is particularly valued by customers, whether this is low cost or some unique dimension which can command a premium price, then it may be able to sustain a higher profit than the industry average. A company is then said to possess a **competitive advantage** over its rivals.

To achieve competitive advantage, a business should have better resources and/or carry out its key processes and activities better than its competitors. Resource analysis is reviewed in the third section and the assessment of competencies in a fourth section.

When a business has identified the key areas of performance for success in a market, then it should monitor its performance in these areas and compare itself against the performance of others. This is a technique called benchmarking, which will be considered in the final section of the chapter.

Market analysis and appraisal of products and services

The product lifecycle

Product lifecycle theory suggests that all products go through a cycle of development, introduction, growth, maturity and decline, and in Chapter 2 it was suggested that different pricing policies might be appropriate at different stages of this lifecycle. There are other implications in terms of cash flow, profits and the organization's strategy.

Cash flows

Products at different stages of their product lifecycle are also likely to make substantially different demands on cash flow. In the early stages of the product lifecycle, at the development and early part of the introduction stage, there is a heavy net outflow of cash. Cash receipts from sales are low and at the same time there is a heavy outflow of cash required for investment in research and development, production and other facilities. As sales increase in the growth phase, there is likely to be a break-even cash flow situation. Although cash receipts are increasing, there is still a significant investment requirement as capacity is expanded. At the mature stage, little additional investment is required while cash receipts are at a peak. During the decline stage, cash flows can be positive as no investment is required. See Figure 15.1.

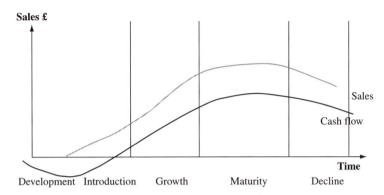

Figure 15.1 The product lifecycle and likely cash demands

Profits

At the development and introduction stages losses will tend to occur, as sales are low and there are high initial set-up costs. Profits and profit per unit are likely to be higher during the growth stage as a result of gaining economies of scale. At the maturity stage, the existence of a large number of competitors is likely to drive down prices and profit per unit. At this stage there is also likely to be a shakeout of competitors as the least efficient operators leave the market. As sales of the product decline, profits and profits per unit will usually continue to decline.

Strategy

Strategy has also been linked to the product lifecycle.

1. A *build* strategy is one in which an organization aims to build market share even if this is at the expense of cash flow and profits. This might occur if a company has a number of products at the introduction and growth stage of the product lifecycle and wishes to grow quickly.
2. A *hold* strategy is one in which an organization aims to maintain its market share and is most likely to occur for organizations with products at the mature stage of the product lifecycle.
3. A *harvest* strategy is one where the organization extracts as much cash as possible, keeps reinvestment to a minimum and potentially sells off the product or service. This strategy is often used at the decline stage of the cycle.

Monitoring competitive position – product portfolio analysis

Ideally, the profitability and sales of individual products and services should be analysed, where possible by market segment. Product profitability analysis is considered further in Chapter 16.

Market size, market share and market growth are also important areas to monitor as these are important drivers for future profits. A number of alternative approaches to mapping the portfolio of products of an organization, along such dimensions, have been suggested in the literature. One that is illustrated here is the growth share matrix, initially developed by the Boston Consulting Group (BCG). See Figure 15.2. The growth share matrix shows the market growth rate on the vertical axis and the relative market share of products on the horizontal axis. The central vertical line identifies the division between high and low market share. In the original version of the matrix, low market share is identified as the point where the share is less than the largest competitor in a particular market segment, while high market share represents a market share that is higher than the largest competitor. The line itself represents the market share of the largest competitor. Where a company does not have any products with a higher market share than key competitors, it may wish to decide on its own definition of 'high' and 'low' share of the market.

Market Growth (%)	High	Cell A STARS	Cell B QUESTION MARKS
	Low	Cell C CASH COWS	Cell D DOGS
		High	Low
		Market share (%)	

Figure 15.2   The growth share matrix (or BCG matrix)

The matrix has four cells and using this matrix, all products are analysed into one of these cells.

Cell A – products which have a high market growth but also have a high market share when compared with their competitors are called STARS. Even though such products have a high market share, little cash (if any) is being generated because of the need to plough cash back into the business. Additional plant and equipment is required in order to meet the increased sales demand.

Cell B – products which are operating in a market with high growth but where the market share of the company is low are called QUESTION MARKS. They usually require large amounts of cash spent on them as it is necessary to invest additional resources in order to increase share.

Cell C – products which are in a low growth market but have a high market share are called CASH COWS. These products generate significant amounts of cash as they are profitable and little reinvestment is needed.

Cell D – products in a low growth market and with a low market share are called DOGS.

While the product lifecycle highlights the likely trend in sales, the BCG matrix provides a picture of the current situation. Note that there may be a relationship between the cells of the BCG matrix and the stage in the product lifecycle. 'Question marks' are often products at the introduction stage of the product lifecycle, while 'Stars' are likely to be the growth stage of the product lifecycle. 'Cash cows' are usually products at the mature stage of the product lifecycle, while 'Dogs' may be at the decline stage of the product lifecycle. However, the above may not necessarily be the case as they are based on different parameters.

Strategic implications of BCG analysis

An implication for the strategy of an organization is that it should have a balanced portfolio of products, which are most likely at different stages of their product lifecycle. For the future success and survival of the business, new products and services should be being developed and launched. However, since these are net users of funds, in order to avoid additional outside financing, these new products will need to be funded by products at the mature stage that are generating a net cash inflow. If all the products of an organization are 'question marks' (e.g. at the introduction stage of their lifecycle), there is a danger that there will be insufficient cash resources to fund the long-term development of the new products. Many small businesses that are developing a new product or service face this problem of funding expansion.

An alternative problem is faced by a business in which most of its products are at the mature/decline stage. At this stage there is a danger that there are no new products to provide future growth and that total sales and profits will start to decline.

The extent to which an organization is prepared to invest in 'question marks' or 'star' products or to sell off 'dogs' will depend on whether it is following a *build*, *hold* or *harvest* strategy.

An illustrative example of the BCG product market matrix is shown in Figure 15.3.

Burnaby PLC manufactures a range of four main products for four different market areas.

	Sales (£)	Market share (%)	Market growth (%)
Product Alpha	100,000	10	1
Product Beta	20,000	4	-2
Product Gamma	80,000	10	5
Product Delta	15,000	3	10

In identifying products with cells in the BCG matrix, the managers of the company have decided that the low growth is considered to be 3% and under. Rather than using a comparison vs. largest competitor, they will identify a low market share as less than 6%. In the analysis below each circle represents one of the company's products, with the area of each circle proportionate to the share of the company's sales represented by that product.

Figure 15.3   Analysis of the products of Burnaby PLC using the growth share matrix (or BCG matrix)

For Burnaby PLC there appears to be a relatively balanced portfolio. Product Alpha is the largest selling product and a 'cash cow' that is generating funds which can selling product and a 'cash cow' that is generating funds which can be invested into product Delta, which is the 'question mark' and project Gamma, which is the star. The company may consider whether it is worth disposing of product Beta, which appears to be a 'dog'

Note that the circles drawn to represent each of the products are approximately in proportion to the size of sales. Thus the circle representing sales of product Alpha (£100,000), which is shown as a 'cash cow' in cell C, is approximately twice the size of the sales of product Beta (£50,000), which is shown in cell A.

Under these assumptions, the BCG matrix of Burnaby PLC will look as follows:

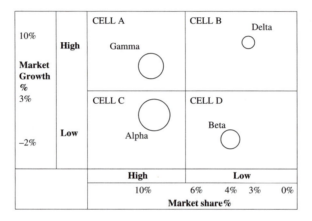

Figure 15.3 (*Continued*)

Problems with using techniques such as BCG analysis

Like many tools and techniques that may help in the analysis of a situation, there are also problems with using the BCG matrix.

Firstly, there is the practical problem of deciding what is a 'high' or 'low' market share or 'market growth'. Using the measure to be a comparison against the largest competitor could be misleading for smaller companies. This approach might lead to classifying all products as either 'dogs', if there is a low market growth, or as 'question marks', if there is a high market growth.

Secondly, managers can use the matrix in a prescriptive manner. For example, they may feel that if a product is classified as a dog then it should be harvested, i.e. there should be no investment and potentially it should be sold off. However, many so-called dogs, as analysed by the matrix, can continue to provide a useful contribution to profits for many years. They may also be necessary in order that the company provides a full product range.

Thirdly, the BCG matrix is a very simple tool that takes account of a limited number of factors, in particular the firm's market share and the growth of the market segment. There may be other factors that are important and should be taken into account when designing a matrix to identify a portfolio of products. For example, the BCG matrix focuses on revenue, it does not consider the profitability or contribution generated by individual products.

Fourthly, there is the choice of the market segment in which the product operates. For example, what is the geographical region chosen – market share in a town or a county or country? A company might have a large market share in a particular county or area, but a small share in an entire country.

Activity 15.1

Able Ltd has identified the following information concerning the sales and market share of its three main products. It has also identified information about market growth of the segment in which each of the products is sold.

	Sales	Market share	Market growth
	(£'000)	(%)	(%)
Product X	1,000	20	7
Product Y	50	4	0
Product Z	800	8	8

High market share is considered to be over 10% and high market growth over 5%.

Required:

1. Provide an analysis of the three main products of Able Ltd using the growth share matrix.
2. Comment on the relevance of your findings.

Achieving competitive advantage

The remainder of this chapter first focuses on the need to identify the factors where success is crucial if an organization is to gain competitive advantage in a particular market or industry. Having identified these factors, it is necessary to identify how well the organization is equipped to deliver these features.

Identifying the attributes that customers value

In order to achieve an improved level of performance, the products or services of an organization must be providing value to customers. The attributes that supplying companies provide to create loyalty and satisfaction in targeted customer segments are called value propositions. Different customers or business segments may well value different attributes. Kaplan and Norton (1996) identify three categories of value propositions: product/service attributes, customer relationships and image and reputation.

Product/service attributes

Certain customers may be particularly interested in product/service attributes. These may include performance dimensions of functionality, quality, price and time.

(i) *Functionality.* For some customers the product or service features are the key attributes required. A particular car may be faster or provide particular technological facilities, such as superior sound systems or navigational devices. In the airline industry, for example, British Airways gained a temporary advantage through the comfort of its accommodation (the provision of seating that could convert into a bed in first class accommodation).

(ii) *Quality.* This can mean different things to different customers, however, one view of quality is a product that is free of defects. Many motorists desire a reliable car, i.e. it gets them from A to B. For some customers, quality from this perspective is more important to them than features such as acceleration or top speed.

(iii) *Price.* For some customers a low price is the key attribute required.

(iv) *Time.* It may be crucial that a product or service is delivered at short notice and on time.

Customer relationships

A strong customer relationship may be an alternative way of achieving competitive advantage. This might include convenience of access and/or knowledgeable employees who can quickly and correctly deal with customer enquiries.

Image

Yet other customers might be influenced by the image and reputation of the company. For example, some consumers prefer certain brands of designer clothes, such as Nike.

Competitive advantage through strategic positioning

Porter (1980) has suggested that competitive advantage can be gained through either cost leadership or differentiation strategies. The strategic target for which this advantage can be gained can be either industry-wide or through a particular marketsegment. See Figure 15.4.

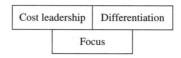

Figure 15.4 Three generic strategies

(1) Cost leadership

   The value proposition or critical success factor for the customer may be a cheaper price and therefore to achieve a reasonable profit, it will be necessary for the organization to have lower costs than the competitors.

(2) Differentiation

   The generic strategy of differentiation means creating some unique dimension that is valued by customers and which can command a premium price. These features might be a product feature, quality, reliability or on-time delivery. Examples from the car industry include Mercedes, who differentiate their cars on the basis of reliability.

(3) Focus

   An organization might not be able to compete in the whole market. Rather, it may choose to focus on a particular market segment employing a differentiation or low-cost strategy. In the car industry, for example, Morgan cars makes no attempt to produce cars for the mass market, rather it aims to be successful through product differentiation in the sale of specialist sports cars.

Confrontation strategy

Cooper (1996) argues that in some industries it is impossible to compete on strict differentiation or cost leadership strategies, rather organizations can only gain temporary advantages. For a period of time, for example, it might be possible to gain a competitive advantage through the provision of superior product features and capabilities (functionality), however, other firms are likely to quickly catch up and provide similar features. Any competitive advantage gained through cost leadership and superior quality is also likely to be temporary. In such a competitive environment it is necessary to carefully balance the provision of the product service attributes of functionality, cost and quality. For this to take place it is essential that firms have a close relationship with their suppliers, including sharing information in order to combine ideas of research, product development and cost reduction.

The strategy of different airlines is considered in Figure 15.5.

Airlines need to first decide whether they are to be a global airline competing in all markets, an example being British Airways. Alternatively, an airline can decide to operate in a niche market, for example a particular geographic area or type of route – e.g. short- (500–1000 miles) or long-haul. Smaller domestic airlines, will often decide to compete in a particular geographic area, while new airlines will tend to compete on specific short-haul routes.

Having decided whether to operate in all markets or in a niche market, it is then necessary to decide on a strategy of cost leadership or product differentiation.

British Airways, following a policy of differentiation on its long and medium haul routes in the 1990's, identified the business passenger as a key market segment prepared to pay premium rates. It set out to provide additional services to those provided by other airlines, for example it was the first to introduce seats that converted into flat beds in first class.

Figure 15.5   Airline strategies

In the UK, EasyJet and RyanAir and in the USA, Southwest Airlines have in contrast been successful with a strategy of cost leadership. This has been possible because they have managed to reduce costs below those of the major competitors.

Doganis (2001) suggests that the collapse in 1999 of Debonair, one of the first European low-cost carriers, was due in no small measure to confused corporate objectives. It was trying to operate as a low-cost, low-fare carrier but offering frills, such as a business class or more leg room, which increased costs.

Despite the above comments, the experience of competing airlines may provide some support for the argument proposed by Cooper. Although price is of key importance for many customers, for the business traveller on-flight frequency and punctuality is of greater importance. Southwest Airlines, for example, has consistently won prizes for the fewest delays, the fewest complaints and the fewest mishandled bags, and this level of service has helped it achieve considerable client base amongst business travellers. Attempting to differentiate a product can also be an ongoing battle. For example, although British Airways gained a temporary competitive advantage with the introduction of the flat bed, other airlines soon copied this feature and eliminated the advantage.

Figure 15.5 (*Continued*)

Sources of competitive advantage

Competitive advantage can arise from two main sources, its resources and the competencies of the organization. See Figure 15.6.

(1) A resource audit will involve an assessment of the financial, physical, human and intangible resources or assets of the organization. It will compare the resources against those of the main competitors and identify those that are superior or unique or those that are inferior.

Sometimes a resource might be sufficient on its own to enable competitive advantage to be achieved. For example, a publicly quoted drug company with a patent on a new drug for a major disease is likely to see its share price rise significantly. Increased sales and profits are almost guaranteed for a significant period of time until alternative treatments come to market.

In other instances, as suggested by Cooper, the competitive advantage may be more transitory and it is likely that both superior resources and competencies are required. For example, a car or television company may construct a new factory that can produce a superior product more cheaply than the competitors. However, the benefit from this new resource may well be only temporary in competitive consumer industries such as these, and competitors will quickly catch up. In such an environment, as well as having superior resources, it is likely that organizations will need to continuously improve their competencies – i.e. the way they use their resources.

(2) The second source of competitive advantage is the set of competencies of the organization. Competencies are the activities and processes involved and used in

linking the resources. The organization needs to be able to undertake these activities and processes in a more efficient (cheaper) or more effective way (can add more value) than their competitors.

Resource audit

Resources can be considered under four categories:

- Financial performance and funds.
- Physical.
- Human resources.
- Intangible assets.

Financial performance and funds

The performance of the company should be considered. For this it is possible to review the current and past financial statements such as the Balance Sheet, Profit and Loss Account and Funds Flow Statement.

The assessment of financial performance can also be assisted through the identification and interpretation of key financial ratios (considered in Chapter 11). Ratios over a number of years can be calculated and compared in relation to the profitability of the business, the efficiency in the use of assets such as working capital and a number of other financial areas. This can help in identifying whether performance is improving or getting worse. It is also possible to benchmark against competitors, to see which companies are performing relatively well or badly.

As well as considering financial performance in terms of profitability and efficiency in the use of assets, the financial situation in terms of funding to support short-term and long-term operations is also important. Funding issues were considered in Chapter 12.

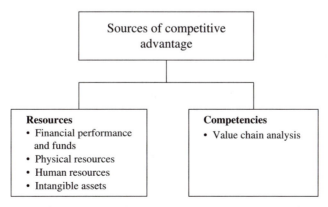

Figure 15.6 Sources of competitive advantage

Human resources

This covers a consideration of the skills of the human resources of the organization. In assessing these resources, it might be possible to identify measures of both the efficiency and effectiveness in which these resources are used. An efficiency measure would be labour productivity. Effectiveness measures could involve an appraisal of the skills and experience of the management and the workforce, employee attitudes and commitment, and how skills give the organization a source of competitive advantage.

Physical resources

A review of the physical assets would include a consideration of the age, suitability and valuation of the assets and the suitability of the location of the existing business for customers, suppliers and employees.

Intangible assets

Intangible assets would include the intellectual capital of the organization. Typical examples include brand names, relationships with partners and customer databases. The use of management accounting information for brands is discussed in Chapter 16 and the valuation of intangible assets and measurement of intellectual capital is discussed in more detail in Chapter 22.

Intangible assets such as patents and trademarks, know-how and important brands often provide longer-term competitive advantage as they are more difficult to copy. A limited illustration of a resource audit of Southwest Airlines is shown in Figure 15.7.

Resource analysis of Southwest Airlines
Southwest Airlines in the United States is the model for most low-cost airlines that have been set up subsequently in the United States and Europe, such as EasyJet and Ryanair.

Financial resources

Except in the initial set-up years in the early 1970s, Southwest trading has never posted a loss. This is exceptionally good performance as the airline industry suffers from major cyclical downturns, with many competitors recording substantial losses during these downturns. In large part, this level of performance has been achieved through steady growth. The airline has traditionally only added a few routes each year and then focused on increasing market share on these routes to the point where it has market leadership. This steady growth has also limited the funding demands caused by rapid growth.

Human resources

Southwest is regularly voted one of the 'best companies to work for in America'. The staff are flexible and highly motivated and labour productivity is high. Motivated staff also leads to a customer-friendly environment.

Figure 15.7   Resource analysis of Southwest Airlines

Physical resources

Aircraft are generally newer than the industry average. Depreciation costs are higher, however maintenance costs are lower because of this and the fact that the airline also only uses one type of aircraft, the Boeing 737.

Intangible assets

The brand name of Southwest is associated with low fares and a quality service.

A resource analysis of Southwest Airlines would therefore suggest that the company has many strengths and relatively few weaknesses when a comparison is made against its major competitors.

Figure 15.7   Resource analysis of Southwest Airlines

Competencies

Competencies are the activities and processes involved and used in linking the firm's resources. Core competencies are the activities or processes that fundamentally underpin the value in the product or service feature and provide the competitive advantage. A firm's competencies will enable innovation, efficiency, quality and customer responsiveness. In this section, value chain analysis will be considered as well as issues related to resource utilization and control

Value chain analysis

The value chain of an organization consists of the resources and activities that link an organization together and are of two types, primary and secondary. The primary activities are those activities that are provided by the organization to transform inputs into outputs. A broad category of activities would suggest that all organizations consist of inbound logistics, operations, outbound logistics, marketing and sales and service. In Chapter 6, the value chain for a 'typical' manufacturing organization was considered. The value chain is shown in Figure 15.8.

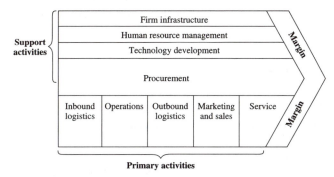

Figure 15.8   The value chain
Source: Porter, M.E. (1985) *Competitive Advantage: Creating and Sustaining Superior Performance*. (c) 1985, 1988 by Michael E. Porter. Reprinted with the permission of The Free Press, a Division of Simon and Schuster Adult Publishing Group.

Each type of organization will have its own value chain, for example the primary activities of an airline are as shown in Figure 15.9.

No product is produced, rather a service is provided to customers. The value chain might be considered to include:

1. Inbound logistics.
   Provision of fuel and catering supplies to the aircraft.

2. Operations.
   The process of moving passengers from one location to another involves a number of activities.
   Prior to arrival at the airport:

   A ticketing/reservations activity.

   Operations at the airport:

   (i) Ticket counter operations. (The customers will be checked in at the airport.)
   (ii) Gate operations. Passengers will be checked onto the airplane.
   (iii) Baggage handling.

   Flight activities:

   (i) Costs associated with the aircraft.
   (ii) Flight operations – pilots and flight crew.
   (iii) Cabin operations – flight attendants.

3. Outbound logistics. Usually these are limited as the passengers will make their own way from an airport.

4. Marketing and sales.
   This will include advertising and promotion.

5. Service. There should be no post-sale service required.

Figure 15.9 Value chain of an airline

Support activities are those that support the primary activities. In organizations there needs to be a firm infrastructure, human resource management, technology development and procurement or purchasing activities.

Cost and value drivers

Each activity needs to be viewed from the point of view of the customer. All activities will add cost and it is necessary to view the value that is added by those activities.

Where competitive advantage is being achieved through cost leadership, then it is essential that activities which do not add value are eliminated and where little value is added, expenditure should be reduced.

Where differentiating a product is crucial for success then the features that add value, for example on-time delivery, product quality or durability, need to be identified. The actions that lead to the provision of these features are known as value drivers.

Low-cost airlines have grown throughout the world because, for a significant proportion of passengers, value is provided by low fares and arrival at destinations on time. In order to deliver these key value propositions, the successful low-cost airlines have developed a value chain that is significantly different to the value chain of traditional airlines. These differences are discussed in Figure 15.10.

Inbound logistics

Traditionally airlines developed their own engineering, catering and other support services and over the years purchased a range of aircraft from different suppliers. Low-cost airlines in contrast have focused on the core activity of providing an airline service and buy in support services as and when required. The range of types of aircraft purchased has been limited.

Operations

(i) Ticketing/reservations activity

For traditional airlines, the majority of fares were booked through travel agents using a limited number of customer reservation systems. Most customers would approach the agent and ask for a flight to a particular location. Airlines would need to make sure that their flights were available on these reservation systems or they would lose bookings. In the 1990s, in particular, the companies running the systems were highly profitable as the airlines were forced to pay high commission fees in order to get customers on their flights. In contrast, low-cost carriers have used direct booking and have increasingly eliminated the need to use travel agents as customers have become more used to booking over the internet.

(ii) Turnaround of aircraft while at the airports

Operations on traditional airlines have often been hampered by strict demarcation lines between the various sets of workers involved in turning round an airplane. Successful low-cost airlines have introduced new working practices such as the involvement of cabin crew in clearing rubbish from aircraft, prior to the airplane landing at its destination and groups of workers, such as baggage handlers cooperating in undertaking a wide range of activities. These new working practices have speeded the turnaround time at airports, which has in turn resulted in greater flight frequency, greater revenue generation and reduced costs.

Gittell (2002) notes that Southwest Airlines is not cheaper in all aspects of the service. For example, in some traditional airlines, one member of staff (an operations agent) will be responsible for the turnaround of up to 15 flights at the same time and will be based in a location that is remote from individual airplanes. At Southwest an operations agent has responsibility for only one flight at a time, ensuring that there is a close relationship maintained between the different operational functions. This additional investment is one of the factors, which it is claimed has led to an improved service and added value to customers.

Flight activities

(i) Costs of the aircraft

To reduce purchase or lease cost, low cost airlines have tended to acquire a limited range of aircraft. For example the fleet of over 500 airplanes of Southwest airlines in the USA are Boeing 737's. Large low-cost airlines such as Southwest, EasyJet and Ryan Air have very strong

---

Figure 15.10 The value chains of traditional and low cost airlines

purchasing power and can negotiate extremely favourable terms for bulk orders. The acquisition of a limited range of aircraft has also reduced maintenance costs as procedures can be standardised.

(ii) Flight operations

Traditional airlines have tended to have higher running costs than their low-cost competitors. Pilots tend to be paid more and work fewer hours and there are additional maintenance and training costs associated with flying a range of planes. Although the planes of some of the successful low-cost competitors may also often be newer (because of significant expansion in recent years) causing higher depreciation costs, this can be at least partly offset through greater fuel economy. Staff working practices are often considered to be more flexible than is associated with many traditional airlines and a further factor reducing flying costs is the practice of operating from low-cost airports. Rather than flying to the main city airports, many low-cost operators have negotiated favourable terms with secondary airports. For example Ryan Air has its main London base at Stansted.

(iii) Cabin operations

Once on the plane, traditional airlines have included a wide range of services, which were traditionally included in the cost of the fare. This includes differing classes of seats with first class and business class passengers having a range of benefits including additional seating space, seats that can convert into beds, free meals and drinks. Even economy passengers have had a number of benefits including free meals. The model with the low-cost airlines is to offer a single class service and to not provide free meals.

Infrastructure

A small corporate headquarters.

Figure 15.10   (*Continued*)

Activity 15.2

Review the activities described in Figure 15.10. Identify the changes that might be considered to support:

(a) A strategy of cost leadership.
(b) A strategy of product differentiation.

The introduction of low-cost flights has resulted in the removal of activities that do not add value to specific customer segments. For example, many customers are happy to book flights themselves using the internet. In exchange for a lower price, they are content to not have a specific seat reserved or a free meal or drinks on the flight.

Identifying linkages between activities of an organization and also between the value chains of different organizations

(i) Linkages between the activities of the organization

Linkages exist between activities and processes of an organization and these linkages can either provide cost advantage or can be a basis for differentiation. At Southwest Airlines, the single operations agent for each aircraft is a linkage that has enabled a close relationship to be maintained between the different operational functions and has contributed to a very low level of delays, complaints and mishandled bags. Gittell (2002) argues that the added value provided to customers has more than offset the added cost.

(ii) Supplier and customer linkages

The organization's value chain should also not be considered in isolation. The customer is often provided with a product or service that has been processed through the value chains of a number of organizations. The linkages between these operations should be considered in order to ensure that operations run efficiently and effectively. Actions that have a favourable impact on the value chain of one organization considered in isolation may have an adverse impact on other companies involved in the total value chain. A decision to implement a just-in-time system in a manufacturing company, for example, may lead to cost reductions in that organization, but introduce added problems and costs for the supplier of raw material and the net effect may be an overall increase in costs.

In recent years the impact of globalization, increasing competitive pressures, rapid technological change and complexity of products has increased pressures to cooperate with other organizations.

Comparative analysis

If an organization is to be successful and gain competitive advantage, then it must be better in respect of the factors that are of key importance to customers. It is also important to compare the performance of the organization against other organizations. This is a process called benchmarking, which involves:

- Regularly comparing aspects of performance with best practitioners.
- Identifying any gaps in performance.
- Seeking fresh approaches to bring about improvements in performance.
- Following through with implementing improvements.
- Following up by monitoring progress and reviewing the benefits.

There are various different forms of benchmarking: competitive, functional, generic or internal.

Competitive benchmarking

Competitive benchmarking involves the comparison of performance characteristics of the organization with those of competitors. Ideally, it is important to identify the information that is of key importance to the customer and then compare how well your organization performs on these criteria in comparison with key competitors. Figure 15.11 provides an example of the type of competitive information that would be of help for an airline if safety, price, on-time arrival performance and customer complaints were considered to be key criteria.

A comparison of performance of three airlines

Airline	Safety (accidents per million flight hours)	Price	On-time departure performance	Consumer complaints to airline user council
Airline X	4.5	£40	84%	132
Airline Y	3.6	£50	91%	77
Airline Z	0.8	£60	88%	44

Figure 15.11

Activity 15.3

Given the information provided in Figure 15.11, which is the best performing airline?

Functional or generic benchmarking

Sometimes it may not be possible to benchmark against competitors, or particular activities are performed best in a totally different industry. Functional benchmarking or generic benchmarking is used when organizations look to benchmark with partners drawn from different business sectors or areas of activity to find ways of improving similar functions or work processes. A number of companies in the airline industry have benchmarked activities such as maintenance, refuelling and aircraft turnaround to formula one racing.

Internal benchmarking

Where there are a number of different business units in an organization, it is also possible to use internal benchmarking. Handelsbanken is a Swedish bank that collects key performance information on similar business units across the group. Organizations can produce league tables of performance based on regions, countries, branches, service centres and portfolio of customers, products or services. The idea of internal benchmarking is to produce pressure for continuous improvement. A potential danger of internal benchmarking is that individual units will not compare themselves against best in class. They may be performing well against internal standards, but poorly against key competitors.

Summary

This chapter has identified key areas of performance that should be reviewed in undertaking an *internal appraisal* of the organization.

An assessment should be undertaken to identify the profitability, market share, market growth and stage of the product lifecycle of individual products. The portfolio of products should also be analysed using techniques such as the growth share matrix. A comparison should be made of the performance of the products and services of the company against those of competitors.

Successful firms that can sustain a higher profit than the industry average are said to possess a **competitive advantage** over their rivals. This can only be achieved through the provision of some feature that is particularly valued by customers, whether this is low cost or some unique dimension that is valued by customers and which can command a premium price.

To achieve competitive advantage, a business should have better resources and carry out its key processes and activities better than its competitors.

When a business has identified the key areas of performance for success in a market, then it should monitor its performance in these areas and compare itself against the performance of others. This is a technique called benchmarking.

Further reading

Bowman, C. (1998) *Strategy in Practice*. Prentice-Hall, Harlow.

Gittell, J.H. (2002) *Southwest Airlines Way: The power of relationships for superior performance*. McGraw-Hill.

Grant, R.M. (2007) *Contemporary Strategy Analysis: Concepts, techniques and applications*, 7th edn. Blackwell Publishing.

Johnson, G. and Scholes, K. (2002) *Exploring Corporate Strategy, Text & Cases*, 6th edn. Prentice-Hall.

Shank, J.K. and Govindarajan, V. (1992) Strategic cost management and the value chain. *Journal of Cost Management* **Winter**: 5–21.

Shields, M.D. and Young, S.M. (1992) Effective long-term cost reduction. *Journal of Cost Management* **Spring**: 16–30.

Answers to activities

Activity 15.1

Product Y generates very low sales. It would be possible to harvest the product, but it will release few funds.

Products X and Z have high sales and sales growth is significant. It is likely that both products are absorbing cash. At present the company appears to have an unbalanced product portfolio, with heavy demands on cash.

Activity 15.2

Most of the activities described in Figure 15.10 have led to a reduction in costs. The appointment of individuals to act as a link for each flight appears to be leading to an improved service and therefore differentiation of the product from a number of other airlines.

Activity 15.3

Each is better on at least one dimension, i.e. airline X on price, airline Y on on-time departure and airline Z on safety. It will depend on which factor is most important to the consumer. Airline Z also has the lowest number of complaint letters, though this may be a function of the size of the airline in relation to the other two companies.

Discussion questions

1. For this question you should choose a social club with which you are familiar, e.g. a students' union or sports club.

   The club is currently making losses. Members are not using the bars or other social facilities; rather, they go to the local night clubs and public houses.

(a) What product/service attributes should your club be promoting in order to gain a competitive advantage? Note that on ethical grounds, the club will not enter a price war on drink prices with the local competition.

(b) Undertake a resource analysis and consider key competencies and then identify strengths and weaknesses of the club, when comparison is made against competitors.

(c) If benchmarking was to be used, what form of benchmarking would be appropriate and what performance measures could be usefully collected?

2. What are the attributes of the products or services provided by the following organizations which should be reflected in their value chain?

(a) A supermarket.
(b) A restaurant.
(c) A fast food outlet.
(d) A chain of bookshops.

3. For Siegmund Ltd:

(a) Using the information provided in table 1 of the case, undertake a product analysis using the share–growth matrix. Comment on the findings, including the implications for the strategy of the company.

(b) Review the actual and forecast sales information provided in table 2. The sales manager has cast doubt on the accuracy of this sales forecast. Why do you think this might be the case? What further information would you wish to know before accepting the sales forecast?

(c)

(i) As far as the information allows, identify the main primary activities carried out in the organization.

(ii) Review the activities completed for the manufacturing process. Consider how on-time delivery performance could be improved. Note that this question can be reconsidered after completing Chapter 22 of the book.

(d) Identify the strengths and weaknesses of the organization as far as the information allows.

4. Undertake an internal appraisal of the assembly division of McLoed Ltd as far as the information allows. Identify the further information that you would need to collect for a full appraisal of the organization.

ACCOUNTING AND STRATEGIC ANALYSIS

16

Objectives

At the end of this chapter students should be able to explain the potential use of management accounting information in the strategic analysis process:

- Assessing the competitive position of an organization through identifying

  - Potential future profitability in target markets through undertaking an industry profitability analysis.
  - Current profitability in target markets.

- Identifying information needs given different strategic positioning and strategies.
- Analysing resources.
- Analysing the value chain of the organization and comparing it with that of competitors.
- Assessing the impact of changes in the external environment.

Introduction

Much of the management accounting information considered in Parts 1 and 2 of the book focused on the internal performance of the organization, for example, full costing approaches and traditional accounting controls. For strategic management purposes, Chapters 14 and 15 have emphasized the importance of knowledge about the external environment of an organization and the organization itself in relation to its markets and competitors.

This chapter will consider the potential application of management accounting information to approaches introduced in the last two chapters, including:

1. Accounting information that can assist in the assessment of the current and likely future competitive position of the organization in target markets.
2. Accounting information appropriate for differing strategic positions (e.g. cost leadership or differentiation) and at different stages of the business lifecycle.

3. Analysis of the tangible and intangible resources of an organization. A particular illustration for the analysis of brands will be provided.
4. Analysis of the value chain of the organization and a comparison with that of competitors.
5. Assessing the potential impact of external environmental change on the organization.

Competitive position in target markets

Monitoring competitive position – industry profitability analysis

In the five forces analysis, discussed in Chapter 14, Porter identified five strategic forces that determine the future profitability of a market segment to an organization, these being competitor rivalry, potential new entrants, supplier bargaining power, buyer bargaining power and threat of substitute products.

For a financial evaluation of different strategies, it is important that the potential impact of each of these forces on sales volume, prices, costs and the required level of investment is understood. The strength of competitive rivalry, for example, is likely to be influenced by financial factors such as:

1. *Availability of funds.* If a competitor has ready access to funds, then choosing a strategy of price competition or an advertising battle is less likely to be successful than if the competitor has few funds available.
2. *Cost structures.* The cost structure of competitors is likely to influence the desire to compete at low prices and to enter or exit a market segment (see further discussion below and in the section on value chain analysis).

Entry and exit barriers

In evaluating different strategies, it is also important to have an understanding of entry and exit barriers to the market. If investing in resources means that an organization can achieve economies of scale or learning curve effects and this then results in potential new entrants being discouraged from entering the market, there is an incentive to undertake the investment. If the additional investment will not result in barriers to entry then it will be a less attractive option.

An organization may also undertake a very expensive competitive strategy (e.g. heavy promotion of products or services and low pricing) and find that despite this, competitors do not leave the industry. This may be because of exit barriers. Closing a company, for example, will result in staff being made redundant and in industries such as mining or quarrying there are also costs of re-landscaping the surrounding area. In some industries, the operational gearing (discussed in Chapter 1) may be very high and assets may have a low resale value. In such a situation even generating a low contribution may be preferable to leaving the industry.

In Chapter 14 a five forces analysis was undertaken for the airline industry. A review of that section will highlight the range of potential changes that could have a major impact on the financial success of a chosen strategy. For example, the ease of entry for new competitors who can challenge the existing routes of an airline; a change in the bargaining power of key aircraft suppliers (particularly influenced by the economic environment and the consequent impact on demand); substitute products such as the development of alternative transport systems (for example, high-speed train links).

Activity 16.1

You are considering opening a coffee shop in a popular student area (it is expected that the majority of sales will be to students). There is already one coffee shop in that area. What type of competitor information would be helpful for your decision?

Sources of information

Information about competitors can be gained from a number of sources, including:

(i) *Recorded data.* This is available in published form from sources such as competitor annual reports, product brochures, newspaper articles, press releases.
(ii) *Observable data.* This follows observation of pricing policy, advertising campaigns and sales promotions.
(iii) *Opportunistic data.* This might be obtained from meetings with suppliers, feedback from the sales force, recruiting ex-employees or social contacts.
(iv) *Market research.* A company can also commission market research information.

Market segment and customer account profitability analysis

In Chapter 15 the focus moved to a consideration of the organization and how well it is performing in its chosen market and in comparison with competitors. This section considers a further analysis of costs to incorporate a market and customer focus. Figure 16.1 illustrates the analysis of sales and profits from two products sold in two different market segments.

Activity-based costing and customer account profitability

The analysis in Figure 16.1 assumes that it is only possible to identify variable costs by market segment. Some market segments or customers, however, may require a greater use of overhead resources such as marketing, administration or distribution costs than others.

Alpha Ltd produces two products, product X and product Y, and sells these two products in two market segments. The cost accountant has prepared an analysis showing revenue and profits for the last year. The managing director has asked for your advice as to whether product Y should no longer be sold in market segment B.

Market	Segment A		Segment B		Total		
Product	X	Y	X	Y	X	Y	Total
	£'000	£'000	£'000	£'000	£'000	£'000	£'000
Sales	20	15	8	12	28	27	55
Cost	16	14	7	12	23	26	49
Profit	4	1	1	0	5	1	6

Activity 16.2

What further information would be needed to answer this question?

Answer

Contribution analysis

A traditional management accounting response would be to first calculate the contribution that would be earned by each product in each market segment.

The analysis below shows that a positive contribution to overheads is in fact earned by product Y in market segment B. If sales of the product to this segment ceased then the overheads would need to be apportioned to both product X and Y in all market segments.

Market	Segment A		Segment B		Total		
Product	X	Y	X	Y	X	Y	Total
	£'000	£'000	£'000	£'000	£'000	£'000	£'000
Sales	20	15	8	12	28	27	55
Variable cost	10	9	4	8	14	17	31
Contribution	10	6	4	4	14	10	24
Share of fixed costs	6	5	3	4	9	9	18
Profit	4	1	1	0	5	1	6

Further information that would assist in the decision

(i) A longer-term strategic perspective may also be important and for this it would be beneficial to have further information on, for example, size and growth of each market segment and of the market share of each product. If a market segment is growing then this may overcome short-term contribution implications.

(ii) The firm may also be concerned about abandoning a market segment if the product is just one of a range of products sold by the company. Customers may wish to buy a full product range from one company and therefore a decision to drop the product may have a knock-on effect on sales of other products.

(iii) A strategic opportunity may also be provided for a competitor wishing to expand.

(iv) The costing situation may not be giving an accurate position. Is the analysis accurate in assuming that the 'fixed' costs will not change if a market segment or customer is dropped? A more detailed costing approach may be required, for example through an analysis of costs by activity.

Figure 16.1   Contribution analysis by market segment

Accordingly, an analysis of those activities and their cost drivers may be necessary in order to more accurately assess profitability. As an example, a further analysis of overhead costs incurred in the supply of product X to two customers is considered in Figure 16.2.

Product X is sold to customers 1 and 2 at £6 per unit. Variable cost per unit is £3.

Customer 1

- 100 orders a year with an average of 10 units of product X with each order.
- Each order has to be shipped so that it arrives at a specific time.
- Any minor problems with the delivery result in a complaint that needs to be dealt with by the customer complaints department. Normally there are 10 complaints in a year.

Customer 2

- 10 orders a year with an average of 100 units of product X with each order.
- Only 8 deliveries a year required as it is often possible to combine orders into single deliveries.
- There are never any complaints from customer 2.

Cost of activities

An activity-based costing exercise has been undertaken and the following have been identified:

1. Cost per order is £10.
2. Cost per delivery is £20.
3. Cost per complaint is £50.

Analysis of profitability of the two customers

	Customer 1	Customer 2
Sales units	1000	1000
	£	£
Sales revenue	6000	6000
Variable product cost	3000	3000
Contribution	3000	3000
Order cost	1000	100
Delivery cost	2000	160
Complaint cost	500	=
Customer profit/(loss)	(500)	2740

This analysis suggests that although the contribution per product is the same, when a more detailed analysis of costs takes place, customer 1 generates a loss, while customer 2 is profitable.

The reason is that a range of costs can be identified at customer level that would have been general overheads if a product-level analysis had been undertaken. In this analysis order, delivery and complaint costs are included. Finance costs such as different levels of credit extended to different customer groups might also be relevant in a real customer profitability analysis.

Figure 16.2   Customer account profitability

The provision of market and/or customer profitability reports can assist in decision-making for both the short and longer term. Such reports can focus the attention of decision-makers on the profitability of key segments or customers and help identify where additional investment or corrective action is required or whether a decision to withdraw should be taken.

As always, costing and profitability reports need to be treated with care. In Figure 16.2, for example, the decision might be taken to discontinue sales to customers who generate a loss after deducting the cost of overheads activities. Before taking such action, the company should consider:

1. Whether the costs will be saved or whether some of these overheads will remain and will therefore be recharged to other customers.
2. Whether all the customer purchases generate a loss or low profitability or whether it is just some of them. A customer will make a number of purchases in the year and an analysis might identify that on average a customer is unprofitable. However, this average might disguise the fact that while some orders are very unprofitable, others are profitable. Johnson and Brohms (2000) recommend the use of order-based profitability analysis. Rather than following a strategy of eliminating apparently unprofitable customers, it would be better to learn how the purchases of these customers differ from those of others. Action could then be taken to eliminate unprofitable orders or resolve the problems that cause them to be unprofitable.

Activity-based management

In this section attention has been given to the use of activity-based costing as a tool for ascertaining the costs of different cost objects, e.g. customer or segment profitability. Later in this chapter and in Chapter 22, the measurement and analysis of the costs of activities, cost driver usage and performance within each activity area of an organization will be considered.

Value analysis

The use of value engineering in target costing was discussed in Chapter 2. With value engineering, each component of a new product or service is examined to see if it is possible to reduce costs without losing functionality.

Strategic positioning, strategy and accounting information

Strategic positioning and management accounting information

In order to gain competitive advantage, it is important that organizations identify the key product or service attributes that create loyalty and satisfaction in targeted customer segments. Having identified the key attributes, Porter (1980) argues that a positioning strategy of cost leadership or product differentiation should be chosen. Shank (1989) has proposed that, in order to be relevant, the management accounting control information that a firm provides should also vary according to the strategic position.

Accounting information given a cost leadership strategy

To a firm following a cost leadership strategy, Shank argues that a focus on cost analysis and control is necessary. Accordingly the type of costing and control systems that have been described in parts one and two of this book would be appropriate.

(a) *Product costing and analysis of competitor* costs would be of key importance. Costing systems (whether traditional or activity based costing) will be required in order that the profitability of products, customers and market segments can be identified. This information can be used in considering selling prices, identifying how well a product or service is performing in its chosen market segment, pinpointing areas where cost reduction activity is required and highlighting where the organization should consider outsourcing or replacement.

The value proposition or critical success factor for the customer is price and therefore to achieve a reasonable profit, it will be necessary for the organization to have lower costs than the competitors. Knowledge of the cost structures of these competitors would therefore also be extremely helpful.

(b) *Control techniques* could include standard costing, comparison against flexible budget in a manufacturing environment and comparison against original budget in other environments.

Accounting information given a product differentiation strategy

To a firm that is following a product differentiation strategy, attributes such as on-time delivery, product features and quality are likely to be crucial to the financial success of the organization. A traditional budgetary control/standard costing control system and product and competitor cost analysis, where the focus is on cost, is therefore likely to be less relevant. Greater emphasis should be given to the optimal use of marketing costs to support and promote key product benefits.

Confrontation strategy

A firm enjoys a sustainable competitive advantage if it has a permanent advantage over other companies. Cooper (1996) argues however, that in some industries such as computing or automobiles, the competition is always innovating and improving so fast that firms are unable to maintain such an advantage. Accordingly for organizations following for example, a position of cost leadership, it would be inappropriate to rely solely on costing techniques and operational controls such as standard costing. There are minimum levels of functionality, quality and price that must be achieved by all competing firms and if the products or services offered by a firm falls below certain minimum standards on any of these attributes, it will not survive. Cooper argues that in a rapidly changing competitive environment it is therefore necessary to develop six cost management techniques to support the management of both existing and future products.

(a) Supporting the management of existing products

Product costing systems and operational control techniques such as standard costing can remain important in order that costs are accurately identified and controlled. Cooper also recommends the use of Kaizen costing, which is a means of ensuring continuous improvement activities during the manufacturing stage of the product life cycle. With Kaizen costing, workforce teams identify specific areas of performance and investigate how improvements can be achieved. Short-term cost and other operational targets, such as quality and safety are set and then performance against target monitored.

(b) Supporting the management of future products

In a rapidly changing environment where competitors are continuously improving the product features offered, it is vital that the company at least meets or exceeds minimum standards of functionality required by consumers. To assist in this process, Cooper recommends the use of target costing, value engineering and interorganizational cost management systems.

Target costing and value engineering were discussed in chapter 2. With target costing it is recognised that a certain level of functionality and quality must be achieved in a new product, at a selling price that will be accepted by the market. Having identified this target selling price, a desired profit margin is established and a target cost set. Value engineering can then be used, which involves an examination of each component to see if it is possible to reduce costs without losing functionality.

Interorganizational cost management systems consider cost improvement throughout the supply chain from raw materials through to the customers. Cooper and Slagmulder (1999) argue that in 'lean' organizations in particular, where much of the work is outsourced, it is essential that there is a blurring of the boundaries between organizations, with the aim of creating relationships and sharing organizational resources. These can fulfill simple objectives, such as lowering material and coordination costs or more complex purposes, for example a long-term partnership where suppliers become a critical source for creativity and innovation.

Strategy, life cycle stage and financial control information

In Chapter 15 it was noted that three different strategies of *build*, *hold* and *harvest* are linked to different life cycle stages. At each stage there are different objectives and different information needs.

(1) A *build* strategy will require considerable resources to fund investment, build operations and infrastructure and develop customer relations. Gaining market share will be at the expense of cash flow and profits.

(2) For a *hold* strategy the level of investment in new resources will decline and there will be an increased expectation that the unit will deliver an improved financial performance.

(3) Finally a *harvest* strategy where the organisation extracts as much cash as possible and keeps reinvestment to a minimum.

Kaplan (1983) and Kaplan and Norton (1996) argue that the accounting measures used by organizations should change according to stage of the product life cycle. At early stages of the life cycle and with a build strategy it is important to develop customer relations and gain market share. For this to occur the product must provide the level of functionality required by customers and to achieve this it may be necessary to undertake additional expenditure in the short term. If managers are evaluated on the basis of cost minimisation at an early stage of the life cycle of a product, there is a danger that the product design will be frozen too soon.

As a product moves through its life cycle, different control techniques may become more relevant. For example at the maturity stage, there maybe an expectation that the product will be delivering profits. There are likely to be a large number of competitors and so cost control and cost control techniques will be more relevant.

As well as differing cost control techniques, other accounting methods may need to be reviewed. In chapter 4 a range of investment appraisal techniques were discussed including payback, Accounting Rate of Return and the discounting techniques of Net Present Value and Internal Rate of Return. The use of payback and Accounting Rate of Return may be most appropriate for later stages of the life cycle where cash and profits should be expected. They might not be so appropriate at the development and growth stages if worthwhile investments generating positive N.P.V.'s are rejected because of low initial cash flows.

Activity 16.3

(i)   CD Ltd continues to manufacture video tape players as part of its product range.
(ii) LM has just launched a new type of electronic 'book' that will store up to 500 books downloaded from the internet in a lightweight case.
(iii) AS Ltd is the manufacturer of a popular range of printers.

What type of financial control information may be appropriate for each type of company and why?

Resource analysis and accounting

It has been noted in Chapter 15 that competitive advantage arises from two main sources, the resources and the competencies of the organization. In this section, the role of accounting in the analysis of resources will be considered.

The assessment of financial performance using ratio analysis was discussed in Chapter 11. Much of the value of a business is, however, not necessarily due to the physical assets that are owned by a business, rather it is in the form of **intangible assets**, which can be defined as 'identifiable non-monetary assets without physical substance'. Examples can include computer software, patents, copyrights, customer lists, brands, customer and supplier relationships and marketing rights. In Chapter 21, the assessment of intangible assets by means of non-financial performance indicators will be considered. This chapter will consider the potential use of management accounting for one particular intangible asset, that of brands.

Management accounting for brands

A **brand** is a name, logo, slogan and/or design scheme associated with a product or service and a successful brand can be extremely important to an organization as it can create a strong and lasting impression in the mind of a buyer (for example Rolex or Cartier).

Despite the value of brands for a business, no attempt is made to value internally developed brands in accounting statements and it has been argued that some method of valuation would be helpful for brand-related decision-making. Roslender and Hart (2006), for example, identify three complementary sets of information (marketing, accounting and inter-functional information), which they argue will provide an understanding of the value creation capacity of a brand and how additional expenditure would increase brand value.

(i) Marketing information could include details of historical market shares of each brand and projections of anticipated brand turnover, market growth and competitor performance. As well as sales-related data, brand loyalty information can be collected and include measures such as customer retention rates, length of relationship and customer satisfaction.

Marketing information should also be collected on the value attributes that provide customer satisfaction and a competitive advantage for an organization. A number of the benefits relating to brands are difficult to quantify, however, as they are intangible and relate to image and reputation. A particular brand of sports car, such as Ferrari for example, might offer similar tangible product benefits as other cars but may convey a particular emotional appeal to the consumer. Some organizations have attempted to quantify such factors in terms of the premium price that can be earned by the brand or the market share. If it is impossible to provide a quantitative measure of such a benefit, then it may be possible for it to be described.

(ii) Accounting information could include brand profitability information, which could be identified in a similar manner to that of customer account profitability. Cost information can also be collected and analysed according to its impact on brand developments. Generally Accepted Accounting Principles dictate that marketing expenditure is treated as an expense in the year that it occurs. Much of the expenditure on brands however, such as that related to marketing campaigns, maintaining customer databases and customer service to ensure long-term retention, might be considered to be an investment as it will have benefits that will last more than one year. Roslender and Hart suggest the use of the residual income method (discussed in Chapter 10) in order to more accurately identify brand profitability.

This proposal is illustrated in Figure 16.3 and considered further in Chapter 21, with a discussion of a technique called economic value added.

Brand X generates a contribution after deducting variable production costs of £1,000,000. Market share has declined in recent years and a marketing campaign costing £750,000 is planned in the coming year in order to relaunch the brand and regain market leadership. The benefit of the campaign is expected to last two years. The company cost of capital is 10%.

Required:

Calculate the profit using:

(i) 'Generally accepted accounting principles', i.e. all marketing costs treated as an expense of the period.

(ii) If the marketing campaign is treated as an investment to be written off over two years.

Answer:

(i) Following generally accepted accounting principles:

	£
Brand contribution	1,000,000
Write-off of marketing expenditure	750,000
Brand profit in year	250,000

(ii) Using a residual income approach:

	£
Brand contribution	1,000,000
Write-off of marketing expenditure	375,000
Brand profit before deducting cost of capital	625,000
Interest charge on additional investment	
= 10% of £375,000 (£750,000/2)	37,500
Brand residual income	587,500

By treating marketing expenditure that will have longer-term benefits as an asset, it may be easier to identify the impact of the expenditure on brand value.

Figure 16.3   Evaluating brand income using the residual income method.

(iii) Interfunctional information would require the development of close cooperation between the marketing and accounting functions. An understanding of the impact of various factors on long-term brand sales and value creation should be developed, for example an understanding of the sensitivity of demand to changes in price or adverse or favourable publicity about environmental or ethical issues. It is also necessary to develop an understanding of projections on a business's stock of brands and the lifecycles of individual brands so that informed decisions can be made on whether it is necessary to dispose of unsustainable brands or invest in brands at earlier stages of the lifecycle.

Identifying organizational competencies – value chain analysis and accounting

A second method of achieving competitive advantage is through the competencies or capabilities of the organization. A business which wishes to outperform its competitors by differentiating itself through higher quality will have to perform its value chain activities better than the opposition. A cost leadership strategy will require a reduction in the costs associated with the value chain activities, or a reduction in the total amount of resources used.

Shank (1989), Shank and Govindarajan (1993) have recommended that accounting systems should be changed to provide a more sophisticated understanding of a firm's cost structure and that this can go a long way in the search for sustainable competitive advantage. They refer to a need for **strategic cost management**, which results from the blending of three themes from the strategic management literature of value chain, cost driver and strategic positioning analysis.

In detail:

1. The activities of the value chain and costs of each of the activities should be assigned.
2. The cost drivers of each activity should be identified.
3. Sustainable competitive advantage can be achieved by rearranging the value chain or by taking action on the cost drivers in order to achieve the chosen strategic position of cost leadership or product differentiation.

Assigning costs to each activity

A first step is to assign costs to the various activities of the value chain. Shank and Govindarajan (1992a) illustrated the use of costing the value chain analysis with an example from the airline industry. Using publicly available data, the value chains of United Airlines (a traditional airline) and People Express (a low-cost airline) were compared. The cost per seat mile at People Express was $1.35 less than at United Airlines due to strategic decisions in the following five areas:

1. Pre-arrival operations and operations at the airport (ticket counter, gate operations, baggage handling) ($0.42 less per seat mile).
2. Costs associated with aircraft ($0.18 per seat mile).
3. Flight operations (pilots and flight crew) ($0.40 per seat mile).
4. Cabin operations ($0.32 per seat mile).
5. Marketing and sales ($0.03 per seat mile).

The analysis provided a starting point in the estimation of the benefit obtained by customers from each activity relative to the cost of provision. For a discussion of the differences between low-cost and traditional airlines, see the consideration of the value chain in Chapter 15 (Figure 15.10).

Cost driver analysis

Having identified the costs of each activity, the next step is to diagnose the cost drivers that explain the variation in cost. If an understanding of costs given changes in the key cost drivers can be understood, then this may go a long way to identifying profit improvement opportunities.

Shank (1989) divided cost drivers into two categories:

1. **Structural cost drivers**. These derive from the company's choice of economic structure and include economies of scale, scope, experience, complexity and technology.
2. **Executional cost drivers**. These are the cost drivers that cause activities and processes to be completed in a more efficient manner.

Structural cost drivers

Economies of scale
Economies of scale are those that arise because of high volumes of production. In a number of industries such as chemical and steel production, for example, large-scale production is required to achieve low costs and any competitor wishing to enter the market will need to commit themselves to a very high level of investment. Barriers to entry will therefore exist for new entrants. The impact of scale on costs needs to be understood by an organization in order that appropriate action can be recommended.

Economies of scope
These can occur where a range of products might be offered. For example, a sales force might benefit from selling a number of products as costs could be shared across these products rather than purely charged to one. Economies of scope can also occur with vertical integration. In the holiday industry some companies own a charter airline as well as a charter holiday company. This means that a 'guaranteed' income for the airline can be predominantly provided by the company's own tour company. For example, TUI own a number of holiday companies throughout Europe including Thomson Holidays as well as airlines such as Thomson fly.com.

Experience
The experience curve effect occurs through learning and has been observed in a number of industries such as aircraft manufacture. Every time an experience is doubled, hours worked and costs incurred per unit can decline by between 10 and 30%. This is because at the start of production, procedures are unfamiliar and staff may not be fully trained. As production continues, there are major benefits as best practice becomes identified and familiarity with this best practice is gained. This can give a huge advantage to the company that is the first to achieve high levels of output. A typical experience curve is shown in Figure 16.4.

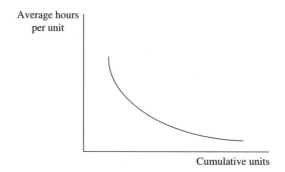

Figure 16.4   The learning or experience curve

Assuming that the time to make the first unit was 10 hours, and every time the number of units manufactured doubles, an 80% learning curve would lead to the following expectation of the time required to make subsequent units:

	Average time per unit (hrs)	Total time to make (hrs)	Additional time to make extra units (hrs)
1 unit	10	10	–
2 units	(10 × 0.8) = 8	8 × 2 = 16	6 (1 unit)
4 units	(8 × 0.8) = 6.4	6.4 × 4 = 25.6	9.6 (2 units)
8 units	(6.4 × 0.8) = 5.12	5.12 × 8 = 40.96	15.36 (4 units)
16 units	(5.12 × 0.8) = 4.096	4.096 × 16 = 65.536	24.576 (8 units)

Activity 16.4

It takes 20 hours to make the first unit. An 80% learning curve is in operation. How many hours would be required to make 4 units?

Activity 16.5

Given the information in activity 16.4 the material cost per unit is £40. The labour cost per hour is £6.

(a) What would be the cost per unit if 1 unit were made?
(b) What would be the total cost if 4 units were made and what would be the average cost per unit?

The learning percent is usually determined by statistical analysis of actual cost data for similar products. The effect in the aerospace industry is estimated to be 85%, for shipbuilding 80–85% and complex machine tools for new models 75–85%.

If a learning curve exists for a product and current competitors are already benefiting from the learning effect, new entrants might hesitate from entering the market. In the latter part of the twentieth century, a number of UK companies found that they could not compete in the car, motorcycle and electronics industries. Although it was claimed that foreign companies were dumping goods at below-cost prices, a counterclaim was made that costs were low due to the benefits of learning and the companies importing goods had driven costs further down the learning curve.

Complexity

Growth often also leads to increased complexity as the number of work units, distribution channels, vertical levels in an organization, product lines, operating facilities all increase. Additional costs often occur with this increased complexity.

Many organizations have tried to take action on costs by reducing the number of levels of management between the shop floor and top management and reviewing business processes. Increased attention has been paid to the potential use of activity-based management, which is the management use of activity information in order to identify the costs of individual activities.

Technology

The process technologies used can also have an impact on cost. Shank and Govindarajan (1992c, 1993) note the choices that logging companies can use to cut down trees. One system involves the mass clearing of a section of a wood, which means that trees of a range of ages are cut down. This is a cheaper technology than an alternative, which more specifically chooses the trees to be felled. The latter, while more expensive, results in less destruction to the forest and the collection of higher-value timber.

Executional cost drivers

These cause activities and processes to be completed in a more efficient manner and include:

(a) Workforce involvement, with the workforce committed to continuous improvement.
(b) Total quality management.
(c) Improving plant layout.
(d) Improving linkages with customers and suppliers.
(e) Designing the product effectively.

In Chapter 22, a range of cost measurement and cost management techniques, which have been developed with the purpose of improving activity and process efficiency, will be discussed.

Developing sustainable competitive advantage

Having identified the key cost drivers for each activity, the third step is to develop sustainable competitive advantage.

For each activity the key questions are:

(i) Can cost be reduced, holding value (and revenue) constant? If so, action should be taken to reconfigure the value chain or control the drivers of cost better than competitors. Action on the cost drivers (such as economies of scale or scope or learning effect), in particular activities, may mean that an organization may be able to sustain a competitive advantage for some period of time. Competitors who currently cannot achieve the economies of scale or whose costs have not been reduced through the experience effect in key areas of activity may be discouraged from entering a particular market segment.

(ii) Can value (and revenue) be increased, holding costs constant? If so, efforts should be made to act on those areas where a payoff is significant.

Activity 16.6

It is noted above that the existence of structural barriers such as economies of scale, learning curve effects and economies of scope and complexity drivers can lead to a competitive advantage for some organizations and act as barriers to entry for new companies.

Do you think that there are any of these structural barriers in existence in the airline industry?

Activity 16.7

How have a number of new airlines achieved a competitive advantage through cost leadership?

Activity 16.8

Many new companies are entering the low-cost airline market, but few are successful. Why do you think this is?

Shank and Govindarajan (1993) provide a number of examples to illustrate the benefits of strategic cost management in comparison with traditional management accounting analysis.

In one example, the Baldwin Bicycle Company (a manufacturer of high-quality bicycles) had been offered a large contract by a discount store to sell a version of their bicycle at a lower price. The bicycle company was operating at 75% capacity and acceptance of the order would have generated a positive contribution to overheads. Viewing the contract from a strategic cost management perspective highlighted how acceptance of the contract would contradict the strategy of product differentiation that the company had been following. Customers in the current market segments in which the company was operating would be likely to be attracted away from the current dealerships who were selling the company's existing product range. This would result in lost sales in the current market segments and alienation of the existing sales network, who might decide to sell the bicycles of other manufacturers.

In a second example, a packaging company was considering whether to invest in a market segment that was growing. Using the growth share (BCG) matrix, the market segment seemed an attractive area for further development. An analysis of the value chain of the existing products supplied by the company to this market area, however, identified that it was currently only able to extract 2% of the total value created in the chain. The reason was that there were only a few large and very powerful customers for the packaging who were able to exert their market strength to affect prices. The expected continuing power of these purchasers seemed likely to limit the opportunity for the packaging company to make substantial profits and so the company decided to not invest further resources in the market segment.

Operational gearing and competitive strength

Improving executional cost drivers will always improve overall performance. This is not the case with structural cost drivers.

Organizations which are capital-intensive and where fixed costs are high as a proportion of total costs are considered to have high operational gearing and during periods of high sales, such companies will be able to produce goods and services cheaply. During periods of low sales, such as occurs with a prolonged recession, such companies are at greater risk and low geared companies will be able to survive more easily. This is assuming that heavy capital investment and high operational gearing is not a prerequisite for production to take place.

The example of the airline industry is discussed in Figure 16.5.

The profitability of the airline industry fluctuates widely over the years. A key problem is that many airlines are highly geared, with aircraft either owned by companies or subject to long-term leases. During times of high demand for air transport, profits have been high, however during recessionary periods, large losses have occurred in a number of airlines.

Southwest Airlines is the only airline in the United States that has remained profitable throughout the last 30 years. It has achieved this, in the main, through following a strategy of slow organic growth and ensuring that where new air routes are added, capacity utilization of aircraft is high.

Other airlines have expanded very quickly during times of high demand, but this has meant that they have been more vulnerable when this demand has faded, as aircraft have had to fly with low levels of occupancy.

Figure 16.5 The impact of operational gearing on airline industry profitability

Assessing the potential impact of changes in the external environment

An organization should be scanning the environment in order to assess the effect that environmental change may have on the organization. PESTEL analysis will have identified a range of political, economic, social, technological, environmental and legal changes that are or may be about to occur. Different scenarios can be identified for the next five or so years. The financial impact on existing and alternative strategies, given these scenarios, can then be evaluated.

In relation to changing attitudes to environmental damage, the potential impact of different strategies on contingent liability costs should be considered. These would arise if fines for non-compliance with regulations were to occur and legal claims for remedial action were made. Different strategies may also lead to less tangible costs, such as the cost of responding to increasing consumer demands for environmentally friendly products. Additional expenditure to meet consumer demands may reduce the likely level of liability costs to be expected, improve relationships with regulators and facilitate faster approval of expansion. In Chapter 13, it was also noted that corporate social responsibility (CSR) goes beyond good citizenship. Recognition of the social dimension of strategy may be an appropriate strategic response in some market segments and should be assessed.

Strategic management accounting – 'a figment of academic imagination'?

Strategic management accounting has been defined as 'management accounting information in which emphasis is placed on information which is related to factors external to the firm, as well as to non-financial information and internally generated information' (Chartered Institute of Management Accountants). Although the exact scope of strategic management accounting is subject to some debate, it would normally be considered to incorporate topics that have been discussed in this chapter. The extent to which organizations should need to implement strategic management accounting systems has, however, been subject to some discussion.

Lord (1996) undertook a case study analysis of a bicycle manufacturer based in New Zealand. This company had pursued a very successful strategy based on product differentiation and Lord wished to know whether strategic management accounting information, such as that suggested above, had been used by the management of the organization in the achievement of the strategy.

Given the bicycle company followed a strategy of product differentiation, the work of Shank and Govindarajan would suggest that traditional cost control information would be of less relevance than marketing information. This was not found to be the case, however, and the use of accounting information was not found to conform to the structure that might have been expected.

Competitor information was collected, however, this was not undertaken by the management accounting function. Rather, information had been gathered from sales representatives, through informal conversations with retailers and through observation of competitors' products. Competitor costs were estimated based on the knowledge that the company had of its own costs and through observation of the components used in its competitors' products. In practice, it might be questioned how often it is possible to obtain more accurate estimates of competitor costs using alternative methods.

The company also achieved cost reductions and product differentiation benefits by exploiting linkages in the value chain and increasing executional cost drivers. Again, this was the natural outcome of effective operational initiatives with operational managers and staff identifying key actions to take rather than it being the result of the provision of detailed accounting information about the relative costs of activities throughout the value chain.

In her conclusions, Lord suggests that the characteristics that are being ascribed to strategic management accounting are likely to be carried out already in many firms by other functions and without the need for detailed accounting information. She questioned whether in fact 'strategic management accounting' was just a 'figment of academic imagination'.

Summary

Management accounting information may be of use in the strategic management process. Examples include:

- The analysis of the profitability of market segments, customers, brands and product attributes.
- Control information given different strategic positioning and strategies.
- Analysis of the resources of the organization.
- Costing of the value chain and identification of cost and value drivers.
- Analysis of the impact of external environmental change on the strategies of the organization.

The extent to which strategic management accounting information is needed to assist in the strategic management process has been questioned. Information can be obtained from a number of sources, and the level of analysis required for decision-making may not be as detailed as suggested in some of the accounting literature.

Further reading

Ackinson, A.A., Kaplan, R.S., Matsumara, E.M., Youngs, S.M. (2007) *Management Accounting*, 5th edn., Prentice-Hall.

Bhimani, A. and Langfield-Smith, K. (2007) Structure, formality and the importance of financial and non-financial information in strategy development and implementation *Management Accounting Research* **18** (1): 3–31.

Hoque, Z. (2002) *Strategic Management Accounting: Concepts, processes and issues*, 2nd edn. Spiro Press, Rollinsford.

Lord, B.R. (2007) 'Strategic Management Accounting', in T. Hopper, D. Northcott and R. Scapens (eds), *Issues in Management Accounting*. FT/Prentice Hall, Harlow.

Shank, J.K. and Govindarajan, V. (1993) *Strategic Cost Management: The new tool for competitive advantage*. Free Press, New York.

Ward, K. (1992) *Strategic Management Accounting*. Butterworth-Heinemann, Oxford.

Answers to activities

Activity 16.1

Information might include market research findings on prices, the level of sales, whether there are long queues at busy periods – so demand not met? Market segmentation – e.g. whether facilities used by students or middle-aged lecturers, ambience, etc. Whether it is part of a chain of shops or a sole trader; likely fixed overheads of the shops; whether the competing shop has a long-term lease on its premises (high exit barrier if there is a long-term lease).

Activity 16.2

The answer is provided in the continuation of Figure 16.1.

Activity 16.3

CD Ltd manufactures video tape players which are at the decline stage of the lifecycle. The company might consider control information relevant for a harvest strategy.

LM has launched a product at the growth stage and might consider techniques that focus less on cost control and more on revenue growth.

AS Ltd appears to be at a mature stage of the lifecycle. A sustain or hold strategy is likely to be followed and traditional accounting controls may be more appropriate in these circumstances.

Activity 16.4

The average time per unit would be $20 \times 0.8 \times 0.8 = 12.8$ hours.

The total time therefore $= 4 \times 12.8 = 51.2$ hours.

Activity 16.5

(a) Labour cost £120 (20 hours × £6) + material cost £40 = £160.
(b) Labour cost £307.2 (51.2 hours × £6) + material £240 (4 units × £40 per unit) = £547.2.

Activity 16.6

As discussed in Chapter 14, there appear to be low structural barriers to entry in the airline industry. To survive in the longer term however it will be necessary to achieve an acceptable level of passenger occupancy.

Activity 16.7

They have reduced or removed services that do not add value. For example, on short-haul flights in-flight catering is not provided. A sizeable market segment prefers low cost on short-haul flights than additional services. They also have a high passenger occupancy percentage.

Activity 16.8

They are unable to achieve the desired occupancy rates needed for the airline to be profitable and/or they are not as efficient in completing the 'executional' cost drivers.

Discussion questions

1. If a customer profitability analysis indicates that 10% of customer accounts are not generating a profit, should the company close down those accounts?
2. What is a brand? Why should the management accountant be concerned about expenditure on brands?
3. Why might it be helpful to understand the cost structure of competitors?
4. You operate a bus company based in one county and are considering launching a new low-price service into the neighbouring counties, which will be in direct competition with local companies who currently operate those routes. What type of competitor information would be useful for you in deciding whether to proceed with this plan?
5. What is meant by strategic positioning? Why might it be important for the management accountant to understand the positioning strategy being followed by an organization?
6. What is the difference between a structural and an executional cost driver?
7. Is it always a good idea to try to achieve economies of scale? If not, why not?
8. Why is it important to consider the environment when assessing different strategies?
9. Why has it been suggested that strategic management accounting is a 'figment of academic imagination'?
10. Undertake a comparison of two fast food outlets, night clubs or other entertainment outlets which you use.

   (i) What are the attributes that add value?
   (ii) Where could they spend additional funds in order to add value or where is there expenditure which could be reduced as it does not add sufficient value?
   (iii) What information do you need to undertake this analysis properly?

Exercises

(Questions with numbers in bold have answers at the back of the book.)

Q16.1 Siegmund Ltd is considering the development of its toaster product range. The variable cost of the basic model is €16 and this will be sold to the retailers for €18. The retailers will in turn sell the product to customers for €36. For an additional cost it is possible to build in additional features such as an ability to toast four slices of bread, a defrost ability, superior styling.

As well as introducing the basic model, the company has decided to introduce one other model and so is trying to identify which features should be included in this second model. To help in the decision a market research exercise has been undertaken and a sample of potential customers have been asked to estimate how much more they would be prepared to pay for additional features. The cost of providing these additional features has also been identified and the information is provided below.

Feature	Additional cost prepared to pay (€)	Cost of manufacture (€)
Ability to toast four slices	10	6
Defrost ability	4	1
Superior styling	4	5

Required:

What additional features (if any) do you recommend should be included in the additional model of toaster? Identify the additional information that you require for your analysis.

For the following questions it is necessary to review the information provided in the case 'Siegmund Ltd'.

Q16.2 You have been asked to advise the general manager of Siegmund Ltd on ways in which the accounting information system might be developed in order to assist in the strategic analysis process.

Required:

Provide a report on potential applications.

Q16.3 The general manager of Siegmund Ltd has been reviewing the information provided in Table 4 of the case. This table provides a profile of cost information of the company and two major competitors.

Required:

Provide a report to the general manager of key issues that should be of concern to the company. Critically evaluate the use of the information that is provided. What further information would be helpful for a deeper analysis of the problem?

Q16.4 The operations director of Siegmund Ltd has expressed the opinion that the existing budgetary control system might be detrimental to the well-being of the organization. Strict attention has been paid over recent years to achieving a good profit margin from all products and she feels that this has meant that expenditure on new product development has suffered.

Required:

Explain why this might be the case.

Q16.5 To what extent do you consider that the positioning strategy of Siegmund Ltd should be taken into account when considering the type of information that should be monitored by the management accounting information system?

Q16.6 Albion Ltd is a wine merchant that supplies the retail trade (off-licences, independent public houses). It has produced a profitability analysis for two of its customers:

	Customer A (£)	Customer B (£)
Sales	9000	9000
Cost of sales	4000	4500
Gross profit	5000	4500
Other costs (30% sales)	2700	2700
Net profit	2300	1800

An allowance of 30% of sales has traditionally been allowed to cover the costs of marketing and distribution.

Albion has decided to undertake a more detailed cost analysis and has identified the following usage of key activities:

	Customer A	Customer B
Number of purchase orders	5	70
Number of deliveries	10	25
Number of miles per delivery	5	25

It has also identified the costs of a number of areas of activity and a cost driver rate for each activity.

Activity centre	Costs (£)	Cost driver	Activity usage	Activity cost driver rate (£)
Purchase orders	80,000	Number of orders	2,000	40
Delivery cost (1)	55,000	Number of deliveries	2,200	25
Delivery cost (2)	100,000	Miles travelled	100,000	1

Delivery costs consist of two cost pools. Delivery cost pool 1 consists of the supervisory costs of the delivery department. Delivery cost pool 2 consists of the costs of actually delivering goods to a customer. The activity driver of the first is the number of deliveries, while for the second it is miles travelled.

Required:

Calculate a revised profitability statement for the two customers in the light of the information that has been revealed and comment on the results of this analysis.

Q16.7 Elvedeer Ltd is investigating the profitability of two customers, X and Y. Elvedeer's sales to customer X are £30,000 and to customer Y, £15,000. Costs of sales are on average 50% of revenue and an allowance of 25% of revenue is allowed for other costs.

A more detailed analysis of the marketing, delivery and sales effort that is needed to deal with each customer is as follows:

	Customer X	Customer Y
Number of sales orders	100	30
Number of sales visits	30	15
Number of deliveries	30	15
Special deliveries	40	2

The information on costs of each activity is:

Activity	Cost driver rate (£)
Per sales order	70
Per sales visit	100
Per delivery	200
Per special delivery	300

It is considered that other general overheads cannot be identified to product level.

Required:

Calculate the contribution each customer makes to general overheads using the traditional method of identifying costs to customers and a more detailed activity-based analysis.

Q16.8 Brand Y generates a contribution after deducting variable and identifiable fixed costs of £1,400,000. A marketing campaign costing £800,000 is planned in the coming year in order to relaunch the brand and regain market leadership. The benefit of the campaign is expected to last two years. The company cost of capital is 10%.

Required:

Calculate the profit assuming:

(i) 'Generally accepted accounting principles', i.e. all marketing costs treated as an expense of the period.
(ii) If the marketing campaign is treated as an investment to be written off over two years.

Q16.9 A customer has approached company X and asked for a quote to manufacture 8 units of a component. It takes 20 hours to make the first unit. The material cost per unit is £60 and labour is paid at £9 an hour. It is believed that an 80% learning curve would be achieved.

(a) How many hours would be required to make 8 units and what price should company X quote if it plans to achieve variable cost plus 25%?
(b) The customer accepted the first quote and the contract has been delivered. The customer has now returned and advised that a further 8 units is required and the customer is prepared to pay a further £1100 for the new contract. Should company X accept the contract at this price? Provide a financial evaluation and identify further factors that your company should consider in making a decision.

Q16.10 A customer has approached company Y and asked for a quote to manufacture 4 units of a component. It takes 8 hours to make the first unit. The material cost per unit is £70 and labour is paid at £10 an hour. It is believed that a 90% learning curve would be achieved.

(a) How many hours would be required to make 4 units and what price should company X quote if it plans to achieve cost plus 20%?
(b) The customer accepted the first quote and the contract has been delivered. The customer has now returned and advised that a further 4 units is required and the customer is prepared to pay a further £600 for the new contract. Should company Y accept the contract at this price? Provide a financial evaluation and identify further factors that your company should consider in making a decision.

Q16.11 The Wilber Corporation is considering whether to manufacture a product that will cost £10 per unit in material. The company is currently considering whether to lease a machine for £10,000 per annum or a machine for £20,000 per annum. The additional variable cost per unit with the former is £4, while with the latter it is £2. The selling price per unit is expected to be £19. Advise the company.

IDENTIFYING SUITABLE STRATEGIC OPTIONS

Objectives

Having studied this chapter you should be able to:

- Explain how opportunities and threats (identified in the external environmental appraisal) and strengths and weaknesses (assessed in the internal appraisal) can be brought together in a SWOT analysis matrix to help identify strategic options.
- Identify strategic options using Ansoff's product/market matrix.
- Describe the advantages and disadvantages of different methods of achieving growth (acquisition vs. organic).
- Explain the need to assess the extent to which different strategic options provide a fit with the desired strategic direction of the organization.
- Explain the need to assess the extent to which new investment is consistent with the desired strategic direction of the organization.

Introduction

Having undertaken a strategic analysis, management will now have an understanding of the environment in which the organization operates as well as of the organization itself. They should also have identified objectives for the next few years and the gap between these objectives and the expected performance, if the organization continues with its current strategies. It is now necessary to consider how to close the planning gap.

To generate ideas for alternative strategies there are a number of tools/techniques that can be used and two popular techniques are considered in the first section of this chapter. The first is known as the SWOT analysis matrix. This can be prepared following the completion of a SWOT analysis (Strengths and Weaknesses of the organization in comparison with competitors and Opportunities and Threats in the environment). The second technique that will be demonstrated is Ansoff's product/market matrix.

In a second section different methods by which the various options can be achieved are identified, for example either by acquisition through development of a joint venture, merger with or acquisition of another business or through organic growth, i.e. internal development.

Having identified a range of possible options that could be pursued, the need to evaluate each option in terms of its fit with the existing strategy of the organization is discussed in a third section. In a final part of the chapter, the need to treat long-term investment in assets as a strategic decision will be reviewed.

Identifying strategic options

SWOT analysis and the TOWS analysis matrix

SWOT stands for Strengths, Weaknesses, Opportunities and Threats.

Strengths and weaknesses

A strength is something that an organization is good at doing or something that gives it particular credibility. It can be a particular attribute of a product or service that provides a competitive advantage, a resource such as a strong financial position or new production facilities, or superior competencies or capabilities. A weakness is something an organization lacks or performs in an inferior way in comparison to others.

Strengths and weaknesses are identified by completing an *internal appraisal* of the organization and comparing how well the organization performs in key areas of the business when compared with competitors. As discussed in Chapter 15, in order to identify strengths and weaknesses, techniques such as the product lifecycle and portfolio analysis can help in the analysis of markets and products or services, a resource audit can be completed and an assessment of the competencies of the organization undertaken.

Opportunities and threats

An opportunity is a condition in the environment that is helpful, while a threat is a condition that is harmful to the achievement of the objectives of the organization. Opportunities and threats can be identified by completing an appraisal of the external environment. As discussed in Chapter 14, the appraisal of the external environment can include an assessment of the general or macro-environment, a market analysis involving an identification of the key consumers in each market segment in which the organization is operating, and an assessment of the competitor forces in these market segments.

Undertaking a SWOT analysis

To provide an illustration of a SWOT analysis, a simple case scenario will be provided in Figure 17.1. A SWOT analysis representing key strengths, weaknesses, opportunities and threats will be drawn from this case and will be shown in Figure 17.2.

Rominska Airlines

Overview of the company and its main markets and services

Rominska Airlines operates in an Eastern European country. Previously a state company, it has recently been privatized. The airline operates two principal services: firstly, long-haul international flights from the country's capital city to the main cities in Europe and to America and secondly, short-haul flights which are within the main cities of the country and to neighbouring countries.

For the international flights it has on average a 40% market share, which is twice as large as its largest competitors. Market size has been growing at 5% per annum in a number of recent years, however, in the last year – following terrorist attacks – there has been no growth in the market. Although the average age of the aircraft is more than for the main competitors, the company has had a good reputation for the quality of its in-flight service and as the national airline, is the first choice for many citizens of the country.

For the short-haul flights the market share varies according to specific routes, however, the market has grown at 15% in the last year as a major overseas low-cost competitor has entered the market and low prices have generated extra sales. In two years the competitor has managed to secure 35% of the market, which is the same size as Rominska Airlines. The market share of Rominska Airlines is shrinking fast as its fares are more expensive than those of the low-cost competitor.

Summary findings of an internal review of the company

Financial resources: Rominska Airlines is making good profits on the international flights, but such significant losses on the short-haul flights that overall Rominska Airlines is in a loss situation. On the positive side, the company has good holdings of cash and low debts.

Personnel resources: Traditional working practices mean that there is a lack of flexibility in working, and restrictive practices operate. This means that turnaround time, for example, is much slower for the airline than for recent new competitors. The management, although experienced in operations management, do not have strong marketing skills.

Physical resources: The average age of the fleet is older than the average for other traditional airlines. There are a number of different types of aircraft, which need a wide range of skills from pilots and maintenance crews.

Summary findings of a review of the general external environment in which the company operates

A number of Rominska Airlines competitors have recently been privatized and many are in a worse financial condition. They have inherited large debts and are running at a loss.

The market situation is fairly uncertain at the moment. Deregulation is spreading. Currently, some international routes are protected by bilateral agreement, which means that there are entry barriers to new competitors on those routes. However, these barriers are soon to be removed. Further, as identified above, there is no growth in the international long-haul market and fast growth in the short-haul market. Airlines had been anticipating continued growth in the long-haul market and additional aircraft had been purchased and are on order to meet the anticipated growth. Without this growth there is overcapacity in this key market of the company. In the face of the general uncertainties in the market, a number of other airlines have been forming alliances. For example, offering benefits (e.g. frequent flyer benefits) to consumers who fly with members of the alliance. Existing customers of Rominska Airlines are being attracted to airlines which are members of the alliance to take advantage of the benefits. (Note that alliances are discussed in greater detail in the next section of this chapter.)

A number of high-speed train links are currently being proposed within the country and some neighbouring states. An upgrade in roads and construction of a number of motorways is also anticipated, and this seems likely to result in reduced travelling time within the region.

Figure 17.1 Description of Rominska Airlines and its external environment

Market research carried out for Rominska Airlines has identified that a significant number of international customers, though not prepared to pay a first class fare on long-haul air travel, would be prepared to pay more than the current economy fares for more space and more comfortable seats than currently provided by Rominska Airlines or its existing competitors.

Although overall inflation is low, fuel costs have risen considerably in recent years and this new higher price level is expected to continue into the foreseeable future. On the other hand, with the current downturn in the market there are a number of new airplanes available to be leased at competitive rates as other airlines have not taken up their options to lease these planes.

The airline has traditionally taken bookings through travel agents, however, it is noted that consumers are increasingly learning to book on-line and it is expected that this trend will continue.

Figure 17.1 (*Continued*)

Activity 17.1

Read the information provided in Figure 17.1 and identify the strengths, weaknesses, opportunities and threats for Rominska Airlines.

The SWOT analysis

With a real company there would be many more findings, however, the above is sufficient for illustrating the use of a SWOT analysis. A common mistake is to list all the strengths, weaknesses, opportunity and threats, however, it is recommended that only the key variables that could be of crucial significance to the strategic direction of the business be identified. A review of the information revealed for Rominska Airlines has been summarized in the SWOT analysis in Figure 17.2.

From reading the sections 'Overview of the company and its main markets and services' and 'Summary findings of an internal review of the company' it is possible to identify the following strengths and weaknesses.

Strengths
(S1) The long-haul international routes of Rominska Airlines are profitable.
(S2) Holdings of cash are high and debts are low.

Weaknesses
(W1) Traditional working practices mean that there is a lack of flexibility in working, and restrictive practices operate. This leads to poor performance in areas such as aircraft turnaround time.
(W2) The average age of the fleet is more than the average for other traditional airlines.
(W3) There are a number of different types of aircraft, which need a wide range of skills from pilots and maintenance crews.
(W4) The marketing function in the company is recognized as weak.
(W5) A number of short-haul routes are making losses.

Figure 17.2 SWOT analysis for Rominska Airlines

From reading the sections 'Overview of the company and its main markets and services' and 'Summary findings of a review of the general external environment in which the company operates' it is possible to identify the following opportunities and threats in the environment.

Opportunities

(O1) Market research carried out for Rominska Airlines has identified that a significant number of international customers are not prepared to pay a first class fare on long-haul air travel but would be prepared to pay more than the economy fares for more space and more comfortable seats than currently provided by existing competitors.

(O2) With a current downturn in the market there are a number of new airplanes available to be leased at competitive rates as other airlines have not taken up their options to lease these planes.

(O3) A number of recently privatized competitors have financial problems.

(O4) The short-haul market is expanding very fast in this region.

Threats

(T1) There is currently a downturn in the world economy and there is overcapacity in the key market for this company (the international routes).

(T2) Fuel costs are rising.

(T3) Deregulation is spreading. Currently some international routes are protected by bilateral agreement, which means that there are entry barriers to new competitors on those routes. However, these barriers are soon to be removed.

(T4) Consumers are increasingly learning to book on-line, which means that in future they are less likely to use the travel agents who have provided most of the sales for Rominska Airlines.

(T5) A number of other airlines are forming alliances. For example, offering benefits (e.g. frequent flyer benefits) to consumers who fly with members of the alliance. Existing customers of Rominska Airlines are being attracted to airlines which are members of the alliance to take advantage of the benefits. (Note that alliances are discussed in greater detail in the next section of this chapter.)

(T6) Development of alternative transport systems, e.g. high-speed trains, may threaten some of the short-haul and long-haul routes.

Figure 17.2   (*Continued*)

TOWS analysis matrix

The TOWS analysis matrix can be used as an extension of SWOT analysis. Having identified the key strengths and weaknesses of the organization and the opportunities and threats in the environment, this information can be used to help identify possible strategies. With the TOWS matrix the following analysis is undertaken to suggest strategies that:

1. Use a strength identified from an internal appraisal of the organization to

   (a) take advantage of an environmental opportunity, or
   (b) combat an environmental threat.

2. Can help the organization correct a weakness identified from an internal appraisal of the organization to

   (a) take advantage of an environmental opportunity, or
   (b) combat an environmental threat.

In order to assist in this exercise the key strengths, weaknesses, opportunities and threats identified in the analysis of Rominska Airlines are summarized into a TOWS analysis matrix in Figure 17.3.

TOWS analysis matrix for Rominska Airlines

Note that in the figure below, rather than listing each of the factors noted in Figure 17.2, an identifier is used in the TOWS analysis matrix. Thus S1 represents the strength 'long-haul international routes are profitable', T4 represents the threat 'consumers are increasingly learning to book on-line'.

	Strengths S1 S2 S3	Weaknesses W1 W2 W3 W4 W5 W6
Opportunities O1 O2 O3	*Cell A* Strategies based on using strengths to exploit opportunities (e.g. S1 + S2 + O1).	*Cell B* Strategies based on correcting weaknesses to exploit opportunities (e.g. W2 + W3 + O2).
Threats T1 T2 T3 T4 T5	*Cell C* Strategies based on using strengths to exploit opportunities (e.g. S1 + S2 + T1).	*Cell D* Strategies based on correcting weaknesses to combat threats (e.g. W1 + T1).

A number of options are listed below.

Cell A

S1 (long-haul routes profitable) + S2 (holdings of cash high) + O1 (market segment prepared to pay more for a service better than economy but not as expensive as first class).

Strategy suggested – modify fleet on long-haul routes to provide this improved service.

Cell B

Option 1: W2 (old fleet) + W3 (different types of aircraft) + O2 (availability of new airplanes on cheap leases). Strategy suggested – look to greater standardization of the fleet with the replacement of older planes with suitable new aircraft.

Option 2: W1 (poor performance in areas such as aircraft turnaround time due to restrictive practices) + O4 (fast growth in short-haul market).

Figure 17.3   TOWS matrix for Rominska Airlines

Strategy suggested – overcome restrictive practices and expand services in short-haul market to recover market share.

Cell C

S1 (long haul routes profitable) + S2 (holdings of cash high) + T1 (overcapacity in the market).

Strategy suggested – consider acquiring competitors to reduce competition and gain new routes.

Cell D

W4 (marketing weak) + T5 (existing customers increasingly flying with competitors who have formed into an alliance).

Strategy suggested – review marketing activities and consider joining the alliance or an alliance with other competitors who are not in the existing alliance.

Note that in a full analysis of an organization and its environment, it may be possible to identify a long list of strengths, weaknesses, opportunities and threats. In such a situation, it is important that only the key factors (say the top three to five) that are of strategic importance to the organization are considered.

Figure 17.3   (*Continued*)

Activity 17.2

Referring to the TOWS matrix in Figure 17.3, suggest one additional option for each of cells A, B, C, D.

Ansoff's product/market matrix

Ansoff's (1957) product/market matrix can help to specify the direction in which a company intends to develop its strategic portfolio – see Figure 17.4. Virtually every possible strategic option can be located in one or other of the cells.

	Existing products	New products
Existing markets	Strategies based on existing markets and existing products. CONSOLIDATION/ PENETRATION	Strategies based on launching new (or improved) products into existing markets. PRODUCT DEVELOPMENT
New markets	Strategies based on finding new markets for existing products. MARKET DEVELOPMENT	Strategies based on launching new products into new markets. RELATED OR UNRELATED DIVERSIFICATION

Figure 17.4   Ansoff's product/market matrix

Existing products/existing markets

Strategies might involve policies of consolidation, penetration or retrenchment. They are usually considered to be the least risky of the options as they do not involve major new expenditure by the organization.

Consolidation
Maintenance of the current position: this may be appropriate when trading conditions are difficult. For example, the firm may be uncertain of the future and may wish to preserve its existing cash holdings and withhold from investing in new ventures.

Penetration
This might involve the firm in an attempt to increase the market share of its existing products in existing markets through greater marketing effort. Alternatively, a firm may buy up some of its competitors and gain market share through such means.

Retrenchment
Dispose of parts of the business where the performance is poor.

New products/existing markets

Product development may be particularly required where the product lifecycle is short. With a rapid cycle of introduction, growth, maturity and decline, it is necessary to have new products being developed to replace the existing products. In the car industry, new products are introduced on a regular basis in order to compete against competitors.

Existing products/new markets

This could involve the marketing of products to new geographical areas, new channels of distribution and new users of the product or new uses of the product. This strategy is often used where there are significant economies of scale, with high fixed costs and inflexible facilities.

Diversification

Diversification is the most risky as it involves developing new products and selling into new markets. There can be *related* diversification through forward or backward integration. As illustration, a manufacturer who decided to open up a number of retail shops to sell the products it manufactured would be involved in forward integration. A retailer who decided to manufacture the products it makes would be involved in backward integration. A number of tour operators such as Thomson have undertaken related diversification by setting up airlines to fly their clients to their destinations.

Alternatively, an organization might be involved in *unrelated* diversification, where it develops into a number of new and unrelated areas. For example, the Virgin group started in the retail sector selling records and has expanded into a number of diverse areas, including insurance and the airline industry. As discussed earlier, EasyJet has undertaken undifferentiated diversification through expanding into new market areas such as low-cost cruises and low-cost hotels.

As illustration, Ansoff's product/growth matrix has been applied to the airline industry in Figure 17.5.

Existing products/Existing markets

Penetration Successful low-cost airlines frequently follow a policy of market penetration. They identify a specific route between two airports and then aim to gain market share on that route, a key competitive factor being the frequency of flights. As discussed later in the chapter, a policy followed by several traditional airlines, such as British Airways, is to achieve market penetration through acquiring other airlines and franchising routes to small airlines with a lower cost base.

Retrenchment When faced with severe competition from low-cost airlines, a number of traditional airlines have withdrawn from particular market segments because they are unable to compete due to their high cost base. Where they have not withdrawn totally from a route, they may reduce capacity, for example British Airways reduced its North Atlantic capacity in 2003 in response to a fall in demand for air travel.

New products/Existing markets

New product development could include the introduction of new type of aircraft onto a route, for example, the introduction of the super sonic jet Concorde by British Airways and Air France onto the transatlantic route. A smaller scale example is the provision of seats that can convert into full-length beds, which provided British Airways with a temporary competitive advantage in the late 1990s. A number of airlines have announced the launch in 2008 of business-only flights from London to the US.

Existing products/New markets

Successful low-cost airlines such as Southwest in the USA have followed a policy of growth and expansion onto new routes. From a start up position in the 1970's, Southwest Airlines is now the sixth largest airline in the USA.

Diversification

A number of holiday tour operators have undertaken related diversification (backward integration) by setting up or acquiring airlines to fly their clients to their destinations.

Alternatively an organization might be involved in *unrelated* diversification, where it develops into a number of new and unrelated areas. For example, the Virgin group started in the retail sector selling records and has expanded into a number of diverse areas including insurance and the airline industry. EasyJet has undertaken undifferentiated diversification through expanding into new market areas such as low-cost cruises (EasyCruise) and low-cost hotels (EasyHotel).

Figure 17.5 Applying Ansoff's matrix to the airline industry

Activity 17.3

Use Ansoff's product/market matrix to identify a range of options that Rominska Airlines might consider.

Identifying methods for achieving different options

Having used Ansoff's matrix and/or the TOWS analysis matrix to identify possibly alternative strategies to consider, the firm now needs to further refine the ideas by identifying an appropriate method for achieving these options. Growth can be achieved through internal development, otherwise it can be gained through acquisition. Acquisition can be the result of merger with or acquisition of another organization or it can be through joint development and strategic alliances. See the illustration in Figure 17.6 for British Airways.

Internal development

Many firms like to achieve growth through internal development because this is often the best way of gaining the necessary abilities to develop new products and also to sell into new markets. This is known as organic growth. The advantage of internal growth is that it is relatively inexpensive to achieve if the business can expand by doing more of what it is good at doing. However, it can take a long time to achieve the required size.

Merger and acquisition

Acquisition is where an organization takes over another organization. Mergers tend to be the result of organizations coming together voluntarily. It is quicker to enter new product or market areas by merger or acquisition. A company may find it too difficult or time-consuming to develop the appropriate production, research and development, marketing or other skills. Further, if a market is fairly static then firms may buy out others in order to gain market share and reduce the level of competition. An existing firm may also have achieved significant cost efficiencies and economies of scale and it would be worth purchasing these benefits rather than having to achieve such economies through long and painful development.

However, acquiring other organizations can cause problems in that the organizational culture and traditions of organizations that merge can be very different. In practice, it often takes a considerable time for financial performance to improve from the combined company.

Joint development and strategic alliances

An **alliance** is where two or more firms agree to cooperate on certain activities. In the airline industry, a marketing alliance could involve giving frequent flyer benefits to passengers who fly on any aircraft of another member of the alliance. Another marketing benefit can be gained through 'code-sharing' agreements. A code-sharing agreement is when one airline lists another's flights as its own in reservation systems to boost market share.

A more permanent form of alliance is a **joint development**. This is where organizations share resources and activities to pursue a strategy. Joint ventures are where the organizations remain independent, but a newly created organization is jointly owned by the parents. For example, airlines may jointly own a computer reservation system, terminal facilities or aircraft.

A **consortium** is where a number of organizations come together on a major contract. In the aircraft manufacturing industry there are two major manufacturers, Boeing in the USA and the European Airbus. The European Airbus is a consortium of four European partners, Aérospatiale (37.9%), Dasa (37.9%), British Aerospace (22%) and Casa (4.2%).

Other methods of development include **franchising**, where the franchisor sells a franchise to a franchisee. Examples of franchises include McDonalds, where the franchisor provides a number of the central services – e.g. the brand name, the food, marketing and training – and the franchisee provides the service. In the airline industry, smaller airlines will act as the franchisee and adopt the livery, brand and service standards. The benefit of the franchise agreements to the franchisee is that they gain a reliable source of revenue, while for the franchisor it is a relatively quick means of adding or retaining market share. Larger traditional airlines also often find that a small franchisee can provide a service on a short-haul market more cheaply than they can themselves.

Licensing is common in science-based industries, where the right to manufacture is granted for a fee. In the bicycle industry, some Moulton bicycles are manufactured by Pashley Cycles.

Subcontracting is where part of the work is completed by another organization. Some organizations identify core and non-core businesses. If an organization identifies itself as an airline, then it might identify services such as cleaning or catering as non-core work that can be subcontracted to other organizations.

British Airways had a global strategy for its airline, which involved growth based on three key objectives:

1. Dominate the UK market.
2. Ensure a presence in the other major European markets.
3. Establish a global presence.

In the 1990s it set out to achieve this through a number of the methods discussed above.

In order to dominate in the UK market it took a share in – or bought outright – a number of smaller airlines including Brymon Airlines, British Caledonian (the UK's second largest airline) and Dan Air. It also entered into a number of franchise agreements. The benefit of the franchise agreements to British Airways was that it was a relatively quick and potentially cheaper means of adding a substantial number of additional destinations to its network. The agreements also meant that there were additional domestic routes to feed its international routes. When, after 1995, low-cost new entrants such as EasyJet and Ryanair created a new challenge to British Airways, it set up its own low-cost airline, Go.

To ensure a presence in the other major European markets, British Airways acquired a number of small airlines based in other European countries such as Germany and France.

To achieve its third strategic objective of establishing a global presence it used a number of approaches. Initially, it tried to form a strategic alliance with firstly USAir and then American Airlines. These alliances were unsuccessful and a weaker marketing alliance, 'Oneworld', was formed, initially with four other airlines and later more. British Airways did also continue with some joint ventures, for example, the scheduled freighter service between Singapore and London is operated jointly by BA and Singapore Airlines.

Figure 17.6 **Methods of achieving growth by British Airways**

As discussed in Chapter 13, in setting the mission statement, it is necessary to consider whether the airline is in the airline business, i.e. flight operations, or is in the aviation business. Traditionally, medium and large-sized organizations have seen themselves as in the aviation business and have retained control of non-aviation activities such as cargo services, engineering, sales and distribution, revenue accounting, in-flight catering, ground handling and information systems. The new start-up airlines, such as EasyJet, have identified themselves as airlines and have subcontracted the other activities. Unusually for a traditional airline, British Airways has decided to follow suit and has also subcontracted 'non-core' activities. For example, in-flight catering at Heathrow was sold to Gate Gourmet.

Other traditional airlines have stayed with the 'traditional' model and retained control of these activities. Others, such as Lufthansa, have separated the different activities into separate core businesses.

Doganis (2001) suggests that the strategy of subcontracting has left British Airways vulnerable to the impact of recessions. In 2000, while Lufthansa saw profits from its airline activities decline, these were offset by good performance from the other business units. British Airways suffered large losses on its airline activities that led to a declining share price and eventually the resignation of the Chief Executive.

Figure 17.6 *(Continued)*

Activity 17.4

If Rominska Airlines wished to achieve growth objectives, advise the company on options that it could consider.

Evaluating the suitability of different options

Techniques such as the TOWS matrix and Ansoff's product/market portfolio will have helped identify a range of options that an organization might consider pursuing. The extent to which the proposed strategy is 'suitable', i.e. fits with the desired strategic direction of the organization, should now be checked.

Market analysis and competitive position

In Chapter 15, the use of the growth/share (BCG) matrix was recommended as a means of assessing the balance of the product portfolio of a company. The implication of the product lifecycle of products on the cash flow and profitability of the organization was also discussed. The impact of potential new strategies on the balance of the portfolio of the organization and on cash flows and profits should be assessed.

Fit with strategic position

Options can be analysed in terms of the extent to which they are consistent with the strategic position of the organization. Shank and Govindarajan (1993) quote the example of the 'Baldwin Bicycle company'. The company followed a product differentiation strategy and sold high-quality bicycles. At one time the company had spare capacity in the factory and was offered a contract to supply bicycles to a department store at low prices. Although the contract would have led to a contribution, accepting the contract would have meant that the company was forced into the competitive low-cost market and would also have undermined the quality image of the existing products.

Fit with competencies

The extent to which the strategy fits with the competencies of the organization should also be reviewed. A company with the competency to produce low volumes of high-quality bicycles, for example, will not necessarily have the capability to compete on a long-term basis in a low-cost market.

For Rominska Airlines, having undertaken a SWOT analysis and analysed services using the TOWS matrix, an option identified was to 'overcome restrictive practices and expand services in the short-haul market to recover market share'. The assessment of the suitability of this option is discussed in Figure 17.7.

Fit with existing competitive positioning in target markets

Product lifecycle

The product lifecycle highlights how products follow a similar pattern of growth and decline.

In considering the option to expand in the short-haul market, the product lifecycle highlights the danger of assuming that sales of this market segment will continue to grow indefinitely. At present, growth is being achieved due to the existence of one low-cost competitor. This growth may continue for some time to come, however, there is a danger that further competitors may enter the market. The product lifecycle indicates that at some stage there will be a point at which sales will stop increasing (maturity) and then a decline stage. This might well occur in the short-haul market in the country in which Rominska Airlines operates. Decline might well set in if the alternative transportation methods develop due, for example, to faster trains and better roads and motorways.

Product portfolio
There are many different product portfolio matrices discussed in the strategic management literature – one of these, the BCG matrix, was introduced in Chapter 15. A key implication of the BCG matrix is that organizations should aim for a 'balanced' portfolio. It is desirable to have products as cash cows since these products are generating cash, which can be reinvested into the business. It is also important to have question marks and then stars, as these are the future of the business. Options should therefore also be judged on the basis of the contribution that they make to rectify any perceived lack of balance in the product range.

Using this analysis, it might be suggested that the international long-haul routes for Rominska Airlines are a cash cow. The short-haul routes appear to be currently a question mark and theory would suggest that one option is for the cash cow to fund the question mark. However, if market share of Rominska Airlines continues to decline further, with aircraft flying on with significant unused capacity and ever-increasing losses, then the viability of pursuing such an option would seem to be doubtful.

Figure 17.7 Assessing the suitability of entering the short-haul market for Rominska Airlines

Fit with positioning strategy

Rominska Airlines is a traditional airline, which has not previously provided low-cost flights. It appears to have relied on a differentiation strategy (superior in-flight service) and has relied on its image as the national carrier. If it is now aiming for a cost leadership strategy in the short-haul market, this may be seen as a strategy in conflict with Porter's view of the need to follow a generic strategy of cost leadership, product differentiation or focus. Arguably, Rominska Airlines could say that it is following a different strategy within specific market segments. As indicated earlier (see Figure 17.6), rather than attempting to follow a low-cost strategy on some routes and product differentiation on others, an alternative that a number of airlines have followed is to franchise the short-haul routes to another airline or to set up a separate low-cost airline to deal with certain of the short-haul routes.

Fit with competencies – value chain analysis

The comparison of the competing low-cost airline and Rominska Airlines reveals that Rominska Airlines is significantly more expensive on a number of processes. The management of Rominska Airlines need to realistically assess the likelihood that they will be able to reduce costs for the short-haul routes in line with the low-cost competitor. Evidence from around the world suggests that many traditional airlines struggle to compete against low-cost competitors such as EasyJet or Southwest Airlines.

Figure 17.7 (*Continued*)

Activity 17.5

Consider the option 'look to greater standardization of the fleet with the replacement of older planes with suitable new aircraft'.

To what extent do you consider that this is a 'suitable' option to pursue?

A strategic perspective to investment appraisal

The impact of an investment on the total value chain

Shank and Govindarajan stress the importance of considering the impact of an investment on the total value chain, i.e. on the value chain of suppliers and customers, as well as that of the firm. The example of a choice of technology for the timber industry was mentioned in Chapter 16 and further information is provided in Figure 17.8.

A further illustration of the need to consider the impact of an investment on the value chain was also mentioned in Chapter 16. Shank and Govindarajan (1992b, 1993) reported on a company considering an investment in new production facilities to supply high-quality packaging. Although it was likely that this was a growth area, an analysis of the value chain identified that the end purchasers had high purchasing power. It was therefore likely that these purchasers would have an ongoing opportunity to force downward pressure on the high-quality product profit margins of the packaging company.

The value chain of the timber industry typically involves three separate sets of organizations:

- The landowners who own the forests.
- The logging companies who cut the trees.
- Customers for the cut logs.

Two technologies can be used by the logging companies to cut logs. One system involves the mass clearing of a section of a wood, which means that trees of a range of ages are cut down and leads to damage to both the land and the delivered timber. The other is ecologically sounder and involves the choice of specific trees to be felled and the careful felling and cutting of these individual trees. From the perspective of the landowners and the customers of the timber, there are financial benefits from the use of the ecologically sound technology, however, there are no financial benefits for many logging companies. The logging companies have no incentive to take a broad view of the benefits to the whole value chain by taking advantage of the linkages between the three sets of organizations; rather, they solely view the investment decision from their own perspective and invest in the technology that provides the greatest return to them.

In order to take advantage of the linkages in the value chain, one option is for the suppliers and customers of the logging company to make some kind of financial inducement to the logging companies, in order that the environmentally friendlier technology is used. Alternatively, the suppliers or customers of the logging companies could consider a strategy of vertical integration by entering the logging business in order to exploit the linkages in the value chain.

Figure 17.8 Strategic implications of different technologies in the timber industry (adapted from Shank, J.K., Govindarajan, V. (1992c), Strategic cost analysis of technological investments, *Sloan Management Review*, 34, 39–51)

Fit with positioning strategy

The positioning strategy of the organization should also be taken into account when undertaking an investment. For example, Shank and Govindarajan note one logging operation that was following a differentiation strategy which required the use of high-quality timber. This required mature trees whose size and type met the current processing needs of the mills. The higher value that was extracted from the higher technology and more ecological system justified the additional cost. For a logging company following a low-cost strategy, the benefit was insufficient to justify the investment.

Assessing hard-to-quantify strategic benefits

Viewing an investment from a strategic perspective may help identify a range of costs and benefits that might be ignored using a conventional analysis. Many benefits, however, remain difficult to quantify. For example, investing in new manufacturing technology may result in enhanced manufacturing flexibility and shorter factory cycle times. This in turn could lead to a significant increase in sales if shorter delivery time was a value proposition of key importance to customers. Quantification of the level of additional sales may, however, be difficult.

In assessing the costs and benefits of investment projects, a first step should involve the listing of all benefits and costs that are likely to arise as a result of the project. Bromwich and Bhimani (1991), in referring to investments in advanced manufacturing technology, suggest that these should be identified with three different categories:

1. Those that can be directly quantified in precise financial terms.
2. Those that can be converted to less precise financial terms.
3. Those that cannot be quantified.

A similar approach could be taken for most investments. Where benefits can be quantified in monetary terms, then this should be done. Where quantification is not possible, then an item could be scored on a 'points' scale (1 to 10). Management can then assess the weighting, which should be given to financial and non-financial factors.

The use of risk analysis to assist in the evaluation of investment projects will be considered in Chapter 18.

Kaplan (1986) also argues that when undertaking an investment appraisal, the impact of not investing may be ignored. For example, assume that 1000 units of an existing product are sold each month and it is expected that additional investment to upgrade the product will lead to 1200 units being sold per month. If the investment appraisal is made on the basis that *an extra* 200 units will be sold each month, this might underestimate the true benefit. If the existing product is approaching the decline stage of its product lifecycle, then it is likely that sales would decline from the current level. Consequently, the additional number of units sold would be greater than 200 and the net benefit therefore greater than that shown in the analysis.

Acceptability and feasibility

This chapter has considered the need to identify potential strategies that will close the gap between existing performance and the level required. It has identified that strategies should be assessed in terms of their fit with the strategic logic of the organization. Strategies should also be reviewed on further grounds of their *acceptability* and *feasibility*.

- Acceptability is an option acceptable to key stakeholders, e.g. for shareholders is the return and risk acceptable?
- Feasibility is whether an option can be implemented successfully. Does the organization have the resources?

The two issues of acceptability and feasibility will be considered in Chapter 18.

Summary

In order to close the gap between the desired expected long-term performance and the actual performance, it is necessary to identify and evaluate strategic options. This chapter has been concerned with techniques that assist with the identification of suitable strategic options that will improve the competitive position of an organization.

Identifying strategic options

Within the framework of an overall generic strategy, a number of techniques can be used. These include:

- The TOWS analysis matrix (drawing on a SWOT analysis).
- Ansoff's product/market matrix.

Methods of achieving options

Having identified different strategic options, the method through which these objectives can be achieved should be considered:

- Internal development.
- Merger/acquisition.
- Joint venture.

Suitability of options

Porter has suggested that to be successful and achieve competitive advantage, organizations need to identify a generic strategy of cost leadership, product differentiation or focus. A broad assessment as to whether the proposed options will improve the competitive position of the organization should be undertaken. The strategy should fit with the existing positioning strategy, resource availability and competencies.

A strategic perspective for investment appraisal exercises

The need to take into consideration a strategic perspective when appraising investments has been identified.

Further reading

Bowman, C. (1998) *Strategy in Practice*. Prentice-Hall, Harlow.
Doganis, R. (2006) *The Airline Business*, 2nd edn. Routledge.
Grant, R.M. (2007) *Contemporary Strategy Analysis: Concepts, techniques and applications*, 7th edn. Blackwell Publishing.
Johnson, G., Scholes, K. and Whittington, R. (2005) *Exploring Corporate Strategy: Text and Cases*, 7th edn. FT/Prentice-Hall.
Porter, M.E. (1980) *Competitive Strategy: Techniques for analysing industries and competitors*. Free Press, New York.

Shank, J.K. (1996) Analysing technology investments: from NPV to strategic cost management (SCM), *Management Accounting Research* **7**(2): 185–197.

Shank, J.K. and Govindarajan, V. (1993) *Strategic Cost Management: The new tool for competitive advantage*. Free Press, New York.

Answers to activities

Activity 17.1

This is answered in the next section in the chapter.

Activity 17.2

Cell A. S2 + O3 + O4. Consider acquiring a competitor to act as a low-cost airline operating in the short-haul market.

Cell B. W4 + W5 + O4. Review marketing activities for short-haul market to achieve greater market penetration.

Cell C. S1 + S2 + T3. Review new routes for development in addition to or as an alternative to some of the existing (and less profitable) long-haul routes.*

Cell D. W4 + T4. Invest in new web site and on-line booking system.

* Note that a threat for one company may be an opportunity for another!

Activity 17.3

A range of options are likely to be suggested. Many will already have been suggested with the use of the TOWS matrix. Other options will be similar to those suggested in Figure 17.5.

Activity 17.4

Internal development will be slower than other alternatives, though airlines such as Southwest Airlines have benefited from slow but continuous organic (i.e. internal) growth. In a deregulated world there may be benefits in a merger, though an option which will mean that the airline remains independent is to form an alliance with two or more other airlines. If it wished to focus growth on core activities it might consider selling non-core activities (such as catering) and reinvesting the funds in the core activities.

Activity 17.5

There should be operational cost savings. It is necessary to consider whether the consumer will lose benefits that they value by the loss of variety of aircraft. Presumably, for routes of a similar distance and capacity, it should be possible to have greater standardization.

Exercises

Questions 17.1 to 17.3 can be undertaken for either of the case scenarios Siegmund Ltd or the assembly division of McLoed Ltd. Questions 17.1 and 17.2 can be answered for Sunshine Sites discussed in the case scenario in Coopers Leisure Resorts Ltd.

Q17.1 Undertake a SWOT analysis and identify a range of options that are suggested using the TOWS matrix.

Q17.2 Identify a range of options which might be suggested using Ansoff's product/market matrix.

Q17.3 Discuss the relative merits for the company to achieve growth through:

1. Internal development.
2. Merger or acquisition.
3. Some form of joint development, e.g. joint venture or licensing.

EVALUATING STRATEGIES AND WRITING THE BUSINESS PLAN

18

Objectives

Having studied this chapter you should be able to:

- Undertake a financial evaluation of different strategic options.
- Use appropriate techniques to evaluate the impact of different assumptions on the values of key input variables. These include sensitivity analysis and risk techniques of:

    - Expected value.
    - Expected value using decision tree analysis.
    - Simulation.

- Use different criteria for dealing with uncertainty – maximin, maximax.
- Explain how resource implications need to be considered in assessing strategies.
- Explain why it is important to prepare a business plan and the contents and structure of a business plan.

Introduction

In Chapter 17, the need to identify a range of possible suitable strategies has been identified. These strategies should now be subject to a detailed evaluation. This should include a financial evaluation in terms of:

 (i) An analysis of the expected return.
 (ii) The risk associated with the strategy.
(iii) The feasibility of the investment project. Feasibility would include a consideration of the funding requirements of a strategy and whether this was affordable to the organization.

Different strategies should also be evaluated in terms of their acceptability to the various stakeholders of the organization and feasibility in terms of their use of non-financial resources, including people and equipment.

This chapter also includes a consideration of reasons for completing a business plan and an outline of topics that would be found in a business plan.

Evaluation of return of different strategies

The financial evaluation of different options, both short and long term, was considered in Part 1 of the book. In the last chapter, one option considered for Rominska Airlines was to start a new route in the short-haul market. In this section of the chapter it will be assumed that the management of the company have decided that this option fits with the existing and intended strategy of the company and a further financial evaluation should therefore now take place. Relevant information for the investment appraisal of this strategy has been collected and is shown in Figure 18.1.

Rominska Airlines is considering flying on a new route, between two cities in its country. It plans to purchase two second-hand airplanes for €10,000,000 (€ = euros). It is expected that these two airplanes would fly for 8 years and at the end of this period could be sold for €500,000.

It is anticipated that the planes will be flying with on average 80% of seats occupied, which would generate funds of €500,000. Other additional costs to the airline due to operating on the new route will be €330,000 per month. The contribution per month to general overheads (i.e. after deducting the identifiable costs of €330,000) will therefore be €170,000 per month, or €2,040,000 per annum.

The cost of capital of the company is 10%.

The cash flows associated with this project are therefore as follows:

Column 1	Column 2	Column 3	Column 4 (Col 2 + Col 3)
Year	Purchase and sale of airplanes €'000	Contribution per annum €'000	Net cash flow €'000
0	(10,000)		(10,000)
1		2,040	2,040
2		2,040	2,040
3		2,040	2,040
4		2,040	2,040
5		2,040	2,040
6		2,040	2,040
7		2,040	2,040
8	500	2,040	2,540

Figure 18.1 Market developments – evaluation of a new route for Rominska Airlines

The investment can be appraised using payback, ARR, net present value and internal rate of return and a summary of the results of the appraisal are shown in Table 18.1. The calculation of these returns is shown in the Appendix at the end of the chapter and if you wish to revise the techniques then see Chapter 4 of the book.

Table 18.1 Financial return expected for new route if 80% occupancy achieved

Percentage occupancy on flights	Contribution per annum from the route	Payback (years)	ARR on *initial* investment	NPV	IRR
80%	€2,040,000	4 years 11 months	8.5%	€1,116,500	13%

The project produces a positive net present value and if this is the main criteria used by the company then it should be accepted. Payback is nearly 5 years and if cash flow is important to the company then payback period may be a key factor to consider.

Evaluation of strategic options taking account of risk or uncertainty

The financial appraisal of the option to start flights on a new route has been based on certain assumptions about revenues, costs and the life of the airplanes. If these assumptions are wrong then there may be serious consequences for the viability of the project.

The chapter begins with an explanation of sensitivity analysis, which is a commonly used technique for assessing the impact on outcome of changes in key variables.

Risk is where there are several possible outcomes and there is evidence to predict the probablility of these different outcomes occurring. Risk techniques explained in this chapter are expected value, expected value using decision tree analysis and simulation. Criteria for choosing an option given a certain level of risk need to be identified and these will vary according to the attitude of the decision-maker.

Sometimes a range of different outcomes is known, but the likelihood of any one outcome occurring is not known. This is *uncertainty* and, given uncertainty, it is necessary to use a decision rule which does not use probability in making a choice. The criteria of maximin and maximax are discussed.

Sensitivity analysis

Sensitivity analysis involves varying the assumptions on key variables. For example, of key importance to the commercial success of the new route considered above is the level of occupancy on flights and in the main analysis the best estimate of the company of an occupancy level of 80% has been assumed. It would be useful to know the profitability, if this occupancy was higher or lower. Table 18.2 shows the contribution, payback period, ARR, NPV and IRR at 72%, 80% and 88% occupancy levels.

Table 18.2   Contribution of new route given different flight occupancy percentages

Percentage occupancy on flights	Contribution per annum from the route (€'000)	Payback (years)	ARR (%)	NPV (€'000)	IRR (%)
72	1,440	6.9	2.5	−2,084	4
80	2,040	4.9	8.5	1,116.5	13
88	2,640	3.8	14.5	4,317	21

This analysis shows that the return generated by Rominska Airlines is very sensitive to small changes in occupancy rates. Further sensitivity tests show that there will be a zero net present value when occupancy falls to 77%, which means that there is a small margin of safety.

Sensitivity analysis is a simple technique that can be carried out on all input variables in order to identify the key variables that will have an impact on the project viability. The effect of a 10% change in the cost of capital is shown in Table 18.3.

Table 18.3   Contribution of new route given 10% change in the cost of capital

Cost of capital (%)	NPV (€'000)
9	1,542.0
10	1,116.5
11	715.1

The cost of capital needs to rise to over 13% before a negative net present value will occur.

Dealing with risk

Expected value

If a problem has been faced many times before then it will be possible to identify the probability of particular outcomes occurring based on historical information. If it is a new situation then market research or the opinion of experts may be sought. Once the probability of an event occurring has been estimated, it is possible to calculate the expected value by multiplying each payoff by its probability and summing for all possibilities.

In Figure 18.2 the expected value approach is illustrated for the problem faced by Rominska Airlines discussed in Figure 18.1. Rather than assuming an 80% occupancy rate, a review of the problem has identified that this occupancy rate could vary according to different uncontrollable factors (known as *states of nature*). Based on the experience of opening other routes, Rominska Airlines consider that there is a 40% probability that flight occupancy will be 75%, a 40% chance that it will be 80%, and a 20% chance that it will be 85%.

The management of Rominska Airlines have asked for an analysis of the expected contribution and net present value that will be generated by the route. This calculation is shown in Figure 18.2.

(i) Calculation of contribution
The revenue at 80% occupancy was expected to be €500,000 per month. For every additional 1% in occupancy on flights, it is therefore expected that revenue will increase by €500,000 / 80 = €6250.

Revenue at 75% occupancy is (75 × €6250) = €468,750
Revenue at 80% occupancy is (80 × €6250) = €500,000
Revenue at 85% occupancy is (85 × €6250) = €531,250

Contribution to *general* overheads can be calculated by deducting *identifiable* costs of €330,000 per month from the revenue at each occupancy level. For example, the contribution at 75% occupancy = €468,750 − €330,000 = €138,750. This contribution is weighted by the probability of this event occurring to provide the payoff based on expected value.

Outcome	(1) Contribution per month	(2) Probability of outcome	(3) = (1) × (2) Payoff (expected value)
75% occupancy	€138,750	40%	€55,500
80% occupancy	€170,000	40%	€68,000
85% occupancy	€201,250	20%	€40,250
			€163,750

A contribution of €163,750 a month is €1,965,000 per annum.

(ii) Given an expected contribution of €1,965,000 per year, the investment can be re-evaluated using the different investment appraisal techniques, giving the following returns.

Method	Return
Accounting rate of return	7.8%
Payback	5 years 1 month
Net present value	€716,330
Internal rate of return	11.9%

Figure 18.2 Expected value given different probabilities of the route occupancy

Criteria for making a decision given risk

To make a decision, it is necessary to understand the criteria of the decision-maker. If the decision-maker is risk-neutral then the above decision will be taken based on the expected value. Given the probabilities provided, the expected net present value of the project is €716,300. Since the expected net present value is positive, a risk-neutral decision-maker would decide to progress with the project.

Expected value takes into consideration the probability of different outcomes occurring. A disadvantage is that with some potential outcomes, large losses could occur and this is taken into account in a way that may be unacceptable to the decision-maker. With the above decision, for example, a risk-averse decision-maker may be concerned that at a flight occupancy of 75%, the contribution of the route to general overheads would only be €138,750 per month, which would lead to a negative present value of €884,000. There is a 40% probability that this state of nature could occur and the decision-maker may decide that the risk of this loss means that the project should not be undertaken. On the other hand, a risk-taker would note that there is a 60% probability (40% + 20%) that the project will generate a positive net present value that is greater than the expected value.

Decision tree analysis

Sometimes the problem can be more complex than that demonstrated in Figure 18.2, where the only level of risk considered is related to the average occupancy on the aircraft. In other problems, there may be concern about more than one variable and the value of some variables may be dependent on others.

In Figure 18.3 a more complex scenario is considered.

The operations manager feels that if Rominska Airlines decides to open the new route, there is a 60% chance that *no* other airline will start a new service on the same route. The same probability on occupancy will occur as before, i.e. there is a 40% chance that flight occupancy will be 75%, a 40% chance that it will be 80%, and a 20% chance that it will be 85% occupancy.

The operations manager identifies that there is a 40% chance that another airline will start a new service on the same route. If so, then that there is a 30% chance that flight occupancy will be 60%, a 40% chance that it will be 70%, and a 30% chance that it will be 75%.

Figure 18.3   Further information on risks associated with a new airline route

Given more complex problems, a decision tree approach may be of assistancein two key ways:

(i)   A visual representation of the problem is provided. This can be helpful, both for those trying to structure the problem and for those trying to understand it after the diagram has been prepared. A tree diagram for the problem is provided in Figure 18.4.

(ii) Having structured the problem, probabilities and expected payoffs can be evaluated for each possible outcome. An overall expected value can then also be calculated. This will be shown in Figure 18.5.

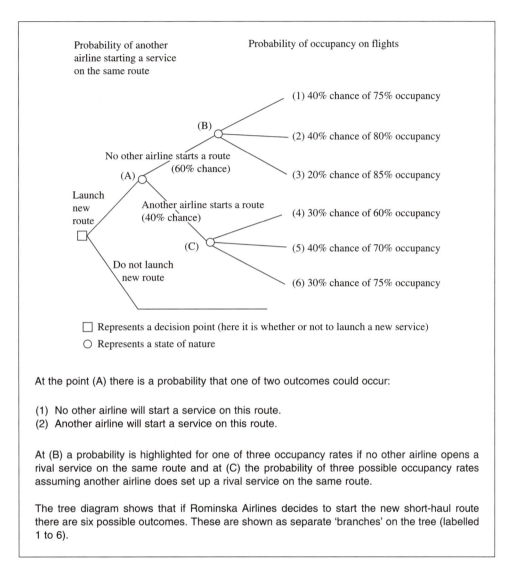

Figure 18.4 Tree diagram showing the structure of the problem

Having drawn the tree diagram, the contribution that will be generated given each outcome can be calculated. By taking into consideration the probability of each outcome occurring, the expected value can be calculated.

The expected value, given the various alternative scenarios that could occur and the probability of each occurring, is €137,500 per month or €1,650,000 per annum. Given a need to purchase aircraft for €10,000,000, the financial returns would be as shown in Table 18.4:

		(1) Contribution	(2) Probability	(3) Expected value
Probability of airline starting a service	Probability of occupancy on flights			
		(€)	(%)	(£)
		138,750*	24*	33,300*
	40% of 75% occupancy	(note 1)	(note 2)	(note 3)
	40% of 80% occupancy	170,500	24	40,800
	20% of 85% occupancy	201,250	12	24,150
	30% of 60% occupancy	45,000	12	5,400
	40% of 70% occupancy	107,500	16	17,200
	30% of 75% occupancy	138,750	12	16,650
			100	137,500*
				(note 4)
do not launch new route		0	100	0

(B) no other airline (60% chance) (1)

(A) (2)

another airline starts a route (40% chance)

(C) decision to start new route

Flight occupancy (%)	Revenue (€)	Cost (€)	Contribution to general overheads (€)
1	6,250	330,000	−323,750
60	375,000	330,000	45,000
70	437,500	330,000	107,500
75	468,750	330,000	138,750
80	500,000	330,000	170,000
85	531,250	330,000	201,250

The calculation of revenue, probability and expected value per month for the top 'branch' in the decision tree is explained below.

Note 1. If there is a 75% flight occupancy then the expected contribution to general overheads is €138,750.
Note 2. There is a 60% chance that no other airline will start a service on this route and there is a 40% chance that, if there is no other airline, there will be a 75% occupancy rate on the flight. The combined probability of this occupancy rate occurring is therefore 60% × 40% = 24%.
Note 3. This is the expected contribution given a 75% occupancy and the probability of this event, i.e. €138,750 × 24% = €33,300.
The same exercise can be undertaken for each of the branches of the tree.
Note 4. The expected contribution of proceeding with the new route is €137,500 (€33,300 + €40,800 + €24,150 + €5,400 + €17,200 + €16,650).

Figure 18.5 Evaluation of a decision using a decision tree

Table 18.4 Financial return from new route

Method	Return
Accounting rate of return	4.6%
Payback	5 years 1 month
Net present value	−€964,200
Internal rate of return	7.4%

With a negative net present value of €964,200 the project is not worth undertaking given the assumptions on occupancy and the probability of events occurring. In addition, a review of the decision tree highlights the range of values that can occur. In the tree diagram in Figure 18.5, for example, it can be seen that there is a 64% chance that flight occupancy will be 75% or less (branches 1, 4, 5 and 6 with probabilities of 24%, 12%, 16% and 12% respectively).

Rominska Airlines should consider reviewing the project to identify whether it is possible to raise prices on the route or to reduce costs further.

Simulation

A method of simplifying the handling of probabilities is to use a technique called simulation. A possible project outcome is calculated many times, but each time the input variables can be different. The value of the input variable is chosen based on the probability associated with that value. A simulation will be carried out for the exercise shown in Figure 18.2 (for illustration purposes, the possibility of another airline opening on the same route will be ignored). As well as probabilities associated with the different flight occupancy rates there are also probabilities assumed to be associated with the likely monthly cost of flying on the proposed route. The analysis is shown in Figure 18.6.

---

(1) Information on flight occupancy from Figure 18.2

Flight occupancy	Revenue at that occupancy	Probability
75%	€468,750	40%
80%	€500,000	40%
85%	€531,250	20%

If a simulation were to take place 100 times, then 40% of the times the flight occupancy selected would be 75%, 40% of the time it would be 80% occupancy, and 20% of the time there would be an 85% occupancy. When using the simulation technique a random number generator can be used to allocate a number to each value, as is explained below:

Figure 18.6 Simulation of expected contribution on new route

Flight occupancy	Revenue at that occupancy	Probability	Identification number
75%	€468,750	40%	1 – 40
80%	€500,000	40%	41 – 80
85%	€531,250	20%	81 – 100

(2) Information on probability of the costs of flying the route

Although the initial estimate on the cost of flying the route was €330,000, the operations manager has re-analysed the information and realized that there are various risks associated with the operating costs. His more recent analysis suggests the following costs and probabilities associated with those costs. An identification number can also be identified to probabilities associated with the costs.

Cost	Probability	Identification number
€280,000	30%	1 – 30
€300,000	50%	31 – 80
€350,000	20%	81 – 100

(3) Running the simulation

The input value is chosen based on the identification number.

Assume the computer is used to generate random numbers, first for flight occupancy % (revenue) and then for costs, and that the first two numbers chosen are 45 and 60. The first simulation will produce the following result:

Iteration 1
The random numbers chosen are 45 and 60

Random number		Value (€)
45	Revenue	500,000
60	Operating costs	300,000
	Contribution	200,000

The random number 45 is within the identification number range of 41–80, which signifies an 80% occupancy and revenue of €500,000.

The random number 60 is within the identification number range of 31–80, which signifies a cost of €300,000.

The contribution is calculated by deducting operating costs from revenue.

Figure 18.6 *(Continued)*

Iteration 2
The random numbers chosen are 20 and 29

Random number		Value (€)
20	Revenue	468,750
29	Operating costs	280,000
	Contribution	188,750

Iteration 3
The random numbers chosen are 35 and 89

Random number		Value (€)
35	Revenue	468,750
89	Operating costs	350,000
	Contribution	118,750

Iteration 4
The random numbers chosen are 60 and 27

Random number		Value (€)
60	Revenue	500,000
27	Operating costs	280,000
	Contribution	220,000

The analysis shows that after four simulations the contribution ranges from €87,500 to €220,000 with an average of:

$$\frac{€200,000 + €188,750 + €118,750 + €220,000}{4} = €181,875$$

Figure 18.6   (*Continued*)

Activity 18.1

With reference to the exercise in Figure 18.6, calculate the contribution after iterations 5 and 6 assuming that the next random numbers generated are 2, 35, 92 and 54.

The result of a simulation of 100 iterations that has been carried out separately on a spreadsheet is shown in Figure 18.7 as a frequency distribution.

The simulation indicates an average contribution of €163,425 per month.

Contribution (€)	Percentage frequency	Percentage cumulative frequency
110,000	0	0
130,000	10	10
150,000	33	43
170,000	30	73
180,000	0	73
210,000	24	97
230,000	0	97
250,000	3	100
270,000	0	100

The frequency distribution also suggests that, based on a simulation of 100 iterations, there is a 10% chance that the contribution earned will be between €110,000 and €130,000 and a 33% chance of the contribution being between €130,000 and €150,000. This gives a 43% chance of the contribution being less than €150,000 per month.

It has previously been calculated that the net present value of the project is zero when the contribution is €152,600 per month. From the table it can be seen that there is a 43% probability that the contribution will be €150,000 or less, so there is at least a 43% probability that the choice to fly on the new route will result in a negative present value.

Figure 18.7   Frequency distribution of contribution given a simulation of 100 iterations

Activity 18.2

Given the information in Figure 18.7, what is the probability that a contribution of greater than €180,000 per month will be generated?

Simulation can be used to calculate an expected value, but can also provide an indication of the range of values that might occur.

A simulation exercise can be undertaken on many computer spreadsheets, for example using the @risk facility on Microsoft EXCEL.

Dealing with uncertainty

In some situations it is not possible to assign probabilities to different outcomes and so the decision must be taken in a situation of uncertainty.

Assume that Rominska Airlines has reviewed the investment in another short-haul route, see Figure 18.8.

The managing director of Rominska Airlines is concerned about the possible reaction of a competitor on another route that Rominska Airlines is thinking of entering. He feels that if Rominska Airlines provides a service on the route then the competitor might take one of three different actions:

1. Prices would be left at the existing level.
2. The competitor might decide to withdraw from the route.
3. The competitor might decide to reduce prices.

The managing director dismisses the idea that it is possible to place probabilities on any particular event occurring (i.e. there is complete uncertainty) and has asked for an estimated net present value given that Rominska Airlines could invest in two different types of aircraft. Type 1 is a larger, more expensive airplane than type 2.

Net present value earned by Rominska Airlines given different competitive response			
	Competitor reduces prices (€'000)	Competitor leaves prices at current level (€'000)	Competitor withdraws from the market (€'000)
Purchase of type 1 aircraft	−€3100	€1500	€4100
Purchase of smaller type 2 aircraft	−€1000	€550	€1480

Figure 18.8 Net present value when using different types of aircraft and given different scenarios

When faced with a problem such as that produced in Figure 18.8, a number of different criteria can be used and two of these will be illustrated below.

Maximin and maximax criteria

A risk-averse decision-maker may use the **maximin criterion**. This involves the choice of the option which will maximize the minimum gain (or minimize the maximum loss). In this example a negative net present value of €3,100,000 can occur if the airline chooses a type 1 airplane, while it will only be a negative €1,000,000 given the choice of a smaller airplane. The smaller airplane will therefore be the preferred choice given the maximin criterion.

A risk-taker might use the **maximax criterion**, which is based on the desire to choose the option that will potentially provide the largest payoff. For Rominska Airlines this would be the choice of the type 1 airplane, which provides a payoff of €4,100,000 if the competitor were to withdraw from the market.

Acceptability of strategic options to stakeholders

The above analysis has considered the assessment of different strategies given financial return, risk and uncertainty. In Chapter 13 the requirement to consider stakeholders' interests and power and business ethics, as well as the organizational culture, were also discussed. For example:

- An additional investment may mean that additional share capital is required, which is unacceptable to existing shareholders.
- A major investment could involve high levels of pollution. This might contravene the organization's policy on social responsibility and also be unacceptable to key stakeholders such as the local community or local authorities.
- A closure of a production site or department may be unacceptable to a powerful group of employees.

Feasibility of different options – resource use and the decision-making process

In Chapter 15, the need to undertake a resource audit was indicated. In considering whether different options are feasible, the resource implications for the organization, whether financial, physical, human or intangible, should be considered.

Funding

Are sufficient funds available if large initial cash outflows are required or if competitor reaction leads to severe price competition?

Some investments may have the potential of a high return, but there may be a high risk of non-achievement of the targets. The growth share (BCG) matrix was discussed in Chapter 15. Using this matrix it is possible to analyse products according to the rate of growth of the market that they are operating in and by comparison with the market share of competitors, see Figure 18.9. Organizations with a significant proportion

		Relative market share	
		High	Low
Market growth	High	Cell A Star (may be cash generator or absorber)	Cell B Question mark (high risk and cash absorber)
	Low	Cell C Cash cow (lower risk and large cash generator)	Cell D Dog (modest cash generator or absorber)

Figure 18.9   Cash implications given different market growth and market share

of 'question mark' products and few 'cash cows' to fund these 'question marks' are likely to be considered high risk. This is because 'question marks' are at the early stage of their product lifecycles and are heavy absorbers of cash. They are riskier ventures than products at the mature stage of the lifecycle, when little additional investment is required and cash is being generated.

Given the existence of a large number of cash absorbers and few cash generators, an organization might wish to avoid a high-risk strategy that takes it into conflict with a stronger competitor.

In Chapter 12, it was also noted that as a general guideline, *if an investment is high risk*, then it would be safer to consider *low-risk funding*, e.g. raising equity capital. Although high profits may be earned, there is also a considerable risk that if the investment fails, then the long-term future of the business is also at risk, as it will not be able to fund any interest payments. Firms such as new biotechnology companies, which are undertaking very high-risk investment, have almost universally raised money from a share issue. This can be through a sale to a venture capital company or, if the company is listed on a stock exchange, through the issue of further shares.

If an investment is *low risk* then *higher-risk funding* could be considered. Utility companies, such as water or electricity and gas, have traditionally been considered to be safe investments. They are assured a steady flow of cash payments from consumers. Much of their funding can be raised through the issue of loan capital.

Physical

Are sufficient materials and other services available, will the existing assets be suitable to cope with increased demands?

Human resources

Does the workforce have the relevant expertise, for example, marketing or technological?

Intangible assets

Is the patent protection sufficient to provide a protection from new competitors entering the market?

Preparing the business plan

Why prepare a business plan?

Having decided on a strategy for the coming years, many organizations prepare a business plan, which can be used to serve a number of purposes:

1. A business plan can clearly explain key aspects of the strategic analysis that has taken place and reasons for the choice that has been made.
2. The plan can be used to communicate with a wide range of stakeholders. It can be distributed to staff in order that they can appreciate the strategic direction of the

organization and their role in this strategy. It can also be used for communication to other stakeholders of the business.

3. If the organization wishes to raise finance, the plan will provide a detailed analysis which can be reviewed by potential funding bodies. Investors will be particularly interested in a cash flow forecast indicating the amount of funding needed and the purpose for these funds. Contingency funds that might be required in the event of adverse trading conditions should be highlighted. Investors will also be interested in identifying how a loan will be repaid and how credit, expenditure, stock planning and control, trade receivable and trade payables will be managed. A financial forecast for three to five years should be provided.

The preparation of a budgeted cash flow, Profit and Loss Account and Balance Sheet is explained in Chapter 8 and the preparation and interpretation of key financial ratios are considered in Chapter 11. Chapter 12 should also be reviewed for a discussion on how organizations can meet the funding requirements and manage working capital.

It should be noted that it has been suggested that many business plans that are produced are unnecessarily detailed. Many investors, for example, are more influenced by the perceived quality of the management team than a detailed and lengthy paperwork exercise.

The contents and structure of a business plan

There is no standard guide as to the exact content and layout of a business plan, although the following will provide an indication of some of the content that is usually provided. It can be seen that some of the information will have been revealed in an internal appraisal of the organization, some from an external appraisal of the environment, while yet further information discusses the detail of how objectives will be achieved, for example through the implementation of a marketing strategy.

- *A title page*
- *A contents page*
  This should list the contents and page references.
- *An executive summary*
  An executive summary might only be one to two pages long and should summarize the plan, including conclusions, recommendations, actions and information on the financial return on investment. It should be written to catch people's attention, because if that does not happen there is a danger that potential investors will not read further!
- *Business background*
  A brief history of the business might be provided.
  Details of the company ownership and the legal set-up, e.g. whether it is a sole trader, a partnership or a company.
  Information on the senior management team, which gives details of their skills and experience.
  The financial background of the business, including details of the existing funding.
- *Business aims and objectives*
  The writing of a mission statement and business objectives was discussed in Chapter 13.

Internal appraisal of products and services

Product or service description

A clear description of the product or service, identifying the key features and benefits and how these provide a competitive advantage (see Chapter 15 for a discussion of the need to identify attributes that customers value). These benefits will guide the decision on the strategic positioning of the product or service, whether through product differentiation or on cost leadership.

Manufacturing and production processes

This should cover the facilities, suppliers and materials and processes that will be used.

Appraisal of the market and competitive environment

External influences

Consider the use of a PESTEL analysis.

Market analysis and market research

Investors will be particularly interested in the market research that has been undertaken, with information provided about the market size and growth of key market segments.

Competitive environment

Five forces analysis would help identify key competitive forces in the market.

Information about competitors and customers should also be provided.

Marketing[1]

Having completed an analysis that has drawn on information obtained from the strategic analysis phase of the strategic management process, it is now important to consider in detail how objectives are to be achieved.

The marketing strategy should support the positioning of the products or services of the organization, whether this is in the form of cost leadership or differentiation. The marketing strategy can incorporate the pricing, promotion, distribution and sales strategy.

Alternative approaches to pricing were discussed in Chapter 2. The relative merits of cost- and market-based approaches were identified, along with alternatives such as target costing. Consideration was also given in Chapter 12 to the use of discounting the selling price in order to encourage faster payments for goods and services. Investment in brands should also be considered (see Chapter 16 for a discussion of branding and the use of management accounting information).

The business plan should provide information on the promotion strategy, with details provided about the advertising, sales promotions and public relations activities that will be undertaken to support the strategic position of the organization.

---

[1] Preparing a marketing plan has not been considered in this book.

A sales forecast should be provided and the sales plan should identify how the product will be distributed, whether through a wholesaler, retailer, dealer or alternative method. The sales organization to support the level of sales required should also be explained.

The financial plan

The financial plan should indicate how the business is expected to perform over the coming (say three) years. The key statements, the cash flow, Profit and Loss Account and Balance Sheet should be provided. Key financial ratios can also be calculated and should indicate sound financial management. Break-even analysis information may be of benefit.

Summary

Having identified a range of strategies that fit with the strategic logic of the organization, a further evaluation is required to ensure that the strategies are acceptable to the various stakeholders of the organization.

A financial evaluation should take account of the return and the risk, or uncertainty, associated with particular strategies. A range of techniques can be used, including sensitivity analysis and risk techniques such as expected value, decision tree analysis and simulation. With uncertainty, where it is impossible to identify probabilities, criteria such as maximizing the minimum gain, maximizing the maximum gain or minimizing the regret might be used.

The feasibility of the investment project should also be considered. Feasibility would include a consideration of the funding requirements of a strategy and whether this was affordable to the organization. The ability of the organization to meet other resource requirements should also be considered.

In order to inform various stakeholders of the organization or to raise funds, a written business plan should be provided. There is no set guidance on the content of a business plan, though the chapter has provided an indication on possible contents. It is suggested that many investors give more weight on their assessment of the skills of the management team and their ability to see through ideas to completion than they do to a comprehensive business plan.

Further reading

Consideration of risk techniques:

Drury, C. (2004) *Management and Cost Accounting*, 6th edn. Thomson Learning, Chapter 12 (pp. 451–460).

Horngren, C. T. *et al.* (2005) *Management and Cost Accounting*, 3rd edn. FT/Prentice Hall, Chapter 8.

Writing a business plan: see links on web site.

Answers to activities

Activity 18.1

Iteration 5

The random numbers chosen are 2 and 35

Random number		Value (€)
2	Revenue	468,750
35	Variable costs	350,000
	Contribution	118,750

Iteration 6

The random numbers chosen are 92 and 54

Random number		Value €
92	Revenue	531,500
54	Variable costs	300,000
	Contribution	231,500

Activity 18.2

The probability of a contribution greater than €180,000 per month is 27%.

Discussion questions

1. Identify the difference between risk and uncertainty.
2. (a) What are the advantages of the analysis of a problem using expected value?
   (b) Which of the following decisions would be most appropriate for the use of the expected value rule, explain your choice:

   - A new product launch.
   - Deciding on the optimum daily purchase of a perishable item.

3. What are the advantages of the analysis of a problem using a decision tree?
4. What methods can be used in order to assess the risk associated with outcomes? Which is the best method?

5. A decision-maker is concerned with what will be the most likely outcome of a decision. He/she would be described as:

(A) a risk-seeker/taker
(B) risk-averse
(C) risk-neutral
(D) a risk reducer?

Exercises

Q18.1 Able Ltd is considering undertaking an investment. The management consider that the probability of success is 60% and the return if successful will be £500,000. If the investment is not successful, then the return will be £50,000.

The advertising department have proposed an advertising campaign costing £100,000, which they believe will boost the chance of success to 75%.

Is it worthwhile undertaking the advertising campaign, given these probabilities of success?

Q18.2 Apple Ltd is considering manufacturing cricket balls. The cost to purchase a machine to manufacture the cricket balls is £40,000. The balls can be sold for £4 each and the variable cost of manufacture is £2.50 each.

Expected sales per annum for the next four years are as follows:

Probability	Sales (units)
0.1	7,000
0.3	9,000
0.3	11,000
0.2	13,000
0.1	15,000

(a) Calculate the net present value of the project given a cost of capital of 10%.
(b) Would your decision be affected if:

- This was a very large company?
- This was a small company?

Q18.3 A company can earn £40,000 by undertaking a project. The project can be completed in three alternative ways and the likely costs of using each method are as shown below:

Option A		Option B		Option C	
Probability	Cost	Probability	Cost	Probability	Cost
	(£)		(£)		(£)
0.5	28,000	0.2	25,000	0.3	24,000
0.5	33,000	0.4	30,000	0.5	31,000
		0.4	35,000	0.2	33,000

Which option should lead to the best return?

Q18.4 Mr Ring has invented a new type of car-telephone. He can manufacture the phone himself, be paid on a royalty basis by another manufacturer, or sell all his rights in the invention for a lump sum. Future sales of the car-phone can be high, medium or low.

The profit that can be expected in each case is as follows:

£'000			
	Manufacture himself	Royalties	Sell all rights
High sales	750	350	150
Medium sales	250	200	150
Low sales	−100	100	150

The probability of high sales is 0.1, of medium sales is 0.3 and of low sales is 0.6.

Required:

(a) Advise Mr Ring of the best option (use a decision tree to answer this question).
(b) On further discussions with Mr Ring it appears that there are further potential advantages of the choice to manufacture the product. If sales are high or medium then there is a possibility of developing a new version of the phone and he estimates that there is a 50% probability of successful development. The cost of development would be £100,000 and the additional profits for high sales (after deducting the development costs) are £600,000 and for medium sales, £200,000. Sales of the new phone would not have an adverse effect on sales of the original phone. If the development of the new phone is not successful, then the project will be abandoned having spent the £100,000 on development work.

Given this new information, advise Mr Ring on the best option.

Q18.5 X Ltd can choose from three mutually exclusive projects. The projects will each last for one year only and their net cash inflows will be determined by the prevailing market conditions. The forecast annual cash inflows and their associated probabilities are shown below:

Market conditions	Poor	Good	Excellent
Probability	0.2	0.5	0.3
	£'000	£'000	£'000
Project A	1,000	940	1,100
Project B	800	1,100	1,140
Project C	900	800	950

Required:

(a) Based on the expected value of the net cash inflows, which project should be undertaken?
(b) Identify the preferred project if the maximin and maximax criteria were used.

Q18.6 Farlington Ltd is preparing its strategy for the year ahead and has to make a choice between various products it can take to market. It can only make two of three product lines. It is expecting that there will be a general election shortly and this will have an impact on the contribution generated by each of the product lines. At present, opinion polls indicate an equal chance that any of the parties will be elected. The contributions earned by each product line given the policies of each party are as shown below:

	Contribution (£'000)		
	A's policies	B's policies	C's policies
Product line			
Tourism-based	900	800	700
Construction-based	600	1,000	700
Defence-based	1,000	450	800

Required:

Identify which two products should be selected if the decision-maker was:

(i) Risk averse?
(ii) A risk taker?

Q18.7 A new project is being considered and there is considerable risk associated with some of the input values.

The selling price per unit is £40.

Sales volume	Probability	Volume
	25%	10,000
	60%	13,000
	15%	15,000

Manufacturing margin	Probability	Volume
	35%	30%
	25%	40%
	40%	50%

Fixed cost	Probability	Volume
	20%	£15,000
	30%	£20,000
	50%	£25,000

Required:

Calculate the expected profit given five iterations and given the following random numbers:
2, 70, 60, 45, 31, 26, 46, 90, 65, 89, 23, 12, 43, 56, 67

Q18.8 Ambling PLC is considering launching a new product. It has undertaken a simulation of 200 iterations and has identified the following distribution of the expected net present value:

Net present value (£)	Percentage frequency
−60,000	0
−40,000	5
−20,000	10
0	15
20,000	35
40,000	17
60,000	11
80,000	4
100,000	3

Required:

(i) What is the probability of the project resulting in a negative net present value?
(ii) What is the probability of the project resulting in a net present value of greater than £60,000?

Appendix: Calculation of payback, ARR, NPV and IRR for new route for Rominska Airlines

Payback method

The payback method identifies how many years it takes to recover the initial investment.

Year	Cash flow	Remaining to be paid back at end of year
	(€'000)	(€'000)
0	(10,000)	
1	2,040	7,960
2	2,040	5,920
3	2,040	3,880
4	2,040	1,840
5	2,040	−200

The payback will therefore be in 4 years 11 months.

Accounting Rate of Return (ARR)

The Accounting Rate of Return (ARR) is the average annual after-tax profit divided by the investment. ARR is very similar to other accounting-based measures of performance such as return on assets and return on investment.

Stage 1. Calculate the average profit:

	€'000
Net cash flows for years 1–8 from trading = 2,040 × 8	16,320
(i.e. excluding capital-related cash flows)	
Deduct the loss in value of the aircraft = €10,000,000	
(purchase price) – €500,000 (resale value)	9,500
Gives a profit over the five years of	6,820

It is now necessary to calculate the average annual profit, which is the profit for the life of the project divided by the number of years of the project.

$$\text{Average profit} = £6,820,000/8 = £852,500.$$

Stage 2. Calculate the accounting rate of return:
If the initial investment is used

$$\frac{\text{Average profit}}{\text{Initial investment}} = \frac{€852,500}{€10,000,000} = 8.53\%$$

Net present value

Column 1	Column 2	Column 3	Column 4
Year	Net cash flow €'000	Discount factor @ 10%	Present value €,000
0	(10,000)	1	(10,000)
1	2,040	0.9091	1,854.5
2	2,040	0.8264	1,686.0
3	2,040	0.7513	1,532.7
4	2,040	0.6830	1,393.3
5	2,040	0.6209	1,226.7
6	2,040	0.5645	1,151.5
7	2,040	0.5132	1,046.8
8	2,540	0.4665	1,184.9
Net present value			1,116.5

Since this is +€1,116.5, i.e. positive, this indicates that the project is worthwhile.

Internal Rate of Return (IRR)

Calculate the Internal Rate of Return (IRR) using interpolation.

The net present value at a 10% discount rate is €1,116,499 and at a 20% discount rate is −€2,055,890, i.e. a range of €3,172,393 over a 10% range.

$$\text{IRR} = 10\% + 10\% \times \frac{€1,116,499}{(€1,116,499 + €2,055,890)} = 10\% + 3.5\% = 13.5\%$$

PART 4

Issues in Management Control

In Part 2 of the book, key features of traditional management accounting control systems were covered. It was noted that traditional controls have focused on the medium and shorter term (up to one year) and included the preparation of the annual budget and the design of budgetary control systems. Control in a range of different organizations, including manufacturing and decentralized organizations, was considered. In Part 3, the strategic management process was reviewed.

Part 4 develops from the material previously covered in the book. The focus of this part is to consider in more detail the relevance of different approaches to control in a range of organizational and environmental circumstances, and in particular the design and operation of performance management systems.

Chapter 19 identifies potential limitations of budgetary control as a performance management system and highlights additional design features that may be required. These will be examined in more detail in Chapters 20 to 23. Chapter 19 also considers how the management style employed with budgetary control systems can lead to inappropriate action being taken by managers and reviews different styles that may be more suitable. Different approaches to control are also noted.

Chapter 20 investigates the interrelationship between control and strategy. Budgetary control systems focus on financial performance; they do not take into consideration other strategic objectives or the means by which these objectives are being achieved. The chapter explains additional frameworks that may be used to provide strategic direction.

A key criticism of traditional accounting measures of performance, such as profit and return on capital employed, is that the measures lead to a focus on short-term financial results. In Chapter 21, alternative measures of financial performance are reviewed, including economic value added, shareholder value analysis and market value added. The extent to which these provide an improved measure of shareholder wealth is considered.

Traditional accounting controls have also usually focused on the performance of functional units of organizations. Less attention has been given to monitoring whether the business is providing the value propositions desired by customers or the internal business processes that support the achievement of these key value propositions. Chapter 22 explores alternative ways to measure and improve these internal business processes.

Finally, Chapter 23 considers the differing control needs of organizations operating in environments of different degrees of complexity and uncertainty. The chapter begins with a review of the different methods of control that have been discussed in the book. It then considers how such approaches to control, organizational structures and management accounting systems may all need to adapt to changing circumstances.

Budgetary Control, Performance Management and Alternative Approaches to Control

19

Objectives

At the end of this chapter you should be able to:

- Describe key requirements of a performance management system.
- Explain key issues and limitations of budgetary control as a means of measuring and managing performance.
- Explain design issues and potential solutions to be considered when developing a performance management system.
- Explain how alternative styles of management and approaches to control may be appropriate when operating budgetary control systems.
- Explain alternative approaches to control, including internal and cultural controls.

Introduction

In part 2 of the book, the design and use of traditional management accounting control systems[1], to assist in the measurement and management of performance were explained.

---

[1] A range of terminology is used in the management control literature. It is possible to distinguish between a management accounting control system, a performance measurement system, a performance management system and a management control system.

A management accounting control system involves the reporting on financial results or outputs. A budgetary control system, for example, reports on actual financial results compared with budget.

A performance management system is one in which performance of business units is measured and performance managed based on the achievement of results. It is likely to involve the measurement of a number of performance dimensions, including financial ones. A management accounting control system could form part of a performance management system.

A management control system is a collection of methods which have the aim of inducing people in an organization to do certain things and refrain from doing others. It includes performance management systems, but also includes other controls such as internal controls and personnel and cultural controls.

This chapter will begin with a review of the requirements for a successful performance management system. This provides a framework against which budgetary control systems can be considered and potential deficiencies identified.

One approach to overcoming potential deficiencies of a performance management system is to change key design features. A number of issues that are explored in more detail in later chapters are introduced. These include the need to monitor:

(i) Key strategic objectives and strategies.
(ii) Alternative measures of financial performance.
(iii) Key processes as well as the performance of functional departments.
(iv) Key strategic uncertainties.

As well as design issues, problems may arise due to the style of management employed and the reaction of staff to being measured and managed using budgetary control and other performance measurement systems. These 'behavioural' issues and the relative merits of alternative approaches to setting budgets and evaluating performance are discussed in the next section of the chapter.

In the final section of the chapter, two further methods of control, internal controls and cultural or clan controls, are explained.

Requirements of a successful performance management system

Otley (1999) proposed a framework for analysing the operation of performance management systems structured around five central issues. These related to objectives, strategies and plans for their attainment, target-setting, incentive and reward structures and information feedback loops. He then tested this framework against three major systems of organizational control, namely budgeting, economic value added and the balanced scorecard to 'highlight neglected areas of development and fruitful topics for research'. This framework is adopted in this chapter, initially with the identification of the requirements of a performance management system:

(1) Identification of the key performance dimensions

Performance dimensions should be identified that reflect:

(i) The key objectives of the organization. For example, dimensions such as profitability and market position.
(ii) The processes and activities that will reflect the successful implementation of the strategies and plans that the organization has adopted. For example, if an organization has decided upon a positioning strategy of product differentiation through the provision of high-quality (say highly reliable) products, then the processes and activities that lead to that high quality should be monitored.

(2) Identification as to how these performance dimensions should be measured

Having identified the key performance dimensions, appropriate measures of these dimensions need to be agreed upon. Traditional measures of profitability are profit or return on capital employed. Market position could be measured in terms of market share. Quality might be measured in terms of level of defects or cost of quality.

(3) A target for the chosen performance measurement must be established

It is important for an organization to consider:

(i) The method used to ensure that appropriate performance targets are set.
(ii) The reward for achievement/punishment for non-achievement of targets. What rewards will managers and other employees gain by achieving these performance targets or, conversely, what penalties will they suffer by failing to achieve them?

Organizational rewards are based on the achievement of performance against formal performance measures. It is crucial therefore that the formal measurement system accurately reflects the crucial performance dimensions of the organization. Hopwood (1976) highlighted the dangers that can occur when a measurement system and the rewards associated with such a system are based on imperfect measures. The problem is illustrated in Figure 19.1.

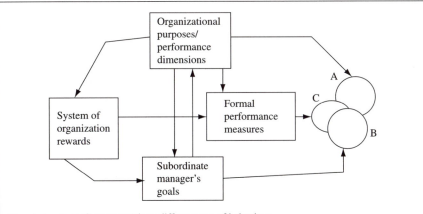

The circles A, B, C represent three different sets of behaviour.

Circle A represents the behaviour necessary to achieve the organization's purposes.

Circle B represents the behaviour that subordinate managers are likely to concentrate on, in order to fulfil their personal goals.

Circle C represents the behaviours that are monitored by the information system of the company.

Figure 19.1   The measurement reward process
Source: Hopwood, A. (1976) *Accounting and Human Behaviour*, p. 113. Prentice Hall. Reproduced by permission of A. Hopwood.

In Figure 19.1, it can be seen that circles A, B and C are not aligned. In this case, the behaviours measured by the formal measurement system do not fully reflect the behaviours necessary to achieve the objectives of the organization and it is also clear that the managers have yet another set of objectives.

Hopwood argued that for a performance management system to be effective, the three circles must be aligned – i.e. the formal performance measures must accurately reflect the key performance dimensions that represent the purpose of the organization and the managers should be motivated to achieve these performance measures.

(4) Identify the information flows (feedback and feedforward loops) that are necessary to enable the organization to learn from its experience

The final step of a results control system is to monitor the actual performance and identify whether this is in line with the target performance and whether the organization needs to adapt its current behaviour in the light of that experience.

Issues of budgetary control – limitations as a system of performance management

In this section of the chapter, the limitations of budgetary control as a performance management system are considered. In the subsequent two sections, ways of overcoming these limitations will be reviewed.

(1) Key dimensions of performance may not be monitored

Issue (i) *Budgetary control systems focus on financial performance and objectives*
Many organizations consider that it is important that a range of non-financial, as well as financial objectives and performance dimensions are monitored.

Issue (ii) *Strategies and plans not monitored*
Although budgets are based on plans of action, the activities and processes through which strategies and plans are to be achieved may not be monitored.

Issue (iii) *Budgetary control reports often focus on functional/departmental performance rather than internal business processes*

A measurement system that focuses on the performance of individual parts of the system may result in the functional departments acting to improve their own performance results at the expense of an overall improvement for the organization. An example might be the purchasing department buying cheap raw materials, this resulting in favourable material price variance, but having an adverse impact on customer satisfaction and labour efficiency variances. To provide customers with the product or service attributes that they value, it is necessary to ensure that internal business processes are improved and these are likely to cross functional boundaries.

(2) Performance measures may not accurately reflect the performance dimension

The measures of financial performance, such as profit, cost and return on capital employed for the coming months and year may not accurately reflect an objective such as increasing shareholder wealth. If a manager is set a target that is expressed in terms of the achievement of short-term (annual and monthly) financial results, it may be unsurprising if he/she then focuses on the achievement of such goals. Potentially, short-term profits may be achieved through inappropriate management action that is detrimental to long-term corporate objectives. For example, by cutting research or expenditure on members of staff who are essential for the development of new products and projects.

For the activities in this chapter, reference should be made to the case of Dundee Bicycle Division provided in the section on 'case scenarios' at the end of the book.

Activity 19.1

The works manager has approached Jack Jones and requested that £100,000 be spent on a quality improvement programme. Although there will be a net reduction in profit in the current year, he anticipates that it will lead to a net improvement in profits of £50,000 in all subsequent years.

(i) Should Jack Jones authorize the expenditure on the quality improvement programme?
(ii) Why might he not take this action?

(3a) An appropriate performance target may not be set: the method used may not be appropriate

Issue (i) *Budgets may become out-of-date due to environmental change*
Budgets have to be relevant for both planning and control purposes. A budget that is set for the new planning year may well have been prepared some 3 to 6 months prior to the start of the budget period. Accordingly, by the end of the budget period the gap between preparation of the budget and the actual events occurring could be nearly 18 months. If the environment in which the organization operates is changing rapidly, there is a significant chance that the budgets and the plans on which they were based are out-of-date and need revising.

With a budget that is out-of-date, variance information – i.e. comparing actual to budget – will also become less relevant. For example, if sales demand is significantly reduced, then each month there will be an adverse sales volume variance. It may well be the case that there is also an adverse sales price variance, as sales staff will need to discount prices to achieve sales in an increasingly competitive market. Although both sales volume and sales price variances might be adverse, given the adverse trading conditions, the performance might well have been as good as could be expected. Care is therefore needed in the interpretation of variances and to assume that an adverse variance is necessarily a reflection of poor performance could be misleading.

Issue (ii) *Approaches such as incremental budgets that are based on historic allocations may not reflect current needs*
Budgeting approaches used, such as incremental budgeting, will not take account of changed circumstances.

Issue (iii) *The management style may not be appropriate*
The level of difficulty of the target and management aspirations has been identified as one set of factors to consider in setting budgetary targets. The extent to which managers should be involved in the budget-setting process (participation) has also been subject to much debate. For example, it has been argued that higher results can be achieved if a manager is involved in budget preparation. These issues will be considered further in the fourth section of this chapter.

Activity 19.2

The engineering manager at Dundee Bicycles has been provided with a cost budget based on last year's expenditure plus a 5% allowance for inflation. A number of breakdowns have occurred in the factory and that will mean that outside technical support needs to be bought in immediately, however, if this is done the cost budget will be exceeded.

(i) What action should the engineering manager take and why might he not take it?
(ii) What are the potential problems with the existing way that the budget is set?

(3b) The reward system of the organization may lead to inappropriate action by managers

Issue (i) *A reward system based on measures that (a) do not reflect the key performance dimensions of the organization or (b) become out-of-date*
   (a) If rewards are linked to performance, a guide is being given by the organization about the amount of time that should be given to the different areas. An inappropriately designed reward system may lead managers to spend excessive time on improving performance in areas that are not central to the desired objectives and strategies of the organization.
   If a reward system is based on a broad range of measures, it is also necessary to consider how to penalize non-achievement of any of these measures! The problem of judging trade-offs between targets becomes an issue. For example, is it better to just achieve all targets or exceed most targets by a significant amount, but marginally fail to achieve some, possibly less important, targets?
   (b) If there have been significant changes in the markets or other external aspects of the external environment of an organization, then the budget and a reward system based on budget achievement may be inappropriate.

Issue (ii) *Budget gaming by managers may occur*
Budget 'gaming' by managers includes efforts to bias the performance-setting process by ensuring that easy targets are set. If an easy budget target is set, it will be easier to achieve favourable budget variances and a manager will achieve a reward for 'gaming' rather than actually performing well. Lowe and Shaw (1968) also noted that managers who are insecure are also likely to attempt to bias the budget-setting process. These issues will also be considered further in a later section.

Activity 19.3

The sales manager has been given a sales target based on sales revenue and will be given a bonus if this target is exceeded. A customer has offered to award a large order, however, the price that the customer is prepared to pay is much lower than for other customers in the region.

 (i) Why might the sales manager not act in the interests of the organization?
 (ii) How might the existing system be changed in order to overcome this problem?

---

(4) The information flows may not be adequate to inform management of key areas of performance requiring action

Issue (i) *Long-term trends requiring changes to strategy may not be highlighted*
With a budgetary control system:

(a) Feedback information is provided with variance information to budget.
(b) Feedforward control takes place through means of a revision of the budget estimate for the remainder of the year.

While this information can be of assistance in identifying short-term operational issues, it may be of less help in informing management of longer-term trends or changes in the environment that should indicate a requirement to reconsider key strategies.

Issue (ii) *The information provided to managers may be presented in a format that makes it difficult to identify action that is required*

In producing variance reports it is necessary to aggregate data and there is always a balance between providing too detailed or too aggregated information. If the data is too aggregated, it is difficult to identify where the problem is occurring, however, too much detail runs the risk of overwhelming management. The principle of management by exception, which has been discussed in Chapter 7, results in aggregated information being provided for senior managers, while more detailed information is provided for intermediate-level departments and managers.

Issue (iii) *Information may be provided some time after the relevant events have occurred*
If information is provided several weeks after the events have occurred, there is a danger that this will be too late for management to take corrective action. A common criticism made of standard costing systems (discussed in Chapter 9) is that in a manufacturing

environment, the reporting of monthly standard costing variances is both too late and the information is provided in a form that is too aggregated for operational management to use.

Issue (iv) *Manager and subordinate behaviour may be inappropriate*
The way that the information is used may lead to inappropriate action and great stress for managers. This issue is considered further in a later section.

Performance management systems – potential design changes

The previous review has provided a long list of reasons as to why care needs to be taken in the design and use of performance management systems. Although the focus was on the deficiencies of budgetary control, similar problems can occur with any system that measures aspects of performance and then manages based on that information.

In Figure 19.2 the problems of budgetary control systems are noted in the left hand column. Potential design changes that may overcome each of these problems are identified in the adjacent column. The chapter where these design changes are discussed further, are noted in the right hand column.

Problems of budgetary control	Potential design changes to the performance management system to overcome this problem	Where explored further
(1) Key dimensions of performance may not be monitored, leading to inappropriate focus and action		
(i) *Budgetary control systems focus on financial performance and objectives*	A broader set of performance dimensions reflecting the strategic objectives of the organization should be monitored.	Ch. 20
(ii) *Strategies and plans not monitored*	As well as monitoring performance dimensions that reflect strategic objectives, means and relationships should also be monitored.	Ch. 20
(iii) *Budgetary control reports focus on functional/departmental performance rather than internal business processes*	Consider approaches that measure the impact of actions on processes that cross functional boundaries.	Ch. 22 (see also note 1)
	Identify potential changes to the organizational processes and the management accounting/information system that might be appropriate in complex environments. The use of the budget for performance management purposes should be reduced. See also the discussion on 'management by means rather than results'	Ch. 23

Figure 19.2 Design issues and potential developments

(2) Performance measures may not accurately reflect the performance dimension		
Performance measures may not accurately reflect the performance dimension	In relation to the measurement of financial performance, for example, alternatives to profit and return on capital employed may provide a closer link with the objective of increasing shareholder wealth. Options to consider include economic value added, market value added and shareholder value added.	Ch. 21
(3a) The method used may not be appropriate		
(i) *Budgets may become out-of-date due to environmental change*	Revise budgetary control reporting. A range of alternatives have been used by different organizations:	
	(a) Use rolling budgets.	Ch. 7
	(b) Abandon the annual budget and use flash forecasts.	Ch. 23
(ii) *Approaches such as incremental budgets that are based on historic allocations may not reflect current needs*	Consider alternative techniques for setting budgets. For example, for overhead budgets, consider approaches such as zero-based, priority-based or activity-based budgeting.	Ch. 8
(3b) The reward system of the organization may lead to inappropriate action by managers		
A reward system may be based on measures that do not reflect the key performance dimensions of the organization	Reward system design should be reconsidered, see discussion on EVA and reward systems designed on achievement of longer-term objectives.	Ch. 21
	Rewards based on relative improvement targets. (See the 'beyond budgeting' debate.)	Ch. 23
(4) The information flows may not be adequate to inform management of key areas of performance requiring action		
(i) *Long-term trends requiring changes to strategy may not be highlighted*	Consider potential mechanisms, e.g. interactive controls (Simons, 1995)	Ch. 20
(ii) *The information provided to managers may be presented in a format that makes it difficult to identify action that is required.*	Mintzberg (1975) made a number of recommendations for improvements in information systems.	See note 2
	Consider the development of the decision support system (DSS).	See note 3
(iii) *Information may only be provided some time after the relevant events have occurred*	Provide real-time systems.	See note 4

Figure 19.2 (*Continued*)

Note 1. Changing the design of the management accounting system may be only one of a range of solutions that may be tried. In Chapter 22, it is noted that different organizational structures may also ease the problems of managers taking a functional view of objectives.
Note 2. Mintzberg noted that:

1. Managers need broad-based formal information systems, to include non-quantitative and non-economic data.
2. Information systems need to contain intelligent filtering systems, more sophisticated than mere aggregation, to avoid the problem of overloading.
3. Appropriate channels of communication need to be geared to the manager's pattern of activity. Much of the work of a manager involves reacting to events and 'fire-fighting'. Proper consideration of long-term issues is also required, and the information system should be designed to take account of the needs of managers given this type of working environment.
4. The information systems should have a capability for in-depth search.

Note 3. Turban (1995) defines a DSS as 'an interactive, flexible and adaptable computer-based information system, especially developed for supporting the solution of a non-structured management problem for improved decision making. It utilizes data, provides an easy-to-use interface and allows for the decision maker's own insights'. A range of commercial specialist computer-based software is available. It is also possible to develop systems in spreadsheets, with an interface or 'front-end' written in Visual Basic to provide an easy-to-use system.

Note 4. In recent years, developments in computer technology have resulted in more 'user-friendly' systems that are increasingly flexible in meeting the needs of managers. Many such systems can report 'real-time' information. Rather than having to wait for the monthly accounts to be prepared and published, managers can view their expenditure to date via on-line access.

Figure 19.2 *(Continued)*

Issues of budgetary control – 'behavioural' implications and improving budgeting processes

As well as changes to the design of a performance management system, it may be possible to overcome some of the problems with budgeting through changing budgeting processes. The potential impact of alternative management styles on the setting of budgets and budget targets, and the evaluation of performance of managers, should be considered.

Target setting and budgeting

Level of difficulty and the aspiration level of managers

A defined quantitative goal or target is likely to motivate higher levels of performance than would be achieved if no such target was set. Hofstede (1968), however, has suggested that if there is little chance of a budget being achieved because the target is too difficult, then the manager will lose that motivation. The manager has to believe that there is a reasonable likelihood that the budget can be achieved in order for him/her to 'aspire' to achieve it.

Following a study of an organization in which budgets of varying levels of difficulty were set, Hofstede concluded that:

1. Budgets have no motivational effect unless they are accepted by the managers involved as their own targets. Since different managers have different aspiration levels, if a

budget is being used as a target then the aspiration level of the manager will need to be taken into account in the setting of the budget.

2. Up to the point at which a budget is no longer accepted, the tighter the budget the better the result achieved. After that point, results are likely to decline. As a guideline, Hofstede suggested that managers should feel they have at least a 50% chance of achieving a target, although this is likely to vary depending on the aspiration level of the manager.

3. The acceptance of budgets is facilitated when good upward communication exists.

The effect suggested by Hofstede is illustrated in Figure 19.3.

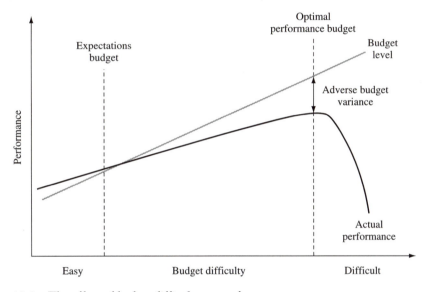

Figure 19.3   The effect of budget difficulty on performance
Source: Otley, D. (1987) Accounting Control and Organisational Behaviour, p. 45. Prentice Hall.

Figure 19.3 illustrates how actual performance can exceed budget performance given an easy budget. As budget difficulty increases then so can actual performance, though it should be noted that with increased budget difficulty the actual performance may well be less than budget. When the budget becomes too difficult to achieve then actual performance is likely to decline as managers no longer aspire to meet the budget target.

Participation in the budget-setting process

There have traditionally been two main approaches to budgeting, the top-down approach and the bottom-up approach.

Budgets can be prepared centrally and the operational managers advised of their budgets. This is called a *top-down* approach. The benefit of the top-down approach is that it can be produced quickly and involve less management time than other options. However, there are significant dangers of inaccurate budgets being set that are also not acceptable to the subordinate managers.

An alternative to a top-down approach is for the operational/subordinate managers to participate in the preparation of their own budgets and then for these budgets to be reviewed by senior management. This is called a *bottom-up* approach.

Many researchers, e.g. Hofstede (1968), have recommended that the bottom-up approach involving participation is a preferable method of preparing a budget. The reasons for this are that:

(i) The manager has the best understanding of his own objectives and the resources required to achieve them.
(ii) A manager is also likely to have greater motivation if he has participated in the preparation of his own operational budget.

Other studies have suggested that participation is not a panacea that will solve all problems. Figure 19.4 highlights factors that have been suggested in different studies as influencing the effectiveness of participation. The right side of the table indicates the situations in which participation is likely to be less effective and relevant.

Study	Factors influencing the effectiveness of participation	Participation is less effective and relevant
Vroom (1960)	Personality	With managers who are more highly authoritarian.
Hopwood (1978)	Work situation	In a highly programmed and technologically constrained environment.
Brownell (1981)	Locus of control	For those individuals who feel they have a low degree of control over their destiny.
Mia (1989)	Job difficulty	Where job difficulty is low.
Bruns and Waterhouse (1975)	Types of organizational structure	In a centralized organization.

Figure 19.4   Factors influencing the effectiveness of participation

Figure 19.4 would indicate that participation is less relevant if a subordinate manager has an authoritarian personality, the work is highly programmable, there is low job difficulty, the manager feels that he has a low degree of control over his destiny and the organization is centralized. In such a situation, a top-down approach to budgeting may well be appropriate.

The top-down approach might not be appropriate in an alternative situation where a manager is less authoritarian, the work situation requires flexibility, innovation and the requirement to deal with unexpected problems, the job is complex, individuals feel they do have control over their destiny and the work is in a decentralized organization. With such a scenario, a bottom-up, participative approach is likely to be preferable.

Budget gaming

A potentially adverse consequence of allowing subordinate managers to participate in the setting of their own budget is that they can bias the information to gain the greatest personal benefit. Managers can best achieve their own goals in an easy or slack environment and may therefore try to attain *slack budgets*.

Lowe and Shaw (1968) suggested three main reasons for budget bias:

(i) The reward system of the organization.
(ii) The influence of company practice and the style of management.

The weight of evidence suggests that if company expectations are that budgets should be strictly adhered to and managers are 'punished' for non-achievement of budget, then bias in the budget-setting process is likely to occur.

(iii) The insecurity of certain managers. An insecure manager will wish to limit the chance that he or she is not meeting management expectations. Staying strictly within budget guidelines is one way of achieving this goal.

To reduce the chance of bias, management can consider two sets of action:

(i) Senior managers need to review the budgets of subordinates in order to check whether the corporate targets have been fully considered and whether the assumptions used are realistic.
(ii) The way that senior managers use budgetary control information for performance evaluation purposes can be reviewed. This is considered further in the next section.

Activity 19.4

What are the advantages and disadvantages of introducing participation into the budget-setting process?

Performance evaluation and the budget

Hopwood (1974) highlighted the problems that can occur when budgets are used as a basis for performance evaluation. He studied how budgetary control information was used in a number of cost centres in the manufacturing division of a large US company and proposed that three distinct management styles could be observed, these being budget-constrained, profit-conscious and non-accounting.

The **budget-constrained style** involved the assessment of the performance of junior managers based primarily upon the ability of junior managers to continually meet the budget on a short-term basis. Short-term cost overspends would result in punitive action and pressure to rectify the situation to ensure achievement of budget. The **profit-conscious style** involved an assessment based on an ability to meet the long-term purposes of the organization, even though this might lead to a short-term overspend. The **non-accounting style** occurred when accounting information played a relatively insignificant role in the evaluation of a manager's performance.

Hopwood was particularly concerned with the budget-constrained style of management, which he felt led to manipulation of accounting data, job tension and poor relations between colleagues and superiors. He argued that senior managers should adopt a 'profit-conscious' style of management. Rather than focusing on ensuring that managers achieve their budgets, a profit-conscious style is more flexible and recognizes the need to overspend budget if it leads to long-term benefits. Hopwood suggested that only the profit-conscious style succeeded in attaining the involvement of managers without incurring either emotional costs or defensive behaviour.

Use of the budget control information in a budget-constrained manner could result in severe tension, manipulation of data and poor relationships. A summary of Hopwood's findings is presented in Figure 19.5.

	Style of evaluation		
	Budget-constrained	Profit-conscious	Non-accounting
Involvement with costs	High	High	Low
Job-related tension	High	Medium	Medium
Manipulation of accounting information	Extensive	Little	Little
Relations with superiors	Poor	Good	Good
Relations with colleagues	Poor	Good	Good

Figure 19.5   A summary of the effects of three styles of management
Source: Hopwood, A. (1976) *Accounting and Human Behaviour*, p. 113. Prentice Hall. Reproduced by permission of A. Hopwood.

It should be noted that not all research evidence supports the view that the budget-constrained style of management always results in a negative impact on the organization and people within the organization. A number of writers (e.g. Hirst, 1981; Govindarajan, 1984) have supported a contingency viewpoint in suggesting that different circumstances may lead to different approaches being appropriate.

Environmental uncertainty may be an important influencing factor. In situations of high certainty, it is possible to place reliance on accounting information as an appropriate level of budget expenditure for an expected output can be accurately estimated. A style of management that focuses on budget achievement may well be acceptable for such circumstances. However, where there is high uncertainty, it is much more difficult to evaluate performance in terms of the extent to which a budget has been achieved. A style of management that focuses on budget achievement is therefore less likely to be appropriate for such circumstances. The contingency theory of management accounting is discussed further in Chapter 23.

Theories of motivation

In attempting to identify appropriate management styles in order to ensure improved results from the budgeting process it is relevant to identify the factors that will cause motivation.

'Content' theories of motivation suggest that to be motivated, it is necessary to meet the needs of individuals. Maslow (1954) suggested that there is a hierarchy of needs with physiological needs, such as food and drink, etc. at the lowest level. Once these are met then higher-level needs such as safety, belonging and esteem from others is required. At the highest level individuals have a need for self-expression and fulfilment. See Figure 19.6.

Figure 19.6 Maslow's hierarchy of needs

Although the idea that there is a hierarchy of needs has been criticized, the existence of group reward systems provides support for the view that social and belonging needs are considered to be important in many organizations. They would also support the view that the involvement of people in the budget-setting process is important for many individuals.

McGregor (1960) considered that managers tend to hold divergent views about the mechanisms needed to motivate staff. A first set of assumptions, which he termed theory X, is that people are lazy and lack ambition and need to be led and told what to do. Such people are motivated by economic considerations. A second set of assumptions he termed theory Y, where it was assumed that people enjoy work and are motivated by self-control and self-development. The view held by managers is likely to influence the style of management they consider appropriate and this will also be evident in the setting of budgets and evaluation of performance against budget.

'Process' theories of motivation, such as expectancy theory, suggest that the probability that planned work will be achieved is also important for motivation to occur. Hofstede's findings may be considered to be consistent with expectancy theory. While the work itself and advancement may be important, managers also need to accept the budget as a reasonable target that can be achieved. If budgets are set at too high a level, then managers will not be motivated to aspire to achieve them.

Activity 19.5

If a manager believes that people are lazy and lack ambition, how do you think this might influence his style of management in relation to the budgetary control process?

Alternative forms of control

In this chapter to date, the focus has been on the design and operation of performance management systems. Such systems are only one mechanism of control that is used in organizations. Ouchi (1979), for example, classified different types of control into three different mechanisms:

1. The *bureaucratic mechanism* incorporates measures which are widely used in the traditional hierarchical rule-based organization. These include:

   (a) Internal controls to prevent inappropriate *behaviour*.
   (b) Measures of *output* such as provided by budgetary control systems and performance management systems such as the Balanced Scorecard (discussed in Chapter 20).

2. Output measurement using the *market mechanism*. Prices can be attached to goods produced or services provided and this mechanism then leads to the allocation of resources between units and divisions of an organization. The market mechanism was discussed in Chapter 10.

3. *Clan (or cultural)* control. These are controls based on the development of shared norms and values for the employees of the organization. If staff support the values and beliefs that are necessary to achieve the goals of the organization, then it is far more likely that those goals will be achieved and the need for other methods of control is reduced.

Measures of output involving the bureaucratic and market mechanisms have been discussed already in this book. Internal controls and clan (or cultural) controls will be discussed below.

Internal controls

Internal controls are measures an organization adopts in order to prevent inappropriate action and to help provide direction to staff. The aim of these controls is to encourage adherence to organizational policies, promote operational efficiency and effectiveness, safeguard assets and ensure the reliability of accounting data. Internal controls include the following.

Physical and administrative constraints

Physical constraints include locks on desks, passwords, limits on access to areas. Administrative constraints can include:

(i) Restrictions set on the decision-making authority of subordinate managers. For example, a junior manager may be authorized to spend up to £50 without needing the authority of a more senior manager. The next level of management may be authorized to spend up to £1000.
(ii) The separation of duties, which means that tasks are divided up so that it is difficult to undertake certain tasks that should not be completed. For example, in a shop, refunds for goods can often only be authorized by a shop senior. Although it does not eliminate the chance of fraud occurring, it does reduce the risk as more than one person has to participate in order for it to occur.

Personnel controls

Personnel controls are those implemented by an organization to ensure the recruitment and training of appropriate personnel. The recruitment process should 'weed' out candidates who will not meet the requirements of the organization. Having recruited the right candidates, they should be trained so that they are able to perform well in their jobs.

Organization and supervision

There should be clear lines of responsibility and employees should be aware of their specific responsibilities and to whom they are responsible.

Supervision of the activities of staff should take place. Where staff need direction there may be scrutiny of the action plans of the individuals being controlled (these can be for the coming day, week or even month). A reviewer can then approve or disapprove of the proposed action plans. Having agreed plans for the coming period, employees can then be held accountable for the actions they take. For action accountability, it is necessary to:

1. Define what actions are acceptable. This may have been identified in the pre-action review. It could also be identified in work rules, policies and procedures.
2. Communicate those definitions to employees.

3. Observe or otherwise track what is happening.
4. Reward good actions or punish actions that deviate from the acceptable.

Cultural/clan controls

Cultural or clan controls are based on the development of shared norms and values for the employees of the organization. If staff support the values and beliefs that are necessary to achieve the goals of the organization, then it is far more likely that those goals will be achieved. Miles and Snow suggested that organizations typically have one of four types of organizational culture – defenders, prospectors, analysers and reactors (discussed in Chapter 13). The culture of an organization should be suitable to its needs. For example, in an environment and organization where innovation and creativity is required for success, a defender culture, involving a conservative inward-looking and risk-averse style of management, may not be appropriate.

Merchant (1998) suggests that there are five important methods of shaping culture, these include codes of conduct, reward systems, inter-organizational transfers, physical and social relationships and good example from top management.

(i) *Codes of conduct*. These formal, written documents provide broad, general statements of corporate values. They can identify the behaviour required of employees towards the organization and to other stakeholders, including customers, service providers, suppliers, competitors and other employees as well as the law, rules and regulations.
(ii) *Reward system*. Group reward systems are often recommended as these can encourage collective achievement. Although the link between individual effort and the results being awarded is weak, group rewards can act to assist in the communication of expectations and mutual monitoring of staff.
(iii) *Intra-organizational transfers*. If staff are transferred between different functions and different units, this is likely to increase the extent to which those members of staff can understand and relate to organizational rather than sub-unit goals.
(iv) *Physical and social arrangements*. Physical arrangements include office plans and social arrangements such as dress code. In a number of airlines, for example, cabin crew rosters are changed in order to create 'families' of staff.
(v) *Good example from top management*. Top managers need to serve as role models.

Personnel controls and the supervision process can also be important in fostering an appropriate culture.

Summary

In designing a performance measurement and management system, four steps are required:

- Identification of key performance dimensions.
- Identification of how these dimensions will be measured.

- The establishment of targets for these measures. There also needs to be a consideration of how these targets are set and the rewards for achievement/punishment for non-achievement.
- The comparison of actual performance to target and the provision of feedback information to enable the organization to learn from its experience.

A budgetary control system acts as a key element of the performance management system in many organizations, but a number of limitations can be noted when comparison is made to the four steps discussed above.

To perform the functions of a performance management system it is likely that it will be necessary to:

(a) Provide additional design features.

It may also be necessary to

(b) Review budget processes and the style of management.

A management control system can incorporate a range of other control techniques. These can include internal controls and cultural/clan control.

Further reading

Emmanuel, C., Otley, D. and Merchant, K. (1990) *Accounting for Management Control*, 2nd edn. International Thompson Business Press, London.

Merchant, K.A. (2003) *Modern Management Control Systems: Performance Measurement, Evaluation and Incentives: Text and Cases*, Prentice-Hall.

Otley, D. (1987) Accounting Control and Organizational behaviour. Heinemann.

Otley, D. (1999) Performance management: a framework for management control system research. *Management Accounting Research* **10**: 363–382.

Ouchi, W.G. (1979) A conceptual framework for the design of organisational control mechanisms. *Management Science* **25**: 833–848.

Turban, E. (1995) *Decision Support and Expert Systems: Management support systems*. Prentice Hall, Englewood Cliffs, NJ.

Answers to activities

Activity 19.1

(i) It is necessary to know the cost of capital to answer the question, though it does seem likely that a cost saving of £50,000 a year will be worthwhile on expenditure of £100,000 as this is only a two-year payback. It is therefore likely that Jack Jones should authorize the quality improvement programme.

(ii) A very short-term view might mean that the decision is not taken as the programme will have an adverse impact on profits in the current year.

Activity 19.2

(i) The contribution of the factory is increased by the additional expenditure, then it would seem appropriate to buy in the outside technical support.
(ii) The engineering manager may not do this if he believes that this will mean that his budget is exceeded and he is measured strictly on budget achievement.

Activity 19.3

The sales manager should find out the contribution that is generated from this order and then consider whether it is sufficient for the company.

However, a reporting system with an incomplete measurement system and an inappropriate management style may again result in different action being taken. If the manager is monitored on the basis of sales generated rather than contribution earned, then the information system will not be accurately measuring key measures that reflect the objectives of the business. Further, if the reward system is based on exceeding budget, then the reward system is providing further motivation to accept sales that may not be in the interests of the organization.

Activity 19.4

Participation is thought by many to be beneficial in the budget-setting process as the budget holder will often have a better understanding of the budget needs for his responsibility centre. A manager is also more likely to be motivated to achieve a target if he/she has been involved in the establishment of the target.

A disadvantage of participation is that a manager will have more opportunity to bias the budget in order to set an easy target.

Activity 19.5

There is no certainty in this answer, though it may be that a manager who believes his staff are lazy and lacking ambition may employ a less participative and a top-down approach to budgeting. The manager may also use a budget-constrained style of management in evaluating performance.

Exercises

For Questions 19.1 to 19.6 you can draw on the case information from Dundee Bicycle Division parts a and b.

Q19.1 Jack Jones relies heavily on budgetary control information as a major method for assessing the performance of Dundee Bicycle Division and the performance of the management team. Cost centre managers are expected to keep within budget and he expects the division to achieve the budgeted return on investment.
Critically review the benefits and potential dangers of this approach to management.

Q19.2 Can you recommend any changes to the *design* of the performance management system for Dundee Bicycle Division?

Q19.3 In Dundee Bicycle Division part B it is noted that a bid for a new automated welding machine had been made on the grounds that this could achieve a faster and better weld than could be achieved with the current labour-intensive welding approach. Mr Jones had requested an investment appraisal and this showed a positive net present value. However, the payback was greater than two years and there was a negative accounting rate of return in the first year. Mr Jones turned down the investment proposal.
Should Mr Jones have accepted the investment proposal, and if so on what grounds?

Q19.4 Should Jack Jones change his management style when involved in the budget-setting and review process? If so, why?

Q19.5 Hopwood has referred to three different styles of management. Which style do you think Jack Jones follows and do you feel this is the most appropriate style to use at Dundee Bicycles?

Q19.6 Ouchi has proposed a range of different control mechanisms. Which mechanisms are mainly used by Jack Jones? Review the alternative types of control and assess the relevance of those controls to Dundee Bicycle Division.

Q19.7 Participation has sometimes been referred to as a 'double-edged' sword. Why should it be viewed as such?

Q19.8 Why is aspiration level important in budget setting?

STRATEGY AND CONTROL SYSTEM DESIGN

20

Objectives

After studying this chapter you should be able to:

- Explain ways in which performance measurement systems should take account of the strategic dimension.
- Explain and apply key elements and strengths and potential weaknesses of one well-known performance management system – the Balanced Scorecard.
- Explain and apply key elements of the control framework of Simons (1995) for implementing strategy.

Introduction

This chapter explores how a performance management system should take into account the strategic objectives and strategies of the organization.

The first part of the chapter explores the need for a system to not only guide organizations towards planned objectives, but also measure the processes and activities that will reflect the successful implementation of strategies and plans. A well-known performance management system called the Balanced Scorecard is then reviewed, incorporating a consideration of strengths and potential limitations of the approach.

The second section considers the extent to which a performance management system such as the Balanced Scorecard is sufficient for the implementation of strategy. Simons (1995), for example, argues that to ensure the successful implementation of strategies, three further control elements are required. Firstly, a 'boundary system' which includes internal controls and codes of behaviour is required to ensure that inappropriate actions and behaviours are avoided by managers. Secondly, there is a requirement for senior managers to inspire subordinate managers and other employees towards a commitment to a clear set of core values. Finally, a system that monitors the external environment and enables organizations to respond to environmental change.

Performance measurement systems

Identifying performance dimensions

In Chapter 15, key methods of achieving competitive advantage were identified. In particular it was noted that Porter recommended that organizations could achieve a competitive advantage through following one of three positioning strategies – low cost, product differentiation or niche. Before deciding on the most appropriate positioning strategy, it is important to clearly understand the key attributes that customers value and the ability of the organization to deliver them. These attributes could be product or service attributes such as quality, price or time, or customer relationship attributes or image and reputation. An example of an airline is considered in Figure 20.1.

An airline has analysed its customer base and identified that they are mainly business users who expect a high-quality service. The key product attributes that they value are: on-time arrival, comfort of the seats, cabin service and quality of the food.

The company has decided that in order to achieve a competitive advantage and gain market share and increase profitability, it should follow a positioning strategy of product differentiation through providing a better service, e.g. comfort of the seats, cabin service, food, on-time departures and arrivals.

Figure 20.1 Key value propositions for an airline

In order to understand how well the airline is trading, it would be helpful to measure the outcomes that are achieved in terms of profitability and market share. It would also be extremely useful to know how well the airline is performing in delivering on the key drivers of performance. In this case, the airline believes that the cabin service, comfort of seats, on-time departures and arrivals are driving improved market share and hence financial results. In the long term, the airline will only deliver profitability and high market share if it delivers a superior performance on the key dimensions that are important to the customer. A performance measurement and management system should therefore provide information on both:

1. The desired 'ends', i.e. the *objectives* of the organization. In this case the airline wishes to achieve increased market share and improved profitability.
2. The 'means', i.e. the key processes of *strategies and plans* for achieving these objectives.

The Balanced Scorecard

Kaplan and Norton (1992, 1996, 2004) proposed the **Balanced Scorecard** as a performance measurement system that can help translate vision and strategy into specific strategic objectives. This involves the measurement of approximately 25 measures across four perspectives – Financial, customer, internal business process, and learning and growth with ultimately all measures linked to financial objectives. The four perspectives are shown in Figure 20.2.

Performance dimensions can be set for each of the perspectives and appropriate measures identified for each dimension. Targets for these measures over a 3 to 5 year period can then be set and strategic initiatives aligned.

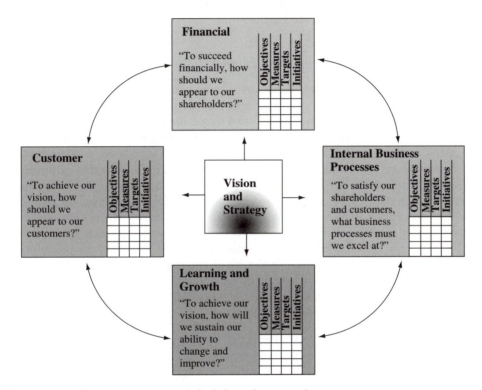

Figure 20.2 The four perspectives of a balanced scorecard
Source: Kaplan, R.S. and Norton, D.P. (1996) Using the Balanced Scorecard as a Strategic Management System. *Harvard Business Review*, January-February 76. Reprinted with permission.

Financial perspective

Kaplan and Norton argue that financial performance must remain a key feature of a performance measurement system. While improvements in customer and internal business process measures are important, they can only be fully relevant if they are contributing to bottom-line financial improvements.

In Chapter 16, it was noted how financial measures might be tailored to fit with the positioning strategy of the firm. The relevance of different measures at different stages of the life of a business was also discussed. In Chapter 21, a range of possible financial performance measures, including shareholder value analysis and economic value added, are considered in more detail.

Customer perspective

To achieve the financial objectives of the organization, the company must achieve certain market objectives. Companies need to identify the customer and/or market segments in which they have chosen to compete and then measure how well they are doing along a number of performance dimensions. These can be dimensions related to outcomes such as market share or could be drivers of performance, for example the product/service attributes that will lead to the outcomes.

(a) Outcome performance (lagging measures)

An organization will wish to achieve certain outcomes. For example, in order to achieve market growth, one important objective might be to acquire new customers. A key *performance dimension* that might be monitored would therefore be customer acquisition and a suitable *measure of performance* would be the number or percentage of new customers.

If a true measure of customer performance is required, then it is likely that performance across a number of dimensions is needed. If only a limited number of performance dimensions are monitored, a misleading picture of actual events may be provided. Customer acquisition may be of little benefit to a company if these new customers are sold goods or services at very low prices and so contribute little or no profit. To bring greater balance, other performance dimensions might be monitored. For example, customer profitability would involve measuring the profit generated by the new customers. There is also little point in performing well in gaining profitable new customers if the existing customers are currently dissatisfied with the product or service. New customers may be gained, but this could be offset by the loss of existing customers to competitors.

A range of potentially important performance dimensions that should be maintained by market segment is shown in Figure 20.3.

Potential performance dimensions	Potential performance measures of those dimensions
Customer acquisition	The number or percentage increase in new customers
Customer profitability	Net profit
Market share	Proportion of business in a given market
Customer retention	The rate at which a business maintains a relationship with its customers
Customer satisfaction	Satisfaction level measured along specific performance criteria

Figure 20.3   Customer outcome performance dimensions and measures

Outcome performance measures are lagging measures. A high market share, for example, may reflect the fact that the company has achieved competitive advantage in the past in the key market segments in which it operates. If this competitor advantage has now been lost and other competitors are better meeting the needs of customers, then market share and other outcome measures may start to deteriorate. To gain a fuller picture of the current performance of the organization, it is therefore necessary to monitor performance on the areas crucial to the provision of a competitive advantage in the future.

(b) Measurement of performance drivers (leading measures)

In order to achieve improved performance of outcome measures, the products or services of an organization must be providing value to customers. In Chapter 15, three categories of value propositions were identified: product/service attributes, customer relationship, image and reputation. Having identified the key dimensions necessary for improved outcomes to occur, measures for these dimensions need to be developed by the organization.

Product/service attributes

Certain customers may be particularly interested in product/service attributes. These may include performance dimensions of functionality, quality, price and time. Performance measures for these dimensions are required and measurements of quality, time and price are particularly widely used in many organizations.

(i) Functionality. For some customers, the product or service features are the key attributes required. Measurement of the value provided by product and service attributes is difficult, though market research and customer survey information may be of assistance. The potential for costing the attributes and comparing that to the benefits was discussed in Chapter 16.

(ii) Quality. This can be measured in various ways, for example parts-per-million defect, returns by customers, warranty claims.

(iii) Price. For some customers a low price is the key attribute required and it might be possible to use a performance measure by providing a comparison of prices against key competitors. An appropriate measurement for low price is not always easy to identify, however, as low initial cost may be at the expense of high costs later in the lifecycle. An inexpensive imported car, for example, may have higher costs throughout the product life due to the costs of replacing parts.

(iv) Time. It may be crucial that a product or service can be delivered with a short lead time and at the time promised. Lead time for delivery and/or the percentage of products delivered on time may be appropriate measures to use for the time dimension.

Customer relationship

A strong customer relationship may be an alternative way of achieving competitive advantage. This might include convenience of access and/or knowledgeable employees who can quickly and correctly deal with customer enquiries. Performance along this dimension may be identified through customer satisfaction surveys or use of 'mystery' shoppers, who judge how well a service is performed.

Image and reputation

Other customers might be influenced by the image and reputation of the company. For example, some consumers prefer certain brands of designer clothes, such as Nike.

Figure 20.4 considers an example of the airline industry, with different customers valuing different value propositions.

Value propositions – choosing your airline
As an example, consider the following scenario of three different customers choosing between one of a number of airlines flying on a particular route.

Customer 1 – choice is based on product/service attributes
Customer 1 might choose an airline on the grounds of functionality/attributes (e.g. comfort of accommodation, price and safety). The decision is based on superior product attributes.

Customer 2 – choice is based on customer relationship
Customer 2 might have compared the attributes of two airlines and decided that, although airline 'A' seemed to him to be very similar in terms of product attributes, the customer relationship value proposition of airline 'B' is better. For example, staff seem friendlier and more helpful. Airline 'A' is more impersonal while airline 'B' seems to go out of its way to build a relationship with the customer. For customer 2, the crucial 'performance drivers' are the factors related to customer relationship.

Customer 3 – choice is based on image
Customer 3 has compared the two airlines and prefers the perceived image resulting from the portrayal of people by airline 'A'. For example, one advertising campaign for British Airways promoted the image of itself as 'The world's favourite airline'. If a customer chose the airline on this basis, the performance driver is the image of the airline.

Figure 20.4 Alternative customer value propositions in the airline industry

As has been discussed in earlier chapters, a company can be successful through achieving competitive advantage in its key markets. The value that customers can gain from a product or service may vary according to the customer or market segment, and these differences should be reflected in the performance measurement system. The performance dimensions, where high performance should lead to successful achievement of required outcomes, are the dimensions that should be measured.

Activity 20.1

What is the difference between a product or service attribute and customer relationship?

Activity 20.2

Suggest a performance dimension to represent the value proposition 'image and reputation'. How should it be measured?

Internal business process perspective

In Chapter 15, the two main sources of competitive advantage were identified as the resources and competencies of the organization. Sometimes a resource on its own is sufficient to enable a competitive advantage, for example a patent on a product or superior production facilities. At other times it is because an organization is better at doing things, i.e. has superior competencies. Because of either set of factors, an organization is able to provide a product or service at low cost or provides additional value and can be differentiated from its competitors. Kaplan and Norton argue that to ensure that the organization continues to provide the attributes that provide value, the internal business processes that deliver the advantage should be measured. Three principle business processes should be the focus of attention, namely the innovation, operations and post-sale processes.

The innovation process

The innovation process is crucial for the long-term survival and success of an organization and is concerned with identifying the market and creating the product or service offering. It requires:

  (i) Basic research to develop radically new products and services.
 (ii) Applied research to exploit existing technology for the next generation of products.
(iii) Focused development efforts to bring new products and services to market.

Innovation is particularly important in fast-changing markets. The lifecycle of products is often short and companies are likely to need to be continually updating the products and services provided. Although a company might be currently profitable, if this is due to a large proportion of mature products and there are few new 'star' or 'question mark' products being developed, then in the longer term the company is unlikely to be able to provide the attributes required by customers. When the company no longer offers value, whether this is in the form of attributes, customer relationship or image and reputation, it will lose market share and profitability will fall. Measures such as percentage of sales from new products and time to develop new products will provide advance warning of potential problems to come. The payback time is also likely to be an important measure. In Chapter 2 the role of target costing in new product development and lifecycle costing was discussed.

Operations

The set of processes that have traditionally been monitored by organizations are the operations processes which start with the receipt of the customer order and finish with the delivery of the product or service.

Traditional measures that have been discussed in previous chapters include standard costs, budgets and variances. These performance measures have been criticized because they may provide a limited perspective of potential cost savings throughout the value chain and also ignore criteria related to quality and time and the cost of processes. Chapter 22 will discuss this area in much greater depth.

Post-sale service

Post-sale service is the service to the customer and includes warranty and repair activities, treatment of defects and returns. Products that become faulty after delivery to the customer are likely to lead to a high cost for customers. Firstly, there are the direct costs of repairing or replacing defective products and secondly, there is the loss of future sales following customer dissatisfaction, though the true cost of the latter is often difficult to quantify. Time, cost and quality metrics that may be applied to the post-sale service are also discussed further in Chapter 22.

Learning and growth perspective

The learning and growth perspective focuses on the infrastructure of the organization. If a business is to achieve the objectives set for the financial, customer and internal business processes, then it is necessary for this to be underpinned by appropriate capabilities in terms of people, systems and organizational processes. Relevant measures therefore need to be developed for each of these three areas.

Employee capabilities

A key objective for many organizations is to retain skilled and motivated staff. Appropriate output measures of performance could be collected to reflect employee satisfaction, retention and productivity.

It is also crucial to develop existing and new staff. There should be measures of the actual skill levels against which the achievement of financial, customer and internal business process objectives is required. Where necessary, retraining should take place.

Information systems capabilities

To be effective, employees need to have excellent information on customers (e.g. customer profitability) and on internal processes. The information system should be assessed in terms of the extent to which it meets the information needs of the employees.

Motivation, empowerment and alignment

Employees must be motivated to contribute to organizational success and appropriate measures could include:

(i) The number of suggestions per employee and the number of suggestions implemented.

(ii) Measures of improvement. For example, the time it takes for performance in terms of cost, quality or time to improve by 50%. If scrap costs were 5% of material costs, the half-life would be the time it takes to reduce to 2.5%.

(iii) Measures of team performance. Many organizations look to team work to implement new initiatives and so measures such as the percentage of team projects which have achieved key targets might be of relevance.

Activity 20.3

Is the financial objective more important that the learning and growth perspective?

Linking multiple scorecard measures to incorporate cause-and-effect relationships

In the above section, the need to identify a range of performance dimensions across four perspectives with measures related to these performance dimensions has been identified.

To be effective, it is essential that there is a cause-and-effect relationship linking the performance dimensions and measures to the objectives and the strategy to achieve these objectives.

Figure 20.5 shows the performance dimensions identified by Southwest Airlines that relate to the performance of the ground crew at Southwest Airlines.

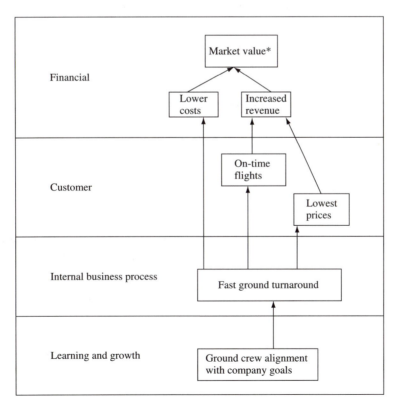

Figure 20.5 **Identifying the performance dimensions relating to ground crew performance of Southwest Airlines**
Source: Southwest airlines Balance Scorecard – The Balanced Scorecard. By: Anthes, G.H. *Computerworld*, 2/17/2003, **37**(7), p. 34. Reproduced by permission.

In the cause-and-effect diagram, the key financial performance dimensions are identified as market value, lower costs and increased revenue. Increased profitability will follow lower costs and increased revenue.

The diagram shows that Southwest Airlines believe that there is a cause-and-effect relationship between increased revenue and the customer dimensions of on-time flights and lowest prices. It can be noted that output measures such as customer loyalty or market share are not included. Rather it is two performance drivers – the product attributes of on-time flights and lowest prices – that are considered to be the most relevant.

A key factor in ensuring 'on-time flights' is the internal business process of fast ground turnaround. This is the time taken between an aircraft's arrival and departure from an airport. Fast ground turnaround will also mean that aircraft will spend a greater proportion of time in the air, leading to a lower number of aircraft required and therefore lower aircraft leasing costs and an improved ability of the airline to charge the 'lowest prices'.

The Balanced Scorecard for Southwest Airlines indicates that there is a belief that there is a cause-and-effect link between fast ground turnaround and the learning objective 'ground crew alignment with company goals'.

Activity 20.4

What do you think might be the weaknesses of the Southwest Airlines Balanced Scorecard?

Figure 20.6 shows the performance measures of the key performance indicators and also the performance targets. The measure of profitability used by Southwest Airlines is market value and the target used, at the time the Balanced Scorecard was drawn up, was a 30% annual growth rate. To underpin this extremely large market value growth target, the target for sales revenue growth was 20% compound growth, while growth in plane lease costs was to be limited to 5%.

For the customer perspective, the objective of on-time flights was measured by the Federal Aviation records of on-time arrival and the target of the airline was to be number 1. To measure lowest prices, the airline was to be number 1 as ranked in customer market surveys.

The internal perspective dimension of fast turnaround time was measured by 'time on the ground', where there was a target of 30 minutes and on-time departure, where the target was 90%.

Finally, for the learning perspective objective of 'ground crew alignment with company goals' there were two measures, percentage ground crew as shareholders and percentage ground crew trained. The target was that in three years, 100% performance would be achieved on both measures.

PERSPECTIVE	OBJECTIVE/DIMENSION	MEASURE	TARGET
Financial	Profitability	Market value	30% AGR*
	Increased revenue	Seat revenue	20% AGR
	Lowest cost	Plane lease cost	5% AGR
Customer	On-time flights	FAA on-time arrival rating	No. 1
	Lowest prices	Customer ranking (market survey)	No. 1
Internal	Fast turnaround time	Time on ground	30 minutes
		On-time departure	90%
Learning	Ground crew alignment with company goals	Percentage ground crew shareholders	Year 1: 70%
		Percentage ground crew trained	Year 2: 90%
			Year 3: 100%

* AGR = annual growth rate.

Figure 20.6 Objectives, measures and targets for the Southwest Airlines Balanced Scorecard for ground crew operations
Source: Southwest airlines Balance Scorecard – The Balanced Scorecard. By: Anthes, G.H. *Computerworld*, 2/17/2003, **37**(7), p. 34. Reproduced by permission.

The airline has a range of operational measures that focus on the performance of the ground crew, monitoring details such as baggage delivery. However, while supervisors might need these detailed measures, senior management just need a 'dashboard' that displays the key measures. If top management need further information on why on-time departures or time on ground are not achieving target measures, then it is possible to ask more detailed questions of the supervisors.

Strategic initiatives

Having identified target measures for the key outcome and performance driver measures, an organization can then consider whether the targets can be achieved through existing initiatives or whether new ones are required. For example, for the Southwest Airlines Balanced Scorecard to achieve the learning objectives, additional training may be required or to achieve the customer performance targets a new quality initiative or customer loyalty programme may be required.

Strengths of the Balanced Scorecard

1. The need to measure both outcomes and drivers of performance is recognised. For the customer, internal business process, and learning and growth perspectives, a series of outcome and performance driver measures are identified.

2. The Balanced Scorecard can be used in a manner that recognizes the objectives of a number of the different stakeholders of the organization. This increases the chance that the range of dimensions considered will be complete. The objectives of shareholders and customers can be recognized, with the establishment of performance measures under the financial and customer perspectives respectively. The objectives of employees can be recognized in the innovation and learning perspective. Other objectives might usefully be incorporated into the development of balanced scorecards for specific organizations in both the public and private sector. It should be noted that some stakeholders, such as suppliers, governments, local communities and the environment, are not explicitly recognized by the four perspectives.
3. The sequence of hypotheses about the cause and effect relationships between outcome measures and the performance drivers of those outcomes can be made explicit.

Potential limitations of the Balanced Scorecard

Applying Otley's framework introduced in chapter 19:

Performance dimensions and measures to be monitored

(1) Norreklit (2000) argues that the linear cause-and-effect model identified in the Balanced Scorecard, which leads from learning and growth through to financial objectives is plausible, but may be a simplification of reality.

In the illustration of the Southwest Airlines Balanced Scorecard, a clear set of cause-and-effect links is shown, with causal links shown from employee skills, leading to improved internal business processes of product development and operations process cycle and then onwards, with the final effect being improved financial performance.

In reality, the cause-and-effect relationship between measures may not always be as clear-cut. Other factors are likely to have an effect, and while a driver may have some impact on output, the exact relationship may be difficult to establish and may change over time.

(2) Even if there is a strong causal link, there may be a long lead-time between management and staff taking particular action and this action resulting in financial benefit.

(3) The measures of performance may not accurately reflect the performance dimensions. For example, how should customer loyalty be measured and how certain can an organization be that an improvement in the measure chosen, actually fully reflects an improvement in performance? For Southwest Airlines, it may well be that percentage ground crew shareholders and percentage ground crew trained are appropriate measures of the learning and growth performance dimension 'ground crew alignment with company goals'. This might not be the case for other organizations, where staff may have been trained and a significant proportion may be shareholders, but for other reasons are not aligned with company goals!

Setting of targets and the reward for achievement/punishment for non-achievement of targets

With a large number of performance dimensions to monitor, it is likely that on occasions some will be achieved while others are not. Each organization will need to identify the importance of non-achievement in specific areas of performance. Otley (1999) also argues that organizations need to consider how achievement on some performance measures and non-achievement on others will impact on the reward and punishment system.

Information on how the above should be achieved is not made clear in the framework introduced by Kaplan and Norton.

The information flows that are necessary in order that feedback/feedforward control can operate effectively

Actual information on the 25 or so key variables should be shown with comparison provided against target. Explicit guidance on how management should react to this information is again not given.

Otley (1999), Norreklit (2000) highlight a concern that the top-down nature of the control process will lead to managers always focusing actions on improving areas of performance that are measured by the Balanced Scorecard. In a dynamic environment, rather than conforming to the existing strategy, a rapid review of the strategy may be needed in order to respond to competitor action. This is likely to require fast decisions taken by local managers, with strategy evolving in an unstructured rather than a structured manner. Dealing with 'emergent' strategies is considered further, later in the chapter.

Performance measurement and the service sector

Measurement systems such as the Balanced Scorecard can be used for both the manufacturing and service sectors, including the public sector.

Fitzgerald *et al.* (1991) developed an alternative framework for the service sector, which also identified a need to measure both results – i.e. the objectives of the organization and the means or determinants for achieving those results.

They suggested that results measures relate to two dimensions, those of financial performance (e.g. profitability, liquidity, market ratios) and competitiveness (e.g. market share, sales growth).

Identifying the determinants or means of achieving results can be difficult in the service industry. Fitzgerald *et al.* suggested they could, however, be categorized under four main areas:

(i) *Quality of the service.* This may involve a range of attributes such as reliability, comfort, courtesy and friendliness. Services are intangible and it may be difficult to clearly identify the attribute that provides competitive advantage, accordingly a number of measures of performance might be collected.

(ii) *Flexibility.* This may be a flexibility to deal with changing workloads, delivery speeds and specifications.

(iii) *Resource utilization.* A service cannot be stored, for example a restaurant may be half empty during an evening or an airplane may fly with few passengers. Productivity and efficiency measures such as occupancy percentages would be useful for such organizations.

(iv) *Innovation.* Innovation can be as important for the service sector as the manufacturing sector.

In the service sector, measures of satisfaction after the service frequently include surveys of customers and letters of complaint. Measures of satisfaction during the service can include mystery shoppers or unannounced visits by the managers.

Strategy implementation and control

Simons (1995) has argued that a performance management system, such as the Balanced Scorecard, is insufficient in isolation for strategy implementation and control. He refers to the need for **'levers of control'**, which consist of a set of control systems used by managers to implement intended and emergent strategies. He considers the Balanced Scorecard to be an example of a **'diagnostic' control system**, which he defines as a performance measurement system that measures the critical performance variables required for achievement of the intended strategies. Simons has recommended that a strategy review process should also consist of a further three 'levers' of control, which he called boundary, belief and interactive systems.

The role of the four 'levers of control' in the strategy implementation process is illustrated in Figure 20.7.

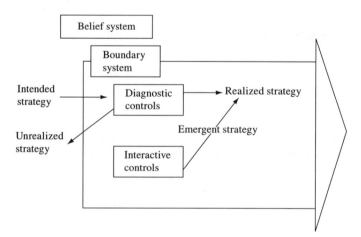

Figure 20.7 The strategy review process
Source: Adapted from Simons (1995).

Diagnostic and boundary controls are both in place to constrain behaviour in line with the intended strategy and to allocate scarce resources required in order to achieve these intended strategies.

Boundary system

Boundary controls form a second lever of control and will help managers identify the specific actions and behaviours that are *off-limits*.

(i) Ethics, corporate social responsibility and corporate governance. Managers often face intense pressure to achieve high results and may also be motivated to take risks. The role of business ethics, the organization's view of corporate social responsibility and corporate governance can all act to ensure that risk-taking takes place within acceptable parameters. Contravening laws and acting in unethical ways, for example, are unacceptable practices that should not be followed and managers should recognize the boundaries of behaviour that are acceptable.

(ii) Internal controls (discussed in Chapter 19).

Belief systems and interactive control systems are in place to motivate staff to search creatively for opportunities.

Belief systems

In Chapters 13 and 19, the importance of cultural control has been discussed. The culture in existence will have a significant impact on the objectives and strategies set and the operation of control systems. A number of organizations have seen organizational culture 'change' as necessary if organizational goals are to be achieved and strategies are to be successfully implemented. Simons refers to the need to ensure that employees engage in the right type of activities and stresses the importance of managers inspiring commitment to a clear set of core values. **Belief systems** are the explicit set of organizational definitions that senior managers should communicate formally and reinforce systematically to provide the core values of the organization, i.e. the basic values, purposes and direction for the organization.

Interactive controls

In Chapter 13 it was noted that realized strategies are not always the result of a *planned* and rational process in which events unfold in a logical and ordered manner. Environmental change can occur rapidly and opportunities or threats may result that require employees to respond rapidly to these changes. Strategies that arise as a result of the spontaneous reaction of employees are called *emergent* strategies. A view of strategy formulation in which employees play a key role requires a further consideration of the constraints and guidance that should be provided to employees to ensure that action and strategies followed are in line with organizational goals.

Interactive controls are different from diagnostic control systems and focus on the identification of the emerging threats and opportunities that could invalidate the assumptions upon which the current business strategy is based. They are the particular controls that senior management focus on and use in ongoing (often face-to-face) dialogue with subordinates.

Activity 20.5

What are the differences between diagnostic and interactive controls?

Figure 20.8 identifies different potential strategic uncertainties and the appropriate response for the interactive control system depending on whether the uncertainty is high or low.

Strategic uncertainty	If uncertainty is high then interactive control system	If uncertainty is low then interactive control system
Technological dependence (Example 1)	Focuses on emerging new technologies	Focuses on changing customer needs
Regulation and market protection (Example 2)	Focuses on socio-political threats and opportunities	Focuses on competitive threats and opportunities
Value chain complexity (Example 3)	Uses accounting-based measures	Uses input/output measures
Ease of tactical response (Example 4)	Has a short-term planning horizon	Has a long-range planning horizon

Figure 20.8   Strategic uncertainties and the response of organization systems
Source: Adapted from Simons (1995).

Example 1.   The aircraft manufacturing industry is dependent on a particular technology and so close monitoring of new technological developments is required. In contrast, for fashion goods, technological uncertainty is low and the key strategic uncertainty is the changing demands of consumers.

Example 2.   The airline industry was, until recent years, highly regulated, which limited the opportunities for new low-cost airlines to enter the market. Regulation throughout the world has been significantly reduced and so the focus of attention has moved from a concern with socio-political threats and opportunities to a concern with competitive threats and opportunities.

Example 3.   High-technology consumer goods will require complex interaction between research and development, production, distribution and marketing activities. Simons argues that in a complex value chain, interactive profit-planning systems can be used to measure trade-offs in a business (for example, transfers between different parts of the value chain can be priced using a transfer pricing system). In a relatively stable and well-understood value chain, simple input/output measures can be used such as brand volume and market share. The need for different approaches to control given varying degrees of complexity will be discussed further in Chapter 23.

Example 4. Where a competitor's tactics can easily be copied, the planning time horizons are short and tactical responsiveness is the key to competitive success. The focus of attention and debate between senior and subordinates will be on the consideration of response to and from competitor action. Where competitive action has to be lengthy due to technological or market constraints, the extent to which competitor action requires constant review is reduced.

Activity 20.6

Your company is a security company that currently offers a limited range of security services to the prison service. These include transporting prisoners from prison to court and back again to prison. What type of interactive controls might be appropriate for this company?

Summary

The chapter has considered the implications of strategy upon the control system.

The Balanced Scorecard is an example of a 'diagnostic' control system. It recommends the measurement of approximately 25 measures across four perspectives – financial, customer, internal business process, and learning and growth.

The Balanced Scorecard has been adopted by many companies internationally and appears to meet a number of the criteria necessary for a performance management system. A number of potential strengths and weaknesses have also been identified.

Simons (1995) provides a framework that suggests that four integrated control systems are required in order to implement strategy. These he calls diagnostic control systems, interactive control systems, belief systems and boundary systems.

Diagnostic control systems involve the monitoring of critical performance variables to identify whether the existing strategy is being achieved.

Boundary controls will help managers identify the specific actions and behaviours that are off-limits.

Interactive control systems are the particular controls that senior management focus on and use in an ongoing dialogue with subordinates. The key concern is with the key strategic uncertainties that could invalidate the assumptions upon which the current business strategy is based. Uncertainties include technological or regulatory and market protection uncertainty, value chain complexity and the ease with which it is possible for an organization to make a tactical response. Emergent strategies are likely to arise from this debate, in response to change in competitive dynamics and internal competencies.

Belief systems are the explicit set of organizational definitions that senior managers communicate formally and reinforce systematically to provide the core values of the organization, i.e. the basic values, purposes and direction for the organization.

Further reading

Bhimani, A. and Langfield-Smith, K. (2007) structure, formality and the importance of financial and non-financial information in strategy development and implementation *Management Accounting Research* **18** (1): 3–31.

Kaplan, R.S. and Norton, D.P. (1996) *The Balanced Scorecard: Translating strategy into action.* Harvard Business School Press, Boston.

Kaplan, R.S. and Norton, D.P. (2004) *Strategy Maps: Converting intangible assets into tangible outcomes.* Harvard Business School Press, Boston.

Otley, D. (1999) 'Performance Management: a framework for management control system research', *Management Accounting Research* 10: 363–382.

Simons, R. (2000) *Performance Measurement and Control Systems for Implementing Strategy. Text and Cases.* Prentice Hall, Upper Saddle River, NJ.

Answers to activities

Activity 20.1

A product or service attribute is a 'tangible' feature of the product or service such as the price, quality or on-time delivery. Customer relationship is more service-oriented and concerned with the relationship with customers and suppliers, for example, how the customer feels about purchasing from the company.

Activity 20.2

It was noted in Chapter 16 that some organizations have attempted to quantify such factors in terms of the premium price that can be earned by the brand or the market share. If it is impossible to provide a quantitative measure of such a benefit, then it may be possible for it to be described.

Activity 20.3

It may depend on the organization. For a commercial organization, the financial results could be argued to be the overriding objective of the organization. The learning and growth perspective is concerned with measuring and managing key skills and resources that are concerned with the longer-term success of the organization.

Activity 20.4

The causal link between the various performance dimensions may be questioned. Weaknesses are discussed further later in the chapter.

Activity 20.5

Diagnostic control systems are a tool for transforming intended strategies into realized strategies. They measure outcomes with preset plans and performance goals.

Interactive control systems focus on strategic uncertainties and involve face-to-face discussions between senior and subordinate managers. From debate and dialogue about the key strategic uncertainties, new business strategies may emerge.

Activity 20.6

The strategic uncertainties suggested by Simons cover technology, complexity of the value chain, each of tactical response and regulation, and market protection. The key strategic uncertainty for a business providing private security services is likely to be related to regulation and market protection. At present, a number of services traditionally performed by staff of the prison service are being put out to tender with private companies. There is a great deal of resistance to this change from trade unions and other sources, who will be interested in identifying and publicizing failures on the part of private contractors. Private contractors would therefore be particularly concerned with socio-political threats and opportunities. As particular services are increasingly contracted out to private-sector organizations, the interactive control system will increasingly focus on competitive threats and opportunities.

Exercises

Q20.1 Is an interactive control system or a diagnostic control system better for ensuring that management maintain control in an organization?

Q20.2 Why would organizations wish to implement a system like the Balanced Scorecard?

Q20.3 Is it inevitable that improvements in organizational performance will result from the introduction of a Balanced Scorecard?

Q20.4 Why might different types of financial objectives, e.g. sales growth, return on capital employed, be relevant for different organizations?

Q20.5 Your company is an agricultural merchant that provides a number of standard products such as seed and fertilizer to the farming industry. There are many competitors and price competition is severe. Discuss the type of strategy that might be followed by your company if it is to be successful in this industry, and what are the implications in terms of the information that should be provided by the management accounting system?

Q20.6 Ellemore consultants used a Balanced Scorecard to help in the assessment of its performance. The following information has been produced for the last two years:

Financial perspective	Current year	Previous year
Revenue	£1,950,000	£1,850,000
Net profit	£450,000	£380,000

Customer perspective	Current year	Previous year
Number of clients	202	225
Repeat customer percentage	15%	35%
Average customer satisfaction measure*	4.2	6.7

Internal business perspective	Current year	Previous year
Tender success rate	14%	32%
New services	1	5

Learning and growth perspective	Current year	Previous year
Employee turnover – managers	80%	25%
– staff	30%	20%
Employee satisfaction*	3	4
Skill rating*	40%	75%

* Higher measures are better.

Required:

Using the information available, assess the performance of the business and its future prospects.

Q20.7 Hilcrest PLC owns and manages a chain of international airport hotels. A new CEO has been appointed, who has immediately conducted a review of the business with a view to developing a new strategy. The hotels had been aspiring to the luxury end of the market but had suffered chronic under-investment, with the result that infrastructure, service and reputation had all become poorer than those of immediate competitors. The CEO has authorized the raising of further funds and is aiming to restore earnings and the share price to their previous levels, following a strategy of:

1. Restoring the existing hotels to the luxury end of the market.
2. Investing in training and computer systems.

Required:

 (i) Design a Balanced Scorecard for the organization. Explain your assumptions.
(ii) Apply the framework of Simons (levers of control) to the organization. What would be appropriate diagnostic and interactive control systems, belief and boundary systems?

Q20.8 *This question can be undertaken for any of the case scenarios Siegmund Ltd, Coopers retail outlets or Dundee Bicycle Division.* Drawing on the information in each respective case:

(a) Design a Balanced Scorecard for the organization. Explain your assumptions.
(b) Apply the framework of Simons (levers of control) to the organization. What would be appropriate diagnostic and interactive control systems, belief and boundary systems?

Q20.9 Design an appropriate performance management system for Sunshine Sites, discussed in the case scenario of Coopers Leisure Resorts Ltd.

MEASURING SHAREHOLDER VALUE

Objectives

At the end of the chapter you should be able to:

- Explain the advantages and disadvantages of alternative measures of income, economic value and shareholder wealth, including:

  - Residual income.
  - Economic value added.
  - Cash flow models and shareholder value analysis.
  - Market value added.
  - Measurement of intellectual capital using non-financial measures.

Introduction

Traditional economic theory assumes that profit maximization and therefore increase in shareholder wealth is the goal of the firm. The deficiencies of short-term profit and return on capital employed as measures of an increase in shareholder wealth were discussed in Chapter 10 and alternative approaches are considered in this chapter.

In the first section, the measure of residual income is revisited. A number of criticisms have been made of residual income, in particular the fact that it is a single-period model and is drawn up using accounting statements based on Generally Accepted Accounting Principles (GAAP). **Economic value added (EVA®)**, a refinement of the residual income model, is explained.

A second popular approach considered is shareholder value analysis. This method is based on the principle of identifying future cash flows and discounting those cash flows to identify a present valuation of the business.

A third approach is based on the identification of the market value added. This compares the market valuation of the equity and debt of a business to the book value that has been identified in the Balance Sheet.

Finally, the measurement of intangible assets is considered. Intangible assets include the skills of employees, patents, brand names and the value of internal structures such as

IT systems. The value of these internally generated 'assets' is not included in the Balance Sheet and is a key reason that the market value of most organizations is different from the book value as indicated in the Balance Sheet. A number of companies are paying attention to – and attempting to measure – these intangible assets, even if a value is not attached in accounting statements. One approach is considered in the final section of the chapter.

Potential problems of residual income

In Chapter 10 the apparent advantage of the residual income method, compared with the ROI method, was discussed. Despite this, relatively few organizations in the latter part of the 20th century changed the measurement system from return on investment to residual income. A key reason is that despite its disadvantages, ROI provides an easy method for comparing divisions and companies. As demonstrated in Chapter 11, it is possible to also use a range of ratios to compare performance on a range of areas of performance. There are also two potential deficiencies with residual income:

1. It is a 'single-period model', i.e. only the performance of the current year is measured. If a key purpose is to measure management performance and its impact on shareholders' wealth, then it is ideally necessary to consider the impact of decisions over future periods in order to gain a more valid assessment of performance in the current year. The residual income generated by an organization or division in one year may not provide a true indication of performance or future wealth. Managers may indeed be able to improve current performance at the expense of future years.
2. As with the return on investment measure, residual income incorporates information drawn from the financial statements, the Profit and Loss Account and the Balance Sheet. These statements are prepared using 'Generally Accepted Accounting Principles' (GAAP) and at the heart of these guidelines there are a number of accounting concepts. One of these concepts requires accountants to be **prudent**, which means that assets and income shall not be overstated and liabilities and charges shall not be understated. Some argue that this can lead to the profit figure stated in the Profit and Loss Account being a conservative estimate of the true 'economic profit' earned by a business in a year. The Balance Sheet may also provide a conservative view of the value of a business. For example, the market value of Dell computers was nearly 15 times greater than its published book value at the end of 2005. One reason for these large differences is that much of the value of many modern organizations is in the form of intellectual capital such as patents and trademarks and in the skills of the employees of the organization. Some expenditure, such as marketing and basic research, *may* have a benefit over a number of years. However, because it is difficult to objectively verify that future benefits will take place, applying the prudence concept, accepted accounting practice is to treat such costs as an expense in the current year.

Although there are sound reasons for taking a prudent view, an unfortunate effect may be to discourage managers from undertaking such expenditure, particularly if the performance measurement system places a significant emphasis on current year profit performance.

Activity 21.1

Division M expects to generate a profit of £500,000 in the year and the current capital employed is £2,000,000. The division is considering expenditure of £300,000 on research related to nanotechnology. Because this is basic research, this must be treated as an expense to be written off against current profits. The weighted average cost of capital of the division is 15%.

Required:

(i) Calculate the expected return on investment of the division given:

    (a) The additional expenditure on research does not occur.
    (b) The additional expenditure does occur.

(ii) Calculate the expected residual income given:

    (a) The additional expenditure on research does not occur.
    (b) The additional expenditure does occur.

Note: Net residual income = operating profit – interest charge for using the capital invested in the organization.

    The methods of calculating return on investment and residual income were covered in Chapter 10.

Note that GAAP does permit the treatment of some expenditure as capital, to be amortized/depreciated over a number of years. As well as physical assets such as plant and equipment, goodwill and some development expenditure, where the recovery of costs can reasonably be regarded as assured, can also be treated as capital. The treatment of goodwill and expenditure on research and development is discussed further in the Appendix at the end of this chapter.

Economic value added

In the early 1990s, an approach called economic value added (EVA®) gained increased popularity. EVA® was promoted by the consultancy group Stern Stewart. EVA® is similar to residual income, in that a charge for cost of capital is deducted from divisional profit and can be calculated using the following formula:

$$EVA^® = NOPAT - (R \times C)$$

where:
NOPAT = net operating profit after tax
R = required returns of investors
C = capital invested

A number of further initiatives have been recommended in order to address the problems caused by the use of GAAP to prepare accounting statements and the use of single-period residual income to measure and reward performance.

Adjustments to GAAP

Stern Stewart advocates the capitalization of all intangible investments in such things as goodwill, research and development and marketing. Approximately 120 potential adjustments to GAAP are identified by Stern Stewart, although they report that typically only 10 or so adjustments might be needed. As indicated above, a key driver for making these adjustments is that accounting statements are based on prudent principles and this distorts management behaviour away from what is good for the shareholders. Divisional or company managers, who are particularly concerned about the profit or residual income of the current year, are reluctant to undertake a decision where all the costs are written off in the current year, while benefits come in subsequent years. The goal of the adjustments is therefore to produce a Balance Sheet that reflects the economic value of the organization's assets more accurately and an income statement that provides a fairer reflection of economic income. An example is shown in Figure 21.1 to illustrate the principle.

Company A currently earns operating profits in the year of £1,200,000, corporation tax is £200,000 and net capital employed is £4,000,000. The company has run a marketing campaign costing £200,000 and the management of the company believe that the benefit from this campaign will take place over two years.

Generally accepted accounting principles would indicate that marketing expenses are treated as a period cost, i.e. charged to the year in which the expenditure took place. Using EVA®, the argument could be made that since the benefit accrues over two years, the cost should also be capitalized over two years. The impact on the company's net operating profit after tax (NOPAT) in the year and the Balance Sheet valuation of the business is shown below:

	£'000
Operating profit	1,200
Less corporation tax	200
	1,000
EVA® adjustment:	
Marketing costs	100
Adjusted NOPAT	1,100
Net capital employed from Balance Sheet	4,000
Add:	
Marketing costs	100
Adjusted net capital employed	4,100

Figure 21.1 Adjusting net operating profit and net capital employed required for the calculation of EVA®

From this it can be seen that company profit has risen by £100,000 as only half the £200,000 cost of advertising has been written off as an expense. The remaining £100,000 has been capitalized and is shown as an asset on the Balance Sheet, thus increasing the book value of the business. The impact of the marketing expenditure is spread over the two years in which it is claimed the benefits are received. It is argued that this change will reduce the incentive to company management to avoid such expenditure because of its impact on single years.

Figure 21.1 (Continued)

Activity 21.2

Given the information in Figure 21.1, calculate the EVA® of company A, given a cost of capital of 10%.

Activity 21.3

Consider the example in Activity 21.1. The management feel that the benefit from the research will last four years and therefore feel that only part of the expense should be actually charged to the profit account in the period, with the balance capitalized and shown in the Balance Sheet.
     Calculate a revised EVA® for year 1 of the investment.

The fact that, given the adjustments to the accounts, the book value of the business will now be closer to its economic value is seen by Stern Stewart as only an incidental benefit of the method. The main reason is to avoid penalizing managers who invest resources for the future.

Changes to the bonus system

A second initiative advised by Stern Stewart is a change to conventional bonus systems. With conventional schemes it may be possible to maximize the manager's bonus by achieving short-term results, which may come at the expense of results in subsequent years. Stern Stewart recommends that bonus awards should be passed through a bonus bank before being paid out. Part of the bonus bank can be paid out in the form of a bonus in the year; however, the balance of the bank should be carried on to subsequent years. If in subsequent years results are good, then a further bonus can be paid out. However, if the results are poor, much of the bonus bank will be eliminated before it is paid out.

Strengths of EVA®

It is argued by Stern Stewart that the adjustments made to residual income mean that the delivery of an increased EVA® is now congruent with the objective of maximizing shareholder value.

EVA® has also overcome some of the problems of traditional reward systems, by ensuring that a full bonus is only achieved if performance is maintained into the future.

Potential problems associated with the EVA® measure

EVA® is a single performance measure and arguably, as such, remains an incomplete measure:

1. It measures past not future performance. Until the EVA® of future earnings can be measured, EVA® does not truly measure the economic value added by current decisions.
2. It is arguable whether, even with the adjustments, EVA® provides a reliable measure of financial performance. Deciding what items should be capitalized and by what method is subjective, and O'Hanlon and Peasnell (1998) highlight the ad hoc character of the adjustments that are made. There is limited empirical data to support the view that the EVA® method of accounting provides a superior measure of economic performance.
3. It is a single measure of performance and does not measure the means of achieving the objectives of the organization. This allows subordinates a great deal of discretion over their operating activities, which potentially could mean actions that are at the expense of the longer term. (This is not necessarily a problem, however, if EVA® is used in conjunction with other techniques, such as the Balanced Scorecard.)

Cash flow models

A key criticism of the methods discussed to date is that they do not attempt to measure future cash flows.

In Chapter 4, the discounted cash flow technique was introduced. With this technique, the future cash flows of an investment are calculated and these cash flows then discounted at the company's cost of capital. An investment is worthwhile if it generates a positive net present value. One approach that has applied this concept to the whole organization is 'shareholder value analysis', which was proposed by Rappaport (1986). This is concerned with analysing how decisions affect the net present value of cash to shareholders.

Shareholder value analysis

Rappaport (1988) departed from methods based on accounting statements and has recommended **Shareholder value analysis (SVA)** as a process of analysing how decisions affect the net present value of cash to shareholders.

He identified three sets of management decisions: operational, investment and financing, which he argued are the key drivers of shareholder value. Using his approach, two stages can be considered:

1. Identify the free cash flows that are generated from operations. These cash flows are affected by *operational* and *investment* decisions.
2. Calculate shareholder value by discounting the free cash flows calculated in step 1 at the weighted average cost of capital. This will identify the net present value of the cash flows and from this deduct the value of any debt. The cost of capital and value of debt are influenced by *financing* decisions.

Calculating the free cash flows from operations and investments

Free cash flow (FCF) represents the cash that a company is able to generate after deducting cash payments for tax and investments in working capital and non-current assets. This can be calculated as shown in Figure 21.2.

Cash flows from operational decisions	Net profit
	+ Amortization/depreciation
	= Operating cash flows
	− Cash tax
	= Operating cash flows after tax
Cash flows from investment decisions	+/− Changes in working capital
	+/− Changes in non-current assets
	= Free cash flows

Figure 21.2   Calculating free cash flows

Cash flow from operational decisions

In order to calculate the 'free cash flows' that will result from operational management decisions over future years, a number of key value drivers should be identified:

1. Expected operating cash flows (earnings before interest, tax and depreciation) for the coming years. Existing margins and the impact of new operational strategies should be taken into consideration.
2. The tax rate that will be expected for the coming years, in order that profit after tax can be calculated.
3. The expected sales growth (if any).
4. The period of time over which sales growth will occur (value growth duration).

Cash flows of investment decisions

If sales growth is taking place then it is likely that there will also be increases in fixed capital and working capital investment.

The cash flows that result from operational and investment decisions are illustrated in Figure 21.3.

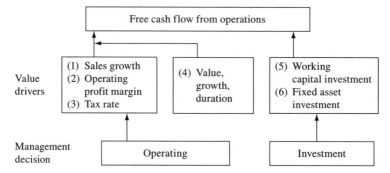

Figure 21.3   Identifying free cash flows
Source: Adapted from *Creating Shareholder Value: A Guide for Managers and Investors*, revised and updated by Rappaport, A. © 1986, 1998 by Alfred Rappaport. All rights reserved. Adapted with the permission of the Free Press, a Division of Simon and Schuster Adult Publishing Group.

In Figure 21.4 a worked example calculating the operating (free) cash flows is shown for Appleyard PLC.

The management of Appleyard PLC wish to calculate the operating/free cash flows for the foreseeable future:

1. Sales for the coming year are expected to be £5,000,000 and it is planned that these will grow at 10% over the following four years. After five years, information is limited and it is assumed that sales will continue at the year 5 level for all future years (in perpetuity).
2. Expected operating cash flows for the coming year are £1,000,000, which is 20% of sales. This operating margin is expected to continue at this level into the future.
3. The tax rate is currently 30% and it is expected that this will continue at this level.
4. Additional investment in fixed assets is expected to be £500,000 a year for the next five years. After five years' investment there will be no additional new investment.
5. Additional investment in working capital is expected to be £300,000 a year for the next five years.

Required:

Calculate the expected free cash flows of Appleyard PLC.

Answer:

Year	1	2	3	4	5	6 onwards
	£'000	£'000	£'000	£'000	£'000	£'000
Sales	5,000	5500	6050	6655	7320.5	7320.5
Operating cash flows (note 1)	1000	1100	1210	1331	1464.1	1464.1
Tax (30%)	−300	−330	−363	−399.3	−439.23	−439.23
Operating profit						
After tax	700	770	847	931.7	1024.87	1024.87

Figure 21.4   Calculating free cash flows

Fixed capital investment	−500	−500	−500	−500	−500	
Working capital investment	−300	−300	−300	−300	−300	
Free cash flows (note 2)	−100	−30	47	131.7	224.87	1024.87

Note 1. In identifying cash flows, non-cash expenditure, such as depreciation, has been added back to the operating profit margin.
Note 2. At year 6 it is assumed that the business operates in a steady state. Sales continue at the level of year 5. With no growth, no additional investment in new fixed assets or working capital is expected.

Figure 21.4 *(Continued)*

Calculating shareholder value

Having identified the free cash flows, the next step is to calculate theshareholder value. To do this it is necessary to:

1. Discount the free cash flows at the company discount rate to calculate the net present value of the cash flows. The discount rate will depend on the company cost of capital, which will in turn be affected by the financing decision. See Chapter 12 for an explanation of how to calculate the weighted average cost of capital.
2. Deduct the value of debt from the calculated net present value.

The steps required for the calculation of shareholder value are shown in Figure 21.5.

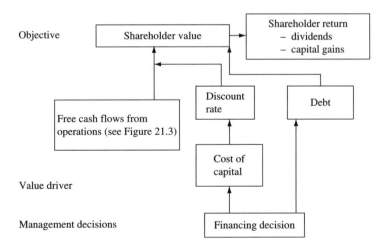

Figure 21.5   Identifying shareholder value

The free cash flows for Appleyard PLC were identified in Figure 21.4. The calculation of the shareholder value for Appleyard PLC is shown in Figure 21.6.

The weighted average cost of capital of Appleyard PLC is 12%.
The value of its debt is £900,000.
The first step is to calculate the net present value of the free cash flows identified in Figure 21.4.

Year	1 £'000	2 £'000	3 £'000	4 £'000	5 £'000	6 onwards £'000
Free cash flows	−100	−30	47	131.7	224.87	1024.87

For year 6 onwards the free cash inflow is calculated at £1,024,870 in perpetuity. To calculate the present value of these steady state cash flows it is necessary to divide the annual cash flow by the cost of capital of:

$$12\% = \frac{£1,024,870}{0.12} = £8,540,583$$

The cash inflows of £1,024,870 in perpetuity from the end of year 6 onwards is equivalent to a single cash payment of £8,540,583 at the beginning of year 6 (i.e. end of year 5).
These future cash flows now need to be discounted at the weighted average cost of capital.

Year	1	2	3	4	5	5	NPV
Free cash flows £'000	−100	−30	47	131.7	224.87	8,540.58	
Discount factor (12%)	0.8929	0.7972	0.7118	0.6355	0.5674	0.5674	
Present value £'000	−89.3	−23.9	33.5	83.7	127.6	4846.2	4977.7

Net present value of future cash flows is £4,977,700

Shareholder value is after deducting the value of the debt from the net present value of future cash flows = £4,977,700–£900,000 = £4,017,700.

Figure 21.6 Identifying shareholder value

Activity 21.4

Referring to Figure 21.4, calculate the shareholder value if the sales growth after year 1 was only 5% per annum, while the other assumptions remain the same.

Strengths of shareholder value analysis

The model has the advantage that it is relatively simple to use and highlights the key decision areas that will have the greatest impact on shareholder value. These are:

- Sales revenue growth.
- Operating margin growth.
- Cash tax rate.
- Working capital.
- Expenditure on non-current assets.
- Weighted average cost of capital.

By using the model, managers are guided to consider the impact of operational, investment or financing decisions on the key value drivers. Decisions that may have a favourable effect on one value driver may have adverse consequences on others, leading to an overall decline in shareholder value. Some examples of potential interrelationships between value drivers, given different generic strategies, are provided below:

(a) Cost leadership

- A drive might be made for sales growth; however, the beneficial effect is more than offset by the reduced operating margins that are required for this to be achieved.
- Tight controls are implemented on inventory levels, but this has an adverse impact on customer service and leads to lower sales growth.
- A decision may be made to invest in new equipment that will provide economies of scale at high volumes. The benefit may be offset by additional expenditure on non-current assets and an increased investment risk having an impact on the cost of capital.

(b) Product differentiation

- A company may decide to diversify its product range and introduce new product features. An assessment of the increase in funding required for working capital and non-current assets plus the impact of risk on the cost of capital may mean that this is not acceptable.
- More favourable credit terms might be offered to increase sales; however, this has an adverse impact on the level of accounts receivable.

The model may also help highlight decisions that may be appropriate given one generic strategy, such as cost leadership, but may not be suitable if the organization is following another, e.g. product differentiation.

For performance measurement purposes it is possible to identify operational value drivers that will underpin the main drivers. For example, unit volume, sales price, overhead cost analysis at business unit level can all help identify trends at lower levels that will have an impact on the main value drivers of the organization as a whole. Rappaport also suggests the assessment of management performance by comparing expected versus actual SVA.

Potential problems of shareholder value analysis

A key disadvantage is the subjectivity of the analysis. If assumptions underpinning any of the key variables are incorrect then the use of shareholder value analysis for valuation purposes will be inaccurate.

A range of other cash flow models have been promoted by different consultancies. These include price–cash flow (PCF) and enterprise value–cash flow (EVCF) ratios, cash recovery rates (CRR) and cash flow return on investment (CFROI). No one model appears to have achieved universal acceptance as a 'best approach' for either valuation or performance measurement purposes.

Market value added

Another method used for evaluating the performance of the management of a company is based on market value added:

Market value added = Current market value of shares and debt − (total capital raised + retained earnings)

To evaluate the performance of the management of a company it is possible to consider the change in market value added over the years. If the market value added in one year is £500,000 and in the next year it is £700,000, then it can be argued that this reflects good management action and management should be rewarded on the basis of this performance

The example of Bramble Ltd is considered in Figure 21.7.

Reference can be made to the Balance Sheet of Bramble Ltd in Chapter 11.

From the Balance Sheet as at 31 March 2008:

	£
Issued share capital	1,000,000
Retained profits	412,000
Loan capital	100,000
Invested capital	1,512,000

Market value
Assume the following information:

1. That the current market price per share of Bramble Ltd as at the end of March 2008 is £2.10 per share. The market value of the shares of Bramble Ltd can be calculated, based on the market price per share multiplied by the number of shares as £2.10 multiplied by 1,000,000 = £2,100,000.
2. The nominal value of the debt is £100,000, but the actual market value of the debt is £90,000. Therefore:
3. Current market value of shares and debt = £2,100,000 + £90,000 = £2,190,000.

Market value added
$$£2,190,000 - £1,512,000 = £678,000.$$

Figure 21.7   Market value added

Activity 21.5

Refer to the information in Figure 21.7. Assume that as at the end of March 2009:

1. The market price per share of Bramble Ltd has risen to £2.20.
2. The market value of the debt is £980,000.

From the Balance Sheet as at 31 March 2009:

	£
Issued share capital	1,000,000
Retained earnings	482,000
Loan capital	1,000,000
Invested capital	2,482,000

Calculate the market value added at the end of the year and therefore the change in market value added since the end of 2007/8.

Activity 21.6

To what extent do you consider that an increase in market value added will reflect good management action? What other causes might there be for an increase in the value?

A key drawback of market value added is that share price can reflect other influences apart from management actions. Environmental changes such as economic change can affect the whole or particular market sectors. Market value added gained popularity when share prices were rising, particularly with managers who might have bonuses paid based on increases in market value added. However, during periods of falling stock markets, the measure may be less popular, particularly with managers!

Intangible assets

As discussed earlier, the Balance Sheet may bear little relationship to the market value of many organizations and one reason for this is that much of the value of many modern organizations is in the form of intangible assets. An **intangible asset** is an 'identifiable non-monetary asset without physical substance'. Examples can include brands, patents, copyrights, computer software, customer lists, customer and supplier relationships and marketing rights.

To overcome this problem, approaches such as EVA® have recommended that a number of adjustments be made to accounting statements. Expenditure on areas such as marketing or research and development can be written off over a period of time to reflect the period of time over which the benefit of the expenditure is experienced. However, many potential adjustments can be hard to objectively justify. Further, where money is spent on training staff, although the purpose is to generate future profits through increasing the competence of staff, this cash is being spent on 'assets' that the company does not own.

Alternative approaches such as shareholder value analysis aim to identify the future cash flows that will be generated by all assets, however the identification of future cash flows is very subjective.

Rather than attempting to quantify intangible assets into a common denominator expressed in money terms, an alternative approach is to develop a system of non-financial measurement. A purpose is to gain a judgement as to whether the business performance in terms of these assets is improving or getting worse. Sveiby (1997) has proposed that as well as monitoring the performance of tangible assets, performance in three categories of intangible assets should also be identified:

(i) *External structure*. This consists of relationships with customers and suppliers, brand names, trademarks and reputation or 'image'. A good relationship with customers is a source of value as they can spread the word and improve the image of the company. Their demands encourage the development of new products and contacts with customers provide further training and development for staff.

(ii) *Internal structure*. This includes the capital incorporated into the organizational structure, such as the investment in IT systems and administrative systems and also includes patents. These have been created by the employees of the organization and are therefore generally 'owned' by it. The internal structure is in effect the key structure of the organization.

(iii) *Competence*. This is also often called human capital and incorporates the knowledge and capabilities of the employees of the organization, their experience, level of training and education.

An 'Intangible Assets Monitor' (IAM) can be developed as a method for measuring intangible assets. This involves the presentation of a number of relevant indicators for measuring intangible assets collected in four categories of growth, innovation, efficiency and stability. The idea is to gain an insight into how the intangible assets are developing, 'by designing indicators that correlate with: the *growth* of the asset in question, its renewal pace (*innovation*), how efficient we are at utilizing it (*efficiency*), and the risk that it ceases to exist (*stability*)'. See Figure 21.8.

Examples of possible measures of the three forms of intangible assets are shown in Figure 21.9.

Celemi, a Swedish-based company, has published an audit of its intangible assets since 1995, based on the model of Sveiby. The purpose is to inform the shareholders of the assets that Celemi possesses and to advise them whether the intangibles are growing or being used efficiently.

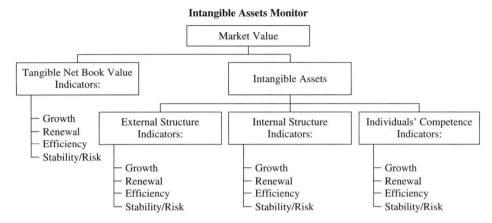

Figure 21.8   Intangible Assets Monitor
Source: http://www.sveiby.com. Printed with permission.

There are some similarities between the measurement of intellectual capital and performance measurement and management systems, such as the Balanced Scorecard. With the Balanced Scorecard, however, the objectives and measures are derived from an

External structure	
Growth	The increase in the number of customers or in sales value due to organic growth. (Note that any increase in sales value due to the acquisition of other companies should be excluded.)
Renewal	The volume of sales to high image customers or sales to new markets.
Efficiency	Profitability per customer or sales per customer.
Stability/risk	Satisfied customers index; proportion of big customers; length of time as a customer; frequency of repeat orders.
Internal structure	
Growth	The level of investment in the internal structure and investment in information processing systems. These can be measured in absolute terms or as a proportion of sales or value added.
Renewal	The proportion of assignments devoted to customers that improve the internal structure of the company or the number of new processes implemented.
Efficiency	The proportion of support staff.
Stability/risk	Values and attitudes of staff (measured through surveys), age of the organization, support staff turnover, proportion of people with less than 2 years' employment.

Figure 21.9   Possible measures of intangible assets

Individuals' competence indicator	
Growth	The number of years that professionals in the organization have worked in their profession, the level of education of staff (and therefore the potential to achieve future success).
Renewal	The proportion of time spent with customers that contribute to competence developments, training and education costs.
Efficiency	The value added per employee or per professional.
Stability/risk	Analysis by age, seniority, employee turnover rate (broken down by category, e.g. professionals or administrative staff).

Figure 21.9 *(Continued)*

organization's vision and strategy. Sveiby argues that in a knowledge economy, people should not be regarded as costs, but rather as revenue creators. Human actions are converted into both tangible and intangible knowledge 'structures', which are directed outwards (external structures) and inwards (internal structures). For each of the three types of intangible assets, it is necessary to obtain indicators as to how they are developing, in terms of growth, innovation (renewal), efficiency and stability (risk of losing it).

Summary

This chapter has been particularly concerned with different approaches to measuring shareholder value.

Residual income had been identified in Chapter 10, as a possible alternative measure to return on capital employed. Potential problems, however, exist with residual income as it measures performance for the current accounting period only and also relies on accounting statements prepared according to GAAP. Critiques argue that this will lead to managers who are investing for the future being penalized.

Economic value added (EVA®) has developed from the residual income approach and involves two key innovations. Firstly, the requirement to conform to GAAP is removed for some major items of expenditure and secondly, the recommendation is made to change the incentive scheme to reward performance over the longer term. EVA® can still be criticized on the grounds that it measures performance in a single accounting period and the objectivity of the adjustment to the accounting information is open to question.

Shareholder value analysis aims to value the business based on the identification of future free cash flows. The approach can be helpful in highlighting the key decision areas that will have the greatest impact on shareholder value, though in identifying future cash flows there is inevitably a high degree of subjectivity.

Market value added = current market value of shares and debt − (total capital raised + retained earnings). It has been noted that this may be flawed as a measure of managerial performance because of the distorting impact of uncontrollable variables such as economic and other environmental changes.

The market value of many companies is substantially more than the book value, often because of the existence of intangible assets. Rather than attempting to provide a financial valuation for all intangible assets, an alternative approach has been taken by Sveiby, who recommends the use of performance measures as indicators of how these intangible assets are developing.

Further reading

Otley, D. (1999) 'Performance Management: a framework for management control system research', *Management Accounting Research* 10: 363–832.

Economic value added:

O'Hanlon, J. and Peasnell, K. (1998) 'Wall Streets contribution to management accounting: The Stern Steward EVA® financial management system', *Management Accounting Research* **9**: 421–444.
Stern, J. and Shelly, J. (2001) *The EVA Challenge*. John Wiley & Sons Inc., New York.

Shareholder value analysis:

Barker, R. (2001) *Determining Value: valuation models and financial statements*. FT/Prentice-Hall: Harlow, Essex.
Black, A., Wright, P. and Davies, J. (2001) *In Search of Shareholder Value Managing Performance Drivers*. Price-Waterhouse-Coopers.
Rappaport, A. (1988) *Creating Shareholder Value: A guide for managers and investors*. Free Press, New York.

Financial reporting and acounting standards:

Elliott, B. and Elliott, J. (2006) *Financial Accounting and Reporting*, 11th edn. Pearson Education, London.

Intangible assets:

Kaplan, R.S. and Norton, D.P. (2004) *Strategy Maps: Converting Intangible Assets into Tangible Outcomes*. Harvard Business School Publishing Corporation, Boston, MA.
Mouritsen, J. (2005) Intellectual capital and knowledge resources. In Berry, A., Broadbent, J. and Otley, D. (eds), *Management Control: theories, issues and performance*. Palgrave MacMillan, Basingstoke, pp. 205–229.
Sveiby, K.E. (1997) The New Organisational Wealth, Managing and Measuring Knowledge-Based Assets. Berrett-Koehler, San Francisco.

Answers to activities

Activity 21.1

(1a) Division M return on investment without the research expenditure:

$$\frac{£500,000}{£2,000,000} = 25\%$$

(1b) Division M return on investment with the research expenditure:

$$\frac{£200,000}{£2,000,000} = 10\%$$

(2a) Residual income without the expenditure:

	£
Divisional profit	500,000
Interest charge £2,000,000 × 15% =	300,000
	200,000

(2b) Residual income with the expenditure:

	£
Divisional profit	200,000
Interest charge £2,000,000 × 15% =	300,000
	(100,000)

Both ROI and the Residual Income measure will decline in the year given the investment.

Activity 21.2

	£'000
Adjusted NOPAT	1,100
Less interest charge on capital invested £4,100 @ 10%	410
EVA®	690

Activity 21.3

Revised profit:

The expenditure of £300,000 to be spent on research will be written off over 4 years = £75,000 per annum. The revised profit will therefore be £500,000 – £75,000 = £425,000.

Revised net capital employed:

At the end of year 1, if the expenditure of £300,000 is to be treated as capital expenditure to be amortized over four years, then following the amortization of £75,000, the closing Balance Sheet value of the research is £225,000.

The revised net capital employed will be £2,225,000.

$EVA^®$ will be:

	£
Divisional profit	425,000
Interest charge £2,225,000 × 15% =	337,500
$EVA^®$	87,500

Activity 21.4

Year	1	2	3	4	5	6 onwards
	£'000	£'000	£'000	£'000	£'000	£'000
Sales (note 1)	5000	5250	5512.5	5788.1	6077.5	6077.5
Operating profit	1000	1050	1102.5	1157.6	1215.5	1215.5
Tax	−300	−315	−330.8	−347.3	−364.7	−364.7
Operating profit After tax	700	735	771.8	810.3	850.9	850.9
Fixed capital investment	−500	−500	−500.0	−500.0	−500.0	
Working capital investment	−300	−300	−300.0	−300.0	−300.0	
Free cash flows	−100	−65	−28.3	10.3	50.9	850.9

The present value of the constant cash flows of £850,900 from year 6 onwards is £850,900/0.12 = £7,090,833.

This should be discounted at the discount rate for the end of year 5.

	1	2	3	4	5	5
	£'000	£'000	£'000	£'000	£'000	£'000
Free cash flows £'000	−100	−65.0	−28.3	10.3	50.9	7090.8
Discount factor (14%)	0.8929	0.7972	0.7118	0.6355	0.5674	0.5674
Present value £'000	−89.3	−51.8	−20.1	6.6	28.9	4023.5

Shareholder value after deduction of the value of the debt = £3,897,700 − £900,000 = £2,997,700.

Activity 21.5

Market value of Bramble Ltd:

The market value of the shares of Bramble Ltd = £2.20 multiplied by 1,000,000 = £2,200,000. The market value of the debt is £980,000.

Therefore current market value of shares and debt = £2, 200, 000 + £980, 000 = £3,180,000.

Invested capital in Bramble Ltd is £2,482,000.
Market value added = £3,180,000 − £2,482,000 = £698,000.
Change in market value added between 20 × 8 and 20 × 9 = £20,000

Activity 21.6

Market value is likely to vary for a range of reasons. General economic changes may be as important a cause of changes in share price as management action. A change in market value added may not therefore be a good guide of management decision-making skills.

Discussion questions

1. In what ways is residual income a better measure of performance than return on capital employed (see Chapter 10)? Why was this measure not more widely adopted by businesses?
2. What are the strengths and weaknesses of economic value added as a measure of performance?
3. If a company were to publish information on shareholder value, using shareholder value analysis (SVA) to calculate this value, what use would this value be to a potential investor? What questions would you have before you accepted the value as true reflection of shareholder value?
4. Should market value and shareholder value analysis produce an identical valuation of an organization?
5. What are the similarities and differences between the measures suggested with the intangible assets monitor, proposed by Sveiby and the Balanced Scorecard?
6. The new operations manager of a company is determined to reduce the level of investment in inventory in the factory. The managing director has indicated his desire to follow a strategy of product differentiation, emphasizing customer service as the key value proposition that should be pursued. Discuss any potential contradictions in the objectives of the two managers and consider how these might be overcome.

Exercises

(Questions with numbers in bold have answers at the back of the book.)

Q21.1 Omega Ltd expects to earn profits of £2,500,000 before tax in the year, budgeted taxation is £500,000 and the expected Net Capital Employed is £10,000,000.

The following expenditure has taken place and been expensed to the Profit and Loss Account.

(i) Research of £250,000 has been expensed in the year.
(ii) Another business was purchased in the year and Omega paid £1,000,000 in goodwill. This goodwill is being written off over 5 years, i.e. £200,000 per year.

The management believe that the existing accounting statements understate the profit and value of Omega Ltd. They believe that the research will lead to benefits over the next five years. They also consider that the goodwill should not be written off as an expense because the value of the intangible assets, for which goodwill was paid, is believed to be at least as great as it was when the assets were acquired.

Required:

(a) The new Profit and Loss Account and Net Capital Employed if the proposed adjustments are made.
(b) Calculate the current EVA® if no adjustments are made and the EVA® if the proposed adjustments do take place. The weighted cost of capital of the business is 10%.
(c) Discuss the advantages and disadvantages of making the adjustment to the accounts.

Q21.2 Altringham Ltd achieved sales of £2,454,000 in the last year and is aiming to achieve the following in relation to its key value drivers:

1. *Sales growth.* With the additional investment currently being undertaken, it aims to achieve sales growth of 5% per annum for the next 5 years, at which time a steady state will be achieved.
2. *Operating profit margin.* It is budgeting to achieve an operating profit margin of 20% for the foreseeable future.
3. *Cash tax rate.* Is expected to be 25%.
4. *Fixed assets investment (FAI).* In order to achieve the growth rate, additional investment in fixed assets will run at 20% of the increase in annual sales.
5. *Working capital investment (WCI).* The sales growth will also require an increase in working capital of 8% of sales growth.
6. *Weighted average cost of capital.* The WACC is 10%.
7. The value of its debt is £900,000.

Required:

Calculate the shareholder value.

Q21.3 Alpha Ltd is aiming to achieve the following results in relation to the key value drivers. Sales in the last year were £3,300,000.

1. *Sales growth.* With the additional investment currently being undertaken, it aims to achieve sales growth of 6% per annum for the next 3 years, at which time a steady state will be achieved.
2. *Operating profit margin.* It is budgeting to achieve an operating profit margin of 15% for the foreseeable future.
3. *Cash tax rate.* Is expected to be 20%.
4. *Non-current/fixed assets investment (FAI).* In order to achieve the growth rate, additional investment in fixed assets will run at 20% of the increase in annual sales.
5. *Working capital investment (WCI).* The sales growth will also require an increase in working capital of 10% of sales growth.
6. *Weighted average cost of capital.* The WACC is 12%.

Required:

Calculate the shareholder value.

Q21.4 Refer to the information in Question 21.2. The managing director of Alpha Ltd has decided that the company should aim for an increased market share and has advised that additional discounts should be offered in order to generate extra sales. He believes that to achieve an additional 1% sales growth for the next 3 years it will be necessary to reduce the operating profit margin to 13%. After 3 years the profit margin can revert to the existing 15%. To provide the additional production capacity it will be necessary to increase investment in non-current assets to 25% of the increase in annual sales.

Required:

Advise the management of Alpha Ltd whether this proposal is worthwhile.

Q21.5 The following information has been provided on Able Ltd:

1. The market price per share is £3.50. 1,500,000 shares (nominal value £1 each) have been issued.
2. The nominal value of the debt is £1,000,000, but the actual market value of the debt is £1,200,000.
3. The book value of the company is £5,535,000.

Required:

Calculate the market value added.

Q21.6 The managing director of Bramble Ltd has recently read about EVA®. He has asked the chief accountant to prepare an EVA® statement for Bramble Ltd for

20X7/8 and the 20X8/9 budget. The chief accountant has investigated the accounts (see Chapter 11 for the actual Balance Sheet and Profit and Loss Account for 20X7/8 and the budget for 20X8/9), prepared an EVA® statement for 20X7/8 and identified further information relating to the 20X8/9 budget. Assume that the cost of capital for Bramble Ltd is 7%.

(1) EVA® statement for 20X7/8

	£'000
Operating profit (profit before interest and tax)	425
Taxation	160
Net operating profit after tax (NOPAT)	265

(The chief accountant does not believe that any adjustments should be made to the 20X7/8 accounts in calculating NOPAT for EVA® purposes.)

Net capital employed as per the accounts	£'000
	1,512
	£'000
Adjusted NOPAT	265.00
Less interest charge on capital invested	
£1,512 @ 7%	105.84
EVA®	159.16

(2) Budget information for 20X8/9

  (i) Research and development expenditure was significantly increased in 20X8/9. Planned expenditure of £100,000 is treated as a budgeted expense in the year, although the benefit is expected to last 8 years.

  (ii) Marketing expenditure is high due to a major campaign that is expected to boost sales for the next 3 years. The cost of the marketing campaign is anticipated to be £120,000.

Required:

Prepare an EVA® statement for 200X8/9 and comment on the results of 20X7/8 and budget 20X8/9.

Q21.7 Advise on the possible use of Sveiby's intangible asset monitor for Ellemore consultants (see Question 20.6). What measures of performance might be relevant for the organization?

APPENDIX: ACCOUNTING FOR INTANGIBLE ASSETS

International Accounting Standards (IAS) and International Financial Reporting Standards (IFRS) lay down guidelines on how to account for revenues and costs.

Intangible assets – International Accounting Standard 38 (IAS 38)

IAS 38 is concerned with accounting for many intangible assets where an **intangible asset** is an 'identifiable non-monetary asset without physical substance'. Examples can include computer software, patents, copyrights, customer lists, brands, customer and supplier relationships and marketing rights.

IAS 38 requires an enterprise to recognize an intangible asset, whether purchased or self-created (at cost) if, and only if:

(i) It is *probable* that the future economic benefits that are attributable to the asset will flow to the enterprise.
(ii) The cost of the asset can be measured reliably.

If these guidelines are followed it should be possible to ensure that assets and income shall not be overstated and liabilities and charges shall not be understated.

Research and development

Research and development is covered by IAS 38. The guideline provided is that the classification of expenditure should be dependent on the type of business and its organization. However, it is generally possible to recognize three broad categories of activity, namely pure research, applied research and development.

- Expenditure on pure and applied research (unless it is expenditure on fixed assets, which should be capitalized and amortized over their useful lives) should be written off in the year of expenditure through the Profit and Loss Account.
- Development expenditure should also be written off in the year unless the technical and commercial feasibility of the asset has been completed, i.e. it can be demonstrated that the asset will generate future economic benefits.

Internally generated brands, customer lists and similar items

IAS 38 identifies that brands, publishing titles, customer lists and similar items that are internally generated should not be recognized as assets, i.e. the general rule is that this expenditure should be charged to the Profit and Loss Account.

Computer software

Purchased computer software can be capitalized. If software is internally generated then it must be expensed until sufficient criteria have been fulfilled. This would include the completion of the technological feasibility, confirmation of probable future benefits, ability to measure cost, resources to complete and the intent and ability to sell the software. The cost can then be amortized over the useful life of the asset.

Goodwill resulting from business combinations – International Financial Reporting Standard 3 (IFRS 3)

Goodwill occurs when one business acquires another and is the excess of the cost of the purchase over the value of the assets and liabilities of the business that has been acquired. As an example, if one business were to purchase another business for £4,000,000 and the net fair value of the assets and liabilities of the business being purchased was £3,000,000, then the acquiring business would be paying £1,000,000 goodwill. The reason for paying more is because the purchaser believes that the business is worth more than is reflected in the tangible asset value. The purchaser expects the intangible assets to lead to future profits that can justify the additional investment. *Note that it is only possible to show goodwill in the Balance Sheet if it is purchased goodwill. Internally generated goodwill is not allowed.*

IFRS 3 identifies that goodwill should be treated as if it has an indefinite life and should be tested annually for impairment. For example, if goodwill of £8 million has resulted from the acquisition of an organization and following an annual review it is decided that it is still worth £8 million, then it should still be shown in the Balance Sheet at £8 million. If a review identifies a lower valuation, then the reduction in value should be written off to the Profit and Loss Account and the Balance Sheet valuation should be reduced accordingly.

MEASURING AND IMPROVING INTERNAL BUSINESS PROCESSES

Objectives

When you have completed this chapter you should be able to:

- Explain a number of approaches to measuring internal business processes:

  - The use of activity-based management to measure process costs.
  - Measures of time.
  - Measures of quality.

- Explain a range of approaches that target process improvement and cost reduction.

  - Total quality management.
  - Business process re-engineering.
  - Theory of constraints and throughput accounting.
  - Kaizen costing.
  - Linkages with customers and suppliers.
  - Changing organizational structures.
  - Plant layout efficiency.

- Explain the role of accounting reports in process improvement.

Introduction

To achieve the key objectives of a business it is necessary to meet customer needs and in previous chapters it has been noted that different attributes, such as price, time and quality, can provide value to customers. If the goods and services of an organization are superior to those of competitors in the delivery of key attributes that give value then this will lead to customer satisfaction and loyalty.

A criticism of traditional accounting controls is that these have often been concerned with the measurement of short-term financial performance of functional business units and departments. Less attention has been given to monitoring whether the business is providing the value propositions desired by customers or to the internal business processes that support the achievement of these key value propositions. See Figure 22.1.

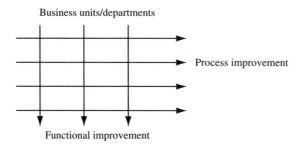

Figure 22.1 **Functional and process improvement**

Following the identification of the main internal business processes of organizations, this chapter initially reviews some measures of internal business processes (in particular along the dimensions of cost, time and quality) and then considers a number of approaches that may assist in process improvement.

The internal business process perspective

Three main internal business processes in organizations were discussed in Chapter 20, these being innovation, operations and post-sale service.

(a) *Innovation processes.* These include basic and applied research and the development efforts required in order that new products and services can be brought to market. Basic research is fundamental research undertaken in order to develop radically new products and services, while applied research is that which exploits existing technology for the next generation of products.

(b) *Operations.* Operations processes are those which start with the receipt of the customer order and finish with the delivery of the product or service. These are the processes that have traditionally been monitored by organizations.

(c) *Post-sale service.* Post-sale service is the service to the customer and includes warranty and repair activities, treatment of defects and returns. Products that become faulty after delivery to the customer are likely to result in a high cost because:

  (i) There is the direct cost of repairing or replacing defective products.
  (ii) There is the loss of future sales following customer dissatisfaction. The cost of lost sales is often difficult to quantify.

To achieve a competitive advantage, an organization must provide these activities and processes in a more efficient (cheaper) or a more effective (add more value) way than their competitors. In order that an organization can identify whether it is achieving such aims, it may be helpful to measure the activities and processes in terms of the key attributes of cost, time and quality. In the next section of the chapter some measures of these attributes are discussed.

Measuring internal business processes

Process cost measurement: activity-based cost management

In recent years, increasing attention has been paid to the use of activity-based cost management, which is the management use of activity information.

Activity-based costing: a cost assignment view

ABC has traditionally been concerned with cost assignment. As described in detail in Chapter 6, this requires that key activities of the business are identified, costs assigned to these activities to form cost pools, cost drivers for each activity determined and then a cost per unit calculated.

Figure 22.2 illustrates the activity-based costing approach, which involves a cost assignment view.

Figure 22.2   ABC: a cost assignment view

Activity-based management (ABM): a 'process' view

As with ABC, activity-based management focuses on:

1. The identification of activities and assignment of costs to cost pools for each activity.
2. Identification of the cost drivers that cause the costs of different activities to change.

Activity-based management is also concerned, however, with the measurement and analysis of key areas of performance in each of the activities. With **activity-based management**, the main emphasis is not on the costing of products or services, but rather on the analysis of activities, cost driver usage and performance within each of the activity areas. The process view of activity-based management, as well as the cost ascertainment view of activity-based costing, is illustrated in Figure 22.3.

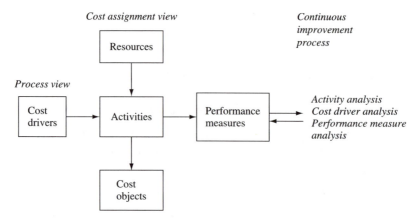

Figure 22.3   ABM: a process and cost assignment view
Source: Turney, P.B.B. (1996) Activity Based Costing: The Performance Breakthrough. Kogan Page, Figure 4.2, *The activity based model*, p. 81. Reproduced by permission of Turney, P.

Activities and activity analysis

Some activities may add a great deal of value to a product or service, while others may add little value. Some organizations have attempted to classify activities according to whether they do or do not add value. A non-value-added activity does not contribute to customer value and a key focus, once a non-value-added activity has been identified, is therefore to reduce or eliminate the cost.

Figure 22.4 identifies the cost pools for Milton Ltd, discussed in Chapter 6.

Activity	Activity cost £
Machining	37,871
Welding	46,656
Set-up/progress chasing	21,132
Purchasing components	14,137
Receiving components	10,602
Issuing components	10,602
	141,000

Figure 22.4   Cost of activities of Milton Ltd

Having assigned costs to the activities, the company would consider which of these activities adds value. It could be argued that the set-up/progress chasing activity does not add value to the customer and this should be subject to particular attention by the management and employees of the company.

As described in Chapter 15, in assessing activities it is also important to compare performance against best practice through benchmarking and to examine the links between activities in order to minimize time and duplication of work and/or to identify areas where value can be added.

Cost driver analysis

If the driver of costs has been identified, then an organization can look to act upon this cost driver to improve efficiency and effectiveness of operations. In Milton Ltd, the number of set-ups is the main cost driver of the set-up cost pool. The set-up process should be analysed in order to identify where inefficiencies are occurring in this activity area and these should then be eliminated.

Performance measurement

Performance measurement targets should be set for activities and should be related to the objectives of the organization. A number of internal measures are the subject of attention in this chapter.

Criticisms of ABM

It has been suggested that ABM is different from old-fashioned management accounting. Traditional techniques such as standard costing and expense budgets define the goal and the emphasis is on managing the numbers while paying little attention to the underlying activities. At the heart of ABM is the activity and its use of resources. Reducing costs is only one of the focal points of the approach as improving quality, flexibility and service are all also central to its purpose.

In contrast, Johnson (1992) questions the extent to which activity-based management does, in practice, change management behaviour in many organizations. He argues that this is because ABM does not generate process maps and does not necessarily have a customer focus. Activity is not systematically linked with the satisfaction of customer wants. In the example of Milton Ltd, having identified a cost for the set-up activity and from this a cost per set-up, it might be hoped that managers and other staff would investigate ways to reduce the cost per set-up. A danger is that rather than take this action, particularly if the accounting control system rewards departmental 'cost savings', individual managers may reduce costs to their own department by reducing the number of set-ups. From a customer viewpoint it might be preferable that an increased number of set-ups and production changes should take place as it would improve lead time for deliveries.

It is further argued that it is often difficult to clearly differentiate an activity according to whether it is *non-value-adding* or *value-adding*, and a better method of classification may be the efficiency with which the activities are completed. Activities, which are deemed to be inefficient, would be highlighted for cost reduction activity.

In practice ABM may also be used as an instrument of management that is used in a 'top-down' manner employing abstract rules. Instead, decisions should be made by those who are directly observing and participating in the process.

Measuring quality

The quality of a product or service may be a key attribute in customer purchasing decisions. If so, poor quality products and services will result in lost sales as customers switch to competitors.

Poor quality also leads to additional costs due to waste, scrap and costs of rework. Kaplan and Norton (1996) recount the story of a division of a major US company that investigated the amount of products that passed through the manufacturing process, without requiring some rework. On finding that the answer was only 16%, the company implemented improvements and within 6 months had increased the percentage of first-pass yields to 60% whilst reducing the workforce from 400 to 300. In effect, 100 people had been employed at the plant to produce and then to inspect, detect and rectify defective products.

Non-financial measures of quality

Quality failures can occur within the organization (internal failures) and measures of internal performance, such as first-pass yields, can have a major beneficial effect on reducing costs. Other non-financial measures of quality related to internal failures can include:

- Process parts-per-million defect rates.
- Yields (ratio of good items produced to good items entering the process).
- Waste.
- Scrap.
- Rework levels.

Quality failures can also occur once the product has left the factory (external failures). Poor quality products delivered to customers will lead to warranty claims and the cost of dealing with customer complaints. By introducing measures to monitor these areas, it will be possible to highlight where improvement action is required.

The cost of quality

Some organizations have attempted to measure the cost of quality. Quality costs can be found in virtually every department and can be divided into four main categories: internal failures, appraisal, external failure and prevention.

(1) Internal failure costs are the additional costs incurred and identified during the operations phase of the value chain. These are associated with materials and products that fail to reach the required standard before they are sent to the customer and include waste, scrap and rework.
(2) External failures costs occur once the product has been sent to the customer. Examples include expenditure involved in dealing with customer complaints, warranty claims for replacement or repair of goods.

(3) Appraisal costs will be incurred as the product or service proceeds through the value chain, from receipt of raw materials to transfer of the goods at the end of the production process, or at the point that the product or service is provided to the customer. They include the costs of inspecting materials at arrival, during the production process and quality control audits.

(4) Prevention costs are those involved in preventing poor quality production or service. This includes the expense of training staff, preventative maintenance (this is maintenance work carried out on key machines, in order to ensure that they do not break down) and quality planning.

Prevention and appraisal costs are known as *conformance costs* as they relate to ensuring that the product conforms to specification. Costs due to internal and external failures are *non-conformance costs*.

A third category added by some academics is the cost of lost opportunities. This is extremely difficult to quantify, but would include the contribution that would have been generated from sales that have been lost for a quality-related reason. This could be because of inadequate delivery time or poor quality reputation.

Although many organizations are content to use non-financial measures to identify areas where corrective action is required, others have attempted to measure the cost of quality. Some have introduced a report, which aims to trace and categorize quality costs from all departments, under the four headings identified above. Such reports can be produced for both the manufacturing and non-manufacturing sectors.

Figure 22.5 illustrates a cost of quality report for an organization. Costs are shown before and after a quality improvement programme has taken place. The analysis highlights a number of changes that should occur as a result of quality improvement policies introduced by organizations:

- Prevention costs are unlikely to decrease and may well increase.
- A reduction in appraisal cost due to detailed checking being minimized. The workforce themselves are given responsibility for ensuring that work is of a high standard, rather than having inspection of products at each stage by independent inspectors.
- A significant decrease in internal and external failure costs because of reduced errors.

Activity 22.1

Identify whether the following costs should be identified as prevention, appraisal, internal failure, external failure or cost of lost opportunity.

Scrap; training in quality techniques; machine downtime; warranty repairs; handling customer complaints; proofreading product brochure; rectifying a product before it leaves the factory; cost of testing equipment; developing instructions manual and procedures; undertaking a quality audit; inspection of materials received from a supplier; order cancelled because of late delivery of a previous order.

	Current situation		Costs after quality improvements	
	£'000	% sales	£'000	% sales
Prevention costs				
Employee training	100		150	
Preventative maintenance	50		100	
Quality circles	50		120	
	200	3.0	370	5.8
Appraisal costs				
Raw material inspection	80		30	
Work-in-progress inspection	70		20	
Finished goods inspection	70		10	
Field testing	90		50	
	310	4.7	110	1.7
Internal failure costs				
Scrap cost	100		40	
Rework	120		60	
Lost time	80		60	
Disposal costs	90		40	
	390	5.9	200	3.1
External failure costs (note 1)				
Product recalls	150		80	
Warranty work	180		90	
Returns	100		45	
	430	6.5	215	3.4
Total	1330	20.0	895	14.0

In this report, the cost of quality would be analysed in detail within the four categories of prevention, appraisal, internal and external failure costs. High costs should be investigated to see how they could be reduced. Expressing costs as a percentage of sales also highlights areas where cost reduction activity would be particularly valuable.

Note 1. Sometimes it is suggested that the opportunity cost of lost sales should be included as an external failure cost. For example, if it is estimated that sales of 1,000 units of a product are lost because of reported quality problems, then the contribution that would have been gained for these sales should be identified as a cost. Thus if each unit would have made a £10 contribution to overheads, the opportunity cost of these lost sales is 1,000 units × £10 = £10,000.

Figure 22.5 Cost of quality report

Traditionally it has been argued that there is a trade-off between conformance costs (appraisal and prevention) and non-conformance costs (internal and external failure). Initially, non-conformance costs will decline faster than expenditure on conformance will rise. However, after a period of time it becomes very difficult to reduce non-conformance costs and so additional expenditure on prevention and appraisal will not be worthwhile. In more recent years, some have argued (e.g. Johnson, 1992) that it is possible to increase quality while at the same time reducing both conformance and non-conformance costs if a programme of aiming for zero defects and/or continuous improvement is followed. To manage costs, however, it is necessary to empower workers to manage processes. It is not possible to achieve an improvement through a top-down management system, if that occurs it will just become another excuse for workers to manipulate processes, not to reduce costs. Johnson also argues that once people understand how to manage the quality improvement process, it will not be necessary to provide information that quantifies ongoing savings.

Time

A third potential customer proposition value is time, so in order to meet customers' needs, the focus in some organizations will need to be on improving the time to develop products and the operations process cycle time.

Improving the development time

The development cycle time is the time span required at the innovation stage, to develop and produce a new product. In a competitive environment, where product features are a key to success, then time to market can be a major source of competitive advantage. If the development time, from concept to market, in one company is 18 months, then it has potentially a key competitive advantage over a competitor who requires 30 months to bring a product to market. Products released by the former company will potentially reflect 12 months of technological and commercial advances over the latter.

Improving the operations process cycle time

Cycle time during the operations stage is the total time from the beginning to the end of a process. Operating cycle time includes process time, which is the actual time in which work is taking place and delay time, during which a product or service is waiting for the next process.

In some organizations a product or service can take many weeks to complete. Much of the time is involved in *waiting* at the end of one part of the process, before it is moved to the next stage of the process or in non-value-adding activities, such as being *inspected* for quality. For some manufactured products, the actual time spent being *processed* can be 5% or less.

A measure that has been used to help identify whether time is being lost is called manufacturing cycle efficiency. Cycle efficiency measures the amount of time that a product or service is being actively processed compared with the total time (throughput time) it takes the product to be manufactured or a service provided.

$$\text{Cycle efficiency} = \frac{\text{Processing time}}{\text{Throughput time}}$$

where:

Throughput time = Processing time + inspection time + movement time + waiting/storage time.

In an ideal world a manufacturing cycle efficiency of 1 would be achieved. An example of measuring the manufacturing cycle efficiency is shown in Figure 22.6.

A company manufactures a range of products.

Each product is typically in the factory for 3 weeks (the factory works 40 hours a week), although processing time per unit of one of these products is 3 hours. The remainder of the time is involved in inspecting, moving the product between the various cost centres in the factory and in waiting/storage time at various stages during the manufacturing process.

Machine cycle efficiency would be:

$$\frac{3}{40 \text{ hours} \times 3 \text{ weeks}} = \frac{3}{120} \times 100\% = 2.5\%$$

Figure 22.6 Machine cycle efficiency

Similar measures can be introduced in the service industry. For example, a member of the public applying for a loan from a bank might have to spend many days waiting for a loan to be agreed. The actual working time spent on deciding whether a loan can be advanced is likely to be relatively short, most of the time would be spent in waiting for the appropriate information to arrive and for various individuals to see and formally agree to the application. If time to agree a loan is crucial to customers and the bank would lose customers because of the delay, it might then be in the interest of the bank to introduce a similar measure of cycle time efficiency. This would highlight the problem and very likely encourage action to eliminate the non-value-added time of the application waiting to be processed.

Activity 22.2
_____

A customer applies for a mortgage from a bank and on average it takes 30 days for the bank to confirm that it will advance money to the customer. The working week for staff is 40 hours. The processes that are undertaken include:

• Step 1. The lender interviewing the customer and writing up notes on the meeting (1 hour).

- Step 2. Once the notes are prepared, details of the applicant are sent in order that employment can be verified. An investigation of credit and banking history of the applicant is undertaken (1 hour).
- Step 3. A loan decision is now made (30 minutes).
- Step 4. Having agreed the loan decision, an appraisal of the intended property is arranged (30 minutes).
- Step 5. The valuer takes 1 hour to visit the property and a further 1 hour to prepare the report.
- Step 6. Assessing the report from the valuer and writing an offer to lend funds on the property to the customer (30 minutes).

Calculate the cycle efficiency of the mortgage process.

Improving business processes

Measuring process costs, quality and time can help highlight areas where inefficiencies are present and corrective action is required. In order to compete, it is necessary for the workforce to improve the processes that lead to customer satisfaction.

Total quality management (TQM)

The International Organization for Standardization (ISO) defines **TQM** as 'a management approach of an organisation centred on quality, based on the participation of all its members and aiming at long-term success. This is achieved through customer satisfaction and benefits to all members of the organisation and to society.' TQM is used to describe a situation where all business functions are involved in achieving continuous quality improvement.

TQM is not a system, a tool or even a process. However, systems, tools and processes are employed to achieve the various principles of TQM. A number of techniques that may be considered to be compatible with a TQM philosophy are considered in the next few sections.

Continuous improvement – Kaizen costing

Kaizen costing is a means of ensuring continuous improvement activities during the manufacturing stage of the product lifecycle.

Key to the success of Kaizen is work force involvement. The assumption is that the workforce has superior knowledge of the processes it is working with and is therefore in the best position to view how improvements can take place. Workforce teams will identify specific areas of performance and investigate how improvements can be achieved. Short-term cost and other operational targets are set and then performance against target monitored.

Kaizen operates outside any standard costing system. A comparison of standard costing and Kaizen costing is considered in Figure 22.7.

Purpose of standard costing	Purpose of Kaizen costing
A key aim is for cost control.	The aim is cost reduction.
Actual costs are compared against standard to see if they are in line with expectation.	Actual costs are compared against target to see if the improvement target has been achieved.
Variances will be investigated when standards are not met.	Investigation will occur when target Kaizen amounts are not attained.
Standards are set annually or semi-annually.	Targets are set monthly. Kaizen improvement is implemented throughout the year.
It may be assumed that the existing manufacturing approach will continue for the budget period.	Cost reduction will be achieved through continuously improving the manufacturing process.

Figure 22.7   Contrast between the purpose of standard costing and Kaizen costing

---

Activity 22.3

Identify the difference between cost control and cost reduction.

If Kaizen costing is combined with target costing then an organization will have in place approaches to reduce costs throughout the lifecycle of a product (see for example Cooper and Slagmulder, 2004a). Target costing takes place at the product design stage, while Kaizen costing occurs during the manufacturing stage.

Business process re-engineering

In order to achieve customer satisfaction, it is essential to identify the key processes that lead to this satisfaction and then target improvements to these processes. Business process re-engineering (BPR) is concerned with the identification and improvement of key business processes. While different approaches can be followed, they usually incorporate steps such as those indicated in Figure 22.8.

Step
1. Identify key processes.
2. Target customer improvements.
3. Analyse the current process.
4. Redesign the process and measurements.
5. Implement the improved process.

Figure 22.8   Steps in business process re-engineering

Assume that a key process identified for process improvement was purchasing.

Step 1. The process should be scoped to identify key activities. These would include determining the materials required, selecting the suppliers, determining the price and placing the order, confirming receipt of the goods at the factory.

Step 2. Key value propositions to the customers of the company should be identified; these might include time, cost and/or quality. If time was the key value proposition, for example, then the company might target improving the time taken for each activity from the time for identifying that materials are required to receiving the goods at the factory.

Step 3. The process should now be analysed, using techniques such as process flow charting. See Figure 22.9.

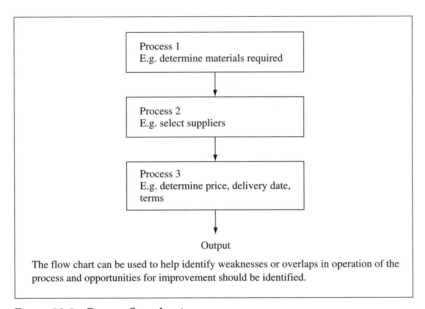

Figure 22.9   Process flow charting

Step 4. The processes that have been identified in Figure 22.9 should be redesigned to eliminate weaknesses and take advantage of opportunities.

Organizations have made a number of changes to purchasing and stock ordering procedures over the years. One approach that is being increasingly adopted involves electronic data processing or EDP systems. A common arrangement with such systems is that for a small premium in the price and a guaranteed annual order level, a supplier will guarantee to despatch raw materials and parts at short notice on receipt of an electronic order (email). An invoice is automatically generated and payment made electronically. Such systems automate a number of the stages outlined in Figure 22.9 and significantly reduce the lead time that is required for production. Although a premium may be paid to the supplier to ensure parts are available at short notice, this will be at least partly offset by reduced ordering costs and a major benefit/competitive advantage may well accrue due to the improved delivery time that can be offered to customers.

Step 5. The improved processes should be implemented and performance should be monitored to ensure that targets are being achieved. Responsibility for the key activities must also be identified.

Activity 22.4

The time to complete the mortgage application process was discussed in Activity 22.1. An analysis of the processes has identified that the average time to complete the process is 30 days, 10 pieces of paper need to be completed in all and that there is usually a backlog of applications that delays the start of the process.

On what areas of activity could improvement targets be set? How might the cycle efficiency be improved?

Changing organizational structures – the matrix structure

Figure 22.1 illustrated the difference between a drive for functional improvement and process improvement. A functional structure will organize activities by function such as production, marketing and accounting. A matrix structure recognizes the need for activities and structures to also be organized along process lines. For example, an organization that frequently sets up project teams to carry out activities is likely to require a matrix structure. Individuals will report to functional areas, however they will also be appointed to individual projects and report to a project leader. Mintzberg (1979) called this form of structure an adhocracy, because of the flexibility of the structure with the organization changing shape on a regular basis with jobs transformed and titles changed according to the work that needs to be completed.

Changing plant layout – just-in-time (JIT)

As identified in Chapter 9, JIT in manufacturing organizations incorporates a change in the factory layout with a simplified routing of products, through the use of linear organization and a simplification of the product line. Through simplifying the work it has been found possible to reduce the time to get a job done and introduce greater flexibility into the organization. JIT has also been pursued in service organizations.

JIT has also often coexisted with a simplification of the organizational structure. Rather than continuing with large central support departments, many organizations have reduced bureaucracy, by dedicating staff to look after specific product lines.

Theory of constraints – increasing throughput through a process by eliminating constraints

The output that can be achieved in organizations of all types is often limited by constraints. In service organizations these constraints may be a particular grade of skilled labour, while in a manufacturing process it may also be due to a lack of capacity on certain machines. The theory of constraints argues that the focus of attention in organizations should be on increasing flexibility and throughput through working to eliminate these constraints. In discussing the theory of constraints, Goldratt and Cox (1984, 1996) argue that in order to achieve improvements the focus should be on:

(i) Increasing throughput through the factory.
(ii) Decreasing inventories.
(iii) Decreasing operating expenses, in that order.

Where:

- 'Throughput' is defined as the rate at which the system generates money through sales. It is sales minus material cost.
- 'Inventory' is the money the system invests in purchasing things the system intends to sell.
- 'Operating expense' is all the money the system spends in turning inventory into throughput. Operating expense includes all labour and other overheads.

While the theory of constraints is relevant to all types of organization, the discussion in this section will consider the application in a manufacturing environment. In a factory, late delivery of products is often due to a constraint in a particular work station (a capacity constraint resource or CCR), which means that inventory is waiting in a queue to be processed. To improve performance, rather than spending equal time on all areas of the factory, analysis and action should be focused on eliminating these CCRs. In a factory, for example, a company might seek to acquire another machine that will increase potential capacity in the constraint area or take action to minimize time lost through breakdown or idle time.

Decreasing inventories is the second priority stressed in the theory. One of the problems in many factories is that inventory is built up in work stations where there is no constraint as there is a natural tendency to produce goods rather than having staff idle. While a buffer of inventory may be required for the constraint resources to ensure that they are operating to capacity, it does not need to be held in other non-constraint resources, as any increase in demand can be quickly pushed through those areas. The only impact of producing inventory in these areas is to tie up cash.

Throughput accounting developed from the theory of constraints. Terms used have the same meaning as for the theory of constraints, with decision-making based on the principle of maximizing the contribution-per-bottleneck-hour (see also Chapter 3 for examples of limiting factor questions). Material costs are assumed to be variable, with labour costs assumed to be fixed in the short term and included in factory costs.

It has also been argued, however, that throughput accounting does not incorporate the theory of constraints thinking. The philosophy of the theory of constraints is that in order to increase throughput, it is necessary to continuously work to identify and eliminate constraints. These constraints are constantly changing, because as soon as one constraint has been identified and eased, another one will often come into existence – i.e. a bottleneck is something that is temporary. Employing throughput accounting might lead accountants and others to focus on maximizing throughput through a particular constraint area, without appreciating that this bottleneck is a temporary blockage in the process and should be eliminated through taking appropriate rectifying action.

Activity 22.5

The following information is provided on products A and B:

	Product A	Product B
	£	£
Sales	25	18
Materials	10	6

Both products A and B are processed on a constraint machine. Product A requires 20 minutes on this machine and product B requires 15 minutes.
   Which product should be manufactured?

Improving linkages with customers and supplier

Taking a local view of costs and benefits can lead to the impact of decisions on other parts of the supply chain being ignored. There is little point, for example, in implementing a JIT system, requiring frequent deliveries of raw materials in the organization, if this creates major problems for suppliers, adds to overall costs and does not add value to the customer. Suppliers and customers should be treated as partners and joint problem-solving should take place in order to achieve required improvements and improved linkages throughout the value chain. Cooper and Slagmulder (1999, 2004b) have argued for the application of a range of interorganizational cost management techniques including resource and information sharing, joint cost investigations including target costing and increased bilateral agreements.

The role of management accounting information in process improvement

The extent to which traditional management accounting reports can help in achieving process improvement has been questioned on a number of grounds.

(1) Accounting reports may provide an incomplete set of measures that do not consider processes. Traditional reporting systems such as budgetary control and standard costing variance analysis do not report on processes. Even activity-based cost management reports lack a customer focus and do not generate process maps.

(2) Assumption of status quo. The status quo, including constraints, is often assumed in the analysis that is undertaken. With contribution analysis, an assumption is made

that fixed costs will not change given different options. With throughput accounting, the aim is to optimize given a contribution (after deducting material costs from sales) per limiting factor. Such approaches potentially go against a philosophy of continuous improvement. The theory of constraints, for example, is concerned with the elimination of constraints, not optimizing given constraints. Standard costing variances are concerned with cost control, not cost reduction.

(3) The impact of inappropriate styles of management. In Chapter 19, the potential adverse impact of budgetary control reports and other management accounting information on people was considered. This is particularly due to inappropriate styles of management, with accounting information often used in a 'top-down' manner. Current thinking is that for process improvement to take place it is necessary for the workforce to control the processes that lead to customer satisfaction.

Summary

Process measurement and improvements can be as important as the measurement and management of functions.

Key measures of internal business processes that support customer value propositions are time, quality and process cost.

With activity-based management, the main emphasis is not on the costing of products or services, but rather on the analysis of activities, cost driver usage and performance within each of the activity areas.

Cost of quality reports aim to quantify the financial cost of internal and external failure costs as well as prevention and appraisal costs.

A number of cost management and other techniques can help improve process efficiency. These include Kaizen costing; business process re-engineering; the theory of constraints and throughput accounting; just-in-time manufacturing; improving linkages with suppliers and customers.

An organization may need to change its organizational structure. A functional structure may not be sufficiently flexible to deal with project work, for example, and a matrix structure may better meet the needs of the organization.

Further reading

Chenhall, R.H. (1997) Reliance on manufacturing performance measures, total quality management and organisational performance, *Management Accounting Research* 8(2): 187–206.

Cooper, R., Slagmulder, R. (1999) *Supply Chain Development for the Lean Enterprise: Interorganizational Cost Management (Interorganizational Cost Management)* Productivity Press.

Glad, E. and Becker, H. (1995) *Activity Based Costing and Management.* John Wiley & Sons.

Johnson, H.J. (1992) *Relevance Regained: From top-down control to bottom-up empowerment.* Free Press, New York.

Kaplan, R. and Cooper, R. (1998) *Cost and effect: using integrated cost systems to drive profitability and performance*. Harvard Business Press.

Kaplan, R. and Anderson, S. (2007) Time-driven Activity Based Costing Harvard Business Press.

The theory of constraints and throughput accounting:

Dugdale, D. and Jones, T.C. (1998) 'Throughput accounting: transformation practices?' *British Accounting Review* **30**(3): 203–220.

Noreen, C., Smith, D.A. and Mackey, J.T. (1995) *The theory of constraints and its implications for management accounting*. Institute of Management Accountants.

Answers to activities

Activity 22.1

Prevention:

Training in quality techniques; proofreading product brochure.

Appraisal:

Cost of testing equipment; undertaking a quality audit; inspection of materials received from a supplier.

Internal failure:

Scrap machine downtime; rectifying a product before it leaves the factory; developing instructions manual and procedures.

External failure:

Handling customer complaints; warranty repairs.

Cost of lost opportunity:

Order cancelled because of late delivery of a previous order.

Activity 22.2

Processing time =	
customer and writing up notes on the meeting	1 hour
verifying employment, etc.	1 hour
making loan decision	30 minutes
arranging appraisal of property	30 minutes
valuer's visit	1 hour
preparing report	1 hour
writing offer to customer	30 minutes
Total processing time	5 hours 30 minutes

Total time available: 30 days × 8 hours per day = 240 hours.
Therefore cycle efficiency = 4.2%.

Activity 22.3

Cost control is concerned with ensuring compliance with budget or standard. Standards may only be set annually or semi-annually. Cost reduction is a more active process of reducing costs to targets that are frequently updated.

Activity 22.4

Improvement targets could be set on the number of pieces of paper required; time waiting between stages.

Cycle improvement could be aimed at:

- Reducing the pieces of paper needed, or aim for a paperless system?
- Clearing the backlog of applications? For example, rather than waiting for completion of each step before commencement of the next step it might be possible to start steps 2 and 4 at an earlier stage.

Activity 22.5

The following information is provided on products A and B:

	Product A £	Product B £
Sales	25	18
Materials	10	6
Contribution to labour and overhead	15	12
Time to process	20 minutes	15 minutes
Contribution per hour	£45	£48

Given the contribution per limiting factor, product B should be made first in preference to product A.

Discussion questions

1. What are the key differences between measures of functions and measures of processes?
2. Which are the most important performance areas to measure: time, quality or cost?
3. What is Kaizen costing?
4. How is Kaizen costing different from standard costing?
5. What is business process re-engineering?
6. What is the difference between the theory of constraints and throughput accounting?
7. Why is the achievement of high quality a key element necessary for a just-in-time system?
8. Alpha Ltd have employed specialist consultants to undertake a business process re-engineering exercise. The consultants have redesigned the processes and management

have advised the workforce that the revised processes should be put into operation, with immediate effect. To what extent do you consider that the organization is operating a total quality management system?

Exercises

(Questions with numbers in bold have answers at the back of the book.)

Q22.1 Ambledon Ltd produce two products, A and B. Details about the two products and the production processes are shown below.

Expected demand for product A is 100 units and for product B, 60 units.
Expected selling price and cost information:

	Product A	Product B
	£	£
Selling price	37	39
Material cost per unit	15	12

Each product goes through two processes, the time in each process is:

Process 1	15 minutes	20 minutes
Process 2	15 minutes	10 minutes

Each process is operated by one operator who works only one shift (40 hours) and is paid £360 for this weekly shift. No overtime is worked and the workers are specialized and cannot be transferred from one process to the other.

Other overheads are charged to products on a labour hour rate, which is £30 per hour.

Required:

(i) Calculate the variable, full cost and profit per unit of each product.
(ii) Suppose production is allocated based on profit per unit, determine what the production plan would be.
(iii) What is the production plan that actually maximizes profits per week? What is the profit at this output level?
(iv) Critically evaluate your analysis in part (iii). Identify areas of action that the management of the organization might consider undertaking.

Q22.2 Apple Ltd is trying to increase its cycle efficiency and has decided to employ a just-in-time manufacturing strategy that incorporates a change in the factory layout. Data from the existing system and the JIT system is shown below:

Time category	Traditional system	JIT system
Processing	3 hours	2 hours
Inspection	40 minutes	5 minutes
Movement	2 hours	30 minutes
Waiting/storage	16 hours	5 hours

Calculate the manufacturing cycle efficiency for the traditional system and for the JIT system.

Q22.3 Axel Ltd manufactures electric kettles. Over the last two years it has collected information on 'quality' costs and now wishes to present the information in a format that would be helpful to the management:

	20X6 £'000	20X7 £'000
Sales	4,300	4,500
Disposal costs	130	90
Employee training	100	120
Field testing	90	80
Finished goods inspection	70	90
Lost time	80	75
Preventative maintenance	80	70
Quality circles	100	120
Raw material inspection	80	70
Scrap cost	100	120
Warranty work	180	160

(a) Classify these items into the four categories of quality cost: prevention, appraisal, internal failure and external failure.
(b) Construct a cost of quality report for the two years.
(c) Compare the cost and comment on any action that should be taken by the company.

Q22.4 The following relates to the performance in 2007 of Arlington Ltd:
  Sales were £5,000,000.
  Employee training for the new total quality management initiative cost £200,000.
  The quality inspection team consists of eight people, who cost £250,000 to employ when on-costs are considered. 10% of time is spent on inspecting raw materials, 35% on inspecting each of work-in-progress and finished goods, with the remaining 20% of time on field testing.
  The company only makes one product (product X), of which 100,000 units were sold. Variable cost per unit is £30 (material £15 and labour £15). Fixed costs are £1,000,000.

5000 units had to be reworked at a cost of £10 per unit. 5000 units were scrapped. All the material, but only 50% of the work, in terms of labour input, had been completed at this stage. The material had no scrap value.

A product recall cost £400,000 and warranty claims amounted to £100,000.

As a result of poor publicity because of the product recall and warranty claims, the marketing department estimate that sales of product X were 10,000 units lower than would otherwise have been achieved.

Required:

Produce a cost of quality report for Arlington Ltd for the year 2007.

Q22.5 Elpington Ltd manufacture two products, A and B. The manufacturing process is illustrated in the diagram below.

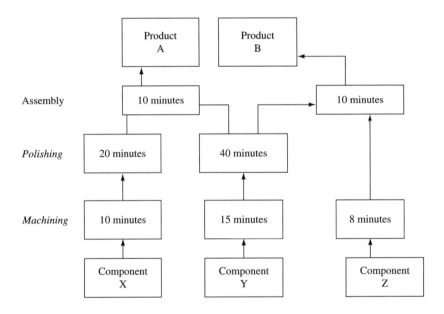

The time shown for machining and polishing is the time per component. For assembly it is the time to assemble the completed product, e.g. for product A two units of component X and one unit of component Y are combined to form the completed product.

Product A requires two units of component X and one unit of component Y. Each component is processed in the machine shop, it is then passed to the polishing department before being transferred to the assembly department. Expected demand for product A over the coming weeks is 40 units a week.

Product B consists of one unit of component Y and one unit of component Z. While component Y goes through the same process as described above, component Z is machined in the machine shop and is then transferred to the assembly department. No polishing is required. Expected demand for product B over the coming weeks is 30 units a week.

The maximum time that can be worked is 40 hours in each department and the labour and overhead cost per hour is £25 for all three departments.

The material costs of component X are £25, component Y £15 and component Z £20.

The selling price of product A is £130 and the selling price of product B is £70.

Required:

(i) Calculate the variable and full cost and the profit per product.
(ii) What is the production plan that actually maximizes profits per week?
(iii) Critically evaluate your analysis in part (ii).
(iv) Identify areas of action that the management of the organization might consider undertaking.

Q22.6 The training department of South Stone Bank provides a number of training courses for the bank. It has provided the following analysis of costs and time for 20X8:

	(£,000)
Salaries	250
Other costs	100
Total costs	350

An analysis of the percentage of time spent by professional staff on various activities gives the following data:

Interviewing clients to identify training requirements for	
agreed future courses	10
Delivering courses	25
Writing course material	25
Proofreading and correcting errors found in the course material	10
Filing and general administration	20
Research for potential new areas requiring training courses	10

Required:

(a) How much of the total costs in 20X8 is value-added, non-value-added or difficult to classify on that basis?
(b) If non-value-added time could be reduced by 50% what would be the impact on the operating profit of the bank?
(c) How has the analysis helped the management of South Stone Bank.

Q22.7 Review the activities completed for the manufacturing process at Siegmund Ltd (see cases section). Consider how on-time delivery performance could be improved.

COMPLEXITY, UNCERTAINTY AND CONTROL

23

Objectives

When you have completed this chapter you should be able to:

- Explain the need for alternative control methods given different environmental and organizational circumstances, including:

  - Varying degrees of knowledge of the transformation process and ability to measure output.
  - Increasing complexity at different stages of the organizational lifecycle.
  - Different levels of interdependence of business units and departments and problems arising from the pursuit of local performance targets.
  - Varying degrees of environmental uncertainty and complexity.

- Explain reasons why some organizations have abandoned budgeting and describe alternative controls that have been adopted in their place (beyond budgeting).
- Identify and explain organizational and environmental reasons for different approaches to the design of management accounting systems.

Introduction

Throughout the book, different methods of giving direction and control to the activities of people within organizations have been examined. Following a review of the various control methods covered so far in the book, four frameworks that argue for alternative forms of control, given different organizational and environmental circumstances, are discussed.

In the second section of the chapter, the 'beyond budgeting' debate will be reviewed. One of the key conclusions from the first section is that output measures in isolation are inadequate and in some instances comparison of performance against preset targets may be an inappropriate means of control. A number of organizations have in fact abandoned operating a budgetary control system because they have found that the costs of running the systems have outweighed the benefits. This section will review the types of controls that have been used when budgetary control systems have been abandoned.

In the third and final section of the chapter, the contingency theory of management accounting will be discussed. This will review academic theory on the impact of different organizational and environmental factors for the design of the management accounting systems.

Control methods

A range of control methods have been reviewed so far, including budgetary control and other performance management systems, the use of market mechanisms (transfer pricing of goods), changing organizational structures, internal controls, cultural/clan controls and environmental monitoring systems.

In Part 2 of the book, traditional planning and control systems were reviewed. The operation of budgetary control systems was explained, including the preparation of the budgets for the organization and its departments, the use of responsibility accounting and the preparation of budgetary control reports. Planning and control in a number of organizations, including manufacturing and decentralized organizations, were discussed. In Chapter 19, the impact of budgets on people was considered.

The design and use of performance management systems were also discussed in a number of chapters. In Chapter 19, a framework was provided that identified key features that should exist in such systems. This was progressed in Chapter 20, with a more detailed consideration of system requirements that incorporate a strategic perspective; in Chapter 21, with a review of alternative measures of financial performance and shareholder value; and in Chapter 22, with a consideration of measures of internal processes.

The use of market mechanisms in organizations was considered in Chapter 10. In order to allocate resources, a system of transfer pricing can be used, with prices based on market price, cost or negotiations between trading partners within the organization (often divisions).

In Chapter 19 it was noted that a range of internal controls can act to constrain the behaviour of members of an organization to prevent inappropriate action. These would include suitable physical and administrative constraints, personnel policies, organization structures and supervision of staff.

Cultural controls were discussed in Chapters 13, 19 and 20. These are controls based on the development of shared norms and values for the employees of the organization. If staff support the values and beliefs that are necessary to achieve the goals of the organization, then it is far more likely that those goals will be achieved.

A final set of controls are those which involve the monitoring of the environment. Environmental change can occur rapidly and opportunities or threats may result that require employees to respond swiftly to these changes. Simons (1995) refers to the need for 'interactive controls' (see Chapter 20), which focus on the identification of the emerging threats and opportunities that could invalidate the assumptions upon which the current business strategy is based. While budgetary control and performance management systems involve the development of formal reporting mechanisms, Simons considers that these environmental monitoring controls need greater face-to-face dialogue. Key environmental areas to be monitored were identified in Chapter 14.

Complexity, uncertainty and control methods

The extent to which different sets of controls might be used in organizations may vary according to the circumstances facing the organization. Four frameworks are discussed in this section. Ouchi (1979) argues that different controls will be required given different knowledge of the transformation process and ability to measure output. Simons (1995) contends that additional 'levers of control' are necessary as the business matures and passes through different stages of the lifecycle. Johnson and Brohms (2000) are concerned at the extent to which many organizations manage through the use of localized output measures in organizations. They argue that control in complex natural systems does not operate in such a manner and organizations that will perform well are those that adopt a natural systems approach. The final framework, that of Mintzberg (1979), identifies five different control mechanisms that are likely to be used in organizations and links these mechanisms with different forms of organizational structure, which are in turn relevant for different levels of environmental stability and complexity.

Knowledge of the transformation process and ability to measure output

As discussed in Chapter 19, Ouchi (1979) identifies three types of control in organizations: the bureaucratic mechanism, the market mechanism and clan/cultural control.

1. The *bureaucratic mechanism* incorporates measures, which are widely used in the traditional hierarchical rule-based organization. These include:

   (a) Internal controls to prevent inappropriate *behaviour*.
   (b) Measures of *output* such as provided by budgetary control systems and performance management systems, e.g. the Balanced Scorecard.

2. Measures of output using a *market mechanism*. Prices can be attached to goods produced or services provided and this mechanism then leads to the allocation of resources between units and divisions of an organization.
3. *Clan (or cultural)* control. Controls based on the development of shared norms and values for the employees of the organization.

Ouchi suggests that organizations often use all three types of control, however, each type may be more prevalent according to different abilities to measure output and knowledge of the transformation process. His conclusions about the appropriate type of control to use in different situations are illustrated in Figure 23.1.

Cell A: High ability to measure output and perfect knowledge of the transformation process

In a situation where output can easily be measured and the method for achieving that output is known, control can be achieved using behaviour and/or output measurement, whichever is the cheapest.

Ability to measure output		Knowledge of the transformation process	
		Perfect	Imperfect
	High	*Cell A* Behaviour and/or output measurement	*Cell B* Output measurement
	Low	*Cell C* Behaviour measurement	*Cell D* Clan element

Figure 23.1   Conditions determining the measurement of behaviour and output
Source: Ouchi, W.G. (1979) A Conceptual Framework for the Design of Organisational Control Mechanisms. *Management Science*, 25, 843, 833–48.

 (i) Behaviour measures, e.g. monitoring the actions of the workforce to ensure that the work is being completed efficiently (internal controls).
(ii) Output measurement through means of (a) a bureaucratic or (b) a market mechanism.

  (a) A bureaucratic control such as budgetary control and in a manufacturing organization, standard costing.
  (b) A market mechanism, as provided by a transfer pricing system (see Chapter 10). Simons (1995) argues that the market mechanism is more likely to be used in organizations where the value chain involves complex interaction between research and development, production, distribution and marketing activities. In relatively stable and well-understood value chains, simple input–output measures can be used.

Ouchi provides the example of sending a spacecraft to the Moon to illustrate a situation where there is perfect knowledge of the transformation process and a perfect ability to measure output. It is possible to specify each step of the transformation process which must occur and this can be controlled through the use of hundreds of ground controllers monitoring every step of the process (behaviour control). It is also possible to measure successful output as the space rocket either gets to the Moon or it does not! A choice of behaviour or output control is available, and behaviour control will be chosen as it is the lowest-cost mechanism. The reason is that the cost of one failure is prohibitive.

Cell B: High ability to measure output and imperfect knowledge of the transformation process

If it is easy to measure the desired output but difficult to specify the best method of achieving this output or observe exactly how it is being achieved, then output rather than behaviour measurement will be most appropriate. For example, a salesperson will not be under direct observation of supervisors at all times and it will be impossible to always observe the actions that are being followed in the selling process. However, it will be possible to identify the success of a salesperson by monitoring the results achieved, e.g. sales generated in a period or gross margin on sales.

Cell C: Low ability to measure output and perfect knowledge of the transformation process

In some instances it may not be possible to identify the output of individual members of staff, but it is possible to monitor the actions and activities taking place. For example, one member of a team providing a catering service might work hard to ensure customer needs are met, plates and glasses cleaned, and generally a high-quality service is provided. Another member of a team does the bare minimum amount of work. The actual output of each person is difficult to measure, however it is possible to observe the work of each person and behaviour measures are therefore appropriate.

Cell D: Low ability to measure output and imperfect knowledge of the transformation process

With some work it is extremely difficult to measure output or actions. If scientific research is being undertaken, the required results may take years to achieve. Short-term results may not be meaningful and direct observation is also of little benefit. The control that will work best here is clan or cultural control, in which shared norms and values will mean that the employees will wish, and act, to achieve organizational objectives.

Business lifecycle and the levers of control

In Chapter 20, the 'levers of control' framework provided by Simons (1995) was explained. Simons considered that a performance management system (diagnostic control) such as the Balanced Scorecard, was, in isolation, inadequate as a means of control for organizations. There was also a need for an additional three 'levers of control', namely boundary controls (internal controls, codes of conduct, etc.), belief systems (i.e. core values of the organization) and interactive controls (these focus on identifying emerging threats and opportunities). Simons has further argued that the extent to which an organization uses these different controls will in fact change as organizations develop through the business lifecycle, in effect with increasing complexity.

Early stage of the lifecycle of a business

The organizational structure is informal and controls mainly involve internal controls, for example, separation of duties and direct supervision of staff. The requirement for more sophisticated control systems is limited because of the small scale of the operation and the ability to control through informal methods.

Growth stage of the lifecycle

Initially a functional organization structure and then, with increasing size and range of products and markets, a decentralized (e.g. divisional) structure is likely to develop. With increased size, there will also be greater delegation of authority to subordinate managers and there will therefore be an increased need to develop appropriate internal, output measures and 'cultural' controls.

Improved internal controls and codes of conduct (i.e. boundary systems) are required to ensure that managers are aware of the boundaries within which they should operate and the limits on risk to which the organization should be exposed. Planning and control systems will become increasingly sophisticated, with the introduction and development of a system of responsibility accounting. Techniques such as economic value added and the Balanced Scorecard might be used. Top managers will also need to create and communicate core values (belief systems), and the organizational culture will be important to ensure that subordinate managers act in the best interests of the organization.

Mature stage of the lifecycle

Senior managers must learn to rely on the opportunity-seeking behaviour of subordinates for innovation and new strategic initiatives. Mechanisms to ensure that the environment is monitored (interactive controls) to identify threats and opportunities should be implemented.

Pursuit of performance targets, particularly where there is a high level of interdependence between departments

In contrast to Simons, Kaplan and many others, Johnson and Brohms (2000) indicate their concern with the widespread use of performance management systems and in particular, localized output measures in organizations. A problem with individual units of an organization operating such systems is that they lead to people focusing on optimizing the measured results of these sub-units, rather than on the means of achieving these results and the overall objectives of the organization.

Johnson and Brohms suggest that the thinking in most businesses is held back by the mechanistic view that has prevailed since the 1700s, which is the Newtonian view in which each part of a business achieves local targets. Such a view is appropriate for a mechanical system such as an aircraft engine, but is not appropriate for running an organization. Techniques of strategic planning, financial analysis, budgeting, cost management and management accounting, such as those covered in this book, form part of the standard material taught in most business schools. However, such techniques and the measurement that they recommend give no understanding of the internal operations of a natural system. Companies that **manage-by-means** recognize the importance of financial well-being, but they believe it is best achieved by attending to factors such as quality assurance, employee development and environmental responsibility. Instead of trying to control or regulate financial results by manipulating parts with quantitative measurements or scorecard targets, the task of management should be to nurture relationships and help people master natural-system principles.

The management-by-means framework reflects three principles that influence natural systems: self-organization, interdependence and diversity.

Self-organization refers to the capability of all living entities to define and sustain their own unique identity. Johnson and Brohms suggest that the Toyota production system, for example, achieves self-organization in its factories through a number of means, including standardization of work in which workers define and document the steps they perform in any work they do.

Interdependence refers to the principle by which interdependent natural systems interact with each other through a web of relationships. The continuous flow line at Toyota is an example of a company following this principle. In a typical North American auto assembly plant, various parts tend to be made at different plants, which are geographically separated from final assembly. Such a system requires an expensive information system that schedules the manufacturing process. At Toyota, production of all parts, as well as assembly, is under one roof. It produces to order and achieves this through local control of work, rather than employing an expensive 'information factory'. All departments are closely linked, with each production line containing some 12 segments of about 30 workstations. Each of these workstations is separated by a buffer of about five cars. A just-in-time system is in operation, incorporating kanban stock control, which helps reduce parts supply costs. To reduce the chance of bottlenecks, it sequences production as evenly as possible and has achieved improvement in changeover times.

Diversity. At Toyota and Scania, a great variety of products are produced at very low cost. To achieve this diversity has required patience and to refrain from intervening every time results fall short of expectation. One approach used by both companies is to use patterns again and again in the design of products and services. Nature achieves immense diversity from surprisingly few patterns. Reflecting nature, Scania use a modular design system to produce a wide variety of vehicles. Trucks (heavy goods vehicles) produced by Scania consist of four self-contained modules: the chassis of the truck, the driver compartment, the dashboard (left- and right-hand drive) and the engine. Each of these modules contains smaller self-contained modules. A result of this system is that Scania requires a much smaller number of different parts than any of its major competitors, who make an equivalent variety of models. Having fewer parts means that longer production runs are possible. With greater commonality there are fewer design costs, less work and confusion in manufacture. Large variety in the end product is still maintained, however, because of the modular approach to design.

A danger of management by results is that this will lead to a mechanistic response in which people are driven to reach planned financial results by aiming for a target regardless of means. Relationships are subordinated to abstract financial goals. Persuade and sell is dominant rather than build customer loyalty; build for scale and size rather than for flexibility; specialize and decouple processes rather than enhance continuous flow. Johnson and Brohms quote a number of examples, including that of the American heavy goods vehicle (HGV) market, where purchasers traditionally had a short-term focus and were concerned with minimizing the purchase cost of the vehicle. Low purchase costs meant that HGV manufacturers took cost-cutting action, which resulted in higher costs later in the lifecycle of the vehicles. Small- and medium-term transport companies, in particular, experienced high service problems. Scania did not enter the market until it was sure that it would succeed in its strategy of building long-term customer loyalty through the provision of dependable products.

A concern is that a number of the new management techniques, such as activity-based cost management and business process re-engineering, will lead to an obsession with results, regardless of the means.

Control mechanisms and organizational structure

Mintzberg (1979) argues that the appropriate organizational structure and associated control mechanism is influenced by environmental circumstances, in particular two distinct factors. Firstly, the degree of stability, with high uncertainty caused by events such as unpredictable changes in the economy, a changing technology and changing client demands. Secondly, the level of complexity, with some organizations operating in simple environments, for example companies providing a limited range of standard products or services, with other organizations operating in more complex environments, for example a research establishment developing a range of new products.

Environmental uncertainty, complexity and the control mechanism

Mintzberg suggests that five different control mechanisms are used in organizations: direct supervision, standardization of work processes, standardization of outputs, standardization of skills and mutual adjustment. The use of these different control mechanisms given different levels of environmental stability and levels of complexity is illustrated in Figure 23.2 and discussed below.

 (i) In a highly stable environment with low complexity, the work is relatively simple and there is little change and so it is possible to increase the level of bureaucratic controls, for example through the *standardization of work processes.*
 (ii) In an uncertain environment though one with low complexity, control through the use of standardization is less possible because of the existence of change. *Direct supervision* may be the best form of control given such circumstances.

As the level of environmental complexity increases, it is more difficult to control through direct supervision as it becomes impossible for senior individuals to understand all the issues that need to be considered. If the environment is also uncertain, then control through standardization of work processes is also not possible. The three further mechanisms of control identified above should therefore be considered.

 (iii) Control through standardization of outputs. When an organization faces a complex environment, for example, it produces a range of products for different market areas, senior managers may increasingly rely on measures of performance against financial or other performance targets.
 (iv) In some organizations such as universities, hospitals, schools, accounting firms and craft production firms, while the environment is complex, it is difficult to rely on output measurement and a key element of control is through standardization

of skills. For example, at a university a business strategy and marketing course can be integrated without the different lecturers meeting, as long as the courses are standard and each teacher knows more or less what the other teaches. In such organizations, therefore, trained and 'indoctrinated' specialists are employed and usually given considerable control over their own work.

(v) In a complex and rapidly changing environment it may become impossible to achieve coordination through the standardization of skills; rather, the experts must amalgamate their efforts and work together through informal communication to achieve the organizational goals. Mintzberg calls this control mechanism 'mutual adjustment'.

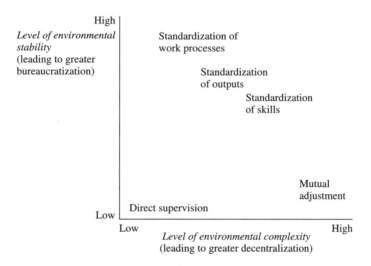

Figure 23.2 Coordinating mechanisms on scale of decentralization and bureaucratization
Source: Mintzberg, H. (1979) *The Structuring of Organisations*, p. 275. Prentice Hall.

Control mechanisms and organizational structure

As well as identifying different control mechanisms, given varying degrees of environmental stability and complexity, Mintzberg has also identified the need for different organizational structures:

(i) Direct supervision and the simple structure
The simple structure typically has few support staff and a small managerial hierarchy. Decision-making is flexible as there is centralization of power and the control mechanism in such structures is direct supervision. New organizations at the early stage of their lifecycle will tend to adopt the simple structure.

(ii) Standardization of work and the machine bureaucracy
The next organizational structure is the machine bureaucracy in which the organizational activities are grouped on a functional basis, for example production, marketing and

finance. Rules and regulations and standardization of work processes form the main method of control in this form of structure.

(iii) Standardization of outputs and the divisionalized form

The divisionalized form consists of a number of quasi-autonomous organizational units (divisions) coupled together by a central administrative structure (headquarters). Direct supervision by top managers of subordinate (divisional) managers is not an appropriate means of control. Control through measurement of outputs is the prime control mechanism for such organizations. This may be through the use of bureaucratic controls, though the market mechanism has also been widely used in divisionalized organizations.

(iv) Standardization of skills and the professional bureaucracy

This is a structure common to universities and schools, where there is little direct supervision of the operators (lecturers/teachers) and few managers at the level of first-line supervisor. The main form of control is the standardization of skills.

(v) Mutual adjustment and the adhocracy

As described in Chapter 22, the adhocracy is a highly flexible structure that will be continually changing. Individuals will report to functional areas, however, they will also be appointed to individual projects and report to a project leader. The adhocracy is required in innovative situations and so standardization and all the trappings of bureaucracy are not appropriate mechanisms for control. The adhocracy must hire and give power to experts with coordination through informal communication (mutual adjustment).

Although central control through output measurement becomes extremely difficult if not impossible given greater degrees of environmental uncertainty and complexity, a danger may persist that with delegation of authority to lower levels, the subordinate management will combine to achieve their own goals, potentially at the expense of those of the organization.

The relevance of output measurement (including accounting information) for the control process

The management accounting controls covered in this book have emphasized the use of standards and output measurement. Each of the four frameworks discussed above have highlighted circumstances where such approaches to control might at best form only a limited part of the control approach of an organization. Simons argues that given increasing levels of complexity, there is a need to supplement output measurement with a range of other forms of control. These include belief systems, boundary systems to prevent inappropriate behaviour and interactive systems which will assist in the understanding of environmental change and strategic opportunities. Ouchi, Mintzberg, and Johnson and Brohms have all gone further in questioning the role of output measurement as a means of control. Ouchi and Mintzberg both quote the example of control in a research environment, where short-term output measures will give little indication of long-term success and where the complexity of the work is such that the organization requires a great deal of sophisticated knowledge in order to judge success. In such circumstances, Ouchi has highlighted the need to carefully select workers who are capable and committed to achieve organizational goals and has argued that cultural or clan controls, which will lead to the internalization of values, should become a main control mechanism. In similar manner, Mintzberg has identified that, given an environment that is both dynamic and complex, control should be achieved through a process of mutual adjustment, with highly skilled professionals achieving control through informal communication.

Johnson and Brohms have highlighted the problems of judging success when there is a high level of interdependence between departments. Output measurement of sub-units of an organization can result in sub-optimization, as the individual parts of a business may strive to achieve higher results for their units at the expense of the whole organization. Management accounting systems report on a limited range of results of these sub-units, rather than the means by which overall organizational goals will be achieved.

Beyond budgeting

A potential implication of theory reviewed in the previous section is that control through means of an output measurement system employing comparison against preset targets, such as budgetary control, may not be appropriate for all organizations. Indeed a number of organizations, such as the bank Svenska Handelsbanken in Sweden, have either abandoned or significantly reduced the time spent on preparing budgets and reporting against such budgets.

Hope and Fraser (2003) advise organizations to consider moving 'beyond budgeting'. This requires decentralization and the empowerment of subordinate managers to make decisions. Instead of having a budget established through an annual planning process, action planning should be a continuous process. Given these changes, it is argued that managers should be able to focus their time on responding to changing events through monitoring actual results and trends against strategic and key performance indicators and/or league tables rather than reporting against budget.

These ideas will now be examined in more detail.

Planning and control without budgets: the use of flash forecasts

The organizations studied by Hope and Fraser have generally operated in fast-changing environments and have found that this environmental change has caused budgets to become out-of-date. The time and cost of preparing and reporting against budget has not been proportionate to the benefit achieved. Volvo cars, for example, have changed the annual planning process to one in which a more limited flash forecast for the next month and three-month period is produced. Targets are now more broad-brush and include a number of non-financial indicators such as market share, customer satisfaction, product costs, warranty costs, dealer profitability.

Decision-making on expenditure when budgets are abandoned is also delegated and subordinate managers are expected to use their judgement on such decisions without being constrained to some plan or agreement.

Control, performance evaluation and motivation: the use of relative improvement measures

(i) *Setting stretch goals aimed at relative improvement.*
   Rather than setting and reporting against budget targets that have become out-of-date, **relative improvement targets** based on external or internal benchmark standards and aspirational medium-term goals need to be established. A range of external standards can be used, incorporating comparison against the performance of competitors and the market. Internal benchmarks comparing performance against similar business units can also be particularly valuable, as managers do not like to be in the lower quartiles when compared with their colleagues. Comparisons against prior year on a range of critical variables that provide the organization with a competitive advantage will also be helpful.

(ii) *Rewards based on relative improvement contracts.*
   Traditional incentive schemes (see Chapter 7), which are set in advance with reward linked to a fixed agreed outcome, can lead to gaming on the part of managers. If a reward is based on budget, then there is a major incentive to managers to introduce slack into the budget to create an easy target. Budget targets are also affected by changes in the environment, so that if trading conditions are worse than expected at the planning time, then a budget target may be impossible to achieve, while an improved competitive environment could lead to the reverse occurring.

Hope and Fraser argue that because of problems caused through the use of preset targets, rewards should be based on relative improvement targets. These can be either external or internal benchmark standards. Hope and Fraser also observe that the practice, in the case organizations they have reviewed, was for rewards to involve the whole team rather than individuals.

Head office control: based on effective governance and a range of relative performance indicators

Given this level of decentralization of decision-making to business units and the abandonment of control through agreement of budgets, a central head office and the board of directors now need to use alternative mechanisms to ensure that local managers are working to achieve organizational objectives.

The way that the centre can still be involved in the development of strategy is to ensure that:

(i) Business units will operate within a framework of clearly stated corporate governance principles and ethical values.
(ii) Control from the centre can be maintained through the use of a number of organizational tools and techniques, such as the Balanced Scorecard and value-based measurement systems, for example shareholder value models (discussed in Chapters 20 and 21, respectively). Alternatively, some organizations maintain control through the establishment of a large number of profit centres, with benchmarking and peer-to-peer competitive league tables ensuring that continuous improvement takes place.

Contingency theory of management accounting

The argument that the use of output controls, including budgetary control systems, may not be appropriate in some situations will be considered further in this section, with particular reference to the contingency theory of management accounting. This aims to identify how accounting information systems should be adapted in order to meet different environmental and organizational circumstances.

With contingency theory, variables that have been identified as important to consider when designing an accounting information system include:

(a) Factors external to the organization, i.e. uncertainty and complexity in the external environment.
(b) Factors specific to the organization. For example:

  (i) The level of interdependence between departments.
  (ii) Organization size and structure.
  (iii) Competitive strategy.
  (vi) Organizational culture.
  (v) Technology.
  (vi) Industry type.

Factors external to the organization: external environment

A number of researchers, e.g. Hirst (1981), Govindarajan (1984), Gordon and Miller (1976), have emphasized the relevance of environmental factors.

Environmental uncertainty

Govindarajan has identified environmental uncertainty as a key determinant that should influence the operation of the accounting system.

 (i) If the environment is stable, Govindarajan argues that it is possible to use a formula-based approach based on financial performance. A budget-constrained style of management can be appropriate as it is easier for top management to understand and apply a formula to calculate the level of financial performance that might be expected.
(ii) If the environment is dynamic (low stability), then a subjective performance appraisal is appropriate and a budget-constrained style of management inappropriate. The reason is that there are likely to be many changes occurring in the environment and therefore the budget is likely to become out-of-date fairly quickly.

Hopwood (1976) argued against the use of the budget-constrained style of management. Govindarajan, however, suggests that Hopwood may have been examining units that were operating in an uncertain environment and therefore did not identify a key contingent factor that could influence the design of the accounting system.

Uncertainty and complexity

A number of other researchers have emphasized both uncertainty and complexity. Gordon and Miller (1976) hypothesized that environmental characteristics could encompass three main environmental characteristics: dynamism, hostility and heterogeneity.

In a dynamic environment budgetary control variance information, which reports on past financial results compared against a budget (that is very possibly out-of-date), is likely to be less relevant than updated forecasts highlighting likely future trends. Non-financial information is also important in order to identify other key factors that will have an impact on the organization. A hostile environment can be considered to be a 'subset' of uncertainty and is one in which there is strong competition and therefore non-financial information about critical threats will be of especial relevance to managers.

A heterogeneous environment is one that is complex due, for example, to a company operating in a number of different product market areas. Gordon and Miller recommended a decentralized control system for such an environment, with independent responsibility centres. The management accounting information for independent responsibility centres has been discussed in Chapters 10 and 21.

Factors internal to the organization

As well as environmental factors, the contingency theorists have tried to identify factors internal to the organization that may lead to a change in the management accounting system that is operated. Potential factors discussed below include the level of interdependence between departments, organization size and structure, competitive strategy, culture, technology and industry type.

(i) Level of interdependence between departments

Organization structure and the degree to which close interaction is required between different sections of the organization may be an important factor that can influence the design of the accounting system. In some companies, separate business units can almost operate as autonomous units and intra-company dealings may be relatively low. The Svenska Handelsbanken Bank, discussed by Hope and Fraser, was an example of such a company with different branches operating in different areas largely independently of each other. In other companies, the actions and decisions of one department are closely interrelated and the decisions of one will have a major impact on others. Decision-making and operational activities will therefore require close cooperation between such departments.

Weber and Linder (2003) suggest that the extent to which an organization might decide to improve or abandon its budgeting system depends on two factors: one that is external to the company is market stability, while a second factor that is internal to the company is the level of interdependence between departments. See Figure 23.3.

Many of the case organizations that have abandoned budgeting in the Hope and Fraser studies appear to have operated in dynamic environments and have also been business units which could operate largely independently of others. In other words, a low level of environmental stability and low interdependence with other business units.

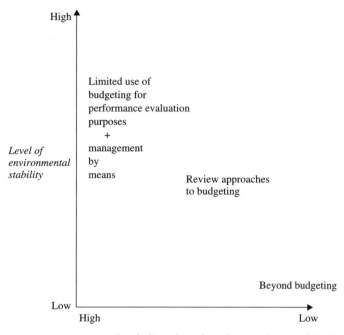

Figure 23.3   Environmental stability, interdependencies and budgetary control
Source: Adapted from Weber and Linder (2003).

For other organizations the environment may be more stable, it may also not be as easy to establish decentralized business units. In such circumstances, and where problems are found with existing budgeting processes, it is likely to be preferable to review and adjust existing budgeting practices rather than abandon budgets. This could be through some limited 'design' changes or through changing budgeting processes. In Chapters 7, 8 and 19, a number of problems with budgeting were identified. For example, with a changing environment, budgets can become out-of-date and some organizations have introduced a system of rolling forecasts (see Chapter 7). In an attempt to link outputs to inputs, zero (and priority)-based budgeting and activity-based budgeting (Chapter 8) have been implemented by some organizations (though not always with success). As well as design changes, revisions to budgeting processes can be made – in particular changes in the style of management involved in setting budgets or evaluating performance may be considered (as discussed in Chapter 19).

Where there is a high degree of interdependence between departments, there could be significant dangers of using budgets for performance evaluation processes. The effect of such an approach may lead to individual units focusing on the results of their own departments or units, potentially at the expense of other parts of the organization. Budgets might still be used by managers for forecasting rather than performance evaluation purposes, and management-by-means may also be particularly relevant to such organizations.

(ii) Organization size and structure

It is perhaps not surprising that large organizations tend to be more associated with 'sophisticated' accounting systems that incorporate a range of new approaches such as activity-based costing, the Balanced Scorecard and other techniques described in earlier chapters. Larger organizations tend to be more complex and deal with a heterogeneous environment involving a range of different products and markets. They also have more resources to spend on the development of new accounting information systems!

(iii) Competitive strategy

Changing information requirements given different strategies were considered in more detail in Chapter 16.

Much of the literature on competitive strategy and management accounting has been influenced by the work of Porter, who examined the need for organizations to pursue strategies of cost leadership or product differentiation. Most studies highlight the importance of cost control for organizations following a strategy of cost leadership. With such a strategy, traditional techniques such as budgetary control and standard costing and further process improvement techniques such as those described in Chapter 22 may be appropriate methods to use.

If, on the other hand, a product differentiation strategy is required, then performance dimensions other than cost are likely to be crucial to the financial success of the organization; for example, time, quality and flexibility. Traditional features of a budgetary/standard costing control system are likely to be less relevant, while information on performance in the other dimensions is likely to be more relevant.

It was noted in Chapter 16 that organizations at different stages of the business lifecycle are likely to require different strategies, which will also necessitate different information requirements. Traditional accounting controls such as short-run profitability and return on investment may well be appropriate for organizations at the mature stage of the business lifecycle, where strict cost control, profit and cash generation are important. Such controls are less appropriate at earlier stages of the lifecycle, where a build strategy is required and achieving criteria for the long-term growth of the organization is important.

(iv) Organizational culture

In earlier chapters, the importance of organizational culture has been highlighted. In Chapter 13 it was suggested that different organizational cultures may be suited to different strategies. For example, Miles and Snow identified a typology of four organizational cultures: defender, prospector, analyser and reactor. Organizations with a defender culture are more likely to follow a strategy involving strict cost control maintained through a centralized organization. In such cultures a budgetary control system can form a key feature of the control arrangements. Prospector companies, on the other hand, are likely to set objectives and strategies that emphasize new product and service development and innovation to meet new and changing customer needs and demands. A prospector organization is likely to be decentralized, have few levels of management and encourage collaboration among different departments and units. Budgetary control information is likely to be of less importance to such organizations and for success, the focus of attention should be on other issues. Imposition of control through analysis of variances and top-down approaches to budgeting could be damaging to the success of the organization and is likely to lead to dissatisfaction from staff.

Another factor that may influence the success of control systems is the power relationships that exist within and between organizations. Markus and Pfeffer (1983) identified a number of organizations in which new control systems were thwarted by those who considered that their positions were threatened.

(v) Technology

In Chapter 9, a range of different production technologies were noted, including mass production, batch production, just-in-time production methods and use of advanced manufacturing technology. Different production management systems and technologies are likely to make different demands on managers and employees.

Chenell (2003) hypothesized that task uncertainty and the extent to which processes can be standardized are key contingent variables that influence the design of the accounting system. Applying Ouchi's framework, where there is low task uncertainty and where technologies are standardized, as with a traditional mass production system, then behavioural controls and bureaucratic controls, such as budgets and standard costing, can be applied. Where there is less certain knowledge of the transformation process and where there is a high degree of interdependence between departments, then there should be less reliance on accounting information and greater reliance on cultural/clan controls and interaction with colleagues.

(vi) Industry type

Different organizations will have different cost structures and therefore different techniques will be appropriate. In manufacturing organizations, a significant proportion of cost *may* be variable (for example, material costs) and be identifiable to specific products. It is possible to identify a link between input and output, hence the relevance of techniques such as budgetary control and standard costing. In a service organization, many costs are likely to be fixed and it may be difficult to directly link the costs to specific outputs. Expenditure on overhead departments, such as marketing and administration, is also discretionary in nature and management judgement on appropriate levels of expenditure is often required.

Implications of contingency theory

The contingency theory of management accounting is helpful in highlighting that no one system of management accounting is appropriate for all circumstances. Despite all the criticisms that have been made of traditional accounting controls, there are still likely to be many circumstances in which such controls can play an important role, even though in other circumstances the use of such techniques may be of less benefit.

There are, however, dangers in blindly following guidelines based on contingency models. As an example, consider the literature on competitive strategy and accounting systems. It might be possible to read the literature and suggest causal models moving from left to right, as indicated in Figure 23.4. Here a mutually exclusive mode of control is suggested (if A then B).

Environment	Positioning strategy	Appropriate organizational culture	Accounting information system
Stable →	Cost leadership →	Defender →	Standard costing/cost control
Dynamic →	Product differentiation →	Prospector →	Non-financial/ marketing information

Figure 23.4 Possible links between contingent variables and the accounting information system

In practice, the links may not be as strong as the diagram implies. Coad (2005) notes how Eurocorp and Johnson and Johnson used different control approaches to deal with similar control problems, even though both organizations faced environmental uncertainty.

- Johnson and Johnson formally introduced (using the terminology of Simons, 1995) diagnostic and interactive controls. The latter involved extensive and formalized discussions between superiors and subordinates.
- Eurocorp operated a traditional responsibility accounting system. However, in order to deal with the uncertainty of the environment, there was extensive informal and horizontal communication between managers of different units.

Similarly, as discussed in Chapter 16, Lord (1996) identified an organization (Cyclemakers Group (NZ) Ltd) that followed a differentiation strategy, but detailed marketing information and analysis was not required from the accountants. Rather, information and analysis was obtained informally from discussions with sales representatives and other contacts.

The evidence suggests that contingency theories may provide an indication of alternative approaches that can be employed given different environmental and organizational circumstances. The contingency models should not, however, be used as a guide to be strictly followed. The cases identified by Coad and Lord provide examples of organizations that have responded to changing needs through different patterns of communication or through using information sources that were outside the accounting system or through both methods. While a contingency model may highlight potential deficiencies, the need for major change to the accounting system should be considered on a case-by-case basis. Other changes to the control system and minor changes to the accounting system may be more cost-effective.

Summary

Four frameworks highlighted different circumstances which indicate a need for alternative control mechanisms.

Ouchi argues that the two key issues in determining the appropriate mechanism are the ability to measure output and knowledge of the transformation process.

Simons notes that as organizations progress through the lifecycle, additional control requirements come into effect.

Johnson and Brohms criticize the use of output measures, particularly where there is a high level of interdependency between departments. They argue that complex organizations should observe and learn from the way that natural systems achieve control. This is through units of organizations self-organizing, liaising with other parts of the organization through a web of interrelationships and achieving divergency through means of repeating patterns in the design of products and services.

Mintzberg traces the source of uncertainty and complexity to environmental conditions and from there to the design of appropriate organizational structures and control mechanisms.

All four frameworks cast doubt on the use of output controls for all circumstances and identify the need for alternative or additional mechanisms given increasing uncertainty and complexity.

The 'beyond budgeting' movement argues for the abandonment of budgets and their replacement with measures such as the use of flash forecasts and use of relative improvement indicators.

The contingency theory of management accounting aims to identify how accounting information systems should be adapted in order to meet different environmental and organizational circumstances. Contingency theory may help identify accounting systems that may not be ideal for the circumstances that are faced by an organization. An exact causal link between specific circumstance and required accounting system can, however, be difficult to establish. A number of organizations appear to have adapted to changed circumstances by using a range of control approaches, of which a change to the accounting system is just one option.

Further reading

Emmanuel, C., Otley, D. and Merchant, K. (1990) *Accounting for Management Control*. Chapman & Hall, London.

Hope, J. and Fraser, R. (2003) *Beyond Budgeting: How Managers Can Break Free from the Annual Performance Trap*. Harvard Business School Publishing Corporation.

Johnson, H.T. and Brohms, A. (2000) *Profit Beyond Measure: Extraordinary results through attention to work and people*. Nicholas Brealey Publishing, London.

Macintosh, N.B. (1994) *Management accounting and control systems: an organizational and behavioural approach*. John Wiley & Sons Ltd, Chichester.

Mintzberg, H. (1979) *The Structuring of Organisations*. Prentice Hall, New Jersey.

Otley, D. (1987) *Accounting Control and Organisational Behaviour*. Prentice-Hall.

Ouchi, W.G. (1979) A conceptual framework for the design of organisational control mechanisms. *Management Science* **25**: 833–848.

Porter, M.E. (1985) *Competitive Advantage: Creating and Sustaining Superior Performance*. Free Press, New York.

Simons, R. (1995) *Levers of Control: How Managers Use Innovative Control Systems to Drive Strategic Renewal*. Harvard Business Press.

Discussion questions

1. To what extent is Ouchi's theory that knowledge of the transformation process and ability to measure output are key determinants of the control mechanism consistent with Simons' view that different levers of control are appropriate at different stages of the business lifecycle?

2. To what extent are the reforms recommended in the 'beyond budgeting' debate consistent with Simons' theory of 'levers of control'?

3. Johnson and Brohms (2000) have emphasized the need to manage by means not results. Explain the relevance of this statement for the design of a management accounting control system.

4. Given the information on Dundee Bicycle Division Part A and Part B:

   (i) Apply Ouchi's method of classification in a discussion of the control mechanisms that would be appropriate for the organization and the various responsibility centres in the organization.

   (ii) Using appropriate theoretical frameworks, critically evaluate the potential strengths and weaknesses of the control system operated at Dundee Bicycle Division.

5. Given the criticisms of accounting controls, why do you think that budgetary control systems are still widely used and considered to be helpful?

6. Discuss the view that the contingency theory of management accounting provides clear guidelines that should be followed by accountants when they are designing a management accounting system for their organization.

7. Although the economy of the former socialist republic of Ruristalia has undergone many changes in recent years, the education control system has remained virtually unchanged. The government still sets a five year plan, a key component of which is an increase in the proportion of young people with degrees. The colleges in the country are each set a target for the recruitment of students and their retention through to completion of course and failure to achieve these targets results in the withdrawal of funding.

The quality system operated by the central education council is largely based on assessment of how well individual colleges comply with pre-set procedures. The central council sends in inspectors to assess whether compliance with procedures occurs, with the date of these visits set many months in advance of the actual date of inspection. Instructors at the colleges set the exams for the courses that they teach and external verifiers are appointed from other colleges to ensure that the papers set and results are consistent with standards in other colleges.

The instructor promotion system in the colleges is based on principles of job matching. For example, all instructors with similar duties such as course leadership will be given the same grading and will be set on the same pay scale.

All instructors are required to undertake teacher training at the start of their teaching careers. This training syllabus consists of three main components, ideology, teaching theory and practical skills. The balance of these components varies between colleges.

The President of a college within Ruristalia has approached you and asked for your advice on possible revisions to the design of the planning and control system in operation at her college. She is particularly concerned about academic standards on some courses and believes that the existing systems are not promoting a culture of high achievement or excellence among instructors or students.

Required:

Why do you think that the existing systems in place may not be encouraging the level of excellence that the President wishes to achieve?

Given the constraints that the college operates within, and using appropriate theoretical frameworks, advise on the elements of a control system that you would wish to see in place at the college that might help achieve desired improvements.

INDICATIVE ANSWERS TO QUESTIONS

Further answers and in some cases, more detailed answers than those shown below are available on the student web site for the book

CHAPTER 1

Q1.4 i) B.E. Point 1000 shirts and margin of safety = 33.3%
   ii) 1400 shirts
   iii) The contribution on existing sales = £5 per shirt x 1,500 shirts = £7,500

The contribution given a new price = £4 per shirt x 1,900 shirts = £7,600. Therefore assuming that fixed costs and other assumptions remain the same it would be worthwhile reducing the price as the contribution increases by £100.

CHAPTER 2

Q2.3 Quote will be £480
Q2.4 The optimum price is £32

CHAPTER 3

Q3.1 a) Contribution given existing price is £1500. Contribution given price recommended by marketing manager £1360. Therefore it is not worthwhile reducing the price.
   b) The additional contribution from sales is 25 units x £10 per unit = £250.

Additional fixed costs	£200
Additional contribution to general overheads	£50

Therefore it is worthwhile placing the advertisement

Q3.2

Existing policy	£	£
Selling price per unit		4
Variable costs		
materials	1.4	
labour	1	2.4
Contribution per unit		1.6

Total contribution = £1.6 x 25,000 units = £40,000

a) Break-even point = $\dfrac{\text{Fixed costs}}{\text{Contribution per unit}} = \dfrac{£35,000}{£1.60} = 21,875$

Margin of safety = $\dfrac{25,000 - 21,875}{25,000} \times 100 = 12.50\%$

b) Proposal of the sales manager

	£	£
Selling price per unit		3.6
Variable costs		
materials	1.4	
labour	1	2.4
Contribution per unit		1.2

Total contribution = £1.2 x 31,250 units = £37,500

The proposal is not worthwhile as it reduces the contribution and profit

c) Proposal of the personnel manager

revised contribution	£1.4
Total contribution = £1.4 x 30,000 units =	£42,000
less additional fixed costs	£10,000
Revised profit	£32,000

Therefore not worthwhile

Q3.4 £9.50

Q3.11 b) Relevant cost is £67,600. The company can gain a contribution on any price above this minimum level. If the contract is important for strategic reasons or if demand is very low then a low price may be quoted. The management will need to make a commercial judgement of the importance of the contract.

CHAPTER 4

Q4.3 It would be better to invest in the new machine as that produced a positive net present value of £147,200.

Q4.4 The purchase of the machines should lead to a positive net present value of £1,531,000.

CHAPTER 5

Q5.4

	Total		Machining	Assembly	Finishing	Stores
Traced costs	Total £	Allocation basis	£	£	£	£
Indirect wages	17,000	Traced	4,500	7,500	2,000	3,000
Power	3,300	Traced	2,400	600	300	0
	20,300		6,900	8,100	2,300	3,000
other costs:	£					
Rent and rates	7,800	area	2,340	3,510	1,560	390
Lighting and heating	2,400	area	720	1,080	480	120
Depreciation – plant and equipment	50,100	P&E at cost	42,000	6,000	1,800	300
Factory administration	21,300	No employees	6,798	9,064	4,532	906
Insurance – plant and equipment	5,010	P&E at cost	4,200	600	180	30
Canteen subsidy	10,650	No employees	3,399	4,532	2,266	453
	117,560		66,357	32,886	13,118	5,200
Reallocate canteen subsidy		No employees	1,733	2,311	1,156	–5,200
Overhead by production department £			68,090	35,197	14,273	0
machine hours			4,800			
labour hours				2,800	1,400	
hourly rate £			14.19	12.57	10.20	

CHAPTER 6

Q6.1

a) Tradtional costing approach

	Alpha	Beta
	£	£
Direct materials	56.00	75.00
Direct labour	4.00	8.00
	60.00	83.00
	23.53	47.06
Cost per unit	83.53	130.06

Overheads are £2,000,000 and 68,000 hours are worked giving an overhead absorption rate of £29.41 per hour.

b) Activity based costing approach

	Alpha £	Beta £
Direct materials	56.00	75.00
Direct labour	4.00	8.00
	60.00	83.00
	144.00	32.00
Cost per unit	204.00	115.00

The calculation of the overhead per unit using ABC is shown in the next table:

	Total cost per product		
	Total £	Alpha £	Beta £
Purchase orders	84,000	28,000	56,000
Scrap/rework	216,000	72,000	144,000
Product testing	450,000	120,000	330,000
Machinery	1,250,000	500,000	750,000
Total	2,000,000	720,000	1,280,000
units		5,000	40,000
Overhead cost per unit £		144.00	32.00

CHAPTER 7

Q7.1 i)

Sound Sleepers

I) Sales	Standard cost units £	Original budget 1 £	Flexed budget 1,000 £	Actual 1,100 £	Variance 1,100 £	
Sales	100	100,000	110,000	107,800	(2,200)	a
Direct material	50	50,000	55,000	57,475	(−2,475)	a
Direct labour	12	12,000	13,200	15,750	(−2,550)	a
Fixed overheads	6	6,000	6,000	7,000	(−1,000)	a
Total cost		68,000	74,200	80,225	(−6,025)	
Profit	32	32,000	35,800	27,575	(8,225)	a

Q7.1 ii)

	£	
Budgeted profit	32,000	
sales volume variance	3,800	(F)
Budgeted profit at actual volume	35,800	

operating variances:	Favourable	Adverse		
	£	£		
sales price		(2,200)		
direct material		(2,475)		
direct labour		(2,550)		
fixed overhead		(1,000)		
		(8,225)	(A)	
Actual profit		27,575		

CHAPTER 8

Q8.1 a)   Cash budget – Milton Ltd

	£	£
	May	June
opening balance	20,000	45,450
ADD RECEIPTS		
from trade	175,450	151,800
receivables		
CASH AVAILABLE	195,450	197,250
LESS PAYMENTS		
labour	30,000	30,000
raw materials	100,000	85,000
Overheads	20,000	20,000
capital expenditure		100,000
TOTAL	150,000	235,000
PAYMENTS		
Closing balance	45,450	–37,750

Q8.1 b)   Increase sales by providing discounts or other incentives, provide cash discounts for prompt payment. Reduce purchases; delay capital expenditure or lease rather than purchase outright.

Q8.3 Venus ltd – summary budget information

a) Production budget (units)

	May	June	July	August	September
Sales	4,000	5,200	7,200	7,500	8,000
closing stock	2,600	3,600	3,750	4,000	
Required	6,600	8,800	10,950	11,500	
opening stock	2,000	2,600	3,600	3,750	
Production	4,600	6,200	7,350	7,750	

b) Production budget (cost)	£409,200
c) Net profit	£136,800
d) Budgeted closing cash balance	£60,800

CHAPTER 9

Answer

Q9.1

	Favourable	Adverse	£	
Budgeted profit			32,000	
Sales volume variance			3,800	(F)
Budgeted profit at actual volume			35,800	
operating variances:	Favourable	Adverse		
Sales price		(2,200)		
Direct material usage		(5,500)		
Direct material price	3,025			
Direct labour rate		(1,750)		
Direct labour efficiency		(800)		
Fixed overhead		(1,000)		
			(8,225)	(A)
Actual profit			27,575	

Q9.2

	Favourable	Adverse	£	
Budgeted profit			156,000	
Sales volume variance			(10,500)	(A)
Budgeted profit at actual volume			145,500	
Operating variances:	Favourable	Adverse		
Sales price		(11,500)		
Direct material usage		(28,000)		
Direct material price	23,000			
Direct labour rate		(47,200)		

Direct labour efficiency	13,200		
Fixed overhead		(4,000)	
		(54,500)	(A)
Actual profit		91,000	

Q9.6 Sound sleepers

Sales margin volume variance = (1000 – 1100) x £32 = 3,200 favourable
Fixed overhead volume variance = (1000 units – 1100) units x £6 = £600 (favourable) over absorption of overhead

CHAPTER 10

Q10.2

	Fairdoo	B division	Cheapbuy
	£	£	£
Price	90	95	85
contribution from division c	16		
additional cost to company	74		

a) Cheapest from division A managers viewpoint is Cheapbuy
b) From Aldo Ltd's perspective the best option is to buy from Fairdoo as the additional cost to the company is £74. £90 to purchase the component less £16 contribution earned by Division C which is not operating at full capacity.
c) Could introduce some method for sharing the contribution earned e.g. dual pricing or negotiated price.

CHAPTER 11

Q11.1

	20X6/7	20X7/8
Return on capital employed	40.4%	27.1%
The budgeted net profit margin % age	25.4%	20.1%
The budgeted capital turnover ratio	1.59X	1.35X
The budgeted gross profit margin % age	50.0%	47.9%
The budgeted current ratio	1.59:1	2.37:1
The budgeted quick ratio	1.0:1	1.61:1
The budgeted trade receivable days	76 days	119 days
The budgeted trade payable days	63 days	68 days
The budgeted number of days stock held	97 days	108 days
The budgeted inventory turnover	3.75x	3.37 x
The gearing ratio	19.9 %	34.6 %
The budgeted interest cover	12.2 X	7.25 X

Commentary

Profitability

In 20X7/8 Digiprint earned a 27% return on capital employed compared to 40% in 20X6/7. This was due to a deterioration in net profit margin (reducing from 25% to 20% and an reduction in capital turnover from 1.6X to 1.35X due to a significant increase in capital employed of 43% at a time when sales "only" increased by 20%.

Liquidity

There was an increase in both the current ratio (1.6:1 improving to 2.4:1) and in the liquid ratio which improved from 1:1 to 1.6:1. Both ratios may be higher than necessary in 20X7/8 and reasons for the increase should be investigated. A comparison v industry norms would be helpful.

Efficiency

Average time to collect debts days declined from 76 days to 119 days. Stock holding rose from 97 days to 108 days and time to pay creditors rose from 63 days to 68 days. The increase in stock holdings in particular is significant and reasons should be identified.

Solvency

The gearing ratio has increased from just under 20% to nearly 35% and the interest cover has declined from 12.2 x to 7.25 x. Although this is not at levels to cause concern, it would be helpful to identify forecast profits before raising significant additional funds through loan capital.

Summary

The company has expanded significantly this year with sales increasing from £2.4 million to £2.88 million, however the increased investment in assets has led to a lower return on capital employed. It needs to be investigated whether the investment will lead to increase sales in the coming year.

To achieve additional sales the company may be allowing longer credit terms to customers and there has also been a deterioration in other efficiency ratios. A consequence is an increase in funds held in working capital which now appears to be at an unnecessarily high level, unless reasons for this increase can be provided. Solvency ratios remain at a reasonable level though the raising of significant further funds through the issue of loan capital may not be desirable.

CHAPTER 12

Q12.1

Cost of debt	i) £1,000,000 of debt at 8% = £80,000.
	Cost of Interest = £80,000 × (1–0.35) = £52,000

$$\text{ii)} \quad \frac{£52,000}{£1,200,000} = 4.33\%$$

$$\text{Cost of equity} = \frac{\text{dividend}}{\text{market price}} = 6.67\% \text{ (no dividend growth assumed)}$$

Weighted average cost of capital

Source of finance	Market Value £	Proportion	Cost of Capital	Weighted average
Equity	3,000,000	71.43%	6.67%	4.8%
Debt	1,200,000	28.57%	4.33%	1.2%
				6.0%

CHAPTER 16

Q16.9

Quote for first 8 units	£
Material cost	480.00
Labour cost (note 1)	737.28
	1,217.28
Mark-up @ 25%	304.32
Selling price	1,512.60

Note 1 Labour hours per unit for 8 units. Average time = 20 x 0.8 x 0.8 x 0.8 = 10.24 hour per unit so for 8 units at £9 per hour = 10.24 hours x 8 units x £9 = £737.28.

Next 8 units with 25% mark-up:

	£
Material cost	480.00
Labour cost (note 2)	442.37
	922.37
Mark-up @ 25%	230.59
Selling price	1,152.96

Note 2 Labour hours per unit for 16 units. Average time = 8.192 hours per unit so labour cost for 16 units = 16 x 8.192 hours x £9 per hour = £1,179.65.

Additional labour costs for the extra 8 units = £1,179.65 - £737.28 = £442.37.

A price of £1,100 would not achieve the desired 25% mark-up on variable costs however it would generate a contribution of £177.63 towards general overheads. The company should consider the assumptions and identify further commercial benefits. For example are there long-term benefits from obtaining this contract?

CHAPTER 21

Q21.2 The cash flow table that identifies the free cash flows, reflecting operational and investment decisions is shown below.

Decisions		yr 1	yr 2	yr 3	yr 4	yr 5	Terminal value
		£'000	£'000	£'000	£'000	£'000	£'000
Operating decisions	Sales	2576.70	2705.54	2840.81	2982.85	3131.99	3131.99
	operating profit (20%)	515.34	541.11	568.16	596.57	626.40	626.40
	Less cash tax (25%)	128.84	135.28	142.04	149.14	156.60	156.60
	Cash flow from operations	386.51	405.83	426.12	447.43	469.80	469.80
	less						
Investment decisions	F.A.I	*24.54	25.77	27.06	28.41	29.83	
	W.C.I.	**9.82	10.31	10.82	11.36	11.93	
	Free cash flow	352.15	369.76	388.24	407.66	428.04	***4698.0

*Sales in year 1 are assumed to increase by 5% i.e. from £2,454,000 to £2,576,700, an increase of £122,700. The increase in new fixed assets is assumed to be 20% of the increase in sales i.e. £24,540.
** Working capital is 8% of the increase in sales.
***Note that if a steady cash flow is anticipated forever (in perpetuity) it is possible to calculate the value of this future stream of cash flows by dividing the annual cash flow by the cost of capital.
For CD Ltd it is assumed that a cash flow of £469,800 will be generated each year from year 6 onwards. Since the cost of capital is 10% the value of the future cash flows is £469,800/ .01 = £4,698,000. These are now discounted at the company cost of capital.

		yr 1	yr 2	yr 3	yr 4	yr 5	Terminal value
		£'000	£'000	£'000	£'000	£'000	£'000
	Free cash flow	352.15	369.76	388.24	407.66	428.04	4697.99
Financing decision	Discount factor	0.9091	0.8264	0.7513	0.6830	0.6209	0.6209
	Present value	334.64	319.43	304.91	291.05	277.82	2917.08

The enterprise value is the sum of the present values of the cash flows yielded from years 1 to 5, plus the terminal value.

The shareholder value is the enterprise value less the market value of debt.

	£'000
Enterprise value	4,378.71
Less market value of debt	900.00
Shareholder value	3,478.00

CHAPTER 22

Q22.1

	A	B	
	£	£	
selling price	37	39	
variable cost	15	12	
contribution	22	27	
Time required	A	B	
units	100	60	
time per unit process 1 (minutes)	15	20	
time per unit process 2 (minutes)	15	10	
			Total
Total time process 1 (hours)	25	20	45
Total time process 2 (hours)	25	10	35

Time available is 40 hours so there is a constraint on process 1 but not on process 2.

i) Calculation of profit

	A	B
	£	£
Selling price per unit	37.0	39.0
Variable cost	15.0	12.0
Full cost*	19.5	19.5
Total cost per unit	34.5	31.5
Profit per unit	2.5	7.5

* Labour cost of each process is £360 hours for a 40 hour shift = £9 an hour.
The overhead is £30 per hour. Total overheads are £39 per hour. Since each
product requires 30 minutes processing the overhead cost per unit is £19.50

ii) Calculation of time per unit and identification of production plan

Based on profit per unit, product B would be manufactured first, followed by product A. Only 40 hours are available in process 1

Product	units	time (hours)	cumulative time (hours)
B	60	20	20
A	80	20	40

60 units of product B would be manufactured plus 80 units of product A.

iii) The optimum production plan based on maximising the contribution per limiting factor

	A	B
	£	£
Selling price per unit	37	39
Variable cost	15	12
Contribution per unit	22	27
time in constraint area (process 1)	15 mins	20 mins
Contribution per hour in process 1	£88	£81

Based on contribution per unit, product A would be manufactured first, followed by product B.

Product	units	time (hours)	cumulative time (hours)
A	100	25	20
B	45	15	40

100 units of product A will be manufactured first followed by 45 units of product B

Profit at this volume of activity	A	B	Total
	£	£	£
Selling price per unit	£37	£39	
Variable cost	£15	£12	
Contribution per unit	£22	£27	
Number of units sold	100	45	
Contribution	£2200	£1215	3415
Total labour cost			720
Overhead (£30 per hour for 80 hours)			2400
Profit			295

iv) This calculation is correct given the assumptions, for example that the selling price for each unit will remain the same, material cost per unit and time through each process will remain constant.

Management should investigate how process improvement action could eliminate the constraint. Improving the method of production or introducing new machinery might reduce the time required to produce each part in process 1. Other ways to eliminate the constraint would be to train the workers so that they could work on each process, therefore if one worker had spare capacity, he/she could work on the other process.

Q22.4

	Cost of quality report for Arlington Ltd	
	£'000	%sales
Prevention costs		
Employee training	200	4.0
Appraisal costs		
Raw material inspection	25	0.5

Work-in-progress inspection	87.5	1.75
Finished goods inspection	87.5	1.75
Field testing	50	1.0
Internal failure costs		
Scrap cost	187.5 (Note 1)	3.75
Rework	50	1.0
External failure costs		
Product recalls	400	8.0
Warranty work	100	2.0
Future lost sales	200 (Note 2)	4.0
Total cost of quality	**1,387.5**	**27.75**

Note 1   5,000 units scrapped with material content of £30 per unit and labour content of £7.50 (half labour cost of £15 per unit.)

Note 2   calculated by multiplying lost sales of 10,000 units by contribution of £20 per unit.

For the purpose of review some changes have been made to market share information for the year shown as '20X8'

CASE INFORMATION

DUNDEE BICYCLE DIVISION – PART A

Introduction

McLoed Holdings is a large company that is organized along divisional lines. One of those divisions is the Dundee Bicycle Division, which produces a single type of specialist high-quality bicycle frame for the bicycle assembly division of McLoed Holdings and for a number of other bicycle manufacturers.

Jack Jones was appointed the general manager of Dundee Bicycle Division in 20X5. Reporting to Jack Jones is a production manager who has responsibility for the operation of the factory, an accountant and a commercial manager who has responsibility for the marketing and sales of the division.

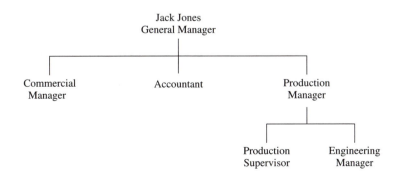

The budgeting and accounting system

An outline review of key features of the budgeting and accounting system is provided below, including:

(i) The procedures followed in preparing the budget for each financial year.

(ii) The budgetary control system. With this system actual results are compared against budget. In the factory a standard marginal costing system is in operation.

(iii) The review process that takes place every three months throughout the year, when a revised forecast for the financial year is identified.

A number of problems and issues arise as a result of the use of a budgetary control system, and some of these issues are noted below.

Preparing the budget for the financial year April 20X8 to March 20X9

Individual managers produce their own budgets and these are reviewed by the general manager and the accountant.

Commercial department

The commercial manager, in liaison with the sales supervisor, produced the sales budget in November 20X7 for the financial year April 20X8 to March 20X9. The commercial manager also produced a budget to cover the costs of the sales and marketing administration staff and any other marketing costs.

Production department

The sales budget was then passed to the production manager, who, in liaison with the accountant, then produced the budget for the expected costs to produce the planned output. Any new capital expenditure required for the following year was also identified at this point.

Engineering

Given the likely level of production and the machinery that would be used, the engineering manager produced a separate budget to cover the expected costs of the maintenance staff and material costs to repair and maintain the factory machinery during the year.

Accounting

The accountant produced a budget to cover the costs of his own staff. The budgets were then consolidated to prepare a budgeted Profit and Loss Account. For the year to March 20X9, sales, cost and net profit for the division was budgeted as follows:

	£
Sales	2,460,000
Costs	2,235,000
Profit	225,000

Further information on the budgeting process is provided in Chapter 7. A detailed explanation on how to prepare a set of operational budgets – as well as the budgeted Profit and Loss Account, Balance Sheet and cash flow – is included in Chapter 8. Chapter 8 also discusses different approaches to budgeting for overheads.

Budgetary control system – reporting variances from plan

Early in each month, the accounts for the division for the previous month and a review of results for the financial year to date are considered. In early July 20X8, senior management of the holding company of Dundee Bicycle Division requested that:

- A review of the financial results of the first three months' trading should be forwarded to head office.
- The accounting statement should identify differences (or variances) from budget.

The summary statement in Table 1 shows that in the first three months of the financial year, actual profit was £41,798 less than the budgeted profit for the period April to June 20X8.

Table 1

	April to June 20X8		
	Budget **£**	**Actual** **£**	**Variance** **£**
Sales	660,000	598,000	(62,000) (A)*
Costs	585,000	564,798	20,202 (F)
Profit	75,000	33,202	(41,798) (A)

*In the table above (A) stands for an adverse variance. An adverse variance is also shown in brackets. (F) stands for a favourable variance.

As well as providing a summary variance report, such as that shown in Table 1, variance reports are also provided to departmental managers. Managers of the various departments of the company are provided with monthly accounts that show actual financial results for each month and for the year to date. This actual information is compared against the budget for those periods. For the factory, a standard costing system is in operation and detailed variances from standard are calculated.

Guidelines that identify recommended best practice for the presentation of financial reports are discussed in Chapter 7. More detailed information on the design of a standard costing system is provided in Chapter 9.

As well as providing financial reporting statements that show variation from budget and standard, at the division a written report to explain the cause of variances from budget was also provided.

Details of the factors causing variances at Dundee Bicycle Division are highlighted in Chapter 9, along with a written report to management.

Undertaking budget reviews

Every three months, a review of the budget takes place and a revised estimate for the profit for the year is produced. The first review takes place in July. At this time, the results for the first three months of the financial year (April to June) are compared against budget. Sales and costs for the remaining nine months of the year are then reviewed and, by combining the actual results for the first three months with the revised forecast for the final nine months of the financial year, it is possible to identify a revised profit forecast for the financial year. The budget review of July 20X8 identifying a revised profit forecast for 20X8/9 of £123,202 is shown in Table 2.

Table 2

	Actual April–June 20X8 £	Estimate July 20X8– March 20X9 £	Revised estimate April 20X8–March 20X9 £
Sales	598,000	1,700,000	2,298,000
Labour	211,558	623,400	834,958
Material	143,240	417,600	560,840
Fixed production overhead	132,000	398,000	530,000
Production cost	486,798	1,439,000	1,925,798
Gross profit	111,202	261,000	372,202
Accounting	35,000	115,000	150,000
Commercial	43,000	56,000	99,000
Net profit	33,202	90,000	123,202

The budget review process and the preparation of the revised forecast are explained in more detail in Chapter 7.

Issues related to the use of accounting information for measuring performance

A key measure of performance for the division is return on capital employed and the original budget target and revised estimates for profits, capital employed and return on capital employed are shown in Table 3.

Table 3

	Budget 20X8/9	Revised estimate 20X8/9
Profit	£225,000	£123,202
Capital employed		
Fixed assets	£1,000,000	£1,100,000
Working capital	£200,000	£250,000
Net capital employed	£1,200,000	£1,350,000
Return on capital employed = Profit / Net capital employed	18.8%	9.1%

As soon as Jack Jones, the general manager, saw that it was likely that the revised profit forecast was now £123,202 instead of the original budgeted profit of £225,000, and that the expected return on investment was 9.1% instead of the expected 18.8%, he immediately demanded an across-the-board reduction in expenditure from all departments in order that the original budget result be achieved. Jack is a blunt man who believes in managing by results and he strongly believes that it is important that they achieve their agreed budget. He is often quoted as saying 'if a member of my staff has a budget to achieve then I expect it to be achieved. If it is, that member of staff will be rewarded, if it is not achieved, I expect them to start looking for alternative employment'. Since joining as general manager, Jack has sacked one subordinate for not achieving budget target and has also introduced an incentive scheme based on achievement of results.

It has been observed that the manner in which budgets are prepared and budgetary control reports used can have a significant impact on human behaviour. This will be considered further in Chapter 19.

Following each budget review, Jack Jones has to report to head office on the year ahead and on reasons for variances from budget. He is concerned about a number of the items included in the accounts, which he feels are at least partly to blame for the shortfall, and has asked his accountant to investigate. For example, some bicycle frames are transferred to the assembly division at variable cost and he feels that this is unfair as it means the assembly division receives all the profit on the sale. Some of the costs charged to his department are also allocations from head office and he has no control over this expenditure.

Chapter 10 considers the financial measurement of performance of divisions. The use of ratio analysis to measure performance is considered in Chapter 11.

DUNDEE BICYCLE DIVISION – PART B

Preparing for the annual planning round

Jack Jones has called in his managers for a review of the plans for the coming year. A number of issues and requests for funding need to be resolved.

(a) New capital investment proposals

The production manager had pressed for three investments.

(i) He had expressed his concern about the state of repair of the factory building. The factory site is on a slope and a number of residential houses are in close vicinity. A recent survey had indicated that the apparent movement and cracks in a key supporting wall were probably settlement. However, there was a faint chance that in exceptional circumstances, the wall could collapse and to be on the safe side the surveyor had recommended that repair work be undertaken. The cost of this work would be £100,000 and it is felt that it would not be possible to reclaim this cost from the insurance company. After some debate, Jack Jones decided that given the remote chance of the wall collapsing, no work would be authorized at this stage. The situation should be kept under review and the production manager should report back if he considers that the situation is getting worse.

(ii) A fund of £200,000 had been requested in order to bring the building up to modern standards. The washroom facilities were, in his words, 'primitive' and there were a number of leaks from the roof. Although this was not against health and safety standards, it was unpleasant for the workforce and gave a poor impression of the organization to the employees of the company as well as to visitors. The commercial manager agreed with this last point and noted that during a recent visit from a potential customer there had been a heavy thunderstorm and the 'unofficial flows' of water into the building had been commented upon. He had not heard back from the customer for some time and feared that the general impression gained from the visit had been unfavourable. Jack Jones decided to allow a payment of £50,000 to ensure some basic repairs to the roof and repainting of the main entrance to the building.

(iii) A bid for a new automated welding machine had been made on the grounds that this could achieve a faster and better weld than could be achieved with the current labour-intensive welding approach. Mr Jones had requested an investment appraisal and this showed a positive net present value. However, the payback was greater than two years and there was a 0% accounting rate of return in the first year. Mr Jones has turned down the investment proposal.

Operational policy issues

The production and the commercial managers expressed their concern at a number of the decisions that have been made by Mr Jones in recent months, which they felt were likely to have an adverse impact on the division in future months. The commercial manager spoke for both managers when he outlined the issues that he felt needed further thought.

'Although in the early days of the division we mainly supplied the assembly division with their bicycle frames, we have seen the sales to other customers increase in recent years. This division has gained a high reputation in the past due to its ability to deliver high-quality bicycle frames that could be delivered to customers at the promised due date. These customers have a range of companies that they can choose to deal with, and quality and delivery promises are crucial to success in this market.

We are rather concerned that a number of recent decisions may adversely affect our continued ability to achieve this level of performance.

Firstly, we feel that we have developed a long-term relationship with our existing main supplier of raw materials. This supplier will deliver at short notice and we have no need to inspect the materials on receipt of the goods as we have always been certain of the quality. The new supplier you are proposing to use is cheaper, but has a reputation for poor quality and unreliable deliveries.

Secondly, having spent many years in developing an organizational culture of team work in the factory, we feel that there are signs that the attitude of staff is changing for the worse. For our organization to work well there needs to be flexibility to meet changing demands and workers in one section need to cooperate with those in another in order to resolve issues. In the past, the budget has been sufficient to arrange a number of training courses that have resulted in increased cross-functional skills. This has a number of benefits, for example in a situation of temporary skill shortages, workers from one section will help out other sections. Members of staff from different sections have also worked together in ad hoc teams to resolve quality and other production issues. The cut in the training budget and allowance for team investigations is resulting in a defensive attitude from staff, with each section focusing on its own problems and taking less interest in the implications of their own actions on others. For example, in recent weeks two batches of machined tubes were passed to the welding department which were faulty. This would never have happened in the past. When questioned the staff mentioned that they now had strict time allowances for work and the last time they spent longer on a particular batch of work than the allowance, they were penalized with the withdrawal of a bonus payment. Staff feel that they are no longer consulted on issues and see less point in contributing to the achievement of the organization's objectives.'

Jack Jones responded by noting his concern at the negative attitude of his senior managers to the changes that he considered to have been needed in the division for a long time. Under the 'lax' management style of his predecessor, financial results had been allowed to stagnate. He had promised the main board a 20% increase in return on capital employed every year for the next five years and he was determined that this would happen. Suppliers needed to be squeezed and unnecessary overhead costs needed to be cut.

The commercial manager responded by agreeing that financial results were important, but that this would not be achieved in the longer term if the level of complaints from customers continued to increase at the present rate. Letters of complaint had previously never been received, but now there were at least two a month, 100 bicycle frames had been returned by a disappointed customer for rework and 1% of frames were now being rejected before being sent out to customers. 5% of deliveries were now late and again this had only very rarely occurred before.

THE UK BICYCLE MARKET[1]

Some general background to the market

Recent years have seen ever-increasing numbers of car sales. With low inflation and interest rates and increasing wages it seems likely that this trend will continue.

Despite the increase in car use, cycling has increased in popularity over recent years and according to a recent survey nearly 10% of adults had participated in cycling in a recent four-week period compared with only 2% in 1980. 40% of people use their bikes for leisure and more people would use their bicycles if the environment for cycling was better.

In response to public opinion, concerns about environmental damage caused by the increasing number of cars and costs involved in expansion of the road network, government initiatives have been introduced to encourage bicycling:

- In 1996, the Conservative Government launched a National Cycling Strategy and this was ratified by the New Labour Government in 1997. This aimed to increase to 10% the use of bicycles for all journeys. The strategy included a range of government-sponsored cycle-friendly initiatives, including the expansion of the National Cycle Network.
- The introduction of congestion charges for cars in London in 2002, is reported to have increased cycle use by 16% on the previous year and a similar impact might be expected elsewhere with the wider introduction of congestion charging.
- The creation of bodies such as Cycling England in 2005 to oversee the implementation of a range of initiatiues throughout the country.

The population is also becoming increasingly health-conscious and cycling is recognized as an excellent fitness exercise. It will also benefit from the desire of young people for adventurous, beach, fun and extreme sports.

Worries about the safety of cycling have discouraged many people. In response to such concerns, the government has introduced new legislation, for example the 2006 Road Safety Bill has increased penalties for dangerous driving. A number of cities have also lowered speed limits within city boundaries.

Approximately 40% of households overall own a bicycle. The proportion is greatest for social class groups C1 and C2 (30% of the population and expected to grow in future years). In terms of

[1] Adapted from Department of Transport website and publications (2007), Department of Transport report, Cycling in GB (1998), *Bikebiz* statistics retrieved 24th June 2004, from http//www.bikebiz.com/statistics.plp

life stage approximately 70% of those with two or more children, own at least one bicycle. Cycling is also likely to benefit from the ageing population and the increase in leisure time. The number of people in the third age (children left home) and retired stage is increasing and in 2004, a fifth of all journeys on the National Cycle Network were made by the over 60s.

Market sales information

There are no 'official' UK breakdowns of sales by categories, but sales of bicycles are thought to be about 2.5 million a year and about 30% of all bikes are sold in the last three months of the year, in the run-up to Christmas.

Imports of bicycles to the UK, which were only 27,000 units in 1970, were approximately 2 million by the end of the century. Anti-dumping duty was charged on bicycles till 2005, though these have now been removed.

An approximate breakdown of sales in 20X8[2] can be assumed to be as follows:

Road bikes	5%
Mountain bikes	27%
Hybrid/city bikes	18%
BMX bikes	7%
Others	8%
Children's bicycles	35%

The mountain bike boom is over. In the UK, the so-called hybrid or city bike is the fastest growing category. A large proportion of purchasers are price-conscious, and many of the mountain bicycle sales have traditionally been made on a low price basis. With the increasing use of bicycles for work, higher quality has become more important and with an ageing population, greater concern for comfort is also becoming evident.

The category of 'others' includes the market share of comfort, folding and electric bicycles. Comfort bikes permit a more upright and comfortable ride and may be becoming more popular, even though they are not as rugged as mountain bikes or as fast as hybrid bikes. Although market

---

[2]
- A road bicycle is a bicycle designed for use primarily on paved roads, as opposed to off-road terrain. Sometimes the term is used as a synonym for the more specific term 'racing bicycle'. In general, road bicycles have drop handlebars and multiple gears, although there are single and fixed varieties.
- Mountain bikes have tough frames, good brakes, lots of gears and knobbly tires and are perfect for riding off-road.
- The hybrid is a relatively new style and is ideally suited to most leisure riders and a good deal of commuters. Designers took the best elements from mountain bikes, tourers and racing bikes and built a bike which met the requirements of the average rider.
- BMX bikes tend to be stronger, due largely to their small frames, and because they have only a single gear, they tend to need less maintenance. This style of bike became very popular with the younger rider.
- Folding bikes are designed to be easier to store and transport than normal bikes. You can fold them up to put them in the back of a car, store them in a closet, and take them by train or bus.
- Electric bikes use a small electric motor driven by a rechargeable battery pack.

share is small, folding bikes are also increasingly widely used for travel to and from work and the implementation of congestion charging is likely to lead to a further increase in demand. Interest is increasing in the potential for electric bicycles, although new technological developments are awaited for the development of longer-life batteries.

Industry analysis

World supply of bicycles has exceeded demand in recent years and there are many manufacturers of equal size operating in the low-price/high-volume market. Increasingly, manufacturing companies in this market sector have been making investments in new machinery in an attempt to offset the low labour costs of competitors. These efforts have not been effective for all companies. The few remaining UK-based companies that manufacture complete bicycles operate in small niche markets (e.g. Pashleys, Brompton and Moulton).

In the past, cheap components were easy to obtain, however in recent years prices have been affected due to scarcity of raw materials and high demand on suppliers.

Most sales are through large multiples and supermarkets such as Halfords, Toys R Us, Motorworld, Asda and Tesco. These outlets are increasing market share over time as they are able to offer very low prices and they find that consumers are generally very price-sensitive. Individual customer loyalty to particular brands is fairly low, and the cost to buyers in swapping from one supplier to another is low. There are up to 4000 bicycle shops (Independent Bicycle Dealers – IBDs), but sales from these shops are declining (less than 30% of total sales) and many will not be saleable when the owner eventually retires. There remains some customer loyalty to specialist high-quality UK-based manufacturers such as Pashleys and Moulton. These bicycles are sold direct to customers or through specialist independent bicycle retailers.

McLOED LTD – ASSEMBLY DIVISION

Traditionally, 70% of the sales of the assembly division came from the high-volume/low-price market, which includes its main road and mountain bicycles. Sales have been declining as trade barriers previously protecting bicycle assembly companies have been withdrawn and imports of pre-assembled bicycles, that are cheaper than can be produced by the assembly division, have increased. 15% of sales come from the sale of a hybrid/city bicycle (Dundee Bicycle Division supplies the bicycle frame). The company employs some talented engineers who have designed a number of new bicycles, including a lightweight folding bicycle and an electric bicycle. The remaining 15% of sales comes from these products.

Due to the intense competition, profits have declined to £500,000 on sales of £5 million. The company is currently working at 70% capacity. In recent years increased maintenance costs have been required to repair machinery, much of which is now more than 30 years old.

Interest rates are low at present and the company has managed to arrange a loan of £2 million, which would enable it to either:

(i) Purchase new machinery in order to set up a highly automated production line for its main low-price mountain bike range of products, or
(ii) Introduce a production line for the folding bicycle range, or
(iii) Develop further the electrical bicycle range and set up part of a production line to manufacture this product.

The following information is available about market growth and market share of the two main products of the assembly division:

(a) The sales of road bicycles are declining at about 5% per annum with a UK market share of about 6% of the market segment.
(b) Mountain bicycle sales are decreasing at 8% annually and the division has a market share of 5% of the market segment.
(c) The hybrid/city bicycle market is growing at 7% per annum at present and the division has a market share of about 10%.
(d) The market growth of both the folding and electric bikes is approximately 8% per annum, though production and sales of these bicycles are currently very low.

A market share of greater than 6% is considered to be high by the Assembly division.

The management team of assembly division is now considering its strategy for the coming years.

SIEGMUND LTD

Siegmund Ltd is a manufacturer of kitchen appliances (for example kettles and food processors), based in the Central European country of Ruritania. The company is considering its future strategic direction and has asked for your help in undertaking the analysis. You have identified the following information.

The external environment of Siegmund Ltd

With the fall of the Eastern Bloc, there has been significant change in Ruritania in recent years. The economy has been growing at a significant rate and consumer wealth has increased.

Until recently, interest rates and inflation have been low, however over the last year wage and price inflation has risen and the government has responded by increasing interest rates. It is expected that because of this, consumer demand will fall over the next two years.

Trade barriers that protected the local companies of Ruritania have been gradually reduced and all barriers to the market for kitchen appliances were removed last year. Accordingly, a number of competitors from the Far East and Western Europe have entered the market. These companies have benefited from years of international competition, most produce much higher volumes than Siegmund Ltd and have achieved economies of scale.

The retail and wholesale sector is changing rapidly as foreign companies move into the country, acquire the main wholesalers and also construct large out-of-town hyper- and supermarkets. These organizations expect improved performance, with on-time delivery of products. The hyper- and supermarkets have also been following an aggressive pricing policy, which has contributed to the undercutting of value across the market.

In Ruritania women remain the main decision-makers in the purchase of kitchen appliances. The media is playing a role in changing attitudes, however, and men are becoming more involved. A recent report has suggested that to encourage men in the kitchen it is necessary to make appliances more fun and more of a 'high-tech' gadget. Healthy eating is also seen as more important and the diet of the population is slowly changing, with less meat eaten, more vegetables and greater variety in meals. In recent decades, because of a need to work, less time has been spent in preparing meals, but attitudes are changing and time-saving aids are likely to be popular. In recent years the number of appliances owned by consumers has increased.

The population of Ruritania is ageing and in the future they are more likely to spend heavily on well-designed appliances that tap into their culinary preferences. Socio groups AB tend to be 'early adopters' for many new ideas. These groups also tend to buy on the internet and this bodes well for manufactures selling direct to customers. 35% of the young people of Ruritania now go to university, and sets of appliances are proving popular gifts when leaving home.

In the longer term, it is expected that global sales of kitchen appliances will rise due to increasing prosperity in the Third World and growing home demand for both existing and new, modern (though more complex) equipment. In the immediate future it is not foreseen that substitute products will become available, and raw materials are in ready supply with a large number of component companies ready to deliver high-quality components at very competitive prices.

Consumers and government have become more concerned in recent years about the environmental impact of different products and the government has been introducing new waste directives, which could impact adversely on sales of kitchen appliances. New products should conform to high standards, for example low electricity usage. The government has also recently introduced a minimum wage and new health and safety legislation.

Products and markets of Siegmund Ltd

Originally Siegmund Ltd manufactured a limited range of relatively simple appliances such as kettles and toasters using mass production techniques to produce large numbers of standard products. In recent years, it has found it difficult to continue with this policy of volume production and has broadened the portfolio of products it manufactures. With a greater product range and lower production volumes, it has changed the production process to the use of batch production techniques. The market in which the division operates is constantly changing and there is a need to frequently update the product range in order to meet new requirements.

The company now manufactures five main groups of products: ice-cream makers, food processors, coffee makers, kettles and toasters. There are a number of other products, though sales of these products are low. A product group consists of a number of models of a product, for example a range of versions of food processors with different capacity, power and speed facilities.

Siegmund Ltd was traditionally a market leader, but this is no longer the case for all product groups. Information on current sales, market share, market share of largest competitor and market growth analysed by product group for the company is shown in Table 1. Past sales and sales forecast information is shown in Table 2 and a product profitability analysis is provided in Table 3.

Table 1   Sales and market share information for Ruritania (Siegmund Ltd)

Product group	Sales 20X7 (euro m)	Market share (%)	Market share of largest competitor (%)	Market growth (%)
Food processors	13	15	15	2
Ice-cream makers	7	12	18	8
Coffee makers	11	10	12	2
Kettles	11	6	10	5
Toasters	6	7	12	4
Other	5			
	53			

Food processors have traditionally been a key product area of the company. The sales manager is concerned that the product range has not been upgraded in recent years and market share has been lost to the two main competitors of the company, who have been changing their designs in line with current trends. The market growth has slowed significantly in recent years, though there is still some limited growth.

With growing affluence in the country, consumers have been able to afford to purchase a number of different appliances and two years ago the company launched a range of ice-cream makers. From a low start, sales of the product have increased rapidly.

The coffee maker range was introduced four years ago. A major competitor has just introduced a new product to compete against this product and the sales manager is concerned that because of lack of investment, sales of the Siegmund range may begin to decline.

Sales of kettles are declining. This product range is old and no development expenditure has taken place for some time. Competitor 1 upgraded its product range last year, rapidly achieving market leadership.

The traditional customers of Siegmund Ltd are very price-conscious and prices of most of its appliances are similar to those of the major competitors and are dictated by the large hyper- and supermarkets. Sales of Siegmund's products are particularly high to the over-40 age group, however market share is falling amongst younger consumers who are showing less brand loyalty and are more demanding in expecting value for money. They are also more aware that competitors' products often have additional product features, and are more reliable.

Sales forecast information

The general manager of Siegmund Ltd has provided the sales forecast shown in Table 2.

Table 2 Sales forecast by product group

	Actual sales (euro m)				Forecast sales (euro m)		
	20X4	20X5	20X6	20X7	20X8	20X9	20Y0
Food processors	11	12	12	11	14	15	15
Ice-cream makers	–	6	12	13	17	20	23
Coffee makers	19	16	13	11	11	15	15
Kettles	3	6	9	11	12	12	12
Other	15	13	9	7	8	8	8
Total	48	53	56	53	62	70	73

The sales director of Siegmund Ltd has privately cast some doubts as to whether the company will be able to achieve the expected sales forecasts.

Current product profitability

Information on product profitability is provided in Table 3.

Table 3   Current average profitability of main product groups

Product group	Sales (euro m)	Production costs (note 1) (euro m)	Share of other costs (note 2) (euro m)	Product profit/loss (euro m)	Profit (% sales)
Food processors	11.0	8.0	4.25	−1.25	−11.4%
Ice-cream makers	13.0	6.0	5.03	1.97	15.2%
Coffee makers	11.0	4.5	4.25	2.25	20.4%
Kettles	11.0	5.0	4.25	1.75	15.9%
Toasters	2.0	2.0	0.77	−0.77	−38.71
Other	5.0	6.0	1.95	−2.95	−139.00%
Total	53.0	31.5	20.5	1.0	0.9%

Note 1. On average, 40% of costs are variable and the remainder considered to be fixed.
Note 2. Other costs are apportioned on the basis of sales revenue.

Analysis of the organization

Over the last 10 years the company managed to update the product range due to the work of a small dedicated team in the research and development department. For a time the new products of the division that were developed became recognized as being more innovative and of higher quality than those of the main competitors. However, several members of staff in the research and development department are approaching retirement age and it has proved difficult to recruit new staff of the right calibre. Given the volume of work that needs to be undertaken, upgrading of a number of current products and development of new products has been delayed.

The company management has also delayed investment in additional research and development, because of an adverse impact on short-term profitability and limited cash resources. Budgetary control is seen as an important control technique and variance information is seen as a key measure of performance.

The production workforce is highly skilled. However, several new businesses have moved into the area recently and as a consequence a number of key members of staff have left, leading to some skill shortages in the factory. The management of Siegmund attribute a recent deterioration of quality to this factor. Additional problems have also occurred because patterns of team work have broken down as members of staff have left. The number of products that complete the manufacturing process without some form of rework has deteriorated from 90% to 80% over the last year, and customer returns have deteriorated from 3% to 6% of sales.

A process of modernization is taking place, but it is estimated that a further €30 million is required to bring the factory up to world-class standards. Siegmund does not have the financial resources required to upgrade the facilities, except on a slow and piecemeal basis.

The management of Siegmund Ltd lay a great deal of emphasis on departments meeting their budget. Apart from this, the accounting department provides limited management accounting information, with minimal analysis of the cost of products or the efficiency or effectiveness in the use of resources. Production overheads are absorbed on the basis of a factory overhead labour hour rate and other costs are allocated to products on the basis of percentage of sales. The accountant has, however, undertaken an analysis of the revenue and costs of the company and two of its major competitors, which are both wholly owned subsidiaries of overseas companies, with a manufacturing base in Ruritania. This is shown in Table 4.

Table 4 Competitor cost analysis

	Siegmund Ltd	Competitor 1	Competitor 2
Sales revenue (€m)	53.0	40.0	50.0
Production costs (€m)	32.0	18.0	27.0
Marketing costs (€m)	1.5	3.0	2.8
Research and development (€m)	4.0	6.0	5.0
Other costs (€m)	15.0	9.0	10.0
Net profit (€m)	0.5	4.0	5.2
Assets employed (€m)	€35m	€30m	€28m

Competitor 1 in particular has been investing in new capital equipment and in process improvements.

Manufacturing process

Products are manufactured using a batch production system. Over the last year there have been some complaints about the delivery time for a number of the products of the company. An analysis of the manufacturing cycle time for a recent order is shown below.

Inbound logistics

On receipt of the order, one copy is forwarded to the purchasing officer who prepares a breakdown of the parts required. Orders for the accessories that need to be supplied by outside suppliers are prepared and passed to the production manager to sign, at which point they are posted to the suppliers. Time elapsed, 2 weeks.

Suppliers then deliver the raw material and components. Time elapsed can vary from 2 days to 4 weeks. The 4-week delivery date is for one of the major overseas suppliers, who can provide the goods at a very competitive price, but needs to deliver the parts from the Far East.

Operations

On receipt of the final part required for the order, manufacture of the part can commence. The order has to be fitted in with other orders and there are a number of stages in the production process that need to be undertaken. Time to manufacture an order can be up to 4 weeks. Although only 8 hours might be spent in manufacturing a batch of 100 products, the remainder of the time is spent in waiting for the batch to be moved from one manufacturing area to the next and to wait its turn to be processed further. At each stage the batch is inspected by independent inspectors. With the increasing number of products manufactured by Siegmund Ltd, the level of inventory has been increasing. The information systems used by the company are limited and it is considering investing in a material requirements planning (MRP) system to help with the scheduling of work in progress through the factory.

Outbound logistics

Finished products are inspected and then stored. Time elapsed, 1 week.

The distribution company picks up the order and takes it to their central warehouse. Smaller vans then take the orders to the individual retail outlets. Time elapsed, 1 week.

COOPERS LEISURE RESORTS LTD

In late 20X7 Sue Cooper, the founder of Coopers Leisure Resorts Ltd, purchased 'Sunshine Sites'. 'Sunshine Sites' is a holiday centre that includes a restaurant, a small shop, a dozen chalets that are rented out on a weekly basis and a two-acre campsite attached to the park. It is based in Dorset, England, some 20 miles from the sea in a green belt area.

The restaurant adjoins a busy main road and is open throughout the year, although currently approximately 75% of revenue is taken during the busy April to September period. The restaurant provides 'family' food similar to that of Harvester and Pizza Express.

The chalets are also available for rent throughout the year. Occupancy is currently on average 90% during the period July and August, 60% during the months April, May, June and September, and 10% during the other months of the year with the exception of a two-week period at Christmas when occupancy is approximately 80%.

The campsite and shop are only open during the period April to September.

Current organizational structure of 'Sunshine Sites'

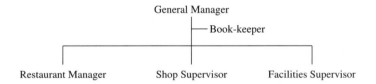

Reporting to the restaurant manager is a head chef plus three kitchen staff as well as waiting and bar staff. The shop supervisor has two members of staff reporting to her and the facilities supervisor is responsible for a number of part-time cleaners as well as administrative staff responsible for checking in new arrivals and leavers.

Current accounting and other information

Historically, quarterly accounts for the business have been provided by the book-keeper for the business. Table 1 shows the Profit and Loss Account for quarter 1 (April to June) of the financial years 20X6 and 20X7 for 'Sunshine Sites'.

Table 1 Profit and Loss Accounts for Sunshine Sites

	Sunshine Sites Profit and Loss Account for quarter 1	
	20X6	20X7
	£	£
Sales	171,600	148,900
Cost of goods sold	42,500	36,300
Gross profit	129,100	112,600
Wages	55,000	57,000
Rent/rates	17,000	18,000
Electricity	11,000	12,000
Other costs	24,000	23,000
Net profit	22,100	2,600

Table 2 key performance information for quarter 1 for the last three years:

		Quarter 1 20X5	Quarter 1 20X6	Quarter 1 20X7
Restaurant	Gross profit on sales % (note 1)	65	67	69
	RoS (note 2)	2.1	2.2	1.6
	ASP £ (note 3)	17	18	17
	Turnover £	98,500	109,300	89,200
Chalets	Average revenue per chalet per week (note 4)	240	245	250
	Average list price per chalet per week	260	280	300
	Average occupancy %	70	65	60
Camping	Average daily caravans	22	18	15
	Average daily tents	16	18	14
	Average daily number of gusts	115	98	90

Note 1. Gross profit on sales % is after deducting the cost of food and drink.
Note 2. RoS = rate of seat turnover. (If a restaurant has 30 seats, 90 customers served = seat turnover of 3.0.)
Note 3. ASP = average spending power, or average spend per head.
Note 4. The average revenue per chalet is £250 per week. To achieve the 60% occupancy rate in quarter 1 20X7, the manager of the park has had to discount from the average list price of £300 for the weekly rent of a chalet.

The future

Sue Cooper is concerned that although 'Sunshine Sites' generates significant profits during quarter 2 of each year, in quarter 1 there is only a marginal profit and in quarters 3 and 4 a loss usually occurs.

Little has been spent on the business in recent years, so that the chalets are now rather old-fashioned. The facilities offered at the campsite are limited to two toilet/shower blocks, which also need upgrading. Other holiday centres and resorts have been upgrading facilities and offering special deals during off-peak seasons.

Traditionally the main clients of the business have been families with young children taking their main holiday of the year, for either one or two weeks. Despite a national trend for families to take more holidays, visitor numbers have been decreasing over the last three years and a number of clients have indicated that there is little to do at the site (e.g. no play park or facilities such as a swimming pool, sports facilities for the family). Marketing of the site has recently been very limited.

Sue is convinced that 'Sunshine Sites' has not been identifying or reaching its potential market and proposes to commission an investigation of the market.

Currently the general economic situation is deteriorating, with interest rates and unemployment both rising.

APPENDIX – PRESENT VALUE TABLE

The table provides the present value of receiving £1 in a number of years time given different discount rates

Years	1%	2%	3%	4%	5%	6%	7%	8%	9%	10%
1	0.9901	0.9804	0.9709	0.9615	0.9524	0.9434	0.9346	0.9259	0.9174	0.9091
2	0.9803	0.9612	0.9426	0.9246	0.9070	0.8900	0.8734	0.8573	0.8417	0.8264
3	0.9706	0.9423	0.9151	0.8890	0.8638	0.8396	0.8163	0.7938	0.7722	0.7513
4	0.9610	0.9238	0.8885	0.8548	0.8227	0.7921	0.7629	0.7350	0.7084	0.6830
5	0.9515	0.9057	0.8626	0.8219	0.7835	0.7473	0.7130	0.6806	0.6499	0.6209
6	0.9420	0.8880	0.8375	0.7903	0.7462	0.7050	0.6663	0.6302	0.5963	0.5645
7	0.9327	0.8706	0.8131	0.7599	0.7107	0.6651	0.6227	0.5835	0.5470	0.5132
8	0.9235	0.8535	0.7894	0.7307	0.6768	0.6274	0.5820	0.5403	0.5019	0.4665
9	0.9143	0.8368	0.7664	0.7026	0.6446	0.5919	0.5439	0.5002	0.4604	0.4241
10	0.9053	0.8203	0.7441	0.6756	0.6139	0.5584	0.5083	0.4632	0.4224	0.3855
11	0.8963	0.8043	0.7224	0.6496	0.5847	0.5268	0.4751	0.4289	0.3875	0.3505
12	0.8874	0.7885	0.7014	0.6246	0.5568	0.4970	0.4440	0.3971	0.3555	0.3186
13	0.8787	0.7730	0.6810	0.6006	0.5303	0.4688	0.4150	0.3677	0.3262	0.2897
14	0.8700	0.7579	0.6611	0.5775	0.5051	0.4423	0.3878	0.3405	0.2992	0.2633
15	0.8613	0.7430	0.6419	0.5553	0.4810	0.4173	0.3624	0.3152	0.2745	0.2394
16	0.8528	0.7284	0.6232	0.5339	0.4581	0.3936	0.3387	0.2919	0.2519	0.2176
17	0.8444	0.7142	0.6050	0.5134	0.4363	0.3714	0.3166	0.2703	0.2311	0.1978
18	0.8360	0.7002	0.5874	0.4936	0.4155	0.3503	0.2959	0.2502	0.2120	0.1799
19	0.8277	0.6864	0.5703	0.4746	0.3957	0.3305	0.2765	0.2317	0.1945	0.1635
20	0.8195	0.6730	0.5537	0.4564	0.3769	0.3118	0.2584	0.2145	0.1784	0.1486
25	0.7798	0.6095	0.4776	0.3751	0.2953	0.2330	0.1842	0.1460	0.1160	0.0923
30	0.7419	0.5521	0.4120	0.3083	0.2314	0.1741	0.1304	0.0994	0.0754	0.0573
35	0.7059	0.5000	0.3554	0.2534	0.1813	0.1301	0.0937	0.0676	0.0490	0.0356
40	0.6717	0.4529	0.3066	0.2083	0.1420	0.0972	0.0668	0.0460	0.0318	0.0221

Years	11%	12%	13%	14%	15%	16%	17%	18%	19%	20%	25%
1	0.9009	0.8929	0.8850	0.8772	0.8696	0.8621	0.8547	0.8475	0.8403	0.8333	0.8000
2	0.8116	0.7972	0.7831	0.7695	0.7561	0.7432	0.7305	0.7182	0.7062	0.6944	0.6400
3	0.7312	0.7118	0.6931	0.6750	0.6575	0.6407	0.6244	0.6086	0.5934	0.5787	0.5120
4	0.6587	0.6355	0.6133	0.5921	0.5718	0.5523	0.5337	0.5158	0.4987	0.4823	0.4096
5	0.5935	0.5674	0.5428	0.5194	0.4972	0.4761	0.4561	0.4371	0.4190	0.4019	0.3277
6	0.5346	0.5066	0.4803	0.4556	0.4323	0.4104	0.3898	0.3704	0.3521	0.3349	0.2621
7	0.4817	0.4523	0.4251	0.3996	0.3759	0.3538	0.3332	0.3139	0.2959	0.2791	0.2097
8	0.4339	0.4039	0.3762	0.3506	0.3269	0.3050	0.2848	0.2660	0.2487	0.2326	0.1678
9	0.3909	0.3606	0.3329	0.3075	0.2843	0.2630	0.2434	0.2255	0.2090	0.1938	0.1342
10	0.3522	0.3220	0.2946	0.2697	0.2472	0.2267	0.2080	0.1911	0.1756	0.1615	0.1074
11	0.3173	0.2875	0.2607	0.2366	0.2149	0.1954	0.1778	0.1619	0.1476	0.1346	0.0859
12	0.2858	0.2567	0.2307	0.2076	0.1869	0.1685	0.1520	0.1372	0.1240	0.1122	0.0687
13	0.2575	0.2292	0.2042	0.1821	0.1625	0.1452	0.1299	0.1163	0.1042	0.0935	0.0550
14	0.2320	0.2046	0.1807	0.1597	0.1413	0.1252	0.1110	0.0985	0.0876	0.0779	0.0440
15	0.2090	0.1827	0.1599	0.1401	0.1229	0.1079	0.0949	0.0835	0.0736	0.0649	0.0352
16	0.1883	0.1631	0.1415	0.1229	0.1069	0.0930	0.0811	0.0708	0.0618	0.0541	0.0281
17	0.1696	0.1456	0.1252	0.1078	0.0929	0.0802	0.0693	0.0600	0.0520	0.0451	0.0225
18	0.1528	0.1300	0.1108	0.0946	0.0808	0.0691	0.0592	0.0508	0.0437	0.0376	0.0180
19	0.1377	0.1161	0.0981	0.0829	0.0703	0.0596	0.0506	0.0431	0.0367	0.0313	0.0144
20	0.1240	0.1037	0.0868	0.0728	0.0611	0.0514	0.0433	0.0365	0.0308	0.0261	0.0115
25	0.0736	0.0588	0.0471	0.0378	0.0304	0.0245	0.0197	0.0160	0.0129	0.0105	0.0038
30	0.0437	0.0334	0.0256	0.0196	0.0151	0.0116	0.0090	0.0070	0.0054	0.0042	0.0012
35	0.0259	0.0189	0.0139	0.0102	0.0075	0.0055	0.0041	0.0030	0.0023	0.0017	0.0004
40	0.0154	0.0107	0.0075	0.0053	0.0037	0.0026	0.0019	0.0013	0.0010	0.0007	0.0001

GLOSSARY

Accounting concept   To support the application of the 'true and fair view', accounting has adopted certain concepts and conventions which help to ensure that accounting information is presented accurately and consistently.

Accounting policies   The principles, bases, conventions, rules and procedures adopted by management/a company in preparing and presenting financial statements.

Accounting rate of return (ARR)   The average annual profit divided by the initial investment. Some companies calculate ARR using the average investment.

Accounting standards   Conduct followed by accountants as prescribed by an authoritative body or law.

Accumulated depreciation   The amount of depreciation which has accumulated over time.

Acid test ratio   See quick ratio.

Activity-based budgeting   Budgeting by activities rather than by cost elements. The budgeted output is determined in order to decide how much resource should be allocated to each activity.

Activity-based costing   A system of costing that allocates costs to products and services using cause-and-effect relationships to identify the resources that are consumed.

Activity based management (also called activity based cost management)   A method of identifying, costing and evaluating activities that a business performs. The main emphasis is not on the costing of products or services, rather with the analysis of activities, cost driver usage and performance within each of the activity areas.

Balance Sheet   A financial statement which shows the assets and liabilities of a business at a moment in time.

Balanced scorecard   A performance measurement system that aims to guide current and future performance towards the achievement of planned organizational goals and strategies and involves the measurement of approximately 25 measures across four perspectives: financial, customer, internal business process, and learning and growth. Ultimately, all measures should be linked to financial objectives.

Barriers to entry   Factors that need to be overcome by new entrants to a market if they wish to compete successfully. Reasons can include the high level of investment required or the fact that existing firms in the market are achieving economies of scale, which a new entrant cannot match.

Batch production   A system of production that employs general-purpose machines and functional layout. Batch production is a flexible system, which allows for different types of product to be made in batches of, for example, 10 or 100 units.

Benchmarking   The process of comparing the performance of an organization against other organizations.

Blanket overhead rate   A single overhead rate established for an organisation.

Break-even analysis   The calculation of the point at which revenue equals costs.

Break-even point   The point at which revenue equals costs.

Budget   A quantification of a plan, for a defined period of time.

Budgetary control   The use of the budgets as a method of comparison with actual financial results in order to identify any differences and whether corrective action may be required.

Capital turnover ratio   The level of sales in relation to the capital employed in a business.

Cash cow   A business unit with a high market share in a mature market. An individual product may also be referred to as a cash cow in similar circumstances.

Competitive advantage   Successful firms that can sustain a higher profit than the industry average are said to possess a competitive advantage over their rivals. This can only be achieved through the provision of some feature that is particularly valued by customers, whether this is low cost or some unique dimension that is valued by customers and which can command a premium price.

Computerized manufacturing technology   The use of computers to regulate production processes in industry.

Contribution   Normally defined as sales less variable costs. If additional fixed costs are incurred because of a decision then the contribution to general overheads generated as a result of that decision is sales less variable costs and less *identifiable* fixed costs.

Controllable cost   Those costs which are the responsibility of a manager and can be controlled by that manager.

Controllable profit   The profit that can be identified after deducting controllable costs from divisional revenues. Controllable costs can include fixed costs.

Corporate governance   A term that refers to the rules, processes or laws by which businesses are operated, regulated and controlled.

Corporate social responsibility   The ways an organization exceeds its minimum obligation to stakeholders.

Cost allocation   Costs that are specific to a department, for example indirect wages or power where this is separately metered.

Cost apportionment   Costs that relate to a number of departments and have to be shared on some agreed basis. Examples can include rent where this is paid on a building which is shared by a number of departments.

Cost centre   Responsibility centres where managers are held accountable for the expenses under their control.

Cost driver   Any factor whose change causes a change in the total cost of the activity.

Cost object   Any activity for which a separate measurement of cost is desired. This could be a range of entities such as a product, a service or a department.

Cost-plus pricing   A pricing approach that identifies the full cost of a product or service and adds a mark-up to allow for profit.

Cost of capital   The weighted average cost of capital (WACC) is calculated by multiplying the cost of each capital component by its proportional weight and then summing.

Cost of equity $\dfrac{\text{Dividend per share}}{\text{Current market price per share}} + \text{growth rate of dividends}$

Cost of sales   The cost of sales includes the costs that can be attributed to producing the goods or providing the services the entity sells.

Cost–volume–profit analysis   The relationship between sales volume (in units), sales revenue, costs and profit.

Current assets   The assets which are expected to be sold or otherwise used up in the near future and include cash, inventories (stock) and trade other receivables (debtors).

Current liabilities   The company's debts or obligations that are due within one year. They include short term debt, trade and other payables (creditors).

Customer account profitability   The assessment of the profitability to the business of individual customers or groups of customers.

Debenture   A long-term loan that is frequently divided into a number of units and investors are invited to purchase the number of units they require.

Debtors   See trade receivables.

Demand-based pricing   An approach to pricing that will take into consideration prices and costs at different volumes of sales in order to identify the point at which profit is maximized.

Depreciation   A method of accounting for the consumption of fixed assets over time, in a way that reflects their reducing value. Different methods can be used; for example, the straight line or reducing balance methods.

Discount factor   A technique which enables organizations to take account of the cost of capital. If future cash flows are identified then it is possible to discount these future cash flows in order to identify their *present value*.

Direct costs   The costs that can be exclusively identified with a particular cost object.

Dividends   Payments made by a company to its shareholders.

Dogs   A business unit with a low market share in a low growth market. An individual product may also be referred to as a dog in similar circumstances.

Earnings per share (EPS)   This can be calculated by dividing the profits after tax by the number of shares.

Economic value added (EVA®)   An estimate of true economic profit after making corrective adjustments to Generally Accepted Accounting Principles (GAAP) accounting, including deducting the opportunity cost of capital invested in the business.

Economies of scale   Those that arise because of high volumes of production.

Equity   The owners' residual interest in the assets of an enterprise after deducting all its liabilities.

Equivalent units   Used in process costing. Where there are partly completed units, these are converted into completed units. For example, two units that are 50% complete is equivalent to one completed unit.

Feedforward control   This occurs where a revised forecast of future performance takes place, is compared against the original plan and action is taken to deal with likely divergences.

Financial accounting   The field of accountancy concerned with the preparation of financial statements for decision-makers.

Financial risk   The additional risk a shareholder bears when a company uses debt in addition to equity financing.

Fixed cost   A cost that does not vary with the level of activity.

Fixed overhead expenditure variance   The difference between the budgeted fixed cost and the actual fixed cost.

Flexed budget   The original budget adjusted for the change in the level of activity.

Free cash flows (FCF)   The cash that a company is able to generate after deducting cash payments for tax and investments in working capital and non-current assets.

Full cost per unit   The variable cost per unit plus the fixed cost per unit at a given level of output.

Gearing   This calculates the relationship between long-term liabilities and shareholders' funds. Long-term debt includes debentures and other long-term loans which are falling due after one year.

Historic cost   The original monetary value of an economic item.

Hire purchase   A means of obtaining the use of an asset before payment is completed. An initial down payment is made followed by a series of hire charges at the end of which ownership passes to the user.

Indirect cost (or overheads)   Costs that cannot be exclusively identified with a particular cost object.

Intangible assets   An 'identifiable non-monetary asset without physical substance'. Examples can include computer software, patents, copyrights, customer lists, brands, customer and supplier relationships and marketing rights.

Internal rate of return   The discount rate that gives an NPV equal to zero.

Inventory   Goods and materials held in stock by a business.

Investment centre   Managers have responsibility for revenue, costs and investments. Common measures of investment centres include return on investment and residual income.

Investment risk   The risk that a company or project will not have adequate cash flow to meet its financial obligations.

Issued share capital   Comprises that part of the authorized share capital that has actually been issued, released or sold by the company.

Just-in-time (JIT)   A production method that employs a factory layout which moves away from batch production to one in which products are split into families of similar products each of which is manufactured in a small manufacturing cell. The production system works on flow line principles, so that batches of products can be made from start to finish, without the long wait between stages that often occurs with batch production.

Kaizen costing   A means of ensuring continuous improvement activities during the manufacturing stage of the product lifecycle.

Labour efficiency variance   Difference in the standard number of hours that would have been expected (SH) for the actual production and the actual hours worked for each grade of labour (AH) multiplied by the standard rate (SR) per hour.

Labour rate variance   Calculated by identifying the difference between the standard rate per hour (SR) and the actual rate (AR) per hour of labour multiplied by the actual hours worked (AH).

Liability   These are amounts that the business owes. They can be current liabilities, which are expected to be repaid within a year and long-term liabilities, which are not expected to be liquidated within a year.

Loan capital   Loans are usually over a stated period of time and pay fixed interest to the person making the loan. At the end of the period the capital is repaid.

Management accounting control system   Reports financial results or outputs. A budgetary control system, for example, reports on actual financial results compared against budget.

Management by exception   The attention of managers is focused on those departments and account items where there is a significant variance from budget.

Management control system   A collection of methods which have the aim of inducing people in an organization to do certain things and refrain from doing others. It includes performance management systems, but also includes other controls such as internal controls and personnel and cultural controls.

Margin of safety   The extent to which sales are above the break-even point.

Market value added   The current market value of shares and debt – (total capital raised + retained earnings).

Mass production   A method of production that utilizes a series of single-purpose machine tools organized into a linear sequence that mirrors the order in which operations have to be performed in the progressive conversion of raw materials into finished products. Mass production is particularly appropriate for large volume production of a relatively few number of products.

Master budget   An overall budget for the organisation. It includes the budgeted income statement, the budgeted balance sheet and the cash budget.

Matching principle   Income should be properly 'matched' with the expenses of a given accounting period.

Material price variance   Equal to the difference between the standard price (SP) per kilogram of material and the actual price (AP) per kilogram multiplied by the actual quantity (AQ) of material used.

Material usage variance   Equal to the difference between the standard quantity of material (SQ) that should have been required for the actual production compared with the actual quantity (AQ) of material used multiplied by the standard price (SP) per kilogram.

Mission statement   A statement of the purpose of the organisation.

Net assets   Equal to the total assets less total liabilities. The total assets are made up of non-current assets (plant, machinery and equipment) and current assets, which is the total of inventory, trade receivables and cash. The total liabilities are made up in much the same way, of long-term liabilities and current liabilities.

Net book value   Equal to its original cost less depreciation.

Net capital employed   Fixed assets plus working capital.

Net profit before interest and tax   The gross profit less overheads.

Nominal value   The price of a security (shares, bonds, etc.) when originally issued. This bears no relation to the market price. Also known as face value or par value.

Non-current (fixed) assets   An asset which is not easily convertible to cash or not expected to become cash within the next year.

Operational gearing   The relationship between fixed and variable costs.

Opportunity cost   A measurement of the cost of an opportunity that is lost or sacrificed.

Ordinary share capital   Ordinary shares represent ownership in a limited liability company. Shareholders are entitled to dividends when they are declared by the company board of directors.

Payback period   This is the number of years it takes to recover the initial investment.

Performance management system   One in which performance of business units is measured and performance managed based on the achievement of results. It is likely to involve the measurement of a number of performance dimensions, including financial ones. A management accounting control system could form part of a performance management system.

Period cost   These are non-manufacturing costs that are expensed in the period and are not associated with the costs of products. Examples include marketing and administration overheads.

Preference share capital   Part of the share capital of a company that ranks after secured creditors but before ordinary shareholders in the event of liquidation.

Product cost   Manufacturing cost is treated as a product cost and only the cost of products sold are recorded as an expense of the business. Unsold product is recorded as asset (inventory) in the Balance Sheet.

Profit and Loss Account   This is a financial statement that shows revenue, expenditure and the profit and/or loss resulting from operations for a given period of time.

Profit centre   A responsibility centre where a manager is held accountable for both the revenue and the costs of the centre.

Quick assets   Are assets which can or will be converted into cash fairly soon such as cash and trade and other receivables. Current assets minus inventory.

Quick ratio   (also termed asset test and liquid ratio) compares the quick assets to the current liabilities. It measures the ability of a company to use its quick assets to immediately extinguish its current liabilities.

Relevant cost   The costs that change because of a decision. Irrelevant costs are general overheads and other costs that do not change.

Residual income   A measure of divisional performance where the net residual income = operating profit – an interest charge for using the capital invested in the organization.

Responsibility accounting   A reporting system which provides accounting control reports for individual departments of an organization.

Retained profits   The earnings of preceding year(s), not yet paid out as dividends.

Return on investment   Divisional profit expressed as a percentage of the assets employed in the division.

Rolling budget   A budgeting system in which budgets are updated on a continuous basis to ensure that a 12-month budget is always available.

Sales margin variance   The difference between the budged sales volume (BV) and the actual sales volume (AV) multiplied by the standard contribution per unit (SC).

Sales price variance   The difference between the actual selling price per unit and the standard selling price per unit times the sales volume in units.

Share capital   The portion of a company's equity that has been obtained (or will be obtained) by trading stock to a shareholder for cash or equivalent item of capital value.

Shareholder value analysis   The process of analysing how decisions affect the net present value of cash to shareholders.

Standard cost   A system in which it is assumed that each unit of a product will require the exact same inputs of labour, materials and other resources at all stages of a standard production process. It is predominantly used in manufacturing organizations involving repetitive operations.

Strategy   The course of action by which the objectives of an organization are achieved.

Strategic management accounting   Management accounting information in which emphasis is placed on information which is related to factors external to the firm, as well as to non-financial information and internally generated information.

Sunk costs   Costs that have already been spent or the commitment has been made to spend them. Sunk costs are not relevant to a decision.

Target cost   A target selling price is first established, the desired profit margin of the company is then deducted to leave the target cost at which the product should be made.

Throughput accounting   An approach that emphasizes decision-making based on the principle of contribution-per-bottleneck-hour.

Trade payables (creditors)   Trade suppliers from whom the organization has bought on credit and not yet paid.

Trade receivables (debtors)   Customers who have bought on credit and not yet paid.

Transfer pricing   The pricing of goods and services that are transferred between divisions and other units of an organization.

Value chain of an organization This consists of the resources and activities that link an organization together to produce a product or service.

Value drivers These are the actions that lead to the provision of the product or service features that add value for the customer.

Variable cost A cost that varies with the level of activity.

Working capital Current assets less current liabilities.

Zero-based budgeting A comprehensive approach to budgeting that requires an organization to build up overhead budgets from a zero base as if the organization were starting from scratch.

References

Ansoff, I. (1966) *Corporate Strategy*. McGraw-Hill.

Anthony, R. and Govindarajan, V. (2004) *Management Control Systems*, 11th edn. Irwin.

Arnold, G. (2005) *Corporate Financial Management*, 3rd edn. Financial Times/Prentice-Hall.

Atkinson, A., Kaplan, R.S. and Young, S. (2004) *Management Accounting*, 4th edn. Prentice-Hall, Upper Saddle River, NJ.

Bromwich, M. and Bhimani, A. (1991) Strategic investment appraisal. *Management Accounting (USA)* **March**.

Brownell, P. (1981) Participation in budgeting: locus of control and organisational effectiveness. *The Accounting Review* **October**: 944–958.

Bruns, W.J. and Waterhouse, J.H. (1975) Budgetary control and organisational structure. *Journal of Accounting Research* **13**: 177–203.

Burns, T. and Stalker, G.M. (1961) *The Management of Innovation*. Tavistock Institute, London.

Chennel, R.H. (2003) Management control system design within its organisational context: findings from contingency based research and directions for the future. *Accounting, Organisation and Society* **28**: 127–168.

Coad, A. (2005) Strategy and control. In Berry, A., Broadbent, J. and Otley, D. (eds), *Management Control: Theories, Issues and Performance*. Palgrave MacMillan, Basingstoke, pp. 167–191.

Cobb, I. (1993) *JIT and the Management Accountant: A study of current UK practice*. Chartered Institute of Management Accountants, London.

Cooper, R. (1990) Cost classification in unit-based and activity based manufacturing cost systems. *Journal of Cost Management* **Fall**: 4–14.

Cooper, R. (1996) Lean enterprises and the confrontation strategy. *The Academy of Management Executive* **10**(3): 28–39.

Cooper, R. and Slagmulder, R. (1999) *Supply Chain Development for the Lean Enterprise: Interorganizational Cost Management (Interorganizational Cost Management)* Productivity Press.

Cooper, R. and Slagmulder, R. (2004a) Achieving full-cycle cost management. *MIT Sloan Management Review* **46**(1): 45–52.

Cooper, R. and Slagmulder, R. (2004b) Interorganizational cost management and relational context. *Accounting, Organizations and Society* **29**(1): 1–26.

Crane, A. and Matten, D. (2007) *Business Ethics*, 2nd edn. Oxford University Press, Oxford.

De George, R. (1999) *Business Ethics*, 5th edn. Prentice-Hall, London.

Doganis, R. (2001) *Airline Business in the 21st Century*. Routledge, Florence, KY.

Doganis, R. (2006) *The Airline Business*, 2nd edn. Routledge.

Drury, C. (2004) *Management and Cost Accounting*, 6th edn. Thomson Learning, London.

Drury, C. and Tayles, M. (2000) *Cost System Design and Profitability Analysis in UK Companies*. Chartered Institute of Management Accountants.

Drury, C., Braund, S., Osborne, P. and Tayles, M. (1993) A survey of management accounting practices in UK manufacturing companies. ACCA Research Paper, Chartered Association of Certified Accountants.

Emmanuel, C., Otley, D. and Merchant, K. (1990) *Accounting for Management Control*, 2nd edn. International Thompson Business Press.

Fitzgerald, L., Johnston, R., Brignall, T.L., Silvestro, R. and Voss, C. (1991) *Performance Measurement in Service Industries*. Chartered Institute of Management Accountants.

Gittell, J.H. (2002) *Southwest Airlines Way: The Power of Relationships for Superior Performance*, McGraw Hill.

Goldratt, E.M. and Cox, J. (1984) *The Goal*. Gower, London.

Goldratt, E.M. and Fox, R.E. (1986) *The Race*. North River Press.

Gordon, L.A. and Miller, D. (1976) A contingency framework for the design of accounting and information systems. *Accounting, Organisation and Society* **1**: 59–70.

Govindarajan, V. (1984) Appropriateness of accounting data in performance evaluation: an empirical examination of environmental uncertainty as an intervening variable. *Accounting, Organisation and Society* **9**: 125–135.

Govindarajan, V. and Gupta, A.K. (1985) Linking control systems to business unit strategy: impact on performance. *Accounting, Organisation and Society* **10**: 828–853.

Grugulis, I. and Wilkinson, A. (2002) British Airways: hype, hope and reality. *Long Range Planning* **35**(2): 179–194.

Handy, C.B. (1976) *Understanding Organisations*. Penguin Books.

Hanlon, P. (1999) *Global Airlines*, 2nd edn, Butterworth Heinemann, Oxford.

Hirst, M.K. (1981) Accountancy information and the evaluation of subordinate performance. *The Accounting Review* **56**: 771–784.

Hofstede, G.H. (1968) *The Game of Budget Control*. Tavistock Institute.

Hope, J. and Fraser, R. (2003) *Beyond Budgeting: How Managers Can Break Free from the Annual Performance Trap*. Harvard Business School Publishing Corporation.

Hopwood, A.G. (1976) *Accounting and Human Behaviour*. Prentice-Hall.

Hopwood, A.G. (1978) Towards an organisational perspective for the study of accounting and information systems. *Accounting Organisations and Society* **3**(1): 3–14.

Jaikumar, R. (1986) Postindustrial manufacturing. *Harvard Business Review* **64**(6): 69–76.

Johnson, G. and Scholes, K. (1998) *Exploring Corporate Strategy*, 5th edn. Financial Times/Prentice Hall.

Johnson, G., Scholes, K. and Whittington, R. (2005) *Exploring Corporate Strategy*, 7th edn. Financial Times/Prentice-Hall.

Johnson, H.T. (1992) *Relevance Regained: From top-down control to bottom-up empowerment*. Free Press, New York.

Johnson, H.T. and Brohms, A. (2000) *Profit Beyond Measure: Extraordinary results through attention to work and people*. Nicholas Brealey Publishing, London.

Johnson, H.T. and Kaplan, R.S. (1987) *Relevance Lost: The rise and fall of management accounting*. Harvard Business Press, Boston, MA.

Kaplan, R.S. (1983) Measuring manufacturing performance: a new challenge for managerial accounting research. *The Accounting Review*, **58**(4): 686–705.

Kaplan, R.S. (1986) Must CIM be justified by faith alone. *Harvard Business Review*, **64**(2): 87–95.

Kaplan, R.S. and Norton, D.P. (1992) The balanced scorecard: measures that drive performance, Harvard Business Review, Jan–Feb, 75–85.

Kaplan, R.S. and Norton, D.P. (1996) *The Balanced Scorecard: Translating strategy into action*. Harvard Business School Press, Boston.

Kaplan, R.S. and Norton, D.P. (2004) Strategy maps: converting intangible assets into tangible outcomes, Harvard Business Press.

Lord, B.R. (1996) Strategic management accounting: the emperor's new clothes? *Management Accounting Research* **7**: 347–366.

Lowe, E.A. and Shaw, R.W. (1968) An analysis of managerial biasing: evidence from a company's budgeting process. *Journal of Management Studies* **5**: 304–315.

REFERENCES

Markus, M.L. and Pfeffer, J. (1983) Power and the design and implementation of accounting and control systems. *Accounting Organisations and Society* **8**(2): 205–218.

Maslow, A.H. (1954) *Motivation and Personality*. Harper and Row.

McGregor, D. (1960) *The Human Side of Enterprise*. McGraw-Hill.

Mendelow, A. (1991) Proceedings of 2nd International Conference on Information Systems, Cambridge, MA.

Merchant, K.A. (1985) *Control in Business Organisations*. Ballinger.

Merchant, K.A. (1998) *Modern Management Control Systems: Text and Cases*. Prentice-Hall.

Mia, L. (1989) The impact of participation and job difficulty on managerial performance and work motivation: a research note. *Accounting Organisations and Society* **14**(4): 347–357.

Miles, R.E. and Snow, C.C. (1978) *Organisation Strategy, Structure and Process*. McGraw-Hill.

Mintzberg, H. (1975) *Impediments to the Use of Management Information*. National Association of Accountants.

Mintzberg, H. (1979) *The Structuring of Organisations: A Synthesis of the Research*. Prentice-Hall.

Norreklit, H. (2000) The balance on the balanced scorecard—a critical analysis of some of its assumptions. *Management Accounting Research* **11**(1): 65–88.

O'Hanlon, J. and Peasnell, K. (1998) Wall Streets contribution to management accounting: The Stern Steward EVA® financial management system. *Management Accounting Research* **9**: 421–444.

Otley, D. (1987) *Accounting Control and Organisational Behaviour*. Heinemann.

Otley, D. (1999) Performance management: a framework for management control system research. *Management Accounting Research* **10**: 363–382.

Ouchi, W.G. (1979) A conceptual framework for the design of organisational control mechanisms. *Management Science* **25**: 833–848.

Porter, M.E. (1980) *Competitive Strategy Techniques for Analysing Industries and Competitors*. Free Press, New York.

Porter, M.E. and Kramer, M.R. (2006) Strategy and society: the link between competitive advantage and corporate social responsibility. *Harvard Business Review* **Dec**.

Rappaport, A. (1988) *Creating Shareholder Value: a guide for managers and investors*. Free Press, New York.

Rosslender, R. and Hart, S.J. (2006) Interfunctional cooperation in progressing accounting for brands: the case for brand management accounting. *Journal of Accounting and Organizational Change* **19**: 229–247.

Shank, J.K. (1989) Strategic cost management: New Wine, or Just New Bottles? *Journal of Management Accounting Research (USA)* **Fall**: 47–65.

Shank, J.K. and Govindarajan, V. (1992a) Strategic cost management and the value chain, *Journal of Cost Management*, **6**(3): 5–21.

Shank, J.K. and Govindarajan, V. (1992b) Strategic cost management: the value chain perspective. *Journal of Management Accounting Research* **4**: 179–197.

Shank, J.K. and Govindarajan, V. (1992c) Strategic cost analysis of technical investments. *Sloan Management Review* **34**: 39–51.

Shank, J.K. and Govindarajan, V. (1993) *Strategic Cost Management: The New Tool for Competitive Advantage*. Free Press, New York.

Shaw, S. (2007) Airline Marketing and Management, 6th edn, Ashgate.

Simons, R. (1995) *Levers of Control: How Managers Use Innovative Control Systems to Drive Strategic Renewal*. Harvard Business Press.

Turban, E. (1995) *Decision Support and Expert Systems: Management support systems*. Prentice-Hall, Englewood Cliffs, NJ.

Vroom, V.H. (1960) *Some Personality Determinants of the Effects of Participation*. Prentice-Hall.

Weber, J. and Linder, S. (2003) Budgeting, better budgeting or beyond budgeting? Konzeptionelle eignung und implmentierbarkeit. *Advanced Controlling* **33**: 1–70.

Womack, J.P., Jones, D.T. and Ross, D. (1990) *The Machine that Changed the World*. Rawson Associates, New York.

Wood, S. (1989) The transformation of work? in Wood, S. (ed.) *The Transformation of work? Skill, Flexibility and the Labour Process* (pp. 1–43) Unwin Hyman.

Index

INDEX